OPDB 93   Sine   35—
PB=88
B.0

SO-DTP-399

1ª, signed, to the typist!

To Gladys F. Boggess
with appreciation
from
Matthew Spinka

JOHN HUS
AT THE COUNCIL OF CONSTANCE

Number LXXIII of the
Records of Civilization: Sources and Studies
Edited under the Auspices of the
Department of History, Columbia University

John Hus

at the Council of Constance

TRANSLATED FROM
THE LATIN AND THE CZECH
WITH NOTES AND INTRODUCTION BY

MATTHEW SPINKA

BX
4917
. P413
West

COLUMBIA UNIVERSITY PRESS
New York and London 1965

Matthew Spinka, a church historian, was on the faculty of
the Hartford Theological Seminary before his retirement.

Copyright © 1965 Columbia University Press, Ltd.
Library of Congress Catalog Card Number: 65-11019
Printed in The Netherlands

Records of Civilization: Sources and Studies

EDITED UNDER THE AUSPICES OF THE DEPARTMENT OF HISTORY,
COLUMBIA UNIVERSITY

General Editor: W. T. H. Jackson, Professor of German and History

Past Editors

1915–1926
James T. Shotwell, Bryce Professor Emeritus of the History of
International Relations

1926–1953
Austin P. Evans, Late Professor of History

1953–1962
Jacques Barzun, Seth Low Professor of History

Editors: Oriental Records

Wm. Theodore de Bary, Professor of Chinese and Japanese
Donald Keene, Professor of Japanese
Ivan Morris, Associate Professor of Chinese and Japanese
Burton Watson, Assistant Professor of Chinese and Japanese

Consulting Editors

Gerson D. Cohen, Associate Professor of History
Gilbert Highet, Anthon Professor of the Latin Language and Literature
Paul O. Kristeller, Professor of Philosophy
Gerhart B. Ladner, Professor of History, University of California
at Los Angeles
John H. Mundy, Professor of History
Ihor Ševčenko, Professor of History
C. Martin Wilbur, Professor of Chinese History

IN COMMEMORATION OF THE
550th ANNIVERSARY OF
THE DEATH OF HUS
AND DEDICATED TO
THE SCHOLAR WHOSE LIFELONG
RESEARCHES AND WRITINGS
HAVE MADE HIM
THE OUTSTANDING AUTHORITY
ON HUS AND HUSSITICA
F. M. BARTOŠ

FOREWORD

A few years ago Professor John H. Mundy of Columbia University, then the editor of *The Records of Civilization,* asked me to translate the *Relatio de Mag. Joannis Hus causa* of Peter of Mladoňovice. I gladly consented, wishing to increase the meager number of source materials available in English relating to the Czech reformer. The task of translating this Latin and Czech text, to which I added Hus's letters from Constance, was not without its difficulties. Nor was the essay depicting the historical background altogether a simple matter. It required an interpretative understanding not only of the historical, but also of the philosophical, ecclesiological, and theological conceptions of the fourteenth century, since they exerted a decisive influence on Hus's trial at the Council of Constance. There is, however, a deplorable dearth of scholarly, critical studies in these fields. One lacks solid ground upon which to base his judgment.

To begin with, the nominalist philosophy and theology adhered to by most of Hus's judges, such as d'Ailly and Gerson, have been for the greatest part ignored or insufficiently evaluated by modern scholars, particularly Roman Catholic. This is not surprising when one considers the predominance of neo-Thomism among them. They regard the post-Thomistic period as one of sharp decline from the high peak of Scholasticism. For instance, Étienne Gilson, not the least among them, significantly entitles the last chapter of his massive *History of Christian Philosophy in the Middle Ages* "Journey's End." To him, the development of Christian thought beyond St. Thomas is but a gradual decline from the summit to the morass of the Protestant Reformation. It is not even worth describing. Ockham's nominalism, instead of being viewed as a fresh start resulting in a new era, is considered as a regrettable aberration. Fortunately, a work recently published has proved of great value to me. Professor Heiko A. Oberman, realizing the situation described above, has produced the first of a number of studies in this period entitled *A Harvest of Medieval Theology.*

The same negative attitude is manifested toward that other movement characteristic of the fourteenth and the early fifteenth centuries, conciliarism. It is axiomatic that without a firm grasp of its ecclesiological principles one cannot understand correctly the dominant motives of the Councils of Pisa, Constance, and Basle. Yet this significant phase of church history, with a few exceptions, has not hitherto found a scholar who would treat it adequately and with unbiased, though critical, judgment. The fact that it was a defeated and officially proscribed cause, in its heyday potentially dangerous to the papacy, has encouraged few to treat it with the seriousness it deserves.

Czech historical scholarship has produced during the last half century a remarkable, even monumental number of studies dealing with the Czech reform, particularly with Hus. It has, however, been understandably dominated by a defensive attitude toward the grave misrepresentations and attacks upon him. Among these detractors the chief place may be accorded to Johann Loserth. His book, *Hus und Wiclif: zur Genesis der husitischen Lehre,* denied the Czech reformer the least shred of originality. Loserth flatly charged that Hus had derived his views practically *in toto*, and often verbally, from Wyclif. He declared pontifically that "there is no ground for speaking of a Hussite system of doctrine." [1] It is to be regretted that this thoroughly biased thesis has been widely accepted and has remained to a large degree the stereotyped characterization of Hus's thought even among the English and American historians to this day. No wonder that the Czech scholars reacted energetically against it, although their works, written in a language not widely known, have failed to exert a sufficiently effective corrective influence! For instance, the two-volume biographical work of Hus by Václav Novotný and the three-volume analysis of Hus's thought by Vlastimil Kybal have remained practically unknown.[2]

Furthermore, Czech historical scholarship has been divided into two

---

[1] Johann Loserth, *Hus und Wiclif: zur Genesis der husitischen Lehre* (Prague-Leipzig, 1884), p. xxx. Paul de Vooght writes about this work: "Le plus récente en date des enterprises allemands contre Huss est celle de J. Loserth qui prétendit avec une incroyable légèrité qui toute l'œuvre écrite de Huss n'était qu'une plate copie de celle de Wiclif. Il n'était plus question de réduire Huss aux proportions de quelque *Untermensch* slave, dévoré de la haine du peuple allemand. Cette personnalité même lui était ravie. Loserth réduisit Huss littéralement au néant." De Vooght, *L'hérésie de Jean Huss,* p. ix.

[2] Novotný-Kybal, *M. Jan Hus, život a učení* (5 vols., Praha, Jan Laichter, 1919–31). Since Novotný wrote the biographical part, while Kybal wrote the section on the teaching, the two sections are separate, though interdependent. I propose henceforth to refer to them separately, Novotný, I–II, and Kybal, I–III.

hostile camps, which can be roughly characterized as the Liberal Catholic-Protestant and Roman Catholic. The former group (not including the Protestant František Palacký, who predated this period) comprised such outstanding liberal Catholic historians as Václav Novotný, Vlastimil Kybal, Kamil Krofta, and the Protestant F. M. Bartoš. It was further greatly strengthened by the influence of the Protestant Thomas G. Masaryk, who regarded the Hussite movement, particularly the Unity of Czech Brethren, as the dominant tradition of the Czech cultural and political programs. Opposed to them was the school of Josef Pekař, also a liberal Catholic but not of the Masaryk orientation, and the orthodox Catholic theologian, Jan Sedlák. The writing of these historians, although of inestimable value as historical research, is necessarily more or less polemical. Their spirit is also partly nationalistic, informed by opposition to the Habsburg dynastic rule over the country, which, since the defeat of Czech Protestantism at the Battle of White Mountain in 1620, has been the chief support of Roman Catholicism. This spirit, dominant particularly in the first-named camp, understandably characterizes the otherwise admirable Czech historical scholarship in dealing with the Hussite period. After all, most of it dates from the the time prior to the liberation of Czechoslovakia from the Habsburg regime. Before leaving this subject, it may be of interest to point out that under the present Communist regime its historians have undertaken to reinterpret the whole Hussite period as essentially a revolt of the lower classes against the injustices of the feudal society. Among the most outstanding of such works, devoted particularly to Hus's theology, are those of Milan Machovec, Robert Kalivoda, and J. Macek.[3] Needless to say, these works, dominated by the Marxist view of history, do not qualify as genuine and unbiased research.

Recently, a welcome change in the attitude of Roman Catholic scholarship toward Hus appeared in two books by Paul de Vooght, a Belgian Benedictine.[4] One wonders if it signifies a permanent revaluation of the subject. De Vooght considers Hus as, on the whole, quite orthodox, while regarding his Czech adversaries and the conciliar judges as guilty of gross injustice toward him. Yet, quite inconsistently—as

---

[3] Machovec, *Husovo učení a význam v tradici českého národa* (Praha, 1953); Robert Kalivoda, *Husitská ideologie* (Praha, 1961); J. Macek, *Jan Hus* (Praha, 1963).

[4] De Vooght, *L'hérésie de Jean Huss, Hussiana.*

it appears to me—he still judges Hus to have been a heretic, principally because of Pope Martin's approval of the conciliar verdict.

In translating Peter's *Relatio*, I gratefully acknowledge the help of a number of friends. Among them is my former colleague, Professor Ford Lewis Battles of the Hartford Seminary Foundation; Professor O. Odložilík of the University of Pennsylvania, formerly of Charles University in Prague, who had aided Professor Novotný in editing the text of the *Relatio*; Professor Robert B. Palmer, the classical scholar of the Scripps College of Claremont; and Professor F. M. Bartoš, the recognized authority in the field of *Hussitica*, who even furnished me a copy of the very rare edition of Hus's Latin works, the *Historia et Monumenta*, and many of his own treatises. Above all, I am deeply indebted to the former editor of *The Records of Civilization*, Professor John H. Mundy, and the present editor, Professor W. T. H. Jackson, who devoted unstinted and minute attention to the rendering of the text. Without their care the work could not but have suffered deficiencies. To all these kind friends I express my very real thanks.

It is with more than the usual perfunctory avowal that I assume sole responsibility for the views expressed in the historical introduction and the annotations. This applies particularly to the concept of heresy, wherein my views differ from those of the editors.

I also wish to express sincere thanks to Miss Gladys F. Boggess for the unusual care she exercised in typing the text.

September 1, 1963   MATTHEW SPINKA
Claremont, California

CONTENTS

INTRODUCTION

The Conciliar Movement
and the
Council of Constance

THE RISE OF CONCILIARISM

The conciliar period is one of the most significant eras in the history of Christianity. Had its principles prevailed, the Roman Church would have become a constitutional, instead of an absolute, monarchy. The Council of Constance was the culmination of a daring effort to change the direction of papal development. The conciliar movement assumed an effective form as a result of the Great Schism of 1378. Conciliarism was, however, but the cumulative effect of the long-drawn-out concern of the earlier canonists and reformers with the concept of the Church. Their particular endeavor centered on the nature of the Church universal, usually designated as the *congregatio fidelium*, and its relation to the Roman Church as represented by the pope and the college of cardinals. The immense labors of the decretists and decretalists of the twelfth and thirteenth centuries, followed by the fourteenth-century conciliarists, contitute the theme of the exhaustive and copiously documented study of Brian Tierney, *Foundations of the Conciliar Theory*.[1] He stresses the fact that the writers who derive the conciliarist ideas principally from such radical thinkers as John of Paris, Marsilius of Padua, and William of Ockham tend to follow the radicalism of these

---

[1] The reader is referred for the full argument to the work itself. Also cf. John Hine Mundy's Introduction to Loomis, *The Council of Constance: The Unification of the Church.* Ray C. Petry, "Unitive Reform Principles of the Late Medieval Conciliarists," in *Church History*, XXXI (Chicago, 1962), 164 ff.

authors. In contrast to their method he urges that the conciliar theory be solidly based upon the views of the earlier canonists. He observes that the principal source from which the concepts were derived are Gratian's *Decretum* and the later *Decretales*. The early canonists had patiently and systematically developed the theories from which the conciliarists, prior to and following upon the Great Schism, drew their principles.

The chief concern of the canonists was to make the *congregatio fidelium* superior to the rapidly growing pretensions of the papacy to the absolute authority within the Church. The universal Church had been regarded ever since the time of the Apostle Paul as the mystical body of Christ.[2] As Dr. Tierney tersely summarizes their quest, it was to make "the whole Christian community superior to any prelate, however exalted; the Pope was to be a servant of the Church rather than its master."[3] Huguccio (d. 1210), one of the greatest of the decretists and the teacher of Pope Innocent III, likewise clearly distinguished in matters of faith "between the powers inherent in the whole *congregatio fidelium* and the authority that could be exercised by the local *Romana ecclesia*. Above all, he emphasized that . . . the fact that Peter stood *in figura ecclesie* did not mean that the Pope possessed in his own person all the gifts that Christ had conferred on the Church."[4]

The conciliarists, beginning with the Dominican John of Paris (d. 1306), further developed the ideas of the decretists and decretalists. John was the author of the influential work *De potestate regiae et papali* (1302). He defines the Church as "one Christian people, one mystical body which is not in Peter or Linus but in Christ, who is the proper and supreme head of the Church."[5] Like every other corporate group, it must have a visible head to maintain its unity. This headship in the Church militant is provided by the pope. John nevertheless argues that the pope's office, although universal, is only vicarial, administrative, while that of the prelates is limited to their local dioceses. Furthermore, since Christ granted Peter only spiritual power, the pope's jurisdiction is restricted to the spiritual realm. The state, which also derives its power from God, possesses an independent and separate sphere of activity endowed with the power of coercion. The pope's prerogatives

[2] I Cor. 12:27 and elsewhere.
[3] Tierney, *Foundations of the Conciliar Theory*, p. 6.
[4] *Ibid.*, p. 41.
[5] J. Leclercq, *Jean de Paris et l'ecclésiologie du XIIIe siècle* (Paris, 1942), p. 230.

are to be used for the edification, not the destruction, of the Church. He is the stewart, the *"procurator* or *dispensator*, not *dominus*," of the Church. He administers, but does not own, the property of the Church. Conceiving the Church as a corporation, John declares that "authority in a corporation was not concentrated in the head alone but diffused among the various members . . . [since] the power of jurisdiction, unlike the power of orders, was conferred on a prelate by human delegation in the act of election." [6] Hence, the pope's authority is not absolute: he has no right to define dogmas, although he has jurisdiction in legal cases concerning them. Should he abuse or exceed his powers, he may be called to account by the college of cardinals or the general Council. The latter, as representing the *congregatio fidelium*, is the source of all power. The supreme hierarchical authority is not concentrated in the pope and the cardinals, but resides in the Church universal.

Marsilius of Padua (1275 or 80–1347?), having left his native Italy, moved to Paris. There he taught natural philosophy and practiced medicine. It was during this Paris period that he wrote, with the assistance of John of Jandun, his chief work, the *Defensor pacis*,[7] which he finished in 1324. When his authorship became known two years later, he was forced to flee for protection to the court of Emperor Lewis the Bavarian. His work is of primary significance both for its political and its ecclesiastical principles. For the former, Marsilius was chiefly dependent upon Aristotle's *Politics* and Augustine's *City of God*. For the latter he cites, besides the Scriptures, Augustine, Ambrose, and Jerome. We shall limit ourselves mainly to the consideration of his revolutionary ecclesiological ideas.

In his *Defensor pacis*, Marsilius defines the Church as comprising all true Christians. What distinguishes an ordinary citizen from a member of the *congregatio fidelium* is the latter's faith in Christ. He, Christ, founded the Church and entrusted it with His teachings. He alone has ever been and "has always remained the head of the Church." [8] Since the Church is His body, it derives its unity from Him alone.

The highest tribunal of the Church is not the papal *curia* but the

[6] Tierney, *op. cit.*, p. 165.
[7] Alan Gewirth, trans., *Marsilius of Padua, The Defender of Peace* (2 vols., New York, Columbia University Press, 1951–56).
[8] *Ibid.*, II, xxviii, p. 27.

general Council, which represents the entire body of believers. It is elected by all the members of the Church, both clerical and lay. It is likewise controlled by all the faithful. They "control excommunication, elect the priesthood to its posts, define articles of faith . . . elect the council, make binding its decisions, and elect the pope or 'head bishop.'"[9] Since its deliberations are under the guidance of the Holy Spirit, the Council is infallible in matters of faith. As such, it is superior to the pope and the entire hierarchy of the Roman Church, which forms but part of the Church universal. Prior to Marsilius, only John of Paris held that "the council is greater than the pope" in matters of faith.

As for the organization of the Roman Church, Marsilius sharply differentiates between its "essential" and "accidental" aspects. The former are derived directly from God, while the latter are of human invention and appointment. Moreover, the "essential" powers are shared equally by the entire priesthood. There is, thus, no essential difference between priests, bishops, archbishops, patriarchs, and pope. The distinction of office among them is of purely human origin. Apostle Peter received no greater *essential* authority than the other apostles. Commenting on the crucial text in Matt. 16 : 18, "Thou art Peter . . ." Marsilius asserts that Christ gave to Peter no greater authority or preeminence than to any other apostle. The pope is not, therefore, superior to the rest of the bishops; his claim to absolute power is not of right but of usurpation. Marsilius refers to Christ's saying in Matt. 20 : 25–26, "The rulers of the gentiles lord it over them. . . . Not so shall be among you," in support of his contention that all ecclesiastical power is spiritual, noncoercive. Only the political rulers possess coercive authority. Among the most startling of his exegetical deductions is the conclusion that, since Peter was the bishop of Antioch, not of Rome, the Roman popes are not Peter's, but rather Paul's, successors.[10]

Denying that the papal and hierarchical organization of the Church is of divine institution, Marsilius nevertheless admits its practical usefulness and even its necessity. He argues that the priests of the early Church "in order to avoid scandal and schism, elected one of their number to guide and direct others in the exercise of the ecclesiastical

---

[9] *Ibid.,* I, p. 263, basing his summary on II, vi, pp. 12–13; xxvii, p. 11; xx, p. 4; xxi, pp. 3, 9; xxii, p. 11.

[10] *Ibid.,* II, xvi, p. 15–18.

office and service." [11] For similar reasons such as administrative unity and efficiency, the office has proved beneficial ever since. Furthermore, Marsilius concedes the necessity of sacramental ministration for the salvation of believers and restricts this function to the priesthood. The essential grace of the sacraments, however, is bestowed by God; the priests exercise only a ministerial function that is purely declaratory.

Summarizing his careful and extensive analysis of Marsilian views, Gewirth concludes:

As a consequence of these considerations, the Marsilian church emerges as a purely spiritual congregation of believers, connected by no ties but their common faith and participation in the sacraments. The priesthood which teaches the faith and ministers the sacraments consists of ministers exercising no coercive authority over the believers and maintaining complete equality with one another. Such equality, in the sense of absence of all jurisdictional superiority, is the direct result of Christ's ordainment, which extends only to the essential power traditionally called the power of order. [12]

Associated with, but at the same time critical of, Marsilius was the English Franciscan, William of Ockham (d. 1349). As time went on, he became more influential than Marsilius. He had studied at the University of Oxford, where he also taught as inceptor from 1318 to 1320. Four years later, having been accused of heretical views by the chancellor of the university, John Luterell, he was cited to Avignon. His doctrine, submitted by Pope John XXII to a commission of which Luterell was a member, was found heretical in some articles and erroneous in others. However, the trial did not result in the papal condemnation of Ockham, perhaps because the commissioners could not agree among themselves. In the meantime, while staying at the Franciscan house at Avignon, Ockham became acquainted with the general minister of the Franciscans, Michael de Cesena, and joined Michael in his conflict with the pope over the matter of "apostolic poverty." On this account both Michael and Ockham, along with two other friars, were forced to flee (1328) and all were thereupon excommunicated. Furthermore, Michael, who had been reelected general of the order against the pope's will, was deposed. They found refuge at the court of Lewis the Bavarian in Pisa, and two years later followed him to Munich. There William became renowned for his numerous

[11] *Ibid.*, II, xv, **pp.** 6–7.
[12] *Ibid.*, I, **p.** 277.

treatises—political, philosophical, and theological. He founded the
radical nominalist school based on an exceedingly subtle system of
logic. This made him an innovator, the inspirer of a forward-looking
philosophical and theological system which profoundly influenced the
whole subsequent period. In it are found the principles of the modern
scientific method with its inductive, rather than deductive, study of
objective reality. He also became the most outstanding theological
antagonist of Thomas Aquinas. Étienne Gilson, himself a thoroughgoing Thomist, characterizes Ockham as

a passionate theologian ... a shrewd logician and a clear-headed philosopher ... and a great publicist whose political doctrines, deeply rooted in his
theology, were dangerously shaking the lofty structure of mediaeval Christendom.[13]

Our concern is principally with his ecclesiological views, for they
later inspired many outstanding thinkers such as Cardinal d'Ailly and
Jean Gerson. Not only were these men among the most influential
judges of John Hus at the Council of Constance, but their philosophical nominalism aided their theological animus against the Bohemian
reformer, a philosophical realist. The most pertinent of Ockham's
works for our purpose are his *Dialogus*, begun in 1333 but never
completed;[14] the *Breviloquium de potestate papae* (1339–41),[15] and
the *De imperatorum et pontificum potestate*,[16] written shortly before
his death.

On strictly logical Ockhamist grounds many Christian doctrines and
dogmas are matters of "probable opinions" rather than of rationally
demonstrable proof. The believer, therefore, may attain an apprehension of God and His revealed truths from the teachings of the Church.
The faith of the Church is grounded in the Scriptures. Only those

[13] Étienne Gilson, *The Unity of Philosophical Experience* (New York, Charles
Scribner's Sons, 1937), p. 86.
[14] *Dialogus de potestate papae et imperatoris* (Torino, Bottega d'Erasmo, 1959).
[15] Léon Baudry, ed. (Paris, Vrin, 1937); also Adalbert Hamman, *Le Doctrine
de l'Église et l'État chez Occam* (Paris, aux Editions Franciscaines, 1942). This
is a commentary on the *Breviloquium*.
[16] This treatise is published in Scholz, *Unbekannte kirchenpolitische Streitschriften aus der Zeit Ludwigs des Bayern*, II, 453–80. For further exposition of
Ockham's thought on this subject cf. Philotheus Boehner, "Ockham's Political
Ideas," in his *Collected Articles on Ockham*, edited by E. M. Buytaert (St.
Bonaventure, N.Y., The Franciscan Institute, 1958), pp. 442 ff; also Georges de
Lagarde, *La naissance de l'ésprit laïque*, IV, *Guillaume d'Ockham: Defense de
l'Empire;* V, *Critique des structures ecclesiales* (Louvain et Paris, 1962–63).

truths are catholic which the Holy Scriptures teach. The Christian is not bound to believe "what is neither contained in the Bible, nor can be inferred by necessary and manifest consequence alone from the things contained in the Bible. . . . The pope or the Church can by their declarations alter absolutely nothing in these truths." "Human authority is by no means to be relied on in those things which pertain to faith, because our faith is above the human intellect." "Whoever says that any part of the New or the Old Testament asserts anything false, or is not to be received by Catholics, is to be regarded as heretical and stubborn." [17] It is on these grounds that Ockham accused Pope John XXII of heresy for teaching that the elect shall not see God until after the Last Judgment. Ockham, however, did not teach the doctrine of *sola Scriptura.* In his *Dialogus* he enumerates five sources of Christian truth: the Scriptures and what can be inferred from them; the apostolic and patristic teaching; reputed historical writings; conclusions drawn from the foregoing evidences; and the testimony of divinely inspired revelations received by the universal Church.[18] These two views—(1) that Scripture contains all the truths of faith, and (2) that the tradition *adds* further truths—raise the question: which of these propositions represents Ockham's own convictions? Heiko A. Oberman, whose exhaustive study of nominalism affords a basic revaluation of the movement, concludes that Ockham favored the second position, and was followed therein by other members of his school.

Ecclesiastical traditions, including canon law, are invested with the same degree of authority as that of Holy Scripture. Leading spokesmen for the nominalistic tradition such as Gerson, Occam, d'Ailly—and even more emphatically Biel—will be shown to champion the position of Tradition II,

the designation Oberman adopted for this view.[19] Tradition I—the view that Scripture is the sole source and criterion of faith—he traces from St. Augustine, through Bishop Thomas Bradwardine, to John Wyclif and Hus. This was one of the reasons why d'Ailly and Gerson opposed Hus at the Council of Constance.

Ockham makes a sharp distinction between the *universitas fidelium* as genus and the *Romana ecclesia* as species. Of the universal Church comprising the totality of believers Christ alone is the head. It alone

[17] Quoted from R. Seeberg, *Textbook of the History of Doctrines* (Grand Rapids, Mich., Baker's Book House, 1961), I, 192–94.
[18] *Dialogus de potestate papae et imperatoris,* II, 415–16.
[19] *The Harvest of Medieval Theology,* p. 373.

cannot err in matters of faith. The pope, the cardinals, and the Roman Church can err and indeed have erred. The *universitas fidelium* may, however, elect a vicegerent of Christ. It is the general Council, not the pope, that holds this office. The Council represents all Christendom, both clerical and lay. As such, it is competent to deal with matters that concern all. Ockham remarks: "God is not God of the clerics only, but also of laymen." The Council is convoked ordinarily by the pope; but when the pope is a heretic or is otherwise disqualified, it may be convoked without him, and even against his will. A heretical pope may be deposed by the Council. As Brian Tierney has pointed out,[20] Ockham based this assertion on the long-established interpretation of the canonists who commented on the thesis of Gratian's *Decretum* that "[papa] *a nemine est iudicandus nisi deprehendatur a fide devius.*" Ockham followed Huguccio of Pisa in his interpretation of this passage, although other canonists went much beyond his carefully delimited opinion. Since Ockham regarded John XXII as actually heretical, this matter of the pope's deposition was no mere theory for him but a real issue. Contrary to Marsilius and other conciliarists, Ockham holds that the Council may err. Its fallibility does not, however, nullify Christ's promise that He would remain "with [the faithful] to the end of the world." That promise would be fulfilled even if all believers but one were to fall into error.[21]

In the *Breviloquium* Ockham repeats many of the ideas expounded previously but adds some new ones. He violently denounces the abuses of the Avignonese papacy on the ground that "the Christian law is the law of perfect liberty." He reaffirms the thesis that Scripture is the ultimate criterion of Christian faith and applies historical and dialectical, rather than allegorical, methods of interpretation to it. He thereby combats the defenders of the absolute papal power, such as Augustinus Triumphus of Ancona, James of Viterbo, and Alvarez Pelayo. Ockham further invokes the authority of the Fathers, particularly of Augustine. He defines papal power as limited by natural and spiritual laws. The papal office is not a *dominium* but a *ministerium*. If the pope exceeds his prerogatives, no one is in duty bound to obey him. The true aim of the papal office is the common good, not the benefit of papal or other private parties. "*Bonum commune*

---

[20] "Ockham, the Conciliar Theory, and the Canonists." *Journal of the History of Ideas*, XV (1954), pp. 40–70.

[21] Gewirth, *op. cit.*, I, 289.

preferendum est bono privato." Christ did not entrust the feeding of His sheep to Peter for Peter's benefit, but for the sheep's well-being. Christianity, in contrast to the Mosaic law, is *"libertas evangelica."* The faithful are not slaves (*servi*); to impose obligations on them contrary to or beyond the natural or spiritual laws is tyranny.

In dealing with the power of popes in temporal matters Ockham, in the first place, asserts that Christ did not claim it for Himself and consequently did not grant it to His disciples. In fact, He taught them not to exercise such power as the kings wielded over their subjects. "It shall not be so among you." The authority of the popes and the prelates is, therefore, limited to the spiritual realm. Ockham further cites the provision of the *Decretum*[22] that if a bishop, priest, or deacon assumes secular duties, he should be deprived of his ecclesiastical office. Peter in his first epistle wrote: "Be subject for the Lord's sake to every human institution, whether it be of the emperor as supreme or governors." Likewise Paul instructed the Roman Christians to "be subject to the governing authorities."[23] Thus the seculars possess rule over temporalities by divine authority, just as the ecclesiastics receive from Christ authority in spiritual matters.

In his last tract, *De imperatorum et pontificum potestate,* Ockham justifies his opposition to the Avignonese papacy. He charges it with "doing grave and enormous injuries to all Christ's faithful by attempting to rule all Christians tyrannically and . . . by persecuting those who are so bold as to dispute its power and its good intentions. Hence, in the universities and other schools no doctor or lector dares propose or accept for discussion and determination any question whatever that concerns the power of the pope." He therefore repudiates the papacy in a frank statement:

I confess openly that it can be truly charged against me that I am withdrawing from the obedience of the Avignonese Church and from the society of the multitude of friars minor for no other reason . . . than that the said Church of Avignon holds errors and manifest heresies. It pertinaciously approves, defends, and does not desist from exercising the gravest and enormous injuries and injustices . . . against the rights and liberties of the faithful, great and small, lay and clerical, to the danger of entire Christendom. These injustices the whole multitude of friars minor often actually supports, asserts, and holds.[24]

[22] Friedberg, I, 307.
[23] I Peter 2:13; Romans 13:1.
[24] Scholz, II, 454.

The papacy further injures the Roman Empire by claiming that the pope has the right to dispose of it and to subject it to himself. Ockham charges that by these means the papacy incites wars among the subjects of the emperor by absolving them from obedience to their rulers. He further asserts that the pope deprives the cathedral chapters of their elective rights and disposes of the benefices as he pleases. He declares that "by divine right the pope has no other powers than ... those that are necessary to the salvation, rule and government of the faithful."

After the outbreak of the Great Schism, conciliarism found its most eloquent and effective exponents in some masters of the University of Paris. The movement was then spurred by the urgent need for dealing with the dire situation created by the division of the Church between the two popes. It was initiated by the canonist Conrad of Gelnhausen with his *Epistola brevis* (1379). He called for the assembling of a general Council, but his voice was not heeded. Conrad, thereupon, published another, larger treatise, the *Epistola concordiae* (1380), in which he formulated his conciliar proposals in greater detail. He asserted that the Church does not consist of the pope and the cardinals, but is the *congregatio fidelium*. Of this universal Church Christ alone is the head; the pope holds only a secondary position in it, since he may err. Conrad's chief contribution consisted in the advocacy of the principle of *epikeia*, by which the ordinary canonical provisions might be superseded whenever the needs of the Church demanded the resort to extraordinary measures. *Salus populi suprema lex est*—necessity is above the positive law. Unfortunately, this work was likewise ignored.

Conrad found an ally in another Paris master, the vice-chancellor of the university, Henry of Langenstein. The latter worked out a detailed program for dealing with the schism in his *Epistola pacis* and later in the *Epistola concilii pacis*. The latter treatise was partly dependent on Conrad; it was later used by both Cardinal d'Ailly and Gerson.[25]

We may pass over any extended discussion of the program of these pioneers in order to concentrate on the three outstanding conciliarists who were directly influential in the practical measures adopted for the termination of the schism. They were Pierre d'Ailly, Jean Gerson, and Francesco Zabarella.

[25] Cf. my essay, "Conciliarism as Reform," in *Advocates of Reform, Library of Christian Classics,* XIV, 95, notes 5–7. The complete translation of Langenstein's "Letter on Behalf of a Council of Peace" is found in Cameron's unpublished doctoral dissertation, "Conciliarism in Theory and Practice, 1378–1418," II, 1–92.

Pierre d'Ailly (1350–1420) was born of a family of *"la bonne bourgeoisie"* in Compiègne. He was trained at the College of Navarre of the University of Paris, receiving his doctorate in theology in 1381. A disciple of William of Ockham, whose *Dialogus* he copied in an abbreviated form for his own use, he remained a faithful adherent of his master throughout his life. Nevertheless, he did not accept all of Ockham's radical ideas. He became rector of the College of Navarre and chancellor of the University of Paris. In his early career he was said to have been positively radical in his theological views. As an Ockhamist he regarded the Scriptures, in his *Recommendatio sacrae Scripturae*, as "this Rock (*petra*) upon which Christ's Church is built." [26] Having also been influenced by his colleagues at the university, Conrad of Gelnhausen and Henry of Langenstein, d'Ailly embraced conciliar views. He gave expression to them early in 1381 in his *Epistola diaboli Leviathan*.[27] This savage satire is cast in the form of a letter written by the devil "to all the prelates of the Church of his kingdom." He bids them fight against all who desire to call a general Council for the termination of the papal schism. The "ruler of this world" rejoices in the disunity of the prelates professing themselves partisans of either Urban, Clement, or the future general Council. He ridicules the conciliarists by calling them frogs who "cease not to croak with raucous voice from the depths of their mud, 'General Council, general Council!'" Instead of following the Scriptures, he bids them to "follow . . . the laws of Justinian and the decrees of Gratian because such works of human inspiration are in the present conflict useful for teaching, arguing, and correcting."

D'Ailly was elevated to the episcopacy by Pope Benedict XIII, at first to the see of Le Puy and later to Cambrai. Nevertheless, when in 1408 thirteen cardinals deserted their respective popes, Gregory and Benedict, in order to call a Council to end the schism, he did not hesitate to support the dissidents. On January 1, 1409, he wrote a letter to the cardinals at Pisa, with which he enclosed his treatise, the *Propositiones utiles*. Its translater, Francis Oakley, regards it as the summary of "all the arguments basic to the Conciliar position." [28]

[26] Louis E. du Pin, ed., *Johannes Gersonii Opera omnia* (Antwerp, 1706), I, 656.
[27] Irwin W. Raymond, trans., "D'Ailly's Epistola Diaboli Leviathan" in *Church History*, XXII (1953), 181 ff.
[28] Francis Oakley, trans., "The 'propositiones utiles' of Pierre d'Ailly, an Epitome of Conciliar Theory" in *Church History*, XXIX (1960), 398 ff.

In this treatise d'Ailly repeats the familiar thesis that the mystical body of Christ, of which He alone is the head, comprises the whole Christian Church. Its unity inheres in Christ. The pope, as the vicar of Christ, "can be said to be the head of the Church" as its principal minister; nevertheless, "the unity of the Church does not necessarily depend upon—or originate from—the unity with the pope." The mystical body of Christ possesses its authority directly from its head. This power includes the calling of general Councils, although the Church possesses it as well on the basis of common laws. These laws are contained in the *Decretum* and the *Decretales*, and although the popes succeeded in limiting them, they have never deprived the Church of them altogether. "In certain cases [the Church] can hold a general Council without the authority of the pope ... indeed, against his wishes." In the event of necessity the positive laws, as Aristotle teaches, must give place to the principle of *epikeia*, i.e., equity. Such necessity has arisen in the papal schism; hence, the assembling of the Council of Pisa is legitimate.

In 1411 d'Ailly received the red hat from the hands of Pope John XXIII. Nevertheless, in the Council of Constance he stoutly maintained the conciliar principles that militated against the pope's personal interests. He insisted that the plenitude of power and inerrancy of faith are possessed only by the universal Church. The episcopal and priestly power derives from Christ, not from the pope. The latter's office is administrative, executive, not absolute. He is a minister, not the lord, of the Church. He holds superiority *in* the Council, but not *over* it. He can err, in fact he may be a heretic. Preferably the cardinals should be elected from all the provinces of the Church. They would thus be truly representative of the entire body of the faithful. Contrary to many conciliarists, he held that the Council may err in faith. In fact, he quoted approvingly the opinion "of some great doctors that the general Council can err not only in fact or even in law but, what is greater, in faith." [29] D'Ailly accordingly sedulously refrained from ascribing inerrancy to the Council. He furthermore placed the necessity of reforms as high as its unity. He declared: "There is no

---

[29] "Conclusiones Cardinalis Cameracensis cum quibusdam additionibus," in J. D. Mansi, ed., *Sacrorum conciliorum nova et amplissima collectio* (Florence and Paris, 1757–1927), XXVII, 547. Also Hefele-Leclercq, *Histoire des Conciles,* VII/I, 178; L. Salembrier, in *Dictionnaire de Theologie Catholique,* I, 648.

real union without reformation, but also no real reformation without union." [30]

In October, 1416, d'Ailly read in one of the Constance churches his *De ecclesiastica potestate*; this, in the judgment of Agnes E. Roberts, "contains some of the most important points in d'Ailly's theory of the ecclesiastical polity and also the most striking instances of his debt to Ockham." [31] He likens the pope's and the cardinals' position to that of Peter and of the other apostles. All spiritual powers were common to all the apostles with the exception of the *potestas positionis ministrarum*. Hence, with the same exception, they are likewise common to the Church's ministers, who derive their powers directly from Christ. The pope is but the *primus inter pares* even though the ministerial order to some degree depends on him. The Roman Church's primacy rests on the fact that Peter chose Rome as his see in preference to Antioch; were the pope to move elsewhere, he would forfeit this privilege. The right of election of the pope belongs to the cardinals, but only because the Roman community has ordained it in this manner, not because it is of divine right. Moreover, the Romans act in behalf of the Church universal in electing the pope, since besides being the Roman bishop he also holds primacy in the universal Church. All communities in Christendom have the right to elect their lay and ecclesiastical rulers, although they may and do empower some other body to perform this task for them. The election of bishops, as a matter of fact, has become the prerogative of the prelates; but this does not negate the original right of the community. No community should have a ruler imposed upon it against its will. Miss Roberts regards this as "a startling example of d'Ailly's debt to Ockham." [32] She concludes her essay by asserting that d'Ailly, "the stern prosecutor of John Hus and Jerome of Prague," is revealed in his works as having been inspired by "the arch-heretic of the fourteenth century"—William of Ockham. [33]

In November, 1416, d'Ailly published his *Tractate on the Reformation of the Church*. [34] He urges that Councils be held frequently to deal

[30] Quoted in John H. Mundy's Introduction, Loomis, *op. cit.*, p. 12.
[31] Roberts, "Pierre d'Ailly and the Council of Constance," in *Transactions of the Royal Historical Society* (London, 1935), 4th series, XVIII, 133.
[32] *Ibid.*, p. 136.
[33] *Ibid.*, p. 139.
[34] This treatise, translated by Cameron, is found in his "Conciliarism in Theory and Practice," II, 189–233.

with matters of faith as well as other current problems, such for instance, as the reunion with the Greeks. "It would be exceedingly dangerous," he writes, "to entrust our faith to the will of one man." In proposing the reform of the papal system he warns against elevating unworthy men to the papal throne. They should be both learned and of exemplary morals. The papal exactions should be reduced to a "reasonable" sum from each diocese. Cardinals and prelates should not hold "a monstrous multitude of benefices." He protests against the proliferation of new decretals, canons, and statutes whereby heavy and oppressive burdens are laid on the people. The major excommunication should be imposed only for mortal sins instead of being used as a weapon in defense of papal or episcopal prerogatives. Benefices should not be reserved by the papacy.

In proposing reforms affecting the greater prelates, he complains that the members of the Council resist their own reformation while they eagerly demand reformation of others. The higher dignities should not be conferred "on youths, indiscreet, uncontrollable, carnal, and ignorant of things spiritual, but on men ripe in years and experience, outstanding in spiritual knowledge and teaching." They should "study the Holy Scriptures, not give themselves over completely to legal and practical sciences." D'Ailly advocates the elimination of titular bishops. The Council should compel the bishops to practice frugality, modesty in dress, and devotion to the duties of their office. They should seek to excel in the performance of their spiritual duties rather than in "filling up their treasuries." Simony is to be strictly forbidden. Engaging in warfare on the part of bishops is "a hideous abuse."

The monastic orders must likewise be reformed. For one thing, there are too many of them. The mendicant orders particularly should be limited in their membership and forbidden to usurp the revenues of the clergy. Monks should not be allowed to leave their monasteries except for study, preferably theology. Nunneries "have been disgraced more than I dare say." Nuns should not be allowed to beg or to "run around."

As for the parochial priests, only the well-deserving should be granted the more prominent benefices. Thus "the foolish and ignorant would not be preferred to the learned and wise, or youths to old men, or strangers and those foreign in life, language and customs to the native born." Morals of the clergy must be reformed, for priests "have now been completely corrupted by wrath, gluttony, lechery, pomp, prodigality, sloth and other kinds of vice." Concubinage must be abolished and priests guilty of it must be suspended or excommunicated. The universities training the clergy must grant degrees only for merit, not favor; moreover, clerics must be taught useful doctrines, not novelties. Also there must be libraries in cathedral and larger churches.

And finally, lay members, particularly the nobility and those in civil authority, must again become conscious of their duty to support the Church and to defend the Christian faith against the Moslem and the Jew. D'Ailly concludes the treatise by writing: "Thus it is obvious that a reformation of ecclesiastics is necessary, since the deformation of their practices is so dangerous and so harmful to all faithful people."

It may be noted, however, that as a member of the college of cardinals d'Ailly seems later to have shared his colleagues' resentment of the limitation of their prerogatives, imposed on them by the Council. The cardinals, after all, had only one vote as against the four, and later five, votes of the nations comprising the Council. One such indication of his resentment may be seen in his refusal to attend the session which adopted, on April 6, 1415, the radical declaration of the Council's supreme authority in the decree *Sacrosancta*. Salembrier explains it on the ground that d'Ailly doubted the validity of "those schismatic decisions" and never submitted to them. This seems scarcely in harmony with his lifelong advocacy of the Council's superiority to the pope and the curia. Another such indication is afforded by d'Ailly's arguing in behalf of the authority of the cardinals when the decree *Frequens*, subjecting the papacy to the periodic meetings of the Councils, was adopted. He claimed that the prerogatives of the cardinals were thereby unduly limited.

Jean Charlier de Gerson (1363–1429) was educated at the College of Navarre under Pierre d'Ailly. He was henceforth associated with him, particularly in the conciliar movement. Although he was a nominalist, he successfully combined this system with mysticism.[35] Mystical theology was for him superior to the scholastic, because it dealt with the heart, not only the intellect. In 1395, at the age of thirty-two, Gerson succeeded d'Ailly as chancellor of the University of Paris; he was also appointed canon of Notre Dame. His influence at the Council

---

[35] Heiko A. Oberman, "Gabriel Biel and Later Medieval Mysticism," in *Church History*, XXXI (1961), 264 ff. Also his *Harvest of Medieval Theology*, pp. 331–40.

of Pisa is evidenced by his *Tractatus de unitate ecclesiastica* (1409), which almost constituted that Council's reform program. He warned the Council against electing a new pope before it made certain that the two popes, Benedict XIII and Gregory XII, deposed as schismatics and heretics, were deserted by the nations supporting them. In his treatise Gerson argues that "the mystical body of the Church, perfectly established by Christ has, no less than any civil, mystical, or truly natural body, the right and power to procure its own union. It is not in accordance with the absolute and immutable law, divine or natural, that the Church should be unable to assemble or unite without the pope." He observes further that "the unity of the Church in one vicar of Christ does not require for its attainment at the present time a literal observance of the outward terms of positive law.... This general Council may proceed summarily, and with the good and important [principle] of equity. It shall have sufficient judicial authority to use the *epikeia*."[36]

When the English delegation on the way to Pisa stopped at Paris, Gerson preached a sermon before it in which he stresses that the Church is established by God, while the papacy, although a permanent institution, "fluctuates" with the succession of the popes. "Popes pass, the papacy endures."[37] After the Council of Pisa, Gerson sought to justify its action by his treatise, the *De auferabilitate papae ab ecclesiae*.

Among the greatest services rendered by Gerson to the conciliar cause was the preaching, on March 23, 1415, immediately after Pope John's flight, of his sermon before the Council of Constance.[38] He declared that the Church is united to its head, Christ, by the bond of the Holy Spirit. As such, it is more than a corporation governed by canon law. The general Council representing this Church must be obeyed by all, including the pope; anyone refusing to do so is to be held as "a gentile and a publican." In another sermon, delivered on June 21, 1415, after the abdication of Pope Gregory XII, Gerson declared that

a general Council, although it cannot nor ought to withdraw or diminish the plenitude of papal power entrusted by Christ to Peter and his succes-

---

[36] Du Pin, *op. cit.*, II, 113–18; Spinka, *op. cit.*, pp. 141–43. The entire treatise is translated by Cameron, *op. cit.*, II, 93–114. Gerson's "Tractate on Ecclesiastical Power and the Origin of Right and Law," *Ibid.*, pp. 115–88.

[37] "Propositio facta coram Anglicis," in du Pin, *op. cit.*, II, 123–30.

[38] Du Pin, *op. cit.*, II, 205; E. F. Jacob, *Essays in the Conciliar Epoch* (Manchester, the University Press, 1953), pp. 11–14.

sors . . . can nevertheless limit the use of that power by definite laws and statutes for the edification of the Church.

He further insisted that the Council could decide matters of faith and morals. It could likewise condemn whatever it deemed wrong, even though such an action could not be supported "expressly from the bare text of the Holy Scriptures." [39]

In spite of the assertions to the contrary by such writers as Connolly and Morrall,[40] clearly motivated by the currently fashionable rejection or denigration of nominalism, Gerson remained an adherent of the basic philosophical and theological positions of Ockham. Although he was increasingly dominated by Bonaventura's mysticism, this did not militate against his nominalism, since its chief protagonists were Bonaventura's Franciscans, as against the Thomistic Dominicans. Gerson, nevertheless, went beyond d'Ailly in advocating the permanent necessity of supervision of the papacy by general Councils. This tutelage and subordination of the papacy to the Councils, as provided by the decree *Frequens*, went beyond the doctrine of *epikeia*, which contemplated an extracanonical action only in times of exceptional crises. Perhaps Gerson was motivated by the assumption that, once the schism was terminated, the papacy was likely to repudiate the conciliar theory. In this prevision he was right.

Finally, it is important to consider briefly the views of Francesco Zabarella, cardinal-deacon of Florence, because of the important role he played both before the calling of the Councils of Pisa and Constance and during their sessions. He was the most distinguished canonist among the conciliarists of that period.[41] His *Tractatus de schismate* was based on the views of the earlier decretists and decretalists, including the earliest conciliarist, John of Paris. His views, in Tierney's judgment, "seem essentially the same as those put forward by John of Paris . . . although modified to meet the particular problems of the Schism." [42] As a jurist, Zabarella regarded the Church as a corporation presided over by the pope. The views held by such men as Wyclif and Hus seemed to him to threaten "the very foundations of medieval

[39] Du Pin, *op. cit.*, II, 247, 279.
[40] James I. Connolly, *John Gerson, Reformer and Mystic* (Louvain, Libraire universitaire, 1928), p. 352.
[41] A. Kneer, *Kardinal Zabarella; ein Beitrag zur Geschichte des abendländischen Schisma* (Münster, 1891); and particularly Tierney, *Foundations of the Conciliar Theory,* chap. IV.
[42] Tierney, *op. cit.*, p. 221

Catholicism." Zabarella regarded the concept of the Church as an authoritative, canonically regulated corporation best fitted to combat the current subversive tendencies. It sufficed to deal with the schism as the immediate problem as well as its later developments, which he perhaps did not clearly envisage but correctly anticipated. The general Council, then, was the best means for realizing his principles. He held that although the canon law required that the pope call the Council, the right devolves on the cardinals when he refuses to do so. Should they fail to act in such an emergency, the duty falls upon the emperor as the representative of the whole *populus*. Zabarella's whole treatise was thus centered in the idea that the papal power is of "a limited and derivative authority conferred upon the head of the corporation by its members." [43] Thus the concept of the *congregatio fidelium*, subtly transformed by him into a legal corporation, represented the supreme authority of the Church. The pope possessed only such powers as were conferred upon him, and must not go beyond them. The idea was most forcibly expressed by him in the dictum "[*Universitas*] *totius ecclesiae non habet superiorem nisi Deum et papam cum bene administrat*." [44] He is, therefore, a worthy member of the company of the illustrious conciliarists of the Council of Constance.

Among the prominent and influential members of the Council deserving to be mentioned along with the judges of Hus was Dietrich of Niem (1340–1418).[45] He was a high official of the curia who, toward the end of his life, served Pope John XXIII. Despite the close curial ties, he became a radical exponent of the conciliar principles. His most important treatise, published first in 1410, was entitled *De modis uniendi ac reformandi ecclesiae*.[46] It was revised just before the meeting of the Council of Constance for use by that assembly. At the Council Dietrich strenuously advocated not only the deposition of all three popes but also a radical reform of the curia and the Church generally. He urged that, even if the schism were terminated, no appreciable improvement could be achieved unless the curia were drastically reformed. Professor E. P. Jacob summarized his estimate of Dietrich in the following judgment:

[43] *Ibid.*, p. 225.
[44] *Ibid.*, p. 226.
[45] Jacob, *op. cit.*, pp. 24–43.
[46] H. Heimpel, *De modis uniendi ac reformandi ecclesiae*, in *Dialog über Union und Reform der Kirche* (Leipzig, 1933). It is translated by Cameron, *op. cit.*, II, 226–348. My quotations are taken from the translation.

Of Dietrich two things may be affirmed. Nobody before him had stated the case for the Council so completely from the legal and administrative point of view; and no man of his period burned with a fiercer desire for that justice apart from which every kingdom is nothing but robbery on a large scale.[47]

Dietrich's reform program as detailed in his *De modis* clearly shows his dependence on William of Ockham and Marsilius of Padua. Like them, he distinguishes between two churches, the Catholic and the Apostolic. They stand to each other in the relation of genus and species. The former is composed of "the Greeks, Latins, and barbarians who believe in Christ." They constitute one body the head of which is Christ. "The pope cannot and ought not be called the head of this Church, but only the vicar of Christ, his vicegerent on earth," so long as he does not err. Salvation is found in the Catholic Church. Christ has communicated his teaching to it and has endowed it with the power of binding and loosing sins. It can never err, and it has never suffered schism or heresy.

The Apostolic Church, on the other hand, is a particular Church; and, as such, is included in the Church Catholic. It comprises the pope, the cardinals, the bishops and the lay members. It is commonly called the Roman Church. "It may err and may have erred, may deceive and be deceived, may suffer schism and heresy, and may even cease to exist." Since for the time being the Apostolic Church is torn among the three rival popes, there is in it "a complete abandonment of good moral practices, for simony, avarice, the sale of benefices, tyranny and cruelty hold sway." Dietrich adds: "Is is hard to think that the son of a Venetian fisherman [Pope Gregory XII] should occupy the papacy to the detriment of the common good of the whole Church . . . and that he should be the cause of so much discord and scandal." "It is ridiculous to think that one mortal man should say of himself that he has the power of binding and loosing of sins in heaven and on earth, and yet be a son of perdition, a simoniac, a miser, a liar, an exactor, a fornicator, one who is proud, pompous, and worse than the devil." Dietrich thus imposes character qualifications on the pope, just as Hus did. Dietrich cites Pope Alexander as having, prior to his election to the papacy, desired to reform the Church. "He even used to speak of this to me. . . . But when he was made pope he did not strive to let it see the light."

[47] Jacob, *op. cit.*, p. 43.

The reforms must be enacted at a general Council convened at a safe place. "I say that the faithful of Christ are not slaves under the law but free men under grace." They are not bound to come "to a place that is not safe." The reform must take the form of a return to the ancient canons. "Let her [the Catholic Church] limit the misused papal power contained in the *Decretum* and the *Decretales* and the pretended power in the *Sext* and *Clementines,* not to mention other papal constitutions." Papal power must be restricted to the spiritual realm, for Christ did not empower Peter "to bestow benefices, to possess kingdoms, castles and cities, and to deprive emperors and kings [of their rule]." As for the pope, he must be "learned in the highest degree." It is his supreme duty to teach the Christian faith and to use wisely the keys of knowledge and spiritual power. The Council should enact "the limiting and moderation of the power of this one shepherd which is now excessive and which has deprived the other prelates [of their rights]. . . . Let there be a reformation and renewal of the ancient laws, decrees, and customary procedures of the primitive Church." This reform must extend to the cardinals, bishops, and all other prelates as well. The abusive privileges granted to the four mendicant orders should be rescinded and all monasteries and nunneries be reformed. The universities must likewise be regulated "lest doctors and masters be easily promoted."

These reforms, urged by a high curial official, show clearly the need of them, and go far to justify similar efforts on the part of Hus. In fact, it is difficult to understand why such earnest reformers as Dietrich, d'Ailly, and Gerson could assume a condemnatory attitude toward Hus, for their own reforms were in many aspects not very different from his, and in some cases even exceeded those of Hus. This applies particularly to Dietrich, who, in 1411, urged a forcible extermination of the Bohemian "heretics" without even a papal investigation.

LEADERS OF THE CZECH REFORM PRIOR TO JOHN HUS

Into this background of the conciliar movement the Czech native reform movement, both prior to and under the leadership of John Hus, must be integrated. The Czech reform was not conciliar in its basic character, but primarily stresed moral virtues. As such it was akin to the "*devotio moderna*" of the Rhineland and the Low Countries, or to the radical reform program of Dietrich of Niem. It was not interested in theological reformation for its own sake, but only as this was necessitated by the demands of the truly Christian life. This purpose, however, was closely associated with the emphasis upon the Scriptures, upon preaching, and upon "apostolic poverty," such as that advocated by the spiritual Franciscans. All these features remained characteristic of the Czech reform movement throughout its course.

The movement was initiated by an Austrian preacher, Conrad Waldhauser,[48] who was called to Prague in 1363 by Emperor Charles IV. An Augustinian canon, Waldhauser emphasized preaching and the study of the Scriptures. Among those who were deeply influenced by his earnest preaching and blameless life was Milíč of Kroměříž (d. 1374),[49] known as the father of the Czech Reformation. He had originally served in the imperial chancery as a notary. In 1361, however, he was appointed a canon of St. Vitus Cathedral. He then received the priestly ordination and soon obtained another lucrative position. Two years later, he surrendered these posts to devote himself exclusively to evangelizing, and began his ministry at the St. Nicholas Church. At first he met with scant success because, being a Moravian by birth, he amused his Czech audiences by occasionally falling into his native dialect. By perseverance he overcame these initial difficulties and later captivated his hearers by his burning eloquence and evident earnestness. After this initial success he preached also in German and Latin, delivering from two to five sermons a day. His sermons were thoroughly biblical rather than scholastic. His strict ascetic manner of life also attracted adherents, since it was in sharp contrast to the loose, licentious, and avaricious life common among the clergy. He stressed voluntary poverty and the subjugation of the body in a manner reminiscent of the early spiritual Franciscans. He was likewise tireless in the service of the poor, ill, and sinful. He held that the true Church is the congregation of the elect, predestined to salvation before all ages. The Scriptures are the supreme rule of doctrine and life, and the sacrament of the altar is the spiritual medicine of the soul. Because of his insistence on clerical poverty and the denunciation of immorality, he came into conflict with the higher clergy and the monks. The woeful moral state of the clergy of all ranks and their determined antagonism to his reform induced him to entertain the then popular

---

[48] F. Loskot, *Konrád Waldhauser* (Praha, 1909).
[49] Odložilík, *Jan Milíč z Kroměříže* (Kroměříž, 1924); also F. Hrejsa, *Dějiny křestanství v Československu* (Praha, 1947), I, 183 ff.

speculation about the imminent coming of Antichrist. By computing the Danielic prophecy (as many before and after him have done), he concluded that Antichrist had appeared in 1365–67. He was, however, uncertain of his identity. At first he dared to consider Emperor Charles IV for the post, and in 1366 actually pointed him out from among his hearers when the emperor happened to attend his preaching. For this daring act he was arrested by the order of the archbishop, but was released when Charles magnanimously intervened in his behalf. Milíč then decided to go to Rome to consult Pope Urban V in the matter. While waiting for the pope, who delayed his departure from Avignon, he wrote him a letter announcing the appearance of Antichrist and nailed it on the door of St. Peter's. Thereupon he was thrown in jail. When Urban arrived in Rome on October 16, 1367, Milíč was released. The pope quieted his fears. Milíč then no longer looked for a personified Antichrist, but identified him with the evils of the Church. Thus reassured, he returned to Prague, and threw himself into his work with renewed enthusiasm. His concern for fallen women was particularly great. In order to restore them to moral life, he secured from his friends means for the building of a house of refuge as well as for supporting some three hundred of them there. He named the refuge Jerusalem.

His reform zeal, however, and particularly his insistence on apostolic poverty, aroused stubborn clerical opposition against him. His enemies composed twelve articles charging him with heresy and sectarianism and sent them to Pope Gregory XI at Avignon. In 1374 Milíč undertook the journey to the papal residence to clear himself of the accusation. Before the trial was concluded, he died there on June 29, 1374.

Another outstanding representative of the Czech reform is the learned master of the University of Paris, Matthew of Janov (c. 1355–93)[50] who, before his sojourn in Paris, was deeply stirred by Milíč. He studied there from 1373 to 1381. Having received his master's degree, he entered the theological faculty for another six years' study and devoted himself to the study of the Scriptures. From Paris he went to Rome, where he secured from Pope Urban VI a reservation to a benefice in Bohemia. Returning to Prague, he was indeed received as a titular canon of the cathedral, but others preceded him in actual occupancy and deprived him of the benefice. In 1381 the archbishop

---

[50] Kybal, *Matěj z Janova, jeho život, spisy a učení*; also Novotný, *Náboženské hnutí české v 14. a 15. století*, I, 146 ff.

appointed him a confessor at the cathedral and seven years later granted him a poor, pastoral charge. He kept it until his death, but entrusted its duties to a vicar. Instead, he preached in Czech at two Prague churches, basing himself on the Bible in the true spirit of Milíč. These reform efforts raised an outcry against him. He denounced formalism in worship, an excessive veneration, if not worship, of images and the saints, and avarice of the clergy. He deplored the increasing resort to legal concepts in the administration of the Church; to him, the Church was the communion of believers, the body of Christ. He also urged frequent communion by laymen—a practice strictly forbidden in 1388, when a synod restricted it to one communion a month. At the clerical synod held the next year he and his followers were placed on trial. He was induced to recant his opposition to images, to the veneration of the relics of saints, and his urging of daily communion by laymen. As a punishment, he was forbidden to preach for a half year. Later he regretted this act as a craven weakness and inwardly remained convinced of the truth of his position. One of his adherents, Priest Jacob, had to recant his assertion that the Virgin or the saints can afford aid to no one; that prayers for the dead profit them nothing; that anyone may forcibly take the elements from the priest refusing to grant him communion; and that relics of the saints could be burned or trampled upon without guilt. He dared to say that he would use a statue of the Virgin as wood for boiling his peas. He was suspended from the ministry for ten years.

This harsh experience taught Matthew to devote himself even more assiduously to the study of Scripture and made him its resolute defender and persuasive exponent. He writes, "When I read Augustine . . . and Jerome . . . immediately my soul adhered to the Scriptures with an eternal love; and I confess that from my youth until my old age . . . it did not leave me, neither while traveling nor at home, neither while working nor at leisure." [51] It became his almost exclusive source of doctrine and preaching. This profound study resulted in his great work, for which he is particularly remembered, the five-volume corpus entitled, the *Regulae veteris et novi testamenti*.[52] This vast work served as the source of inspiration for the subsequent leaders of the Czech reform movement, particularly Jakoubek of Stříbro. Matthew included

[51] Novotný, *Náboženské hnutí*, p. 159.
[52] Kybal, ed., *Regulae veteris et novi testamenti* (Inspruck, 1908–13), Vols. I–IV; Odložilík, ed., *Regulae* (Praha, 1926), Vol. V.

in it treatises of earlier reformers, such as Milíč's *Prophetia et revelatio de Antichristo* and William of Saint-Amour's antimonastic *De periculis novissimorum temporum*. He asserts that the supreme teacher of truth is Jesus Christ, while the Holy Spirit suffices to lead men into a fuller apprehension of Christ's revelation of God. The law of love is found in the Holy Scriptures. Only by faith working through love, not by scholastic learning, may a man apprehend spiritual truths. This faith must be manifested in a holy life of apostolic poverty. Such as possess it are the elect, chosen by God's predestinating grace. Matthew distinguishes between the Church comprising both the elect and the foreknown, and the communion of saints, of which only the elect are members. The elect alone constitute the one congregation of saints, the mystical body of Christ, of which He is the head. The foreknown, on the contrary, are the body of Antichrist. The Church had continued in its pristine purity until about 1200; thereafter it degenerated, a state which culminated in the Great Schism of 1378. The awakening began about 1350 with the appearance of the true preachers of Christ. Since then the Church has been gradually renewed by them. In Avignon the supreme see has been occupied by Antichrist, beginning with Clement VII. Matthew relied upon the secular lords and the people, not the general Council, for reforming the Church, since the spiritual arm has been wielded by Antichrist. But this is not enough. A return to Christ and His gospel must also take place in order that the entire Church be reformed in head and members. Furthermore, to make the "law of God"—Scripture—available to all, either Matthew himself or his circle translated the entire Bible into the Czech. Just a year before his death, he was cited before the general vicar of the archbishop, John of Pomuky, to clear himself of charges of heresy. He was requested to bring with him two of his works, one Latin and the other Czech. Professor Bartoš assumes that the latter could be none other than the Czech translation of the Bible.[53]

This brief survey of some of the chief representatives of the Czech reform provides a certain indispensable amount of background enabling us to place Hus in the "apostolic succession" of the movement. It would, nevertheless, be inexcusable to leave this preliminary subject without a mention of John Wyclif (1328–84).[54] Wyclif's teaching had

---

[53] Bartoš, *Čechy v době Husově* (Praha, 1947), p. 251.
[54] Of the extensive literature dealing with Wyclif, Herbert B. Workman's *John Wyclif* (2 vols., London, 1926), still ranks as the standard reference.

become so closely integrated with the native Czech reform, particularly from the 1390s on, that a brief treatment of his thought is essential. We need not take time to recount the familiar story of his life and service in the employ of the English crown prior to the Great Schism. It was during this time that he developed the double-edged thesis of the "lordships," both secular and ecclesiastical. They were granted by God, the absolute suzerain, on condition that the possessors remain "in grace." Once that condition was broken, the holder of the privilege no longer retained it by divine right; hence, in the case of ecclesiastical lordship, he should be deprived of it by secular authority.

We shall concern ourselves principally with Wyclif's theologically far more important reaction to the Great Schism, which called forth his radical repudiation of the then current thought and practice of the Church. His reform proposals made a profound impression on the contemporary thinkers in general and the Czech religious leaders in particular.[55] As a presupposition of his entire theological system, how-ever, one must bear in mind that Wyclif was a philosophical realist, an adherent of the Augustinian-Anselmic realism, and thus stood in sharp contrast to the ruling nominalism that regarded universals as constructs of the mind without independent existence. As S. Harrison Thomson defines Wyclif's philosophical views:

To sum up briefly his doctrine of read universals, then, we may say that distinct, productive archetypes (*ydee, raciones exemplares*) make up the divine mind. They are created by, coeternal with, yet inferior to God. They partake of his being. They therefore are real. They can and do communi-cate their content, which is being modified, to God's other and different creatures. These creatures then possess being in varying and diminishing degrees. Insofar as they possess being, we call them identical with God, always remembering their temporal, individual nature.[56]

Accordingly, no real thing can be annihilated: for instance, the sub-stance of the bread in the sacrament of the altar (as we shall see later).

Along with his philosophical realism, Wyclif's basic principle was that the Scriptures are the sole criterion of faith and practice. The work in which Wyclif stated his Scriptural principles most cogently is the *De veritate sacrae Scripturae* (1378), which abounds in references to St. Augustine, who held the same view. He quotes other great

[55] Spinka, *op. cit.,* section on "Wyclif as Reformer," pp. 21 ff.

[56] Thomson, "The Philosophical Basis of Wyclif's Theology," *Journal of Reli-gion* (1931), pp. 86–116.

Augustinian theologians—Anselm, Hugh of St. Victor, Grosseteste—in support of the Scriptural all-sufficiency.[57] Since his initial task was to find an authority indisputably superior to that of the pope and the scholastic theology, he, as all the reformers before and after him, elevated the "law of God" to the place of supreme authority. Although the Church likewise recognized the Scriptures as normative, it was in practice governed more by the canon law and papal decisions than by Scriptural authority. For Wyclif, the Bible is "the standard of faith," "the supreme organ of divine revelation." It contains all truth. All dogmatic teaching and practice must conform to it.

In considering the concept of the Church from this Scriptural-Augustinian point of view, Wyclif defines it in his *De ecclesia* as "the universality of the predestinate." We shall frequently meet this definition among the Czech reformers, including Hus. The Church is composed of all the predestinate, present, sleeping, and triumphant, who have existed from the beginning of the world and shall exist to its end. Christ alone is the head of this His mystical body. Outside this invisible Church there is no salvation. To be sure, the foreknown are *in* the visible Church, but are not *of* it. Thus Wyclif repudiates the extreme papalist view that the Church consists of the pope and his cardinals. His doctrine of predestination undercuts all hierarchical, sacerdotal, and sacramentarian pretensions. As such, it is truly radical.

As for the papacy, he writes in the *De potestate papae* that, although Peter held the primacy among the apostles, it was on account of his preeminent faith and qualities of character. The primacy of the pope likewise rests on his character: if he is truly a follower of Christ and of Peter, he then rightly holds his office. If not, he is Antichrist. Nevertheless, even a worthy pope possesses only spiritual, not temporal, authority. At first Wyclif conceded that a pope might be of the predestinate and thus rightfully the head of the Roman Church. After 1380 he reached the radical, though illogical, conclusion that the pope is Antichrist.[58] The papal office should, therefore, be altogether abolished. Moreover, there is no difference between priests and bishops. All ecclesiastical offices, save that of deacon and priest, are of papal invention.

To theologians of his day the most offensive of his conclusions is

---

[57] William Mallard, "John Wyclif and the Tradition of Biblical Authority," *Church History* (1961), pp. 50 ff; William Stacey, *John Wyclif and Reform*.

[58] R. Buddensieg, ed., *John Wyclif's Polemical Works* (London, 1883), II, 691.

his repudiatiton of the dogma of transubstantiation adopted by the Fourth Lateran Council in 1215. This view is stated in *De eucharistia*. He claims for it the authority of three great doctors of the Church—Augustine, Ambrose, and Anselm. He also appeals to the recantation of Berengar of Tours made at the synod of Rome under Pope Nicholas in 1059, from which it was clear that the dogma of transubstantiation had not been held by the Church at that time.[59] In other words, what Wyclif denounces is the "modernity" of the dogma, in his day only some 165 years old, in favor of the ancient teaching of the Church. He considers himself not an innovator, but a restorer of the older and, in his estimation, purer doctrine. In brief, he teaches that the consecrated elements remain outwardly and materially what they are—bread and wine—but become sacramentally, inwardly, Christ's body and blood. He writes: Christ's body is "sacramentally, spiritually, and virtually [present] in every part of the consecrated host, even as the soul is in the body." He also cites Augustine's statement, "What is seen is the bread and the cup which the eye renounces; but what faith demands to be taught is that the bread is the body of Christ and the cup is his blood. These are called sacramental elements for the reason that in them one thing is seen and another is understood." [60] The believer then receives the elements spiritually, not materially. Only thus do they possess saving grace.

As for baptism, Wyclif distinguishes between baptism with water, blood, and the Spirit. Only the last-named is a saving ordinance. He rejects the other five sacraments—those of confirmation, priestly ordination, penance, marriage, and extreme unction. He also repudiates the rites of excommunication and of indulgences.

Although quite insufficient as a comprehensive treatment of Wyclif's tenets, this brief summary must suffice for our purpose. When the teaching of Wyclif became known in Bohemia, it powerfully affected the native movement already some three or four decades old. It quickly gained enthusiastic supporters among some outstanding leaders, particularly of Stanislav of Znojmo, Stephen Páleč, Stephen of Kolín, and Jakoubek of Stříbro; the latter, however, was more definitely influenced by the teaching of Matthew of Janov. The three first-named were members of the faculty of theology of the University of Prague.

---

[59] Spinka, *op. cit.*, pp. 67 f.

[60] *Ibid.*, pp. 61–62, 69. Augustine's statement is quoted from Friedberg, *op. cit.*, I, 1336.

Stanislav and Stephen of Kolín were Hus's revered teachers, while Stephen Páleč and Jakoubek were his intimate friends. Nevertheless, Hus, who at first had known only the philosophical works of Wyclif, which, as he said, "had opened his eyes," never completely adopted the Wyclifite tenets of his teachers. For that reason Hus played a subordinate but none the less important role in the movement until Stanislav and Páleč, having repudiated Wyclif, ceased to stand in the forefront of the party.

HUS'S LEADERSHIP OF THE REFORM MOVEMENT

After receiving his master of arts degree, Hus became a member of the faculty of arts, and from 1396 lectured for the next two years on Aristotle. Thereafter he chose to deal with Wyclif's philosophical works and, for that reason, copied for himself four treatises of the Oxford doctor. That they had a powerful effect on him is evident from the remark he wrote in the margin of one of the treatises still preserved at Stockholm: "Wyclif, Wyclif, you will unsettle many a man's mind!" Hus's original intention had been to become a priest. During his early student years his aims do not appear to have been noticeably different from those of the majority of similar aspirants who regarded the priesthood as a lucrative career. He used to join his fellow students in the merry pranks customary among them. He describes one such occasion when he had taken part in the shockingly blasphemous "Feast of the Ass." [61] In his "Last Will" sent before his departure for Constance to his friend and former pupil, Master Martin of Volyně, he bewails his former fondness for splendid apparel by writing: "I, too, a miserable wretch, am being rebuked for having made use of such things"; and further: "You know that, alas!, before becoming a priest, I gladly and often played chess, wasted time, and by that play have frequently provoked to anger both myself and others." [62] Hus does not mention when he became an earnest adherent of the reform movement, but it is clear that he did so before he was ordained. He became deacon in 1400 and received the priestly ordination a year later. When chosen preacher at the Bethlehem Chapel (1402) by the Czech university

---

[61] Hus, "Výklad modlitby Páně," in Žilka, *Vybrané spisy Mistra Jana Husi* (Jilemnice, n.d.), II, 419–20. Also Eustace J. Kitts, *In the Days of the Councils* (London, 1908), pp. 46–47.

[62] Cf. Part I of Peter's *Account*, p. 95.

masters, he began to take a prominent position among the leaders of the native reform. By that time he was acquainted to some extent with Wyclif's theological works. Jerome of Prague, who had studied at Oxford and had copied many of the works of the Oxford doctor, brought them back to Bohemia in 1401.

As the preacher of the Bethlehem Chapel, the already famous center of Czech reform, Hus succeeded the eloquent moderate realist, Stephen of Kolín. His preaching in the early years was traditionally orthodox. His sermons from the years 1401–03,[63] with the exception of later interpolations dealing with the communion in both bread and wine and with the Council of Constance, show no trace of Wyclif's influence. They are addressed almost exclusively to his lay hearers, exhorting them "to follow Christ," demanding of them true repentance and the pursuit of holiness. In these demands he does not spare even kings and nobles. As for the clergy, he mentions them sparingly and criticizes them mildly. Throughout these sermons the Church is not defined extensively. Hus refers, nevertheless, to "the elect" as constituting its membership. In commenting on the Prologue of John's Gospel, he writes: "But the Scripture says: Those that are born of God, namely by His election from eternity, are born of Him." [64] The doctrine that the predestinate alone are the sons of God is, of course, orthodox; Augustine and Thomas Aquinas, as well as Wyclif and Hus, were predestinarians.

The next volume of his sermons, entitled the *Collecta*,[65] contains ninety-nine sermons for the church year of 1404–05. Hus wrote them in Latin and used them as aids in his Czech preaching, since they comprised numerous biblical and patristic quotations which he wished to use exactly. They were addressed for the greater part to his lay audiences, exhorting them earnestly to pious life by proceeding "from virtue to virtue." The supreme aim of religion, he taught, was to love God absolutely. He denounced pride, luxury, avarice, and immorality, both of the lay and of the clerical members of the Church. As in the previous sermons, there is no explicit discussion of Hus's concept of

---

[63] Šimek, ed., *Mistr Jan Hus, Česká kázání sváteční*. These Czech sermons for the holy days are published for the first time. Hus did not write his sermons in Czech at that time; the editor supposes that they were taken down in shorthand by one of the hearers from Hus's spoken words.

[64] *Ibid.*, p. 89.

[65] Schmidtová, ed., *Magistri Joannis Hus, Sermones de tempore qui Collecta dicuntur*.

the Church. He comes closest to it in the sermon dealing with Hagar and Sarah (Gal. 4 : 30): "Cast out the slave and her son; for the son of the slave shall not inherit with the son of the free woman." Hus asserts that the Apostle "calls the holy Church and her son all the multitude of the elect; the slave and her son as the Church of the wicked, the multitude of the foreknown." [66] Both are at present in the Church militant, but shall be separated from each other in the Day of Judgment. He refers to the elect in these sermons many times, declaring that the true Church is composed of them. He never uses for that Church the term *congregatio fidelium*. This concept, doctrinally unimpeachable, Hus later elaborated in his polemical works and defended at the Council of Constance.

It is surprising, therefore, to find that, in the sermon preached at Zbyněk's invitation before the synod held at the archiepiscopal palace on October 19, 1405,[67] Hus takes the clergy severely to task. He now defines the Church as consisting, in one sense, of the congregation of the faithful, and in another of the Roman as a particular church. The latter comprises the pope and his cardinals "when they had entered through the door" [i.e., Christ]. There are other particular churches, such as the Prague Church with the archbishop and his clergy, provided they, too, are qualified in the way similar to that of the pope and the cardinals. Nevertheless, his basic definition is that of "the totality of the predestinate." As such, the Church is the mystical body of Christ and the kingdom of heaven. Hus further speaks of the familiar division of the Church into the triumphant, the militant, and the dormient, but all three are composed of the predestinate. Those who have not "entered through the door" are the church of Antichrist.

In his dealing with the clergy, Hus declares that those worthily performing their office are "the best part of the Church." He castigates the priests severely, however, when they fail to live up to their high calling. He particularly denounces the clergy living in concubinage or committing adultery, calling them "sons of the devil" and reminding them that such as they cannot enter the kingdom of heaven. They should indeed be suspended from their office in accordance with the Church's canons. He further lashes against the unscrupulous exactions

[66] *Ibid.*, p. 150.

[67] "Sermo M. Joannis Hus, 'Diliges Dominum Deum ...' " in *Historia et Monumenta Joannis Hus atque Hieronymi Pragensis, confessorum Christi* (Nuremberg, 1715), II, 39–47. This work is the principal collection of Hus's Latin works. It was published originally in 1558; the 1715 edition is a reprint of the original.

of the laity both by the secular and the ecclesiastical lords. He is particularly bitter against the monks, but does not spare the prelates, either, on account of simony. Finally, he quotes Bernard's denunciation of the papacy itself. If the sermons previously mentioned show but little, if any, of Wyclif's influence, this cannot be said of the synodical sermon of 1405!

Similarly the sermon Hus preached before the synod in 1407 dealt largely with the duties of the clergy and the denunciation of their vices.[68] It was, indeed, fitting that he should address his clerical brethren in such direct and uncompromising terms, since the occasion itself sugested it and his reformatory zeal demanded it.

Besides his strenuous labors as the preacher of the Bethlehem Chapel, Hus continued his academic career as a member of the faculty of arts, having even been chosen its dean during the winter semester of 1401–02. At the same time he continued his studies in theology as a candidate for the doctoral degree, having attained the rank of *baccalaurius* in 1404. He began to lecture on the Bible during the years 1404–06. When he gained the degree of *baccalaurius sententiarius*, it gave him the right and duty to lecture on Peter Lombard's *Sentences*. He performed this duty in a wholly orthodox fashion during the years 1407–08. Thereupon he attained the degree of *baccalaurius formatus*. When the anti-Wyclifite struggle broke out at the university in 1403, it resulted in the victory of the German masters, who had an overwhelming numerical majority over their Czech colleagues. They forbade the teaching of Wyclif's forty-five articles, twenty-four of which had already been condemned at London in 1382. Hus became quite prominent in the defense of Wyclif's philosophical realism against the Germans, who, as a rule, adhered to nominalism, which was now primarily a theological rather than a philosophical system. The theological tenets of Wyclif, however, were defended chiefly by Stanislav of Znojmo and Stephen Páleč. Hus defended the theses mainly by repudiating the indiscriminate and illogical manner of their condemnation by the German masters, without declaring explicitly whether or not they were orthodox or heretical.

The first denunciation of Stanislav's Wyclifism occurred in 1405 after the publication of his treatise defending remanence. The case was brought to the attention of Archbishop Zbyněk by a Cistercian, John Štěkna, then professor at Cracow in Poland. The archbishop was

---

[68] *Ibid.*, II, 47–56.

a well-meaning young noble, a soldier by profession who, at the age of fourteen, had become canon of Prague and provost of Mělník. Since he possessed but a smattering of theological education, he submitted the treatise to a commission. This body, as could be expected, found it heretical. Nevertheless, Zbyněk contented himself on this occasion with Stanislav's lame excuse that he had propounded the thesis in an incomplete form merely as a subject of academic discussion, and not as his personal belief. He promised to complete it in an orthodox manner. Zbyněk nevertheless issued a proclamation (1406) ordering all priests to teach that, after the words of consecration, nothing remains in the sacrament but the body and blood of Christ. In fact he went so far as to forbid even a mention of the word "bread." Hus was painfully conscious of the unheroic conduct of his revered teacher and by no means shared his views. He wrote a treatise, *De corpore Christi*,[69] in which he set forth the orthodox catholic doctrine that, after the consecration, the bread and wine do not cease to exist altogether by becoming the body and blood of Christ, but become *transubstantiated* bread and wine. He wrote and preached on this subject many times afterward. His enemies subverted this perfectly orthodox view by asserting that he taught remanence. This charge was repeatedly used against him at Constance. It remained one of the thirty final charges on the basis of which he was condemned as a heretic.

Hus succeeded to the leadership of the reform party after 1407. By that time he had become more thoroughly acquainted with Wyclif's theological views, since two young students, Nicholas Faulfiš and George of Kněhnice, had brought some of the most important of Wyclif's works from England. In 1408 the antireformist faction, having Ludolf Meisterman, a bachelor of theology, for their spokesman, laid charges against the leaders of the movement at the papal court. Stanislav and Páleč were particularly singled out, although Hus was included as well. Thereupon Pope Gregory XII issued a bull strictly forbidding all adherence to Wyclifism and citing Stanislav to appear within sixty days at his court. The Czech university masters, at the behest of the archbishop and the king, met in May of that year at "The Black Rose," their usual meeting place, and passed a resolution implying a criticism of the papal order: they agreed that no one was to teach the articles of Wyclif "in their erroneous sense." In June the synod of the clergy ordered that Wyclif's books be submitted to the

[69] *Ibid.*, I, 202 ff.

archbishop "for examination." Moreover, Stanislav and Páleč, who were on their way to Rome, were imprisoned at Bologna by Cardinal Baldassarre Cossa (the future Pope John XXIII). Upon their release and return, because of fear of the consequences, they became the pre-eminent antagonists of Wyclif. This brought Hus to the forefront and also involved him in a conflict with Archbishop Zbyněk.

The primary cause of disagreement between Hus and Zbyněk was the question of papal obedience, although it was preceded and pre-cipitated by the fundamental change in the constitution of the univer-sity. King Wenceslas IV and the university, together with the arch-bishop and the clergy in general, had hitherto recognized Gregory XII as the legitimate pope. In an effort to terminate the long-drawn-out schism which had caused untold damage to the Church ever since its outbreak in 1378, thirteen cardinals of both Gregory XII and Benedict XIII abandoned their respective popes. Supported by the French king and the University of Paris, they adopted the radical plan of deposing both popes in a general Council and electing a new one. The French then sent an embassy to Wenceslas to win him over to the cause. The Czech king decided to adhere to the revolutionary conciliar program. The German university masters, however, refused to accept the new policy and, together with the archbishop, remained faithful to Gregory. The king, incensed at what he regarded as an act of disobedience, decided on a radical change of the constitution of the university. This he effected by reversing the provision whereby the three "foreign nations" wielded three votes, while the Czechs, who embraced the king's papal policy, had only one vote. This basic change was pro-mulgated by the famous decree of Kutná Hora (January 18, 1409). Although Hus had not been principally instrumental in securing this change, he was brought into the resulting conflict with the German masters by being elected the first rector of the reorganized university in October of that year, a dangerous honor which the senior professors apparently did not care to accept. The Germans now took an oath, reinforced by severe penalties, that under no circumstances would they recognize the changed status. When all their efforts to reverse the king's decision failed, they left Prague *en masse* and founded the Uni-versity of Leipzig. Henceforth, they became bitter enemies of the University of Prague, of the Czechs in general, and of Hus in particu-lar. They made their hatred effective at the Council of Constance, where their biased testimonies greatly aggravated the case against Hus.

They charged him not only with Wyclifite heresies, but with their expulsion from the university.

When the Council of Pisa met (March 25, 1409) to act for the first time on the theory that a general Council is superior to the pope, it deposed and excommunicated both Gregory XII and Benedict XIII as heretics and schismatics. Then in June they elected a new pope, Alexander V. Unfortunately, this action only added a third pope to the previous two, thus aggravating the schism and making the confusion worse. The two deposed popes retained the support of certain rulers, while Alexander gained the recognition of the rest, among them the French and the Czech kings. Unfortunately, Archbishop Zbyněk and many of the higher clergy, particularly the ambitious and influential Bishop John of Litomyšl, remained loyal to Gregory. It was this event that caused the major rift between the archbishop and Hus. The opponents of the latter—who resented his scathing denunciations of the vices of the clergy—took advantage of the disagreement to instigate the young archbishop against Hus and the whole reform party. They charged them with Wyclifite heresies. Hus, who proved his orthodoxy in his commentary on Lombard's *Super IV sententiarum*, completed that very summer, was actually not guilty of any Wyclifite heresies, even though he defended some of the forty-five articles "in their good sense." In spite of that, however, Zbyněk fell completely under the sway of Hus's enemies. By taking severe measures against the archbishop, the king, however, forced him in the end to abandon Gregory and, on September 2, to recognize Alexander as the rightful pope. Moreover, the archbishop was required to declare to the papal curia that there existed no heresy in the land. Smarting under the humiliation caused him by the forced recognition of the Pisan pope, Zbyněk now took further active measures against Hus. He secured from Pope Alexander a bull (December, 1409) ordering him to extirpate the Wyclifite heresy and particularly to prohibit preaching in any place except the cathedral, parochial, and monastic churches. This was done ostensibly as a measure in the fight against heresy. Although no persons were named in the bull, it was obviously directed against Hus's preaching at the Bethlehem Chapel, since it was not a parochial church. By obeying the order, he would not only have lost his own pulpit, but was certain to be barred from any other.[70] He refused to obey the com-

[70] Part II, Nos. 1–3 of this work where the events are decribed quite fully and the reasons for Hus's appeal are given in detail.

mand, appealing first to Pope Alexander and, after that pontiff's death, which occurred soon after, to his successor, John XXIII.

We can form an opinion of Hus's preaching during the years 1410–11 from his sermons published by V. Flajšhans.[71] They differ considerably from those preached by him previously. He still addresses himself primarily to his lay hearers, and deals for the most part with themes aimed at exhorting them to a life of piety and virtue. He stresses faith as basic, but it must be "faith formed by love." If it does not issue in holy life, "then we believe no more and have no greater faith than the devil." "Let our hope then be grounded on faith wherewith man first of all trusts that he is predestinated ... in the second place, that he will be of the elect; and in the third place, that he will escape eternal damnation and, finally, that he will be eternally nourished." [72]

Hus nevertheless deplores the spiritual condition of the inhabitants of Prague, "where so much preaching is done but so few people are improved." He, therefore, fiercely lashes out against the vices of the people, devoting many sermons to the castigation of their various sins. He strikes out at worldliness in general, and at fornication, adultery, and drunkenness in particular. He denounces the current superstition connected with the fabled miraculous appearance of Christ's blood in the host at Wilsnack in Germany and in various places in Bohemia. He also warns against superstitious pilgrimages, worship of images, and other transgressions of the law of Christ.

In these sermons, which fall into the period of Hus's increasing resistance to the current evils of the Church, especially among the clergy and the hierarchy, the influence of Wyclif is already clearly discernible. He mentions Wyclif by name, defending him against unjust calumny.[73] Although he exalts good priests who faithfully perform their office as servants of Christ, and declares them "in the spiritual office to be worthier than the secular king," he assails unworthy clergy far more frequently and vigorously than in the previous sermons. He is likewise more explicit in defining the concept of the Church, on which he bases his disobedience of the archbishop and the pope in refusing

---

[71] Flajšhans, *Mag. Io. Hus, Sermones in Bethlehem.* These sermons are translated, twenty-two in full, others in part, by A. Císařová-Kolářová, *M. Jan Hus, Betlemské poselství.*

[72] Flajšhans, *op. cit.,* I, 90.

[73] *Ibid.,* IV, 278; I, 58.

to desist from preaching at their command. His polemic against his theological opponents is likewise clearly discernible. But since these are subjects to be treated later in the systematic exposition of his concept of the Church, we shall defer their fuller treatment until then.

In addition to forbidding preaching in chapels, Archbishop Zbyněk ordered the surrender of all Wyclif's books "for examination," but then had them hastily burned, in July, 1410, irrespective of their nature, whether philosophical or theological. Hus, who had personally surrendered his books, now protested against this arbitrary act. Thereupon Zbyněk promptly excommunicated him and laid charges against him at the curia. The pope, who refused to accept the findings of his own commission of four cardinals that the burning of *all* Wyclif's books, irrespective of their nature, was unjustifiable, now turned the case against Hus over to Cardinal Odo de Colonna. The cardinal declared in favor of the archbishop by confirming the latter's excommunication of Hus. He ordered Zbyněk to take further measures against heresy and cited Hus to appear before him at Bologna, where the papal court then resided. He moreover refused to heed the pleas of the Czech king and queen, the nobles, the university, and the officials of the Old and New Towns of Prague, who had besought him to send papal legates to Prague to examine the charges. Zbyněk thereupon declared Hus under an aggravated excommunication (*in causa fidei*). When Hus, who had sent his legal representatives to the curia on three separate occasions, did not obey the citation to appear personally at the papal court, Colonna pronounced him contumacious and excommunicated him (February, 1411). A month later, the papal secretary, Dietrich of Niem, wrote that it would be useless to examine the case any further; suspicion of heresy, he declared, is sufficient to decide the case. His advice was that the "Wyclifites" of Prague be jailed, degraded, and turned over to the secular arm. When the papal bull announcing Colonna's verdict reached Prague, it excited immense public indignation. The king's favorite, Voksa of Valdštejn, organized a procession, parading a young man dressed as a prostitute, with a mock papal bull hanging about his neck, loudly denouncing the pope. The populace jeered when the document was burned. Charges of heresy were now aggressively urged against Hus at the curia by Michael de Causis, a notorious priest in the service of Zbyněk and the antireformist party. Hus protested that, since no one should obey a superior in a command contrary to the law of God, both the accusations and the excommunication were unjust. Hus's principal procurator, sent to plead his cause, Dr. John of Jesenice, was accused by Michael of Wyclifism and was imprisoned in March, 1412, but succeeded in escaping. The other two representatives were likewise unsuccessful in their effort to quash the demand for Hus's personal appearance.

The trial had taken a turn for the better when the pope appointed a commisison of four cardinals, headed by the famous jurist, Francesco Zabarella of Florence (June 11, 1411). He declared Colonna's decision unjust and precipitous on the ground that Hus's procurators should have been heard. Nevertheless, Michael was able to induce the pope, through intermediaries, to transfer the case to Cardinal Rainald de Brancacci, who chose to take no action in the matter and refused to receive Hus's representatives. In fact, he forbade any further pleading on their part. Thus Hus's excommunication and citation remained in force. Moreover, the case now entered upon the critical stage. Zbyněk, still defying the king's Pisan policy, had not fulfilled the conditions required of him by the king the previous year and fled to his estate at Roudnice. This drew the king's wrath upon him. Wenceslas ordered the ecclesiastical property of the clergy supporting the archbishop to be seized, citing nonperformance of their priestly duties. Zbyněk, in turn, pronounced a ban on the executors of the king's behest and in June, 1411, placed Prague and its environs under an interdict. The king, however, ordered it ignored. In July, 1411, the controversy between the archbishop, the university, and Hus was submitted by the king to an arbitration commission. This body proposed to the archbishop that as a condition of peace he submit to the king, annul the excommunication of Hus, and withdraw the interdict. If he fulfilled these conditions, the confiscated benefices of the clergy would be restored to them. Furthermore, the archbishop was requested to write to the pope that no heresy existed in Bohemia and to petition him to terminate the trial of Hus. Hus was likewise enjoined to write a respectful and conciliatory letter to the pope, professing his orthodoxy and promising obedience. He wrote the letter declaring that by the good offices of the king and the arbitration commission he had been fully reconciled with the archbishop. To this letter was attached the testimony of the university witnessing to Hus's uprightness both in faith and conduct.[74] Zbyněk, however, found these conditions unac-

[74] The decision of the arbitrators is found in Palacký, *Documenta Mag. Johannis Hus*, pp. 437–39. For the testimonial of the university cf. Part I, pp. 146–49.

ceptable and humiliating. Instead of performing them, he took counsel with Bishop John of Litomyšl, called "The Iron," who advised him to reject the terms. Zbyněk then wrote the king that to inform the pope of the nonexistence of heresy in Bohemia and to lift the interdict would be contrary to his conscience and honor. Thereupon, without waiting for an answer, he fled the country, seeking "redress of the coercion against himself and his clergy" at the court of Wenceslas' younger brother, Sigismund, king of Hungary. On the journey, he died unexpectedly at Bratislava (September, 1411).

The archbishop's death put an end to his three-year-old struggle with Hus and with the reform party. Unfortunately, the respite proved of short duration. A new and much more dangerous struggle, followed by disastrous results for Hus, broke out over indulgences. The very month in which Archbishop Zbyněk died, Pope John XXIII issued a bull calling for a crusade against King Ladislas of Naples, who had driven him out of Rome, and against Pope Gregory, then residing in Rome, whom the king continued to support. The bull also promised indulgences to all who would contribute toward the expenses of the campaign. The pope ordered all prelates, under pain of excommunication, to declare Ladislas a perjurer, schismatic, blasphemer, and heretic, and, as such, an excommunicate. A second bull, commissioning the indulgence sellers, excommunicated Gregory XII as a heretic and schismatic. Of the indulgence sellers appointed for Bohemia, one was Wenceslas Tiem, a German, born at Mikulov in Moravia. He was then dean of Passau and held an astonishing number of other benefices besides. He proceeded to carry out his commission by farming out whole archdeaconries and parishes to unscrupulous collectors, who in turn exploited the people mercilessly. They beat drums and offered their wares for as much as the traffic would bear. Such nefarious commerce in forgiveness of sins could not but arouse Hus's most determined opposition, in which he was joined by other members of the reform party. He did not denounce indulgences in principle, but only the abuse accompanying their sale and the objectionable terms of the "crusading" bull. In two treatises he openly repudiated this papal document (June, 1412) as inciting Christians against their brethren in a fratricidal war and as trafficking in the forgiveness of sins without demanding the basic requirement of repentance. He denied the right of the pope or any priest to make war.[75] Only God forgives sins, he

[75] *Historia et Monumenta*, I, 215 ff. The text of the two bulls, pp. 212–15.

asserted, and does so of His free grace to such as are of contrite heart. Well might the latest Catholic author dealing with the subject, Dom Paul de Vooght, declare Hus's position "perfectly catholic!" [76] Unfortunately, King Wenceslas, always impulsive and unpredictable in his decisions, now refused to oppose the papal bull. The fact that he had been granted a considerable portion of the proceeds of the sale might well have influenced his decision. Accordingly, Hus's action lost him the king's support and henceforth he stood defenseless against his enemies. At first even Páleč acknowledged that there were "palpable errors" in the bull's "articles of absolution." But later he, along with the rest of the theological faculty under his rectorship, openly defended the papal prerogatives, including the right to issue the bull against Ladislas. Hus sadly commented: "Páleč is a friend; truth is a friend; and both being friends, it is holy to prefer the truth." [77] In spite of the prohibition, however, Hus now held a debate at the university (June 17, 1412) denouncing the "crusading bull." Páleč had forbidden any member of the theological faculty to take part in it, and when that attempt to stop the discussion failed, he appealed to the king. Moreover, the populace, stirred by the preaching of Hus and other members of his party, broke into open defiance. This made the king furious. He instructed the royal council to convoke the theological faculty and Hus to the house of Conrad of Vechta, the bishop of Olomouc, at Žebrák. The faculty recommended that the forty-five articles of Wyclif be again condemned and any further adherence to them be punished by expulsion from the country. Moreover, in seven additional articles they demanded that the right of the pope to proclaim indulgences be acknowledged and all opposition to them forbidden.[78] These proposals were accepted by the royal council, and the king issued a decree embodying them. In spite of the royal decree, however, the popular disturbances continued. At the Týn Church on the Old Town Square and in several other churches three young men loudly protested against the preachers' exhorting the congregations to buy indulgences. They were seized and taken to the Old Town Hall. Hearing of it, Hus, accompanied by some university masters, promptly went there to offer himself in place of the three youths, declaring that they had acted in accordance with his protests. The councilmen assured him that no

---

[76] De Vooght, *L'hérésie de Jean Huss,* pp. 194, 196.
[77] Hus, "Contra Paletz," in *Historia et Monumenta,* I, 330.
[78] Palacký, pp. 451–57.

serious punishment would be inflicted upon them. Nevertheless, immediately after he left, they ordered the youths beheaded. Thereupon an immense crowd gathered in front of the Town Hall; the bodies of the unfortunate youths were lifted and reverently carried to the Bethlehem Chapel in a solemn procession chanting *Ita sunt martyres.* Although Hus had taken no part in the procession, he did hold the next day a martyrs' mass instead of the ordinary mass for the dead, and allowed the bodies of the three youths to be interred in the chapel.

The theological faculty now demanded that the Žebrák decisions be made public and put into effect. King Wenceslas, infuriated by the continuing defiance of his orders, called a meeting of the clergy, the prelates, and the university masters at the Old Town Hall (July 16). It was presided over by the titular patriarch of Antioch, V. Králik, and Bishop Conrad of Vechta. Hus, however, had left Prague the day before and consequently was not in attendance. The inquisitor of Prague, Bishop Nicolas of Nezero, thereupon read the resolution adopted at Žebrák. It decreed that anyone defending any of the forty-five articles of Wyclif, or denying that the pope has the right to grant indulgences and to demand subsidy from the faithful, or preaching against the bull of indulgences, was to be excommunicated and exiled from the country. Rector Mark of Hradec was commanded to announce to the whole university that any further discussion of the matter was forbidden. When he was personally called upon to affirm his acceptance of the decision, he demurred on the ground that not *all* the forty-five articles were heretical, and demanded Scriptural proof against them. But only two other masters supported him. All the rest dared not withhold their consent.

After his return, Hus continued to preach and even dared, along with several other masters, to hold a new disputation at the university about the theses. He himself chose to defend five of Wyclif's theses that he regarded as capable of an acceptable interpretation. This was a direct challenge not only to the theological faculty but to the king as well. By this act he burned his bridges behind him. Stanislav and Páleč now, for the first time, went so far as to condemn Wyclif altogether. Stanislav preached at the Týn Church (August 28, 1412) against five articles of Wyclif, three of which had been defended by Hus, particularly the thesis that the civil power may deprive the prelates and priests in mortal sin of their possessions. He called it an insane doctrine and declared that all possessions of the Church are sacred and to touch them were a sacrilege. This he did in spite of the fact that the year before he had supported the king when he had impounded the goods of the clergy supporting Zbyněk.[79] On September 4, Páleč preached that *all* forty-five articles of Wyclif were heretical, erroneous, and scandalous. He thus ignored the carefully delimited sense in which Hus had defended five of these theses and in effect condemned Hus along with Wyclif.[80] Thus the rupture with Hus was now complete.

On April 12, 1412, Pope John convened a Council at Rome which condemned not only Wyclif, but also dealt with the case of Hus. Cardinal Peter degli Stephaneschi, who had replaced Cardinal de Brancacci, on July 29 placed Hus under the major excommunication. He furthermore threatened that unless Hus took proper steps to avoid it within twenty days, the interdict would once more be imposed upon Prague. The cardinal also solemnly forbade all the faithful to afford Hus food, drink, salutation, discourse, purchase, sale, or hospitality. The verdict was announced at the meeting of the synod (October 18). Since the king no longer interposed his prohibition of the action, as he had done before, the dreaded consequences of the measure became grimly real. Seeing no further use in appealing to the pope, Hus now solemnly appealed to Christ.[81] Furthermore, to spare the city the horrors of the interdict, he left Prague the same month. The crowning irony of the situation was that the original cause, the papal sale of indulgences, no longer existed. John XXIII had concluded peace with Ladislas in June; it was proclaimed in Prague the very month Hus left it.

While in hiding at a castle of one of his noble protectors, Hus petitioned the supreme court of the land, the king and the queen, for protection. The court met in December and, complying with his request, instructed the new archbishop, Conrad of Vechta, who had hitherto held the episcopal see of Olomouc, but had purchased the see from Albík of Uničov, the successor of Zbyněk in the archiepiscopal office,[82] to call a meeting of the synod for January 3, 1413. The king, however, invited the university as well to submit its opinion as to how

---

[79] Bartoš, *op. cit.*, pp. 346–47.

[80] De Vooght judges Páleč culpable in the matter; cf. de Vooght, *op. cit.*, p. 220.

[81] Palacký, pp. 464–66; cf. Part II, No. 1 of this work.

[82] Bartoš, *op. cit.*, p. 363; Novotný, *M. Jan Hus, život a učení*, II, 176. Hus himself refers to it in his treatise on simony (cf. my translation, "Hus on Simony" in *Advocates of Reform*, pp. 213, 219, 222).

the conflict could be pacified. The synod met later, on February 6, and was presided over by Archbishop Conrad. The faculty of theology, represented by eight of its members, drew up a *consilium*,[83] demanding that all must "think and believe as the Roman Church does and not otherwise." Furthermore, they declared that all must hold that the pope is the head and the cardinals the body of the Roman Church, "the manifest and true successors in the ecclesiastical office of the blessed Peter, the prince of the apostles, and of the company of the other apostles of Christ." All' must likewise confess that they are ready "to obey the prelates in everything whatever that does not prohibit pure good or enjoin pure evil."

Hus's party among the university masters, on its part, demanded that the conciliation between Archbishop Zbyněk and Hus concluded by the royal commisison in 1411 be accepted as still valid. Its conditions, not fulfilled by the archbishop, were now to be carried out by the theological faculty. Hus was, furthermore, to be allowed to face his opponents in person and, if no heresy were proved against him, the faculty was to report the result to the curia and the interdict be lifted. This then produced an impasse, promptly and gladly utilized by the archbishop by returning the case to the crown council. This body thereupon appointed a four-member commission, composed of the rector of the university, Christian of Prachatice, a long-time supporter of Hus, Dr. Albík of Uničov, the former archbishop and now the king's physician, and two other persons. This group was, on the whole, well disposed toward Hus. It called upon the representatives of both parties to present their case before the commission. The theological faculty chose four of its members for the purpose, while Hus was represented by his legal councilor, John of Jesenice, and three others. The result of the conference was not essentially different from that of February 6. The hopeless impasse was, however, broken by the provision previously accepted by the parties that they would abide by the decision of the commission, whatever it might be. In case of refusal, they were to be fined one thousand *grossi* or exiled from the country. Thereupon the commisison ruled that the conciliation adopted in 1411 be regarded as binding and its conditions be carried out. The four theological members were required, therefore, to write to the curia that no heresy had been found in Bohemia. This they refused to do. They chose rather to go into exile. All four were thereupon deprived of their

[83] Palacký, pp. 475–88; for Hus's reply, offering his own terms, cf. pp. 491–92.

benefices and left the country, finding refuge in Moravia. The commission had to begin all over again by securing other members of the theological faculty to continue the negotiations. None of them, however, was willing to risk the fate similar to their exiled colleagues. Although it is not clear just what happened, it seems probable that the theological faculty demanded as the price of attendance that the February *consilium* be accepted as the basis of any further negotiations. When this was presented by Christian to Hus (according to Bartoš in July), he spiritedly and decisively rejected it. In a letter written clearly with deeply stirred emotions, Hus asserts that he would not accept the *consilium* even if it were to cost him his life. He hopes that

death will sooner direct me or those two turncoats from the truth [i.e., Páleč and Stanislav] either to heaven or to hell before I agree with their opinions. I have indeed known both of them formerly as rightly confessing the truth according to Christ's law; but out of fear they succumbed and became the pope's flatterers. . . . Páleč calls us Wyclifites as if we deviated from all Christianity. Stanislav calls us infidels, perfidious, and insane. . . . I hope, however, by God's grace, to oppose them until I am consumed by fire. . . . It is better to die well than to live evilly; one should not sin in order to avoid the punishment of death. . . . Truth conquers all things.[84]

Hus's letter made any further attempts at conciliation useless. Henceforth, no other attempt was made. The parties then engaged in a literary duel that was not terminated until Hus's departure for the Council of Constance. It was in reply to the *consilium* that he changed the plan of his treatise *De ecclesia*. The text shows that chapters xi–xxiii of that major work of Hus are his reply to the pronouncement of the eight doctors of the theological faculty.[85] The book was completed about the middle of May, 1413, at Kozí Hrádek, the castle of one of his noble protectors where he had taken refuge. It was read at the Bethlehem Chapel early in June.

Hus continued to preach in the neighborhood where he resided, and occasionally secretly visited Prague. His principal occupation, now that he no longer could preach at the Bethlehem Chapel, consisted of

[84] Novotný, ed., *M. Jana Husi Korespondence a dokumenty*, No. 63. He expresses the opinion that the letter was sent to Master John of Rejnštejn, called "the Cardinal." Bartoš, *op. cit.*, p. 368 argues that it was the last letter sent by Hus to the member of the commission, Christian of Prachatice. This illustrates the uncertainty which characterizes the interpretation of the events of this period. I followed Bartoš' opinion, although without prejudice to Novotný's view. In the absence of decisive data I cannot form an independent judgment.

[85] Thomson, ed., *Magistri Johannis Hus Tractatus de Ecclesia*, pp. xv–xvi.

writing some of his most important Czech treatises intended for the instruction of the common people. They comprised the *Postilla*, a collection of his sermons; *The Exposition of the Faith*; of *Decalogue*; and of *The Lord's Prayer*. Furthermore, he wrote *Concerning the Six Errors*; and particularly his most determined attack on simony, in a treatise bearing that title.[86] He also devoted much time to the writing of Latin works in defending himself against his theological antagonists. Among these men the Carthusian prior of Dolany, Stephen, and the Benedictine monk of Břevnov, John of Holešov, played a conspicuous part.[87] But other writers, less voluminous but equally acrimonious, attacked him. Above all, the writings of Stanislav of Znojmo and of Stephen Páleč were of preeminent importance; they served, along with Hus's own *De ecclesia*, as the principal source of the charges against him at the Council of Constance. It is, therefore, to the treatises of those two former friends of his that we shall devote special attention.

THE BATTLE IS JOINED

Stanislav of Znojmo wrote his *Tractatus de Romana ecclesia* and *Alma et venerabilis* in 1412 and 1413 respectively. Both works seem to have been almost exclusively devoted to the defense of the tenet that the Roman Church is "the mystical and ecclesiastical *compositum*" of which the pope is the head and the cardinals the body.[88] Christ on

[86] My translation of the treatise, in *Advocates of Reform*, pp. 196–278. All Czech treatises mentioned in the text are found in Erben; *Mistra Jana Husi Sebrané spisy české*; also Jeschke, ed., *Mistr Jan Hus, Postilla*.

[87] Stephen wrote, in 1408, a book against Wyclif, and in 1414 against Hus, the *Antihussus* and *Liber epistolaris ad Hussitas*. His *Dialogus volatilis inter Aucam et Passerem adversus Hussum* was addressed to Bishop John of Litomyšl. Cf. Pez, *Thesaurus anecdotorum novissimus*, IV, 149–706. For John of Holešov, cf. de Vooght, *Hussiana*, pp. 116 ff.

[88] Stanislav's *Tractatus de Romana ecclesia* was published by Sedlák in *Hlídka*; the *Alma et venerabilis . . .* was edited by J. Loserth in *Archiv für österreichische Geschichte* (Vienna, 1889), LXXV, 344–413. In *de Romana ecclesia* Stanislav writes:

Sancte igitur et iuste a Christo et a spiritu sancto ordinata est sancta katholica et apostolica *Romana ecclesia* semper permanens eadem quoad formam, *in qua caput est papa, cuius corpus est collegium cardinalium,* existens manifesti et veri successores principis apostolorum Petri et reliquorum apostolorum Christi *in officio ecclesiastico* ad auctoritate illuminandum . . . in tota materia fidei et universa ecclesia katholica et auctoritative cognoscendum et diffiniendum in omni tali materia et errores circa talem materiam *corrigendum* et purgandum et ad potestative regendum et dirigendum omnes alias ecclesias et universitatem christianorum ac curam talium habendi in tali materia. Pp. 91 f.

leaving the world "constituted on the earth . . . in a mystical and ecclesiastical *compositum* the official source of the light of faith manifested to all the world." [89] At first it consisted of Peter and the other apostles. In order to preserve this source of light after His departure, Christ provided another such *compositum* in their successors, the pope and the cardinals of the Roman Church. He entrusted to them the supreme authority. To that end the pope receives for his official function "the sacrament of papal unction." "There cannot be found or provided any other such mystico-ecclesiastical *compositum* aside from the *compositum* of the mystico-ecclesiastical head, namely, the pope and the college of cardinals, which *compositum* assuredly is and is called the Roman Church." It possesses the identical form [essential being] it had in Peter's time. This Church is the fount of the fullness of power for "the ruling and directing of all particular churches and the universality of Christ's faithful in all matters catholic and ecclesiastical." Stanislav likens it to the human body in the unity of its psycho-physical organism. The pope and the cardinals constitute the corporeal, visible members of the mystical body, while Christ is its invisible soul. The corporeal part may and does change. In fact, the Roman Church may exist for a time without the visible head; for instance, when the pope dies. Then the plenitude of power passes temporarily to the college of cardinals. In its essential being, however, the Church remains ever the same. Moreover, the pope and the cardinals, considered separately and individually, may "gravely err in morals and fall into errors concerning the faith." The Roman Church, however, considered as a mystical *compositum*, "cannot be polluted by errors in morals nor by errors against the faith. Therefore, the Roman Church remains ever the same as to its form and its fundamental essence. Thus it ever remains holy and immune from all pernicious errors in morals and faith." When Christ's faithful resort to the Roman Church, they do not come primarily to the pope and the cardinals. They come rather "through them to that form and fundamental essence of the Roman Church itself which directs Christ's faithful by them and through them in matters catholic and ecclesiastical." Christ, then, as the soul of His mystical body, residing in that Church, is the source of all power. The pope and the cardinals may be occasionally

---

[89] For this and the subsequent quotations, unless otherwise designated, cf. Stanislav's *de Romana ecclesia* in Sedlák, *op. cit., passim,* especially pp. 85–86. Also cf. Kybal, *M. Jan Hus, život a učení,* II, 112–28.

sinful. Nevertheless, through them Christ direct and rules His body in all doctrinal and ecclesiastical matters.

The Roman Church, therefore, alone is universal and not a particular Church. There is only one apostolic see—that of Rome. The Church is one in spite of its divisions into particular churches. Authority, to be complete and properly exercised, "must be supreme, visible, and unique (*plenitudo non est divisibilis*)." [90] Consequently, there is only one rightful and true pope, although there may exist antipopes. Hus objected that no one knows or can know whether or not he is of the predestined. Therefore, if the pope or the cardinals are not of the elect, they cannot judge truly in matters catholic and ecclesiastical. Stanislav curtly remarked that in such a case there is no other body on earth where the necessary authority can be found. "It is foolish, therefore, to say such a thing." This is, by the way, the only reference to the elect found in the two treatises of Stanislav. Hus, on the other hand, regarded predestination as of fundamental importance. Likewise it is inappropriate, Stanislav continues, to demand that all matters concerning the faith should be judged exclusively on the basis of the Scriptures or the teaching of the Fathers of the Church. This he designates as "the Armenian heresy." "Infinite errors and infinite schisms" may thus be engendered. The Church possesses the teaching authority whereby it alone has the right to define Scriptural doctrine or saving faith in general. The believer is bound to accept its interpretation instead of resorting to and relying on his own understanding. Thus in effect the Scriptures are subordinated to the Church; consequently, they cease to possess supreme authority. He sums up his argument:

Therefore the holy catholic and apostolic Roman Church was holily and justly ordained by Christ and the Holy Spirit, ever and permanently the same as to form, of which the pope is the head, and the college of cardinals the body, being the manifest and true successors in the ecclesiastical office of the prince of the apostles Peter and of the other apostles of Christ, authoritatively and universally illuminating the totality of Christians dispersed over the world . . . in all matters of faith.

These concepts of the Church are for the greatest part repeated in Stanislav's *Alma et venerabilis.* . . . There are, however, a few notable additions. One of these states that as Christ was the chief pastor of

[90] De Vooght, *Hussiana*, p. 126. "L'Église universelle est donc régie par une autorité universelle: le pape et le collège des cardinaux." Also his *L'hérésie*, pp. 266 f.

His sheep, and the apostles were "vicarial pastors," so likewise is Christ the principal head and the pope the vicar of the Church. He writes:

sic Christus est caput per se auctoritativum tocius sue ecclesie super terram, papa vero est eiusdem ecclesie vicarium, officiale et ministeriale, misticum et ecclesiasticum caput secundum fontalem et capitalem illam in eo plenitudinem potestatis ecclesiastice officialis vicarie et ministerialis.[91]

Accordingly the papal office may be held even by a foreknown pope existing in mortal sin. It is not of merit, but of Christ's appointment.

It is extraordinarily difficult to analyze and interpret Stanislav's views of the Church. By no stretch of the imagination can anyone regard his ideas as lucid. As a convinced papalist, he totally ignores or deliberately denies the usual concepts of the conciliarists, i.e., that there exist both the *congregatio fidelium* of which Christ alone is the head and which is represented by the general Council, and the *Romana ecclesia* of which the pope and the cardinals are the vicegerents, subject to the over-all supervision and control of the general Council. He elevates the Roman Church above the universal, for this Roman Church by Christ's appointment rules and directs all particular churches in the world and all Christ's faithful. The *congregatio fidelium* as a separate entity comprising, rather than being comprised in, the *Romana ecclesia*, disappears. In fact, since the pope is the head and the cardinals are the body of this Roman-universal Church in the sense that they alone possess the "power of the keys"—the legal right to rule all Christendom—it is difficult to see what else is left for the Church universal but absolute passive subjection to this rule. Christ is still said to be its "principal head," but He rules it by and through the vicarial *compositum* of the pope and the cardinals. These human agents can and do err both in morals and in faith; but the Roman Church cannot err. Nevertheless, since the Roman Church is constituted of the pope and the cardinals, it is difficult to understand why the Church does not err when they do. To say, as Stanislav does, that in such a case there is no infallible authority on earth in matters of faith is no solution. One can only wonder in what concrete way Christ can rule His Church when His vicar and the college of cardinals fall into error. Who decides that they have fallen into error? The general Council? Stanislav makes no mention of it. Needless to say the con-

---

[91] Stanislav, *Alma et venerabilis . . .* , in Loserth, *op. cit.,* pp. 370 f.

ciliar fathers summarily rejected such overweening papalism, even though Stanislav's treatises presumably did not come to their attention. As for the Roman Church today, it, too, repudiates his view. It is the pope who is infallible in matters of faith and morals, not the Church.

There is no doubt that Hus understood Stanislav to teach that the pope is the vicarial head of the Church universal, since the mystical body of the pope with his cardinals is identical with Christ's mystical body, which is the Church. He denies this concept by insisting that for the attainment of the mystical status the grace of predestination must be added to the natural status. He challenges Stanislav to prove his assertion by a Scriptural proof, but declares in advance that he would never succeed in doing so. He taunts Stanislav by asserting that he would never be able to prove that "Pope John XXIII with his twelve cardinals are Christ's mystical body unless he is able to prove that the pope with his cardinals are linked [to Christ] by the bond of predestination." Hus bluntly declares that Stanislav imagines such a view "*secundum Pharisaicam et inanem fallaciam.*" [92]

As for Hus's own views, he holds that Scripture teaches that Christ alone is the head and the predestinate are the body of the Church universal. "This mystical universal Church is truly constituted of Christ and the company of the predestinate, inasmuch as it has the similitude to the human body according to the saying of the Apostle in I Cor. 12, 'As the body is one, although it has many members . . . so it is with Christ.' " [93] Further Hus asserts in the same passage that "not in the pope somewhere outside Christ, but in Christ Himself are the predestinate one mystical body." He recognizes the pope, if he is of the predestinate, as the true vicar of Christ. He admits that the Church militant is composed of both the predestined and the foreknown; the latter, however, although they are *in* the Church are not *of* the Church. The mystical body of Christ is in reality the *only true* Church. This distinction between the Roman Church as composed of both the predestinate and the foreknown and the mystical body of Christ as the Church universal proved to be the bone of contention between Hus and his theological adversaries. It also constituted the charge repeatedly brought against him at the Council. In fact, throughout the trial it was placed foremost among the accusations, and he was condemned as if he had denied the Church militant altogether.

[92] "Contra Stanislaum," in *Historia et Monumenta,* I, 336.
[93] *Ibid.,* p. 335.

Has Hus correctly interpreted Stanislav's definition of the Church as applying to the Church universal as well as to the Roman? Sedlák denies it without substantiating his assertion. He insists that Stanislav was defining the Roman Church, *not* the Church universal. It is difficult, however, to agree with him. Stanislav clearly asserts that, since the Roman Church is the only universal Church while all the rest are merely particular churches, it follows that the pope is the vicarial head of the whole universal Church. He has absolute authority both in doctrine and governance not only of the Roman but of the universal Church. Thus Stanislav reverses the concept generally held by outstanding decretalists and conciliarists that the universal Church—the *congregatio fidelium*—is the genus while the Roman Church is one of its species. He writes that Hus "errs if he refuses to believe that the pope is the vicarial, official and ecclesiastical head also of the entire company of Christ's churches on earth." [94] This still leaves the principal headship of the universal Church in some innocuous fashion to Christ. The actual governing authority of that Church, however, is exercised by His vicar, the pope, and his cardinals. Together they form what Stanislav designates by his everlastingly iterated favorite phrase as the "mystical-ecclesiastical *compositum.*" Had Stanislav and Sedlák acknowledged the saving distinction between the *congregatio fidelium* as a separate entity having Christ for its head and the Roman Church with the pope as Christ's vicar, the problem dealt with would not have arisen. It is the terms "universal-Roman" and the "mystical-ecclesiastical *compositum*" that confuse the issue. The first certainly implies a commingling of two entities, while the second makes the pope and the cardinals the exclusive members of the *body* of the Church. Dr. Sedlák is manifestly in error by insisting that the Church universal is not involved in the definition.

As for Páleč's polemics, in 1413 he wrote three treatises against Hus: the *De equivocatione nominis ecclesia*, the *Tractatus de ecclesia*, and the *Antihus*.[95] In his *De ecclesia* he answers point by point the first ten chapters of Hus's own *De ecclesia*, while the remainder of the work is devoted to Hus's answer to the *consilium* of the synod held on

[94] Sedlák, *M. Jan Hus*, p. 283; Stanislav, *de Romana ecclesia*, pp. 403 f. Cf. also Kybal, *op. cit.*, II, 112–27.

[95] Two of these works were published by Sedlák, "Pálčův spis proti Husovu traktatu 'De ecclesia' " in *Hlídka*, and the "Antihus" in the same periodical's supplement. Selected portions of Páleč's *Tractatus de ecclesia* are published in Sedlák's *Jan Hus*, supplement, pp. 203–304. It is a remarkable fact that this

February 6, 1413. Into the third of his polemical treatises, the *Antihus*, Páleč inserts passages from Stanislav's and Prior Stephen's writings. Even de Vooght declares that these polemics contain many "unjust judgments."

There is no great difference between Páleč's and Stanislav's views. Limiting the discussion principally to Páleč's concept of the nature of the Church and of the papacy, we may note, first of all, how he interprets the crucial text in Matt. 16:18, "Thou art Peter, and on this rock will I build my Church." He proposes a novel, truly Solomonic exegesis by asserting that the verse possesses all three traditionally acknowledged meanings. Being aware of Augustine's interpretation of the text that the "rock" upon which the Church is to be built is Christ Himself,[96] Páleč holds that Christ is the "principal rock (*petra*)," while Peter is to be understood as the rock in a secondary sense. He writes that Christ did not say that He would build His Church *super me, petram,* or *super hanc petram, quam confessus es,* or *super te, petram,* but *super hanc petram.* This he lamely explains as meaning that "Christ wished to inculcate all the above-stated three senses as catholic."[97] No wonder de Vooght characterizes this astonishing exegesis as "specious"![98] He thinks that Páleč resorted to it because he did not wish to repudiate the traditional interpretation, which affirmed that the "rock" was Christ Himself. He made, therefore, the term *petra* do service for *both* Christ and Peter.

Furthermore, Páleč, in contrast to Stanislav, distinguishes three senses in which the concept of the Church is to be understood. On the one hand, there is the Church universal consisting of the totality of the predestinate; on the other hand, there is the Church militant comprising both the predestinate and the foreknown; and finally he includes in the concept the Roman Church. Christ was indeed the *caput supremum* of the Church universal and militant while He was on the earth. Nor did He cease to be the pope, as Páleč expressly calls

latter work of Páleč was not known in its complete text until Dr. Sedlák had found it in 1912 at Cracow. Unfortunately, he himself published only selections, so that the complete text is still not known. The incomplete Prague ms. had formerly been ascribed to Stanislav. These writings are dealt with in considerable detail in Kybal, *op. cit.,* III, 112–28, 203–74; also in de Vooght, *Hussiana,* pp. 124–47.

[96] Augustine, *Sermones de Scripturio novi testamenti,* LXXVI, i, 1.

[97] Páleč's "De ecclesia" in Sedlák, *op. cit.,* supplement, p. 240.

[98] De Vooght, *Hussiana,* p. 143.

Him, of the Church militant after His ascension, but in a different sense. He ceased to be present corporeally, since "by His ascension He withdrew from it [the Church militant] His intercourse and corporeal presence." In his stead Peter became the vicarial head of the entire Church militant and likewise of the Roman Church, since he was the head of the apostles and the supreme vicar of Christ.[99] Thus the pope as the true successor of Peter is the *caput vicarium, ministerialium,* of the visible Church. Besides, the pope, as the head of the Roman Church, possesses "the sacrament of unction" which makes him the supreme source of sacerdotal authority in all the earth." [100] Páleč declares that Hus "gravely errs" in asserting that the true Church is composed only of the predestinate and refuses to acknowledge the Church militant as likewise being the true Church. He accuses Hus of denying thereby the reality of the latter Church. Páleč supports his assertion by referring to Paul's journeying to Jerusalem to visit Peter (Gal. 1 : 18). Paul did not go merely to see Peter *corporaliter,* but

because Paul knew that there is one universal Church of God on earth.
. . . He also knew that that Church on earth had one head, namely, Peter . . .
in which head existed the plenitude of power on earth of discerning and
defining in every cause on earth in respect of the salvation or of the danger
to souls according to the forementioned two keys of the kingdom of heaven.

This power extends not only over matters ecclesiastical, but civil as well.[101] He adds further that for more than a thousand years this has been acknowledged by the saints and the learned men of both the Church and schools. This belief has likewise been confessed by "the community of all the clergy of the world and the entire Christendom; they have ever professed that the ecclesiastical and mystical *compositum* of the pope as the head and the cardinals as the body of the Roman Church . . . are the fount and source of the plenitude of ecclesiastical power on earth." [102] He quotes the decree *Unam sanctam* of Boniface

[99] "Antihus," in Sedlák, *op. cit.,* supplement, pp. 37–38.

[100] Kybal, *op. cit.,* I, 256–58, discusses Páleč's view extensively and illustrates it in diagramatic form. The references to the "sacrament of unction" are found in Páleč's "Antihus," p. 56. De Vooght also asserts that this sacrament is received by the pope alone, and is thereby endowed with supreme power over all other bishops. Cf. his *Hussiana,* pp. 153, 156.

[101] Páleč's "De ecclesia," in Sedlák, *op. cit.,* pp. 217–18. He writes further: "Est enim potestas et auctoritas sedis apostolice universalis, habens ut est sepe dictum non parcialiter et particulariter sed universaliter et totaliter cognoscere et diffinire non solum in causa ecclesiastica, sed in civilibus causis i.e. secularibus."

[102] *Ibid.,* p. 219.

VIII to affirm that "to submit to the Roman pope is a neccessity for salvation for all rational creatures." [103] It is an *error insanus* to declare that a foreknown pope is not the head of the Church. Even a wicked pope, if rightly elected, is the legitimate vicar of Christ. Peter was not chosen as the first among the apostles and Christ's vicar on account of his exceptional faith or virtues. In 1412, when preaching against Wyclif, Páleč had admitted that a pope might be a heretic. Now, however, he rejects the very notion of it, asserting that the Roman Church with the pope and the cardinals has never erred in matters of faith.[104] Hus pointed out that, since there existed three popes at the time, there were three infallible judges in matters of faith. To that Páleč replied that Pope John XXIII and his cardinals alone constituted the true Church militant, the other two popes having no valid claim to papacy. Yet John derived his authority from the Council of Pisa that upheld principles contrary to those of Páleč! Finally Páleč, although he professed to recognize the Scriptures as inspired by the Holy Spirit, yet argued that they are *res inanimata* while the Church possesses the "living authority" to interpret them. It is, therefore, an error to limit doctrinal tenets to the contents of the Scriptures (*quoad in Scriptura veteris et novi testamenti continentur*). The Roman Church has passed on to the faithful a great deal of tradition not contained in the Scriptures.[105] This view had been held by Henry Totting de Oyta, formerly professor of the theological faculty in Prague. He taught that, since the Church is infallible, whatever it teaches necessarily corresponds to the Scriptural doctrine. This, as de Vooght remarks, amounts "practically to giving the Church a *carte blanche*."

When Páleč arrived at the Council of Constance, he must have anticipated that the conciliar fathers would not agree with his and Stanislav's papalism so radically negating their theories. He soon learned that not only the two popes he rejected, Gregory XII and Benedict XIII, but John XXIII as well were to be deposed. Thereupon he promptly reversed his position and acknowledged the authority and infallibility of the Council. In spite of his own change of position, however, he still opposed Hus for repudiating the extreme papalism

---

[103] *Ibid.*, p. 223.
[104] *Ibid.*, p. 228. "Illa enim romana ecclesia, papa et collegium cardinalium, numquam errat in judicio et sentencia, quam tradit fidelibus in quacunque materia, ubi altera pars contradiccionis fideliter et catholice credi debet et teneri." Cf. also "Antihus" in Sedlák, *op. cit.*, p. 109.
[105] *Ibid.*, p. 230; also de Vooght, *Hussiana*, p. 155.

Páleč himself had just abandoned! Be it noted, nonetheless, that the commission appointed to try the case radically reduced Páleč's forty-two articles drawn up against Hus. In fact, only eleven of these were retained, although fifteen others were added. In the final redaction only seven of Páleč's original forty-two articles were kept, and the text of these was corrected. This clearly shows, it seems to me, what the Council thought of his accusations in their entirety.

Since the fiercest attacks upon Hus were concentrated on his views concerning the Church, he, in turn, wrote as his principal defense the treatise *De ecclesia*.[106] This is a radical statement of his opinions, in some few instances going beyond his previously expressed views, but in the main reiterating the views he held from the beginning. This radicalism of the book must be judged, however, against the background of the extreme papalism of his opponents, and not against the views of the conciliarists. In it he rejects the exaggerated tenets of Stanislav, Páleč, and the other members of the Prague faculty of theology. He bases his own statements largely on the teaching of Augustine, Gregory, Chrysostom, and other earlier doctors of the Church. There is, of course, no doubt that he was also influenced by Wyclif, although he avoided the latter's extreme opinions.

Hus defines the Church basically as the totality of the predestinate, past, present, and future, the mystical body of Christ, of which Christ alone is the head. This is, however, his definition of the Church in the strictest sense of the word (*propriissime dicta*) and does not exclude the concept of the Church militant comprising both the predestined and the foreknown, both the kernel and the chaff. Thus he does not deny that in the visible Church there are members, including even popes, cardinals, bishops, clergy, as well as laymen, who are not of the predestinate. Accordingly, Hus does recognize the Church militant, the *congregatio fidelium*. Nevertheless, only the elect within the Church militant are truly members of the mystical body of Christ, which has existed from the beginning of the human race. Consequently, the foreknown are not members of the true Church even though they may temporarily be "in grace." They are like certain bodily substances —such as ulcers and excrements—which although for the time being lodged in the body, in the end are expelled from it. They are like

---

[106] The latest critical edition of this work is that of Thomson, *Magistri Johannis Hus Tractatus de Ecclesia.* For Thomson's reconstruction of the stages of its composition cf. pp. xv–xvii.

Judas, who, although chosen by the Lord Himself, was never truly His disciple or apostle, while Paul, who was not of the twelve, was truly of the elect. No predestinate is ever lost, since the grace of predestination binds him to the head—Christ. Thus Christ alone is the supreme head of the Church universal of which the predestinate everywhere, including those within the Roman Church, are members.

Since the predestinate form an invisible body within the visible Church, does not that concept in reality make impossible a reliable functioning of the Church militant in the exercise of its administrative and sacerdotal offices? Does it not render uncertain all hierarchical and sacerdotal functions? How can one know whether or not the pope and the cardinals, the bishops and the priests, are of the predestinate? Hus does have an answer: by their fruits ye shall know them! If the hierarchy and the priesthood live in accordance with Christ's life and teaching, they are to be recognized and obeyed as legitimately holding their offices. He demands that all Christians live worthily of their calling. Nevertheless, when the prelates and the clergy do not show the fruits of the Spirit, they are still ministering validly, although unworthily. Thus the charge of Donatism does not apply to Hus.

Hus deals further with the assertion of Stanislav and Páleč that it is necessary for salvation that all men be subject to the Roman pontiff,[107] the "earthly god," as Hus calls him in a sermon quoting an unnamed propapal fanatic. He argues that Christ alone is such a pontiff. Likewise he denies for the same reason that the pope is the head and the cardinals the body of the Roman Church *ex officio*. Since the predestinate alone are rightly members, only the prelates who are of their number are rightly rulers of *particular* visible Churches—for Christendom comprises several such particular Churches, as the Eastern, Western, and others. This constitutes his "federal" view of the Church, which nowadays we call "ecumenical." No one, neither the pope nor the cardinals, is the head of the totality of the predestinate, the universal Church, but Christ alone. Following most of the Fathers, especially Augustine, Hus asserts that Peter was not the rock (*petra*) on which the Church was built; it is his confession that Christ is the Son of God that is the *petra* on which Christ founded His Church. Peter was chosen "the prince of the apostles" on account of his faith. The pope is, therefore, Christ's vicar in the Roman Church only, provided he follows Christ and Peter in their lives and virtues. Thus primacy depends

[107] This is the claim of Pope Boniface VIII in his bull *Unam sanctam* (1299).

on the character of the occupant of Peter's see. Neither is Peter's primacy automatically transmitted to his successors, nor does it inhere in the papal office. Hus admits that many popes, cardinals, and bishops have *de facto* exercised their office despite their unworthy or even criminal character and conduct; but they did so unworthily, putatively, not of merit. As such, they were vicars of Judas instead of Peter. He denies that it is necessary to believe that the pope is infallible or *sanctissimus*. Nevertheless, he does not follow Wyclif in advocating the abolition of the papal office altogether. He holds, however, that the Church could exist without it, since it is not of divine institution.

Hus preaches obedience to all to whom it is rightly due. When, however, ecclesiastical authority is simoniacally acquired, or when the pope or prelates order something contrary to the law of God set forth in the Scriptures, then it is the duty of all members of the Church to obey God rather than men. In such a case men do not resist God, but only an abuse of ecclesiastical authority. On this ground Hus himself disobeyed both Alexander V and John XXIII when they prohibited preaching in chapels, or when John issued the "crusading" bull which resulted in the subsequent trafficking in indulgences.[108] Nevertheless, even wicked prelates must ordinarily be obeyed when they exercise their legitimate authority. He is not repudiating ecclesiastical authority as such, but only its abuse.

Hus was likewise charged with elevating the Scriptures to the position of supreme authority and with claiming the right to interpret them according to his own understanding. He indeed elevates the Scriptures above all other doctrinal criteria, but he interprets them according to the expositions of the ecumenical Councils, of the Fathers of the Church, and of reason. He denies that the pope and the cardinals have the right to declare as obligatory anything contrary to Scripture. It is on this ground that he approves the use of the cup in the communion, for it was clearly instituted by the Lord, and he indignantly repudiates the decree of the Council of Constance forbidding its use on the ground of Church custom. He vainly requested times almost without number that the Council prove, even by delegating one of the least of its members for the purpose, that he had ever taught anything unscriptural or contradictory to the teachings of the Fathers. The

---

[108] His "Refutatio scripti octo doctorum theologiae" in *Historia et Monumenta*, I, 366–408, is his reply to this crusading bull and the doctors' defense of it.

Council ordered him to submit unconditionally and without demur on his part.

One of the principal charges against Hus was that he upheld Wyclif's heresies. He was certainly an admirer of Wyclif, although never an indiscriminate or uncritical disciple of his, ever since he had become acquainted with his philosophical works. With the later theological works he exercised perceptible caution. In his earlier preaching at Bethlehem there is practically no trace of Wyclif's influence in his sermons. Although he held in high regard and veneration his teacher, Stanislav of Znojmo, and in sincere esteem his friend Páleč, he never shared their more complete adherence to Wyclif's opinions, including that of remanence. Other members of the reform party, such as Jakoubek of Stříbro, were likewise more radical in their doctrinal views. It is indeed true that he loyally defended Wyclif, in season and out of season—mostly the latter!—against unjust accusations and misrepresentations of his teaching. Thus he argued in connection with the condemnation of the forty-five articles of Wyclif that not *all* of these were "heretical, erroneous, or offensive to pious ears," but that some could be interpreted in an acceptable and orthodox sense. Actually, he regarded many of the theses as having been incorrectly excerpted and given a warped sense not intended by Wyclif. Nevertheless, he carefully discriminated among them and defended no more than seven. One of the most explicit declarations of Hus's attitude toward Wyclif is to be found in his lectures on Lombard's *Sentences.* He there opposes those who declared as a certainty that Wyclif was among the damned in hell.

I, however, not wishing to pass a temerarious judgment, hope that he is of the number of those saved. If he is in heaven, may the glorious Lord, who placed him there, be praised; if he is in purgatory, may the merciful Lord free him soon; if he in hell, may he, in accordance with God's just judgment, remain there until its eternal consumation.[109]

As for the dogma of the sacrament of the altar, Hus was actually more traditionally "orthodox" than Cardinal d'Ailly, for he accepted without any reservation or private interpretation the dogma of transubstantiation in its official sense. The cardinal privately preferred the doctrine of "impanation" propounded by William of Ockham, although he professed the official dogma because the Church so decided. Ock-

[109] Flajšhans, ed., *Super IV. Sententiarum* (Praha, 1904–06), p. 261.

ham privately held that the elements of bread and wine were not transubstantiated, but that beneath or within them the body and blood of the Lord were present, although he actually submitted to the teaching of the Church. Luther, who had been trained in the nominalist tradition of Ockham, d'Ailly, Gerson, and Biel, accepted d'Ailly's private conception of the sacrament as his own. He specifically states this in unambiguous terms in his *Commentary on the Galatians*.[110]

It is significant that Hus indignantly repudiated the ascription of all-embracing Wyclifism to himself as a calumny, particularly when made by Páleč and Stanislav. He retorted that they themselves had indeed been Wyclifites, not he. In his spirited polemic with Páleč he writes:

I indeed confess that I hold the true opinions propounded by Master John Wyclif, professor of sacred theology, not because he taught them but because the Scriptures and infallible reason taught them. If, however, he held any error, I do not intend to imitate in whatever manner either him or anyone else.[111]

At the university debate in 1412 Hus defended only five of Wyclif's theses in their "correct" sense, none of which may be said to be heretical. When he was arrested a few weeks after arriving in Constance, the commission appointed to examine him confidently expected that he would prove himself a Wyclifite, since by common reputation he was regarded as such. When in December, 1414, they presented him with the forty-five articles of Wyclif and demanded his answers to them, it must have been a shocking surprise to them when Hus answered thirty-three of them with a categorical "I do not hold and have never held it." To the remaining twelve he replied that they either might possess a correct sense or qualified them acceptably. He thus converted an undoubtedly erroneous assertion into a true statement. Actually, he was prepared to defend only seven of the theses of which

---

[110] John Dillenberger, ed., *Martin Luther, Selections from his Writings* (Garden City, Doubleday, 1961), p. 265. Luther writes: "Some time ago, when I was studying scholastic theology, I was greatly impressed by Dr. Pierre d'Ailly, cardinal of Cambrai. He discussed the fourth book of *Sententiae* very acutely, and said it was far more likely, and required the presupposition of fewer miracles, if one regarded the bread and wine on the altar as real bread and wine, and not their mere accidents–had not the Church determined otherwise." Also cf. an extensive discussion of Luther's relation to the nominalists in B. A. Gerrish, *Grace and Reason, a Study in the Theology of Luther* (Oxford, 1962), pp. 48, 55.

[111] *Historia et Monumenta*, I, 330.

he wrote prior to his departure for Constance that he "did not dare to condemn them lest he resist the truth and become a liar before God." Thereupon the commission requested Hus to answer the articles in writing.[112] It was only when this initial attempt to convict Hus of the Wyclifite heresy failed that Páleč was requested to draw up charges excerpted from Hus's own writings.

Perhaps the best summary of the contemporary errors which Hus vehemently and persistently opposed and denounced is found in his treatise *The Six Errors*. It was originally inscribed in an abbreviated Latin version (*De sex erroribus*) on the walls of the Bethlehem Chapel. Later (1413) it was translated and expanded by him into the Czech version. When the chapel, which some centuries later had been destroyed, was restored in 1949 to its original form, a very small remnant of the inscription was found on one of the original walls. Professor Ryba was entrusted with the task of reconstructing the text. He edited the critical text of both the Latin and the Czech versions of the treatise.[113] The first of the errors is the boast of the "insane priests" claiming to "create the body of God." They exalt themselves above the Virgin Mary, who gave birth to the body of Jesus once, while they claim to do the same times without number. Hus then teaches that since "to create" is to make something *ex nihilo*, only God can be properly said to be Creator. He supports this by numerous quotations from the Fathers, as he does with every other subsequent error.

The second error concerns the abuse of the term "to believe." Some priests command that men believe in the Virgin Mary, in the saints, and in the pope. We should believe *in* none but God. *Of* God we should believe all that Scripture teaches. To believe God is to hold as true whatever He asserts. Therefore, we should not believe *in* the Virgin Mary, although we should believe about her that no one save Jesus Christ is worthier than she among mankind. Likewise, we should not believe *in* Peter, or *in* the pope, or *in* the saints, but should believe whatever is true about them.

In the third place, Hus deals with the forgiveness of sins. Only God forgives sins of His own absolute right, while Jesus Christ, since He is divine-human, has a correlate right to forgive sins because of His

[112] The text is found in Sedlák, "Několik textů z doby husitské," in *Hlídka*, I, 58–69; also in Flajšhans, *M. Jan Hus, Obrany v Kostnici* (Praha, Otto, 1916), pp. 9–18.
[113] B. Ryba, ed., "De sex erroribus" in *Betlemské texty*, pp. 41–104.

humanity. The third kind of forgiveness is ministerial and belongs to the Church and its priesthood. It is essentially declaratory, for a priest declares that only a man who has satisfied the requirements of such forgiveness—contrition for his sins, confession of them to a priest, and rendering of satisfaction—is pardoned by God Himself.

The fourth error deals with obedience. It refers to those who believe that they must obey their superiors, the bishops, lords, parents, and others placed over them, in everything. Hus insists that a Christian must discern whether the command is good or evil in accordance with God's will as revealed in Scripture. When it is found to be contrary to it, the superior must not be obeyed, as Hus himself refused to obey the papal order not to preach at the Bethlehem Chapel.

The fifth chapter deals with the ban and excommunication, of which the priests in question wrongly teach that it affects all whom the ecclesiastical authority condemns for any reason whatsoever. Hus insists that man is rightly excommunicated only for mortal sin.

And finally the sixth error consists of simony, when a spiritual office is either bought or sold for money or granted for favor or other consideration. In condemning these fragrant abuses, Hus was strictly within the Scriptural and ecclesiastical requirements made even by cardinals such as d'Ailly, university leaders such as Gerson, and papal officials such as Dietrich of Niem.

From this brief summary of his religious and theological views, it is evident that a man of Hus's temperament and of his exceedingly sensitive conscience was of necessity compelled by an overwhelming sense of duty to denounce the sins and vices of all, irrespective of rank or office. Under those conditions, he was bound to be resented and opposed by those who felt themselves rebuked by his fearless preaching. To silence him, his opponents and enemies resorted to calumnies and charges of heresy. Actually, Hus was to a surprising degree "orthodox" in the current sense of the word, a child of his times and of the contemporary Church. He firmly believed, as has already been often mentioned, in the dogma of transubstantiation. He upheld the supreme authority of the Scriptures as interpreted by the ecumenical councils, Church Fathers—particularly those of the first five centuries —and reason. He taught the proper veneration, but not worship, of the saints, particularly of the Virgin Mary, whom he believed to have risen from the dead and been elevated above all the angelic hosts in heaven, where she intercedes for sinners and for the Church in general.

This is a puzzling exception to his otherwise uniformly held conviction that the Scriptures alone are the source of doctrine. After all, this is an extrascriptural tenet, even though it had been generally held. He shared faith in purgatory and the masses, prayers, fasts, and alms-giving as aids for the souls in it. He particularly emphasized the sac-rament of penance fully in accordance with the threefold division into contrition, auricular confession, and absolution as well as properly administered indulgences. He did not deny the efficacy of the sacra-ments even when administered, although unworthily, by priests in mortal sin. He submitted to the constituted ecclesiastical and civil authorities, including the pope, in all things lawful, i.e., in accordance with the Scriptures. He taught that salvation is attained by faith formed by love, understood in the sense that good works were necessary to the saving process. He nowhere discusses the problem that became central to Luther, whether divine grace appropriated by faith is suffi-cient to salvation, so that good works are to be performed by the justified sinner *because* he is saved, not *in order* to be saved. Hus stressed the concept, shared by the greatest theological minds of the ages, of "faith formed by love" (*fides caritate formata*) persistently and strenuously, even though he denounced as vigorously the notion of good works without faith. He was essentially a reformer, aiming at the Pauline ideal of a Church "with no spot or wrinkle or any such thing, that she might be holy and without blemish."

At the same time Hus was ahead of his age in regarding the Church as the body of Christ, composed exclusively of the predestinate, of whom Christ alone is the head, the "rock" on which the Church was built. This did not imply any denial of the mixed character of the visible Church, but it did repudiate the concept of the Church as a juridical corporation. Essentially, he conceived the Church as a spir-itual fellowship, a communion of saints, living in holiness and bound to Christ by the grace of predestination. This necessarily implied that the Church is one and therefore ecumenical. He placed emphasis on the supreme authority of the Scriptures as the norm of faith and prac-tice. He insisted, however, on the right of private understanding and conviction as to what the Scriptures taught, rather than on the exclusive right of the Church to their interpretation. This principle he resolutely applied against the entire hierarchy, including the pope, the cardinals, the general Council, whose infallibility he rejected; he applied it also to his own theological opponents. He declared that both the hierarchy and the priesthood exercise only "ministerial" function in the sacrament of penance, rather than dispensing forgiveness of sins by the authority vested in the Church. Only God forgives sins; the priest's authority is limited to a declaration of God's forgiveness. It is in this devotion to the truth as he understood it, and to which he remained faithful unto death, that he towers above his contemporaries. On this ground he decisively approved, although he did not make the original demand for, the granting of the cup in the communion to laymen. On the same ground he rejected capital punishment for religious opinions. The Scriptural emphasis also implied the duty of preaching as central to the service of worship, rather than the ceremonialism and the outward acts of devotion of which much of the worship then consisted. The preaching of the Word was not only to instruct and confirm the believer in his faith, but to deepen his spiritual life, in which true religion consisted. All these characteristics constitute the total and significant impact of Hus on the subsequent reformation of the Church.

THE PRINCIPLES AND AIMS
OF THE COUNCIL OF CONSTANCE

We need not detain ourselves with recounting the story of the calling of the Council of Constance; it has been competently done by Professor Mundy in his introduction to Louise R. Loomis' recently published book, *The Council of Constance*,[114] or is to be found in many other older works. Moreover, the *Account* of Peter of Mladoňovice, which constitutes the principal part of this work, is devoted to the Council's dealings with Hus. His story is, however, told from the point of view of one who, being convinced of the essential innocence of Hus, regarded many charges against him as false. What is needed, therefore, is to present a brief consideration of the Council's aims and principles governing its procedures and to do so from a sympathetic estimate of the Council's own motives.

When the Council opened its sessions on November 5, 1414, it was confronted with a formidable task. To attain its principal objective, the termination of the schism, it had the obvious choice between recognizing one of the existing popes as the rightful one or of removing all three and electing a new one. Were it to choose the former alternative, the Council almost inevitably would have to decide upon John XXIII.

[114] Loomis, *op. cit.*, pp. 10 ff.

He had succeeded Alexander V, the first pope elected under the conciliar principles. He had consented to the calling of the Council of Constance, having for that very reason hoped to win that Council's approval. Would the supporters of the other two popes, however, be willing to abandon their respective popes and accept John as the sole pontiff? In case they would not, the Council would have failed in its principal task as the Council of Pisa had done. The cardinals and the nations composing the Council must have been aware of this dilemma. They soon concluded that the other alternative, the removal by any means possible of all three existing popes and the election of a new one, was preferable. When John became aware of this trend of events he, at first, sought to win the Council's good will by promising to abdicate, if his rivals would do the same. This conciliatory gesture was greeted with enthusiasm. In less than three weeks, however, John escaped from Constance and summoned his cardinals to follow him. Had they obeyed, the Council would have been in danger of disintegration. It was at this perilous juncture that Gerson preached, on March 23, his sermon boldly advocating that the Council proclaim itself, even in the absence of the pope, the supreme tribunal of Christendom. The Council fortunately plucked up enough courage to follow his advice, and on April 6, 1415, adopted the famous decree *Sacrosancta*. J. N. Figgis, with considerable exaggeration, calls this declaration "probably the most revolutionary official document in the world . . . asserting its [i.e., the Council's] superiority to the Pope, and striving to turn into a tepid constitutionalism the Divine authority of a thousand years." [115] It was indeed revolutionary. Had the attempt succeeded, "the center of gravity of the whole Church would have shifted; the Pope would have been reduced to the position of a limited monarch ruled by the College of Cardinals or by the meetings of the Council. It was a life and death struggle, and the Papacy, during its whole course, never lacked skillful and devoted protagonists who saw this quite clearly." [116] Furthermore, even some cardinals not unnaturally saw in the assertion of the Council, dominated by the four nations rather than by themselves, a curtailment of their own prerogatives. At least they had to share them with the Council. Whether for this reason or some other, Cardinal d'Ailly ab-

[115] J. N. Figgis, *Political Thought from Gerson to Grotius: 1414–1625* (New York, Harper & Brothers, Torchbooks, 1960), p. 41.

[116] L. Elliott-Binns, *A History of the Decline and Fall of the Medieval Papacy* (London, 1934), p. 202.

sented himself from the session of April 6, while Cardinal Fillastre, who had been asked to present the document, refused to do so. It was read by the bishop-elect of Posen, Andreas Lascaris. The text of this famous decree reads in part as follows:

This holy synod of Constance, constituting a general council, lawfully assembled to bring about the end of the present Schism and the union and reformation of the church of God in head and members, to the praise of Almighty God in the Holy Spirit, in order that it may achieve more readily, safely, amply, and freely the union and reformation of the Church of God, does hereby ordain, ratify, enact, decree, and declare the following:

First, it declares that being lawfully assembled in the Holy Spirit, constituting a general council and representing the Catholic Church Militant, it possesses its power directly from Christ, and all persons of whatever rank or dignity, even a pope, are bound to obey it in matters pertaining to faith and the end of Schism and the general reformation of the said church of God in head and members,

Further, it declares that any person of whatever position, rank, or dignity, even a pope, who contumaciously refuses to obey the mandates, statutes, ordinances, or regulations enacted or to be enacted by this holy synod, or by any other general council lawfully assembled, relating to the matters aforesaid or to other matters involved with them, shall, unless he repents, be subject to condign penalty and duly punished, with recourse, if necessary, to other aids of the law.[117]

The task which the Council thus set forth in the declaration comprised, besides the termination of the schism and the unification of the Church, the extermination of heresy and a reformation of the Church in head and members. The first of these objectives was attained in three different ways. Pope John XXIII, after having been seized just as he was on the point of crossing the Rhine at Breisach, was imprisoned at the Castle of Gottlieben only three days after Hus had been taken thence and returned to Constance. He was tried on a large number of charges and deposed on May 29. Now plain Baldassarre Cossa, he submitted to the newly elected Pope Martin V, and was reinstated in the cardinalate. He died in Florence (1419) at the court of Cosimo di Medici.

Pope Gregory XII greatly eased the situation by his voluntary abdication (July 4, 1415). Before taking this step, however, he first insisted on issuing through his plenipotentiary, Duke Charles Malatesta

[117] J. D. Mansi, ed., *Sacrorum conciliorum nova et amplissima collectio* (Florence and Paris, 1757–1927), XXVII, 590 f.

of Rimini, the bull of convocation, thereby legitimatizing the Council in his own name. Having thus exacted from the Council his own recognition as the only legitimate pope and by his action legitimizing the Council, he resigned. The Council by this amazing concession recognized that its sessions hitherto had been illegal, and that Gregory, who had been deposed by the Council of Pisa as a schismatic and a heretic, was, after all, the only legitimate pope! Until the election of Martin V the Council was conducted largely by the cardinals. In gratitude for Gregory's abdication, the Council appointed him cardinal-bishop of Porto, a rank second only to that of the pope.

Pope Benedict XIII refused all inducements offered him by the Council through the mediation of Emperor Sigismund himself. The latter had traveled to Narbonne for a personal interview with Benedict; but his efforts to induce the pope to resign proved vain. Having been abandoned by Spain and Portugal, the obstinate old man took refuge at Peñiscola in Spain. He was then deposed by the Council on July 26, 1417; nevertheless, he continued to claim his sole right to the papal office. He declared in his refuge: "Here is the Noah's ark, the true Church." [118] Thus at last the principal *desideratum,* the termination of the schism, was successfully accomplished thirty-nine years after its outbreak!

This tremendous task concluded, the Council was at last in a safe position to proceed with the election of a pope to be acknowledged as legitimate by the entire Church. The man chosen for the office on November 11, 1417, was Cardinal Odo de Colonna, who thereupon assumed the name of Martin V (1417–31). Cardinal Zabarella, who had aspired to this highest honor, was thus defeated by his Roman colleague.

From the very opening of the sessions the Council had set about dealing with the second problem confronting it, that of heresy. Having then declared in *Sacrosancta* that "all persons of whatever rank or dignity, even a pope, are bound to obey it in matters pertaining to faith . . ." the Council was determined to live up to its resolve to crush all dissidence within the rank and file of the Church membership. The maintenance of the unity of the Church being its most important consideration, it was in no mood to deal more leniently with the lower ranks than it had done with the heads of the Church.

[118] Hubert Jedin, *Kleine Konziliengeschichte* (Freiburg-im-Breisgau, Herder-Bücherei, 1959), p. 68.

The three outstanding cases to be dealt with were those of John Wyclif, John Hus, and Jerome of Prague. The first-named case required no more than an official confirmation of the condemnation long before pronounced by the English authorities and recently at the Roman trial. The conciliar verdict was pronounced on May 4, 1415, but since Wyclif himself had been dead for over thirty years, his body was ordered exhumed and removed from the consecrated ground and his writings burned. Later his remains were likewise burned. His followers, the Lollards, had suffered persecution since 1401, when King Henry IV had passed the statute De haeretico comburendo. This persecution was continued with even greater severity by his son, Henry V. He ordered the outstanding leader of the Lollards, Sir John Oldcastle, Lord Cobham, executed in 1417. A similar persecution of the Lollards and other heretics broke out in Scotland under the inquisitor, Lawrence of Lindores. The most conspicuous example of it was that of the Czech Hussite Paul Kravař (in Scottish sources referred to as "Craw"), who was burned at the stake in St. Andrews in 1433.[119] A marker in the pavement of the market place still commemorates the event.

Since the trial and condemnation of John Hus is the exclusive theme of the Account of Peter of Mladoňovice, any extended treatment of it here would be redundant. We are concerned with the Council's motives as revealed by the trial rather than with Hus's condemnation, with which we shall deal later. A balanced judgment of the conduct of the trial, however, presents considerable difficulties. To begin with, Hus was regarded even before arriving in Constance as having been already condemned by the previous verdicts of cardinals Odo de Colonna, Rainald Brancacci, and Peter degli Stephaneschi. Hence the Council refused to treat him as having come to Constance "freely to give account for his faith" at a public hearing. He had even hoped to be allowed to preach before the Council and had made preparations for the occasion! The cardinals thus ignored the papal suspension of the interdict and of the excommunication of Hus. The justice of the condemnation of Hus by the above-named cardinals had been questioned, however, by Cardinal Zabarella when he had been appointed to head the commission to try Hus. Moreover, since Hus had appealed from the verdict of excommunication, although this appeal had been ignored for over two years, he did not consider himself as acting contumaciously

[119] Spinka, "Paul Kravař and the Lollard-Hussite Relations," in Church History (1956), pp. 16 ff.

when he kept on with his ministry. His final appeal to Christ was indeed a piece of astonishing daring contrary to canonical provisions, for he thereby resorted to an extracanonical procedure. But he felt that he was forced to take this step because the judges refused to grant a hearing to his procurators. Hus was, moreover, ever ready to submit to the judgment of the Council, were he proved wrong from the Scriptures, from the Fathers of the Church, and from reason. The argument that the Council could not argue with heretics in order to prove *to them* their guilt is not valid. Hus had come to Constance for that very purpose, having trusted Sigismund's promise to be granted a free hearing. It is plain that the Council never intended to accord him that privilege.

It may be fully conceded that his judges were sincerely concerned with preserving the *status ecclesiae,* which was threatened by heretical movements, and acted as far as possible in accordance with the then current inquisitorial procedures. In fact, even the granting of the three public hearings to Hus was a concession, doubtless wrung from them by Sigismund. In fairness to the Council it should be mentioned that this body would have preferred to induce Hus to recant voluntarily rather than to condemn him to death. Toward the end of the trial, they either authorized one of their members to make the attempt or he did so on his own initiative. At any rate, an unknown member of the Council, whom Hus addressed in his replies as "Father," made the attempt. This prelate, whom Hus regarded as his sincere well-wisher, argued that even if Hus, being innocent, professed himself guilty, the responsibility for the perjury would not be his but the Council's. This was clearly an ethically irresponsible and morally reprehensible attitude. It is to Hus's credit that he rejected it for reasons of conscience. The denial of what he held to be the truth was to him literally a matter of life and death.

What then did Hus hold that the Council found irreconcilable with its own principles? It is clear from the final thirty articles on the basis of which Hus was declared a heretic that it was, among others, his view of the Church universal as being composed of the predestinate of whom Christ alone is the head. Actually, the conciliarists themselves distinguished between the *congregatio fidelium* and the *Romana ecclesia,* as Hus likewise had consistently done. The tragic conflict between the Council and Hus may be viewed as being essentially the difference in conceiving these concepts: the conciliarists regarded the

congregatio fidelium legalistically and considered themselves as representing it, while the *Romana ecclesia,* likewise viewed as a legal entity,
was the domain of the pope and the cardinals. As Tierney has tersely
formulated it, the change was the result of

> the gradual assimilation into the canonistic theory of the ancient doctrine
> of the Church as the Mystical Body of Christ, with a consequent fusion
> between the theological concept of mystical unity in the Church and the
> juristic idea of legal incorporation. . . . The idea of the Chuch as a corpora-
> tion enabled them to give a more precise and concrete expression to the early
> idea of the ultimate authority inherent in the *universitas fidelium.*[120]

The Council, then, regarding itself as a legal institution, claimed coercive powers over the entire Christendom.

On the other hand, Hus retained and defended the view originally
held by the Church in general, including the early conciliarists, that
the *congregatio fidelium,* which he habitually defined more narrowly
as the *universitas praedestinatorum,* is a spiritual entity, the mystical
body of Christ, the membership in which depended on God's will, not
on man's choice. The two concepts thus differently conceived were at
bottom irreconcilable. The Council, rightly sensing this irreconcilability,
felt forced by its own legal principles to condemn Hus's views as subversive of its authority and destructive of the very essence of the
Church conceived in these legal terms. Viewed from this point of
view, the Council was indeed right. If membership in the Church as
the body of Christ depends on predestination, and since no one can
with certainty determine who is or who is not of the elect, what becomes of the corporate and authoritative structure of the Church militant? How can one tell whether the pope, the cardinals, the rest of
the prelates, and even the priests ministering the sacraments are of the
predestinate and, therefore, worthily exercising the divinely sanctioned
authority? They might exercise their office *de facto,* without possessing
the spiritual qualification, as Hus repeatedly conceded; but in that case
they did so unworthily, not in accordance with the divine will. This
was the real charge against Hus, although actually it was never explicitly formulated or included among the final accusations, but only
implicitly inferred. Hus's spiritual concept of the *true* Church implied,
in the Council's view, a denial of the validity and even the reality of
the Church militant. Such a concept was indeed destructive of the

[120] Tierney, *op. cit.,* p. 246.

Church as a legal corporation, as Apostle Paul's concept of the liberty in Christ had been destructive of the Jewish legalism. The hidden destructive force of Hus's spiritual concept of the Church catholic was plainly demonstrated a century later in the Protestant Reformation.

In Dom de Vooght's judgment Hus stood, on the one hand, for "the affirmation of the rights of individual Christian conscience before the interventions of ecclesiastical authority . . . and, on the other hand, for the exaltation of the Christian tradition (patristic, conciliar, and inspired Scriptural) as the absolute norm to which all Christians, from the pope to the least believer, are in duty bound to submit." [121] As such, his views were certainly in basic discord with those of the Council.

As for Jerome of Prague, who stoutly upheld both Wyclif and Hus as truly evangelical, he had ventured against the warnings of his friends to come to Constance. Realizing that he was in imminent danger of being seized and imprisoned, he promptly left that city. He was, nevertheless, recognized and apprehended at a village near the Bohemian border. Returned to Constance, he was imprisoned, and after Hus's execution was placed on trial. He defended himself so eloquently and successfully as to excite the admiration of the humanist Poggio Bracciolini of Florence, who wrote an account of the trial to his friend Leonardo Aretino.[122] Cardinal Zabarella was able to induce Jerome to repudiate his adherence to Wyclif and Hus. When, however, Jerome was not released from prison, although d'Ailly and Zabarella favored it, he withdrew his recantation. Thereupon, on May 30, 1416, he was declared a heretic and sentenced to death. He was burned at the stake at the same place where Hus had suffered the same punishment the year before.

If the Council regarded its dealing with the three men as tending toward a successful extermination of heresy, it was sadly mistaken. The deaths of Hus and Jerome led to an outbreak of revolt in Bohemia that culminated in the long-drawn-out Hussite wars. They were triumphantly conducted under the leadership of John Žižka, and, after his death in 1424, by his successor Procopius the Bald. The Hussite warriors were astonishingly succesful in their struggle with the imperial

---

[121] *L'Hérésie*, p. 280.

[122] "Poggio Florentini ad Leonardum Aretinum epistola de M. Hieronymi de Praga supplicatio," in *Fontes rerum Bohemicarum* (Praha, 1932), VIII, 323 ff. An English translation is found in *The Portable Renaissance Reader* (New York, The Viking Press, 1953), pp. 615 ff.

and crusading armies of both Sigismund and the pope.[123] Unable to overcome the revolt by force of arms, Pope Martin V finally resorted to the calling of the Council of Basel in 1431. He died, however, before the Council opened its sessions. It was his successor, Eugenius IV, who was confronted with the responsibility of dealing with the Council. He promptly dissolved it before it was really started; but the Fathers refused to obey. They reasserted the decree *Sacrosancta* and proceeded with the task of pacifying the Czechs. Sigismund, whom the Czechs had refused to recognize as the successor of his brother, King Wenceslas IV, who had died in 1419, urged that the negotiations be conducted with the "moderate" Prague party. This party had been led at first by Jakoubek of Stříbro and, later, by the Utraquist arch-bishop-elect, John of Rokycany. As the result of these negotiations, the Council granted, on November 30, 1433, the *Compacts of Prague,* consisting of four articles: the communion in both kinds of bread and wine; the free preaching of the Word of God; the punishment of mortal sins, of the clergy by the ecclesiastical, of laymen by the civil author-ities; and finally the prohibition of ruling over secular matters by priests and monks and their excessive acquiring of property. These *Compacts* having been accepted by the "moderate" party at Jihlava in 1436, this party thereupon organized itself into the Utraquist Church, a spe-cial but nevertheless officially recognized ecclesiastical communion within the Roman Church. This became the dominant religious organ-ization of Bohemia; King George of Poděbrady (1458–71) was its faithful adherent, and the archbishop-elect, John of Rokycany, served as its ecclesiastical head. The latter, however, never succeeded in se-curing the papal approval for his office. Even the modest concessions granted the Utraquists by the Council of Basel proved too much for Pope Pius II. He rescinded the *Compacts* in 1462 on the ground that they had been granted as a temporary measure and possessed validity only for the generation represented by the Czech delegation at Basel! Hus was right; no compromise with Rome was possible.

Even more radical development occurred in the case of the Unity of Brethren (*Unitas Fratrum*) which in 1458–59 separated itself both from the Utraquists and the Roman Catholics. The Brethren were thus among the first to organize themselves as a separate communion, having anticipated the Lutheran schism by more than half a century. They

---

[123] Frederick G. Heymann, *John Žižka and the Hussite Revolution* (Princeton, Princeton University Press, 1955).

ordained their priesthood by the presbyterial laying on of hands, thus dispensing with the episcopal ordination in apostolic succession.[124]

Luther, who at first had no intention of separating himself from the Church and organizing a new communion, but had desired to reform what he had regarded as abuse of the indulgences, quickly found himself in conflict with the Church. Having been excommunicated by Pope Leo X in 1520 and condemned at the Diet of Worms in 1521, he was in the end forced to break with the Church. Thus the Protestant Reformation was fully launched.

Under these circumstances the attempt of the Fathers of the Council of Constance to extirpate all dissent by forcible means proved almost wholly unsuccessful.

The last avowed aim of the Council was "the general reformation of the . . . Church of God in head and members." The German and the English nations had desired to proceed with the reforms before the election of the new pope. Their proposal was, however, defeated in favor of a compromise whereby five reform decrees were promulgated prior to the election, the rest being postponed until after that event. The most significant of the five decrees was the decree *Frequens*, adopted on October 9, 1417, by means of which the conciliar supremacy over the papacy was rendered permanent. By its provisions the next Council was to be held within five years, to be followed by another in seven years, and thereafter the meetings to be held every ten years. Eventually, however, these provisions were disregarded by the popes. Thereupon, the Council, consisting of the cardinals and thirty members chosen by the nations, proceeded with the election of the pope. On November 11, 1417, they chose Cardinal Odo de Colonna, who assumed the name of Martin V (1417–31). Once that final step in healing the schism was taken, no major reforms, formerly regarded as essential as the healing of the schism, were seriously attempted. Certain restrictions of the papal finances were enacted and some administrative measures were adopted. Thereupon, Pope Martin closed the sessions on April 22, 1418, before any adequate measures of thoroughgoing reforms were even considered, not to say passed. As Brian Tierney concludes: "It is probable that in any case the merely constitutional reforms emphasized in the Conciliar program could not have produced

---

[124] Peter Brock, *The Political and Social Doctrines of the Unity of Czech Brethren* ('s-Gravenhage, Mouton & Co., 1957); Spinka, "Peter Chelčický, Spiritual Father of the *Unitas Fratrum*," in *Church History* (1943), pp. 271 ff.

the much-needed regeneration in the whole life of the Church." [125] The subsequent history of the papacy, particularly during the second half of the fifteenth century in the days of the Renaissance papacy and just prior to the outbreak of the Protestant Reformation, proved the extreme need of the reforms neglected by the Council of Constance. This constituted its principal failure, as summarized by a recent scholar:

As a reforming council Constance must be pronounced a failure. Its failure was the more regrettable as there was, in not a few quarters, a genuine desire for reform among its members; but this was neutralized by the clash of separate interests, and, as so often happens in reforming movements, each was anxious to reform his neighbours, but very loath to take any steps which might injure himself.[126]

HUS'S "HERESY"

The answer to the problem of Hus's condemnation for heresy obviously depends upon the presuppositions one brings to it. Hus's "real" heresy was his conception that the *true* Church is limited to the predestinate. Although this charge was always in the forefront of the accusations against him, it was never explicitly formulated or declared heretical, but was regarded as implying Hus's denial of the validity of the Church militant. This latter Church, consisting of both the predestinate and the foreknown, was asserted to be a "true" Church as well. The confusion in applying these two concepts derives from the double meaning with which the term "Church" was employed by the contesting parties. Hus conceded that the Church militant was a "true" Church, meaning thereby the predestinate in its membership. The foreknown were not members of this Church universal, but belonged to the synagogue of Satan. Ultimately, they would be separated from the predestinate as the chaff is from the wheat. Thus the basic conflict concerned the concept of the Church, as to whether it was an authoritative corporation or a spiritual fellowship.

There is nothing heretical about Hus's concept of the Church, limited to this aspect of it. It is thoroughly Pauline as well as Augustinian. For that reason it was never explicitly condemned as heretical by the Council, which could do no more than wrongly to imply that Hus's definition excluded the Church militant from being in *any* sense a

[125] Tierney, *op. cit.,* pp. 246–47.
[126] Elliott-Binns, *op. cit.,* p. 202.

"true" Church. The Council could not but concede, although only implicitly, that the foreknown would not ultimately be saved. Otherwise it would have been guilty of teaching the heresy of universalism. Consequently, although this view of Hus was actually the principal reason for his condemnation, he was not for that reason a heretic. He held the faith the Church had always confessed.

In the second place, only those may charge Hus with heresy who accept the final thirty articles as correctly stating his teaching. Throughout the three hearings granted him and in all the other examinations to which he had been subjected, he was never allowed to state his own understanding of the propositions, or, if he did express it, his statement was either disregarded or disbelieved. He was assumed to be a liar and treated as one. The charges of this nature drawn from *De ecclesia* and his other writings he persistently claimed as not being correctly stated, or as being wrenched from their true context and meaning, or as being totally false. What the Council, therefore, condemned were not actually Hus's own tenets, but charges drawn up by his enemies. His own convictions were thus not condemned, for he had not been permitted to state them freely and fully. Only those who accept as correct, either wholly or in substantial part, the charges on the basis of which Hus was declared a heretic, can hold him guilty.

In the third place, Hus repeatedly declared his readiness to submit to the Council's "instruction and correction," provided he were shown by Scriptural proof that he had been wrong. He refused, however, to abjure what he did not hold. He begged the Council "for God's sake" not to force him to lie and thus to risk the danger of damnation. In reply, both Cardinal d'Ailly and Emperor Sigismund, in utter disregard of his piteous plea, speaking with apparent fatherly and friendly concern for Hus's fate, demanded that he abjure all that he was charged with and thus commit perjury! Unless one is ready to argue that Hus should have abjured what he never taught or believed, and should have submitted to the Council's unconditional, ethically unjustifiable demands, one cannot agree with his condemnation as a heretic. His standards of Christian conduct were higher than those of the Council. Its claims to being directly under the inspiration of the Holy Spirit were contradicted by its own conduct.

In the fourth place, the trial was conducted by men committed to principles based on canon law and scholastic or nominalist theology, which regarded the Church mainly as a legal corporation, while Hus based himself on the Scriptures and the teaching of the ancient Fathers, particularly Augustine. Thus he was indeed in conflict with the pre-suppositions of his judges. It cannot, however, be proved that he repudiated the criteria the Church acknowledged—the Scriptures and the great doctors of the Church. To be sure, his strict Biblicism and the Augustinian and Thomistic doctrine of predestination undercut the then current legalistic concepts of his judges. Nevertheless, his emphasis on the spiritual and ethical norms, and his denunciation of their abuses, do not render him guilty of heresy. To prove Hus guilty, one would have to prove his Scriptural and patristic bases as wrong. This is what Hus persistently demanded of the Council.

Finally, one may regard Hus's condemnation by the Council as justified only if one accepts as valid the conciliar theory that the Council is superior over the pope as promulgated by the decree *Sacrosancta*. Pope Gregory XII at his abdication and Pope Martin V at his election indeed confirmed the Council's acts as legitimate, if for no other reason than that the former's submission to it and the latter's election by it made their approval necessary. Martin's bull *Inter cunctas* (March 8, 1418) [127] confirming and approving the Council, is the basis of the remarkably curious reasoning of Dom de Vooght concerning Hus's "heresy." Although he acknowledges that Hus was "a man profoundly religious" and his theology "on the whole catholic," in fact "utterly traditional," yet judging the matter from the modern Roman Catholic view, he chooses to brand Hus's concept of the Church and of the papacy as heretical. In one instance he assumes that Hus denied the reality of the Church militant. In a number of other instances, how-ever, he concedes that Hus recognized the visible Church, especially the Roman Church, but accorded it only a secondary place in the "order of dignity," reserving the first place for the Church universal. This he declares to be a heresy. He furthermore declares Hus's nonrecognition of the papacy as a "divine institution" established by Christ Himself to be heresy. He bases these conclusions not on the Council's con-demnation of Hus, but on Pope Martin's bull legitimizing the con-demnation. In fact, he makes short shrift of the excuse that the Council acted in accordance with the established legal norms. He asks rhetori-cally, if Hus merited to be burned for his opinions, "what have not his

---

[127] The text is found in *Acta scitu dignissima docteque concinnata Constantien-sis concilii celebrissimi* (Hagenau, Henry Grau, 1500), "Errores Johanem Wiclef et Johanem Hus et Hieronymum"; also Hefele-Leclercq, *op. cit.*, VII/I, 511–28.

judges, the Fathers of the Council, merited for having solemnly proclaimed as the dogma of the Faith the *heretical, impious, and scandalous* opinion as to their superiority to the Sovereign Pontiff?" [128]

Martin, in his bull, forbade an appeal from the pope to the Council, thus indirectly condemning the conciliar theory.[129] Within seventeen years Pope Eugenius IV declared the claims advanced in *Sacrosancta* as "impious and scandalous." Pope Pius II in his bull *Execrabilis* of 1461 prohibited any appeal to a Council. Finally, one hardly needs to point out that Pope Pius IX in his decree of papal infallibility in 1870 declared that the pope by his own authority alone can define matters of faith and morals even without the concurrence of cardinals, bishops, and the Church generally. Thus only a person who accepts the principles of *Sacrosancta* can claim that Hus was tried by a legitimate Council.

On the other hand, those who do not believe that Hus received a fair trial at the Council cannot agree with its verdict as to Hus's "heresy," even though they fully admit that there have existed irreconcilable differences beween his views and those of his judges. Actually, Hus had no chance of receiving a fair trial, because he stood from beginning to end before a biased tribunal, determined in advance to condemn him no matter what he adduced in his defense.[130] The procedure was further unfair and unjust because the validity of Sigismund's safe-conduct was not honored even by him; because Hus was not allowed to state his own views and prove the falsity of the trumped-up charges; because some of the witnesses, as Cardinal Zabarella himself admitted, testified only "from common hearsay," while others, being his enemies, bore false witness against him; and because the then current provision of law did not allow him legal representation or advice.

If a proof of the above comments is required, all one needs to do is to read carefully the final thirty articles condemning Hus for heresy. These charges are also incorporated, with minor omissions, in Pope Martin's bull *Inter cunctas*.[131] The text published by Palacký includes Hus's comments on the charges, although if one would learn his more explicit replies, they must be supplemented by his replies to the forty-

---

[128] De Vooght, *Hussiana*, p. 59, and *L'Hérésie*, pp. 464–68, 470, 473.

[129] Jedin, *op. cit.,* p. 72; F. Dvornik, *The General Councils of the Church* (London, Burns & Oates, 1961), p. 74.

[130] De Vooght, *L'Hérésie*, pp. 460–80, especially p. 467.

[131] Part II, No. 15; the bull *Inter cunctas* in Hefele-Leclercq, *op. cit.*, VII/I, 519–22.

five articles of Wyclif, the forty-two articles of Páleč, and his answers at the hearing of June 8. His whole corpus of writings would, of course, yield far more detailed and extensive refutation of these accusations, but those specified above are sufficient for our purpose.

In summarizing, even at the risk of redundancy, all such refutations made by Hus at Constance, it is evident that the one thing common to all the charges is the subversion of the meaning Hus originally gave them. In fact, it is difficult to see what is heretical about the statement that "Paul was never a member of the devil," or that "the two natures, divine and human, constitute one Christ." After all, the Fourth General Council of Chalcedon (451) expressly taught that identical dogma, and it remains the orthodox definition of Jesus Christ's person to this day. The basic distinction Hus made between the predestined constituting the Church universal and the foreknown who are indeed *in* the Church but are not *of* it is a theological commonplace which the Council dared not explicitly condemn. The Council subverted Hus's assertion (article 1) by formulating it as if he denied the very existence of the Church militant with its mixed membership of both the predestined and foreknown. This he never taught. His severe and, it must be admitted, very frequently iterated denunciation of wicked priests and prelates as *unworthy* servants of the Church was undoubtedly irritating, perhaps even exasperating, to those to whom it applied; but it could not be declared erroneous, not to say heretical. All reformers are, as a rule, annoying. Hus, however, never denied that the sacerdotal ministration of wicked clerics was valid. This is particularly true of article 30, "No one is secular lord, or prelate, or bishop while he is in mortal sin." The thesis is undoubtedly Wyclifite. What the Council, however, left out was the all-important qualifying adjective "worthily": "No one is *worthily* secular lord, etc. . . ." Hus freely admitted that even a wicked prelate must be obeyed if what he demands is not contradicting the Scriptures. The charge of disobedience leveled against him in articles 17–18 is pertinent to his refusal to cease preaching at the Bethlehem Chapel and against the "crusading bull." Since he, however, regarded these orders as "unlawful, fulminated out of malice," he felt justified in his disobedience on the ground that "it is meet to obey God rather than man." Moreover, these cases of ecclesiastical disobedience involved the right or duty of private judgment as to what is the command of God or of man. It is not surprising that, from the point of view of the Council, which regarded the Church as a juridical corporation, such an exercise of private judgment was intolerable. Its own view, however, would require submission to every command of ecclesiastical authority and thus negate the right of individual conscience altogether —a veritable ecclesiastical totalitarianism. Furthermore, Hus's predestinarianism, which underlies many charges against him, is not heretical *per se*. St. Augustine and St. Thomas Aquinas were predestinarians as well. Which general Council has ever condemned it as heresy?

The remaining twelve articles deal with papacy, although they involve in many instances other tenets, such as predestination and the consequent difference in the concept of the Church. Article 9, declaring that "the papal dignity arose from Caesars," is a particularly clear instance of the subversion of Hus's meaning. He taught that the pope received his spiritual authority from Christ, but his temporal possessions and supreme rank from several emperors. Surely no one will argue that "the patrimony of Peter," the "Donation of Constantine," and "the Pseudo-Isidorean Decretals" (though this latter was not granted by an emperor) were bestowed upon him by Christ! In articles 11–13, 21–22, it is again the omission of a key word or a modifier that has changed these statements from innocuous truisms into culpable charges. Hus's insistence (article 23) that only God is *sanctissimus* while the pope is at most *sanctus* is certainly not heretical or erroneous, although it may be "offensive to pious ears," particularly to those of not-so-pious popes! In articles 24 and 26, accusing Hus of denying that an election of the pope, even though formally legitimate, does not necessarily prove that the pope has "entered through the lowly door, Christ," would hardly need much argument if applied to John XXIII! The Council itself acted on that principle in deposing two popes, although it condemned Hus for holding it. Articles 27–29, declaring that the Church did and could live in a state of holiness without the pope, stated an obvious historical fact: it did not advocate abolition of the papacy. Which, then, of the thirty articles as really taught by Hus were unscriptural and therefore heretical? Or were the charges as drawn by the Council true simply because the Council, claiming to act under the authority of the Holy Spirit, asserted them to be true in spite of anything Hus really held and taught?

No wonder that Hus, in his last declaration made to the Council, courageously asserted that "fearing to offend God and to fall into perjury" he was not willing to abjure any of the articles with which he was charged. "For God is my witness that I neither preached, nor asserted, nor defended them."

PETER OF MLADOŇOVICE AND HIS "ACCOUNT" OF HUS'S TRIAL

The present translation of Peter's *Relatio de Magistro Johanne Hus* is based on the critical edition of this work prepared by Václav Novotný [132] and constitutes the first and principal part of the present treatise. The second part comprises documents and letters complementary to Peter's narrative. Since he was an eyewitness of most of the events described by him, his work is generally regarded as the most complete and reliable record of all that is connected with Hus's trial and death. Novotný, who devoted the last years of his life to its editing, pronounced it "the most important of all the information about Hus." [133] Peter also collected many of the letters Hus had written during this crucial period, some of which he incorporated in his work. He also served as the actual writer of the protests of the Czech and Polish nobles, read before the Council or sent to Emperor Sigismund. In them his legal training is particularly, sometimes painfully, evident. In contrast to Peter's ordinary narrative style, they are redundant and replete with the technical legal verbiage indulged in by lawyers of all ages, but particularly in his day. It must be further admitted that his Latin leaves much to be desired and at times is hardly translatable, as will be pointed out at appropriate places in the text. He seems to have been in a great hurry to finish the final copy and, in a number of instances, he can hardly be spared the charge of carelessness. Thus he refers several times to documents to be inserted in the text, but fails to do so at the designated place, although he does insert them elsewhere. Other samples either of his or of his transcribers' carelessness are pointed out in footnotes. Nevertheless, despite his relatively humble station, Peter played an important part in the events he so minutely and faithfully narrated. Were it not for his *Account,* our knowledge of the conduct of the trial of Hus before the Council of Constance, and particularly his martyr's death, would have been not only quite meager, but would have been based on sources inimical to him.

[132] Novotný, "Historické spisy Petra z Mladoňovic a jiné zprávy a paměti o M. Janovi Husovi a M. Jeronymovi z Prahy," in *Fontes rerum Bohemicarum* (Praha, 1932), VIII, 25–120.

[133] *Ibid.,* p. xxi.

The high regard in which Peter's work was held is attested by the fact that the final chapter descriptive of Hus's martyr death was regularly read on July 6, the day which became a national holiday, and remained so observed for more than 200 years thereafter. Besides the Gospel lesson for the day, the farewell letters written by Hus from Constance were read along with Peter's fifth chapter. Under Luther's influence the Latin original of this whole work was published in Nuremberg in 1528 and its German translation a year later. A further mention of this translation will be made later. The work gained a wide circle of readers among the Calvinists when Jean Crespin published it, along with Hus's letters, in his celebrated *Le livre des martyrs* (1554).[134] From Geneva it soon spread into other French-speaking countries and was published in many editions. Later Peter's work was translated into Dutch, German, and Polish. It became immensely influential in John Foxe's successive editions of his *Book of Martyrs,* the first edition of which was published in 1554 and five years later appeared in a greatly expanded Basel edition. Foxe kept on enlarging the initial text until it reached almost monumental proportions.[135] Next to the Bible, his martyrology continued to be the favorite reading of the English churchmen late into the nineteenth century. Palacký's recovery of this work in his *Documenta* was thus a much belated act of justice (1869). The entire work has never been translated into Czech with the exception of Václav Flajšhans' version of the narrative portions (omitting the documents and the quotations from Hus's writings), which was published in Prague in 1917.

Peter was born in the village of Mladoňovice (Bladendorf) in Moravia

[134] Jean Crispin, when he adopted the Reformed tenets, was forced to flee for safety to Strasbourg and later to Geneva (1548). There he established a printing press. In 1554 he published his *Le Livre des Martyrs,* which was translated into Latin by Claude Baduel (1556) and published under the title *Acta martyrum.* Crespin published his *Histoire des vrays témoins de la vérité de l'Evangile depuis Jean Hus jusqu'à présent* (1570).

[135] John Foxe (1516–87), who sought refuge on the Continent during the Marian persecutions, published in Strasbourg a small book (1554), *Commentarii rerum in ecclesia gestarum maximarumque per totam Europam persecutionum a Vuicleui temporibus ad hanc usque aetatem descriptio.* He continued this work, which was then published in Basel in 1559. Returning to England, he translated it into English and published it in London under the title *Actes and monuments of these latter and perillous dayes ... from the year of our Lorde a thousande, to the tyme now present, etc.* The first edition appeared in 1563, but was continually enlarged. By Elizabeth's order, the *Book of Martyrs,* as it was commonly called, was placed in all college chapels and the residences of the higher clergy throughout the kingdom.

some time in the nineties of the fourteenth century.[136] He came to Prague to study at the university. There he became an ardent adherent of Hus, a devotion that is evident throughout his *Account*, the work for which he is best known. He received his B.A. in 1409, on which occasion Hus delivered the promotion address. Two years later we find him among the first members of the college established by Queen Hedwiga of Poland primarily for Lithuanian students. The implementation of the queen's project was entrusted to the wealthy merchant Kříž, who had also been instrumental in the founding of the Bethlehem Chapel. In 1411 Kříž was able to effect a loose affiliation of the two foundations, so that the preachers of the chapel played an important part in the administration of the college. No wonder that Peter, one of the students there, came into close contact wih John Hus, the most celebrated of the preachers of the chapel.

In Constance, as the secretary of Lord John of Chlum, Peter lived with Hus in the same lodging, at "the good widow Fida" in St. Paul's Street (now *Hussenstrasse*). Thus he became the eyewitness of all that befell Hus, to whom he usually refers as "the Master". He kept in close touch with him even after Hus's imprisonment in the Dominican monastery and by generous gifts to the jailers secured Hus's contact with his friends. When, however, Hus was transferred to the Castle of Gottlieben, belonging to the bishop of Constance, all contacts ceased. Hus was kept there in the strictest confinement. He was not able to send out a single letter throughout the period from March 24 to June 3, 1415, at which time he was removed to the prison in the Franciscan monastery in Constance. Among many other significant services Peter rendered the cause of Hus was his notifying of the two Czech nobles, Wenceslas of Dubá and John of Chlum, of the intention of the Council to adjudge the case in Hus's absence. They in turn informed Sigismund of the alleged design, and he forbade it. Moreover, during the hearings of June 8, Peter, along with the two Czech nobles, overheard Sigismund's remarks in a conversation with some cardinals urging that they burn Hus as a heretic even if he should recant. Without this detail contributed solely by Peter, Sigismund's deceitful conduct would not have been as well known to the Czech Hussites as was eventually the

---

[136] This biographical sketch of Peter is based on F. M. Bartoš' article, "Osud Husova evangelisty Petra Mladoňovice," of which the author kindly sent me a typescript copy. It was published in *Křestanská Revue,* supplement (Praha, 1963), pp. 79–85.

case. It contributed to their rejection of Sigismund from succeeding
to the crown of Bohemia after his brother's death. After Hus's martyrdom—an event which Peter described with faithful realism and earnest
piety—he returned to Bohemia to complete the *Account*, partly written
during his stay in Constance. Having received his master's degree in
January, 1416, he began his career at the university.

When King Wenceslas died (1419), the Hussite revolt against his
successor, Sigismund, broke out. It was spearheaded by the radical
Taborite wing under the leadership of John Žižka. Even the "moderate"
party of the Praguers came under attack. The majority of the university
masters, among them Peter of Mladoňovice, although remaining faithful
to Hus's reform program, suffered rough treatment because they opposed the radical innovation of the "left wing" of the Hussite movement. Peter, who served as an assistant to the fatherly friend and
supporter of Hus, Master Christian of Prachatice, pastor of St. Michael's
Church in Old Town, shared the anti-Taborite views. When in 1421
the Hussite armies conquered that bastion of the royal forces, the city
of Kutná Hora, which ranked second in importance only to Prague,
Peter, under pressure from Christian, reluctantly assumed the pastorate
of its principal church. When, however, the city's newly appointed
burgomaster, Peter Zmrzlík of Svojšín, the generous supporter of Hus
who had furnished most of the money for the latter's journey to and
stay in Constance, died, and when shortly afterward Kutná Hora was
retaken by the royal forces, Peter returned to Prague. He thus escaped
sure death at the hands of the conquerors. Since Sigismund had been
deposed at the Diet of Čáslav, and the Polish-Lithuanian prince Sigismund Korybutovič, son of the Polish king Wladislaw III, was elected
king and entered Prague in May, 1422, Peter at last felt safe. Unfortunately, the young and inexperienced new king proved quite unable
to secure peace for the country. When in the end he entered into
negotiations with Emperor Sigismund and agreed to surrender Prague
to him, he was deposed. His downfall had for its consequence the
expulsion, in 1427, of the university masters who had supported him,
among whom Peter of Mladoňovice had taken a prominent part. The
new leader of the "moderate" Prague party, chosen the archbishop-
elect, was Master John of Rokycany. Peter, however, opposed him,
and even though some of the masters soon afterward accepted the new
leadership of the Utraquist Church, Peter remained firm in his rejection
of Rokycana. He secured the pastorate of the church at Batelov in his

native Moravia and remained there until 1438. In the meantime, the Council of Basel granted, although in an attenuated form, the Utraquist demands formulated in the *Compacts*. This agreement was solemnly proclaimed in 1436 by Bishop Philibert, representing the Council, at Jihlava, not far from Batelov. The peace thus reestablished after sixteen years of ceaseless warfare included the recognition of Sigismund as king of Bohemia. He died, however, a year later.

Peter returned to Prague in 1438 and a year later became pastor of St. Michael's Church in succession to his old friend Christian of Prachatice. He was also elected rector of the university and joined the party of Rokycana. His prominence among the Utraquists is attested by his being chosen, in 1446, a member of the delegation to be sent to the curia to negotiate the recognition of Rokycana as archbishop. He did not accept the honor for reasons not clearly known—perhaps because he still refused to believe in the good faith of the papal court. Two years later, however, when he was chosen the principal spokesman of the Utraquists in the negotiations with the papal nuncio, Cardinal Carjaval, who came to Prague to announce Pope Nicholas' rejection of Rokycana, Peter told the cardinal: "Lord nuncio, if you do not confirm to us the communion in both kinds and Rokycana as archbishop, you will hear, before you reach Rome, strange things about this kingdom!" The threat was not an empty one. A few months later the young Lord George of Poděbrady, political leader of the Utraquists, secured control of Prague and became, in 1452, regent of the country during the youth of King Ladislav. After the latter's untimely death, George was elected king of Bohemia. During his remarkably able reign he offered powerful opposition to Pope Pius II in defense of the *Compacts* and of the still unconfirmed Archbishop Rokycana. By that time, however, Peter was dead, having died on February 7, 1451.

Peter originally intended to give his *Account* a form not actually attained by him. Novotný informs us that "only in the single manuscript at the Museum (M) [137] is the whole account contained; but not even there is it in the order in which the author wished to present it to the public." Even the title is not his. He wanted to call it *Historia de sanctissimo martyre Johanne Hus*, or more briefly *Historia M. Johannis Hus*. It was Palacký in his *Documenta* [138] who gave it the title *Relatio*

---

[137] The National Museum in Prague; cf. Novotný's preface to "Historické spisy Petra z Mladoňovic," p. xxxi.

[138] Palacký, pp. 234–324.

de Mag. Johannis Hus causa, and divided it into five chapters. The last of these, dealing with the account of Hus's death, is extant in numerous copies, while chapters I–IV exist only in one, or partly in two, manuscripts. Nevertheless, even the museum text is a copy that does not preserve the original arrangement. Peter gathered the source material of Chapter II at the time the events themselves took place, but chapters III and IV were actually written contemporaneously with the events. Novotný concludes that "parts III and IV, dealing with the hearings, are in fact the oldest definitely written parts of his work." [139] Peter intended to write the whole account while still in Constance, but did not succeed in doing so with the exception of the above-mentioned chapters, which were written probably between June 8 and July 6, 1415. The concluding chapter about Hus's death was added later, while Chapter I, concerning the preparation for the journey and the journey itself, was written last.

Nevertheless, the original form of the book has been preserved in a curious manner. In 1529 Johannes Agricola (1497–1566) published a book at Hagenau, translated into German by Nicholas Krombach under the title *History und wahrhafftige Geschicht, wie das heilig Euangelion mit Johann Hussen ym concilio zu Costnitz durch den Bapst vnd seinen Anhang offentlich verdampt ist ym yare nach Christi vnsers Herren geburt 1414. Mit angehenckter protestation des Schreibers, der bey allen Stucken und Puncten gewesen ist.*[140] The manuscript thus translated did not bear the name of its author, but Agricola judged it to be the work of Peter of Mladoňovice. He was quite right. This is the first redaction of Peter's *Account,* exhibiting the original form that the author intended for it. This German translation omits certain details included in the second redaction and contains some errors. The translator also adds some of his own explanatory remarks.

Palacký's version of the *Account* in his *Documenta* is the first critical edition of the document. It is based on three manuscripts of the first redaction. Novotný's edition differs from it in so far as he has not only used the M version as the basis, as Palacký had done, but expanded it by the additional material from the second redaction, and collated it with all the extant manuscripts. For that reason Novotný's edition is definitive as far as the present available sources allow.

In view of the sincere devotion of Peter to Hus, the question naturally

[139] Novotný, *op. cit.,* preface, p. xxvi.
[140] This German version is found in Novotný, *op. cit.,* pp. 150–221.

arises as to the reliability of his narrative. In Novotný's judgment, it is not biased or deliberately slanted to favor Hus at the expense of factual truth. Peter certainly regarded Hus's opponents, such as Páleč, Michael de Causis, and Bishop John of Litomyšl, as Hus's enemies who deliberately falsified the facts in order to compass his death. In this he did them no injustice. They were Hus's enemies, irrespective of their motives. Such an estimate of Peter's reliability is shared by the majority of the outstanding Czech historians. It is disputed chiefly by the late Dr. Jan Sedlák, whose oft-mentioned book, *M. Jan Hus*, merits consideration, though I for one am not convinced by his adverse arguments. Far less unfavorable, although still written from the Roman Catholic point of view, are the two works of the Belgian Benedictine, Paul de Vooght, already mentioned a number of times. He, nevertheless, shares Sedlák's conviction of the heretical character of Hus's concept of the Church. He admits, however, as Sedlák does not, that the judges were determined in advance to adjudge Hus guilty. He censures them for conducting themselves like bad schoolmasters aiming at humiliating rather than gaining their pupil's heart.[141] In case after case he points out that the accusations against Hus were actually misconstrued, given a wrong meaning, or altogether false.[142]

As for Part II of the present work, it comprises documents and letters, predominantly Hus's own, which are either referred to in Peter's text or furnish Hus's own description of events germane to Peter's narrative. From these letters one derives the best evidence of the Czech reformer's character and personality. They reveal his deep convictions regarding the supreme authority of the Scriptures as interpreted by the Church Fathers in contrast to the legalistic views of his judges, coupled with his profound humility and readiness to be instructed concerning anything that might conflict with his understanding of faith. They also witness to his determination to die rather than betray the truth. They illustrate better than any other available source the tragic conflict between his sincere and faithful desire to reform the Church according to the primitive apostolic pattern, interpreted by the doctors of the Church, particularly Augustine, and between the contemporary Church, far removed from that pattern. They manifest his supreme devotion to the ideal of a church as the body of Christ that exists amid the corruption of the secular society "without spot or

[141] De Vooght, *Hussiana,* pp. 207 f.
[142] De Vooght, *L'Hérésie,* Chap. X.

wrinkle," a fellowship of the redeemed, "unspotted from the world."
If such an ideal was excessively, unattainably high, the contemporary
conditions of the Church were so low as to make the demands for
reform imperative.

PART ONE

Peter of Mladoňovice:
An Account of the Trial and
Condemnation of Master John Hus
in Constance

CHAPTER I

Events Prior to the
Journey to Constance

In the year of our Lord 1414, the most serene prince and lord, Lord Sigismund, king of the Romans and of Hungary, etc., after he, along with Pope John XXIII, had called and ordered to be proclaimed a general Council to be held in Constance,[1] in the region of Swabia, sent from Lombardy certain noble lords of Bohemia,[2] his councilors and familiars, charging them in his royal name to conduct Master John of Husinec, *formatus* bachelor of sacred theology,[3] [to that Council]. They were to assure him of a safe-conduct, in order that he should come to Constance to the said general Council for the clearing of his own evil reputation as well as that of the Bohemian kingdom. The king was also willing to send him a special safe-conduct in order that, having come to Constance, he might return to Bohemia. He also solemnly promised to be ready to take him under his and the Holy Empire's protection and defense. Afterward, therefore, he sent him that safe-conduct in duplicate, written in Latin and German, to be delivered to him on the way.[4] The purport of the Latin version follows in these words: [5]

"Sigismund, by the grace of God king of the Romans, ever Augustus, and king of Hungary, Dalmatia, Croatia, etc., to each and every one

---

[1] The text of these proclamations is found in Loomis, tr., *The Council of Constance: the Unification of the Church,* pp. 70–83.

[2] Particularly lords John of Chlum and Wenceslas of Dubá.

[3] *Baccalarius formatus* was a person who, holding the rank of bachelor of divinity, had completed the study of Peter Lombard's *Sentences,* but had not yet obtained the doctorate.

[4] Hus had already started on the journey; he received the safe-conduct two days after he arrived in Constance.

[5] Novotný, *M. Jana Husi Korespondence a dokumenty,* No. 88.

of the princes ecclesiastical and secular, dukes, margraves, counts, barons, nobles, notables, *ministeriales*, knights, squires, captains, regents, governors, presidents, tollgatherers, tax collectors, and every kind of official, and to the communities, cities, towns, villages, localities, and settlements and their officials, as well as the rest of our own and the Holy Empire's subjects and faithful, to whom these presents shall come, royal grace and all good!

"Venerable, illustrious, noble, and faithful beloved!

"We wholeheartedly commend to you all and every one of yours the honorable Master John Hus, *formatus* bachelor of sacred theology and master of arts, bearer of these presents, journeying from the kingdom of Bohemia to the forthcoming general Council soon to be held in the city of Constance, whom we likewise have received into our and the Holy Empire's protection and defense. We desire, when he comes to you, that you receive him kindly, treat him favorably, and afford him willing help as regards the speed and safety of his journey, both by land and by water. You are in duty bound to aid him with his servants, horses, baggage, weapons [*arneriis*], and his other private possessions at any passes, harbors, bridges, lands, domains, districts, jurisdictions, cities, towns, castles, villages, and every other kind of your localities, without his paying any sort of tax, path toll, toll, tribute, and freeing him from every other burden of payment whatsoever and every kind of impediment; to permit him and his companions freely to go, stop, tarry, and return, and if need be to provide him willingly and out of duty a secure and safe conduct, to the honor and respect of our royal majesty.

"Given at Speyer, in the year of the Lord 1414, on October 18, and in the thirty-third year of our reign in Hungary, etc., and our fifth year as king of the Romans.

"By order of the Lord King.

Michael de Prziest, canon
of Wratislaw" [6]

---

[6] Bartoš, *Čechy v době Husově*, p. 391, asserts that this was a mere pass and not a "safe-conduct." But the two Czech nobles who had been sent to Hus by Sigismund, and Hus himself, regarded it throughout the trial as a veritable "safe-conduct." They regarded it as embodying the promises made to Hus by Sigismund's emissary, Lord Mikeš Divoký, and of Wenceslas' plenipotentiary, Lord Henry Lefl of Lažany. Sigismund himself declared that he had given Hus the safe-conduct. Cf. Chapter III toward the end. Bartoš further states that the canon's name was Michael of Přestanov. *Ibid.,* p. 385.

Master John Hus, seeing and hearing so many and so great promises and forms of assurance, wrote to the king[7] that he would without fail come to the said Council. And before he left Prague, he wrote his public notices in Latin, Czech, and German a sufficient number of days in advance and ordered them posted several times on the doors of the cathedral, parish, cloister, or monastery churches and in many other places, publicly announcing his willingness to go to Constance and his readiness publicly to render account there to anyone for his faith. And if anyone knew of any error or heresy against him, that he should also make ready to go there to oppose him. The purport of it follows in these words:

"Master John of Husinec, *formatus* bachelor of sacred theology, is willing to appear before the most reverend father, Lord Conrad, archbishop of Prague, legate of the Apostolic See, at the fortcoming convocation of all the prelates and clergy of the kingdom of Bohemia, being 'ever ready to render account for the faith and hope that is in him,' to the satisfaction of all who may demand it of him; and to see and hear each and every one individually who wishes to charge him with an obstinate error or any heresy whatsoever, provided they are willing to subject themselves, according to the law of God and of juridical exigency, to a like penalty if they do not legally prove against him an obstinate error or heresy. To all these he wishes to prove his innocence, in the name of Christ, before the said lord archbishop and prelates and also before the forthcoming general Council in Constance, in accordance with the decrees and canons of the holy fathers.

"Given on the Sunday after the feast of St. Bartholomew."[8]

The Czech notice follows:[9]

"I, Master John of Husinec, announce to the entire kingdom of Bohemia that I am ready to take my stand in the court of the priest archbishop at the forthcoming assembly of the clergy in regard to all those accusations by which I am falsely accused and charged. Hence, because in many corners they call me a heretic, contrary to justice and right, let such of you stand forth openly before the priest archbishop and denounce me fearlessly as to which heresies you have heard from me; and if I shall be found in any error or in any heresy, I will not refuse to suffer as being erroneous and a heretic. But if no one who

---

[7] I.e., to Sigismund; cf. Hus's letter in Part II, No. 5.
[8] Novotný, *op. cit.*, No. 75; dated by him August 26, 1414.
[9] Palacký, *Documenta Mag. Joannis Hus*, No. 34.

wishes to accuse me in his own name will stand up, then I again announce to the entire kingdom of Bohemia that I intend to take my stand on this declaration, in order to establish the truth, before the general Council in Constance: if the pope will be present there, before the pope and before the clergy of that Council. And if anyone knows anything erroneous or heretical against me, let him prepare to go there to accuse me in his own name before the said Council. I will not hesitate to reply properly in defense of my truth, whether he be little or great. Therefore, consider this, good people who love justice, if by this writ I demand anything against the divine or human right. But should I not be granted a hearing, then may it be known to the whole Bohemian kingdom that it is not by my fault."

And on the same day: [10]

"To the royal Grace and the Queen, their councilors, the master of the royal court, and the entire royal court: I, Master John Hus, announce and declare that, being well informed by certain people that letters from the pope [11] have come to the King's Grace—sent by whom I know not—wherein it is written that your royal Grace should take care to uproot the widespread heretics from his Bohemian land; and because there is against me an outcry and demand—without my fault, as I hope to God; and in order that your royal Grace should not on my account incur dishonor and the Bohemian land defamation; I sent out and posted many letters, offering to come to the court of the archbishop, being willing to stand first of all an inquiry into my truth. I stated further that, if there is anyone in this entire Bohemian land who knows of any heresy against me, he should announce himself at the court of the archbishop and there in his name stand up against me. Inasmuch as no such person has appeared and the priest archbishop did not allow me and my procurators to appear, therefore I beseech his royal Grace, the Queen, their councilors, and the master of the royal court for justice, that they would be pleased to grant me due testimony that I did make this offer and have publicly posted the letters, and that no one in this land has on that account stood up against me. In spite of all this, I declare a sufficiently long time in

---

[10] Since the archbishop refused to allow Hus to testify before him, he wrote to King Wenceslas and Queen Sophie. To this appeal he received no answer. The term translated "master of the court" refers to the official known in Latin as *magister curiae* and in German *Hofmeister*. Cf. Novotný, *op. cit.*, No. 78, and Palacký, No. 35.

[11] This refers to the letter of Pope John XXIII dated July 11, 1414.

advance to the whole Bohemian land and to other lands that I am willing to take my stand in Constance before the summoned Council; and if the pope should be there, to do so before him and that general Council. If anyone knows of any heresy against me, let him get ready to go to that Council, that he may accuse me there in his own name before the pope and the entire Council as to whatever heresies he has ever heard from me. And if any heresy should be proved against me, I do not refuse to suffer as a heretic; for I fully trust in the dear God that He will not permit slanderous people, opponents of the truth, to be victorious over the truth."

Likewise, he also sent his procurators to the reverend father in Christ, Lord Nicholas, bishop of Nezero [Nazareth],[12] inquisitor of heretical pravity of the city and diocese of Prague, specially appointed by the Apostolic See, to ask of him, Lord Nicholas, if he knew of any error or heresy concerning him to make it known and to declare it publicly. Lord Nicholas acknowledged before the said procurator of Master John Hus and before a notary public and several trustworthy witnesses that he has held several conversations with the said Master John Hus and that he had found him a catholic and faithful man. This will appear more clearly in the record of his inquest to be inserted hereafter. Besides, Lord Nicholas, bishop and inquisitor of heretical pravity, to confirm the aforesaid inquest, gave and presented to the said Master John a letter patent, sealed with his own evident seal appended, in testimony of the said matters. It will also hereinafter be inserted word for word.[13]

Besides, the said Master John Hus in a plenary session of the barons of the Bohemian kingdom, assembled in the St. James cloister together with the archbishop of Prague, Lord Conrad,[14] to discuss matters pertaining to the kingdom, sent the same lord barons a letter or an epistle, sealed with his own seal, petitioning them, among other things, to ask

[12] Although the Latin sources (Peter's *Account* among them) uniformly designate Nicholas as the bishop of Nazareth, this see, which had been captured by the Saracens in 1170, had been transferred to Barletta in Apulia, and was occupied in Nicholas' time by Bishop John Paul (1400–31). Cf. P. B. Gams, ed., *Series episcoporum ecclesiae catholicae* (Ratisbon, 1873), p. 287. Czech historians designate his see as Nezero, perhaps the suffragan see of Larissa in Greece.

[13] See *infra*, Chap. II, pp. 142–44, 151–52.

[14] Conrad of Vechta, a Westphalian by birth, bought the Prague archbishopric from the curia in 1413 and retained it until 1431, having accepted in 1421 the Utraquist tenet of communion in both kinds. He was, however, deposed by Pope Martin V in 1415.

publicly of the said lord archbishop whether he knew of any error or heresy concerning the said Master John Hus, declaring that he, Master John Hus, was still ready to be corrected on its account in Bohemia. But if he knew of none, that he should give him a letter of testimony concerning these matters. Hus himself was nevertheless willing to go to Constance to declare his faith there. Upon being asked, the lord archbishop publicly declared that he knew of no error or heresy against the said Master John Hus, but only that the pope had excommunicated him; and from that excommunication [he said] let the said Master John Hus extricate and clear himself as best he could. This declaration of the archbishop's and also the lord barons' request is clearly contained in the testimonial letter given him, Master John Hus, sealed with the seals of the noble lords Čeněk of Vartemberk or Veselí, the supreme burgrave of the Prague castle; of Boček of Poděbrady; and of William of Vartemberk or of Zvířetice, sealed and inserted hereafter.[15]

Further, when the plenary convocation or synod of all the clergy and prelates of the said kingdom of Bohemia was assembled at the court of the said archbishop of Prague,[16] the said Master John Hus sent his procurator, the honorable Master John of Jesenice, doctor of laws, to the said archiepiscopal court of Prague. He sought to be admitted either in person or by his procurator in order to ask each and every one of the prelates of the said kingdom, if any of them knew of any error or heresy concerning the said Master John Hus, to make himself known and to pledge himself in accordance with the canonical sanctions. Neither Master John nor his procurator, however, was admitted to the said archiepiscopal court or to an audience to make the request in any form, as it also clearly appears from the public record made of it, which will be inserted hereafter.[17]

While all these things as mentioned before were taking place, the said Master John Hus, in the company of the noble lords Wenceslas of Dubá and John of Chlum, took the road to Constance on Thursday before the Feast of St. Gallus in the year of the Lord 1414.[18]

Here follows a copy of the sealed letter which he [Hus] sent to Master Martin before leaving, requesting him not to open it unless he were

---

[15] See *infra*, Chap. II, pp. 152–53.
[16] On August 27, 1414.
[17] See *infra*, Chap. II, pp. 144–46.
[18] October 11, 1414, when he left the castle of Krakovec, where he had found refuge.

certain that he [Hus] had been overtaken by death; it follows in these words: [19]

"Master Martin, dearly beloved brother in Christ! I exhort you in the Lord to fear God, to keep His commandments, to flee consorting with women, and to be cautious while hearing confessions of women, lest Satan beguile you by means of women's hypocrisy. For Augustine says: 'Do not believe devotion; for the more devout, the more lascivious it is, and under the pretext of piety it conceals the birdlime of concupiscence.' [20] Therefore, be on your guard lest you lose the irrecoverable virginity, which I hope you retain. Remember that ever since your youth I taught you to serve Christ Jesus, and if possible would have liked to teach you in one day all I myself knew. You likewise know that I denounced the avarice and irregular life of priests, for which cause by the grace of God I am suffering persecution that will soon achieve my destruction. Nor am I afraid of bearing shame for the name of Jesus Christ. I beg you also from my heart not to be greedy of benefices. Nevertheless, if you should be called to the pastoral office, be motivated by the honor of God, the salvation of souls, and labor, instead of by the ownership of sows or a plot of land. But if you become a pastor, beware of having a young woman for a cook, lest you build up the house more than the soul. See to it that you are a builder of a spiritual building, being kind to the poor and humble, not spending your goods on feasts. I also fear that, if you mend not your life by giving up splendid and superfluous garments, you shall be severely rebuked by the Lord; as I, too, a miserable wretch, am being rebuked for having made use of such things, having been seduced by men's evil custom and praise. By these things I offended God through the spirit of pride. Because you have well known my preaching and public conduct ever since your youth, I do not consider it necessary to write you more. I beg you, however, for the sake of the mercies of Jesus Christ not to follow me in any levity that you have seen in me. You know that—alas!—before I became a priest, I had gladly and

[19] This letter is addressed to Master Martin of Volyně; cf. Novotný, op. cit., No. 86; Palacký, No. 38.

[20] This is not a quotation from Augustine, but from a letter of Pope Alexander III to the archbishop of Canterbury. Cf. Friedberg, Corpus juris canonici, II, 455. Augustine expresses similar views in De conjugiis adulterinis, Book 2, Chap. 21. Patrologia Latina, XL, col. 486. Hus himself repeats a similar warning in the Exposition of the Decalogue, Žilka, Vybrané Spisy Mistra Jana Husi, II, 383.

often played chess, had wasted time, and by that play had frequently unhappily provoked to anger both myself and others. Therefore, on account of countless other faults which I have committed, I entrust myself, by your prayers, to the most merciful Lord for His pardon in that you may not be slow to appeal for His mercy even now, that it may please Him to direct my life, and, overcoming the vileness of the flesh, the world, and the devil, to place me at least in the day of judgment in the heavenly homeland. Farewell in Christ Jesus, along with all who keep His law.

"You may keep the gray gown, if you wish, as a memento; but as I believe that you are ashamed of gray, give it, therefore, to anyone who seems best to you. Give the white gown to my pupil, 'the Pastor.' To George or Georgie also give sixty *grossi* [21] or the gray gown, for he has served me faithfully."

There follows the superscription: "I beg you not to open this letter unless you are certain that I am dead, etc."

The letter to the people, which he left behind upon his departure for the journey to Constance, was translated into Latin at the Council in a malicious fashion. They said that he had left a letter in the following form: "If I should happen to abjure, understand that I do it only with my lips but do not consent to it in my heart." Therefore, observe whether their lie will be thwarted by the letter which follows in the vernacular word for word as he left it: [22]

"Master John Hus, in hope a priest and servant of the Lord Jesus Christ, to all the faithful and dear brethren and sisters in the Lord Jesus, who have heard and received the Word of God through me: grace and peace from God our Father and from the Holy Spirit, that they may remain spotless in His truth.

"Faithful and dear friends! You know that for a long time I have faithfully labored among you, preaching to you the Word of God without heresy and errors, as you are aware, and that your salvation was, is now, and shall remain my desire until my death. I had intended to preach to you before my journey, prior to my departure for the Council at Constance, and in particular to acquaint you with the false testimonies and the witnesses by name, who have lyingly witnessed against me. I have all their names and their testimonies recorded, and will announce them to you in order that if they slander or condemn me to

[21] Sixty *grossi* make one *sexaginta* (in Czech *kopa*).
[22] Cf. Novotný, *op. cit.,* No. 87; and Palacký, No. 37.

death, you, knowing it, may not fear it as if I were condemned on account of any heresy that I held. Also that you may stand without fear and wavering in the truth which the Lord God gave you to know through faithful preachers as well as through me, a weakling. And thirdly, that you may learn to beware of deceitful and hypocritical preachers.

"I have now begun the journey without a safe-conduct, amid very great and numerous enemies—among whom the worst are my country-men, as you will perceive from their testimonies and will learn after the conclusion of the Council. For there will be many more of them against me than there were of the bishops, masters, secular princes, and lawyers against our merciful Redeemer. But I trust in our merciful, wise, and mighty Savior that He will grant me, by reason of His promise and through your faithful prayer, the wisdom and bravery of the Holy Spirit to remain steadfast, so that they would be unable to swerve me to the wrong side, even though He grant me to suffer temptation, disgrace, imprisonment, or death; as He himself suffered and has allowed His dearest servants likewise to suffer, giving us an example that we should suffer for His sake and for our salvation. He is God and we are His creatures; He is Lord and we are His servants; He is the king of all the world and we are but puny weaklings; He lacks nothing while we are in need. Since He likewise suffered, why should we not suffer as well? For our suffering in grace is our cleansing from sins and our deliverance from eternal torments; and death is our purification. Surely His faithful servant cannot perish if, by His help, he remains steadfast. Therefore, dear brethren and dear sisters, pray earnestly that He may be pleased to grant me to undergo the suffering without excessive fear. But if it be better for us that He should restore me to you, pray that I may go there and back undefiled, so that we may edify ourselves in His law awhile longer, and tear asunder Antichrist's nets somewhat, and leave behind us a good example to the brethren in the future.

"You may perhaps not see me in Prague before I die; if, however, the Almighty God should be pleased to bring me back to you, we shall meet each other all the more joyfully. Furthermore, we shall, of course, meet one another in the heavenly joy. May the merciful God, who grants sure peace to His own here and hereafter, Who brought forth the Great Shepherd by the pouring out of His blood,[23] which is the

[23] Hebrews 13:20.

eternal witness of our salvation, be pleased to enable you to do all good, that you may fulfill His will in harmony, without dissension; that possessing peace, you may in virtues obtain eternal peace through our Lord Jesus Christ, Who is eternal God and true man, born of the Virgin Mary. Unto Him is and shall be glory forever with all the elect, with whom persevering in the truth, we shall dwell in joy. Amen.

"Given in the year of our Lord 1414, after the feast of St. Wenceslas,[24] on my departure for Constance."

When he arrived in Nuremberg on Friday after St. Gallus [25] with the said lords, a certain master came to him after dinner—I think it was Albert, pastor of St. Sebald [26]—requesting that he wished to confer kindly with them. And when he consented, some masters came, among whom was a doctor and many of the council of the said city. They conferred for about four hours with the Master about matters of current interest, including the rumors spreading about the Master. And after they conversed about the particulars, they said: "Surely, Master, the things we have now heard are catholic, and we have taught and held the same for many years, and now we hold and believe them; and if no other things exist against you, surely you will depart or return from the Council with honor." Thereupon they parted from each other favorably.

In this and other imperial cities through which the said Master Hus rode, he also procured the posting on the gates and doors of churches the following public notice in Latin and German: [27]

"Master John Hus, who is already on his way to Constance to show the faith he has hitherto held, now holds, and with the help of the Lord Jesus Christ will hold until death, as he had notified the entire kingdom of Bohemia by his notices and letters that he was willing to render account of his faith at the general synod of the archiepiscopal court of Prague, and before his departure to give satisfaction to any opponents, so he now gives notice even in this famous and imperial city that, if anyone wishes to charge him with any error or heresy let him ready himself for the Council, for he, Master John, is prepared to render account for his faith at that Council to any opponent."

---

[24] October 19, 1414.
[25] After September 28, 1414.
[26] Master Albert Fleischmann, pastor of the principal church in Nuremberg.
[27] Novotný, op cit., No. 89.

The letter which he wrote in Nuremberg and sent to his faithful friends in Prague follows: [28]

"Salvation from Jesus Christ! You should know that I never rode with donned hood, but openly with uncovered face. And when I had left Bohemia, even before I arrived at the first town of Bärnau, its pastor with his vicars awaited me. When I entered the room, he immediately gave me a large goblet of wine and received all my teaching very kindly along with his colleagues, and said that he had always been my friend. Later at Neustadt all the Germans were very glad to see me. We passed through Weiden, where a large crowd of people watched me with approval. And when we came to Sulzbach, we entered an inn where a court, *landgericht,* was being held. There I said to the councilmen and elders sitting in the dining hall: 'Look! I am Master John Hus, of whom I suppose you have heard much evil. Question me therefore.' And treating of many things, they received it all with great favor. We then passed through the city of Hirsweld, where they also received me very kindly. Then we passed through the city of Hersbruck and stayed overnight in the city of Lauf. There the pastor, a great jurist, came with his vicars, with whom I conversed; he also received everything with favor. And lo! we came to Nuremberg, where merchants who had preceded us had announced our coming. On that account the populace were standing in the streets, looking at us and inquiring which was Master Hus. Before dinner, Master John Helwel, pastor of St. Laurence, sent me a letter writing that he had long wished to speak to me freely. I answered him on the same letter that he should come. And he came. Because I had already written a notice [inviting interviews], wishing to post it, Lord Wenceslas in the meantime sent me word that the citizens and masters were gathered and wished to see me to confer with me. I rose at once from the table and went. The masters sent me word that we should confer in private. To them I said: 'I preach in public and desire that all who wish may hear me.' And forthwith from that hour we conversed before the councilmen and citizens present until the dusk.

"There was, moreover, a certain Carthusian doctor, a zealous debater. I noticed that Master Albert, pastor of St. Sebald,[29] was displeased

---

[28] Novotný, *op. cit.,* No. 93; and Palacký, No. 39.

[29] It will be noticed that Hus mentions Master Albert all of a sudden, although up to this point he dealt only with John Helwel.

that the citizens agreed with my opinions. Finally all the masters and citizens were satisfied.

"You should know that as yet I have not been aware of any enemy. In every inn I give to the innkeeper as a parting gift the Ten Commandments, and in some places I post them with flourpaste.[30] The innkeepers' wives and their husbands everywhere receive me with great kindness. Nor do they [the ecclesiastical authorities] impose the interdict anywhere; furthermore, all praise the German notices. I declare, therefore, that there exists against me no greater enmity than among the inhabitant of the kingdom of Bohemia. And what more shall I write? Both Lord Wenceslas and Lord John treat me with great kindness and tact; they are as it were heralds of the truth, or, to speak more truly, defenders of the truth, with whom by the help of the Lord all goes well. The king is on the Rhine and Lord Wenceslas of Leštno followed him there. We are going directly[31] to Constance which Pope John is approaching. For we judge it would be useless to follow perhaps sixty miles[32] after the king and then return to Constance.

"Written in Nuremberg on the Saturday before the Feast of the Eleven Thousand Virgins."[33]

Then on the Saturday after [the Feast] of All Saints, November 3, Master John Hus arrived at Constance and was lodged in the street of St. Paul[34] with a good widow named Fida. The next day Lords John of Chlum and Henry Lacembok went to Pope John XXIII in his palace,[35] and told him that they had brought Master John Hus to the Council of Constance under the safe-conduct of the king of the Romans and of Hungary. They asked him that, in consideration of the king, [the pope] would permit no interference with Master John. The pope answered that he had no intention of interfering with him in any way or to permit any interference. Even if he had murdered the pope's own brother, he should be safe in Constance.

In the meantime Master Stephen Páleč came to Constance. Master

---

[30] The short *Exposition of the Decalogue* in Latin or German is no longer extant, although it does exist in Czech. Cf. Žilka, *op. cit.,* II, 397–99. The phrase *"et allicubi applico in farina"* is variously translated; but my rendering seems most reasonable to me. Hus pasted it on doors and walls.

[31] Palacký corrected *"de nocte"* to *"directe,"* which makes sense.

[32] The medieval German mile equals about eight modern English miles.

[33] October 20, 1414.

[34] Now known as *Hussenstrasse*; the house where he lodged was called the Pfister house. Cf. Loomis, *op. cit.,* p. 129.

[35] November 4; the pope resided in the palace of the bishop of Constance.

Stanislav of Znojmo on his ride though Bohemia had been stricken with an abcess at Neuhaus [now Jindřichův Hradec] and had died. Indeed, this Páleč on his arrival in Constance immediately associated himself with Michael de Causis, the instigator against [36] and opponent of Master Hus. They drew up certain articles [37] against Master Hus and others, which they said they took from the treatise *De ecclesia*.[38] Then he, with the said Michael, scurried around among all the principal cardinals, archbishops, bishops, and other prelates. We saw him doing that almost daily. He accused the said Master John to them and urged them to arrest him without fail. Afterward he associated himself with the Dominican friars and members of other orders and showed them the above-mentioned and other articles and incited and urged them— especially the more prominent among them, such as the masters of the Holy Scriptures [39]—against Master Hus. He gave them the articles collected against the said Master Hus and other accusations, from one of whom I later copied them.

This Páleč had indeed been a great friend and companion of the said Master John well-nigh from his youth. But when [the news of] a certain crusade of John XXIII—now since his deposition from the papacy called Balthasarre de Cossa—against Ladislas, king of Naples, reached Prague,[40] the said Master Hus had resisted it, for he regarded it as contrary to and inconsistent with the law of God and with love. The said Páleč, however, dared not oppose his [the pope's] bull, be- cause he had been jailed and robbed by the said Balthasarre Cossa in Bologna,[41] although he had declared at the parsonage of Master Christian,[42] pastor of St. Michael in the Old Town of Prague, before

[36] The French word *agent-provocateur* would best express the meaning.

[37] Palacký, pp. 194–96, entitled "First Articles against M. J. Hus by Michael de Causis presented to Pope John XXIII."

[38] *Ibid.,* pp. 204–24.

[39] The degree of *magister sacre pagine* was superior to that of doctor of laws.

[40] Peter refers to the papal bull proclaiming the crusade in 1412. In *Contra Paletz,* Hus writes of Páleč that he was "once my friend and particular comrade, now indeed the most captious adversary." And further he refers to the reason for the enmity: "Then the sale of indulgences and the raising of the cross against Christians first separated me from that doctor." And he adds: "Páleč a friend, the truth a friend; and both being friends, it is holy that truth be preferred." *Historia et Monumenta,* I, 318, 330.

[41] Páleč was taken captive along with Stanislav of Znojmo when they were journeying to Rome, having been cited to the curia in 1408. Balthassarre Cossa was then Cardinal of St. Eustachius and papal legate in Bologna.

[42] Master Christian of Prachatice was a friend and benefactor of Hus; he came to the Council, representing King Wenceslas.

several masters, bachelors, and students, and in the presence of Master John Hus himself, that it—that is, the bull—contained palpable errors.[43] Hence he fell into dissensions and controversies with the said Master Hus, whom he later persecuted mortally both before this time and at the afore-mentioned Council of Constance.

The said Michael indeed had been at one time pastor of St. Adalbertus in the New Town of Prague. Because he had shown himself as having knowledge of restoring gold mines, Wenceslas, king of Bohemia, gave him a large sum of money to restore the gold mines at Jílové. And he, abandoning his flock and accepting the money, attempted to restore the said gold mines. When, however, he failed to accomplish anything, he secretly fled from the kingdom with the said money to the Roman curia. With that money as well as with other [sums] given him by the opponents of the said Master Hus, he procured the proceedings and citations against Master Hus himself as well as against his adherents. He posted these proceeding on the church doors while the said Master Hus was in Constance.

Here follows a letter and many others, both in Czech and in Latin, written in Constance by Master John Hus to the people, including his special friends: [44]

"Salvation from Christ Jesus! We came to Constance on the Saturday after the Feast of All Saints [45] without any mishap. As we passed through towns, we posted notices both in Latin and German. We reside in Constance in a street near the pope's residence, having come without the safe-conduct.[46] The next day Michael de Causis posted on the church the proceedings against me,[47] and placed above them a lenghty superscription to the effect that these proceedings were against the excommunicated and stubborn John Hus, suspected of heresy, and many other things besides. Nevertheless, with God's help I pay no

[43] Hus mentions this in his treatise *Contra Paletz*. He writes: "For if he would confess the truth, he would acknowledge that he had said that the *articles of absolution* which he himself handed me with his own hand, contain palpable errors." *Historia et Monumenta*, I, 330. Dom de Vooght asserts that this is a reference to "les articles des commissaires" and not to the papal bulls." *Hussiana*, p. 189. But Páleč's own statement asserts that the errors were invented by the indulgence sellers. Sedlák, ed., *Antihus* in *Hlídka*, p. 147.

[44] Novotný, *op. cit.*, No. 69; Palacký, No. 40.

[45] November 3, 1414; it was on this day that the Council was to be opened. But because the pope fell ill, the opening was postponed to November 5.

[46] It was brought the next day by Wenceslas of Dubá. Cf. the text of it at the beginning of the chapter.

[47] This refers to the proceedings issued at Rome.

attention to it, knowing that God sent him to say evil things against me on account of my sins, in order to test my knowledge and willingness to suffer a little. Lord Lacembok [48] and Lord John Kepka [49] were received by the pope and spoke with him about me. He said that he wished to do nothing by violence.

"It is rumored, although vaguely, that the Spanish pope, Benedict, is on his way to the Council.[50] Today we received the news that the duke of Burgundy [51] with the duke of Brabant [52] has withdrawn from the field [53] and that King Sigismund should arrive within three days at Aachen and be crowned,[54] and that the pope and the Council should await him. As Aachen is seventy miles distant from Constance, I suppose that the king will scarcely arrive by Christmas. Accordingly, I suppose that the Council, if not dissolved, will be terminated about Easter.[55]

"Food is expensive: a bed costs half a florin a week. Horses are cheap: one costing six *sexagenae* in Bohemia is bought here for seven florins.[56] We sent the horses with Lord John to a city four miles away, namely Ravensburg. I think that I shall soon be in want of necessities. On that account try to solicit friends whom it would take too long to name and onerous to recall.

"Lord Lacembok is riding today to the king. He enjoined me to attempt no action before the king's arrival. I hope that I shall have a public hearing for my reply.

"There are many Parisians and Italians, but few archbishops as yet, and even bishops are few. The cardinals are numerous; they ride mules, but they are greedy.[57] When riding to Constance on horseback,

---

[48] Lord Henry Lacembok of Chlum, the uncle of Lord John.

[49] Lord John called Kepka of Chlum.

[50] This was Benedict XIII and the rumor proved false.

[51] Duke John the Fearless of Burgundy (d. 1419).

[52] Duke Anthony, brother of Duke John of Burgundy; he fell at the battle of Agincourt (1415).

[53] Refers perhaps to the withdrawal of the Burgundian forces from France after the signing of the Peace of Arras in February, 1415. Cf. *Cambridge Medieval History*, VII, 386.

[54] The coronation took place on November 8.

[55] Sigismund, as a matter of fact, arrived on December 24. But Hus's estimate as to the termination of the Council was certainly far from the mark; it lasted until 1418!

[56] The sum referred to amounted to 360 silver *grossi*; seven florins was about a third of that sum.

[57] This phrase is in Czech: "*ale jsu lační.*" In the margin it is translated "*sed valde ieiuni.*" It may be taken to mean that the cardinals were greedy.

I suddenly heard horsemen—a very great multitude of them. But a
great crowd kept gathering.[58]

"Many of our Czechs have spent on the way all the money they had
and already suffer want. I greatly pity them, but cannot help all. Lord
Přibyslav's horse was taken over by Lord Lacembok; but my horse
Rabštýn indeed excels them all in strength and high spirit. It is the
only one I have with me, if I should chance some time to go out of
town [to meet] the king.[59]

"Greet all our friends, making no exception of anyone, etc. This
is the fourth letter from foreign parts, sent on Sunday night after the
Feast of All Saints in Constance.[60]

"None of the Bohemian knights is in Constance save Lord John
Kepka, who brought me and guarded me like a real knight. He preaches
everywhere more than I do, declaring my innocence. Given in Constance. Pray to God for constancy in the truth."

"Dearly beloved fellow-partisans and friends! [61]

"We remember having sent your friendly selves several letters [62]
describing truthfully the manner of our journey and of our present
lodging in Constance. Now, however, especially to show you, friends,
our abiding affection toward your community, I wish to inform you
that yesterday the auditor of the sacred apostolic palace [63] with the

---

[58] This is one example of the faulty writing—whether Peter's or Hus's. The
Latin text is corrupt; it reads as follows: "*Quando equitavi ad Constanciam in
equo, statim audivi equitantes, permagnam multitudinem equitantem, sed con-
currebat magna multitudo.*" It may perhaps be understood that, when Hus was
approaching Constance on horseback, he heard from a distance the sound of
equestrians—a very large troop of them. But when a great crowd of onlookers
gathered to watch them, this either drowned the sound of hoofs or Hus was
unable to approach nearer.

[59] Perhaps he expected to meet the king on his arrival; but by that time he had
already been a month in prison!

[60] November 4, 1414.

[61] This is a letter written by Master John "Cardinal" of Rejnštejn, the representative of the University of Prague. He was a member of Hus's party. Cf.
Novotný, *op. cit.,* No. 98; Palacký, No. 42.

[62] All such letters are no longer extant.

[63] Novotný, *op. cit.,* No. 98, n. 2, remarks that the identity of the man is
unknown; but Workman and Pope, *The Letters of John Hus* (London, 1904),
p. 161, n. 2, identify him as John of Borsnicz, bishop of Lebus. This is almost
certainly an error for this bishop was never a papal auditor. However, Berthold
of Wildungen, mentioned several times by Peter, did hold this office.

bishop of Constance [64] came to our lodging together with an official of the town of Constance,[65] and told the Master that a great altercation had taken place between the pope and the cardinals over the pretended interdict fulminated against our Master. In brief, they [the pope and the cardinals] decided that they [the auditor and others] should go to the Master and tell him that the pope in the plenitude of his power had already suspended the said interdict and the sentences of excommunication passed on Master John. They were to request him, nevertheless, that in order to prevent popular scandal and gossip, at any rate not to attend their high masses. Otherwise he may freely visit both the city of Constance and the churches and any other places he pleases. We really think that they all fear his preaching to the clergy, which Master John intends to deliver soon. For some person, whether a friend or foe is not known, said yesterday in church that Master Hus would preach next Sunday to the clergy in a Constance church, and would give a ducat to everyone present. Thus we are free in Constance, and the Master daily celebrates the divine office as he had done throughout the journey. The Master accepted the king's advice that in the matter of the truth and his own cause he attempt nothing until the arrival of the king of Hungary. In fact, nothing of the conciliar business has as yet been begun, nor has any embassy from any king or prince come, nor has anything been hitherto heard of Gregory or Benedict [66] or of their embassies. We therefore do not expect the Council to begin for several weeks.

"You should know and tell all [the friends] that all have been personally cited [67] and publicly denounced [by posters], among other means, as is known, on the porches and the doors of the churches, in order that they should look out for themselves. And Michael de Causis loudly [68] proclaims what he has done! Lord John Kepka and Lord Wenceslas of Leštno are fearless and zealous promoters and defenders of the truth.

[64] This was Otto III, Margrave of Hachberg-Sausenberg, a canon of Basel. He was appointed its bishop in 1410. Since he was not then in Constance, he might have sent his vicar, John Tenger. Cf. Ulrich von Richental, "Chronicle of the Council of Constance," in Loomis, *op. cit.,* p. 129.

[65] Richental asserts that this was the bishop's official, Master Conrad Helye. *Ibid.,* p. 130.

[66] These were two of the three popes—Gregory XII and Benedict XIII.

[67] These citations were instigated by Michael de Causis on account of the events of 1412–13.

[68] The word in Czech is *"rycznie."*

"Written at Constance, the Saturday before Martinmas.[69]

"The Goose [70] is not yet cooked and is not afraid of being cooked, because this year the vigil of its celebration falls on the Saturday before St. Martin's feast when geese are not eaten!"

This letter appears to be [written] by Master John Cardinal, pastor at Janovice.

Another: [71]

"Salvation from Christ Jesus! Dearly beloved! Be assured that I fare well in every respect. I came to Constance without the pope's safe-conduct.[72] Pray God, therefore, that He may grant me constancy, for many and powerful adversaries have risen against me, incited particularly by that indulgence vendor, the dean of Passau, now already provost,[73] as well as by Michael de Causis, who ever keeps on posting the proceedings against me. But I fear none of them, nor am I terrified, trusting that after the great battle there will be a great victory, and after the victory a greater reward and the greater confounding of the persecutors.

"The pope does not want to quash the proceedings and said: 'What can I do? After all, your own countrymen are doing it!' But two bishops and a doctor said to Lord John Kepka that I should come to terms by keeping quiet. Thus I know that they are afraid of my public reply and preaching, which I hope by God's grace to secure when King Sigismund arrives. Lord Wenceslas of Leštno told me about him [Sigismund], that he was very glad when he, the noble Lord Wenceslas, told him that I was riding directly to Constance without the safe-conduct.

"We were treated well and honorably in all the cities; and in the imperial cities in which I had conversations with the masters, we posted Latin and German notices. I had a herald on the way, the bishop of

---

[69] November 10, 1414.

[70] "*Auca*" is the designation for Hus, meaning goose, used either for concealment or in playful mood. The postscript was perhaps written by Hus himself. It should be noted that it was customary in Bohemia to eat goose on St. Martin's Day.

[71] Novotný, *op. cit.*, No. 97; Palacký, No. 41.

[72] Hus never had a papal safe-conduct; hence, it is somewhat puzzling why he mentions the fact at all.

[73] Wenceslas Thiem of Mikulov, who was selling indulgences in Prague in 1412, when as yet he was dean of Passau.

Lebus,[74] who always preceded us by a *nocturn*[75] and spread the rumor that they were bringing me chained to a wagon, and that people should beware of me because I was a mind reader! Consequently, whenever we approached any city, crowds ran out to meet me as if to a show. But the enemy was confounded by his own lie, while the people were glad when they heard the truth. Surely 'Christ Jesus is with me as a mightly warrior';[76] therefore, I fear not what the enemy may do.

"Live in holiness, pray devoutly that the merciful Lord may assist me, defending His law in me to the end. Written at night on the Day of St. Leonard.[77]

"I think I shall soon be in want of necessities, if the Council should be protracted. Therefore, ask whomever you know of my friends for a contribution, but at first ask conditionally. Greet all the friends, both men and women, and urge them to pray God for me, for I need it."

In the vernacular to the people:[78]

"Peace be to you from the Lord and Jesus Christ, that you may beware of sins, dwell in His grace, prosper in virtues, and enter after death into eternal joy. Dearly beloved, I pray that, living according to God's law, you would be diligent about your salvation, hearing the Word of God with circumspection, lest you be beguiled by the messengers of Antichrist. They make light of men's sins, do not punish them, flatter their superiors, do not warn the people against sins, extol themselves by boasting of their actions, by magnifying their power, but have no wish to follow the Lord God Jesus in humility, poverty, patience, and labor. Of them the gracious Savior prophesied, saying: 'There shall arise false prophets and shall lead many astray.'[79] And warning the faithful, He says: 'Beware of false prophets who come to you in sheep's clothing, but inwardly are ravenous wolves. By their fruits you shall know them.'[80] There is indeed great need for faithful Christians to guard themselves diligently, for the Savior says that 'even

---

[74] John of Borsnicz (1397–1420), bishop of Lebus, formerly canon of Prague.

[75] "Nocturn" is the time it takes a priest to recite the prescribed three Psalms and three Scriptural passages.

[76] Jeremiah 20:11.

[77] November 6, 1414.

[78] Novotný, *op. cit.*, No. 100; Palacký, No. 43. The Mladoňovic's version is slightly changed.

[79] Matt. 24:11.

[80] Matt. 7:15–16.

the elect would be deceived, if possible.' [81] Therefore, dearly beloved, watch lest the devil's guile overcomes you; be all the more diligent, the more Antichrist assails you. For the Day of Judgment is approaching, death saddens many, and the Kingdom of God is drawing nigh to the sons of God. On these accounts discipline your body, fear not death, love one another, and by your remembrance, reason, and will, stand ever firm in God. Let the Day of Judgment be terrible before your eyes, that you sin not; and the eternal joy, that you may long for it, and the suffering of the Savior, that you may gladly suffer along with Him. For if you keep His suffering in mind, you will gladly undergo opposition, reviling, slander, beating, and imprisonment, and, should it be His will, even bodily death for His holy truth.

"You should know, dearly beloved, that Antichrist has assailed us with slander, but has as yet not hurt even a hair of many of us, not even of me, although he has assailed me sorely. I beseech you, therefore, pray earnestly the Lord God that He may be pleased to grant me wisdom, patience, humility, and bravery to remain steadfast in His truth. He has already brought me to Constance without any hindrance. On the whole journey, riding openly as a priest and announcing myself loudly to the people, I found no open enemy in any of the cities. Nor would I have many of them in Constance, if the Czech clergy, who go about begging for benefices and [in bondage to] [82] avarice, had not led people astray. But I hope in the merciful Savior and in your prayer that I shall remain steadfast in God's truth unto death. You should know that nowhere have they stopped the services on my account, not even in Constance, where the pope himself held a service while I was there. [83] I commend you to the Lord, and to the merciful Jesus, the true God, the son of the pure Virgin Mary, Who redeemed us, undeserving, by His cruel and terrible death from the everlasting torment, from the power of the devil and from sin.

---

[81] Matt. 24:24.

[82] Added by Palacký, p. 83.

[83] The pope celebrated the mass at the opening of the Council on November 5, 1414. The phrase "while I was there" is not altogether clear; the Czech text reads "za mne," literally rendered "for me." Novotný in his M. Jan Hus, II, 366, renders the phrase "in his presence," although this may be understood as meaning "in his presence in Constance." The likeliest interpretation, suggested among others by Dr. O. Odložilík, is that the pope celebrated the mass while Hus was in Constance; I accepted this rendering.

"This letter was written in Constance on the day of St. Othmar,[84] the good servant of our Lord Jesus Christ, who is blessed for ever. Amen.

Master John Hus,
priest and God's servant in hope."

[84] Friday, November 16, 1414.

CHAPTER II

The Trial to the Beginning
of the Imprisonment, and in what
Matter it Originated

When the said Master John Hus had dwelt in Constance for three and
a half weeks, it was rumored throughout the city that he had been
taken out of the city in a wagon in which hay was carried and brought
in. But it was false. For it happened in this way: the servants who
rode out with the said wagon for hay did not remove the canvas or
cover (in the vernacular called *sperloch*) from the wagon, but removed
it for the first time after two or three trips and then again brought in
the hay without that cover. From that then some supposed, or it was
rumored, that Master Hus had already been conveyed out of the city
in the hay and thus had escaped in the hay and had been spirited
away.[1] But in truth there was never even a mention made of the

[1] In Richental's *Chronicle* the same story is told twice and very differently.
In the first place, it is placed in mid-March, and aims at justifying Hus's arrest,
although that event had taken place on November 26 of the previous year. The
first story asserts that lords Lacembok and "Kolenbrat"—apparently John of
Chlum—sounded an alarm after they found him in a wagon, and "gave him up
to the Pope and more than 12,000 people ran after them." Moreover, Richental
asserts that the pope imprisoned Hus in the Dominican monastery "where he lay
until he was burned." The second story places it on March 3 and asserts that
Hus hid in Lacembok's wagon, and was found by the burgomaster's guards; and
when Lacembok was taking him to the pope's palace, Hus jumped off the horse
he was riding and tried to hide among the immense crowd accompanying them.
The papal guards, however, caught him. Loomis, *op. cit.,* pp. 113–14, 130.
Could not Richental, so meticulous in the description of the smallest details,
investigate the circumstances somewhat more carefully? He was apparently
satisfied with the wild stories circulating about the arrest of Hus. But it is still
difficult to understand why he placed that event over three months later than it
had actually occurred. Hefele-Leclercq suggests that he confused Hus with
Jerome of Prague, who did attempt to escape.

matter, as later appeared and is now apparent. Had he then escaped, he would never have been arrested and thrown into chains, or finally condemned by them.

Then on the Wednesday after St. Catherine's Day [2] the cardinals who were then in Constance, having been instigated thereto by the said enemies, namely Páleč and Michael de Causis, sent two bishops —that is, of Augsburg [3] and of Trent,[4] the burgomaster of the city of Constance,[5] and a certain knight, Hans of Poden [6]—to the lodging of Master Hus. They arrived at the hour of dinner and told Lord John of Chlum that they had come on behalf of the cardinals and by command of the pope to Master John Hus. As he had previously desired to speak with them, they were now ready to hear him.[7] And Lord John of Chlum, rising first, quite angrily spoke to them, saying: "Do you not know, reverend fathers, how and under what terms Master John Hus came here? If you are ignorant of it, listen and I will tell you. When we, that is I and Lord Wenceslas of Leštno, were in Friuli with our lord the emperor, and were resolved to return to our kingdom or province, he thereupon commanded us to assure Master John of his safe-conduct, so that he would come to the present Council. On that account be sure that you do nothing against our lord's honor!" And to the burgomaster he said in German: "You know that if the devil himself came to present his cause, he ought to be fairly heard!" Furthermore, Lord John said to the bishops: "The lord king himself then

[2] November 28, 1414.

[3] Frederick II of Grafeneck (1414–18). Cf. Hauck, V, ii, 1139.

[4] George of Lichtenstein (1390–1419).

[5] Hans von Ulm.

[6] Finke, *Acta Concilii Constantientis,* gives his name as Frischhans of Bodman; he was captain of the town guard.

[7] The papal notary, Cerretano, in his *Journal,* describes the circumstances as follows: "John Hus, the Wyclifite, who had been teaching the wicked doctrine of Wyclif in his lodging house at Constance to all who came to meet him there and in spite of warning refused to desist, was taken into custody to prevent his further teaching of that doctrine. This was by order of our lord Pope, with the approval of the lord Bishop of Trent, lord Frederick, bishop of Augsburg, lord Ottobono, doctor of decretals, the envoys of the King, and the burgomaster and consuls of the city of Constance. They brought John Hus in person before our lord Pope and the lord cardinals, against the loud protests of the knight who had escorted him to Constance and who said our lord Pope had given John Hus a safe-conduct, which the pope denied." Loomis, *op. cit.,* p. 469. From this account it appears that John XXIII did order Hus's arrest, although according to Peter's story, he denied it. Moreover, John of Chlum asserted that Hus came under Sigismund's safe-conduct, not the pope's.

went on to say: 'If Master Hus consents to go to Constance with you, then tell him to say nothing of this matter [the charge of heresy] except in my presence, when I with God's help shall come to Constance'." When all those had come heard how roughly he answered them, they said, and particularly the Tridentine, or the bishop of Trent: "Lord John, we have come solely for the sake of peace, not to cause an uproar."

Then Master John Hus, whom, I think, neither of the bishops as yet knew, rose from the table and replied: "I did not come here merely to the cardinals, nor have I ever desired to speak with them by themselves; but I have come to the whole Council and there will I say whatever God grants me to say and whatever I shall be asked about. Nonetheless, at the request of the lord cardinals I am ready to come to them at once ; and if I shall be questioned about any matter, I hope that I may rather choose death than deny the truth which I have learned from the Scriptures or otherwise." Then the said bishops and the others who came to Master John Hus with these fine words invited Master Hus in a friendly way to come to the said cardinals, since they wished to talk with him. In the meantime they had surrounded the dwelling of Master Hus and some other houses of the neighborhood with guards from the said city. As the Master was coming down, the hostess met him, and he took leave of her, saying: "God bless you!" She answered in tears. And those bishops—as some reported—while they were descending, remarked: "You will officiate or say mass no more!"[8] Then mounting a small horse along with the said messengers and with the said Lord John of Chlum, his companion, he rode to the palace of the pope and the cardinals.

And when he came to the cardinals and greeted them, they said to him: "Master John, there is much strange talk about you, that you have held many errors and have disseminated them in the kingdom of Bohemia. For that reason we have called you, wishing to find out from you whether it is so." And he replied: "Most reverend fathers! Be it known to Your Paternities that I would rather die than hold a single error. For indeed I have come freely to this sacred Council and, on being instructed that I have erred in any way, I am ready humbly to be corrected and to make amends." The cardinals said: "Certainly these are good words!" And having said that, they went off to their

---

[8] This remark must be understood in the light of the prohibition of attendance of masses read by Hus forbidden by Otto, bishop of Constance.

own lodgings, leaving the Master there in the custody of the armed guards. And Lord John remained with him.

In the meantime they commanded a certain Minorite friar, Didachus by name,[9] professor of the sacred Scriptures, to ensnare the Master, already held under armed guard. Approaching him, he said: "Reverend master! I, a simple and unlearned monk [*ydiota*], having heard that many devious doctrines are ascribed to you, have come for that reason to you to learn whether or not it is so, and whether you hold those opinions ascribed to you by rumor. First, it is said that you hold and assert that after the consecration and the pronouncement of the words there remains the material bread in the sacrament of the altar." And Master John Hus answered: "I do not hold it." And the friar: "You do not hold it?" The Master replied: "I do not hold it." And when he had so replied three times, Lord John of Chlum, sitting by, exclaimed: "What sort of man are you? Were someone to affirm or to deny something to me once, I would believe him. And look! he has repeated to you three times, saying 'I do not hold it,' and you still keep on asking him!" The friar said: "Esteemed knight, do not hold it against me, an unlearned and simple friar, for I ask in order to be instructed." And when he further inquired of Master John, among other things about the hypostatic union or of the nature of the union of the divine and human in Christ, the Master said to Lord John in Czech: "Indeed, this monk calls himself an unlearned simpleton, but he is not so very simple, since he is asking about the solution of the profoundest problem." And turning to the monk, he said: "You, brother, say that you are simple: but I perceive that you are double-faced, not simple.' And the friar said: "I deny that I am double-faced." Then the Master argued that for a man to be simple it was required, at least as to his moral conduct, that his mind or heart, his mouth or speech, and his acts agreed. "And because these do not agree in you, for your mouth pretends simplicity and professes you to be a simpleton, but your actions show subtlety in inquiring about such moot questions, these do not agree and do not tend to simplicity. In spite of that, however, I will tell you what I think of that question." And when he explained it, [the friar] thanked Master John Hus for his good instruc-

[9] Fra Andreas Didachus de Moxena, a Spanish theologian, was chaplain of King Ferdinand of Aragon. From his question it is clear that Hus was thought to be a Wyclifite, i.e., to deny transubstantiation. And despite his denial of it on this and many other occasions afterward, the Council continued to regard him as a remanentist and he was finally condemned as such.

tion. But that instruction is not stated here because Lord John could not recall it. Thereupon, the monk immediately left.

The armed guards standing about, being in the service of the supreme pontiff, that is, Pope John XXIII, approaching Hus, said: "Do you know who that was?" The Master answered that he did not. They said: "That was Master Didachus, who is reputed to be the subtlest theologian in all Lombardy." And Master Hus said: "Oh, if only I had known it, I should have otherwise punctured him through with Scripture! If only all were like him! With God's help and the support of the Holy Scriptures aiding me, I should fear them not a whit!"

After dinner then, at four o'clock in the afternoon, the said cardinals again gathered in the papal palace to discuss what to do with the said Master John Hus. His opponents, Páleč, Michael, and others, kept on instigating them and the other prelates not to release him under any circumstances, as it appears from the concluding part of the first articles of Michael.[10] And prancing about the dining hall, they gloated, saying: "Ha, ha, we have him now! He shall not escape us until he has paid the last heller!"

At that very moment Páleč went and found Master John Cardinal,[11] who had come with Master Hus, and said to him: "Master John, I am sorry for you that you have let yourself be seduced. You had formerly been esteemed [12] at this curia (namely, the pope's) as the most distinguished of all the Czechs; and now they regard you almost as nothing on account of this sect!" To whom Master Cardinal answered: "Master Stephen, I am even more sorry for you. For if you knew anything evil against me that I did, then you should have felt sorry for me!" Thereupon they promptly parted from each other. Peter of Mladoňovice indeed had an altercation with the monk, *dominus* Peter,[13] at the time preacher at St. Clement in Prague, near the bridge, about a certain sermon,[14] saying: "Dominus Peter! Where was that fight about which you preached, namely, that someone had preached in Prague that one should buckle on a sword, and kill his father and mother!"

[10] Cf. these articles in Palacký, pp. 194–99: *Primi articuli contra M. J. Hus per Michaelem de Causis praesentati Joanni pp. XXIII.*

[11] Master John Cardinal of Rejnštejn came to Constance in the same wagon with Hus; he represented the University of Prague.

[12] This word in Czech is "*wzácný.*"

[13] Master Peter of Uničov, a Dominican.

[14] This refers to Hus's sermon of 1410 on the verse, "Compel them to enter," Luke 14:23, in which he advised his hearers to buckle on the spiritual sword.

He answered: "I do not know what you are talking about!" At that moment Páleč, arriving, told the monk: "Come, leave them!" Peter [said to him]: "Nevertheless, we speak peaceably." Again Páleč cried in a loud voice and with an angry countenance, twirling his hand and repeating it a good three times: "I will 'peaceable' him! Indeed, I will give him a whole ocean of the Scriptures!" To him Peter [of Mladoňovice] replied: "Master, have you ever heard of a goldsmith who, having plenty of gold and silver before his eyes, would be displeased?" He answered: "No." To him Peter [said]: "That's the way with Master Hus if you give him an ocean or two of the Holy Scriptures; he will not be annoyed by reading them, but will rejoice, for they may very well be in his favor." He replied: "No, against him." Then again [Peter] . . .[15] To him Páleč: "Those are words to the Ephesians." And Peter countered: "And yours to the Corinthians." Thereupon, Páleč in a fury, taking the monk along with him, left the house of his father, that is, the palace of the most holy Pope John XXIII, now called Cossa.

But when it grew late, they sent the master of the papal court to tell Lord John that he could leave, if he chose, but that Master Hus must remain in the papal palace. The Lord John, moved by anger that they had taken Hus captive under the guise of such fine words, went immediately to the pope and in the presence of the said cardinals told him: "Holy Father! This is not what Your Paternity promised me or to my paternal uncle, Lord Henry Lacembok. I said to Your Paternity, and still say, that I had brought Master Hus here under the safe-conduct of my lord, king of the Romans. And Your Paternity told me that even if he had killed your own brother, he ought to be safe here and that you would neither interfere with him nor allow any interference with him, nor make a new move against him. And look! he is already arrested under the safe-conduct, and your messenger, one Francis, a member of your own court, was at his lodgings to take the Master away! May Your Paternity know that I will denounce and warn all who have violated the safe-conduct of my lord the king!" And the pope answered Lord John: "See, these my brethren"—pointing to the cardinals—"heard me say that I never ordered him to be arrested.[16]

---

[15] Something is missing here.

[16] It is indeed true that the cardinals, particularly Collona and Fillastre, demanded Hus's arrest from the beginning, for they regarded him as an already condemned heretic and looked upon the suspension of the interdict as a personal affront, since they themselves had been at least partly instrumental in condemning him in the previous trials. When Cardinal d'Ailly arrived at the Council (No-

That Francis is a rascal and is none of mine!" Subsequently he said
to Lord John alone: "You surely know how my affairs stand with them.
They surrendered him to me and I had to receive him as prisoner."
But he lied, as it appeared later from certain letters wherein he said
that "I now hold that heretic, whom that King Sigismund wished to
protect!"—he wrote this, I think, to the king of France from Schaffhausen, after he had escaped from Constance.

When Lord John heard the pope as stated above, he left and Master
John Hus remained in the papal palace in custody of the armed guards.
Later Peter brought him his fur coat and the breviary. And that very
same night, at nine o'clock, as they said, he was led into the house of
the precentor [17] of the Constance church, a house in which a cardinal
lived. He was guarded there for eight days by armed men. Thereupon,
however, he was taken to the Dominican monastery [18] situated on the
Rhine or on the said lake, and there was thrust into a murky and dark
dungeon in the immediate vicinity of a latrine. There he lay or sat
from the said time when he had been incarcerated, that is, from the
Feast of St. Nicholas the Confessor until Palm Sunday.[19] When he had
lain in that prison for several weeks, he fell ill of high fever and con-
stipation of the bowels, so that his life was despaired of. Pope John
XXIII sent his own physicians to the prison and they gave him an
enema.

In the meantime his enemies urged the presidents [of the nations]

vember 17), he became the moving spirit in the prosecution of Hus. As for
Francis—who by the way is not mentioned among those who came to invite Hus
to see the cardinals—the pope simply denied him as being one of his servants.
But since as a matter of fact, Francis of Conzié, archbishop of Narbonne, was
the Chamberlain of the papal court, and as such held the important office of
controller of the papal finances, was he not the "rascal" referred to by John?

[17] The canon who directed the choir; it is asserted (Finke, op. cit., II, 189)
that the pope did not want Hus to stay overnight in the palace because he feared
Lord John's threats. This is also stated in Cerretano's Journal: "But because of
this knight's complaints our lord Pope would not have the said John Hus spend
the night in the apostolic palace. So he was put elsewhere and kept under guard
of the lord Bishop of Lausanne, regent of the Camera." Loomis, op. cit., p. 469.

[18] This was the famous monastery situated on a small island very close to the
shore—in fact at present it is separated from it only by a narrow canal. Hus
was later imprisoned in a round tower attached to the main building on the
lake side. The tower still stands. The monastery served as the residence of many
prominent members of the Council. It was later transformed into a luxurious
modern hotel—the Insel Hotel—the best in town. It has a magnificent view of
the lake.

[19] From December 6, 1414, to March 24, 1415.

of the Council to appoint judges [favorable to them but] opposed and adverse to Master John Hus. They chose for them three commissioners or judges,[20] namely, the patriarch of Constantinople, the bishop of Castello, and the bishop of Lebus.[21] Certain witnesses were cited and examined before them and then were brought to the Master in his prison at the height of his illness that he might see those witnesses take their oath.[22] The names of the witnesses of whom I have learned and whom I have seen are these: the first is Münsterberg,[23] doctor of the-

[20] The papal notary, Cerretano, recorded in his *Journal* that on December 1, twelve cardinals, prelates, and masters were chosen "to examine John Hus, the Wyclifite, and his books and wicked doctrines. Among the twelve were the most reverend lords Cardinals of Cambrai [Pierre d'Ailly], St. Mark [Guillaume Fillastre], Brancacii [Cardinal Rainold], and Florence [Francesco Zabarella], the reverend lord Friar Anthony of Pereto, Master General of the Minorite Order, and Master Leonard of Florence, Master General of the Order of Preachers, and others." Loomis, *op. cit.,* pp. 469–70. This statement does not necessarily conflict with the report of Peter, for there is a possibility that among the twelve the three named by him were included. And yet it is surprising that he left out the names of those recorded by Cerretano.

[21] The three were: John of Rupescissa, a Frenchman, since 1412 the titular patriarch of Constantinople, later a cardinal; Bernard of Città di Castello; and John of Borsnicz (Bořečnice in Silesia), formerly canon of Prague, but since 1397 bishop of Lebus, near Frankfurt on Oder in Brandenburg, and later archbishop of Gran.

This commission examined Hus in December, 1414, concerning the forty-five articles of Wyclif, confidently expecting that by professing his adherence to all or at least the majority of them, he would prove himself heretical. It must have been a shocking surprise to them when Hus answered thirty-three of them by a categorical "I do not hold and have not held it," while to the remaining twelve he replied that they might have a correct sense or by qualifying them acceptably. The commission obviously did not know that Hus had never defended all the forty-five articles of Wyclif. Before departing for Constance, he prepared his defense of seven of them of which he wrote that he "did not dare to condemn them lest he resist the truth and became a liar before God's face." Thereupon, the commission requested Hus to answer the articles in writing. The text is found in Sedlák, "Několik textů z doby husitské" in *Hlídka*, I, 58–69; also Flajšhans, *M. Jan Hus, Obrany v Kostnici* (Prague, 1916), pp. 9–18.

[22] When Pierre d'Ailly arrived (November 17), he was told that the proceedings "had been started against Master John Hus, accused of heresy for the pernicious doctrine that he professed, but that many who might testify against him were deterred by terrifying threats." Cerretano's *Journal,* Loomis, *op. cit.,* p. 476. Since Hus was actually arrested on November 28, it appears that the action had been contemplated and decided upon even earlier. Moreover, the same writer records that Sigismund remarked "that the case of John Hus and other minor problems ought not to interfere with the reform of the Church and the Roman Empire, which was the principal object for which the Council had been convened." *Ibid.,* p. 476.

[23] Master John of Münsterberg, a Silesian.

ology, and Peter Storch,[24] both formerly Prague masters and members of the college, but at present living at Leipzig in Meissen; further, Páleč, and Dr. Zeiselmeister,[25] formerly the official of the Prague diocese; Berounec,[26] a member of Charles College; Peter,[27] monk of St. Clement, of whom the Master said, as he [Peter] himself declared there, that he is [Hus's] principal and great enemy. I myself have seen and observed how pleased he [Peter the monk] was with the remark, as he reported it with glee in front of the prison; further, Adam,[28] a licentiate in canon law, who said before he was called to the prison: "He [Hus] would have done well had he waited for the king in Nuremberg"; also one layman, who had said in Czech before he was called: "I swear to God that I know nothing to witness about!" To whom Michael de Causis remarked: "My dear fellow, you do not know what they are going to ask you, and you swear that you do not know what to witness. As for me, I would willingly testify against my own father as to anything opposed to the faith." [29] To which the layman replied: "That is true; but I know nothing." Peter the monk, at one time the abbot of St. Ambrose in the New Town of Prague, also wished to return to Prague. Michael, however, rebuked him, saying: "But see here, you took the oath yesterday!" At that time when the monk made his deposition, there were present a good fifteen [people] altogether, and not only those [I have mentioned], but many more unknown to us to this time, made their depositions, may the Lord pardon them! Although Master Hus had requested and petitioned for a procurator or advocate to defend him and support him against the said witnesses, for many of them were his principal enemies, they refused him one. They said that it was contrary to their laws, for no one should defend a man suspected of heresy.[30] And they adduced many similar things in their behalf.

[24] Master Peter Storch of Zwickau in Saxony. Both he and Münsterberg had been teaching at the University of Prague, but left in 1409 after the promulgation of the edict of Kutná Hora and settled at Leipzig.

[25] Nicholas Zeiselmeister, canon of Prague, known as an especially bitter opponent of Hus.

[26] John of Beroun, a member of Charles College, pastor of the church of St. Clement in Prague.

[27] Peter of Uničov, a Dominican, a confessed enemy of Hus.

[28] Perhaps Adam of Býchory.

[29] Both these sentences are in Czech.

[30] The denial of legal aid to one suspect of heresy was the standard inquisitorial procedure. But Hus regarded himself as having come to the Council freely, not as one under an excommunication, since he had appealed it. Moreover, John XXIII had suspended the interdict and the excommunication of Hus.

Indeed, Lord John in the days following the arrest of Master Hus complained regarding the pope and the cardinals, asking by what right Master John Hus had been taken prisoner while under the safe-conduct of the king himself. He displayed the said royal safe-conduct and had it read to the counts, knights, lords, bishops, and the principal citizens of the city of Constance. Afterward on the Saturday before the Feast of St. Thomas the Apostle [31] he himself posted letters of complaint against the pope and the cardinals on the doors of the cathedral of Constance adjacent to the papal court, and of other churches, complaining that the pope had not at all kept faith with him and had arrested Master John Hus, who was under the patent safe-conduct of the king, and that he kept him captive. This will appear more clearly from his [Lord John's] said letter sealed with his appended seal, inserted herein, a copy of which follows in these words:

"To all and every one seeing or hearing these presents, I, John of Chlum, make known that Master John Hus, *formatus* bachelor of sacred theology, under the safe-conduct and protection of the most illustrious prince and lord, Lord Sigismund, king of the Romans, ever Augustus, and king of Hungary, etc., my most gracious lord, and under the protection, defense, and guardianship of the most Holy Roman Empire (which letters patent of the said my lord, king of the Romans, etc., he has), came to Constance to render full account for his faith in a public hearing to anyone demanding it. The above-mentioned Master John in this imperial city under the safe-conduct of the said my lord, king of the Romans and of Hungary, was detained and is kept detained. And although the pope and the cardinals have been urgently requested in the king's name by solemn ambassadors of the said my lord, king of the Romans, that the said Master John be released and restored to me: nevertheless, in contempt and defiance of the king's safe-conduct and the security and protection of the empire and the king's majesty, they have so far refused and are still refusing to release him. For which reason I, the above-mentioned John, declare in the king's name that the detention and arrest of the said Master John Hus were carried out entirely against the will of the above-mentioned my lord, king of the Romans, that were done in contempt of his safe-conduct and of the imperial protection, because the said my lord was at the time far distant from Constance. If he had been present, he would have never per-

[31] December 15, 1414.

mitted it. When he arrives, however, all will have cause to feel that he has been most deeply offended by the disrespect shown to himself and for the protection and safe-conduct issued by himself and by the Empire.

"Given in Constance, on the vigil of Christ's Nativity,[32] in the year of the Lord 1414."

A similar notice was issued in the German vernacular translation.

Then after the said Master John had recovered somewhat from his illness, the said commissioners delivered to him soon afterward about forty-four articles which they said had been drawn from his book, *De ecclesia*. Páleč, however, had quoted them falsely and inaccurately by abbreviating some at the beginning, others in the middle, and others at the end, and inventing others that were not at all in the book. The Master later wrote his answers to them in prison with his own hand, as they stood in his books. These articles, together with the answers copied by the Master's own hand, are also inserted here.[33] They begin, "I, John Hus, in hope a priest of Jesus Christ, though unworthy, master of arts and *formatus* bachelor of sacred theology of the University of Prague, do acknowledge that I have written the book *De ecclesia,* etc." He replied to them without [the aid of] books. These replies were later carefully compared with the book written by his own hand and found to agree throughout word for word with the original.

He likewise composed in that prison certain very beautiful little treatises at the request of some of his jailers,[34] having no book to aid him: namely, the small treatise on the Lord's Prayer, an Exposition of the Ten Commandments of the Lord, on Christ's Body, on Marriage, on Repentance, on the Three Enemies of Man, on Sin and its Origin, on Loving and Knowing God, and such others as will likewise be inserted in the present work in their proper place.[35]

Meanwhile, on the Wednesday before Palm Sunday,[36] at three o'clock

---

[32] December 24, 1414; this is therefore the *second* notice, not the one promised on December 15. Pope John himself admitted that Sigismund swore that he would free Hus even if he had to break the prison door. Cf. Van der Hardt, II, 253.

[33] Cf. Palacký, pp. 204–24, where the number is given as forty-two. But Peter did not insert the articles with Hus's responses here; perhaps they have originally been placed here, but removed in this redaction.

[34] Robert, Jacob, and Gregory.

[35] Again Peter failed to insert them; they are found in *Historia et Monumenta*, I, 38–52.

[36] March 20, 1415; Cardinal Fillastre records in his *Diary*: "So the pope,

at night (as it was said) Pope John XXIII fled disguised in lay clothing and secretly escaped from Constance to a certain city of Frederick, the duke of Austria, namely, Schaffhausen,[37] four miles distant from Constance. Later his retinue and the jailers of the said Master John followed him, having delivered the keys of the said prison, in which the Master was confined, to the king and, as it was said, to the Council. Thus they exonerated themselves from any further guarding of Master Hus. The king and the Council accepted the keys and on Palm Sunday[38] gave them to the bishop of Constance,[39] that he might take the Master into his power. Indeed, at that time the king could have honorably freed him [Hus] from the prison and thus could have honored his own safe-conduct, had he acted justly in this matter. The bishop ordered his armed guards the same night to conduct Master John to his fortress or castle. And they, taking the Master at night, chained him and put him in a boat and went or sailed with him on the Rhine as far as the fortress of Gottlieben of the said bishop of Constance, which was about a quarter of a mile distant from Constance.[40] From that Palm Sunday he lay in that fortress in the upper story of an airy tower, walking in chains and at night fastened by iron handcuffs to the wall beside the bed. He thus remained always in chains until the time of his return

realizing his situation, left the city by river during the night between Wednesday and Thursday, March 21, after midnight, under escort provided by Frederick, duke of Austria, and went to Schaffhausen on the Rhine, a city belonging to the duke." Loomis, *op. cit.,* p. 222.

[37] From this city he ordered his curia to follow him within six days on pain of excommunication and the loss of benefices. Cf. Cerretano's *Journal,* in Loomis, *op. cit.,* p. 492. When the cardinals refused to obey, he planned to escape across the Rhine into the territory of his supporter, Duke John the Fearless of Burgundy, but was caught before he could reach safety. He was deposed on May 29, and then arrested and imprisoned on June 3 in the same castle of Gottlieben from which Hus had been removed only a few days earlier. But after resigning the papal office and submitting to the new pope, Martin V, he was again raised to membership in the cardinal college and died in Florence at the palace of Cosimo di Medici on December 22, 1419. For a biographical sketch, cf. Loomis, *op. cit.,* p. 69.

[38] March 24.

[39] Otto III of Hachberg-Sausenberg.

[40] According to an anonymous writer of a letter, Hus was taken to Gottlieben by 170 soldiers and was bound in chains day and night. Gottlieben is now on Swiss territory, the castle being a pleasant, indeed a luxurious place. Hus later wrote his friends some letters from which additional information may be gleaned. Cf. Part II, Nos. 6–9.

again to Constance, where, as will be told later, he then lay in chains
in a certain prison of the Franciscan friars.

However, while he lay in that fortress in chains, as said before,
etc.,[41] he wrote in the first prison with the Dominicans some treatises
and letters to his friends, which will be likewise inserted later. He also
wrote letters to the people in the vernacular in the following form:

"God be with you, that resisting wickedness, the devil, the world,
and the flesh, you may remain steadfast!

"Dearly beloved! I entreat you, lying in prison, of which I am not
ashamed, for I suffer in hope for the Lord God's sake, to beseech the
Lord God for me that He may remain with me. He has mercifully
visited me with a grave illness and again healed me. He has permitted
my very determined enemies [to attack me], men to whom I had done
much good and whom I had loved sincerely. In Him alone I hope and
in your prayer, that He will grant me to remain steadfast in His grace
unto death. Should He be pleased to take me to Himself now, let His
holy will be done; but should He be pleased to return me, likekise let His
holy will be done. Surely, I have need of great help; yet I know that
He will not allow me to bear any suffering or temptation except for
my or your benefit, so that being tested and remaining steadfast, we
may obtain great reward.

"You should know that the letter which I had left behind for you [42]
was, in its Latin translation, greatly falsified by my enemies. They are
putting forth so many articles and charges against me that I have a
great deal of writing to do, frequently replying from the prison. There
is no man who could advise me save our merciful Lord Jesus, Who told
His faithful: 'I will give you a mouth and wisdom which all your adversaries shall not be able to resist.' [43]

"O dearly beloved! Remember how earnestly I labored among you
and that I ever desire your salvation, even now while in prison and
amidst great temptation.

"Written on Saturday, the day before St. Fabian." [44]

Dominus Havlík, then serving the Bethlehem Chapel, himself read

---

[41] This sentence appears to be misplaced, since its sequence refers to the
previous prison in the Dominican monastery. It is likely that it belongs to the
paragraph which follows the quoted letter, as that paragraph begins with the
identical words.

[42] The farewell letter written on Hus's departure for Constance; cf. Chap. I.

[43] Luke 21:15.

[44] January 19, 1415.

this letter to the people during a sermon and showed them the torn paper, saying: "Ha! ha; Hus is already in need of paper!" [45]

In the meantime, while he lay in the said fortress in chains, as mentioned before, the noble lords, knights, and squires of the Czech and Polish nations, moved by the love of truth and of the honor and fame of the illustrious kingdom of Bohemia, then exposed by its enemies and persons of little worth to the derision, gossip, and infamy of foreigners, on that account desired, as heirs of that kingdom, to aid in restoring and recovering it. Likewise they wished to promote the cause of the said Master John Hus, at one time their preacher and preeminent mentor, now bereft of all human aid. And [finally] they desired that the truth might have a freer access to the public. Accordingly, they devoutly wished to come to his aid at least with verbal intercessions, and to make an effort while the necessity of such an act was obvious. Thus concurring in their good zeal and their desire, they decided to present and read publicly the hereafter inserted letter and others to follow to the Council itself, or at least to the deputies of the four nations of the Council, namely, the German, the English, the French, and the Italian. The afore-mentioned lords were personally present at this reading. From the Czech nation in particular the following lords were present: Lord Wenceslas of Dubá alias of Leštno, Lord John of Chlum, Lord Henry Lacembok, Lord Půta of Ilburg, Lord Wenceslas Myška of Hrádek, Lord Bohuslav of Doupov, Lord Skála of Lileč, and other knights and squires then in Constance. From the Polish nation there were: Lord Janusz of Kalisz, Lord Zawisza called Czarny, ambassadors of the Polish king; and Lord Boruta, and Lord Donin, Lord Balicki, and other knights and squires of the said nation then in Constance.

Their first petition to the Council and the said nations was presented by the said lords to the deputies on Tuesday, May 13. It follows in these words:

"Most reverend fathers and lords! The noble lords of the Czech

---

[45] Havlík was appointed a substitute for Hus at the Bethlehem chapel. The letter was written on torn paper, since Hus could not obtain any other. Havlík, who was Hus's former pupil and a faithful friend (as evidenced from Hus's letter to him, Part II, No. 24), is reported in the Czech version as having said "Ha! ha!," an expression understood by Novotný as mockery (cf. his *M. Jan Hus*, II, 389). He assumes that Havlík's stubborn opposition to the granting of the cup to the laity turned him against Hus. Palacký interpreted the expression as *Heu, heu!*, i.e., Alas! alas!. I retain the reading of the Czech text.

and Polish nations here present declare before Your Paternities by
these presents that the most serene prince and lord, Lord Sigismund,
king of the Romans, ever Augustus, and king of Hungary, etc., having
heard a rumor of dissension in the kingdom of Bohemia, and wishing
as it lord and heir apparent to come to the support of its honor, sent
the noble lords, Wenceslas of Dubá and John of Chlum, here present,
to induce Master John Hus and assure him by the royal safe-conduct
and name openly granted and tendered him, since he was willing to
come to the sacred general Council of Constance for the purpose of
purging the kingdom of Bohemia and himself from ill repute, under
the safe-conduct of that lord king and under the public protection of
the most holy empire, to render there a public account of his faith to
any plaintiff demanding it. This the above-mentioned lords did at a
meeting with the above-named Master John Hus. When, however, the
said Master Hus had freely arrived at Constance under the said safe-
conduct, he was arrested and without any previous hearing was harshly
thrown into prison, where he suffered until now not only chains but
hunger and thirst as well. Although the heretics formerly condemned
by the Council of Pisa freely appeared here and afterward freely
departed,[46] he, the afore-mentioned Master John Hus, on the contrary,
neither convicted nor condemned, nor even as yet heard, as mentioned
before, was imprisoned at a time when none of the embassies of any
king, electoral prince, or university had yet arrived here. And although
the lord king along with the noble lords here present demanded with
great urgency that care be taken to honor his safe-conduct, and that
the said Master John Hus be publicly heard, in order that he might
publicly render account of his faith; and if convicted of stubbornly
asserting anything contrary to the Holy Scriptures and the truth, that
he ought then to amend it according to the decision and instruction of
the Council; he could not thus far obtain or hold that [hearing]. On
the contrary, regardless of this, the said Master John Hus is still kept

---

[46] This refers to the plenipotentiaries of Pope Gregory XII and of Benedict
XIII who were sent to the Council of Constance to negotiate concerning their
abdication. These two popes had been condemned and deposed at Pisa "for
schism and heresy." Cardinal Fillastre recorded in his *Diary* that there arose
"a violent dispute as to whether they should be permitted to enter the city wearing
their red hats. For the sake of peace they were permitted to do so and in that
garb they made their entry." Loomis, *op. cit.*, p. 208. The envoys of Gregory XII
made their entry on January 22, after having waited more than two months.
Those of Benedict XIII entered on January 8.

so cruelly chained and reduced to so slender a diet that it is to be feared that, his strength being exhausted, he might be in danger of losing his reason. Furthermore, the lords here present are severely blamed by the people of the kingdom of Bohemia that, when they saw the said Master John Hus thus afflicted in violation of the safe-conduct of the said lord king, they neglected to warn the lord king in their letters concerning his safe-conduct. Then the lord king himself would no longer suffer such conduct verging on contempt and dishonor of the crown of the kingdom of Bohemia and of the afore-mentioned nation. That realm since it first accepted the catholic faith has never departed from the obedience to the Holy Roman Church. The lords have hitherto borne all these things patiently, lest they should appear to give an occasion for any disturbance to this sacred Council. On this account, most reverend fathers and lords, the noble lords by these letters urgently, ceaselessly, and ardently entreat Your Paternities that both on account of honoring the safe-conduct of the said lord king and of conserving the fame of the illustrious kingdom of Bohemia, and at the same time of enhancing your own, you would be willing, by the intervention of divine justice, to bring the case of the said Master John Hus to a speedy end. There is danger for him in delay. Therefore the lords put particular confidence in the eminent rectitude of Your Paternities.

"Furthermore, most reverend fathers and lords, it has come to the hearing of the noble lords of Bohemia here present that certain traducers and enemies of the honor and fame of the already mentioned illustrious kingdom of Bohemia have brought to the ears of Your Paternities that the sacrament of the most precious blood of the Lord is being carried about Bohemia in bottles and that cobblers are now hearing confessions and administering the most holy body of the Lord to others. On that account the Bohemian lords here present ask you to put no faith in such false detractors, for these perverse defamers of the said kingdom tell lies. The lords sedulously petition Your Paternities, however, that you may rather name such defamers of the above-named kingdom, that both the previously mentioned king and Your Paternities will see how the lords of Bohemia will undertake to refute the false and scurrilous accusations so that such defamers will fear to stand before the lord king and Your Paternities."

This petition on behalf of John Hus, bachelor of sacred theology, was presented to the nations on Monday, May 13, before the feast of the Holy Spirit, by the lords of the Czech and Polish nations in Constance in the house of the Brothers Minor.

The names of the lords who presented the above mentioned petition are these in particular: Lord Henry Lacembok, Lord John of Chlum called Kepka, Lord Wenceslas of Leštno and Dubá, Lord Šraňk the Younger and his father, Lord Myška of Hrádek, Lord Kuneš of Chlum, Lord Skála of Moravia, and Lord Beškovec.[47]

Of the Polish, these: Lord Zawisza called Czarny, Lord Kalisz, Lord Boruta, and several others. The reader of this petition was Peter of Mladoňovice, at that time bachelor of arts, but now master of arts.[48]

Recension B: [49]	Recension M:
When the reading came to the last clause, that is, "Furthermore, etc.," the bishop of Litomyšl [50] promptly rose and said: "That concerns me and mine!" [51] and further added: "Most reverend fathers and lords! Because this last article concerns me and my adherents, for that reason I request time for deliberation about it and that the lords appoint a time to hear my reply to it." Wherefore the lord deputies in the end appointed Thursday [52] as the time for hearing the Council's replies to the said document, with which reply they [the nobles] should [they said] be deservedly	When the above-mentioned letter was read and that portion which concerned both the Czechs and the Poles was finished, and the second part was begun that concerned the Czech lords alone, namely: "Furthermore, most reverend fathers, etc.," the bishop of Litomyšl promptly arose and said: "See here! that concerns me and mine!" Likewise in Latin he said: "Most reverend fathers and lords, this last article concerns mine and me." And he requested time for himself to deliberate on the reply, as he also did reply; it will later be given here word for word. But

[47] The two Šraňk nobles were perhaps Wenceslas and Nicholas; Kuneš of Chlum and Beškovec are otherwise unknown.

[48] It is clear that this part of the narrative was written in 1416, when Peter received his M.A.

[49] What follows is presented by Novotný in two recensions, B and M, because of verbal differences.

[50] Bishop John of Litomyšl, called "Iron," was one of the three most formidable accusers of Hus at the Council. Since neither the archbishop of Prague nor the bishop of Olomouc attended the Council, he was the ranking Czech hierarch there.

[51] This sentence is in Czech.

[52] May 16.

content.[53] Further to hear the response of the bishop of Litomyšl to the clause which, as he said, concerned him and his adherents.

So on Thursday before the feast of the Holy Spirit, which fell on May 16, the bishop of Carcassonne in the name of the deputies gave the lords a verbose response to their document, which he divided into a few parts, as will appear more clearly later in the lords' document replying to that response.

Also the bishop of Litomyšl made a reply to the petition of the lords and ordered it read by his [man] Mužík; that reply is as follows:

the afore-mentioned lords of the nations told the Czech and Polish lords that they would be given a reply to the above-mentioned petition the next day wherewith they should deservedly abide and rest content. Their reply will appear later[54] after the reply of the bishop of Litomyšl.

The reply of the lord bishop of Litomyšl to the second article of the afore-mentioned letter, namely: "Furthermore, most reverend fathers," was given on Thursday before the feast of the Holy Spirit.

"Most reverend fathers and preeminent lords! Peter of Mladoňovice, bachelor of arts, has lately in the name of certain nobles of the kingdom of Bohemia set forth in a writing, among other matters, that certain defamers and traducers of the said kingdom, whom they [the nobles] consider false and iniquitous, namely those who have brought to Your Paternities' notice that the most precious blood of Christ is being carried about Bohemia in flasks and that cobblers are hearing confessions and administering the body of Christ to others.

"Most reverend fathers and lords! It is notorious that the wicked sect of Wyclifites, alas! is now spreading pollution in the said kingdom. 'Tis true that to uproot this sect I have labored along with other prelates, doctors, masters, and countless other Catholics of the same kingdom who desire with their utmost strength to defend Christ's faith. Then at long last I have reluctantly related some of these things in my German nation.[55] I did so not to disgrace the kingdom itself, since I, too, am a Czech, but rather for the honor of the kingdom, I stated that

[53] From the context it is clear that this refers to the reply made in behalf of the Council by Gerard de Puy, bishop of Carcassonne.
[54] Actually, Peter left out this reply (cf. Van der Hardt, IV, 209).
[55] The Czech delegation was included at the Council in the German nation.

a new scandal has arisen in the kingdom; for the followers of this sect in many cities, villages, and places of that kingdom, laymen of both sexes, commune in both kinds of bread and wine and persistently teach that this is the way communion must be administered. They stubbornly assert that the clergy who administer it in the contrary manner err and consent to a repugnant sacrilege. This clearly appears from their writings hitherto sent and circulated here.[56]

"Furthermore, on the basis of the report and rumor divulged here in this [German] nation and the writings transmitted [to me] by [our] party, I stated that it had come to my notice that the blood of Christ is being carried about in unconsecrated bottles and receptacles. Indeed, on the basis of the erroneous assertion of the afore-mentioned Wyclifites that it is necessary for salvation that people commune in both bread and wine, it follows necessarily that just as the body of Christ is [carried] in a pyx, so also the blood of Christ should be carried from place to place in bottles and other utensils, particularly for the use of the sick.

"Further, I have not asserted it myself, but have heard it stated by trustworthy and eminent men that a certain woman, a member of that sect, had snatched by force the body of Christ from the hands of a priest and administered the communion to herself, and had asserted that it should thus be done if the priest denied the communion. That selfsame woman, among other errors of which she was convicted, maintained the opinions that a good layman or laywoman consecrated and absolved better than a bad priest; asserting that a bad priest neither absolves nor consecrates. But neither I nor those of mine assisting me in this matter have ever brought to the ears of Your most reverend Paternities that cobblers of the said kingdom are hearing confessions

---

[56] This refers to some treatises advocating the communion in both kinds, most likely the treatises of Jakoubek of Stříbro, which were sent to Constance in March. Jakoubek even urged Hus to approve the usage, but Hus asked that the matter be postponed. It is noteworthy that, as early as January, Lord John of Chlum had asked Hus for his opinion about the matter. Cf. Part II, Nos. 8–9. Moreover, shortly after arriving in Constance, Hus wrote a treatise, *Utrum expediat laicis fidelibus sumere sanguinem Christi sub specie vini,* and answered the question affirmatively. *Historia et Monumenta,* I, 52-54. We also learn from a letter written by Master Peter de Pulka, delegate of the University of Vienna, that Master Christian of Prachatice, representing King Wenceslas of Bohemia, defended communion in both kinds and was on that account imprisoned by the Council. I owe this statement to Miss Louise R. Loomis' unpublished notes quoting de Pulka's letters, published in *Archiv für Kunde österreichischer Geschichts-Quellen* (Vienna, 1856), XV, 22.

and are administering the sacrament of the body of Christ, as had been stated in the document offered by the said Peter on behalf of the said persons. Nevertheless, it is to be feared that if the above-mentioned scandals are not stopped, those things will speedily come to pass.

"Most reverend fathers, the afore-mentioned events were stated by me for the guarding and defense of the honor of the aforesaid kingdom, so that that kingdom would not be further defamed and the faith would not be imperiled by pestiferous sects of this kind. Therefore, I request with all reverence and charity, by the bowels of mercy of our Lord Jesus Christ, that this sacred Council inform itself concerning the aforesaid matters and provide the previously mentioned kingdom with a fitting remedy for it. Let it also declare whether they be the defamers and traducers and false and iniquitous enemies of that kingdom of Bohemia who hinder the purging of the afore-mentioned and many other errors disseminated by the Wyclifites in that kingdom and else-where, and who foster, promote, and defend the teachers [*dogmatistas*] of those errors; or whether they be those who labor and have labored for the extirpation of those errors from the said kingdom, manfully opposing themselves, as Catholic men zealous for the faith, against those who maintain these errors. Such judgment and definition will indeed be truly most useful to the said kingdom, for it will do much to quiet the disturbances. This response with its supporting [evidence] that I have advanced long ago has been presented to Your Paternities on my behalf and on the part of those assisting me, ever submitting myself and those assisting me to the decision and definition of this sacred Council of Constance."

The response to the answer of the deputies of the Council to the [Czech and Polish] lords, which was delivered orally by the bishop of Carcassonne,[57] together with a resumé of the answer to the response of those deputies, which was read in the same refectory on the Saturday before Pentecost: [58]

"Most reverend fathers and lords! Inasmuch as recently, on Thursday, the sixteenth day of the present month of May, at the request of the noble lords of the Czech and Polish nations, Your Paternities responded that the lords had been ill informed on certain points con-

[57] Bishop Gerard de Puy, the contents of which may be reconstructed from Peter's reply.
[58] I.e., May 18, by Peter of Mladoňovice.

tained in the text of the said document; the above-mentioned lords have decided, therefore, to make a more explicit statement relating to the petition presented to Your Paternities. They do not hereby accuse Your Paternities of dissimulation in this matter, but wish that Your Paternities, weighing their views together with those of the other side, may discern and judge about the submitted matter more clearly and effectively.

"First, whereas to the lords' statement that Master John Hus came here to Constance of his own will and freely under the safe-conduct of the lord king and the protection of the most holy empire, Your said Paternities responded that the lords had been ill informed concerning the safe-conduct. For Your Paternities said that they accepted as true the statement of men worthy of being trusted that his own supporters and friends had procured the safe-conduct for Master John Hus only fifteen days after his arrest.

"The lords, and especially Lord John here present, whom this statement especially concerns, answer that not on the fifteenth day, but on the very day of the arrest of the said Master John Hus he, Lord John, when he was interrogated by the lord pope in the presence of almost all the lord cardinals as to whether the said Master Hus had the safe-conduct of his son [Sigismund] the king, replied: 'Most holy father, be assured that he has.' When among other questions he was asked for the second time if he [Hus] had a safe-conduct, he replied that he had. None of them, however, requested at that time that the safe-conduct be shown. Immediately on the next and the third day and thereafter Lord John loudly complained in respect of the lord pope that Master Hus, under the safe-conduct of the said lord king, was detained a prisoner, and showed the safe-conduct to many. Moreover, to verify what he is saying, he calls on the counts, bishops, knights, squires, and the notable citizens of this city of Constance for their confirmation and testimony, for at that time they all saw that safe-conduct and heard it read. Wherefore, the above-mentioned Lord John is ready to pledge himself to whatever penalty with anyone declaring the contrary, clearly to deduce and prove the foregoing. The lords appeal also for the confirmation of certain electors and other princes and bishops and many other nobles who at that time waited upon his royal majesty, as to where and at what time the said safe-conduct was granted by the lord king's special command. Your Paternities can elicit and understand therefrom that it is not these lords who were ill informed concerning

the said safe-conduct, but rather the persons who gave Your Paternities such unfounded reports. For first, it is injurious and damaging
to the lord king and his chancellors, since it alleges that the lord king
together with his chancellors and notaries postdated the time of the
issue of the said safe-conduct by almost ten weeks.[59] They have also
done injustice to the lord knights, as if the latter had surreptitiously
obtained the safe-conduct. The above-mentioned lords, therefore, ask
Your Paternities to put no faith in assertions too readily called trustworthy, but rather to discuss the matter after having heard the other
side. In this way, they feel, the truth will shine forth more clearly.

"Secondly, whereas the lords stated that the afore-mentioned Master
John Hus, not condemned or yet heard, having come here freely, was
imprisoned, etc., Your Paternities replied that he, Master John Hus,
in the time of Lord Alexander V had been condemned on account of
certain errors and had been cited personally to appear [at the curia]
and had been there heard through his procurators. Because he contumaciously did not trouble himself to appear, however, he was excommunicated and in that excommunication, as you said, he has persisted well-nigh on to five years. Therein he is to be regarded not only
as a mere heretic, but as a heresiarch, that is, an inventor and disse-
minator of new heresies. And having arrived here, he has also preached
publicly.

"To this the lords reply that they know nothing about the condemnation and citation—unless to some degree by rumor—since some of
them had then been out of the kingdom. Indeed, about the personal
nonappearance they assert that they have often heard him and other
trustworthy men say he would have gladly appeared at Rome or elsewhere, had he felt himself safe to come and had not his mortal enemies
thwarted it. But, as they heard, he had publicly sent his procurators
to the Roman curia to present the aforesaid reasonable excuses and
several others in respect to his nonappearance. Some of them were
imprisoned and others actually cruelly treated.[60] About the long-
lasting excommunication, then, they have often heard him say that he

[59] The safe-conduct was issued on October 18 and delivered to Hus on November 5. Less than three weeks would therefore have elapsed between these two
dates. But it would appear that the imperial chancery was charged with "post-
dating" the document, although in the case alleged they would actually have predated it.

[60] Cf. Hus's own numerous explanations of these events, both in sermons and
letters, in Part II, Nos. 1–6. He made reference to it on many other occasions.

had borne it not contumaciously, but under an open appeal. He referred in this connection to the records of the trial conducted in the Roman curia, in which this entire matter is more fully contained. As for some points stated above, Your Paternities may learn of them clearly in the present public copy.

"As to the preaching which his enemies allege that Master John Hus had publicly delivered in this city, the lords, and especially Lord John of Chlum here present, reply that he has continuously resided in Constance with the said Master John Hus; and that whoever does or dares to say that he, Master John Hus, has preached or, indeed, has taken a single step outside the house where he has lodged from the time of his arrival in this city to the day and hour of his arrest, as stated above, the said Lord John is willing to pledge himself to any such person who had made such a malicious [charge] to Your Paternities, that he should never be able justly and truthfully to establish and prove it, under pain of any kind of penalty, monetary or other.

"Thirdly, in like manner Your Paternities have said that they did not understand what the lords implied as to the heretics condemned at the Council of Pisa; whether they meant those ambassadors who quarreled over the [claims of the] rival popes who had come here in order to secure the desired unity and for that reason had been tolerated and kindly treated, so that their lords might be more inclined toward unity; or whether they meant any other particular heretics condemned there; adding, that even heretics who came here for the sake of unity should be tolerated and kindly treated.

"Most reverend fathers and lords! irrespective whether the first or the second [kind] were or can be understood, the lords seek nothing else but that he himself, the afore-mentioned Master John Hus, may be able to enjoy liberty similar to that which they enjoy. For he came to this sacred Council of his own will and freely for no other purpose than to acknowledge publicly his faith and to receive instruction if he strayed from the law of God and the unity of the Holy mother Church: for in this matter he wishes to be reconciled and united with her. And not only he himself, but also to induce his supporters and adherents in the truth to do the same, the majority of whom, it is admitted, are in the kingdom of Bohemia. Therefore, he has also come here that he may be able to clear the already mentioned illustrious kingdom of Bohemia from the perverse defamation of which it was accused a short time ago.

"Finally, most reverend fathers and lords, inasmuch as Your Paternities have favorably responded to the principal petition of the lords by being willing to expedite speedily the trial of John Hus and by dispensing divine justice with all clemency, the lords already mentioned out of sincere affection express their thanks to Your Paternities for this gracious action. When with God's help the things desired have been brought to a successful conclusion, they wish, not only in your presence but also before the whole kingdom of Bohemia and elsewhere, wherever they may go, to render great thanks to Your Paternities."

The present document was read in Constance in reply to the lord deputies in the trial of Master John Hus, in the great refectory of the Brothers Minor, by command of the afore-mentioned lords, namely the Czech and Polish, by P.M.,[61] on Saturday, May 18, before the entire German nation and the deputies of all other nations, namely the French, Italian, and English.

There was then offered a transcript of the public testimony sealed with the great seal of the University of Prague, in which Master John Hus professes his catholic faith, refutes many articles falsely ascribed to him, and legally excuses himself for his personal nonappearance. That transcript had been sent to Pope John XXIII [62] in the year of the Lord 1411 and then had been posted on the gates of the church of St. Peter in Rome.

In this document the lords replied to those statements orally delivered to the said lords of the Czech and Polish nations by the bishop of Carcassonne in behalf of the Council. The reply [of the Czech nobles] to the statement of the bishop of Litomyšl, which he delivered on Thursday, May 16, [is as follows]:

"Most reverend fathers and lords! As the other day, on Monday the thirteenth of the present month of May, the noble lords of the Czech and Polish nations offered to Your Paternities a certain document to be read, the last clause of which, when offered and read on behalf of the lords and nobles of Bohemia, states that it has come to the hearing of the said lords and nobles of Bohemia, as mentioned before, that some traducers and enemies of both the honor and the fame of the already mentioned illustrious kingdom of Bohemia brought to the ears of Your Paternities that the most precious sacrament of

---

[61] This is of course Peter of Mladoňovice.

[62] This is the letter of September 11, 1411, which is inserted in this chapter *infra*. Cf. Novotný, *op. cit.,* No. 31; Palacký, No. 9.

the blood of the Lord is now being carried about Bohemia in bottles, as well as that cobblers are now hearing confessions and administering the most holy body of the Lord to others. At once the lord bishop of Litomyšl rose and said that such statements concerned him and his adherents. He offered to reply to it and requested that time be granted him for it. When the time came, he made his response, a copy of which was later presented to the lords.

"In that response, among other matters, he acknowledged this one thing, that he had declared to Your Paternities that the blood of Christ was still being carried about there in unconsecrated bottles or vessels. The other two points in the said document of the lords, which had come to their hearing, he denied to have brought to the ears of Your said Paternities; interspersing among other things into his document some statements which the lords in their aforesaid document, to which he offered to reply, had not stated nor had mentioned.

"The lords, therefore, reply that these assertions which he acknowledges to have declared before Your Paternities, they do not believe at all. They regard them as founded solely on fictitious and imagined tales, unless first, as was said before, the statements defaming the said kingdom be proved true more convincingly, competently, and fundamentally. If these assertions as mentioned previously shall be proved true without a doubt, the aforesaid lords are eager to show themselves, as much or more than he or anyone else anywhere, how deeply pained and grieved they are by the scandal which may be arising in the said kingdom—which God forbid! Furthermore, as true heirs and Catholic Christians of the said kingdom they are willing to devote their powers and to try with all their strength to mitigate and eradicate it.

"Secondly, he stated as a principal charge that those things which he proposed to Your Paternities and commanded to be proposed in the said document, he did for the honor and protection of the forementioned kingdom. He alleged for it the reason that he feared the defamation of this kingdom by the pestiferous sects and the danger to its faith.

"To this the lords reply that if it were true that he has shown himself as doing or as having previously done such things as were proposed by him, as he claims, for the honor and safety of this kingdom and for the extirpation of the sects which he says are spreading there—although in reality he has shown himself as doing or having done otherwise—this the lords gladly and gratefully acknowledge. Indeed, they are willing to labor to the same end by their counsels and aid. But the lords do not and cannot believe that he has proposed these things for the honor of the said kingdom, since the facts teach the opposite, unless he can demonstrate these efforts more effectively than he has done here.

"In the third place, he states that he requests this sacred Council to declare whether those are the defamers and traducers, etc., who, as he says, hinder the extirpation of the afore-mentioned errors and many others which are being disseminated by the Wyclifites in that kingdom and elsewhere, etc.; or whether they are those who labor and have labored for the extirpation of those errors, as he says, from the said kingdom, etc.: as [it stands] in his document.

"The lords reply that there by implication he speaks provocatively and perhaps derogatorily. Since he thus censures the nobles and lords of the kingdom of Bohemia, members of the court of its and their lord, the king of the Romans, as well as others of their friends of the aforesaid kingdom, he slanders them thereby. Were it not for the lords' veneration of Your Paternities and for his episcopal dignity, they would retort more harshly to his accusations and to the other things he has charged against them. For these things which he implies by his provocative assertions he will never be able to demonstrate and prove against them or their friends. It is well known throughout the entire kingdom that the lords present here, as well as the nobles of the kingdom of Bohemia, have never defended errors or the adherents of errors, nor will they ever defend them. Rather, along with their forefathers and predecessors, as Catholic men, they have urged and pressed for the extirpation of those perfidious errors, avoiding no labor and sparing neither their bodies nor their money. They have heard nothing of the sort about his [the bishop's] own progenitors and forefathers, as said before.

"Finally, the above-mentioned bishop demanded to have the names of the lords in writing, that he might know whom to answer. The above-mentioned lords reply that it seems to them that he well knows who and what they are, and by what names they are called. But if indeed he still desires to have their names, they say that they are ready to give not only their own, but also their forefathers' names. They, however, do not ask for his name in writing, knowing well who and what he is, and who his progenitors were." [63]

[63] This is an obvious reference to the bishop's illegitimate birth. It is supposed

The document was signed by the above-mentioned lords of the Czech and Polish nations. It was presented in the great refectory of the Brothers Minor in Constance to the said deputies of the nations of the Council on Friday before Marcellus, the last day of the month of May,[64] with the exception of the first clause, namely, from "To the most serene prince" to the "Most reverend fathers in Christ," and also the last clause concerning the king. Thereafter the same document was presented on the same day to the king, including the first and the last clauses concerning the king. The deputies of the nations decreed that the subscribed letter be edited for the lords into public form by the notary of those deputies.

With these documents was offered the record of the public testimony of the reverend father, Lord Nicholas, the bishop of Nezero, oppointed by the Apostolic See inquisitor of heretics for the city and diocese of Prague. He testified that in many conversations and contacts with Master Hus he had found no error or heresy in him, as it will appear in that record.[65] Also there was offered a letter of the barons of Moravia commending Master Hus, to which eleven seals [were appended]. The documents follows in these words.[66]

It was presented on Friday after the Feast of Corpus Christi to the deputies of the nations by the Czech lords along with the public attestations given below, except for the first and last clauses concerning the king, with a copy presented to the king on the same day:

"To the most serene prince and lord, Lord Sigismund, king of the Romans, ever Augustus, and king of Hungary, Dalmatia, Croatia, etc., our most gracious lord, our sincere and faithful service in all things! Most serene prince and most gracious lord! We declare to Your Serenity by these presents that we, the undersigned, by a unanimous consent and accord, have presented this our petition, reasonable and just, hereinafter described, as worthy of hearing, which we signed with unanimous consent and accord, to the reverend fathers and lords in

---

by Bartoš that Bishop John was the son of Peter of Šternberg and Anne, the illegitimate daughter of Margrave John Henry. Cf. Bartoš, *op. cit.,* p. 472, n. In the episcopal register the bishop's name is given as Joannes V. Bucka (1392–1616). Cf. Gams, *op. cit.*

[64] May 31, 1415.

[65] It is inserted later, although by that time Bishop Nicholas had slipped away from Constance.

[66] This is probably the letter of the Moravian lords assembled at Meziříčí; it is inserted later.

Christ, the deputies of the four nations, and to the whole sacred Council here in Constance. The purport of it follows word for word in this manner:

" 'Most reverend fathers in Christ and lords! Recently Your Paternities were supplicated on behalf of the lords and nobles, knights and squires of the Czech and Polish nations that you would be pleased to take notice that the information given by the enemies of Master John Hus to Your Paternities was insufficient and, to speak with reverence, unreliable in many respects, both as regards the safe-conduct of the king and in other articles, as is more clearly contained in the document then presented. Nonetheless, so far we have had no reply to this document and others then produced and at that time received by the lord bishop of Merseburg [67] for transmission to the deputies of the nations. On that account the oft-mentioned lords supplicate Your Paternities to be pleased now to consider the said document and give an answer to those who presented it as requested and petitioned therein.'

"Further, when you have considered especially the hardships inflicted upon the afore-mentioned Master John which might be inferred from the said document and the previous one, we pray that you might be willing to give merciful attention to the fact that such uncharitable hardships have been brought upon him by his said enemies out of black rancor and hatred. In order, therefore, to confound their wickedness and bring to light the clear truth, may Your Paternities be pleased to know that the barons, notables, nobles, citizens, townsmen, clergy, and the lay people of the afore-mentioned kingdom of Bohemia know that the said Master John Hus has in all his academic and ecclesiastical acts, and especially in his public preaching, repeatedly declared [his orthodoxy] and formulated his protests in the best legal manner and form that he, Master John Hus, could and was able to do. By these repeated declarations he sought to assert their validity against anything to the contrary. This appears quite clear to anyone who looks at the patent protest made and declared by him about the definition of a certain question, as well as in his other protests which, as has been mentioned, were made quite openly. It reads in its legal form as follows: [68]

" 'Because above all things I desire the honor of God, the advance-

---

[67] Bishop Nicholas Lubich, president of the German delegation.

[68] For the rendering of this difficult passage I am indebted to Professor Robert B. Palmer of Scripps College, Claremont, California.

ment of the Holy Church, and because I am a faithful member of the
Lord Jesus Christ, Who is the head and bridegroom of the Holy Church
which He redeemed; therefore, as I have done before, so again I now
declare hereby that I have never stubbornly said, nor wish in future to
say, anything contrary to the truth of faith; and finally that I have held,
now hold, and firmly resolve to hold all the truth of faith to such a
degree that instead of wanting to defend a contrary error, I would
rather suffer, in the hope and with the help of the Lord, the punishment of death. Yea, with the help of God I am ready to expose this
wretched life for the law of Christ, which I believe was given in every
particular by the counsel of the most Holy Trinity and was promulgated
by the holy men of God for the salvation of the human race. Moreover, I believe every single article of that law according to the meaning
in which the blessed Trinity ordained them to be believed. Hence, as
in my disputations and academic acts as well as in my public preaching
I have submitted again and again, and now again I submit and, in the
future I wish humbly to submit, to the ordinance and conciliation as
well as the obedience of this most sacred law, being ready to revoke
whatever I said if I am taught that it is contrary to the orthodox faith
and truth.'

"From these protests and from the expressions and legal forms
observed by John Hus, as has been mentioned before, it can be easily
gathered that his intention was and is that he never wished nor now
wishes, in his books, treatises, teachings, and public preaching to have
written or spoken anything or to have stated in any articles anything
he wittingly knew to be erroneous, scandalous, seditious, offensive to
pious ears, or heretical. Yet he is charged by his enemies, although
illegally, with such things. His chief intention, however, has been and
is to formulate all points and conclusions and articles found in his
books and teachings, with the support of the gospel truth and of the
holy doctors as well as the interpreters of Holy Scripture, in and for
the end expressed in his declaration quoted above. If in course of time
he were informed about these afore-mentioned matters more clearly
by men more able than he; and if he were found in error or insufficiently informed, or if he were not well understood by others, he could
then through such information be guided, corrected, instructed, and
enlightened. He would then by no means defend and stubbornly sustain in any way whatsoever any article against the most holy Roman
Church and the catholic faith.

"However, most reverend fathers, the said matters notwithstanding, his enemies, urged by hatred, draw and have drawn several articles from the books of Master John's teachings in a truncated and abbreviated [form], rejecting or failing to examine the reasons for and elucidations of them and disregarding the distinctions of the ambiguities. They invent fictitious and mendacious articles against him, to the end that, once their uncharitable purpose is reached, hatred may prevail against him and he be deprived of his life and standing. This they do contrary to the safe-conduct justly and patently assigned to him, Master John Hus, by the pious intent of the most serene prince and lord, Lord Sigismund, king of the Romans and of Hungary, for his just defense against all his enemies' attacks and scurrilous accusations. And not only for his own defense, but also of the illustrious kingdom of Bohemia, and for the timely quelling of all enmities arising in the said kingdom or elsewhere. As the heir and lord apparent of the said kingdom, the said lord, king of the Romans, supremely desires and wishes the suppression of such dangerous enmities in the kingdom of Bohemia.

"Wherefore, the said barons, notables, knights, and squires ask that, giving attention to the said matters and considering the infamy which may result to that kingdom and its inhabitants from what has been said, you would be willing on your part to intervene by ordering and directing that the said Master John be fairly heard by learned men and by masters of sacred Scripture now appointed or by others to be appointed, in regard to each and every article laid or to be laid to his charge, in order that he may explain his intention and meaning of the things he has taught in accordance with the expressed design and the numerous distinctions and ambiguities in which his excerptors disagree for the most part with him in many of the articles. By these means he would not be condemned unheard by the testimony of witnesses and the trivial charges of his accusers, many of whom are and have for a long time been his mortal enemies. It is on their account that he is held a prisoner in such a miserable condition as mentioned before. Your Paternities can be clearly informed from his declarations of the truth that he is ever ready to submit to the determination of this most sacred Council. Indeed, most reverend fathers, the greater part of the sacred Council is so misinformed and misled by the fictitious and deceitful persuasions of his enemies, asserting that he, Master John Hus, has been for a long time incorrigibly obstinate in some dangerous articles of his faith, that Your Paternities may clearly perceive therefrom that they are false. To show an ampler evidence of it, we call Your Paternities' attention to the letter of public testimony of the reverend father in Christ, Lord Nicholas, bishop of Nezero and inquisitor of heretical pravity of the city and diocese of Prague, appointed specially by the Apostolic See, to which Your Paternities should pay heed.

"May it, therefore, please Your most reverend Paternities to free the said Master John Hus, neither convicted nor condemned, from the chains and shackles in which he is now cruelly detained, and to place him in the hands of some reverend lord bishops or commissioners appointed or to be appointed by this sacred Council, in order that he, Master John Hus, may regain his strength and thus may be more carefully and readily examined by the said lord commissioners appointed or to be appointed and be at greater liberty to reply to them. The lords and nobles of the said kingdom of Bohemia offer to give a guarantee from the hands of the said lords until his process and trial —as has been mentioned before—have been settled. They promise not to break their faith for anything in the world, no matter what such guarantees might be. Further, they will salutarily provide, in the effecient execution of the foregoing guarantee, for the status, fame, and honor of the said illustrious kingdom of Bohemia and for the safe-conduct of the said most serene prince, the king of the Romans. Nevertheless, lest the enemies of the honor and fame of the said kingdom of Bohemia and the traducers of the afore-mentioned lords may in the future disparage those lords, pretending and casting suspicion on them later, that they have sought and now seek by excessive and illegal petitions, and on behalf of these petitions make insistent demands here in the presence of Your Paternities; for that reason the above-mentioned lords have presented and do present to Your Paternities none but these just and reasonable requests worthy indeed to be seen and favorably heard by Your Paternities. Therefore, they petition Your Paternities, in order to prevent the fore-mentioned evils, to be willing to decree and consent most graciously that the purport of this document and the above-mentioned petition be edited into public form and copied by your notary public, in the best form and manner in which this is usually and customarily done.

"In view of these reasonable and just petitions presented for the consideration of the said lords, we supplicate Your royal Majesty,[69]

---

[69] This paragraph is now addressed to Sigismund, along with the first paragraph. The whole document was sent to him on June 1.

that out of the love of justice and of the fame of the illustrious kingdom of Bohemia, whose heir and lord apparent without doubt we know you are and will be, and to assure the freedom of your safe-conduct, you would be willing on your part to intervene with the said most reverend fathers and lords, in order that they may be willing effectually to hear us in this our just petition presented to them, as previously mentioned. However, lest the enemies of the honor and fame of the said illustrious kingdom of Bohemia as well as our traducers should in the future disparage us, perhaps by pretending that we have made some illegal, unreasonable, and irregular demands on the said most reverend fathers, we therefore requested the said lord deputies that they be willing to decree a public validation of the contents of our document. Similarly we most assiduously beseech Your afore-mentioned Serenity that Your Serenity may deign and be willing to grant us a testimony concerning the said matters."

After this document, therefore, was presented on the aforesaid day and place to the deputies of those nations, the lord patriarch of Antioch [70] replied in the name of the deputies of the Council. Dealing first with the protest, he said that "whether his protest proves to be valid, will become evident during the proceedings of the trial." Secondly, concerning the false abstracting of the articles made by the enemies of the Master, he said: "Whether they are rightly or wrongly abstracted will be seen in the final and definitive sentence, in which, should he be declared right, his foes and enemies will then be shamed." Concerning the offer of a guaranty proposed by the lords for the person of Master John Hus, however, he replied that "even if a thousand such guarantors were offered, it is against the conscience of them, the deputies, to surrender such a man into the hands of the guarantors, for under no circumstances is he to be trusted." [71] Concerning the final petition for a hearing, he replied that the lord deputies had favorably heard the lords' petition and were willing to grant him, John Hus, a favorable public hearing on the next Wednesday, that is the fourth day immediately following, which is June 5, and were willing to deal kindly with

[70] The person referred to is Dr. Jean Mauroux, a French canonist. He at first supported John XXIII; in December, 1414, he wrote him a letter arguing that John was not subordinated to the Council. Cf. Bartoš, *op. cit.,* p. 418.

[71] The patriarch's assertion that Hus was "under no circumstances to be trusted" already constituted his condemnation—and that even before the trial began. Consequently, any further defense on his part was rejected in advance. It is in statements like these that the unfairness of the trial is seen clearly.

him. What, however, and of what sort and how kind that hearing was, is evident from its description in its place along with the other subsequent [hearings]: namely, on the fourth day after Marcellus [72] before the eclipse of the sun; and on the sixth day [73] during the eclipse of the sun; and on Saturday after the eclipse of the sun.[74] Lastly he [the patriarch of Antioch] replied that they decreed to have the said petition of the lords edited and copied into public form by the notary of the Council in the manner they had requested; nevertheless it was not received [by the lords] in that form, etc.

The record of the testimony of the said lord inquisitor of heretical pravity, in which he publicly acknowledged that he knew of no error or heresy against the previously mentioned Master John Hus, is as follows:

"In the name of the Lord, Amen. In the year of His Nativity 1414, the seventh indiction, on Thursday the last day of the month of August,[75] about the time of the *nones*, in the pontificate of our most holy father in Christ and our lord, Lord John XXIII by divine providence pope, of his pontificate the fifth year, in the upper room of the house of the renowned Lord Peter of Svojšín caled Zmrzlík, master of the mint of the most serene prince and lord, Lord Wenceslas, king of the Romans and of Bohemia, situated in the Greater City of Prague near the monastery of St. James the Apostle, and in the presence of me, the undersigned public notary and of the undersigned witnesses who were called and requested specially for this purpose, consisting of the person of the honorable man, John of Jesenice, master of arts and doctor of laws, procurator and in virtue of his procuratorship of the honorable Master John Hus of Husinec, *formatus* bachelor of sacred theology of the University of Prague; and of the reverend father in Christ, Lord Nicholas, bishop of Nezero and inquisitor of heretical pravity of the city and diocese of Prague, appointed specially by the Apostolic See. He [John of Jesenice] appeared there in person and humbly and

---

[72] This should be Marcellinus, whose feast is celebrated on June 2. June 5 was the date of his first public hearing. Hus had been transferred for that reason from the Castle of Gottlieben to the prison of the Franciscan monastery situated between the cathedral and the church of St. Stephen, where the public hearings were held.

[73] June, 7, the date of the second hearing.

[74] June 8, when the last hearing was held.

[75] August 30, 1414.

earnestly asked: 'Reverend father, do you know of any error or heresy concerning Master John of Husinec, otherwise Hus?' Lord Nicholas, without compulsion or coercion, but spontaneously, freely and publicly acknowledged, saying in these or similar words in the vernacular Czech: 'I have conversed in many and several places with Master John Hus, eating and drinking with him,[76] and have often been present at his sermons and have had many conversations with him about various matters relating to the sacred Scriptures, but have never found in him any error or heresy, but in all his words and acts I have ever found him to be a true and Catholic man; nor have I discovered in him anything that savored of heresy or error.' Again for the second time the said Master John, procurator of the above-named, interrogated and requested the same Lord Nicholas, bishop and inquisitor, whether any man accused the said Master John Hus of some heresy before him as inquisitor of heretical pravity and convicted him of heresy. He replied that, from the time he knew him, Master John Hus, and he himself had been made inquisitor of heretical pravity in the city and diocese of Prague, as already referred to, nowhere has anyone to the present time accused or convicted him, Master John Hus, of heresy before him; adding that he, Master John Hus, publicly posted his letters patent of the above-mentioned year in the month of August on the doors of the cathedral church of Prague and other collegiate and parochial churches of the city of Prague, and on the gates of the said lord, lord king and of the archbishop of Prague, stating that he was willing to appear before the Lord Conrad, the archbishop of Prague and all the prelates and clergy of the kingdom of Bohemia, convoked and assembled on a certain day of the said month, ever ready to render account of his faith and hope to the satisfaction of all asking him. Further, in order that he might be seen and heard by each and all who wished to lay any charge of whatever stubborn errors or heresies against him, and to pledge themselves there to a like penalty according to the law of God and the judicial rules; to all such he would reply before the said lord archbishop of Prague and the Lord Nicholas, the afore-mentioned bishop and inquisitor, and the prelates, and also at the forthcoming

[76] Nicholas was on that account known in derision as "Nicholas-sup-with-the-devil." When he arrived in Constance in the middle of February, he was arrested and subjected to an examination by the Council and under duress testified that King Wenceslas had forced Hus to appear before the Council in order to clear the kingdom of Bohemia from the charge of heresy. This gained him freedom, whereupon he secretly fled from the city .

general Council of Constance, standing trial in accordance with the decrees and canons of the holy fathers to demonstrate his righteousness. Concerning each and all these things Master John of Jesenice, procurator and in virtue of his procuratorship, as stated above, asked me, the undersigned notary public, to make and execute for him one or more public records.

"Done this year, indiction, day, month, hour, place, and pontificate as given above, in the presence of the noble and renowned lords William of Zvířetice, baron of the kingdom of Bohemia, and Peter, his son; Lord Hlaváč of Ronov, also a baron; Wenceslas of Lnáře; Oneš of Měkovice, burgrave of the castle of Lichtenberg; Ctibor of Bohdanec, squire; and William of Doupov, knight of the said diocese of Prague; and many other trustworthy witnesses, specially called and requested, as said before.

And I, Michael, son of the late Nicholas of Prachatice, of the Prague diocese, a public notary by the imperial authority, was present at the aforesaid request, interrogation, response, petition, and all and each of the other things described above, along with the above-named witnesses, and I saw and heard all these things; and being occupied by other business, I had it faithfully recorded by another; and here, subscribing with my own hand, I have made it public and edited it into this public form, and I signed it with my usual and customary seal and name as called and requested, to the faith and testimony of all and each of the said matters."

"In the name of the Lord, Amen. In the year of His Nativity 1414, of its indiction the seventh, on Monday, the twenty-seventh day of the month of August, at the *tierce* hour or thereabouts, in the pontificate of the most holy father in Christ and our lord, Lord John XXIII by divine providence pope, of his [pontificate] the fifth year, in the Lesser Town of the city of Prague, in front of the archiepiscopal court of Prague, when the most reverend father in Christ and Lord Conrad, by the grace of God archbishop of Prague and legate of the Apostolic See, and all and each of the lord abbots, priors, provosts, deans, archdeacons, scholastics, canons, and priests, and all the prelates of the city and his diocese of Prague, were holding a solemn convocation for a certain cause in his court, there personally appeared the venerable man and dominus, Master John of Jesenice, doctor of canon law, procurator and in virtue of his procuratorship of the honorable man and dominus, Master John Hus of Husinec, *formatus* bachelor of sacred theology, the mandate of whose [Jesenice's] procuratorship was deemed sufficient to me, the undersigned notary public. Beating upon the gate or door of that archiepiscopal court, he requested that the said Master John, his master, or he himself in the name of the said Master John Hus of Husinec, his master, be admited into the same archiepiscopal court into the presence of the said lord archbishop and the prelates then assembled there, because he, Master John Hus, was ready to render account for the faith and hope that was in him to the satisfaction of all demanding it of him, and to see and hear all and each then assembled there—namely, the lord archbishop himself and the prelates and anyone of them who wished to impute to him whatever stubborn error or heresy —that they might pledge themselves there to a like penalty, according to the demands of the law of God and of the canon law, if they could not legitimately prove any stubborn error or heresy in him. He was willing to reply to all, with the help of God, before the said lord archbishop and also the prelates in the forthcoming general Council of Constance, to stand trial and to demonstrate his innocence in the name of Christ according to the decrees and canons of the holy Fathers. Thereupon, a certain renowned Ulrich, called Šváb of Švábenice, the marshal of the said lord archbishop Conrad, coming out of that court, denied the said doctor John of Jesenice and his party all entry whatever to that court and to the presence of the aforesaid archbishop and prelates assembled there, asserting and saying that the said archbishop was for the time being engaged with the said lord prelates in royal business. Nevertheless, he requested the said doctor to wait in some place outside that court until after the business of the aforesaid royal matter was finished by the lord archbishop together with the lord prelates; that then he [Ulrich] would return to grant him an entry to the said court. The said dominus and Master John, doctor, requesting for some time an entry into that court into the presence of the said lord archbishop and prelates, but not obtaining his request, at once solemnly protested there that he [Ulrich] did not open the entry either to himself or to Master John Hus, his client, to that archiepiscopal court to the presence of the lord archbishop himself and the prelates then assembled; in fact, that access was totally denied him. He requests that I, the undersigned notary public, make and execute one or several public records of the said matters.

"Done this year, indiction, day, month, hour, pontificate, and place as stated above, in the presence of the honorable and discreet men, Simon of Tišnov, bachelor of sacred theology, Simon of Rokycany, Procopius of Plzeň, Nicholas of Stojčín, and John of Příbram, masters of liberal arts; as well as Fráňa Čotrův, Jerome Šroloň of Prague, John of Michnice, and Jerome of Újezd, clerics and students of the Prague and Litomyšl dioceses, witnesses of the said matters.

"And I, James Moleš, son of the late Ambrose of Prague, a sworn public notary by the imperial authority and also of the university masters, doctors, and scholars of the University of Prague, was present at all and every of the above-described matters while the action was taking place, and have seen and heard each and all; but having been otherwise occupied in arduous dealings, I procured their faithful recording by another notary. I subscribed this with my own hand, published and edited it into this public form, and signed it with my usual and accustomed seal and name, as called and requested, to the faith and testimony of all and each of the said matters."

There was also offered a public transcript sealed with the seal of the University of Prague, in which Master John Hus confessed his faith, writing to Pope John, in order to disprove the errors ascribed to him by his enemies, and their subsequent steady reporting of him because of this to the Apostolic See. That transcript follows here word for word in this form: [77]

"In the name of the lord, Amen. In the year of His Nativity 1411, in the fourth indiction, the first day of the month of September, at the hour of vespers or thereabouts, in the pontificate of the most holy father in Christ and our lord, Lord John XXIII, by divine providence pope, in his second year, in the Greater City of Prague, in the office of the faculty of Charles College, where the difficult transactions and negotiations of the University of Prague have usually taken place, in the presence of the undersigned notaries public and of the undersigned witnesses specially called for this, in the presence in person of the honorable and learned man, John of Husinec, master of arts and *formatus* bachelor of sacred theology of the said university and preacher of the Word of God in the chapel called Bethlehem, situated in the said Greater City of Prague, before the venerable man, Simon of Tišnov, master of arts and bachelor of sacred theology, rector of the celebrated University of Prague, himself there present with the masters of that

[77] Novotný, *op. cit.,* No. 31.

university, specially called by him through sworn emissaries, present in a plenary assembly, where that Master John Hus exhibited a paper or document written by his own hand on paper in the form of a letter, whose hand we the undersigned notaries knew and know well, and read the same word for word. The purport of which word for word was as follows:

" 'With the due reverence which should be shown to the Church of Jesus Christ and her supreme pontiff!

" 'Being ever ready to render account for the faith that I hold to the satisfaction of anyone who demands it, I confess with a sincere heart that the Lord Jesus Christ is true God and true man; and that His whole law contains so firm a truth that not one jot or tittle [78] of it can fail. Further that His holy Church is so firmly founded upon the firm rock that the gates of hell cannot in any way prevail against it.[79] And because I am ready in the hope of her head, the Lord Jesus Christ, to suffer the punishment of a dreadful death rather than deliberately to say or assent to anything contrary to the will of Christ and of His Church; therefore, I faithfully, truthfully, and steadfastly assert that I have been wrongfully indicted at the Apostolic See by the enemies of truth. They have without a doubt falsely indicted me and are indicting me that I have taught people that in the sacrament of the altar the material substance of the bread remains. Falsely, that when the host is elevated, it is the body of Christ, and when it is laid down, then it is not; falsely, that a priest in mortal sin does not consecrate; falsely, that lords may deprive the clergy of temporal goods and need not pay tithes; falsely, that indulgences are worthless; falsely, that I have urged that the clergy be smitten with a material sword; falsely, that I have preached or held any error or errors or any heresy, or that I have in any wise seduced people from the way of truth; falsely, that I was the cause why some German masters were expelled from Prague, whereas they themselves refused to adhere to the foundation privilege of the University of Prague [80] or to obey the lawful mandates of the most serene prince and lord, Lord Wenceslas, king of the Romans, ever

[78] Matt. 5:18.

[79] Matt. 16:18.

[80] This somewhat puzzling phrase most likely refers to the foundation document of Charles IV which, among other reasons for the establishing of the university, also includes the emperor's desire "that the sons of the kingdom would have no need of begging for education abroad, but would have a table prepared at home." Novotný, M. Jan Hus, život a učení, I, 333.

Augustus, and king of Bohemia; they imagined that without their presence the University of Prague would not be able to exist, and so returned, no one forcing them, to their native land or wherever they pleased.

"'I acknowledge, moreover, that I appealed from the sentence of the most reverend father in Christ, Lord Zbyněk, to the Apostolic See and also from the legal proceedings which on the basis of wrongful information had been started by the sacred Apostolic See. For the enemies of the truth, unmindful of their honor and salvation, maliciously suggested to the Apostolic See that errors and heresies have sprouted in the kingdom of Bohemia, in the city of Prague, and in the margravate of Moravia, and that the hearts of many have been so infected thereby that because of the multitude of persons infected with such errors it becomes necessary to apply a remedy for their correction. Further, they falsely suggested that the Bethlehem Chapel was a private place, whereas it had been confirmed by the ordinary [81] as an ecclesiastical benefice, and its destruction would diminish somewhat the honor of God among the people, impede the benefit to souls, and create an offense to and greatly stir up the people against its destroyers.

"'When personally cited to the Roman curia, I desired humbly to appear there. But because my life was plotted against both within and without the kingdom, particularly by the Germans; relying, therefore, on the counsel of many friends, I judged that it would be tempting God to expose my life to death when the welfare of the Church did not demand it. So I did not appear personally, but appointed advocates and procurators, since I desired to obey the Apostolic See.[82]

"'Wherefore, Supreme Vicar of Christ, I humbly implore Your Holiness' clemency, that you may deign, for the sake of the mercy of the Almighty God, graciously to absolve me from appearing in person and from the other consequences therefrom, because through the offices of the most serene prince and lord, Lord Wenceslas, king of the Romans and king of Bohemia, as well as of the most reverend fathers and illustrious princes, Lord Wenceslas, patriarch of Antioch,[83] Lord Conrad, bishop of Olomouc,[84] the illustrious prince Lord Rudolph, duke of Saxony and elector of the holy empire, and other princes,

---

[81] I.e., the bishop.

[82] Cf. Part II, Nos. 1–4.

[83] Wenceslas Králík of Buřenice, who held that title until 1413, when he became bishop of Olomouc in Moravia.

barons, and lords, and of the magnificent Lord Ctibor, ambassador of the most illustrious prince and lord, Lord Sigismund, king of Hungary, I am now in complete accord with the aforesaid most reverend father in Christ, Lord Zbyněk.[85] For I offered to reply to all and every objection, appealing also to my whole audience, that if anything were proved against me, I would be willing, if I did not yield, to be corrected even by burning. I am ready today to render account to objections before the University of Prague and the whole assembly of prelates, if anyone should rise to oppose me. But no one, who would bind himself to undergo the retaliatory penalty in accordance with the canonical sanctions, has hitherto been willing to take part against me.

Written in Prague by my own hand on the Day of St. Giles.[86]

John Hus, Your Holiness' least priest.'

"Thus exhibiting and reading this paper or epistle, the aforesaid Master John petitioned that this same document, subscribed by us notaries for the greater evidence and credibility, be transcribed and edited into public form and sealed with the seal of the aforesaid university by the already mentioned dominus rector, doctors, and masters. Rector Simon, having consulted and deliberated with the masters called by him, as mentioned before, and having ascertained the vote of each and all of them, because by their unanimous advice and assent agreeing to the said petition of the said Master John, has ordered the above matters to be transcribed by us the undersigned notaries and to be edited into public form, to promote faith in his, Master John's, dealings. For its greater credibility, he ordered that the seal of the aforesaid University of Prague be appended to that letter or its public transcript.

[84] Conrad of Vechta, at that time bishop of Olomouc, but who in 1412 bought himself the archbisphoric of Prague from Albík of Uničov.

[85] As appears from this declaration, King Wenceslas, desirous of purging his kingdom from the aspersion of heresy, of which Archbishop Zbyněk complained to the pope, appointed a commission of arbitration between Zbyněk and himself, as well as the university and Hus, whose finding he accepted. He then proposed to the archbishop as the condition of peace, that Zbyněk write the pope that he found no heresy in the kingdom; that he release all whom he had excommunicated and lift the interdict. This of course included Hus. As for Hus, he was ordered to write the pope that he had been reconciled with the archbishop, which he did in the present letter. The archbishop at first accepted the conditions, but later, on the way to seek protection of Sigismund in Hungary, he repudiated this submission, but died before he reached his destination. Cf. the text of the letter of Wenceslas' commissioners, in Palacký, pp. 437–39.

[86] September 1, 1411.

Concerning all and each of this procedure the above-mentioned Master John Hus has petitioned that we, the undersigned public notaries, make and execute for him one or more public records.

"Done this year, indiction, day, month, hour, pontificate, and place, as stated above, in the presence of the honorable and discreet men, domini Vitus, provost of Miřín of the diocese of Olomouc, professed of the Order of St. Benedict; James of Tachov, John of Teplá, priests; Matthew of Chlumčany, cleric, by the imperial authority a notary public; John called Zápasník, squire of the Prague diocese; Anthony of Rojc and George Michael of Drenov, clerics of the Zagreb diocese; and many other witnesses of the said matters and called to the said matters.

"And I, Michael, son of the late Nicholas of Prachatice, of the diocese of Prague, by the imperial authority and of the masters, doctors, and scholars of the University of Prague sworn public notary, have been present when the forementioned letter was being shown, read, petitioned, copied, transcribed, and signed by each and all of the above-mentioned persons together with the forementioned witnesses and Nicholas of Matthew of Brno, the undersigned notary public and my colleague, and have thus seen and heard all these things; but being occupied by other dealings, I had it faithfully recorded by another, and when it was done, I have first, along with my aforesaid colleague, diligently listened to the [reading of the] present transcript with that of the original letter, and having found them to agree word for word with it, I have therefore executed the present public transcript, adding, diminishing, or transposing nothing that would change or vary the understanding of the substance of the facts, edited it into this public form and published it, signing it with my usual and accustomed seal and name, appending to it the seal of the said University of Prague according to the will of the rector and masters of that university, and sealed it as asked and requested to the faith and testimony of all and each of the said matters.

"And I, Nicholas, son of the late Matthew of Brno, of the Olomouc diocese, a public notary by the apostolic and imperial authority, have been present while the said letter was being shown, read, petitioned, copied, and transcribed, along with Michael, son of Nicholas of Prachatice, the above-mentioned notary public, my colleague in this matter, and with the afore-mentioned witnesses, and have thus seen and heard each and every thing; but my other arduous dealings hindering, I

procured a faithful recording of it by another, and having first diligently
listened to the present and public transcript with the original letter and
having found them to agree, I edited it into this public form, adding,
diminishing, or changing nothing that would change or vary the sense
of its understanding, and sealed it with my usual and accustomed seal
and name and with the appended seal of the University of Prague by
the order and will of the rector and masters of that university, as asked
and requested, to the faith and testimony of all and each of the said
matters."

A letter of commendation of the bishop of Nezero, inquisitor of
heretical pravity of the city and diocese of Prague, specially appointed
by the Apostolic See, with his seal appended, that he gave to Master
John Hus. I myself have often held this letter with its seal in my hands
and read it. It follows word for word:

"We, Nicholas, by God's grace bishop of Nezero, inquisitor of
heretical pravity of the city and diocese of Prague, specially appointed
by the Apostolic See, declare by the purport of these presents to all,
that for a long time we have quite frequently conversed with the honored man, Master John Hus, *formatus* bachelor of sacred theology of
the University of Prague. We have had with him many and various
discussions concerning the Holy Scriptures and have his replies concerning diverse matters. In all these discourses, acts, and conduct we
found him a faithful and catholic man, and discerned nothing evil or
wrong in any way erroneous in him to this time. Finally, we declare
that the aforesaid Master John, late in the year of the Lord 1414, on
August 27, posted on the cathedral church of Prague and on other
collegiate and parish churches, on the colleges of the university of the
afore-mentioned city of Prague, on the gates and doors of the most
serene prince and lord, Lord Wenceslas, king of the Romans and king
of Bohemia, of the most reverend father, Lord Conrad, archbishop of
Prague, legate of the Apostolic See and chancellor of the University
of Prague, and of other princes and barons then residing in the city
of Prague, his letters patent written in Latin and in the vernacular,
announcing in purport and effect that he, the afore-mentioned Master
John Hus, was willing to appear before the most reverend father, Lord
Conrad, the aforesaid archbishop of Prague, and before all the prelates
and clergy of the kingdom of Bohemia convoked and assembled on the
afore-mentioned day in the said city of Prague by the said lord arch-

bishop, ready ever to render account to the satisfaction of all who should demand it for the faith and hope that is in him; and to see and hear all and each who would wish to charge him with any stubborn error or heresy whatsoever, that they pledge themselves in accordance with the demands of the law of God and the [canon] law, to the same penalty, if they should not legitimately prove any stubborn error or heresy in him. He was willing, with God's help, to reply before the said lord archbishop and us as well as the prelates at the forthcoming general Council of Constance, and there to stand trial, to demonstrate in Christ's name his innocence according to the decrees and canons of the holy Fathers. After these letters, as has already been mentioned, had been made known by the said Master John Hus, in the public place and day as stated above, no man appeared before us to denounce the above-mentioned Master John Hus or to accuse him of any error or heresy. In clear testimony of all of this we commanded the present letters to be written and acknowledged with our appended seal.

"Given in Prague, in the year of the Lord 1414, next to the last day of the month of August."

Concerning the Council of St. James, the letter written by the barons of the kingdom of Bohemia, etc., to the king of Hungary, a mention of which was made at the beginning,[87] sealed with their seals, follows word for word in this manner:

"To the most illustrious prince and lord, Lord Sigismund, king of the Romans and of Hungary, etc., our gracious lord. We, Čeněk of Vartemberg, the supreme burgrave of Prague, Boček of Kunštát, otherwise of Poděbrady; William of Vartemberg, otherwise of Zvířetice, send and profess our faithful service. We declare by this letter that the honorable Master John Hus sent us a letter when we were in a public assembly with many other lords, begging us to ask the priest Conrad, archbishop of Prague, who was there with us, whether he knew of any heresy or of any kind of error against him. He was willing first to be corrected or punished here, if he did not amend, as was fitting and proper. And if the archbishop did not know, that he would likewise state it and give him [Hus] a testimony under his seal to that effect. We have done so; and the afore-mentioned priest archbishop testified saying that he knew of no heresy or error whatever against

---

[87] The Latin text reads "*principum*," but it is clear from the context that it should be "*principium*."

Master Hus; nor did he accuse him. Nevertheless, he said that the pope accused him; 'Let, therefore, Master Hus come to an agreement with him.' In testimony thereof we have appended our seals to this letter. Further also, most illustrious king, our gracious lord, heir of the Bohemian land and defender and lover of its honor, we beseech Your Grace that you be pleased to make a valiant and gracious effort that the aforesaid Master John be given at the Council a public hearing to present his truth, lest he be surreptitiously condemned to the dishonor of our nation and of the Bohemian land. For we trust in the Lord God and Your Grace that we shall thus escape a false aspersion.

"Written in Prague, in the year since the birth of the Son of God 1414, on the Sunday after St. Francis." [88]

The undersigned lords and barons have sent the signed letter in behalf of the liberation of Master John Hus to the king at Constance prior to the Lenten season,[89] in the year of the Lord 1415; it follows in this manner:

"Our service before all to Your Grace, most illustrious prince, king and lord, our gracious lord! The reverend man and preacher of the Holy Scriptures, Master John Hus, voluntarily rode hence to the general Christian Council to Constance on account of a false accusation that had been erroneously ascribed to him, and by that means to the whole Czech crown and the Czech nation. He desired and earnestly requested, for his own purging as well as of the whole Czech crown, to reply at that Council to all and each particularly before the assembly of the sacred Council, and wished there openly, if anyone should accuse him of anything, to show and declare his faith even to all Christendom. And if he were found in error in anything, as we—God grant—know of no such thing against him, except all good, he is ready to amend it in accordance with the correction and instruction of his superiors from the Holy Scriptures. Your Grace sent him a letter of safe-conduct that has been made known throughout the entire land of Bohemia and Moravia. When, however, he arrived in Constance, as we hear, he was arrested, contrary [90] to that safe-conduct, and thrown into prison without any correction or previous hearing, contrary to the truth and right

[88] October 7, 1414.

[89] It occurred on February 13, 1415; but the letter was sent in January, so that the date must refer to its reception by the king. The letter is in Czech, as is the previous one.

[90] The actual phrase reads "seized under the safe-conduct."

and the safe-conduct granted by Your Grace. There is current a great deal of talk here and elsewhere among the princes, lords, poor and rich, that the holy father has done so against the right and truth and contrary to the safe-conduct of Your Grace, and has thrown a righteous and guiltless man into prison. May Your Grace, therefore, be graciously pleased, as king and heir apparent of the Bohemian crown, to secure the liberation of Master John Hus from that illegal imprisonment. And further may Your Grace be pleased, for God's sake, to obtain for him a public and free hearing, so that he may openly reply to anyone accusing him of anything, just as he openly and fearlessly preached the law of God. And if he should be found [guilty] of anything by the due process and lawful right, let whatever is fitting in such a case be done, provided that the safe-conduct of Your Grace be ever observed. For otherwise there might result harm to Your Grace and to the whole Bohemian crown on its account, if something were to befall a righteous man under the safe-conduct. The Lord God knows that we should be loathe to hear if anything were to touch Your Grace's honor for any such reason, since it would afford an excuse to many for distrusting Your Grace's safe-conducts, as indeed it is already currently talked about. Your Grace, as the gracious king and lord, can well put a stop to it and bring about its favorable end. Should Your Grace not allow truth to be illegally trampled upon, You would receive in advance a reward from the Lord God, and honor from men. Given . . .

Subscribers: Lacek of Kravaře, captain of Moravia; Boček of Kunštát, otherwise of Poděbrady; Heralt of Kunštát, otherwise of Skála; William of Pernštejn; John of Lomnice, supreme chamberlain of Brno; Hanuš of Lípa, supreme marshal of the king of Bohemia; Peter of Kravaře, supreme chamberlain of Olomouc; Jodocus Hecht of Rosice; Ulrich of Hlavatec, under-chamberlain of the margravate of Moravia; and other barons now assembled in Meziříčí."

The letter of the king of Aragon that was transmitted, as was said, to the king of Hungary.[91]

"The most serene prince! Among other documents and letters, I sent by my messenger a certain letter written by my own hand to my

---

[91] It may perhaps be surmised that the instigator of the two letters of King Ferdinand was his confessor, Dr. Didachus of Moxena, the "simple friar" who had attempted to catch Hus in some heretical remark before the latter's imprisonment.

ambassadors that they might show it to Your royal Majesty. Its purport
is as follows:

"Most Serene Prince Sigismund, by the grace of God king of the
Romans, ever Augustus, and king of Hungary, Dalmatia, Croatia, etc.,
my dearest brother; Ferdinand, by the same grace king of Aragon and
Sicily, sends greetings in Him 'by Whom kings reign.' [92] Most serene
prince! There have come to my ears the dark words that some false
Christian has been subverting the Church of God by heretical tenets.
I am not a little saddened thereby, because the time has come when
'there shall be lying masters who will introduce sects and perditions
and who deny God who redeemed them, bringing upon themselves
swift perdition.' [93] Nevertheless, it is reported to me that that iniquitous
person had been in your prison for a long time, but not yet judged. I
greatly marvel, if that is so, that Your Majesty has not punished such
a man whom God has judged, saying through Moses: 'If your brother,
the son of your mother, or even your son or your daughter or wife,
who is in your bosom, or a friend whom you love as your soul, desire
to persuade you, secretly saying, "Let us go and serve other gods whom
neither you nor your fathers have known," do not acquiesce nor listen
to him, let not your eye spare him, having compassion and concealing
him, but instantly kill him.' [94] Again saying through the Apostle: 'The
man who is a heretic after one or two corrections avoid, for he is guilty
and subversive, whoever he is and whatever his guilt; by his own judgment is he condemned.' [95] On that account, most serene king, I beseech
you that observing the precepts of God you will not release that wicked
man that he might not persuade the people, nor that his false heresies
be publicly heard, but that he be immediately punished in such a manner that God will not charge you with that and you may not be confounded. For as it is said by apostle John the Evangelist: 'If any one
comes to you and does not bring the doctrine of Jesus Christ, do not
receive him into your house nor give him a greeting; for he who gives
him a greeting shares in his wicked work!' [96] See! It has been foretold
to you so that in the day of our Lord Jesus Christ you may not be
ashamed. Will the pass [pedagium],[97] most serene king, granted by

[92] Proverbs 8:15.
[93] II Peter 2:1, very loosely rendered.
[94] Deut. 13:6–9, loosely rendered.
[95] Titus 3:10–11.
[96] II John, 10–11.
[97] The term "pedagium," usually translated as "traveler's toll," in that sense

Your Majesty, free the man who had been persistently delinquent by reason of his heresy, and had not turned away from it, nor had been contrite for his sin, but had persevered in his iniquity? God forbid! Surely he is worthy of punishment, for one does not break faith with him who has broken faith with God. Written with my own hand on March 27, etc.

"Now, however, most serene prince, I submit that, since the other letters and documents were received, the messenger, by the operation of the devil, lost only the letter written by my hand, and only that one, in order that the devil's iniquitous work might not be impeded. On that account I most affectionately pray Your Majesty, for the love of God, not to permit the most evil work of the devil to prosper, but immediately to inflict punishment on his servant, that it may be reckoned to you for righteousness. And the Lord will grant you eternal reward. Written by my own hand on April 28, in the year of the Lord 1415.

King Ferdinand."

"To the most serene prince, Sigismund, king of the Romans, ever Augustus, and king of Hungary, Dalmatia, Croatia, etc., my dearest brother.

"Most serene prince, Lord Sigismund, by the grace of God king of the Romans, ever Augustus, and king of Hungary, Dalmatia, Croatia, etc., our dearest brother! Ferdinand, by the same grace king of Aragon and Sicily, [sends] greeting in Him 'by Whom kings reign.' Most serene king! It has been reported to me concerning the flight of him who is by some called Pope John,[98] and of the labors and tribulations you have suffered as much from false brethren, enemies of peace, as from the devil and of other sectarians: whom 'resist, firm in the faith,' and know that our 'adversary, the devil' in that holy ministry 'roars like a lion, seeking whom to devour.'[99] But you, most serene, 'be faithful even unto death and the crown of life shall be given you';[100] for 'if God is

---

contradicts the context of the sentence. I therefore adopted the term "pass," since that interpretation is indicated by the statement that Sigismund granted it. F. M. Bartoš concurs in this rendering of the term.

[98] King Ferdinand still recognized Benedict XIII as the rightful pope; therefore he speaks of John as "by some called Pope John."

[99] I Peter 5:8, 9.

[100] Rev. 2:10.

for you, who is against you?'[101] And 'if the Lord is your helper, fear
not what man can do to you.'[102] Hope in the Lord and manfully labor
in such a ministry, being sober in all long-suffering, bearing patiently
all tribulations, 'for through many tribulations must you enter the kingdom of heaven.'[103] Persevere in your holy resolve that it may be
accomplished. And I believe that the Lord on account of His great
mercies and the merit of the most blessed Virgin Mary will illumine us
to such a degree that we will do His will, and He will guide our feet
in the way of peace, so that we may see the desired end of that ministry.
Most serene king, I am ready, whether living or dying, to be ever with
you in the prosecution of such a ministry, bearing equally with you
all tribulations that will befall, 'for God is faithful Who will not suffer
us to be tempted beyond what we can bear, but with the temptation
also makes provision that we may be able to sustain it.'[104] Most serene
king, I beseech you that with the love and fear of God, without growing
weary, you may prosecute that holy undertaking, not retreating back,
lest the example spoken of in the gospel apply to you: 'He began to
build and was not able to finish.'[105] Act ever firmly, constantly and
faithfully, that you may be a victor worthy of meriting that response
of our Lord Jesus Christ: 'He who conquers and keeps my works until
the end, to him I will give power over the nations; and he shall rule
them with a rod of iron, and they shall be shattered like the vessel of
a potter; even as I have received [power] from my Father, I will give
him the morning star.'[106] Most illustrious king, may the Most High
by the most blessed Virgin's regard preserve your most serene person
in her grace! Written by my own hand on April 28 in the year of the
birth of the Lord 1415.

King Ferdinand

"Superscription: To the most serene prince, Sigismund, by the grace
of God king of the Romans, ever Augustus, and king of Hungary,
Dalmatia, Croatia, etc., my dearest brother."

[101] Romans 8:31.
[102] Reminiscent of Heb. 13:16.
[103] Acts 14:22.
[104] I Cor. 10:13.
[105] Luke 14:30.
[106] Rev. 2:26–28.

A copy of the letter to the lord king sent here to Constance by the lords of Moravia: [107]

"Our service before all, most illustrious prince, king and lord, our most gracious lord! We formerly wrote to Your Grace [108] concerning Master John Hus, a righteous man and reverend preacher and publisher abroad of the Holy Scriptures, in whom no evil has ever been found in our lands. That dear master and Christian preacher was charged with false and erroneous accusations by wicked and calumnious men, opponents of the Word of God, and because of the erroneous accusations of that man the whole Bohemian crown and the entire Slavonic tongue [109] have been dishonored, although without any guilt. He rode freely and without compulsion to the general Council at Constance, wishing to clear himself and the Bohemian crown, as a good and faithful Christian, of that erroneous and unjust accusation before the general Council of all Christendom. He went under the safe-conducts [110] granted by Your Grace, although as a good man he had no need of them. Having arrived there, however, he could not secure or obtain a hearing, although he had asked for it and had sought it by all Christian ways. Furthermore, contrary to right and justice, he was thrown into a cruel prison under the safe-conducts. Concerning that safe-conduct, it is rumored in all neighboring lands that this should not have befallen him, and that thereby these safe-conducts are violated and in his case are rendered void. We hear and regretfully accept that which touches the honor of Your Grace, since you are the gracious heir apparent and lord. We had hoped that Your Grace would have deigned to bethink yourself to preserve your safe-conduct in force because of the enemies of your honor, dignity, and reverence, so that no one in the future would fear them. Further we had hoped that that Christian man would obtain a hearing before the assembly of the sacred Council; and if anything erroneous were found in him, it would be publicly corrected and not in a surreptitious manner. If he were found to have held the truth, as we, God grant, so suppose, that he would continue to live in the truth he had received from God.

"Now, alas! we hear that the pope has fled along with those who guarded him [Hus] and that he [Hus] was removed from that prison—

[107] The letter is written in Czech.

[108] That letter is dated in January, 1415, and is given above.

[109] Or nation; the word has both connotations.

[110] The term is used in the plural several times, although without any apparent reason, unless the verbal promises are included.

God knows best by whose authority—and was placed in an even more cruel prison by the bishop of Constance, where his hands and feet were cruelly and in an unchristian manner put in irons, so that he could secure no justice whatever—as even a pagan should not have been so treated! Therefore, gracious king and lord, first of all for God's and the truth's sake, and also on account of your dignity and the good of the Bohemian crown, as well as of your safe-conducts, be yet pleased graciously to obtain and secure that that righteous man be freed from the cruel prison and receive a public hearing, instead of being so surreptitiously and erroneously slandered, contrary to right, justice, and the safe-conducts. For such an action Your Grace will receive honor from men and in the end a reward from the Lord God. And we hope in Your Reverence that on account of our faithful service Your Grace will exert himself [to secure this end] as the gracious and kindly heir and lord apparent of this land.

"Given in Brno, on the vigil of the Ascension of the Lord Christ,[111] in the assembly of the standard-bearing lords of the margravate of Moravia."

The subscription of the lords follows: "Lacek of Kravaře, captain of Moravia; Boček of Poděbrady; Heralt of Kunštát, otherwise of Skála; William of Pernštejn; John of Lomnice, supreme chamberlain of Brno; Peter of Strážnice, supreme chamberlain of Olomouc; Protasius and Aleš of Kunštát, otherwise of Lysice; Jaroslav of Štermberg; Jodocus Hecht of Rosice; Ulrich of Hlavatec, under-chamberlain of the margravate of Moravia; and other nobles and barons now assembled at Brno."

Thereupon, this letter was presented and read by a certain prelate in the assembly of the deputies and all nations, having been translated from the Czech into Latin.

A copy of the letter of the barons of the kingdom of Bohemia to the lord king: [112]

"To the most illustrious prince, Lord Sigismund, king of the Romans and of Hungary, etc., our gracious lord. We the undersigned lords, knights, and squires of the lands of Bohemia and Moravia send our faithful service. Since Pope John XXIII last year sent his bulls and

---

[111] May 8, 1415.
[112] The letter is in Czech.

letters throughout all Christendom [113] calling and announcing therein
the general Council to [be held in] Constance for the unification of the
Christian faith and all other schisms, he granted to all by those letters
and bulls his secure and safe conduct and full and free security, so
that every Christian, good and bad, and even a heretic of any kind
whatsoever could safely come to and return from that Council. Besides,
he commanded under an interdict and the deprivation of all dignities,
honors, offices, and benefices of both the spiritual and temporal estates
that no one should hinder, or as far as he were able, to allow any
hindrance, of anyone who would decide to ride to Constance to that
general Council or return therefrom. Thereupon, the honorable man
and faithful preacher of the Word of God, Master John Hus, voluntarily
rode to that Council on account of the false accusation that had been
ascribed to him without his fault and thereby to the entire Bohemian
crown and nation. At that Council he wished and greatly desired, for
the clearing of his innocence and of the Bohemian crown, to answer
all and each separately and publicly before Your Grace and before the
assembly of that whole Council, if anyone should accuse him of
anything. Further, he wished there to make manifest and to declare
his faith and preaching to all Christendom. If he were found erroneous
in anything—as God knows that we know no such things concerning
him, save all good—he declared his readiness to correct it according to
the rule and instruction of the Holy Scriptures. He was very glad to
do so if thereby he might obtain a public and just hearing. And against
all those witnesses who were produced against him he has and may
have many more good men and witnesses who are more worthy of
belief than those enemies of his, as may God grant!, since in Bohemia
he engaged in or preached nothing evil or erroneous, but the truth
alone and the law of God according to the Word of God and the exposition of the holy doctors. Your Grace despite all that had requested
him by many of your lords that he should go to that Council, and for that
purpose had sent him your safe-conduct and protection; and that [safe-
conduct] has been here made known and broadcast in writing through-

[113] Palacký, pp. 515 ff. Its translation is found in Loomis, *op. cit.*, pp. 72 ff.
There are also added the "Edict of King Sigismund" and John's "Bull of Convocation" issued on December 12, 1413 (pp. 70 f., 75 ff.). But none of these
documents, particularly the bull, contains the promises of safety even to heretics,
as is asserted in this letter of the barons, unless one can so interpret the phrase
in Sigismund's edict, "we . . . can preserve all and every person of whatever rank
who attends the Council in his full liberty."

out the lands of Bohemia and Moravia. Then when he arrived in
Constance, he was seized, although possessing your safe-conduct, and
thrown into a cruel prison without any examination or hearing, contrary
to the truth and law and the safe-conduct granted him by Your Grace.
Concerning that seizure there circulates here and elsewhere among the
princes, lords, knights, and squires, poor and rich, a great deal of talk
that the pope did it contrary to his letters and bulls, contrary to the
right and truth, and contrary to the safe-conduct of Your Grace, by
having thrown into prison Master John Hus, a just and guiltless man,
may God grant it!, without any kind of hearing and any just cause, to
the dishonor and disgrace of us and of all Bohemian land and nation.
Therefore, may it please Your Grace kindly to obtain, as the king and
heir apparent of the Bohemian crown, [that Master John Hus enjoy
the like freedom] [114] as those condemned heretics sent to Constance by
Gregory and Benedict, who have enjoyed and now enjoy peace and
safety. The pope also, leaving Master John Hus there [in prison], rode
away and left him in your power, so that Master John Hus, who had
already without guilt suffered enough, could have been freed and
liberated and could no longer have been kept in prison under duress
and contrary to the right, to the dishonor and disgrace of the whole
Bohemian nation, as Your Grace had cited him there and had granted
him the protective safe-conduct. For otherwise there would result, on
account of such illegal and unjust imprisonment of a just man, first of
all a great injury to Your Grace, and likewise to the entire Bohemian
crown. For, as we hear, he was seized when he was already in your
power and in your city, possessing your promises and your letters of
safe-conduct. It would afford to many a reason to be apprehensive
about Your Grace's safe-conducts—as there is already a great deal of
talk that we dislike to hear about Your Grace. Your Grace can easily
stop all that by obtaining that Master John Hus, who went freely in
accordance with your will, may freely return again to us to Bohemia.
[You can do this] as a gracious and just king and lord, first of all for
the sake of the Lord God and the extension of His truth, for the good
repute of Your Grace, of the peace and honor of the Bohemian land,
and on account of our faithful and for all time ready service of Your
Grace.

---

[114] This sentence is incomplete in the text, but the inserted clause is clearly
implied.

"Written in Prague, in the year 1415 since the divine birth, on the Sunday after the Lord's Ascension,[115] under our seals appended below."

This letter, written in the vernacular, was read in a Latin translation to the deputies of all the nations present, namely, the French, English, German, and Italian, the fourth day before St. Vitus,[116] the glorious martyr and patron of the Czechs, in the greater refectory of the Brothers Minor. Master Stephen Páleč protested against it, saying: "Most reverend fathers! I protest before your reverences that no mention was made or is made concerning our lord king, etc." That letter was attested by two hundred and fifty seals of the lords of Bohemia and Moravia.

Here the text of the safe-conduct given to Master John Hus by Sigismund, king of Hungary, is given.[117]

---

[115] May 12, 1415.
[116] June 12, 1415.
[117] See Chapter I, pp. 89–90.

CHAPTER III

Here Follow the So-called Hearings, but in Truth not Hearings but Jeerings and Vilifications

On the Saturday before Marcellus, which was the first day of the month of June, the noble lords of the Czech and Polish nations presented a letter or document to the deputies of the Council of Constance at the Brothers Minor.[1] In this document they stated that Master John Hus had freely come to Constance wishing to declare his faith "to anyone requesting it" and "to render account" for it, not wanting obstinately to defend or hold anything that had been ascribed to him; but that he was ready humbly to revoke any points, conclusions, or articles for which he would receive instruction from more pertinent Scripture than he himself had taught, written, or stated—as his protest inserted into the said document shows quite clearly. It begins as follows: "Most reverend fathers and lords! The noble lords of the Czech and Polish nations here present, etc."[2]

It is further stated that the lords sought that the Council be willing to grant to the said Master John a public hearing spoken of earlier, so that he could express his mind and intention, and other matters connected with it, as is also quite clearly contained in the said document. The lords asked further that this their petition be edited into public form for the greater credibility to be accorded to them in the future.

To this petition the patriarch of Antioch[3] responded in the name

---

[1] The mention of Marcellus is a mistake for Marcellinus (June 2). The Franciscan monastery stood between the cathedral and the Church of St. Stephen. It was converted in modern times into barracks.

[2] This document is quoted in full in Chap. II, pp. 133–41, and is dated May 31.

of the Council, saying, among many other things, that they were willing
to grant the said Master John Hus a public hearing on Wednesday
next, which was June 5. This they also did grant in the following
manner:

When the said day of the hearing arrived, that is the Wednesday
after Marcellus, certain cardinals, archbishops, bishops, and almost
all the prelates then present in the said city, along with doctors, masters,
bachelors of sacred theology, and many others of lesser status, assembled in the said place in the refectory. In the absence of the said
Master John Hus they ordered the reading of all the articles and testimonies, of which many are and had been mendaciously ascribed to
him, and lastly the articles they said had been drawn from his books.
Of them many, when compared with the copy of the original written
by his own hand, were [seen to be] most falsely drawn—some by an
addition in the beginning, others in the middle, and others at the end.
To some of them in those places were added expressions changing the
sense of the whole. Others, that were found nowhere in his books,
were craftily invented. They then attempted to condemn all these
articles before he, Master John, was heard. When U.,[4] who stood near
the reader, perceived this, he ran out and told it to P., and P. ran to
the lords W. and J.,[5] in order that they might report it to the king.
And they, hastening to him, at once recounted to him each item in
detail.[6]

The condemnation took this form: first they read a verse from the
Psalm, "God of gods has spoken, etc.," beginning with the verse "To
the sinner then God said: why do you expound my justice, and why do you
take my covenant into your mouth? You indeed hate discipline and have
cast my words behind you. If you saw a thief, you ran with him; and with
adulterers you took your portion. Your mouth abounded in malice, and
your tongue concocted deceit. You sat and spoke against your brother,

[3] John Mauroux. Cf. pp. 141–42.
[4] Perhaps Ulrich, one of the retainers of Lord John of Chlum; P. is, of course,
Peter of Mladoňovice.
[5] Wenceslas of Dubá and John of Chlum.
[6] J. Sedlák, the Catholic apologist for the conduct of the Council in the trial
of Hus, asserts that Peter misrepresented the intention of the meeting as if it
were about to condemn Hus without hearing. He asserts that the purpose of the
meeting was merely to inform the members of the charges against Hus. But
from what follows it is evident that Sigismund himself concluded that Hus was
to be condemned without a hearing. Sedlák also points out that Peter was not
present at the meeting on this occasion. Cf. Sedlák, *M. Jan Hus,* p. 336.

and against the son of your mother you asserted slander; these things you have done and I was silent. You have thought, you evil man, that I will be as yourself. But I will rebuke and place the charge against your face." [7] And having finished this, they immediately began [to read] the letter that he [Hus] had left behind when he rode from Bohemia to Constance; but not in the form in which he had left it, for they read it as if he had said and written: "If I should happen to abjure, you should know that even though I confess with my mouth and abjure, I do not agree with these things in my heart." What a lie, Almighty God! Those who have that letter which he sent after his departure know that it contains [a request] that they pray for him and that "if the Lord will grant me help that I may return to you, that we shall be instructed all the more fully in the law of the Lord and His Scriptures and at the same time we shall tear the nets of Antichrist asunder. And you should know that there will be many more bishops and prelates against me than were against our Savior and Lord Jesus Christ," etc., as is contained therein etc. [8]

When the lords repeated these things in detail to the king, as mentioned previously, he immediately dispatched the illustrious princes, Ludwig, Count Palatine of Heidelberg, and Frederick, burgrave of Nuremberg, commanding through them that they [the members of the Council] should condemn or decide nothing in the said hearing before patiently hearing Master John. Then whichever articles they finally settled on with him and adhered to, they should give him [the king] in writing; for he would like to submit them to some doctors for consideration. And in order to show the falsity of those who abstracted the said articles from the books of Master John, the lords and his friends took counsel and decided to offer those books of Master John, written by his own hand—namely the book *De ecclesia* and the treatises *Contra Stanislaum* and *Contra Paletz* [9]—to the Council through the said

[7] Psalm 50:1, 16–21. Hus quotes the same verse in *De Ecclesia* to prove that God "suspends" a sinner on account of a mortal sin. The Church's suspension is valid only if the sinner had first been suspended by God. Thomson, *Mag. J. Hus, Tractatus de Ecclesia*, p. 219.

[8] Cf. the text of the letter in Chap. I, pp. 96–98; also Novotný, *op cit.*, No. 87; Palacký, No. 37.

[9] In a letter written by Hus to his friends on June 5, he chides them: "You have done wrong in presenting the treatise *Against a Secret Enemy* with the treatise *On the Church*." Part II, No. 10. There is no mention in Peter's narrative that the first-named treatise was included. Moreover, it is difficult to see why Hus so emphatically demanded that treatise to be kept from the knowledge of

princes, at that time the messengers of the king. They, however, stipulated the condition that whenever the said lords should ask these princes to request the Council for them, the said books be returned to the princes to be restored afterward to the said lords. This was done. For the said princes, handing over the said treatises to the Council and having delivered the message of the king, departed. And Master John, receiving those treatises and carefully inspecting them, lifted them high and publicly owned them to be his, adding that he was and had been ready humbly to amend, when instructed, whatever in them was stated wrongly or erroneously.

In the meantime someone read the articles and statements of the witnesses. When the Master wished to respond to them, at once many with one voice clamored simultaneously; that [clamor] was heard by his [friends] who had not been able to enter. He turned here and there, now to the right then to the left, then to the back, responding to those shouting and attacking him. And when he wished to explain the ambiguities or different significance of the expressions in the articles charged against him, that those who had excerpted them had repeatedly twisted them into a sense foreign to him, immediately they shouted: "Leave off your sophistry and say 'Yes' or 'No.' " And others mocked him. When, however, he adduced the authority of the holy doctors for certain points and articles, many continued to shout simultaneously, saying that they did not apply or were not to the point. He, then, seeing that to respond to the objections was of no avail, kept still. Whereupon at once others exclaimed, saying: "Look! since you are silent, it is a sign that you consent to these errors!" Seeing thus the tumult, since they were exceedingly wroth with him, being embittered by the preceding frequent repetition of his articles denouncing them, they adjourned that hearing to Friday next.[10]

And when he was led back to the prison by the bishop of Riga,[11] seeing his own [friends], he gave them his hand, saying: "Do not fear for me!" They responded: "We do not fear." He then added: "I know well—I know well!" And ascending the steps, he extended his hand,

---

the Council, since it contains nothing incriminating. The treatises that were offered actually contained matter that could be used against him with far greater effect. Cf. "Contra Occultum Adversarium," *Historia et Monumenta*, I, 168 ff.

[10] Friday, June 7. Cf. the letter of Hus concerning this hearing written on June 5, in Part II, No. 10.

[11] Archbishop John V of Wallenrode of Riga (1393–1418).

blessing the people, smiling and merry, joyfully walking despite that mockery.

Similarly on Friday, on the already mentioned June 7, an hour after an almost total eclipse of the sun, they again brought Master John to a hearing in the said refectory, which was surrounded during each hearing by many city guards armed with swords, crossbows, axes, and spears. In the meantime the king arrived and brought with him Lords Wenceslas and John along with Peter the bachelor. At this hearing were read the articles about which the Prague witnesses had testified before the vicar of the archbishop of Prague and also in Constance, to some of which he responded separately. Among them, when the said lords and Peter arrived, this article was in effect ascribed to him.[12]

It is also stated that the above-named Master John Hus in the month of June of the year of the Lord 1410, as well as before and after, preaching to the people congregrated in a certain chapel of Bethlehem and in various other places of the city of Prague, at various times contrived, taught, and disputed about many errors and heresies both from the books of the late John Wyclif and from his own impudence and craftiness, defending them as far as he was able. Above all, he held the error hereafter stated, that after the consecration the host on the altar remains material bread. To that charge they produced as witnesses doctors, prelates, pastors, etc., as it is stated in the said testimony.[13]

Then he, calling God and his conscience to witness, replied that he had not said or stated it; in reality, when the archbishop of Prague had commanded that the term "bread" be not even mentioned,[14] he [Hus]

[12] Since Peter came while the proceedings were already in progress, he does not report the whole scene.

[13] It must be remembered that Wyclif's teaching and books had been condemned on May 4, so that convicting Hus of Wyclif's chief heresy—remanence—was tantamount to an almost automatic condemnation of Hus as well. It should be noted that despite his repeated and consistent denials of this charge, the article remained among the final charges against him and he was condemned on this, as well as on other counts. Cf. Part II, No. 15. Also cf. de Vooght, *L'Hérésie*, 329–34, where he comments on Hus's answers to Wyclif's forty-five articles and shows the basic differences between Hus and Wyclif.

[14] Cf. Palacký, p. 335, where Zbyněk's mandate is published; it expressly states that after the priest pronounces the words of consecration, "*substantia panis non remanet, sed solum verum corpus Christi.*" The same is asserted about the "*substantia vini.*" Whoever should dare to teach otherwise is a heretic. This is a faulty statement of the catholic dogma, which Hus correctly opposed. He wrote a treatise, *De corpore Christi,* in which he defends the perfectly orthodox thesis

rose to oppose it on the ground that even Christ in the sixth chapter of John eleven times called Himself "the angelic bread" and "giving life to the world," and "descending from heaven," [15] and was so called by others. Therefore, he [Hus] did not want to contradict that Gospel. He asserted, however, that he had never spoken concerning the material bread. Then the Cardinal of Cambrai,[16] taking a paper that, he said, had come into his hands late the evening before, and holding it in his hand, questioned Master John if he regarded the universals as real apart from the thing itself. And he responded that he did, since both St. Anselm and others had so regarded them. Thereupon the cardinal argued: "It follows that after the consecration there remains the substance of the material bread." And he advanced proofs of it as follows: that in the act of consecration, while the bread is being changed and transubstantiated into the body of Christ—as you have already said—either there did or did not remain the most common substance of the material bread. If it did, the proposition was proved; if not, it follows that with the cessation of the particular there also ceased the universal substance itself." He [Hus] replied that it ceased to exist in the substance of that particular material bread when it was changed or passed into the body of Christ, or was transubstantiated; but despite that, in other particulars it was not affected. Then a certain Englishman wished to prove by an exposition of the subject that the material bread remained there. The Master said: "That is a puerile argument that schoolboys study"—and acquitted himself thereby. Then again a certain Englishman, standing beside Master John, wished to prove that after the consecration there remained the form of the substance of the material bread and the primal matter, while that bread was not annihilated. The Master responded that it was not annihilated, but that the particular substance ceased by being transubstantiated into the body of Christ. Again another Englishman—known as Master William [17]—rose

that the bread which prior to the consecration was material, after the consecration is *transubstantiated*. This is *not* the Wyclifite tenet of remanence, which asserts that the material bread remains material. But Pierre d'Ailly and the others mentioned in Peter's narrative accused him of remanence just the same.

[15] John 6:31–35, 41, 47–51.

[16] Pierre d'Ailly, the cardinal-priest of St. Chrysagogus, a consistent nominalist, opposed Hus's philosophical realism as necessarily resulting in remanence. This shows how persistently the charge of remanence was made against Hus despite all his denials and assertions of his belief in transubstantiation. Cf. Part II, No. 15 B, article 17.

[17] This was probably Master William Corfe, who represented the English

and said: "Wait, he speaks evasively, just as Wyclif did. For he [Wyclif] conceded all these things that this man concedes, yet nevertheless he held that the material bread remained in the sacrament of the altar after consecration. In fact, he adduced the whole chapter 'We believe firmly' [18] in confirmation of that erroneous opinion of his." And he [Hus]: "I do not speak evasively, but God is my witness, sincerely and out of my heart." "But, I ask you, Master John, whether the body of Christ is there totally, really, and manifoldly [*multiplicative*]?" And Master John responded that truly, really, and totally that same body of Christ that had been born of the Virgin Mary, had suffered, died, and had been resurrected, and that was seated at the right hand of the Father, was in the sacrament of the altar. And many irrelevancies on the subject of universals were inappropriately mixed with the debate. That Englishman who had insisted on the primal matter said: "Why are irrelevancies that have nothing to do with the subject of faith mixed with it? He judges rightly about the sacrament of the altar, as he here confesses." But the Englishman Stokes [19] said: "I saw in Prague a certain treatise ascribed to this Hus in which it was expressly stated that the material bread remains in the sacrament after consecration." [20] The Master said: "With all respect to your reverence, it is not true."

Again for the confirmation of that article they brought forth witnesses—masters, doctors, and Prague pastors who deposed that at the table in the parsonage of a certain Prague pastor he [Hus] had defended his assertion concerning the remanence of the material bread. And when a certain pastor [21] brought objections against him on the authority

nation on the commission appointed to deal with Hus's case after the papally appointed commission had lost its authority because of Pope John's flight. Cf. Fillastre's *Diary* in Loomis, *op. cit.,* p. 233. Corfe died at Constance and Bishop Richard Flemyng of Lincoln delivered his funeral oration.

[18] This is the designation of the chapter defining the dogma of transubstantiation by the Fourth Lateran Council in 1215.

[19] John Stokes, representing the English king, wished to avenge himself for the humiliation he had suffered in Prague (1411) when Hus had denounced him for his indiscriminate repudiation of Wyclif. The reply of Hus is found in *Historia et Monumenta,* I, 135 ff.

[20] Stokes actually might have seen such a treatise in Prague; but then it must have been written by one of the remanentists, such as Stanislav and Páleč had been, and Jakoubek still was.

[21] John Protiva, pastor of St. Clement in Old Town and the first preacher of the Bethlehem Chapel, was formerly an ardent member of the reform party. His testimony, presented in 1409 to Archbishop Zbyněk, is found in Palacký, pp. 174 f. Before departing for Constance, Hus had secured a copy of Protiva's

of the blessed Gregory, that Master John had responded saying to him that St. Gregory had been a joker [*ioculator*] or a rimester, because he had composed his saying in rime. But Master John said: "[On the contrary], I esteem him to be the most eminent doctor of the holy Church."

When these altercations ceased, the cardinal of Florence [22] said: "Master John, you know that it is written that 'in the mouth of two or three witnesses stands every word.' [23] And look! here are well-nigh twenty witnesses against you—prelates, doctors, and other great and notable men, some of whom depose from common hearsay, others however from knowledge, adducing reasonable proofs of their knowledge. What, then, do you still oppose against them all?" And he replied: "If the Lord God and my conscience are my witnesses that I have neither preached nor taught those things they depose against me, nor have they ever entered my heart—even if all my adversaries deposed them against me, what can I do? Nor does this in the end hurt me."

The cardinal of Cambrai said: "We cannot judge according to your conscience, but according to what has been proved and deduced here against you and some things you have confessed. And you would perhaps wish to call all who out of their knowledge deposed against you, adducing reasonable evidence of their knowledge, your enemies and adversaries? We must believe them.[24] You said that you suspected

charges and wrote comments upon them in order to answer them at the Council. For instance, to the charge about Pope Gregory he wrote: "That is true; I have often said in his praise that St. Gregory the pope was the best poet, a great doctor, whose language is, among the saints, very pleasing; and that he uses beautiful rimes for the sake of right exposition and pleasing expression." When examined by the commission about Protiva's charges, Hus replied that Protiva lied. Cf. de Vooght, *L'Hérésie*, p. 311.

[22] Francesco Zabarella, cardinal-deacon of Sts. Cosmas and Damian, was a famous canonist. He had been formerly one of the principal members of the trial commission appointed in 1411 to try Hus. After Pope John's flight, all members of the papal commission, of which Zabarella was a member, were replaced (April 17) by representatives of the four nations, i.e., by Archbishop Anthony of Ragusa for the Italians, by Bishop Schonelefe of Schleswig for the Germans, by Dr. Ursin of Talevende for the French, and by Master William Corfe for the English. The old commission, consisting of cardinals d'Ailly, Fillastre, and Zarabella, was ordered to turn over its records to the new body. But a conflict arose between the two groups and resulted in the restoration of the three cardinals to the commission.

[23] A reference to Deut. 19:15.

[24] D'Ailly's acceptance of the testimony of the witnesses regarding Hus's re-

even Master Stephen Páleč, who has certainly dealt humanely and very kindly with these books and articles, abstracting them even more leniently than they are contained in the book. And similarly all the other doctors. In fact, you said that you suspect the chancellor of Paris,[25] than whom surely no more renowned doctor could be found in all Christendom."

Further it is stated that the said John Hus obstinately preached and defended the erroneous articles of Wyclif in schools and in public sermons in the city of Prague. He replied that he had neither preached nor wished to follow the erroneous doctrine of Wyclif or of anyone

---

manence is particularly detrimental to his reputation. He privately held the doctrine of "impanation," although he publicly professed the dogma of transubstantiation. He wrote about impanation that *"ille modus est possibilis, nec repugnat ratione nec auctoritate Bibliae; immo est facilior ad intelligendum et rationalibior quam aliquis aliorum."* Cf. article "Ailly(D') Pierre," in *Dictionnaire de Theologie Catholique*, I, 657.

[25] Jean Charlier de Gerson, chancellor of the University of Paris, was reputed to be the most famous theologian. Archbishop Conrad of Prague had submitted to him some of Hus's works, asking for his opinion of them. Gerson's reply, returned on September 24, 1414, took the form of twenty articles (cf. *Historia et Monumenta*, I, 29–30). He declared that the "most pernicious error" was Hus's assertion that the foreknown man in mortal sin does not have dominion or jurisdiction over the Christian community. Since Hus never taught or wrote that, it seems probable, as both Sedlák and de Vooght suppose, that Gerson hastily assumed that Hus shared Wyclif's view without taking the trouble to note Hus's qualification of it. Gerson insisted that these errors be exterminated "by fire and sword." Cf. Palacký, pp. 523–28 and de Vooght, *L'Hérésie*, 298, where the twenty theses of Gerson are discussed. In commenting on Gerson's advice that the heretics be put to death, de Vooght remarks: "On what [teaching of Christ] does he base it? A mystery."

When Gerson arrived at Constance on February 25, 1415, he brought along the twenty articles which in the meantime had been approved by the University of Paris. He assumed that Hus, whose teaching he regarded as identical with Wyclif's, was stirring up riots by inciting men to disobedience of the authorities: "It is clear that in respect of the daring, pertinacy, and the large number of the adherents of the arch-heretic John Wyclif in England, Bohemia, and Scotland, they should be dealt with by judicial condemnation rather than by vain reasoning of which they are not worthy. For they extol themselves impudently against all ecclesiastical and secular dominion by holding the already many times condemned errors and by denying the principles of law, both positive ecclesiastical and civil as well as divine and natural. Finally, brutal and ignorant men who seduce and incite the peasants to vices of every kind of rebellion and sedition, as is known, would be corrected more quickly and effectively by punishment rather than by words." Quoted in Novotný, *M. Jan Hus*, II, 392, n.4. He further remarks that this is "a worthy addition to the advice of Dietrich of Niem, who had long ago as well as now counselled a crusade against the Czech heretics." Cf. Sedlák, *Studie a texty*, I, 53.

else, as Wyclif was neither his father nor a Czech. And if Wyclif had disseminated some errors, let the English see to that.[26]

When they objected to him that he had resisted the condemnation of the forty-five articles of Wyclif, he replied that when the doctors had condemned his [Wyclif's] forty-five articles for the reason that none of them was catholic, but that every one of them was either heretical, erroneous, or scandalous, he dared not consent to their condemnation because it was an offense to his conscience. And particularly of this: "Pope Sylvester and Constantine erred in endowing the Church." Also this: "If the pope or a priest is in mortal sin, then he neither transubstantiates, nor consecrates, nor baptizes"; but he qualified it that he does not do so worthily, but unworthily, for he was at the time an unworthy minister of God's sacraments. And they said: "It is stated unqualifiedly in your book." He replied: "I am willing to be burned if it is not stated as I have qualified it." Afterward they found it so qualified in the treatise *Contra Paletz* at the beginning of chapter two.[27]

He also said that he dared not consent to the condemnation of this: "Tithes are merely [voluntary] alms." [28] The cardinal of Cambrai objected to him: "In order that something be alms, it must be given freely, without obligation and duty; and since tithes are given by reason of obligation and duty, it follows that they are not alms." He denied the argument; for similarly the rich were obligated to perform the six works of mercy on pain of eternal damnation, such as to clothe the naked, or to feed the hungry, and such others as are shown in Matt. 25 [29]—and yet these were received by the indigent as alms. Then the

---

[26] This is another of Protiva's charges made in 1409 (cf. note 21). Hus made essentially the same answer to it. He furthermore writes in *Contra Paletz* that he holds only the true tenets of Wyclif "not because he said it, but because Scripture says it and reason infallibly says it. But if he stated any error, I do not intend to imitate him or anybody else in any fashion whatever." *Historia et Monumenta*, I, 330.

[27] The sentence actually reads as follows: "For we concede that a wicked pope, bishop, prelate, or priest is an unworthy minister of sacraments, through whom God neverteless baptizes and consecrates, or otherwise operates for the benefit of His Church." *Ibid.*, I, 319.

[28] It is interesting to note that in his treatise *De decimis* Hus defends only the first half of Wyclif's article, that "tithes are merely alms," while he says not a word about the second half of the article, that "the parishioners on account of the sins of their prelates can refuse them [the tithes] at will." *Historia et Monumenta*, I, 156 ff.

[29] Matt. 25:35–36.

archbishop of Salisbury, an Englishman,[30] said: "If all are obligated
to perform the six works of mercy, it follows that paupers, having not
whence to give, ought to be damned." And he replied that he limited
it to those who, having [the means] and being able to give, were by
the Gospel obligated on pain of damnation to give alms. Then he began
to explain more fully that at first the givers had been at liberty to give
tithes as alms, but that later they became obligated to do it by reason
of [long] submission; but he was not permitted to speak of it more
fully.

He also said that he did not assent to the said condemnation [of the
forty-five articles] for the reason that the judgment of the doctors was
a copulative syllogism [copulativa], the second part not being provable
in relation to the other parts of the articles: that is, that any one of
them was heretical, erroneous, or scandalous. Then Páleč stood up
and said: "Let the contrary of that syllogism be held as valid: some one
of them is catholic that is neither heretical nor erroneous nor scandalous; which one is it?" The Master said: "Prove that concerning any
part of your syllogism and you will prove the argument." However,
despite that he declared specifically that he had not obstinately asserted
any of those articles, but that he had resisted their condemnation along
with other masters and had not consented to it, because he had wished
to hear Scriptural [proofs] or adequate reasons from those doctors who
had contended for the condemnation of the articles.[31]

It was also stated that the said John Hus in order to seduce the people
and the simple-minded dared with temerity to say that in England many
monks and other masters convened in a certain Church of St. Paul's [32]
against Master John Wyclif but could not convict him; for immediately
thunder and lightning descended on them from heaven and smashed the
gate of the church, so that those masters and monks scarcely escaped
into the city of London. This he said for the confirmation of the

---

[30] Robert Hallam (1407–17), bishop of Salisbury and leader of the English
delegation. He had been chancellor of the University of Oxford and later arch-
deacon of Archbishop Arundel. Cf. Jacob, op. cit., Chap. IV, "English Conciliar
Activity, 1395–1418."

[31] He actually writes in Contra Paletz: "Show the [proofs of] Scripture, assign
true reasons." Historia et Monumenta, I, 324.

[32] The incident refers to the attempted trial of Wyclif at St. Paul's in 1377,
conducted by Bishop Courtenay of London. But since Wyclif was accompanied
by John of Gaunt, the duke of Lancaster, and by Lord Henry Percy, the bishop
did not dare to proceed against him.

statements of John Wyclif, thereupon breaking out at people with the words: "Would that my soul were where the soul of Wyclif is!"

He replied that it was true that, twelve years ago, before his [Wyclif's] theological books had been [available] in Bohemia, and his books dealing with liberal arts had pleased him [Hus] much, and he had known nothing but what was good of his life, he said: "I know not where the soul of that John W[yclif] is; but I hope that he is saved, but fear lest he be damned. Nevertheless, I desire in hope that my soul were where the soul of John W[yclif] is!" [33] And when he said that in the Council, they laughed at him a great deal, shaking their heads.

They also charged that with his accomplices he had defended the books and errors of that Wyclif and had supported other defenders of those errors. He replied that he had defended no error of Wyclif, nor had known of any other Czech who had defended or was defending any errors of Wyclif.[34] Further he said: "I confess that I do not know nor have known any Czech who was or is a heretic; however, on that account I do not deny that some Czechs could be heretics."

They stated among other things that he had opposed the condemnation of Wyclif's books condemned in the city of Prague by doctors assigned to it and also condemned at the Roman Council. He responded that he, along with others, had been ordered by the archbishop of Prague to deposit with him the books of Master John Wyclif [35] and

[33] In the lectures delivered by Hus in 1409 on the fourth book of Peter Lombard's *Sentences,* he writes: "Concerning that I spoke on account of those who with temerarious judgment positively assert and preach that Master John Wyclif is damned eternally in hell. I, however, wishing to avoid temerarious judgment, hope that he is of the number of those to be saved. And if he is in heaven, may the glorious Lord be praised; if he is in purgatory, may the merciful Lord liberate him quickly; and if he is in hell, let him remain there in eternal punishment in accordance with the just judgment of God." Flajšhans, *Spisy M. Jana Husi, Super IV Sententiarum* (Prague, 1906), IV, 621.

[34] This assertion of Hus may be understood only in conformity with the similar declaration which the Archbishop Zbyněk had been required by King Wenceslas to make to Pope John XXIII (in 1411). For Hus knew well that Stanislav of Znojmo and Stephen Páleč had been remanentists. It is remarkable that he did not say so on this occasion, for he writes in *Contra Paletz*: "Don't you remember the arguments of your colleague, Stanislav, who argued in the university assembly that the articles [of Wyclif] be not condemned? Don't you remember how you praised those articles . . .?" *Historia et Monumenta,* I, 324.

[35] The first such examination occurred on July 4, 1408. After the examination of the books, the archbishop publicly declared that he found no heresy in the kingdom. But Zbyněk ordered the surrender of Wyclif's books for the second time, and on that occasion had them burned (July 16, 1410).

himself had carried the book [36] and had given it to the archbishop of Prague, saying: "Look, reverend father! I offer these my books in order that whatever you find erroneous in them, you may command it to be marked, for I am willing to declare it as such before the whole community." And that archbishop with his [officials], not pointing out any such articles, had ordered the books burned, a thing he had not been commanded by the Apostolic See to do. And from that burning, he said, he had appealed, both from the verdict as well as from the proceedings of that archbishop, to the Apostolic See and especially to Alexander V; [37] and while that appeal had been still in force and that Alexander had died, he appealed to John XXIII, now called Balthassarre Cossa. And because no hearing had been granted him through his procurators for well-nigh two years, he therefore in the end appealed to Christ.[38]

When they raised the objection whether he had an absolution from Pope John, he replied that he did not; and likewise whether it was lawful to appeal to Christ, he replied: "I here publicly assert that there is no more just or effective appeal than to Christ." They laughed a great deal at that saying.[39] And he said: "Since 'to appeal' is, as the laws say, seeking or imploring a greater judge for aid from the injustices of a lesser judge, who is more effective or more just judge, who could better lift up the wronged and oppressed and could help them than Christ, Who neither deceives nor can be deceived?"

As to the hearing refused to Master John at the curia, Páleč, rising, said: "Indeed a hearing was granted him at the Roman curia, although not in order to absolve him from the personal citation; for he was exceedingly suspect of heresy. For that reason he was not given a hearing there as to relaxing the personal citation."

They stated among other things that he had advocated that his adversaries be cut down with the material sword according to the example of Moses.[40] He replied that this was falsely ascribed to him for he had rightfully exhorted [the people], preaching on the epistle in which the

[36] This word is in the singular, but immediately thereafter Hus refers to "books."

[37] Cf. Palacký, pp. 387 ff.

[38] Cf. this most famous appeal of Hus in Part II, No. 1, where the reasons for the appeal are more fully explained.

[39] Any such appeal was specifically condemned in the definitive sentence pronounced upon Hus.

[40] Deut. 32:42.

Apostle declared [41] that all ought to gird on the helmet of salvation and the sword to defend the truth of the Gospel. And he added that he had said: "Yea, so that my enemies would not catch me, I do not say with 'the material sword,' but I say 'the sword that is the Word of God.'" And they cried out, saying: "But what has that to do with that Scriptural passage of Moses, to adduce that 'the sword is the Word of God'? We clearly hear that you are here adducing it."

Also they stated subsequently about the same point that immediately the next day notices had been [posted] in many places by his, as it was presumed, order and inducement, that everyone gird on a sword on his thigh most mightily and spare not his brother or his neighbors. And he responded that he knew nothing about that or about the notices.

Also it is stated that the same John Hus had preached various errors from which arose offenses between the prelates and the people of the kingdom of Bohemia, masters and scholars of the Prague school, disobedience of the subjects toward their prelates, and destruction of the above-mentioned Prague school. He replied that it was not on his account, but by reason of the refusal [of the German masters] to adhere to the king's neutrality by abandoning their obedience to Gregory; [42] for since they had refused to agree with the king, the king had justly granted the Czech nation three votes according to the founding letter [43] granted the university by Emperor Charles of holy memory, for he had founded the University of Prague after the pattern of the Universities of Paris and Bologna. And they, not wishing to consent to the king in it, had even taken an oath that sooner than to allow the Czech nation three votes and the other nations one, they would rather leave the University of Prague and not return again to teach there. They had confirmed that oath with four grave penalties—namely, of perjury, loss of faith and honor, excommunication, and of six thousand *grossi*. And pointing his finger at Albert Warentrapp,[44] he said: "And this

---

[41] Eph. 6:17; the sermon was preached in 1410.

[42] This refers to the events during 1408–09, when King Wenceslas transferred his recognition from Pope Gregory XII to the Pisan Pope Alexander V. Because the German masters refused to do likewise, he changed the current usage by the edict of Kutná Hora by granting the Czech nation three votes and the rest only one. It was on this account that the German masters spread rumors of heresy of the Czechs, particularly of Hus. He resolutely denied the accusation, and, in replying to Protiva's charge he wrote: "Christ knows that I love a good German more than a bad Czech, even if he were my own brother."

[43] For our explanation, cf. Chap. II, n. 80.

[44] He was a Saxon, formerly (1409) dean of the faculty of arts at Prague.

man was one of those who swore, as he was then dean of the faculty of arts." And he, [Warentrapp] standing up, said: "Reverend fathers! In order that dominus John Hus's story and assertion be not believed true, be pleased to hear me." He was not, however, granted a hearing.

In the meantime Náz,[45] rising, said: "Reverend fathers! hear me, please. As for the mention he made here concerning the nations, the circumstances are well known to me. For I was then with the king of Bohemia when the masters of the three nations came to the king of Bohemia, then also of the Romans, imploring him to be willing to conserve their rights that they have held from ancient time by the grant of the emperor. And he consented to them. Thereafter, this Hus having come with Jerome [46] and others, persuaded him, the king, to another course. Nevertheless, moved by anger, the king exclaimed: 'You are always making trouble for me with your associate, Jerome; and if those whose concern it is will not take care of it, I myself will burn you!' Be it known to you, reverend fathers, that the lord king of Bohemia had never favored or favors them now, but those favorites of his decide everything. They recently ill-treated even me, who am under his [the king's] safe-conduct." And Páleč, rising, said: "Indeed, reverend fathers, not only strangers, but even doctors of our own nation were expelled on his account and by his order.[47] And some of them are in exile in Moravia to this day." Master John Hus responded: "It is not true that it was on my account; for I was not then in Prague when they went away."

The cardinal of Cambrai said: "Master John, you have recently in the tower [48] spoken more patiently than you do now. And you should know that this is not in your favor [*non est pro te*]." He replied: "Reverend father! because then they spoke fairly with me; but here almost all shout at me. I believe, therefore, that they all are my enemies." The cardinal said: "And who is shouting? On the contrary, when you speak, they hear you in silence." He responded: "If they did not shout, they would not have promulgated [the rule] in the name of the lord king as well as your own that all should keep still on pain of

[45] Dr. John Náz was for many years a diplomatic agent of King Wenceslas, and a canon of Prague.

[46] Master Jerome of Prague was then a prisoner of the Council and was burned at the stake a year later than Hus.

[47] This refers to the expulsion of four doctors, Stanislav and Peter of Znojmo, Jan Eliášův, and Stephen Páleč himself, for disobedience.

[48] The tower of the Gottlieben castle; cf. Chap. II, pp. 121–22.

expulsion and of leaving this place. However, we are at a trial here: the others ought to keep still, for I cannot hear when you speak." [49]

Further it is stated that on account of his erroneous and scandalous preaching in the city of Prague, a great sedition took place, caused by the deceit and fault of John Hus, so much so that notable catholic and God-fearing men were forced to leave and hide outside the afore-mentioned city. Then there arose and followed strife, depredations, sacrileges, and other horrible and execrable deeds by the aid and acts of the aforesaid John Hus with his accomplices. He replied that [this had occurred] not on his account, but on account of Archbishop Zbyněk's nonadherence to the king's and the university's policy of neutrality, and by the archbishop's imposition of the interdict extending for two miles around Prague.[50] For Zbyněk, having robbed the sepulcher of St. Wenceslas, fled to Roudnice and was followed there by the prelates and other clergy. And when they had refused to adhere to the king and to perform divine services and had fled, others appropri-ated their property. "But not by my command," he said, "nor by my inducement."

And Náz said: "No, reverend fathers, not because of nonadherence to the king, but by reason of having suffered spoliation did they pray the said lord archbishop to impose the interdict, and for that reason were plundered."

And the cardinal of Cambrai, at that time the commissioner and judge, said: "Here I also should testify. When I rode from Rome,[51] I was met by certain prelates from Bohemia. And when I inquired what were the news from there, they replied: 'Reverend father, bad! All the clergy are robbed of their prebends and property and are ill-treated.' "

Then the cardinal of Cambrai said to him: "Master John! When you were conducted into the palace,[52] we questioned you how you had come here; and you said that you had come here freely, and if you had not want-ed to come, neither the king of Bohemia nor the lord king of the Romans

---

[49] There is no record of any such order given to Hus; but at the opening of the Council, Pope John prohibited all loud talk, disputation, or laughter, under penalty of being "ejected in utter disgrace from the session . . . and lie under the sentence of excommunication." Cardinal Fillastre's *Diary,* in Loomis, *op cit.,* pp. 205–6. It appears that this prohibition in the case of Hus was observed mostly in its breach!

[50] The interdict was imposed on June 20, 1411. Cf. Bartoš, *op. cit.,* p. 347.

[51] This took place apparently in 1411.
cil in Rome.

[52] On November 28, 1414.

here present could have compelled you to come." [53]   And he, Master
John, replied: "No, rather I said that I had come here freely, and if I
had not wished to come, there are so many and such great lords in the
kingdom of Bohemia who love me, that I could have hidden and con-
cealed myself in their castles so that neither the king of Bohemia nor
the king here present could have forced me to come here." The cardinal, shaking his head and his face as if grimacing with indignation,
exclaimed: "Yea, what temerity!"   And Lord John [54] said to those
standing around, murmuring at it: "Indeed, he speaks the truth and it
is true. I am but a poor knight in our kingdom, but I would have protected him for a year, whether it would have pleased or displeased any
one, so that he could not be seized. And there are many and great
lords who love him, who possess the strongest castles, who would have
protected him as long as they wished, even against both these kings." [55]

Before he was led away, the cardinal of Cambrai said to him:
"Master John, you said not long ago at the tower that you wish humbly
to submit to the judgment of the Council. I counsel you, therefore, not
to involve yourself in these errors, but to submit to the correction and
instruction of the Council; and the Council will deal mercifully with
you."

The king likewise said: "Listen, John Hus! Some have said that I
gave you the safe-conduct fifteen days after your arrest. I say, however, that it is not true; I am willing to prove by princes and very many
others that I gave you the safe-conduct even before you had left
Prague.[56] I commanded Lords Wenceslas and John that they bring
you and guard you in order that having freely come to Constance, you
would not be constrained, but be given a public hearing so that you
could answer concerning your faith. They [the members of the Coun-
cil] have done so and have given you a public, peaceable, and honest

[53] This is another instance of the persistent attempt of the Council to prove
that Hus did not come freely, but was ordered to come by King Wenceslas. The
reference to Sigismund was made obviously with the intention to irritate Sigismund by the seeming affrontery of Hus. But even he testified that Hus had
come freely, since he had given him the safe-conduct.

[54] John of Chlum.

[55] The last of the nobles who gave refuge to Hus at his castle of Krakovec
was Lord Henry Lefl of Lažany, the principal member of the king's council.

[56] Actually, this is incorrect; Hus left the castle of Krakovec (not Prague) on
October 11, while the safe-conduct is dated October 18. Apparently, Sigismund
could not remember the details correctly. But he was right in affirming that he
had not given Hus the safe-conduct fifteen days after his arrest.

hearing here. And I thank them, although some may say that I could not grant a safe-conduct to a heretic or one suspected of heresy. For that reason, as here the lord cardinal has counseled you, I likewise counsel you to hold nothing obstinately, but in those things that were here proved against you and that you confessed, to offer yourself wholly to the mercy of the sacred Council. And they, for our sake and our honor and for [the sake of] our brother and of the kingdom of Bohemia, will grant you some mercy, and you will do penance for your guilt. But if you wish to hold all that obstinately, then indeed they know well what they must do with you. I told them that I am not willing to defend any heretic; indeed, if one should remain obstinate in his heresy, I myself would kindle [the fire] and burn him. But I would advice you to throw yourself wholly on the mercy of the Council, and the sooner the better, lest you involve yourself in graver errors." He then replied to the first statement: "I thank Your Serenity for the safe-conduct that Your Serenity was graciously pleased to grant me." Just then others interrupted his words and he forgot, as it were, to protest his nonobstinacy. Lord John of Chlum, however, standing up, said: "Master John, reply to the lord king concerning the second part." And he [Hus] said: "Most serene prince! Your Serenity knows that I came here freely, not to defend anything obstinately, but having been instructed, humbly to correct wherever I have erred."

Below the cardinal of Florence sat a notary public who, after the reading and the response to each article, noted down whatever the said cardinal ordered him to write; but I am not certain whether or not it included what the Master declared.[57] Nevertheless, I have seen and heard that after their every response or altercation with the Master the cardinal ordered the notary to record something.

Thus charging him with these and many other articles in his presence, they recessed and he was led back in chains. Then he, along with Master Jerome, was placed into the power of the bishop of Riga,[58] to whom the Council committed him.

Although I could not distinctly and verbally remember all the things that, while present there, I saw and heard, I have nonetheless incorporated all matters to the best of my memory; and especially since I did not have the articles to which the witnesses had testified and of which Master John had been accused, if for that reason I stated any-

[57] This public record is not extant.
[58] John of Wallenrode, archbishop of Riga.

thing defectively, I wish to be corrected by those who remember it better; but particularly by those who had been present there, not by those who have heard it from others.

CHAPTER IV

About the Hearing
on the Eighth day of June

On the Saturday after Marcellus [actually Marcellinus], which was June 8, Master John Hus was again conducted to a hearing in the previously mentioned refectory, where the king presided along with certain cardinals, archbishops, bishops, and other prelates.[1] Lords W. and J. and P. the bachelor, the scribe,[2] were also present there. About thirty-nine articles were read, said to have been drawn from the Master's books. Those that were exactly as stated in the books, the Master acknowledged as his; but those indeed that were not excerpted *verbatim* were read or delivered by a certain Englishman as they appeared in the excerpts and the Master's book. When anything they disliked was contained in the book, the cardinal of C[ambrai] said several times to the king and others: "Look! here it reads worse and more dangerously and erroneously than in the excerpt."

Those articles will follow. A certain person[3] who diligently compared them with the original book, [found that] but few of them were so stated in the book. Therefore, those which were stated exactly as in his [Hus's] original book are marked "is" in the margin; while about those, indeed, that were changed in the beginning, in the end, or in the middle he wrote "not exactly" in the margin.

---

[1] Cf. Hus's own account of these events in his letters, Part II, Nos. 11–12.

[2] These are, of course, Wenceslas of Dubá, John of Chlum, and Peter of Mladoňovice.

[3] Almost certainly Peter himself; even Sedlák supposes so. Cf. his *Studie*, II, 15, n. 1.

ARTICLES DRAWN FROM THE TREATISE "DE ECCLESIA" OF MASTER JOHN HUS:[4]

1. "There is only one holy universal Church, and that is the totality of the predestinate." Chaps. I and II in the beginning. Error, as far as it asserts, as it in fact does assert, that the totality of the predestinate alone constitute the holy universal Church.[5]

In the original book written by the hand of Master John Hus this and others following [are stated]:

"The holy catholic Church, that is the universal [Church], is then the totality of all the predestined, present, past, and future. This definition is stated by blessed Augustine *On John,* under his definition 32, question 4, chapter *Recurrat,* which shows that that same Church of the predestinate has existed from the beginning of the world until the

---

[4] These articles are doubtless based on those prepared by Stephen Páleč in January, 1415; they then numbered forty-two. Cf. Palacký, No. 9. But in the present form they were reduced to twenty-six, while those from the other two treatises to thirteen, thus making thirty-nine in all. In fact, only eleven of Páleč's forty-two original articles were retained, although fifteen others were added— some from Gerson's twenty articles drawn up in 1414, but the majority of them new. Cf. Sedlák, *op. cit.,* II, 14.

[5] This definition would indeed be erroneous, had Hus asserted that the Church consists exclusively and only of the predestinate, i.e., that it does not include the Church militant. Hus distinguished between the universal Church, which indeed consists exclusively of the predestinate, and the Church militant, which consists of *both* the predestined and the foreknown. He quotes Christ in speaking of this character of the Church militant as wheat and chaff (Matt. 3:12); as of good seed and weeds (Matt. 13:47). In the *Exposition of the Faith* he asserts that both the good and the bad "form one community and one congregation, as one sheepfold consisting of sheep and goats...." Žilka, II, 39.

In his *Hussina* (pp. 66–92) Dom de Vooght comments on Hus's references to Augustine's works and concludes that of the three senses in which Augustine used the word "ecclesia" Hus chose only one—the community of the predestinate. De Vooght thus agrees with the Council's condemnation of the first article of the final charges as implying the denial of the Church militant. In his *L'Hérésie,* however, he admits that Hus's concept "*l'universitas praedestinatorum* ne suprime ni ne remplace l'Église terrestre avec ses évêques, ses prêtres et ses sacrements, mais à celle-ci Huss attribue seulement la seconde place par rang de dignité." (p. 414.) Further, "Il a enseigné aussi que l'Église universelle, dans le sens le plus strict de mot, est l'assemblée des prédestinés avec toutes les incidences de cette proposition, relevées en plusieurs articles. Mais le concile ne paraît pas remarquer que Huss situe *l'universitas praedestinatorum* dans un ensemble ecclésial où l'Église traditionelle, c'est-à-dire terrestre, visible, hiérarchique, sacramentaire, est entièrement respectée." (p. 422). Dom de Vooght thus contradicts himself and as a result declares Hus a heretic. Were his reasoning to be accepted, Augustine would also be a heretic, for he too held the concept of the *universitas praedestinatorum.*

apostles, and since then until the day of judgment. For he says: 'The Church that brought forth Abel, Enoch, Noah, and Abraham, also brought forth Moses, and at a later time the prophets before the advent of the Lord; and the same that brought forth the apostles and our martyrs and all good Christians. For it has brought forth all who have been born at different times, yet they all have comprised a society of one people. And the citizens of this city had already experienced the toils of this pilgrimage, while some are experiencing them now, and some will be experiencing them even to the end.' " [6]

2. "As Paul was never a member of the devil, although he committed some acts similar to the acts of those evilly-disposed toward the Church; similarly also Peter, who fell into grave perjury by the permission of the Lord, in order that he might rise up the stronger." Chap. III, *Ff.*

As stated below, it stands exactly thus in the Master's book:

"For as Augustine says, it is expedient for the predestinate to fall into such sins. And it is evident from this that there are two kinds of separation from the holy Church: the first is permanent [*indeperdibilis*], by which all the foreknown are separated from the Church. The second, not permanent [*deperdibilis*], by which also some heretics are separated by sins of perdition from the Church, yet are able by God's grace to return to the sheepfold of Lord Jesus Christ. Of such He himself says, John 10: 'Other sheep I have which are not of this sheepfold; and it behooves me to bring them in. And they shall hear my voice, and there shall be one sheepfold and one shepherd.' The same is proved by blessed Augustine in dealing with John 11 concerning this word, that the children of God who are scattered abroad shall be gathered into one, etc. Also in *De penitentia,* distinction 4, question *Hoc ergo* to the end of the chapter." [7]

3. "No part of the Church finally falls away from her, because the predestinating love that binds her together does not fail." Chap. III, page. 2.

Note! It is stated in the book in this manner:

"Thus the purgaments of the Church, namely, the foreknown, proceed

[6] Thomson, ed., *Magistri Johannis Hus Tractatus de Ecclesia,* pp. 2–3; this critical edition of the basic work of Hus differs in minor verbal points from the text of Peter's *Account.* The quotation is from *Decretum Gratiani,* pars II, def. 32, q. 4, c. 2, chap. Recurrat. Friedberg, *op. cit.,* I, p. 1126.

[7] Cf. the text with Thomson, *op. cit.,* pp. 18–19. The passages are not consecutive, but selected from the entire text. Cf. *Decretum Gratiani,* pars II, De penitentia, dist. 4. Friedberg, *op. cit.,* I, 1228 f.

from her; nevertheless, they were not from her as parts. For no part of her finally falls away from her, because the predestinating love that binds her together does not fail, as the Apostle says in I Cor. 13. And this the Apostle proves in Romans 8, saying: 'We know then that all things work together for good to them that love God, to those who, according to His purpose'—that is predestination—'are called saints. For whom He predestined those He also called, and whom He called, those He also justified.' And he concludes concerning the long-tested predestinate, saying: 'I am certain that neither death, nor life, nor angels, nor principalities, nor powers, nor things present, nor things future, nor fear, nor depth, nor any other creature shall be able to separate us from the love of God which is in Christ Jesus, our Lord, etc.'" The remainder is clearly stated in the book; therefore, I abbreviate it.[8]

4. "The predestinate not existing in grace according to present righteousness is ever a member of the holy universal Church." An error, if understood concerning all the predestinate.

It is not so stated in the book, but it stands at the beginning of Chap. V, where it is declared that differend [members] are in the Church by different modes:

"Some are in the Church in accordance with unformed faith and in accordance with predestination, as are the predestinate Christians now in sin, who will, however, return to grace," etc.[9]

5. "No position of dignity, or human election, or any outward sign makes one a member of the holy Church catholic." Chap. V toward the end.

It stands in the book as follows:

"And arguing of this kind will be understood by considering what it is to be in the Church, what it is to be a member or part of the Church; that what makes one a member of the holy catholic Church is predestination, which is the preparation of grace in the present and of glory in the future, not, however, a position of dignity, or human election, or any outward sign. For the devil Iscariot, notwithstanding Christ's choosing and granting him temporary charismatic [gifts] for the apostolate or episcopacy, along with the popular repute that he was

[8] Cf. with the text of Thomson, *op. cit.,* pp. 15–16. The quotation is from Rom. 8:38–39; since it follows the Vulgate, the word "powers" is inserted. Hus had already answered this item in his reply to Páleč's forty-two articles. Cf. Palacký, p. 819.

[9] Cf. with the text of Thomson, *op. cit.,* p. 30.

a true disciple of Christ, was not a true disciple of His, but a wolf clad in sheep's clothing, as Augustine says," etc.[10]

6. "The foreknown is never a member of the holy mother Church." Chap. IV *D* and Chap. V *D*.

It stands otherwise in the book, Chap. IV *D*:

"No foreknown is a member of the holy mother, the Church catholic." And he proved it previously by quoting Augustine on the Psalm,[11] commenting extensively on the word: 'I have been young and now I am old.' And further by the Apostle to the Ephesians 5: 'Christ loved the Church,' etc. Likewise, Bernard *On the Song of Songs,* sermon 12, says: 'The Church is the body of Christ, dearer than that he gave to death,' etc. Also in Chap. V it is said: 'However, it is conceded that the holy Church is the Lord's threshing-floor, in which exist both the good and the wicked according to faith: the predestinate and the foreknown now commingled—the predestinate as wheat, the foreknown as chaff. The first shall be gathered into the granary of the celestial homeland, the rest to be burned in the inextinguishable fire, as says the Gospel and Augustine's exposition' " in the book.[12]

7. "Judas was never a true disciple of Christ." Chap. V.

Note: it stands in Chap. V *G* as follows:

"For he, the foreknown, was never a true disciple of Christ, as Augustine proves, but was a wolf clad in sheep's clothing." Again in Chap. IV *F*, Augustine treating the words of I John 2: 'They went out from us, but they were not of us';[13] and further he says: 'For he knew from the beginning who were believing, and who were to betray him. And he said: 'Therefore I have said to you that no one comes to me except it be given by my Father. On that account many of his disciples went away and walked with him no more.' Were they not for a time called disciples in the words of the Gospel? Nonetheless, they were not true disciples, for they did not abide in His word in accordance with what He said: 'If you abide in my word, you are my disciples.

[10] Cf. with the text of Thomson, *op. cit.,* pp. 35–36.
[11] Psalm 36:25.
[12] Cf. with the text of Thomson, *op. cit.,* pp. 23, 22, 23–24, 33. This statement is quoted from various parts of two chapters and is not consecutive. Again the charge rests on the failure of the judges to recognize Hus's distinction between "the Church catholic," i.e., composed of the predestinate, and "the Church militant," comprising both the predestinated and the foreknown. The quotation is from Bernard's "Sermons in Cantica," Migne, *Patrologia latina,* 183, c. 831.
[13] I John 2:19. Cf. Friedberg, *op. cit.,* I, 1231.

As they were not true disciples of Christ, they did not have perseverance. Thus they were not truly children of God, even when they seemed for a time to be and were so called. And later on: And the same is shown by Chrysostom in *De opere imperfecto,* homily I, who says: 'Those who were of God could not perish because no one can fall away from God.' " [14]

8. "The congregation of the predestinate, whether or not they be in grace according to present righteousness, is the holy Church universal, and in that sense the Church is an article of faith." [15] The same in Chap. VII *B.*

In the book it stands thus:

"But in the third sense the Church is conceived as the congregation of the predestinate, whether or not they be in grace according to present righteousness. And in that sense the Church is an article of faith, concerning which the Apostle spoke to the Ephesians, Chap. 5, saying: 'Christ loved the Church and gave Himself for her, that He might sanctify her, washing her in the bath of water and the word of life, that He might present a glorious Church to Himself, not having a spot or wrinkle or any such thing, but that she might be holy and immaculate.' [16] In the reply written by his own hand it is stated as follows: 'And that is an objective article of faith which we ought to believe firmly with the words of the Creed, I believe in the holy catholic Church.' Concerning that he adduces proofs from the saints at the beginning of the treatise." [17] This does not exclude the other two parts of the distinction about the Church stated later in Chap. VII *B,* toward

[14] Cf. with the text of Thomson, *op. cit.,* 25–26; the last quotation is from Pseudo-Chrysostom, *De opere imperfecto,* homily IX instead of I. It is quoted from Wyclif, *De ecclesia,* p. 74.

[15] Again Hus makes a distinction between "the holy catholic Church," i.e., the predestinate, and the Church militant, which comprises both the predestinate and the foreknown. This is well illustrated by the answer Hus gave to the papal legate before Archbishop Albík when the legate asked him whether he was willing "to obey the Apostolic mandate" [in the matter of Pope John's bull of indulgences]. Hus responded cordially that he was. The legate of course understood this to mean that Hus would obey the *papal* bull. He was by no means pleased to learn that Hus made a distinction between the apostolic mandates—i.e., of the apostles—and the papal. The Council similarly failed, or refused, to understand this distinction. *Historia et Monumenta,* I, 367.

[16] Cf. with the text of Thomson, *De ecclesia,* p. 45; the quotation is from Eph. 5:26. Hus had already answered this charge when he dealt with Páleč's forty-two articles. Cf. Palacký, pp. 206–7.

[17] This refers to Hus's reply to Páleč's articles, where these words appear.

the end, where there is [presented] a full treatment of the intention of the Master concerning that article.[18]

9. "Peter was not nor is the principal head of the holy catholic Church." Chap. IX G.

This is how the same stands in the book:

"It is conceded, moreover, that Peter received from the Rock of the Church, which is Christ, humility, poverty, firmness of faith, and consequently blessedness. But that by the words of the Gospel, 'Upon this rock will I build my Church,' Christ should have intended to build the whole Church militant upon the person of Peter is contradicted by the faith of the Gospel, by the exposition of Augustine, and by reason. For Christ was to build His Church upon the Rock which was He Himself, from whom Peter received the firmness of faith, since Christ is the head and the foundation of the whole Church, not Peter," etc.[19] And further he adduced the sayings of the saints as to the manner in which Christ was the head of the Church and in what manner was Peter; showing the different ways in which one may be said to be the head of the Church."

At this time we hastily arrived [and heard] his subsequent replies to the Council.[20]

10. "If he who is called the vicar of Christ follows Christ in life, then he is His vicar. If in fact he walks in contrary ways, then he is the messenger of Antichrist, an adversary of Peter and of the Lord Jesus Christ, and the vicar of Judas Iscariot." Chap. IX L, H, and XIV G.

This does not stand in the book in that form, but is written in Chap. IX L as follows:

"If then he, called Peter's vicar, walks in the said ways of virtue, we believe that he is truly his vicar and the chief pontiff of the Church he rules. But if in fact he walks in contrary ways, then he is the messenger of Antichrist, an adversary of Peter and of the Lord Jesus Christ.

---

[18] The last sentence was added by Peter of Mladoňovice.

[19] Cf. with the text of Thomson, *op. cit.,* p. 64. This was one of the principal points of difference between Hus and Páleč along with Stanislav, who taught as an article of faith that the Church is built on Peter and his successors.

The quotation from Augustine is from *Sermones de Scripturio Novi Testamenti,* LXXVI, i, 1.

[20] It is evident both from this and n. 23 that Peter, along with the two Czech nobles, had not been present at the hearing up to this point. Consequently, he does not report Hus's own verbal answers, as he does henceforth.

Hence the blessed Bernard in *To Pope Eugenius,* Book 4, writes as follows: 'Among these things you, a shepherd, go forth among the pastures bedecked with gold, clad in multicolored vestments [*tam multa circumdatus varietate*]. What does is profit the sheep? If I dare say so, these [pastures] are of great demons rather than of sheep. Not so did Peter act or Paul frisk about!' And further he continues: 'Either deny to the people that you are the shepherd or show yourself to be such. You will not deny it lest he, whose seat you hold, denies you as his heir,' etc. And further: 'In these things you have succeeded not Peter but Constantine.' " Thus Bernard.[21] Also in Chap. XIV *G* it is written as follows: 'If in morals he lives contrary to Peter, and if he is avaricious, then he is the vicar of Judas Iscariot who loved the reward of iniquity, selling the Lord Jesus Christ.' " [22]

When this was being read, the presidents looked at one another, smiling and shaking their heads.

To [the reading] of these articles we have already come; but we were late for the first nine, for which reason [they are stated here without] [23] the Master's replies to them.

11. "All simoniacs and priests living wickedly [*criminose*], as faithless children, think faithlessly concerning the seven sacraments of the Church, the keys, the offices, censures, morals, ceremonies, and the sacred things of the Church, the veneration of relics, indulgences, and orders in the Church." Chap. XI *D.*

This passage does not agree with the book, but is as follows:

"Also they exercise this abuse of power who sell and buy sacred orders, simonically acquire the episcopate, canonry, and benefices, make extortionate demands for the sacraments, live avariciously, voluptuously, or lustfully, or in whatever other kind of offense they pollute the power of the priesthood. Even if they profess to know God, they nevertheless deny Him in deeds—Titus 1. Consequently, they do not

---

[21] Cf. with the text of Thomson, *op. cit.,* p. 70. The quotation from Bernard is found in his "De consideratione libri quinque ad Eugenium tertium," *Patrologia latina,* 182, cols. 775–76.

[22] Cf. with the text of Thomson, *op. cit.,* p. 115. Hus acknowledges that when the pope possesses the proper moral qualification, he is then Peter's "vicar and the chief pontiff of the church he rules." Thus he does not follow Wyclif in repudiating the pope as Antichrist. Further, Hus speaks of such a pope as the vicar of Peter, not of Christ.

[23] The inserted words are a reasonable conjecture supplying an omission which occurs in this place.

believe in God and thus as faithless children think faithlessly concerning the seven sacraments of the Church, the keys, the offices, censures, morals, ceremonies, and the sacred things of the Church, the veneration of relics, indulgences, and orders in the Church. It is evident that such men despise the name of God according to the [word] of Malachi: 'It is said to you, O priests, who despise my name and say: in what way have we despised your name? You offer polluted bread upon my altar,' etc.[24] The same is shown in I, q. 1, in the chapter *Multi secularium*,[25] and in Hebrews 10, etc., as in the book above." [26]

And when that article had been read, Master John Hus said: "They think faithlessly because they lack faith formed by love and have at that time dead faith." And they said: "And where does that stand in your book?" He replied: "This may be easily gathered from the sayings of the saints in the book."

12. "The papal dignity arose from the Caesars." Chap. XIII *C*. And further on: "The papal preeminence and institution emanated from the Caesar's power."

The first statement is not found there in the book (Chap. XIII), but the second is, and it reads as follows: [27]

"And it is proved in distinction 96,[28] where Constantine speaks as follows: 'We are bestowing upon him power and force and imperial honor, deciding that he should thus hold preeminence over the four sees: Alexandrian, Antiochian, Constantinopolitan, etc., being higher than and the prince above all the priests in the world. See how the papal preeminence and institution have emanated from the power of Caesar.' [29] Further down in the same chapter, *G*: 'Therefore it is truly concluded that the pope has the supremacy of dignity immediately from God and not from man—who is not God—or from a mere man; but it

[24] Malachi 1:6–7.

[25] This is a reference to St. Gregory. Cf. *Decretum Gratiani, pars* II, q. 1, c. 84; Friedberg, *op. cit.,* I, 387.

[26] Cf. with the text of Thomson, *op. cit.,* p. 93.

[27] Actually, even the second statement in Chap. XIII does not read as stated, but is as follows: "For the Emperor Constantine about the year of the Lord 301 thought and commanded that his bishop should be called pope by all and confirmed that name with his Donation." Cf. Thomson, *op. cit.,* p. 104.

[28] This refers to *Decretum Gratiani, pars* I, dist. 96, c. 13–14, Constantinus. Friedberg, *op. cit.,* I, 342–45.

[29] For some reason Jerusalem is not mentioned in Peter's *Account,* although it is implied in the number four; but it is named in the text of Thomson, *op. cit.,* p. 122.

behooves him to merit that dignity by humility, without pomp.' " [30]

When this article had been read, Master John, rising, said: "That is what I say: that as for the outward adornments and the possession of temporal goods of the Church as such, the papal dignity has its origin from Caesar Constantine; and that later other emperors also confirmed it, as is shown in the *Decretum* distinction 96.[31] But as concerns the spiritual administration and the office of the spiritual governing of the Church, such dignity originates directly from the Lord Jesus Christ." And the cardinal of Cambrai said: "Nonetheless, at the time of Constantine a general Council was held and there that decree was ascribed to Constantine on account of his presence and reverence. Why not, therefore, rather say that the preeminence of the pope emanates from the Council rather than from the power of Caesar?" And the Master said: "Because of the Donation, which, as I said, was granted by Caesar." [32]

13. "No one may reasonably assert without revelation about himself or another that he is the head of a particular holy Church." Chap. XIII *G*.

It stands in the book as stated. And it continues as follows: "Although if he live well, he should hope that he is a member of the holy catholic Church, the bride of Christ; for in accordance with Ecclesiastes: 'No one knows whether he is worthy of grace or of hate.' And Luke 17: 'When you have done all that is commanded you, say: We are unworthy servants.' " [33]

14. "It should not be believed that every Roman pontiff whatsoever is the head of every particular Church, unless God predestinated him." Chap. XIII *G*.

It stands in the book exactly so. And it is proved thus: "It is evident

[30] Cf. with the text of Thomson, *op. cit.,* p. 125. It is to be particularly noted that Hus acknowledges that the spiritual dignity of the pope is derived directly from God. Only the temporal power he received from the emperor. Hus had answered in this sense even in commenting on the forty-two charges of Páleč. Palacký, p. 213. By condemning this statement of Hus, the Council condemned an indubitable historical fact.

[31] This is already quoted in n. 28.

[32] It need hardly be pointed out that the Council of Nicaea (325) passed no such legislation. Indeed, the "Donation of Constantine" is a forgery.

[33] Ecclesiastes 9:1, which in the R.S.V. reads: "Whether it is love or hate man does not know." Hus of course follows the Vulgate. And Luke 17:10. Cf. Thomson, *op. cit.,* pp. 107–8, where the text after the phrase "bride of Christ" is widely separated from the quotation from Eccl., and the Lucan quotation is omitted.

because otherwise the Christian faith must be proved deceptive and a
Christian confess a lie; as when the Church was deceived by Agnes." [34]
It is shown by blessed Augustine in his book *De decem cordis*.

15. "The power of the pope as vicar is frustrated, unless the pope
conforms in morals and in life to Christ or Peter; for he received the
procuratorial power from God for no other reason; for no other following [of Christ] is more pertinent." Chap. XIV C.

That proposition or article does not stand exactly as stated, but
otherwise, as follows:

"And as the vicar ought to assume as best he can the place of the
superior from whom he has received the vicarial power, so he should conform as immediately as possible to the works of him whose place he
occupies. For otherwise the power should in this way be frustrated in
him. From this, then, the argument is constructed as follows: that man
is a vicar who occupies the place of him from whom he has legitimately
received the procuratorial power; but no one truly occupies the place
of Christ and Peter unless he follows him in morals. For no other
following is more pertinent, nor has he received the procuratorial power
from God for any other reason. Therefore, there are required for that
vicarial office both the conformity of morals and the instituting authority." And so forth in the book. [35]

When this article was concluded, Master John, rising, said: "You
should understand it in the sense that the power of such a pope is
frustrated as to his merit or prerogative that ought to follow from it
but does not; but not as far as the office is concerned." Then they
said: "Where is that explanation in your book?" He said: "As a matter
of fact it is in the second chapter *Contra Magistrum Paletz*." [36] And
they smiled, looking at each other.

16. "For not because the pope holds the place of Peter, but because
he posseses the great Donation, is he [called] the most holy [*sanctissimus*]."

That proposition does not stand so in the book, but is altered in the
middle and clipped off at the end; it stands in the book as follows:

---

[34] Cf. with the text of Thomson, *op. cit.*, p. 107; this refers to the then generally believed legend that there existed a female pope Agnes (John VIII, c. 855),
that was held even by Gerson. The real Pope John VIII held office in 872—88.
Augustine's *De decem cordis* is in Migne, *Patrologia latina*, XXXVIII, 75–91.
[35] Cf. Thomson, *op. cit.*, p. 112.
[36] Cf. *Historia et Monumenta*, I, 319, where it is so delimited.

"For not because he holds the place of Peter and because he possesses the great Donation, is he the most holy; but if he follows Christ in humility, gentleness, patience, and labor from the great bond of love, then is he holy." [37]

17. "The cardinals are not the manifest and true successors of the college of Christ's other apostles unless they live after the manner of the apostles, observing the commands and counsels of our Lord Jesus Christ." Chap. XIV G.

This is according to the text of the book. It is proved in the same place: "For if they climb up by another than the principal door, the Lord Jesus Christ, then they are thieves and robbers, as is said in John 10: 'As many as came [that way] are thieves and robbers.' " [38]

When that reading was concluded, the cardinal of Cambrai, who was supreme in the Council, said: "Look! it stands worse and harsher in the book than it was formulated." And he said to Master John Hus: "You do not observe moderation in your preaching and writing; for you should have adapted your sermons to the need of the hearers. Why was it necessary or useful, therefore, while preaching to the people to preach against the cardinals, since none of them was present there? Rather you should have spoken and preached it to their faces, and not to scandalize the laymen." And he answered: "Reverend father, I have dealt with such matters because my sermons were attended by priests and other learned men, in order that both the present and the future priests would know beforehand what to guard against." The cardinal retorted: "You are doing wrong; for by such preaching you wish to destroy the status of the Church."

18. "Apart from the ecclesiastical censure, no heretic is to be turned over the secular courts to be punished by corporeal death."

This proposition does not stand in the book, but they added it themselves; the following is in the book:

"They, the doctors, should be ashamed for their apish and cruel comparison, especially as the Lord Christ, the pontiff of both Testaments, neither would judge a civil suit nor would condemn the disobedient to corporeal death. For as to the first He said, Luke 12: 'Man, who constituted me a judge or divider over you?' [39] As to the

[37] Thomson, *op. cit.*, p. 117. Hus insists that only God is "the most holy." The pope, possessing the proper qualifications of character, is to be called "holy."

[38] *Ibid.*, p. 115; the Thomson text adds: "as was declared by the Savior Himself concerning all such." The reference is to John 10:1.

[39] Luke 12:14.

second He said to the woman adulteress, whom the Pharisees declared liable to death according to the law, John 8: 'Neither do I condemn you, etc.' [40] But perchance the doctors would say that this has nothing to do with the case, because the law says: 'He who acts presumptuously, not willing to obey the priest's rule, etc.' [41] I mention a case as an example: for it is said in Matthew 18: 'If your brother sins against you, reprove him between yourself and him; if he does not hear you, take him along with you,' etc. And the following: 'Moreover, if he does not hear the Church, let him be to you as a gentile and a publican.' [42] Note! to whom did the supreme Lord and pontiff speak? Certainly to Peter, the future Roman pontiff after Him, that he might kindly correct the erring and reprove the disobedient before witnesses, that he might make known the persistenly disobedient to the Church, not putting to bodily death the stubbornly disobedient to the Church, but shunning him as a publican and a gentile"; and so forth in the book.

When that and other matters were finished, the Master said: "I say that a heretic, if he is such, ought first of all be fairly, kindly, and humbly instructed from the Holy Scriptures and the reasons derived from them, as did St. Augustine and others while disputing with heretics. If he were in no way willing to desist from errors, providing he has had such instruction, I do not say that such a man should not be punished even corporeally.[43] But I always assert that such instruction from the Scriptures ought to precede," etc. This caused murmuring and tumult.

In the meantime they read a passage from the book in which he attacked such as those above, saying: "In this they are surely like the priestly princes, the Pharisees and scribes who, saying to Pilate, 'It is not lawful for us to kill anyone,' surrendered Jesus to him: and Christ testified that they were greater murderers than Pilate when He said: 'He who surrendered me to you has a greater sin.' Thereupon instantly with a great tumult and noise they shouted at the Master: 'Who are

[40] John 8:11.
[41] Deut. 17:12.
[42] Matt. 18:15–17. Greatly condensed.
[43] Cf. Thomson, *op. cit.*, p. 138. This admission that a heretic could be put to death after he had received and had rejected repeated admonitions is exceptional. Normally, Hus did not grant it. Hus was ahead of his age in advocating that no one be put to death on account of heresy. Even the Protestant Reformers were not ready to accept this position. It would have saved them from severe condemnation in later times.

like them? Is it not those who have turned a heretic over to the secular arm?' And the Master replied: 'Those who have turned an innocent man over to the secular arm to be put to death, as did the priestly princes, scribes, and Pharisees to Christ when they surrendered Him to Pilate.' But they cried: 'No! no! for here you speak of the doctors.' And the cardinal of Cambrai said: 'These words are much harsher than those that were abstracted; for surely they abstracted them leniently.' "

And the reason why there were harsher? Surely because they touched them—the priests—more sorely!

19. "The secular nobles should compel the priests to observe the law of Christ." Chap. XVII B.

That proposition does not stand in the book in that form, but otherwise, as follows:

"And fourthly, our party desires and preaches that the Church militant be genuinely commingled as to the estates that the Lord had ordained: that is, of the priests of Christ serving His law in purity; of the secular nobles for the compelling of the observance of the ordinance of Christ; and of the common people serving both these estates according to the law of Christ." [44]

20. "Ecclesiastical obedience is obedience according to the invention of the priests of the Church beyond the express command of Scripture." Chap. XVII.

In the book it stands in this way:

"Concerning this it is to be noted that obedience is threefold: namely, spiritual, secular, and ecclesiastical. Spiritual is due purely according to the law of God, under which Christ and the apostles lived and every Christian should live. Secular obedience is obedience due according to the civil laws. Ecclesiastical obedience is obedience according to the invention of the priests of the Church beyond the express command of Scripture. The first kind of obedience always excludes what is in itself evil both on the part of the one commanding and the one obeying; and of it is said in Deuteronomy 24: 'You shall do whatever the Levitical priests shall teach you, according to that which I commanded

---

[44] Cf. *Ibid.,* p. 149. When in 1412 Hus defended Wyclif's article XVII about the rightfulness of the deprivation of clerical possessions by nobles, he argued that the secular rulers are entitled to correct clerical corruptions in a brotherly spirit; and furthermore, that since the Bohemian king endowed the church with temporal goods, he could take them away for cause; otherwise he would not be a ruler in his own domain. *Historia et Monumenta,* I, 153–54.

them,' etc.[45] At that time the Master delimited it, saying that this obedience would be such only when the priests commanded something without regard for or beyond the express command of the Scriptures and contrary to the law of God." [46]

21. "A person excommunicated by a pope, who has ignored the judgment of the pope and of the general Council, if he appeals to Christ is thereby protected, so that the excommunication of this type does not affect him in any way." Chap. XVIII L.

This proposition is not in the book. But in that same chapter [Hus], showing the many serious grievances suffered at the curia both by him and his [procurators], including the denial of a hearing to them, says and writes as follows:

"When therefore the appeal from one pope to his successor profited me nothing, and the appeal from the pope to the Council is of long-delayed and uncertain benefit in a serious grievance; in the end I appealed, therefore, to the head of the Church, the Lord Jesus Christ. For in deciding a cause, He is superior to any pope whatsoever, for He cannot err, nor can He deny justice to anyone rightly seeking it, nor can He, if a man has observed His law, condemn him without fault," etc., as it is in the book.[47]

When the reading of this article had been concluded, the Master said: "I confess that I appealed to Christ, as I said before, as the last resort, when my procurators had not been given a hearing for more than two years." The cardinal of Cambrai said: "Do you want to be above St. Paul who, when he was wronged in Jerusalem, appealed not to Christ but to Caesar?" And the Master said: "Very well. But if

---

[45] Deut. 24:8.

[46] Cf. with the text of Thomson, *op. cit.*, p. 156; the following sentence is missing from the text of Peter, which Thomson places after the words, "The first kind of obedience": "For those who command according to the law of God and those who obey, proceed correctly as to obedience, as it is said both to the commanding and the obeying in Deuteronomy 24."

The same statement is made by Hus in his sermon on April 23, 1411, where his intention is expressed more clearly: "The ecclesiastical obedience is obedience in accordance with a command of the priests of the Church. The Scriptures do not state ... that all persons of both sexes should go to confession once a year. Nevertheless, whoever does go, does well; for if he does not obey, he sins thereby; for having sinned, he does not confess it." Císařova-Kolářova, *M. Jan Hus, Betlémské poselství*, I, 220.

[47] Cf. Thomson, *op. cit.*, pp. 165–66. Cf. also Part II, Nos. 1–3, where Hus writes about these matters extensively. In the definitive sentence, Hus's appeal to Christ is explicitly condemned.

someone here had done the same thing, he would have been condemned as a heretic. Nevertheless, St. Paul appealed to Caesar not from his own impulse, but by the will of Christ Who, appearing to him said: 'Be steadfast, for you should go to Rome,' and later repeated it." Therefore, Master John confessed that as the last resort in case of injustice there is no more effective appeal than to Christ. As the reason for it he reiterated the one he had stated before. And they derided him. When they further objected to him that he had officiated and had celebrated the mass while under excommunication, he admitted that he had performed the divine office, but under the appeal. And when they asked whether he had an absolution from the pope, he answered that he did not. The cardinal of Florence, leaning forward, ordered the notary who sat at his feet to record it, as he did in connection with other articles as he saw fit.

22. "If a man is wicked, whatever he does, he does wickedly; and if he is virtuous, whatever he does, he does virtuously." Chap. XIX *D*.

It stands in the book just as abstracted:

"Further be it noted that there is an immediate distinction between human deeds whether they be virtuous or wicked: for it is evident that if a man is virtuous, whatever he does, he does virtuously. And if he is wicked, whatever he does, he does wickedly. For just as wickedness, which is called crime—that is mortal sin—infects all acts of the subject or man; so virtue vivifies all acts of the virtuous, so that, living in grace, he is said to pray and deserve merit while sleeping or doing anything whatsoever, as saints Augustine, Gregory, and others say. It is shown in Luke 6: 'If your eye'—that is, your intention—'be single,' not bent by depraved sins, 'then your whole body,' that is, the sum of your deeds, 'shall be light,' that is, pleasing to God. 'If however it is evil, your whole body shall be dark.' [48] And in II Cor. 10: 'Do all to the glory of God.' [49] In I Cor. at the end: 'Let all things be done in love.' " [50]

When that article was completed, the cardinal of Cambrai said: "However, Scripture says that we all sin; and again: 'If we say that we have no sin, we deceive ourselves.' Thus we must ever act wickedly." The Master replied: "There Scripture speaks of venial sins that do not deprive man of his virtuous status but agree one with the other." And

---

[48] It actually refers to Luke 11:34, and is not quoted exactly.

[49] This is in I Cor. 10:31. Hus (or Peter) obviously quoted from memory.

[50] I Cor. 16:14. Cf. Thomson, *op. cit.*, p. 176.

Master William [51] said: "But these sins are not compatible with a morally good act." The Master then cited Augustine in the passage 'I believe,' *On the Psalm*: "If you get drunk on wine, whatever praise your tongue utters, your life blasphemes." He was not, however, permitted to speak, for they shouted at him saying: "What has that to do with this proposition?" etc.

23. "The priest of Christ living in accordance with His law, having knowledge of Scripture and a desire to edify the people, ought to preach, a pretended excommunication nothwithstanding." And subsequently: "that if the pope or another superior orders a priest so disposed not to preach, he ought not to obey." Chap. XX *H*.

That is proved from what follows; but the first sentence is stated differently, as follows:

"The pretended excommunication notwithstanding, threatened or already imposed, the Christian ought to follow Christ's commands. This is evident from the conclusion of blessed Peter and other apostles in Acts 5: 'Is is more meet to obey God than men.' [52] Consequently it follows therefrom that the priest of Christ, living in accordance with His law, having knowledge of Scripture and the love of edifying the people, ought to preach a pretended excommunication notwithstanding. It is evident that priests are commanded to preach the Word of God, as apostle Peter testifies in Acts 10: 'God commanded us,' he says, 'to preach to the people and to testify.' [53] And Matthew 10: 'Jesus sent out these twelve, commanding them and saying: Go not in the way of gentiles,' etc. And later on: 'Go and preach, saying that the kingdom of heaven is at hand.' [54] And in Luke 9 and 10 the same appears. It also is stated by blessed Augustine in the Prologue to his sermons. He says: 'Few are the priests who rightly preach the Word of God; but many are those who are damnably silent.' Also the same is extensively asserted by blessed Jerome in Ezekiel 3; and by blessed Gregory in *The Pastoral Care,* Chap. XV; [55] and in distinction 43, *Sit rector*; [56] and by blessed Isidore, Book III, *De summo bono,* authorities

---

[51] Perhaps William Corfe.

[52] Acts 5:29.

[53] Acts 10:42.

[54] Matt. 10:5–6.

[55] *Nicene and Post-Nicene Fathers* (Oxford and New York, 1895), XII, "St. Gregory's Pastoral Care," Chap. XV, pp. 38–39.

[56] *Decretum Gratiani,* pars. I, dist. 43, c. 1, *Sit rector.* Friedberg, *op. cit.,* I, 154. The reference to Isidore is in *PL*. 83, 714.

of which are [mentioned] in the text of the book. As for the second particular, the Master said toward the end: 'It is evident therefrom that preaching for the priest and giving alms for the rich are not voluntary works but mandatory.' Further he said that if the pope or another superior orders a priest so disposed not to preach, or the rich not to give alms, the subordinate should not obey," etc.[57]

That being finished and read, the Master said: "Thus I call an alleged excommunication unjust and irregular, promulgated contrary to the order of law and of the precept of God. On account of it, as mentioned before, the priest so disposed ought not to cease from edifying preaching or to fear it as damning him eternally." And they objected (as was said) that such an excommunication was a blessing. The Master responded: "That is true; yet I say that an excommunication unjustly suffered by a man is for him a blessing before God, according to the prophet: 'I will curse your blessings and will bless your cursings,' etc.[58] Or another: 'They shall curse but you will bless!' "[59] The cardinal of Florence remarked: "Nevertheless, there are laws that even an unjust excommunication is to be feared." The Master replied: "That is true; for there are about eight reasons on account of which it is to be feared." The cardinal said: "Are there not more?" The Master said: "Let us admit that there are even more," etc.

24. "Whoever has accepted the office of preacher, and has entered upon the priesthood, ought to execute his mandate, an alleged excommunication nothwithstanding." Chap. XX *H*.

The proposition stands in the book not in that form, but otherwise, as follows:

"When therefore, from what has been said, anyone has accepted the office of preaching in accordance with a mandate and has entered upon the priesthood, it is evident that he ought to execute that mandate, a pretended excommunication notwithstanding. Likewise no true Catholic ought to be in doubt that if a man is sufficiently trained in doctrine, he has greater obligation to teach the ignorant, to counsel the doubtful, to castigate the unruly, and to remit [sins] of the wrongdoers,

---

[57] Cf. with the text of Thomson, *op. cit.*, pp. 190–91. Hus had asserted the same thesis in his defense of one of Wyclif's articles in 1412, when he claimed that a man legitimately ordained by the Church can preach even without further papal or episcopal permission. *Historia et Monumenta*, I, 142.

[58] Malachi 2:2; the text is very different at present, nor does the Vulgate bear it out.

[59] Psalm 109:28.

than to apply them in performing some works of mercy. Since, therefore, he who is capable of administering material alms is bound to do
them under the pain of damnation, as is shown in Matthew 25, much
more is he who is capable of administering spiritual alms!" [60]

25. "The ecclesiastical censures are antichristian, for the clergy
have devised them for their exaltation and for the subjection of the
people, in case laymen are not obedient to the clergy's will." The last
chapter, G.

This statement is not in the book, but its subject is extensively
treated in Chap. XXIII. [61]

Moreover, during the examination at that hearing, they gathered
together conclusions most adverse and irritating to them. After they
had read them, the cardinal of Cambrai said: "Surely these are much
harsher and more offensive than those abstracted." For what reason?
Because they were more damaging to their status, and on that account
were displeasing to them.

26. "An interdict ought not to be imposed on the people, for Christ,
the supreme pontiff, imposed no interdict on account of John the
Baptist or on account of the wrongs done to Himself." The last
chapter, G, H. I.

This statement also does not stand in the book in that form; but it
is indeed said in that same chapter, dealing with the facile fulminations of interdicts, that an interdict is sometimes imposed on account
of an imprisoned clerical thief, and for that reason all good [people]
are deprived of the worship of God. He says in the book:

"Christ, however, the supreme pontiff, when the prophet [i.e., John
the Baptist] 'than whom no greater has arisen, born of women,' was
imprisoned, did not impose an interdict, not even when Herod beheaded
him. Yea, when He himself was robbed, beaten, and blasphemed by
the soldiery, the scribes, the Pharisees, magistrates, and the high priests,
even then He did not utter any curses, but prayed for them saying, in
Luke 23: 'Father, forgive them, for they know not what they do.' [62]
And He passed that doctrine on to His members, saying, Matthew 5:

---

[60] Cf. with the text of Thomson, *op. cit.*, p. 191; the quotation is from Matt.
25:34–36.

[61] It is indeed true that the sentence does not appear in the place designated
in that particular form (Chap. XXIII G); but that paragraph deals with ecclesiastical censures and asserts the substance of the charge.

[62] Luke 23:34.

'Love your enemies and do good to them that hate you, and pray for them that persecute and calumniate you,'[63] etc. Hence, following this doctrine in word and deed, the first vicar of Christ, the Roman pontiff, teaches the faithful in I Peter 2, saying: 'To this you were called, because Christ suffered for us, leaving us an example that we should follow in His steps.' And further on: 'Who, when He was reviled, did not revile; when He suffered, He did not threaten.'[64] And Paul, traveling the same path, says in Romans 12: 'Bless them that persecute you; bless and curse not.'"[65]

And so in other Scriptural passages extensively stated there, from which, however, very few were adduced in the hearing; and choosing only the points which were capable of stirring up anger, they kept proposing them.

ARTICLES DRAWN, BUT VERY SPARCELY, FROM THE TREATISE WRITTEN AGAINST MASTER STEPHEN PÁLEČ

1. "If a pope, bishop, or prelate is in mortal sin, then he is not pope, bishop, or prelate."

It occurs as stated at the beginning of Chap. II; thereafter he says: "I refer him to the saints, Augustine, Jerome, Chrysostom, Gregory, Cyprian, and Bernard, who further say: 'Whoever is in mortal sin, is not a true Christian.' Therefore, let this crass deceiver (*fictor*) learn that such are not truly or worthily at that time according to present righteousness popes, bishops, and prelates, but only nominally; but truly and according to the Gospel of truth, John 10, are they thieves and robbers. And in Matthew, Chap. 7: 'They are ravening wolves in sheep's clothing' of whom Amos 8 says: 'They reigned but not from me, they elevated princes but I knew it not,' etc.[66] And further on: 'For we concede that a bad pope, bishop, prelate, or priest is an unworthy minister of the sacraments, through whom nevertheless God baptizes, consecrates, or otherwise operates for the benefit of His

---

63 Matt. 5:44.
64 I Peter 2:21, 23.
65 Rom. 12:14. The whole quotation is in Thomson, *op. cit.*, p. 226.
66 This is found in Hosea 8:4, not in Amos.

Church.' " [67] That is more fully treated in the text in accordance with the authority of the saints already referred to.

When that article was concluded, the Master said: "Indeed, he who is in mortal sin is not a worthy king before God, as appears from IV Kings 16, where the Lord said through the prophet Samuel to Saul, who should have killed Amalek but did not: 'For this, that you have rejected my word and did not kill Amalek, I will also reject you from being king.' " [68]

In the meantime, then, King Sigismund of Hungary was leaning out of the window of the refectory, for that hearing was held in the monastery of the Minorites. He had risen and was speaking with Count Palatine of the Rhine and the burgrave of Nuremberg,[69] saying to them that in all Christendom there had never been a greater heretic than this—pointing to Master John Hus. When, however, Master John Hus spoke about the king and Saul, as mentioned above, the prelates shouted, saying: "Call the king!" For indeed the king had not heard it on account, as said before, of his conversing about Master John with the princes through the window. Because of that, the presiding judges shouted to those who were near the king: "Draw him, the king, away that he may hear, for it concerns him!" And they made Master John Hus repeat that statement. When he finished and qualified it, King Sigismund said: "John Hus, no one lives without sin." And the cardinal of Cambrai said to the Master, wishing thereby to incite the seculars more against him: "It was not enough for you to despise the spiritual order by attempting to overthrow it by your writings and teachings, and now you also wish to overthrow the status of the royal order and of kings?" And Páleč rising, began to adduce certain laws in order to prove that Saul had still been a king and had been called king, despite the Lord having said these things to him; and that David had not permitted, but had forbidden him to be killed, not on account of the sanctity of life that he did not possess, but because of the sanctity of his anointing. And further, because the Master adduced St. Cyprian, who says: "Vainly does he choose the name of Christianity who does

---

[67] "Responsio Magistri Joannis Hus, ad scripta M. Stephani Paletz," usually referred to as "Contra Paletz," in *Historia et Monumenta,* I, 319. The text differs slightly, inasmuch as Cyprian's name is omitted, while after the reference to Matt. 7 the phrase "are false prophets" is added.

[68] This is found substantially in I Sam. 15:26.

[69] Princes Ludwig and Frederick are meant.

not in the least imitate Christ in morals," [70] Páleč exclaimed: "Yea! what fatuousness! What does it have to do with the matter to allege that if someone is not a good Christian he is therefore not a true pope, bishop, or prelate, or even king? For the learned know that the terms 'pope,' 'bishop,' 'king' are the names of office, while 'Christian' is in fact a name of merit. Thus it is proved that someone may be a true pope, king, or bishop, although he is not a true Christian." And Master John, after a pause, said: "Indeed, this is clear in regard to the already deposed Pope John XXIII, who is now called Balthassarre Coxa or Cossa: if he had been a true pope, why was he deposed?" And King Sigismund said: "Indeed, recently the lords of the Council agreed in the opinion that Balthassarre was a true pope, but because of his notorious crimes, by which he had scandalized the Church of God and had wasted the goods of the Church, was he deposed from the papacy." [71]

2. "The grace of predestination is the bond whereby the body of the Church and every member of it is linked indissolubly with the head." Chap. II, page 2.

"It agrees with the text as stated. And it is proved by the Apostle in Romans 8: 'Who shall separate us from the love of Christ? tribulation, or distress, or persecution?' And further on he concludes in regard to the predestinate, saying: 'I am sure that neither death, nor life, nor angels, nor principalities, nor powers, nor force, nor things present, nor things future, nor terror, nor depth, nor any other creature will be able to separate us from the love of God which is in Christ Jesus, our Lord.' [72] There is no doubt but that the Apostle, a member of the Church, speaks for all members of the Church who enjoy the love of God, which is the grace of predestination, whereby they are joined with Christ the head. Indeed, that Head speaks in John 10: 'My sheep hear

[70] Cf. Roy Deferrari, trans. and ed., *Saint Cyprian, Treatises* (New York, 1958), p. 302.

[71] Sigismund, a layman, did not recognize that this really was the crux of the whole matter: for if, as Páleč consistently urged, papacy was the name of office with which the personal character of its holder had nothing to do, then indeed the Council had no right to depose John XXIII "because of his notorious crimes." And if the Council acknowledged him as the "true" pope, and later in dealing with Gregory XII acknowledged him also as the "true" pope (he is so acknowledged to this day), how could the Council hold that two popes were true at the same time? At any rate, this article was not included in the final charges.

[72] Rom. 8:35, 38–39. Hus is of course citing the Vulgate version, which differs from the *textus receptus*.

my voice and I know them, and they follow me; and I will give them eternal life; and they shall not perish eternally and none shall snatch them out of my hand.' [73] Let the deceiver, therefore, know that the joining of the body of the Church and of Christ the head is not corporeal but spiritual"; [74] and so forth in the book.

When that reading was concluded, the Master said: "By thus limiting the concept of the Church to the congregation or totality of the predestinate, as it is limited in the first articles, every member of that Church as well as the body of the Church is then indissolubly joined to that head by the grace of predestination; as is proved by the authority of the Apostle and of Christ, cited in the text, and by other saints."

3. "If a pope is wicked and particularly if he is foreknown, then like Judas the apostle he is a devil, a thief, and son of perdition, and not the head of the holy Church militant; for he is not a member of the Church militant."

This does not agree with the book in that form, but stands as follows in Chap. II, page 4:

"For if a pope is wicked, and particularly if he is foreknown, then like Judas the apostle he is a devil, a thief, and son of perdition; how then is he the head of the holy Church militant, its corporeal head,— as the deceiver says—since he is not truly a member of the holy Church militant? For if he were a member of the holy Church, then he would be a member of Christ, and if he were a member of Christ, he would adhere to Christ by the grace of predestination and of present righteousness, and would be of one spirit with God, as the apostle argues in I Cor. 6, saying: 'Do you not know that your bodies are members of Christ?' " [75] and so forth in the book.

4. "A wicked or foreknown pope or prelate is not truly, but only

---

[73] John 10:27–28.

[74] "Contra Paletz," in *Historia et Monumenta,* I, 321. This text omits from the quotation of Romans 8 the words from "I am sure" to "nor any other creature . . ." Páleč, in his *Contra Quidamistas,* asserted that Christ was the head of the Church militant during His life; and before His assumption, not to leave the Church without a head (*acephalous*), He appointed Peter to that position. Later he asserted that Christ is the head of *both* the Church militant and Church universal. Páleč's position is contrary even to the official Roman Catholic doctrine. to the official Roman Catholic doctrine.

[75] I Cor. 6:15. In the "Contra Paletz," *Historia et Monumenta,* I, 322; this entire text appears in a slightly different form. Again, as in so many other instances, the disputants argue at cross purposes: Páleč insists that the pope is the head of the Church by virtue of office, while Hus speaks of the foreknown pope who is therefore not a member of the *holy,* i.e., invisible Church.

nominally, a shepherd, for in truth he is a thief and a robber." Chap. II, page 5.

It stands in the book as follows: "For if he is wicked, then he is a hireling of whom the Savior said in John 10: 'A hireling who is not a shepherd, whose own the sheep are not, sees the wolf coming and abandons the sheep and flees.' [76] And so do in the end all the wicked and the foreknown. Such a wicked or foreknown pope or prelate, therefore, is a shepherd nominally, but in truth a thief and a robber." [77] And he proves this extensively in the book; consult there further.

After that was concluded, Master John said: "I have delimited and now delimit all such [statements] that as to merit and thus truly and worthily, before God, are such not popes, prelates, or shepherds, etc.; but as to the office and the reputation of men they are popes, pastors, priests, and others like this."

Immediately a certain monk from Froettstedt,[78] dressed in a black cape over which was draped something shiny black—it appeared to be satin, rose up behind him and said: "Lords, see to it that this Hus does not deceive himself as well as you with these explanations, even if they are in his book. Not long ago at a hearing I also objected to him about these articles and said to him: 'Master, perhaps these wicked popes and such others are not such well and truly as to merit, but are such as to the office. Therefore, he is now employing these explanations that he has learned and heard from me—and not because they are stated in his books.'" Master John, turning to him, said: "Have you not heard that they are in my book and were recently read here? What does it profit to say that the wicked and foreknown bishops, prelates, and priests are not truly and worthily, according to present righteousness, bishops, prelates, or priests, but are unworthy ministers of the sacraments of God, since they are not such truly and worthily as to merit but as to the office? I have stated in my book that they are unworthy ministers of the sacraments, through whom nevertheless God baptizes or consecrates. It remains true that they are such priests, prelates, and bishops and others like them." After a pause the Master added, saying: "That was well shown in [the case] of John XXIII, once pope, now called Balthassarre, whether he were a true pope or actually

---

[76] John 10:12.

[77] "Contra Paletz," in *Historia et Monumenta*, I, 322, slightly changed.

[78] Froettstedt in Thuringia.

a thief and a robber." And they, looking at one another, derided him, saying: "Indeed, he was a true pope." [79]

5. "The pope is not nor ought to be called the most holy even according to office; otherwise a king ought also to be called the most holy according to office, and executioners, public criers, and devils ought to be called holy."

This is not in the book as abstracted, but differently. Chap. II, page 5, it is proved as follows: "The deceiver should say that if someone is the most holy father, then he exercises that paternity in a most holy manner; and if he is the worst father, then he exercises that paternity in the worst manner. Similarly, if he is the most holy bishop, then he is the best bishop. And when he [Páleč, 'the deceiver'] says that to be pope is the name of office, it follows that the wicked and foreknown pope is the most holy man, and consequently as to his office is the best. And since no one can be the best according to office unless he exercises that office in the best [manner], it follows that a wicked and foreknown pope exercises the office the best; but he cannot exercise it the best unless he be morally good. As the Savior says in Matthew 12: 'How can you speak good when you are evil?' [80] It follows that a wicked and foreknown pope is morally good during that particular time or moment, which is a contradiction." Further on it is written: "And if by reason of office the pope is called the most holy, why is not the king of the Romans by reason of his office called the most holy, since the king—according to Augustine—occupies the place of Christ's deity, while a priest like the pope [holds the place] of Christ's humanity? Why also should not the judges and magistrates, yea, the executioners and public criers be called holy, since they hold an office ministering to the benefit and merit of the Church of Christ?" [81] And so forth as is shown in the book where he argues these things against doctor Páleč.

When this article was finished, Master John said: "Indeed, I do not know the ground for calling the pope the most holy, since it should suffice him that he both be called and be holy. For it is read concerning

---

[79] In Páleč's polemic with Hus, he asserted that John XXIII had been appointed by Christ Himself, and that this is required to be believed (*est fides ecclesiae*). *Antihus*, Chap. V, 67–68; Kybal, *op. cit.*, II, 237–38.

[80] Matt. 12:34.

[81] "Contra Paletz," in *Historia et Monumenta*, I, 322–23; the text there is slightly changed.

Christ: 'You alone are holy, you alone are Lord,' [82] etc. And Him I call truly the most holy, and thus about the others."

6. "If the pope lives in a manner contrary to Christ, even if he were rightly, legally, and canonically elected according to human election, he has entered the papacy by another way than through Christ."

It does not agree with the book, but is otherwise, as follows. Chap. III, page 1:

"If the pope lives in a manner contrary to Christ, in splendor, avarice, vengeance, and voluptuousness, how has he not ascended into the sheepfold of the sheep by another way than the lowly door, the Lord Jesus Christ? And granted, as you say, that he has ascended by a rightful and legitimate election—which I call an election accomplished principally by God, not merely according to the common human constitution—it still remains valid that he has ascended by another means. For Judas Iscariot was elected to the episcopate by God Jesus Christ rightly and legitimately, as Christ says in John 6: 'Have I not chosen you twelve, and one of you is a devil?'; [83] nevertheless, he ascended into the sheepfold of the sheep by another way, for he was a thief, a devil, and son of perdition. Has he not ascended by another way when the Savior said of him at the Last Supper before His death, in John 13: 'He who eats bread with me, has lifted his heel against me?' [84] etc. And this same is extensively proved in the book by blessed Bernard to Pope Eugenius toward the end of the chapter."

After this was finished and read, Master John Hus said: "That is what I say; that if the pope or another prelate lives contrary to Christ in the above-mentioned vices, he has ascended by another way, even though he was elected by men to such an office; for he has not ascended into the sheepfold of the Church by the lowly door, the Lord Jesus Christ. Thus it was shown concerning Judas, although he was elected to the apostolate by Christ, he nevertheless did not ascend through Christ, for he was a thief and a miser and son of perdition." Instantly rising, Páleč said: "Yea, what fatuity! Judas was elected by Christ or through Christ—and yet he has entered by another way and not through

---

[82] This reference to Christ is found in Luke 4:34, where the demoniac says of Him: "I know who you are, the Holy One of God"; or in Lev. 19:2, where it is applied to God; "for I the Lord your God am holy" as is so repeated throughout the chapter.

[83] John 6:70.

[84] John 13:18. "Contra Paletz," in *Historia et Monumenta*, I, 323–24; two passages are conflated.

Christ!" And Master John Hus: "Indeed, it is quite true that he was elected by Christ; nonetheless, he entered by another way, for he was a thief, a devil, and son of perdition." And Páleč added: "Someone may be rightly and legitimately elected to the papacy or episcopacy, yet afterward may live contrary to Christ; he did not, on that account, ascend by another way." Master Hus amplified it further: "I say, furthermore, that whoever has simoniacally entered the episcopacy, prelacy, etc., or any other benefice whatever, not with the intention of laboring in the Church of God, but rather in order to live daintily, voluptuously, lustfully and proudly, every such person has ascended in another way; for he has not ascended by the lowly door, the Lord Jesus Christ. And by the testimony of the Gospel, every such person is a thief and a robber," [85] etc.

7. "The condemnation of the forty-five articles of Wyclif pronounced by the doctors is irrational and unjust, and the reason alleged by them is fictitious: namely, that none of them is catholic, but every one of them is either heretical, or erroneous, or scandalous." Chap. IV, page 1.

Is does not agree with the book, but is as follows:

"The forty-five articles are all condemned for this reason, that none of these forty-five articles is catholic, but every one of them is either heretical, or erroneous, or scandalous. O doctor! where is the proof? You are a deceiver, falsely making a case you do not prove, etc.; for you show no Scripture to the contrary." [86] And he argued this extensively in the treatise.

The article being finished, they thereupon read elsewhere, where it appeared to be stated "why do not now the city-hall doctors [87] include in their condemnation that article" about the tithes and offerings; for what they had condemned in writing they approve in deed. For "arriving at the city hall," they requested that their tax [ecclesiastical payment] be refunded to them, since it is alms. And "some of the councilors" responded, "why they should insist on what they had

---

[85] Cf. the extended treatment of this subject in Hus's treatise "On Simony," Spinka, *Advocates of Reform,* XIV, esp. pp. 211–33.

[86] "Contra Paletz," in *Historia et Monumenta,* I, 324.

[87] This refers to the Synod held at the Old Town City Hall on July 16, 1412, at which Wyclif's articles were condemned. The text of the resolutions is found in Sedlák, *Studie* I, 55 ff. The one about the tithes is No. 18, condemning the thesis that "tithes are only alms." Later some of the doctors protested to the City Hall officials against paying the tax. This is what Hus ridicules.

previously condemned as heresy," and added: "They condemned joyfully but paid the tax tearfully." The cardinal of Cambrai said: "Master, you told us that you wish to defend no error of Wyclif, and see! here it is now evident from your books that you have publicly defended those articles. And there certainly is stated much that is scandalous and harsh." And the Master responded: "Reverend father! As I said before, I still say that I do not wish to defend either Wyclif's or anyone else's errors. But because it seemed to me to be against my conscience simply to consent to their condemnation, there being no Scripture to the contrary, therefore it did not seem to me [right] to consent immediately to their condemnations. Especially because their reason, which is nondiscriminating, cannot be verified in relation to any of its particulars, as I said before."

ARTICLES ABSTRACTED FROM THE TREATISE WRITTEN AGAINST MASTER STANISLAV OF ZNOJMO

1. "Not because the electors, or the greater part of them, have assented *viva voce*, in accordance with human rite, to some person, is that person *ipso facto* legitimately elected, or is *ipso facto* the manifest and true successor of Christ or the vicar of the Apostle Peter in the ecclesiastical office; but for the reason that the more abundantly and meritoriously one labors for the benefit of the Church, the more abundant power therefor one has for it from God. *Ibid.,* folio 13."

It stands in the book as follows:

"For the electors are blameless in electing a woman to an ecclesiastical office, as appears [in the case] of Agnes called John, who for more than two years occupied the papacy. Indeed, it may happen that they may elect a robber, a thief, and a devil, as Christ elected Judas, and in consequence they may elect Antichrist. And it happens that they elect a person from love, avarice, or hatred, in which case God does not assent approvingly. It also happens that they elect a wicked person whose passive election God approves. It is evident that not because the electors, or the greater part of them, have assented *viva voce*, in accordance with human rite, to some person, is that person *ipso facto* legitimately elected, or is *ipso facto* the manifest successor or vicar of the Apostle Peter or of another apostle in the ecclesiastical office. Therefore, those alone can make a probable estimate of the elected who elect most conformably with the Scriptures, drawing upon revelation. Hence, whether the electors have chosen well or ill, we should believe the works of the elected. For that reason the more abundantly and meritoriously one labors for the benefit of the Church, the more abundant power therefor he has for it from God. And this Christ Jesus said in John 10: 'Believe the work,' " [88] etc.

It is also evident in the case of John XXIII, whom and what kind of man they elected, from the fifty-four articles issued against him by the Council of Constance at that time [89] when and in what year these things were done, in the same place—that he was a simoniac, murderer, a pirate, and others like this.

2. "The foreknown pope is not the head of the holy Church of God."

That statement is not found in the book, but is stated as follows in Chap. II, folio 9:

"I would gladly receive from the doctor [Stanislav] an effective reason why that question is a faithless one and why he said that I asked faithlessly when I said: 'If the pope is foreknown, in what way is he the head of the holy Church?' [90] Yea, the Truth Who cannot fail in argument, not arguing faithlessly, asked the scribes and Pharisees in Matt. 12, saying: 'You brood of vipers, how can you speak good, when you are evil?' [91] I also inquire of the scribes: 'If the pope is foreknown and thus of the brood of vipers, in what way is he the head of the holy Church of God?' Let the scribes and Pharisees, who were in the council at the Prague Town Hall, respond! [92] For it is more possible that the foreknown would speak good things, since he could be in grace ac-

[88] John 10:38. The entire article is in "Responsio Joannis Hus ad scripta M. Stanislai," usually referred to as "Contra Stanislaum," *Historia et Monumenta,* I, 331–65.

[89] Originally, the Council drew up seventy-two articles against Pope John, which included charges of his having poisoned Pope Alexander V and of heresy. But these charges along with some others were dropped, thus reducing the total to fifty-four. This was done not because the eighteen excluded articles were proved untrue, but because it was feared that they would prove too offensive to the membership of the Church. But this is not to say that all the articles, whether retained or dropped, were actually proved true by a due legal process: the aim was to depose John, not to prove whatever wrongs or crimes he committed. The text is found in Hefele-Leclercq, *op. cit.,* VII/I, 234–39; cf. also p. 230, n. 3.

[90] I.e., whether the foreknown pope is the head of the Church, which Hus denied and on that account Stanislav called him an infidel.

[91] Matt. 12:34.

[92] Cf. note 87 of this chapter.

cording to present righteousness, than that he be the head of the holy Church of God! Also in John 5 the Savior argues, inquiring thus of the Jews: 'How can you believe who receive glory from one another and the glory which is from God alone you do not seek?'[93] And I inquire similarly: 'If the pope is foreknown, who receives the glory from the world, but the glory which is from God alone he does not seek, how can he be the head of the holy Church of God? For it is more possible that the foreknown pope, who receives the glory from the world, would believe than that he be the head of the holy Church of God'," etc. He argues the same extensively in the book.[94]

The Master said: "Considering the Church as the congregation or the totality of the predestinate, I ask at that place where the lector has read: 'If the pope is foreknown, how is the head of *that* holy Church of God?'"

3. "There is not a spark of apparent proof that there should be one head ruling the Church in spiritual matters that would always abide with that Church militant." Chap. V, folio 2.

It is so contained in the book: "The [following] consequence is therefore distorted: the king of Bohemia is the head of the kingdom of Bohemia; *therefore*, a foreknown pope is the head of the entire Church militant. For Christ is the head in spiritual matters, ruling the Church militant. This is much more necessary than that there should be a Caesar ruling in temporal matters. Because Christ, sitting at the right hand of God the Father, necessarily rules the Church militant as its head [*capitaliter*]. And there is not a spark of apparent proof that there should be one head in spiritual matters ruling the Church that always abides with that Church militant, unless an unbeliever should wish to assert heretically that the Church militant should perpetually remain as an abiding city here and not seek a future one. And further the unsuitability of the comparative relation of the analogy is evident in so far as that the foreknown pope is the head of the Church militant even as the king is the head of the kingdom of Bohemia," etc.[95]

When that was finished and read, Master John said: "Indeed, it is true that such a corporeal head with which the doctors have dealt in their statement, need not always be and abide corporeally with the

[93] John 5:44.
[94] "Contra Stanislaum," in *Historia et Monumenta*, I, 339–40. This article was excluded from the final charges; it appears that the judges themselves found it unsupported by evidence.
[95] *Ibid.*, p. 346.

Church militant. For just now we have no such corporeal head, but only the Lord Jesus Christ."

4. "Christ without such monstrous heads, through His true disciples scattered over the circumference of the earth, would rule His Church better."

That agrees with the book in that form, in Chap. V, folio 1:

"And although the doctor [Stanislav] says that the body of the Church militant is sometimes without a head [*acephalum*], we nevertheless truly believe that Jesus Christ is the head over the entire Church, ruling it indefectibly, infusing it with spiritual mobility and sensitivity. I maintain that the doctor will not to the Day of Judgment be able to prove that there is another head of the Church than the Lord Jesus Christ himself. Nor is the doctor able to give a reason why the Church at the time of Agnes had been without a head for two years and five months, living on the part of many members in Christ's grace. Why cannot it in the same way be without a head for many years, when Christ without such monstrous heads, through His true disciples scattered over the circumference of the earth, would rule His Church better?" And so forth in the book.[96]

After this was finished, they said: "Look! he is now playing a prophet!" And Master John Hus said: "I say that the Church at the time of the apostles was infinitely better ruled than it is now ruled. What deters Christ from not regulating it better without such monstrous heads as there have been now, through His true disciples? And see! now we have no such head[97] and yet Christ does not desist from regulating His Church." And they derided him.

5. "Peter was not the universal shepherd of Christ's sheep, nor the Roman pontiff."

That statement is not in the book, but in Chap. V, folio 3, it is written:

"It is evident, in the second place, from the words of Christ that He did not restrict the jurisdiction over the whole world to Peter, or only to one province; nor similarly in regard to the other apostles. Some, therefore, traveled over more regions, others over fewer, preaching the kingdom of God; as Paul, who labored more than all others, personally

---

[96] *Ibid.*, p. 347. In admitting that the Church was occasionally without a head (*acephalous*), Stanislav contradicted Páleč on this point and thus admitted that Hus was to that degree right.

[97] This was true because John XXIII was deposed, Gregory XII resigned, and Benedict XIII was not recognized and was deposed shortly afterward.

visited and converted more regions. Hence, every apostle or his vicar was permitted to convert or confirm in the faith of Christ as many people or lands as he was capable [of doing]; and there was no restriction, except for insufficiency," etc.[98]

6. "The apostles and the faithful priests of the Lord had firmly ruled the Church in things necessary for salvation before the papal office was instituted: they would do so if there were no pope—as is highly possible —until the day of judgment." [99] The fourth sextern, folio 1.

After this was read, they again said: "Yea, he is playing a prophet!" And Master John said: "It is indeed true that the apostles before the institution of this kind of papal office had firmly ruled the Church in matters necessary to its salvation, and certainly better than it is ruled now. Their faithful successors can do the same. And note! now we have no pope, and this situation may last perhaps for two years, or who knows how long a time!" And Páleč said: "Oh, is that highly possible?" And the Master: "Indeed, it is possible!" And Stokes the Englishman said to the Master: "Why do you glory in these writings and teachings, ascribing in vain their title to yourself, since these teachings and statements are not yours, but rather Wyclif's, whose way you follow?" [100]

When, therefore, the already mentioned articles, both of the testimonies and those immediately preceding, were finished and there already ensued near silence, the cardinal of Cambrai said: "Master John! behold, two ways are placed before you, of which choose one! Either you throw yourself entirely and totally on the grace and into the hands of the Council, that whatever the Council shall dictate to you, therewith you shall be content. And the Council, out of reverence for the lord king of the Romans here and his brother, the king of Bohemia, and for your own good, will deal kindly and humanely with you. Or if you still wish to hold and defend some articles of the fore-

---

[98] *Ibid.,* p. 348. Hus asserts that the pope is not the shepherd of the Church universal, for besides the Roman Church there exist other Christian churches— such as the Eastern Orthodox. The pope, however, is the shepherd of the Roman Church, provided he is of the predestinate. If he is not one of the elect, then he may hold the office *de facto,* but not in accordance with the divine will. Páleč and Stanislav held that if the pope had been legitimately elected by the cardinals, he is the head of the whole Church militant irrespective of his character.

[99] *Ibid.,* p. 354.

[100] Actually, Hus did *not* follow Wyclif, who advocated that the papal office be altogether abolished. Hus only asserted that the Church could exist for a long time without a pope as far as things necessary for salvation were concerned.

mentioned, and if you desire still another hearing, it shall be granted you. But consider that there are here great and enlightened men—doctors and masters—who have such strong reasons against your articles, that it is to be feared lest you become involved in greater errors, if you wish to defend and hold those articles. I counsel you—I do not speak as judge." And others added: "Surely, Master John, it were better for you, as the lord cardinal says, that you throw yourself totally on the grace of the Council and hold nothing obstinately." And the Master, inclining his head, replied humbly: "Most reverend fathers! I came here freely, not to defend anything obstinately, but that if in some matters I had stated anything not quite well or defectively, I would humbly submit to the instruction of the Council. I pray, however, for God's sake that a hearing be granted me for the explanation of my meaning of the articles brought against me, and of the writings of the holy doctors. And if my reasons and Scripture will not suffice, I wish to submit humbly to the instruction of the Council." Instantly many shouted, saying: "See! he speaks captiously and obstinately: he is willing to submit to the instruction, but not to the correction and decision of the Council!" And he replied: "Indeed, I wish to submit to the instruction, correction, and decision of the Council. God is my witness that I speak sincerely and not captiously." Then the cardinal of Cambrai said to him: "Master John! since you are willing to throw yourself on the grace of the Council and to submit to its instruction, you should know that the instruction to you by well-nigh sixty doctors —of whom some have already left while the Parisians have just arrived —without anyone contradicting, and from the command and the commission of the Council, is this: that you first humbly acknowledge your error in these articles that you have hitherto held; secondly, that you recant those articles and swear that you will not to all eternity hold, preach, or teach them; thirdly, that you publicly revoke those articles and retract those which were here proved against you that you have held, written, and preached; and fourthly, that you expound, hold, and preach their opposite."

And Master John, other things having been tossed about and brought out here and there by others, said: "Most reverend father! I am ready humbly to obey the Council and be instructed. But I pray for God's sake that you desire not to lay a snare of damnation for me, that I be not forced to lie and abjure those articles of which—God and conscience are my witnesses—I know nothing. The witnesses have borne

testimony against me of what has never entered my heart: and especially
that after the consecration, the material bread remains in the sacrament
of the altar. Those, however, of which I know and which are stated
in my books, if I be instructed as to their opposite, I am willing humbly
to revoke. But that I should abjure all the articles laid against me, of
which many are—God knows—falsely ascribed to me, I should by
lying prepare for myself a snare of damnation. For 'to abjure,' as I
recall having read in the *Catholicon*,[101] is to renounce a formerly held
error. But since many articles that I have never held are ascribed to
me, nor have they entered my heart, it appears to me, therefore, contrary to conscience to abjure them and to lie." And they said: "No!
no! that it not [the meaning] of 'to abjure.' " And the Master said:
"Thus have I read: that is 'to abjure.' " And many shouted when he
called conscience to witness, saying: "And perhaps your conscience has
never told you that you have erred or err?" [102]

In the meantime the king said: "Hear, Hus! Why do you refuse to
abjure all the erroneous articles of which the witnesses, as you say,
have wrongly deposed against you? On the contrary, I am willing to
abjure and do abjure all errors and wish to hold no error. Nevertheless,
it is not necessary that I have first held any of them." And Hus: "Lord
King, that is not what the term or word 'to abjure' connotes." And
the cardinal of Florence said: "Master John! There shall be given you
in writing a sufficiently qualified formula of those articles, in which
form you ought to abjure them; deliberate then what you ought to or
want to do."

Then the king said: "John Hus! behold, there are two ways placed
before you: either that you abjure and revoke the errors here condemned, and surrender yourself to the grace of the Council, in which
case the Council will to some extent grant you grace. Or, if you wish,
that you defend those errors; then the Council and the doctors have
their rules as to what they ought finally to do with you!" And he replied: "Most serene prince! I do not wish to hold any error, but am
willing to submit humbly to the Council's decision. Only [I pray] that
I may not offend God and my conscience, nor say that I have held
those errors that I never held nor did they ever enter my heart. And

---

[101] The medieval theological dictionary similar to such handbooks today.

[102] This is an outstanding instance of the Council's demand of unconditional
submission, even involving perjury, i.e., swearing to something one knows as
untrue, or as Hus expresses it bluntly, to lie.

I also pray that an adequate hearing be granted me that I may explain my meaning concerning certain points and articles brought against me; especially concerning the pope and the heads and members of the Church, in which there exists an ambiguity between me [and them], so that they would be able to apprehend my meaning. For I concede and say that although the pope, bishops, prelates, and others like them, if they are foreknown and in mortal sin, are not such truly as to merit, nor worthy before God at the time; yet they are such as to office: that is, the pope, bishops, prelates, and others like them. When, as I said, they are unworthy ministers of the sacraments."

After many other things had been tossed to and fro, the king again said: "Listen, John Hus! As I told you yesterday, I still say to you and cannot keep on repeating it to you: you are old enough, you could well understand, if you wished. You have already heard that the lords have proposed two ways to you: either that you surrender yourself in all things to the grace of the sacred Council, and that the sooner the better, and revoke all the errors, those written in your books as well as those that you yourself have acknowledged and concerning which they have adduced sufficient testimony against you; which we must believe. For the Scriptures say that 'in the mouth of two or three witnesses stands every word.' [103] And here several and great men have deposed about some of the articles! And for those errors do penance with a contrite heart, not feigned, as the Council will dictate to you. And of those [articles], as the lords say, [you must] expound and write the opposite and swear that you will not further hold them and others. Or, if you wish to hold and defend them stubbornly, then the Council will surely proceed against you according to its laws." And a certain old and bald bishop from Poland said: "The laws concerning heretics are clear in the *Clementines* and in the *Sexts*,[104] how they should be dealt with!"

And the Master replied to the king: "Most serene prince! I have already said before that I came here freely, not with the intention of wishing to hold any error or heresy; but that I wish humbly to submit to the instruction of the Council." And many shouted: "See, he is stubborn! He is willing to submit to the instruction of the Council,

---

[103] Deut. 19:15.

[104] *Liber sextus,* a collection of laws, was promulgated in 1298 by Pope Boniface VIII as a supplement to Gratian's *Decretum* and of the collection begun by Pope Gregory IX in 1230 and promulgated by him in 1234. *Clementina* is a still later similar addition ordered by John XXII in 1317.

and has held those errors for many years; but he will not subject himself to the correction and decision of the Council and revoke those errors!" A certain fat priest, sitting in the window, [clad] in an expensive tunic—he seemed to be a Prussian—shouted: "Do not permit him to revoke, because even if he should revoke, he will not keep it. For he had sent a letter to his supporters and adherents on his departure, to whom it had been publicly read, that even if he were forced to revoke, he would do so solely with his mouth but not with his heart.[105] Therefore do not on any account believe him, for he will not keep it!" And the Master said: "Indeed, I humbly wish to subject myself to the instruction, correction, and decision of the Council. And I made public declarations in the treatise *Contra Magistrum Stanislaum* that I am willing to submit humbly to the decision of the holy mother Church, as every faithful Christian ought to submit." [106] And Páleč, rising, said: "If I protested volubly that I do not want to slap Master Albert [107] sitting here next to me, but nonetheless did slap him, or while I was slapping him, what kind of protest would that be? Thus you, too, protest that you do not wish to hold and defend any error, and especially of Wyclif himself, while you are defending them!" And he [Páleč] continued: "Most reverend fathers! here are nine articles of Wyclif himself"—and he read them *seriatim* from a paper—"against five of which Master Stanislav of Znojmo long ago publicly preached in condemnation in the Church of the Blessed Virgin before the Týn Square [108] in the presence of a multitude of clergy. Duke Ernest of Austria was then in Prague. I similarly preached there against them later.[109] And this Hus with his accomplices stubbornly defended them in schools and in public. And you wrote"—he addressed Master John—"certain treatises in their defense that we have here; and if you do not surrender your writings, we will surrender them." And he [Hus] said: "Surrender them." The king said: "If you have any such writings, it were well if you surrendered them to this Council for their examination; and if you do not surrender them, others will." And he said: "Let them!"

<hr>

[105] This refers to Hus's farewell letter, which was falsified in its Latin translation and its true meaning subverted. Cf. Chap. I, pp. 96–98.

[106] "Contra Stanislaum," in *Historia et Monumenta*, I, 334.

[107] Perhaps Albert Warentrapp.

[108] This is the famous old church, known as Týn on the Old Town square. *Laeta curia* was the ancient market place, known as Tronhof; at present it is called Ungelt. Stanislav preached the sermon on August 28, 1412. Duke Ernest was in Prague later.

[109] Páleč preached the sermon on September 4.

In the meantime, they cited an article [to prove] that he had commented on a certain papal decree.[110] He said that he himself had not made those comments, nor had he ever seen those comments on the said decree until in the Dominican prison, when they were shown him by the commissioners. And they said: "But you know who made the comments? Tell us under oath which you took to tell the truth." And he said: "I do not know for certain who made the comments; but I heard that it was Master Jesenic who commented on that decree." And they said: "However, in the prison you stated that he had made the comment." And he: "I did not assert it, but spoke from hearsay only." And they: "Do you approve that comment or do you agree with it?" And he: "How should I agree with it when, as I said before, I have never seen it?" And they to him: "But do you agree with it now?" He replied: "I do not agree with it." And from so great a harassment he already grew very pale, for—as those said who knew about it—he had spent the whole night without sleep because of toothache and headache, and began to be shaken with fever.[111]

Thereafter, they read an article about the three beheaded [young men] [112] who, as they stated, were beheaded on account of his offensive preaching by which he had induced them to disobedience of the Apostolic See and of the papal letters, so that they were beheaded for loudly denouncing the apostolic letters. He later ordered his priests and disciples to carry them [the three dead men] to the Bethlehem Chapel singing "These are saints," and the next day he ordered that instead of the masses for the dead, the martyrs' mass be sung. Thus he sanctified and, as far as he could, canonized those beheaded youths. Later in a sermon he said that he would not want to surrender them for as great a mass of silver as the certain mass in the said chapel to which he pointed.

The Master replied: "It is true that they were beheaded. But that I ordered them to be carried with such singing is not true; for I was not there." [113]

---

[110] This refers to the papal bull concerning Wyclif issued in 1413, upon which John of Jesenice commented critically. Cf. the text of the bull and John's remarks about it in Palacký, pp. 467–71.

[111] Hus describes it in his letter of June 7; cf. Part II, No. 10.

[112] This refers to the beheading of three young men on July 11, 1412, because they had protested against the papal indulgences.

[113] The procession was led by Hus's friend, Master John of Jičín; Hus was not present.

And Náz, instantly rising, said: "Hear me, I pray—just two words! Since a mention was made about those beheaded, it is well known to me, for I was then with the king of Bohemia—then [king] of the Romans as well—where after this Hus had preached much against obedience to the Apostolic See and to the papal letters and had incited his hearers thereto, directly the said beheaded [youths] shouted during a certain sermon against the apostolic letters. And the king of Bohemia ordered them to be beheaded. After they had been beheaded, [Hus] preached in Bethlehem as he pleased and as you have already heard. Later, on their account, the community rose up against the council and the Prague councilors, saying that they had unjustly ordered innocent men to be beheaded. And there arose a great riot and clamor; for many hundreds of people came to the town hall, saying that they, too, were prepared to die for the truth. Hence, the councilors, being unable to quell the tumult, went to the king and asked what he wanted done, because they could not quell the riot. And the king of Bohemia said: "Even if there were thousand such, let them suffer the same fate as the others! And if there are not enough justices and officers here in the kingdom, I will have them brought from other areas." And the Master said: "Notice, lords, that this doctor slanders the lord king; for the king did not command them [the three men] to be beheaded." And Páleč, rising, said: "Because the king by a public proclamation commanded that no one was to contradict the papal bulls, and these did contradict them publicly, it was, therefore, by virtue of that royal command that they were beheaded—and Hus canonized them! For if you read in his book *De ecclesia*, Chap. XX *Ff*, you will see that he canonized them." [114] And they read a prophecy—I believe from Daniel 11—where it is stated: "And they shall fall by the sword and flame and by captivity for some days, and many shall join them deceitfully." [115] And later this was fulfilled in those three "laymen, Martin, Stašek, and John who," not consenting, indeed "contradicting Anti-

[114] This is actually found in Chap. XXI, where all that Hus wrote about the incident is as follows: "The text makes understandable the facts of experience; for simple laymen and priests, taught by God's grace, teach very many by the example of good life and, publicly contradicting Antichrist's lying words, perish by the sword. This is seen in [the case] of the laymen, John, Martin, and Stašek who, contradicting Antichrist's lying disciples, perished by the sword." Thomson, *op. cit., p.* 201. As to whether the three youths were executed in accordance with the king's proclamation, Páleč is correct in his statement; but not that Hus "canonized" them.

[115] Dan. 11:33–34.

christ's lies," stretched out their necks to the sword. And many others were ready to do the same, while many without conviction associated themselves with them who, frightened by the threats of Antichrist, turned to flight and "went back," [116] etc. When this was read, the presidents looked at each other as if they were in a fashion amazed.

Later the English produced a copy of a certain letter of the Oxford University brought to Prague [117] which, they said, Master John had publicly read in a sermon and the seal of which he had exhibited in order to commend Wyclif. After they had read it, they requested him to say whether he had read it. He replied that he had, since it, bearing the seal of the University of Oxford, had been brought to Prague by two students. Then the English requested him to name those students, saying that the letter had been forged and had not come by true channels. And the Master, pointing to Páleč, said: "My friend over there knows Nicolas Faulfiš,[118] of good memory, perfectly well who, along with another—I do not know who he was [119]—brought that letter." The English questioned him where he [Faulfiš] was. The Master said: "He died, I believe, somewhere between Spain and England." And they laughed at him. And Páleč said: "Oh, that Faulfiš was not English but a Czech. And note, most reverend fathers, that that same Faulfiš brought a piece of stone from the grave of Wyclif himself, which the Praguers later venerated and regarded as a relic. And of all that this Hus was aware."

Later the English read another letter with an affixed seal which contradicted the [previous] one. They said that the seal was that of the chancellor of Oxford. He wrote, not without bitterness of heart, that the disciples and imitators of John Wyclif had disseminated in the kingdom of England many errors from his books. The university, therefore, wishing to prevent such an evil, had deputed twelve eminent doctors and great theologians who, having diligently gone over his books again, drew from them two hundred and sixty articles. The university, having diligently examined them, after a mature deliberation declared that they should be burned. Out of reverence for the faith

---

[116] Allusion to John 6:67.

[117] This letter, commending Wyclif, was brought to Bohemia toward the end of 1408. Novotný, Mladoňovic's *Relatio*, p. 107, n. 27, asserts that "of its authenticity there are no reasons to doubt." The text is found in *Historia et Monumenta*, II, 542.

[118] Faulfiš studied at Oxford in 1407.

[119] The other student was George of Kněhnice.

and for this sacred Council, however, they sent and delivered them here to Constance to be condemned,[120] etc., as it is contained in that letter.

In the meantime, when they had been quiet for a while, Páleč, rising, and as if he had already heard the decision against the Master, said: "Most serene prince and most reverend fathers! I first call to witness Your Serenity and Your Reverences and God, that in those things in which I have proceeded against him [Hus], I did not do it from any malicious zeal or personal hatred—God is my witness—but solely for the reason that I should be true to my oath that I had taken, since I am a doctor of sacred theology, although an unworthy one; on that account have I done it." And Michael de Causis, who sat before the Master, rising, said: "And I likewise." To whom Master Hus replied: "I stand before God's judgment Who will judge justly both me and you according to merit."

And the cardinal of Cambrai said: "Surely he, Master Stephen, as well as the other doctors, has dealt very kindly with those books and articles; for many more and harsher ones than they have abstracted and had been deposed, thus far they always interpreted for the better. Yea, even now it is stated much more harshly in the books than it is formulated by them," etc.

After that the bishop of Riga [121] took charge of Master Hus to conduct him to the prison. As they went by Lord John of Chlum, he greeted him and extended his hand to him, consoling him. Hus was very glad that Lord John was not ashamed and did not hesitate to greet him—already rejected, despised, and regarded as heretic by almost all—and that he [Lord John] publicly extended his hand to him. Hus later wrote this to Lord John.[122]

After his departure, everyone in that place, cardinals and prelates, were about to leave and had already risen. Then the armed guards, who guarded the rear, also left, and our [friends] approached the window. Lord John of Chlum and Lord Wenceslas of Leštno and P. the bachelor [123] were still inside. It appears that the king did not notice it, but supposed them to have gone when the Master was taken to the prison. And the king said: "Most reverend fathers! You have heard

---

[120] The articles are published in Van der Hardt, *op. cit.*, IV, 325–38, and were condemned by the Council. Wyclif himself had been condemned on May 4.

[121] John of Wallenrode.

[122] See the letter to Lord John dated June 8, in Part II, No. 12.

[123] This is of course Peter of Mladoňovice.

that just one of the many things that are in his books and that he has confessed and that are sufficiently proved against him is enough to condemn him. Therefore, if he will not recant his errors and abjure and teach the contrary, let him be burned, or deal with him according to your knowledge of your laws. And be sure, that whatever he would promise, whether he intends to recant or whether he actually recants here, you do not believe him; nor would I believe him. Because, returning to the kingdom, he will go to his supporters and will disseminate those and many other errors, and the latest error will be worse than the previous. Restrain him, therefore, from any kind of preaching, so that he would no longer preach, and also that he would not again return to his supporters, lest he disseminate more of those errors. And send these articles here condemned to my brother in Bohemia, and alas! to Poland and to other lands, where he also already has his secret disciples and many supporters, and say that any people who hold these beliefs will be punished by the bishops and prelates in those lands, and so uproot the branches with the root. And let the Council write to kings and princes that they show favor to their prelates who in this sacred Council have diligently labored to extirpate these heretics. You also know that it is written "in two or three witnesses stands every word"; here, however, a hundredth part would suffice for his condemnation! Therefore, also make an end of others of his secret disciples and supporters, because I shall soon depart. And especially with him, him—and he repeated the term "him"—who is here detained.[124] And they said: "Jerome?" And he: "Yes, Jerome!" [They responded:] "Of him we shall make an end within one day. That will already be easier, because this one is the master (denoting Master Hus), and that Jerome is his disciple." The king said again: "Indeed I was still young when this sect had its origin and inception in Bohemia, and see how much it has grown and multiplied!" Then they left the said refectory, parting from one another and rejoicing.

And at every hearing, there were many armed guards with swords, crossbows, and long axes who, whenever Master John was led out or in, surrounded the said refectory.

These things, therefore, we have put down, what we saw and heard there. And if we stated anything not quite properly, we are willing to revise the account, having been instructed by those who, having also been present, remember it better. However, we have not recorded it

[124] Sigismund obviously forgot for the moment the name of Jerome of Prague.

in order to shame or laud any person, but simply—God is our witness
—to bear witness to the truth, and that we might more effectively stop
the mouths of many in the future who speak solely from contradictory
and uncertain accounts concerning the said hearing and the happenings
and acts that have taken place.[125]

---

[125] It is remarkable that Peter altogether omitted any mention of the reply
which Hus made to the final formulation of the charges against him presented
to him by the Commission on June 18. The text is found in Palacký, pp. 225–34,
and consists of thirty articles drawn largely from Hus's own writings (particularly
from De ecclesia and the treatises against Páleč and Stanislav), and additional
sixteen articles drawn from the testimony of the witnesses. Accordingly, ten
articles with which he had been charged at the public hearing of June 5, 7, and
8 were by that time eliminated. These final articles were submitted to him in
the Franciscan monastery prison, but contrary to the promise, he was not granted
a public hearing to reply to them. Thus he replied only in writing (on June 20).
And although both the charges and Hus's replies are to a large degree repetitions
of the previous accusations, with the exception of some modifications of the
articles retained; yet, for the sake of completeness, they are included in Part II,
No. 15. Also cf. my earlier work, John Hus and the Czech Reform, pp. 56–70.

Hus also received appeals from a friendly member of the Council, to whom
he refers as "Father" and whom he answers. Cf. Part II, Nos. 16–18. The letters
written between June 18 and July 5, descriptive of the events of this intervening
period, are found in Part II, Nos. 19–34.

CHAPTER V

The End of the Saintly and Reverend Master John Hus

In like manner in that year of the Lord 1415, on July 5, the Friday after St. Procopius,[1] the noble lords Wenceslas of Dubá and John of Chlum were sent by Sigismund, king of the Romans and of Hungary, along with four bishops, to the prison of the Brothers Minor in Constance to hear the final decision of Master John Hus: if he would hold the above-mentioned articles which had been, as has already been said, abstracted from his books, as well as those that had been produced against him during the course of the trial, and the depositions of the witnesses; or if he would, according to the exhortation of the Council, abjure and recant them, as has been said. When he was brought out of the prison, Lord John of Chlum said to him: "Look, Master John! we are laymen and know not how to advice you; therefore see if you feel yourself guilty in anything of that which is charged against you. Do not fear to be instructed therein and to recant. But if, indeed, you do not feel guilty of those things that are charged against you, follow the dictates of your conscience. Under no circumstances do anything against your conscience or lie in the sight of God: but rather be steadfast until death in what you know to be the truth." And he, Master John Hus, weeping, replied with humility: "Lord John, be sure that if I knew that I had written or preached anything erroneous against the law and against the holy mother Church, I would desire humbly to recant it—God is my witnes! I have ever desired to be shown better and more relevant Scripture than those that I have written and taught. And if they were shown me, I am ready most willingly to recant." To those words one of the bishops present replied to Master John: "Do you wish

---

[1] See Hus's letters written on July 5, in Part II, Nos. 34–36.

to be wiser than the whole Council?" The Master said to him: "I do not wish to be wiser than the whole Council, but I pray, give me the least one of the Council who would instruct me by better and more relevant Scripture, and I am ready instantly to recant!" To these words the bishops responded: "See, how obstinate he is in his heresy!" And with these words they ordered him to be taken back to the prison and went away.

Then the next day, which was July 6, or the Saturday after St. Procopius, in the octave of the blessed apostles Peter and Paul, the said Master John Hus was led by the archbishop of Riga[2] to the cathedral of the city of Constance, where the general session of the prelates was held, presided over by the king of the Romans and of Hungary wearing his crown.[3] In the midst of that session and church a bench like a table was elevated and on it a kind of pedestal was placed, on which the vestments and the chasuble for the mass and the sacerdotal garments were arranged for the purpose of unfrocking him, Master Hus. When, therefore, he was brought into the church and approached the said elevated bench, he fell on his knees and prayed for a long time. In the meantime the bishop of Lodi,[4] ascending the pulpit, delivered a sermon concerning heresies, declaring among other things how much harm heresies cause in the Church of God and how they tear it asunder, and how it is the duty of the king to extirpate such heresies, particularly the heresy of simony, from the Church of God.

In the meantime Henry of Piro, procurator of the Council, rising, made a motion requesting that the Council continue the trial of Master John Hus until a definite decision [could be reached].[5] Then one of

[2] John of Wallenrode, of the Order of the Teutonic Knights.

[3] The crown was held by Henry of Bavaria; it was not actually worn by Sigismund, as the famous painting of Václav Brožík mistakenly shows. In the Czech version of the *Passio,* composed later, but perhaps by Peter of Mladoňovice (Novotný in *Fontes rerum Bohemicarum,* VIII, 121–49 ascribes it to him), it is added that the archbishop with Hus had to wait in the entrance while the mass was being celebrated within (p. 127).

[4] Jacob Balardi Arrigoni, an Italian Dominican, bishop of Lodi, who preached on the text in Rom. 6:6, which in the Vulgate version reads, "That the body of sin be destroyed." The sermon is found in Novotný, *Fontes,* VIII, 489 ff.

[5] This was the usual procedure at the Council: one of the two procurators— Henry of Piro and John of Scribanis of Piacenza—presented the requests for formal actions agreed upon by the nations. When the request was granted, the proposal was then read. In this instance, it was Henry of Piro who requested the formal action against Hus.

the bishops, deputed by the Council,[6] stood up in the pulpit and read the proceedings of the trial that had been carried on between Master John and the Prague archbishop and the prelates in the Roman curia and elsewhere; and after other matters, read the articles against Master Hus himself, drawn from his books and from the trial proceedings, a copy of which, containing the comments and qualifications from the hand of Master John Hus himself, and signed by him in the prison, were delivered to us,[7] as will be further clearly described. Some of them I shall put in here, as to set down the words which he actually used at the time.

The first of these articles was this: the holy universal Church is one, which is the totality of the predestinate, etc. To that, when it was read and finished, as well as to others subsequently, Master John replied in a loud voice with the same qualifications that he had appended to them and signed with his own hand, as has been mentioned previously.[8] When, however, he answered, the cardinal of Cambrai [9] told him: "Be silent now; it were better that you reply later to all of them together." Master John replied: "And how should I reply to all of them together when I cannot reflect upon them all together?" When, therefore, he again attempted to reply to other charges that were being brought up against him, the cardinal of Florence [10] rose and told him: "Be silent now. For we have already heard you enough!" And again rising, he said to the guard: "Order him to be silent!" Master Hus, clasping his hands, implored in a loud voice, saying: "I beseech you for God's sake, hear me, so that those standing about would not believe that I have ever held such errors; then afterward do with me as you please!" When, on the contrary, he was forbidden to say anything whatever or to respond to the charges against him, he fell upon his knees, and clasping

[6] Berthold of Wildungen, the papal auditor. Peter made a mistake in calling him bishop. The representatives of the other three nations were bishops Anthony of Concordia, Stephen Coevret of Dol, Nicholas of Merseburg, Vitalis Valentini of Toulon, and Patrick Foxe of Cork.

[7] Hus succeeded in sending a copy of this document to his friends; cf. Part II, No. 15, for its translation.

[8] According to the *Passio,* Hus declared: "I doubt not that the holy Church catholic is one which is the congregation of all the elect here on the earth, and of those in purgatory, and also in heaven; they are the secret body of the head Jesus Christ." Novotný, *Fontes,* VIII, 129–30.

[9] Pierre d'Ailly, the president of the Commission and Hus's principal opponent among the cardinals.

[10] Francesco Zabarella, one of Hus's former judges, and a member of the Council's Commission.

his hands and lifting his eyes to heaven, he prayed most devoutly, committing his cause to God, the most just Judge. He did this repeatedly.

After the conclusion of the articles drawn from his books, the articles from the proceedings of the trial were read, which the depositions of the witnesses were said to have proved against him and objected to him. And to each individual accusation they adduced as witnesses pastors, canons, doctors, and other prelates without naming them personally, but mentioning them merely by their official titles and places. Among those articles was the one that after the consecration of the host there remains on the altar the material bread or the substance of the bread. Also another, that a priest in mortal sin does not transubstantiate, nor consecrate, nor baptize; and so forth about others. Then when Master John again arose, wishing to respond, the cardinal of Florence, again shouting at him, forbade him. And he [Hus], responding nonetheless, said: "I pray for God's sake, hear my meaning at least on account of those standing here, lest they believe that I have held those errors. I declare that I have never held, nor taught, nor preached that in the sacrament of the altar the material bread remains after the consecration." And subsequently he responded to other [charges] in accordance with what he had signed with his own hand.

Among other things they also accused him of the article that he wished to be and is the fourth person of the Godhead, as they stated.[11] They attempted to prove that article by [citing] a certain doctor. And the Master cried: "Name that doctor who testified that against me!" But the bishop who was reading it said: "There is no need here now that he be named." And the Master, responding, said among other things: "Be it far from me, a miserable wretch, that I should want to name myself the fourth person of the Godhead, for that has never entered my heart; but I unswervingly assert that the Father, the Son, and the Holy Spirit are one God, one essence, and a trinity of persons."

Thereupon the said lectors read that Master John Hus had appealed to God, and condemned such an appeal as an error. To that Master John responded in a loud voice: "O Lord God, see how this Council already condemns Thy acts and law as an error; and Thou, when Thou

[11] According to Novotný, this fantastically absurd charge represents a twisted deduction from philosophical realism, alleging that there could be more than three hypostates in the Trinity—although Hus neither made any such deduction nor claimed to be the fourth hypostasis of the Godhead!

wast gravely oppressed by Thine enemies, Thou didst commend Thy
cause to God, Thy Father, the most just Judge. Thus Thou hast given
us wretches an example, that in all grave cases we should resort to
Thee, the most just Judge, most humbly asking Thy help in rendering
a righteous decision." And to that he added: "I continue to declare
that there is no safer appeal than to the Lord Jesus Christ, Who will
not be suborned by a perverse bribe, nor deceived by a false testimony,
but will render to each one what he deserves."

Among other things they stated that Master John Hus, although excommunicated, bore it contumaciously, etc. He responded: "I did not
bear it contumaciously, but having appealed, I preached and celebrated
the mass. But although I have twice sent procurators to the Roman
curia,[12] advancing reasons for not appearing personally, I was never
able to obtain a hearing: instead, some of my procurators were incarcerated[13] and others were ill treated. In all these matters I refer you
to the acts of the trial in which all these things are more fully contained. Above all, I even came to this Council freely, having the safe-
conduct of the lord king here present, desiring to show my innocence
and to give account of my faith."[14]

When therefore all the articles offered against him were completed
and read, a certain old and bald auditor, a prelate of the Italian nation
commisioned thereto, read the definitive sentence upon Master John
Hus.[15] And he, Master John, responded, replying to certain points in
the sentence, although they forbade it. And particularly when he was
declared to be obstinate in his error and heresy, he replied in a loud
voice: "I have never been obstinate, and am not now. But I have ever
desired, and to this day I desire, more relevant instruction from the
Scriptures. And today I declare that if even with one word I could
destroy and uproot all errors, I would most gladly do so!" And when
all his books, either in Latin written by himself or translated into

---

[12] In fact, he sent three procurators successively: Mark of Hradec, John of
Jesenice, and Nicholas of Stojčín.

[13] This was John of Jesenice, who was imprisoned and excommunicated by the
machinations of Michael de Causis.

[14] The *Passio* adds: "And when he said that, he turned toward the king; and
the king blushed a great deal and reddened." Novotný, *op. cit.*, p. 135.

[15] This was Anthony, bishop of Concordia. The text is given in Novotný, *op.
cit.*, 501 ff., and its translation is to be found in Part II, No. 35. Cf. also Sedlák,
Studie, I, 349 ff., where two preliminary texts of the sentence are published. The
sentence is correctly summarized by Cardinal Fillastre in his *Diary*. See Loomis,
op. cit., p. 256.

whatever other language, likewise in that sentence condemned as suspect of heresy, were for that reason condemned to be burned—of which some were burned later, particularly the book *De ecclesia* and *Contra Paletz* and *Contra Stanislaum*, as they were called—he, Master John, responded: "Why do you condemn my books, when I have ever desired and demanded better Scriptural proofs against what I said and set forth in them, and even today I so desire? But you have so far neither adduced any more relevant Scripture in opposition, nor have shown one erroneous word in them. Indeed, how can you condemn the books in the vernacular Czech or those translated into another language when you have never even seen them?" While the rest of the sentence was being read, he heard it kneeling and praying, looking up to heaven. When the sentence was concluded, as has already been mentioned concerning particular points, Master John Hus again knelt and in a loud voice prayed for all his enemies and said: "Lord Jesus Christ, I implore Thee, forgive all my enemies for Thy great mercy's sake; and Thou knowest that they have falsely accused me and have produced false witnesses and have concocted false articles against me! Forgive them for Thy boundless mercy's sake!" And when he said this, many, especially the principal clergy, looked indignantly and jeered at him.[16]

Then at the command of the seven bishops [17] who assisted at his unfrocking, he put on the altar vestments as if he were about to celebrate the mass. When he put on the alb, he said: "My Lord Jesus Christ, when He was led from Herod to Pilate, was mocked in a white garment." And when he was already so dressed and was exhorted by those bishops to recant and abjure, he rose, and ascending the table before which he was being dressed, and turning toward the multitude, weeping sorrowfully, he exclaimed: "Behold, these bishops exhort me

[16] On the same day, July 6, the Council sentenced Jean Petit, who had defended (1408) the right of regicide in an effort to justify the duke of Burgundy for his assassination of the duke of Orleans. But while Hus was burned, Petit, who had died in 1411, was declared not guilty when the case was reopened several times at the insistence of John the Fearless, the duke of Burgundy. Both Jean Gerson and Cardinal d'Ailly strenuously opposed this as unjust. In the session held on May 2, 1416, the bishop of Arras, the envoy of the duke of Burgundy, criticized Gerson "and asked for his condemnation as the purveyor of calumny." Loomis, *op. cit.,* p. 509.

[17] They were Bartolomeo de la Capra, the archbishop of Milan; Henry Scarampi, bishop of Belluna-Filtre; Albert Guttuaria d'Agliano, bishop of Asti and abbot of St. Bartholomew in Pavia; Bartholino Beccari of Alessandria; William Barrowe of Bangor; John Belli of Lavour in France; and the suffragan Bishop John of Constance.

to recant and abjure. But I fear to do so, lest I be a liar in the sight of the Lord, and also lest I offend my own conscience and the truth of God. For I have never held those articles that are falsely witnessed against me, but rather have written, taught, and preached their opposite; and also lest I offend the multitude to whom I have preached and others who faithfully preach the Word of God." When he said this, the prelates sitting nearby and others of the said Council remarked: "We see now how obdurate he is in his wickedness and obstinate in heresy."

After he descended from the table, the said bishops at once began to unfrock him. First they took the cup from his hands, pronouncing this curse: "O cursed Judas, because you have abandoned the counsel of peace and have counseled with the Jews, we take away from you this cup of redemption." He replied in a loud voice: "I trust in the Lord God Almighty, for whose name I patiently bear this vilification, that He will not take away from me the cup of His redemption; but I firmly hope to drink from it today in His kingdom." And subsequently taking away from him the other vestments—that is, the stole, the chasuble, and others, etc.—they pronounced in each instance an appropriate curse. And he responded that he humbly and gladly embraced the vilifications for the name of our Lord Jesus Christ. When he was divested of all vestments, as already mentioned, the said bishops proceeded to obliterate his tonsure. Thereupon they began an altercation among themselves, for some wished to shave him with a razor while others asserted that it suffices to obliterate the tonsure merely with scissors; he, turning toward the king presiding on the throne, said: "Look, these bishops so far do not know how to agree in this vilification!" And when they cut his tonsure with scissors into four parts— namely, right, left, front, and back—they spoke during it these words: "The Church has already deprived him of all ecclesiastical rights, and has nothing more to do with him. Therefore, we turn him over to the secular court." But prior to that they placed on his head a paper crown for vilification, saying to him among other things: "We commit your soul to the devil!" And he, joining his hands and lifting his eyes to heaven, said: "And I commit it to the most merciful Lord Jesus Christ." Seeing that crown he said: "My Lord Jesus Christ on account of me, a miserable wretch, bore a much heavier and harsher crown of thorns. Being innocent, he was deemed deserving of the most shameful death. Therefore I, a miserable wretch and sinner, will humbly bear this much lighter, even though vilifying crown for His name and truth." The paper crown was round, almost eighteen inches high, and on it were shown three horrible devils about to seize a soul and to tear it among themselves with claws. The inscription on that crown describing his guilt read: "This is a heresiarch." Then the king said to Duke Ludwig, the son of the late Clem of Bavaria,[18] who then stood before him in his robes, holding the golden orb with the cross in his hands: "Go, receive him!" And the said Clem's son then received the Master, giving him into the hands of the executioners to be led to death.[19]

When so crowned he was then led from the said church; they were burning his books at that hour in the church cemetery. When in passing by he saw it, he smiled at this their act. On his way indeed he exhorted those standing around or following him not to believe that he was to die on account of the errors falsely ascribed to him and deposed by the false testimony of his chief enemies. Indeed, almost all the inhabitants of that city, bearing arms, accompanied him to death.

And having come to the place of execution, he, bending his knees and stretching his hands and turning his eyes toward heaven, most devoutly sang psalms, and particularly, "Have mercy on me, God," and "In Thee, Lord, have I trusted," [20] repeating the verse "In Thy hand, Lord." His own [friends] who stood about then heard him praying joyfully and with a glad countenance. The place of execution was among gardens in a certain meadow as one goes from Constance toward the fortress of Gottlieben,[21] between the gates and the moats of the suburbs of the said city. Some of the lay people standing about said: "We do not know what or how he acted and spoke formerly, but now in truth we see and hear that he prays and speaks with holy words." And others said: "It would certainly be well that he have a confessor

[18] This was Duke Ludwig of Palatine, the son of the one-time king of the Romans, Ruprecht of Palatine, known as Clem (Clement).

[19] The *Passio* adds that Sigismund spoke the words in German and one later Ms. inserts at this place a rather unlikely story that Ludwig, accosting Hus, said to him: " 'Master John, recant now and save your life.' Thereupon Master John said to him: 'And who are you?' He then replied: 'The young Hercules' [i.e., Herr zu Klem]. Master John Hus said: 'Do not hold it against me, that I supposed that you were the executioner.' Thereupon he, blushing and looking at the king, took Master John Hus and turned him into the hands of the executioners." Novotný, *op. cit.,* p. 140.

[20] Psalms 51:3 and 31:2, 6.

[21] It is now on the western outskirts of the city itself in the vicinity of the municipal gas works on the *Alten Graben Strasse*. A large boulder serves as a monument and is inscribed for both John Hus and Jerome of Prague.

that he might be heard." But a certain priest in a green suit with a red silk lining,[22] sitting on a horse, said: "He should not be heard, nor a confessor be given him, for he is a heretic." But Master John, while he was still in prison, had confessed to a certain doctor, a monk,[23] and had been kindly heard and absolved by him, as he himself stated in one of his letters to his [friends] from prison.[24]

When he was praying, the offensive crown already mentioned, painted with three devils, fell from his head. When he perceived it, he smiled. Some of the hired soldiers standing by said: "Put it on him again so that he might be burned along with the devils, his masters, whom he served here on earth." And rising at the order of the executioner from the place where he was praying, he said in a loud and clear voice, so that his [friends] could plainly hear him: "Lord Jesus Christ, I am willing to bear most patiently and humbly this dreadful, ignominious, and cruel death for Thy gospel and for the preaching of Thy Word." Then they decided to take him among the bystanders. He urged and begged them not to believe that he in any way held, preached, or taught the articles with which he had been charged by false witnesses.[25] Then having been divested of his clothing, he was tied to a stake with ropes, his hands tied behind his back. And when he was turned facing east, same of the bystanders said: "Let him not be turned toward the east, because he is a heretic; but turn him toward the west." So that was done. When he was bound by the neck with a sooty chain, he looked at it and, smiling, said to the executioners: "The Lord Jesus Christ, my Redeemer and Savior, was bound by a harder and heavier chain. And I, a miserable wretch, am not ashamed to bear being bound for His name by this one." The stake was like a thick post half a foot thick; they sharpened one end of it and fixed it in the ground of that meadow. They placed two bound bundles of wood under the Master's feet. When tied to that stake, he still had his shoes

[22] Ulrich Schorand, a deputy of the bishop and of the Council. The description written by Richental, who claims to have walked along with the guards and thus was an eyewitness, differs in many details from that of Peter. Cf. Loomis, *op. cit.,* p. 133.

[23] The *Passio* adds: "... which confessor the Council had sent, as he [Hus] himself confessed and wrote in a letter written by his own hand, which he sent, among others, from the prison." Novotný, *op. cit.,* pp. 142–43.

[24] Cf. Part II, No. 21 of this work.

[25] The *Passio* adds that he requested to speak to his jailors; and when they drew near, he thanked them for all the good they had done him. Novotný, *op. cit.,* pp. 143–44.

on and one shackle on his feet. Indeed, the said bundles of wood, interspersed with straw, were piled around his body so that they reached up to his chin. For the wood amounted to two wagon- or cartloads.

Before it was kindled, the imperial marshal, Hoppe of Poppenheim,[26] approached him along with the son of the late Clem, as it was said, exhorting him to save his life by abjuring and recanting his former preaching and teaching. But he, looking up to heaven, replied in a loud voice: "God is my witness," he exclaimed, "that those things that are falsely ascribed to me and of which the false witnesses accuse me, I have never taught or preached. But that the principal intention of my preaching and of all my other acts or writings was solely that I might turn men from sin. And in that truth of the Gospel that I wrote, taught, and preached in accordance with the sayings and expositions of the holy doctors, I am willing gladly to die today." [27] And hearing that, the said marshal with the son of Clem immediately clapped their hands and retreated.

When the executioners at once lit [the fire], the Master immediately began to sing in a loud voice, at first "Christ, Thou son of the living God, have mercy upon us," and secondly, "Christ, Thou son of the living God, have mercy upon me," and in the third place, "Thou Who art born of Mary the Virgin." And when he began to sing the third time, the wind blew the flame into his face. And thus praying within himself and moving his lips and the head, he expired in the Lord. While he was silent, he seemed to move before he actually died for about the time one can quickly recite "Our Father" two or at most three times.

When the wood of those bundles and the ropes were consumed, but the remains of the body still stood in those chains, hanging by the neck, the executioners pulled the charred body along with the stake down to the ground and burned them further by adding wood from the third wagon to the fire. And walking around, they broke the bones with clubs so that they would be incinerated more quickly. And finding

[26] Members of this noble Swabian family held the office of marshal for many generations.

[27] Richental's account is strangely confused, for he seems to have conflated Jerome's trial with that of Hus. He asserts that *both* Hus and Jerome "promised to abandon their wicked beliefs and denounced what they had taught." He dates the death of Hus as taking place on July 8, and of Jerome early in September, 1415, instead of May 30, 1416. Altogether, Richental is surprisingly inaccurate in reporting the trial of Hus and Jerome. Loomis, *op. cit.,* pp. 131–35.

the head, they broke it to pieces with the clubs and again threw it into the fire. And when they found his heart among the intestines, they sharpened a club like a spit, and, impaling it on its end, they took particular [care] to roast and consume it, piercing it with spears until finally the whole mass was turned into ashes. And at the order of the said Clem and the marshal, the executioners threw the clothing into the fire along with the shoes, saying: "So that the Czechs would not regard it as relics; we will pay you money for it." Which they did. So they loaded all the ashes in a cart and threw it into the river Rhine flowing nearby.[28]

Thus I have therefore described clearly and in detail the sequence of the death and agony of the celebrated Master John Hus, the eminent preacher of the evangelical truth, so that in the course of time his memory might be vividly recollected. My principle has been not to dress up the account in a mass of highly embellished diction lacking the kernel of fact and deed, wherewith to tickle the itching ears desirous to feast thereon; but rather to speak of the marrow of the substance of the trial proceedings mentioned above, of what I have clearly learned from what I myself have seen and heard. He who knows all things is my witness that I lie not. I would rather suffer the blame of having used inept and awkward words so that it may be recognized that I have brought forth testimony to the truth, that the memory of the Master, its most steadfast champion, may thus live in the future!

---

[28] The *Passio* adds: ". . . wishing to destroy, as far as they could, his memory among the faithful." Novotný, *op. cit.*, p. 147.

PART TWO

Letters of Hus and Relevant Documents

1. Hus's Appeal from the Pope's Condemnation to Christ.[1]

[October 18, 1412]

Because the Almighty God, one in essence, three in persons, is the first and the last refuge and lord of the oppressed, "guarding the truth forever," "executing justice and loving kindness upon those who suffer wrong,"[2] "is near to all who call upon Him in truth,"[3] "frees the prisoners,"[4] "fulfills the desire of those who fear Him," and "preserves all who love Him, but destroys all 'incorrigible' sinners";[5] and Jesus Christ, the true God and true man, who, surrounded in distress by pontiffs, scribes, and Pharisees, priests, unjust judges, and witnesses, wished by His most cruel and shameful death to redeem from eternal damnation those who have been chosen to be the sons of God before the foundation of the world, left to His followers this most excellent example that in His memory they should commit their cause to the almighty, all-knowing, and all-loving Lord. He said: "See, O Lord, my affliction, for the enemy is risen";[6] for "Thou art my help and my support."[7] "Thou, O Lord, hast made it known to me and I knew; Thou hast shown me their designs. I was as a gentle lamb who is carried to the slaughter, and I did not know that they devised their counsels against me, saying: let us destroy the tree with its fruits and let us uproot him from the land of the living, that his name should be remembered no more. Thou, however, Lord of Sabaoth, Who judgest justly and triest the reins and the heart, let us see Thy vengeance upon them; for to Thee have I laid bare my cause."[8] Indeed, "they who afflict me are multiplied,"[9] and "they consult together, saying: God

---

[1] Novotný, *M. Jana Husi Korespondence a dokumenty,* No. 46; Palacký, *Documenta Mag. Joannis Hus,* pp. 464–66.

[2] Reminiscent of Ps. 146:7.

[3] Ps. 145:18.

[4] Ps. 146:7.

[5] Ps. 145:19–20.

[6] Lam. 19.

[7] Ps. 119:114.

[8] Jer. 11:18–20.

[9] Ps. 3:1.

has forsaken him, pursue and seize him, for there is none to liberate him." [10] See, therefore, O Lord, and consider, because "Thou art my patience"; [11] "snatch me from my enemies." [12] "For Thou art my God, do not depart from me; for tribulation is near, and there is none to help." [13] "O God, my God, look upon me, why hast Thou forsaken me?" [14] "For many dogs surround me, a company of evildoers encircle me." [15] "They spoke against me deceitful words and with hateful speeches they surrounded me; they attack me without cause, and instead of loving me, they draw away from me and reward me evil for good and hatred for my love." [16]

Supporting myself with this most holy and most helpful example of the Redeemer, I appeal to God from the grave oppression, the unjust sentence, and the pretended excommunication of the pontiff, the scribes, the Pharisees, and the judges seated in the seat of Moses. To Him I commit my cause, following in the footsteps of the Savior Jesus Christ, as did the holy and great patriarch of Constantinople, John Chrysostom,[17] from the two synods of bishops and priests. Likewise the blessed in hope Bishop Andrew of Prague [18] and Bishop Robert of Lincoln,[19] when unjustly condemned, humbly and confidently appealed from the pope to the supreme and most just Judge, Who is not terrified by fear or deflected by love, or suborned by a bribe, or deceived by false witnesses.

I desire, therefore, that all the faithful of Christ, and particularly the princes, barons, knights, squires, and the rest of the inhabitants of

[10] Ps. 71:10–11.
[11] Ps. 71:5.
[12] Ps. 59:1.
[13] Ps. 22:10–11.
[14] Ps. 22:1.
[15] Ps. 22:16.
[16] Ps. 109:2–5.
[17] John Chrysostum was deposed for political reasons by two synods in 403 and 404.
[18] Hus is quite mistaken in his high estimate of Bishop Andrew (1215–23). This stubborn prelate had a controversy with King Přemysl I about the prerogatives of the Church, in which he at first had the support of Pope Honorius II. When, however, he refused to accept the conditions of settlement negotiated between him and the king by the papal legate, he broke even with the pope. He retired to Venice, where he died. Of the appeal mentioned by Hus nothing is known. Cf. Novotný, České dějiny, I, ii, pp. 451–532.
[19] Robert Grosseteste of Lincoln defended himself against Pope Innocent IV in an epistle written in 1253. It is reproduced in Wyclif's De civili dominio, i, c. 43. Most likely Hus cites the incident from Wyclif.

our kingdom of Bohemia know and sympathize with me, so gravely wronged by the pretended excommunication, brought about especially by its instigator and my enemy, Michael de Causis, formerly pastor of the church of St. Adalbertus in the New Town of Prague, with the consent and aid of the canons of the cathedral of Prague. The excommunication was declared and promulgated by Peter, the cardinal-deacon of the Roman Church of the Holy Angel,[20] appointed as my judge by the Roman Pope John XXIII. For almost two years he refused to grant a hearing to my representatives and procurators, which ought not to be denied even to a Jew, a pagan, or a heretic; nor was he willing to accept any reasonable excuse for my personal non-appearance. He was not well-enough disposed to receive with fatherly kindness the testimony of the Prague university attested with its seal, and the witness of the public notaries called to testify to it. It is evident, therefore, that I did not incur a charge of contumacy; for I failed to appear, when cited, at the Roman curia not of contempt, but for a reasonable cause. For on the one hand, attacks had been plotted against me on the way from all sides; and on the other, I was warned by the dangers of others—by the robbing and the imprisonment of masters Stanislav and Stephen Páleč.[21] They, wishing to obey a citation, had been robbed of money and of other possessions in Bologna and shamefully imprisoned and treated as malefactors there, without any preliminary hearing at all. Furthermore, my procurators at the Roman curia were willing to undergo the penalty of fire along with anyone wishing on his part to oppose me. In spite of that, my legitimate procurator was imprisoned at the aforesaid curia without, as I suppose, any actual guilt. Moreover, by the grace of the lord king,[22] I was reconciled with the Lord Zbyněk, the archbishop of Prague of holy memory. Between the said Lord Zbyněk and me, as well as other masters, [a reconciliation was affected by] princes and lords and the royal council who declared, appending their seals to it,[23] that the lord archbishop should write to the lord pope that he knew of no heretical errors in the kingdom of Bohemia, in the city of Prague, and in the margravate of Moravia; and that none had been convicted of heresy, and that he was fully reconciled with me and with the other masters.

[20] Peter degli Stephaneschi; the decree of excommunication is published in Palacký, pp. 461–64.

[21] Cf. Bartoš, *Čechy v době Husově, 1378–1415*, p. 294.

[22] King Wenceslas IV.

[23] Palacký, pp. 437–38.

He also should have asked the apostolic lord to absolve me from the appearance, citation, and the excommunication.

Since, therefore, all the ancient laws, both the divine of the Old Testament and the New, and the canons, contain the requirement that the judges visit the place where the crime has allegedly been committed, and there inquire into the charge against the accused or defamed from those who have personal knowledge of the defendants and who are not ill disposed, haters, or enemies of the accused or defamed, but honest men; not transgressors, but fervid lovers of the law of Jesus Christ; and finally that the cited or accused has convenient, secure, and open access to the place, and neither the judge nor the witnesses are his enemies: it is clear that these conditions for my appearance were lacking. I am, therefore, excused before God, by reason of endangering my life, from [the charge] of contumacy and from the pretended and arbitrary excommunication.

I, John Hus of Husinec, master of arts and *formatus* bachelor of sacred theology of the University of Prague, and an appointed priest and preacher of the chapel called Bethlehem, make this appeal to Jesus Christ, the most just Judge, Who knows, protects, and judges, declares and rewards without fail the just cause of every man.

2. Hus Writes to the Lords Assembled at the Supreme Court.[24]

[The place is unknown, before December 14, 1412]

To the noble lords and officials of the kingdom of Bohemia and to other lords who are now in Prague.

May the merciful Lord God be pleased to further you in all good!

Dear lords, heirs of the sacred kingdom of Bohemia! I thank my gracious lord, King Wenceslas, king of the Romans and of Bohemia, before Your Graces, that he has graciously supported me in continuing to preach the Word of God and in the truth as I see it. For he, along with the princes, lords, and his councilors, has reconciled me and other masters with Zbyněk, the archbishop of Prague of holy memory, and has concluded an agreement between us, as Your Graces will learn from its copy.[25] But the Prague canons, disregarding this agreement, engaged Michael, pastor of St. Adalbertus, to continue the lawsuit against me. Thus they secured my excommunication, which, however, I do not fear, but gladly and joyously suffer, as not to offend souls. I

---

[24] Novotný, *Korespondence*, No. 54; Palacký, No. 11. In Czech.
[25] The condition of agreement are found in Palacký, p. 437.

am grieved, however, that I cannot preach the Word of God, since I have no wish to have the divine services stopped and the people distressed. Consider, dear lords, even if I were fully guilty, whether they should restrain the people of God from the praise of the Lord God and grieve them by such excommunications and cessations of the divine services. They do not have [the warrant] of the Holy Scriptures to forbid services whenever they please! They oppress and despoil princes, lords, knights, squires, as well as the poor community and drive them out of their country. Such acts are against the law of God, against the decrees of the spiritual laws, and against the imperial laws.[26] Therefore, dear lords and heirs of the kingdom of Bohemia, strive to stop such mishaps in order that the Word of God may be preached freely among the people of God. As I have ever been ready to stand and used to stand before the priest Zbyněk of holy memory and before his officials, before he rose up against me, by the instigation of the prelates and pastors of Prague, and cited me to Rome;[27] so I am now willing to stand before all the masters, prelates, and even before Your Graces, and gladly hear the charge against me and to answer it, or to suffer judgment, as is fitting for a poor priest, provided the accuser, who charges me, will stand forth. This I have always offered to do, and the king's grace has granted his consent to it. But never has anyone charged me as guilty, except to say that I do not obey. Furthermore, I declare that I am not willing to obey either the pope or the archbishop in their prohibition of my preaching: for it is contrary to God and to my salvation. I know, dear lords, that you are also disobeying the command of the bull of the late pope,[28] which they [Hus's enemies] bought so dearly, that there be no preaching of the Word of God in chapels. I know that many of you have chapels in which you have preaching, as formerly [it was done] even in houses. I did not appear at the papal court because I had my procurators there, whom they threw into prison without cause.[29] They [the procurators] were willing to challenge even to a trial by fire anyone who would accuse me of errors. Furthermore, I myself did not appear because my enemies had

[26] Hus refers to certain rules of the canon law to which he alluded in his appeal to God. Cf. the preceding document.

[27] This happened in 1409.

[28] An allusion to the letter of Pope Alexander V of December 20, 1409; cf. Palacký, pp. 374–76.

[29] This happened to John of Jesenice, who was actually imprisoned in Rome at the instigation of Michael de Causis.

laid snares for me everywhere so that I would not return to Bohemia. I hope that Your Graces, along with the king's and the queen's graces, will do all that the Almightly God has taught you to do for the benefit of your land. May He also confirm you in His grace. Amen.

Master John Hus, an unprofitable priest.

3. Hus Giving his Reasons in Sermons for Refusing to Go to Rome to Answer the Papal Citation.[30]

But there still remains the question as to how Christ is excused [from the charge] that he was afraid to go to the feast of the lamb as prescribed by the law. The answer to it is that those who had been threatened by sworn enemies were excused before God for nonattendance. Because of that custom, I trust God that I am excused for not appearing in Rome, though cited before the pope. First, because I had sent there my procurators, who for three years had never been granted a hearing. They were seized and imprisoned because they desired the truth. Second, because from Prague to Rome is a greater distance than from the region of the Sea of Tiberias to Jerusalem, to which Christ retreated from Jerusalem. Third, that there is no command in God's law that people be compelled to go in vain as far as Rome. Fourth, that there is but little of God's truth at the papal court observed there in accordance with God's law. Fifth, that I would deprive the people of the Word of God, and while on the way what good could I do? And if I came to the court, what kind of holiness would I acquire there? Only quarrels, and if I wished, simony. Sixth, that I would spend to no purpose much alms which I received from the people. Seventh, that the struggle I am engaged in is against the pope's customs and against the power not bestowed on him by God but invented by the devil. For Pope Alexander V issued a bull for money, in which he forbade the preaching of the Word of God to the people in chapels, although they had been founded and confirmed by popes for that purpose. That bull declared that preaching be done nowhere else but in the parochial churches and monasteries. It was secured by the priest Zbyněk of good memory, the archbishop of Prague, along with other prelates. The monk Jaroslav, a titular bishop,[31] was engaged as messenger for obtaining that bull. It stated that

---

[30] Jeschke, *Mister Jan Hus, Postilla*, pp. 131–34.

[31] Literally "sterile." It refers to Jaroslav, bishop of Sarepta *in partibus infidelium*.

the hearts of many in Prague, in the kingdom of Bohemia, and in the margravate of Moravia were so greatly infected by heresy that there was need of supervision and punishment. Accordingly, the bull shows that the pope and the priest Zbyněk opposed God's law: the pope by ordering and Zbyněk by demanding that the free preaching of the Word of God be stopped, contrary to the word and deeds of our Savior Jesus Christ, Who commanded His disciples, Mark 16 : 15, that they go to all the world, preaching the Word to every creature. They preached everywhere, as St. Mark says in Chap. 16 : 20; everywhere, understand, wherever the people were capable of hearing. Our Savior, in today's lesson, preached in the desert, and at another time by the sea standing in a boat, in streets, in small towns without churches, and in villages. He told His disciples to preach even from roofs, and sent His servants among fences and crossroads to invite them to the eternal supper. How then does that bull agree with the word and the deeds of Christ? Not at all! . . . The second part of the bull may be right in so far as it declares that the hearts of many in Prague are infected by heresy—namely, of those who demanded that bull contrary to the Word and against the salvation of men, and of those who consented to it!

Moreover, what good did they desire by demanding that the Word of God be not preached in chapels, or anywhere but in the parochial churches and monasteries? Surely, it was prompted by jealousy, avarice, and wickedness, contrary to the Word of God; it aimed at depriving the Bethlehem Chapel of God's Word. Other archbishops built chapels in order to provide preaching in them, as did the priest John, archbishop of Prague, who had founded and confirmed the Bethlehem Chapel by his own hand. Afterward, however, the late Zbyněk, having been instigated by the canons and priests against Bethlehem, wished to destroy [the preaching of] the Word of God in that chapel and thus to prevent me from preaching altogether! For they concluded that if, according to the pope's command, I did not preach in the chapel . . . and could preach nowhere else but in the parochial churches and monasteries, they agreed among themselves to prevent me from preaching altogether. Accordingly, having discerned this also, I stood up against their unworthy command and evil scheme, taking the merciful Savior to my aid. Finally, I did not appear at the papal court lest I lose my life for nothing. For every place was full of my enemies, both Czech and German, seeking my death. The pope-judge is my enemy, the cardinals likewise are my enemies. I read it in their letters wherein they describe me as a heretic, although they have never heard or seen me. For any preaching against pride, avarice, and particularly against simony touches both the pope and the cardinals. Consequently [if I went to Rome], justice would be denied me, as it had been denied to Jesus, particularly as I learned about the false witnesses and their testimonies which they had brought against me in Prague and sent to Rome. . . . In the letters issued against me by the cardinal, my principal judge, he declares me to be a seducer of the people and an inventor of errors. Furthermore, in the charge by the priest Zbyněk, Michael, pastor of St. Adelbertus in New Town, states that all faithful Christians in the kingdom of Bohemia regard me as a heretic, that I preach errors and heresy every day in Bethlehem, and that I am the prince and the chief of heretics. Nevertheless, I trust gracious Christ, that this does me no harm, nor does it cause me sorrow. For I know that priests have done the same to His Holy Grace and in the end have put Him to death by a shameful and cruel death. To His Holy Grace I committed my cause that He might bring it to an end as He pleases, even by my disgrace and death at the hands of men; only that He would not allow me to fall away from His truth.

Nevertheless, they still keep on saying: let him suffer death and go to Rome, as Christ went to Jerusalem! I reply: if I knew that it is God's will that I should die in Rome, I would go; and if I knew that I would accomplish some good, as Christ did to the people and to the saints both before and after Him, [I would go]. Nevertheless, even He failed to bring the bishops, masters, priests and lawyers to salvation; instead, they from jealousy and because He had rebuked their sins and had denounced them to the people murdered Him as a seducer and a heretic by a cruel and abominable death. Let the bishops and priests of the supreme bishop send after me, as they had sent after Jesus! A beginning of it was made by the Germans when, led by Bernard Chotek, clad in armor, with crossbows, halberts, and swords, they attacked Bethlehem while I was preaching. The Lord God, however, confused their way so that they did not know what to do, as is known to many people. For they came inopportunely. The bishops had sent after the Lord Jesus when He preached; but because His hour had not yet come, therefore the servants of the bishops preferred to listen to Him rather than to seize Him. Likewise the hour of my death has not yet come; hence, they left me alone until the time of God's will. Later the Germans, after consulting together, wished to pull down Bethlehem, having conspired among themselves at the Town Hall. . . . A Czech, Holubář, spoke on their behalf to the Czechs, whether they would agree, as the Germans had agreed, that Bethlehem be destroyed. The faithful Czechs, however, discerning that it was contrary to God and His Word, against the salvation of men, and a shame to the Czechs, and that they had no right to pull down a useful church of God in such a city, refused to agree. Consider the German audacity: they would not dare to pull down a neighbor's oven or a stable without the king's permission, and they would dare to attempt [to destroy] God's Church! But the Lord God did not grant them the power. . . .

This I wrote for the warning of posterity to encourage the good to stand up courageously for the truth; to the blind concerning the truth, that they would beware of such a conduct. Those, then, who do not know about my cause and slander me, [I exhort them] that having learned the truth, they sin not by slandering.

[Hus makes a similar reference to the prohibition of preaching in chapels in the sermon for the second Sunday after the Holy Trinity, preached on the text in Luke 14 : 16–24, dealing with the parable of the great supper.] [32]

In this remark [i.e., "Go into the byways and hedges,"] the Savior points out that, whenever his faithful servant can call the people to the supper in any place whatsoever, he should do so. He clearly commanded it in the sixteenth chapter of St. Matthew: "Go into all the world, preaching the Word to every creature." And they went, preaching everywhere, that is, where they could find those who would hear them. But alas! this kind of preaching has been restricted by pride, avarice, and jealousy, so that God's Word does not have freedom as before. Antichrist is already extending his nets and narrowing those of Christ. For Christ commanded Peter to spread his nets for fish, of which he caught many. The draught signified the draught of souls with the net, which is the Word of God, as He told him immediately afterward that he would be catching men. Peter spread the nets extensively, as did the other holy apostles. The apostles of Antichrist, however, now promptly attack those who wish faithfully to call men to the Supper in accordance with the divine command. They do not allow them to be called, unless they be willing to preach in accordance with their will, flatter them, and refrain from castigating their sins. The priests of the Prague archbishop, the priest Zbyněk, were of that Antichrist's crew;

[32] Jeschke, *op. cit.,* pp. 281–82.

for they obtained the bull . . . ordering that the Word of God be preached nowhere save in the parochial churches, monasteries, and their
cemeteries. Nevertheless, the Lord God gave me the desire to stand
up against that bull and to disobey its command as contrary to His
Word. Therefore, I preached with His help until my excommunication
and the unjust stopping of the services. I still preach and will continue
to preach, if His Holy Grace will grant it, that I may bring any of the
poor, weak, blind and lame to the Supper in Christ's house. At first I
preached in cities and streets, but now I preach among the hedges,
outside the castle called Kozí, and in the byways of towns and villages.
For Christ says: "Go into the byways and hedges,"—understand thereby
among the hedges—"and constrain them to enter so that my house be
filled." He says "constrain," that is by the threat of eternal pains; and
"to enter," that is, that they come "that my house be filled," that is,
by the number of the elect to everlasting bliss.

[Another reference to Hus's refusal to stop preaching is in his sermon
on the fifth day after Trinity.] [33]

The priest, Zbyněk, archbishop of Prague, along with the canons,
bought a bull from Pope Alexander V, in which the pope ordered that
the Word of God be preached nowhere—not even in the chapels approved by popes—except in the parochial, monastic, and cathedral
churches. From that bull, with God's help, I appealed to the pope
[Alexander V]; but he, as well as his chancellor, died immediately
after issuing the bull. Thereupon, I appealed to his successor, John
XXIII. When I found, however, no help in him for preaching the Word
of God freely, I appealed to the Lord God, to Jesus, the venerable and
just bishop, that He might judge me. Now I preach in cities, castles,
fields, and forest, and if I could do as the Savior did, Who gave us
such an example, I would preach from the shore and from a boat.

4. Hus Preaching against the Wrong Interpretation
of the Eucharist.[34]

Such a blasphemy the priests commit who talk as if they were the
creators of their God, and as if they created the body of God in the
mass. That is a lie: for they do not create Him Whom the Virgin Mary
bore. He was created by God alone and was given birth by the Virgin
Mary. . . . Nor do they create another body of Christ, for He never

[33] *Ibid.*, p. 306.
[34] *Ibid.*, p. 411.

had another body, nor will He ever have. "To create" is to make something that did not exist before so that it may exist. Thus God alone is Creator, because He made this world out of nothing; for it had not existed before. Therefore, we believe in the Almighty God, Creator of heaven and earth, but do not believe that priests are creators.

5. Hus Announces to Sigismund that He Is Ready to Go to Constance.[35]

[At the castle of Krakovec (?), September 1, 1414]

To the most serene prince and lord, Lord Sigismund, king of the Romans and king of Hungary, etc., his most gracious lord, [I send] my humble prayer with ardent desire in my heart that "his salvation, peace, and grace may be multiplied" and that, after guiding his present life, he may be granted eternal life of glory!

Most serene prince and most gracious lord! As I contemplate with all my heart and soul the favor with which Your Benignity most graciously regards me, a poor man, I cannot respond adequately; nevertheless, I feel constrained to implore the mercy of the omnipotent Lord, Who rewards every man worthily, for Your Majesty's happy reign.

Recently I sent by the hand of Stephen Harnsmeister[36] my reply to Your Serenity, that in accordance with the message of Lord Henry Lefl of Lažany,[37] I intend humbly to bend my neck to Your Majesty's desire, and under the protection of your safe-conduct, with the aid of the Most High Lord, to appear before the forthcoming Council of Constance. Therefore, wishing to proceed properly, I have posted notices, both in Latin and in Czech, throughout all Prague. I also have sent copies to other cities to be posted and announced in sermons. I humbly beg Your Majesty, supplicating you in the Lord, that for the honor of God, the welfare of the holy Church, and the honor of the kingdom of Bohemia, of which the King of kings has willed to make Your Serenity the heir, and thus disposed you by a natural inclination to desire its welfare and honor, that you deign to extend to me the grace that, coming in peace to the general Council, I may be able to profess publicly the faith I hold.

I have taught nothing in secret, but in public, for my ministry was

---

[35] Novotný, Korespondence, No. 81; Palacký, No. 36.

[36] He was in the royal service.

[37] He was the owner of the castle of Krakovec, where Hus was staying at the time, and the principal member of the king's council.

attended mostly by masters, bachelors, priests, barons, knights, and many others; I thus desire to be heard, examined, and to preach not in secret, but at a public hearing, and to reply with the aid of the Spirit of God to all who should wish to argue against me. I will not, I hope, be afraid to confess the Lord Christ, and, if need be, to suffer death for His most true law. For He, "the King of kings and the Lord of lords,"[38] the true God, being poor, mild, and humble, "suffered for us, leaving us an example that we should follow in His footsteps." He, "who committed no sin, on whose lips no guile was found,"[39] Who humbled Himself, having by His death destroyed our death, has placed us under an obligation to suffer humbly and not in vain. For He said: "Blessed are those who suffer persecution for justice's sake, for theirs is the kingdom of heaven."[40]

I, His servant in hope, although unprofitable, after turning this over in my mind, have desired to induce both the clergy and the people toward His imitation. On that account I became hated, not indeed by all the people, but by those who oppose the Lord by their behavior. Having been very often cited by them to the archiepiscopal court, I have always proved myself innocent. When I was finally cited to the curia,[41] I have never been able to secure a hearing through my representatives and procurators. Thus I committed myself into the hands of the most just Judge, for Whose glory, I trust, Your Clemency will obtain for me a safe and public hearing under the protection of the Lord Jesus Christ. Finally, I am consoled by what the noble and courageous lord, Mikeš Divoký,[42] Your Majesty's illustrious messenger, told me, that Your Highness so kindly and steadfastly keeps me in remembrance as to wish to bring my trial to a laudable end: which you will also accomplish to the glory of the King of kings.

Written with my own hand on the Day of St. Egidius.

I, Master John Hus, Your Majesty's humble petitioner in the name of the Lord Jesus Christ.

[38] I Tim. 6:15.
[39] I Peter 2:21–22.
[40] Matt. 5:10.
[41] In 1410.
[42] Alias Divůček of Jemniště.

6. *To Lord John of Chlum.*[43]

[Constance, the Dominican monastery, between
December 25, 1414, and January 3, 1415]

Gracious Lord!

Acquire for me a Bible and send it by this good man.[44] If your
scribe, Peter, has any ink, let him give me some, as well as several pens
and a small inkwell.

I know nothing about my Polish servant,[45] nor about Master Cardinal;[46] I only hear that your lordship is here and is with the lord king.
Accordingly, I beseech you to pray his royal majesty, both for my sake
and for the cause of the Almighty God, Who has so magnificently endowed him with His gifts, as well as for the sake of manifesting justice
and truth to the honor of God and the welfare of the Church, to liberate
me from captivity, that I may prepare myself for and come to a public
hearing. You should know that I have been very ill and was given an
enema, but am already convalescing.

I pray, greet the Czech lords who are at the court of the lord king.

Written with my own hand, which your scribe Peter knows well.
Given in prison.

Remember the *Auca*[47] you my friends!

7. *To His Friends in Constance.*[48]

[Constance, in the Dominican prison, January 3, 1415]

Almost the whole last night I wrote responses to the articles formulated by Páleč.[49] He labors directly for my condemnation. May God
forgive him and strengthen me!

---

[43] Novotný, *Korespondence,* No. 103; Palacký, No. 45. Hus was arrested on
November 28 and imprisoned in the Dominican monastery on December 6, 1414.

[44] Perhaps one of Hus's guards.

[45] There is no mention of him elsewhere.

[46] Master John of Rejnštejn, known as "Cardinal," was a faithful friend of
Hus; he represented the University of Prague, and accompanied Hus on the
journey to Constance.

[47] Latin for Hus (goose); perhaps a cryptogram employed for reasons of
caution.

[48] Novotný, *Korespondence,* No. 104; Palacký, No. 50.

[49] It is difficult to determine which articles Hus refers to: the first accusations
were prepared by Michael de Causis (Palacký, No. 7); the second were drawn up
by the commissioners of the Council (*Ibid.,* No. 8). Hus replied in writing only
to the forty-two articles prepared by Páleč (*Ibid.,* No. 9). It is in these last-
mentioned that the articles referred to are found, except the one concerning the
deprivation.

Further, they say that the article "concerning the deprivation"[50] is heretical. Inform the lord king[51] that if this article be condemned as heretical, he himself will then be involved in the condemnation as a heretic for having deprived the bishops of temporal possessions,[52] as did his father, the emperor and king of Bohemia,[53] before him. Do not entrust the letters to be carried by anyone except a man in whom you have as much confidence as in yourselves, who would carry them without prating.

Further, tell Doctor Jesenic[54] and Master Jerome[55] on no account to come [to Constance], nor any one of ours.

I marvel that the lord king has forgotten me and sends me no word. Perhaps I shall be sentenced before I speak a word with him. Whether that will be to his honor, let him see for himself.

Noble and gracious Lord John,[56] our gracious benefactor and staunch protector, do not be perturbed on my account or on account of the losses you are sustaining. The Almighty God will give you more. I pray that you greet the Czech lords, I know of none; I suppose, however, that Lord Wenceslas of Dubá is here and Lord Henry of Lacembok, who remarked: "Good man, do not try to puzzle it out!"[57]

Inform me if you have decided what stand you wish to take.

John Bradáček,[58] pray God for me, dearly beloved, along with others. Arrange that the king requests my replies that are written with my own hand, both as regards the articles ascribed to Wyclif and those ascribed to me.

Have those replies copied, but show them to no outsider. Have them so copied that the articles stand well separated.

I do not know whether my petition, which I gave to the patriarch[59]

---

[50] That is, the deprivation of priests of their property.

[51] King Sigismund is meant.

[52] Both Wenceslas and Sigismund did that: the latter in 1403–04 in both Hungary and Bohemia, the former in 1409 and 1411 in Bohemia.

[53] Emperor Charles IV.

[54] Doctor John of Jesenice, Hus's procurator and legal adviser.

[55] Master Jerome of Prague, who came to Constance nevertheless, was arrested, tried, and burned at the stake a year later than Hus.

[56] John of Chlum, to whom this portion of the letter is addressed.

[57] The words are in Czech: "*Dobrý muži, nehlúbej!*" Its meaning is not clear, unless it is regarded as a word of encouragement.

[58] He was a staunch supporter of Hus; he later wrote a *Passio,* dealing with Hus's martyrdom. Cf. Novotný, *Fontes rerum Bohemicarum,* VIII, 14–24.

[59] John of Rupescissa, patriarch of Constantinople (1412–24), a member of the commission for Hus's trial.

that he might present it to the Council, will be considered. I think he will not present it. If it will please God, the king—if he would have some [good] reasons [for it]—could cancel one or two [articles] of the decisions of the Prague doctors; i.e., the one regarding the deprivation, and the other about the donation of Constantine,[60] and the third about the tithes; for I did not intend to deny them. The reasons, however, should be given him by someone else than by one of our party. If I were free, I would myself tell him: "See to it, King, that your affair, which you love, be not secretly taken away, so that you would no longer be able to see it!"

I pray that Master John Cardinal be careful, for all those who appeared to him as friends were *agents provocateurs* [against him]. I overheard those who examined me to remark: "A certain John Cardinal calumniates the pope and the cardinals, saying that they are all simoniacs." Let Master Cardinal attach himself to the king's court as closely as he can, so that they would not seize him, as they did me.

No one does me more harm than Páleč. May the Almighty God forgive him! He, Páleč, is the ringleader of them all, a [veritable] pointer dog.[61] He insisted that all my adherents be cited and recant. He said in the prison that all who had attended my preaching hold that after the consecration the material bread remains.

I marvel that none of the Czechs visits the prison. Perhaps they do it for the best.

Tear up this letter immediately.

Send me another shirt by this messenger.

Lord John, insist along with the other Czechs that the citation of those who were summoned be canceled,[62] and that the king have compassion on his inheritance and does not permit it to be needlessly harassed on account of the one trouble-maker.[63] Further [I wish] that at all events I may speak at least once with the king before I am con-

---

[60] The notorious assertion of the Forged Decretals that Constantine gave the papacy certain territories comprising the West. It was demonstrated as forgery by Laurentius Valla in 1440. Hus, of course, did not know of the falsification, but only the fact that Constantine and other emperors had created the temporal rule of the papacy.

[61] The last phrase is in Czech: "*sledník*" is a term used for the pointer dog that scents the game.

[62] This refers to those men mentioned in the letter of John Cardinal, dated November 10, 1414. Cf. Peter's *Account*, Chap. I, pp. 104–6.

[63] Perhaps Páleč, although it is not certain as to who is meant.

demned; for I came here at his wish and under his promise that I should safely return to Bohemia.

8. To John Hus from Lord John of Chlum.[64]

[Constance, January 4, 1415]

Dearest friend in Christ!

You should know that today the king spoke with the delegates of the nations of the entire Council about your affairs, and especially concerning your public hearing. They all answered him finally and conclusively that you will be granted a public hearing without fail. Your friends likewise want to urge and do urge that you be placed unfailingly in some airy place where you can recover and inwardly restore yourself.[65] Therefore, for the sake of God, of your salvation, and of the spread of the truth, do not retreat from it on account of any fear of the loss of miserable life. For God has visited you by this His affliction solely for your great good. Our friends in Prague are faring very well, especially Lord Škopek, who rejoices greatly that you have already obtained the persecution for the truth which you desired. We pray you earnestly that you reply on the enclosed paper, if you deem it proper, giving your reasoned and final opinion concerning the communion of the cup, so that we may show it to friends at an appropriate time. For there is still some disagreement among the brethren, and many are disquieted on that account, referring to you and your decision in accordance with some treatise of yours.[66] Friends, and especially Jesenic, are particularly sorry that you were examined in the prison. But the past cannot be recalled. They praise your constancy profoundly and most appreciatively.

9. To Lord John of Chlum.[67]

[Constance, January 4, 1415]

As regards the recovery, I know not how I can recover or how else

[64] Novotný, *Korespondence,* No. 105; Palacký, No. 46.

[65] Hus was actually transferred to a better room near the refectory (January 9, 1415).

[66] Hus replies to Lord John in the following letter that he gave his opinion on the granting of the cup to the laity in the treatise *Utrum expediat laicis fidelibus sumere sanguinem Christi sub specie vini,* written before his imprisonment. Cf. *Historia et Monumenta,* I, 52–55. The reference to the "disagreement among the brethren" applies particularly to Havlík, Hus's substitute at Bethlehem, who vehemently opposed the granting of the cup to the laity.

[67] Novotný, *Korespondence,* No. 106; Palacký, No. 51.

to conduct myself; for I do not know what the public hearing to be given me will deal with. I petitioned, with a [legal] protestation before notaries, and wrote a supplication to the whole Council, which I gave to the patriarch. In it I request that I may respond to any article as I have responded in private and have written in my own hand. Or if I am granted a hearing, that I may respond in the due academic form [*more scholastico*]. Perhaps God will grant me a hearing at which I may deliver a sermon. I hope that by God's grace I shall never retreat from the known truth. Pray God that He may preserve me.

Regarding the sacrament of the cup, you have the treatise I wrote in Constance, in which the reasons for it are given.[68] I know not what else to add, except that the Gospel and St. Paul's letter[69] sound definite and that it had been practiced in the primitive Church. If at all possible, try to have it granted by a bull, at least to those who request it from devotion, having regard to circumstances.

Our friends should not be disturbed on account of the private examinations.[70] I did not see how else it could be done, since the Council had so decided before I was seized. The commissioners had issued a bull, which was read before me, in which I am called a heresiarch and a seducer of the people. I hope, however, that what I have spoken in secret [*sub tecto*] shall be proclaimed from the housetops [*super tecto*].

The day before yesterday—the day on which I saw my brother John Barbatus[71]—I was again interrogated about each of the forty-five articles. I replied with the same responses as previously. They questioned me about each article separately, if I wished to defend it. I replied that I would abide by the decision of the Council, as I had declared before. To each of the articles I replied as I had done previously. About some I said: "This is true in such and such a sense." They said: "Do you wish to defend it?" I replied that I did not, but that I would abide by the decision of the Council.

Truly, God is my witness that at the time no other response seemed to me more appropriate, because I had previously written with my own hand that I did not wish to defend anything obstinately, but was ready to be instructed by anyone.[72] The interrogation was granted me because someone had told them that I had reported to the king that I

---

[68] This is the treatise referred to in note 66.

[69] Cf. Matt. 26:28; Mark 14:24; John 6:54; I Cor. 10:16.

[70] I.e., in the prison.

[71] This is the same person referred to formerly as John Bradáček. Cf. note 58.

[72] Such a declaration from the earlier period of his imprisonment is not extant.

wished to defend three or four articles. For that reason they questioned me whether I had informed him of anything. I said that I did not, because I had never thus informed the king, but as you know, etc.

Michael[73] also stood by holding a letter, urging the patriarch that I reply to the questioning. In the meantime some bishops came. Again Michael cooked up something new. God permitted him and Páleč to rise up against me because of my sins. Michael pries into my letters and other things, while Páleč composes articles from those ancient matters which we had discussed many years ago.

The patriarch insists a great deal in front of everyone that I have a large amount of money. Hence, an archbishop told me at a hearing: "You have 70,000 florins." Michael exclaimed in front of all: "Ha, ha, what has become of the bag full of florins? How much money do the barons in Bohemia owe you?" Indeed, I had sore trouble that day!

One bishop said: "You have established a new law." Another bishop said: "You have preached all these articles." And with the help of God I answered also quite sternly, saying: "Why do you wrong me?"

You write me nothing about those who have been cited.[74] Have no steps been taken in their behalf either by the king, or the citizens of Prague, or by the cited men themselves?

10. To His Friends in Constance.[75]

[In the Franciscan prison, June 5, 1415]

The Almighty God today gave me a courageous and stout heart. Two articles are already deleted. I hope, moreover, that by the grace of God more will be deleted. Almost all of them shouted at me like the Jews had done at Jesus. So far they have not come to the principal point—namely, that I should confess that all the articles [charged against me] are contained in my treatises.

You have done wrong in presenting the treatise *Against a Secret Adversary* with the treatise *On the Church*. Present none but the treatises *Against Stanislav* and *Against Páleč*. It is well that the princes[76] demanded that my book be restored to them. For some, and particu-

---

[73] These lies were spread by Michael de Causis to induce the members of the Council to demand a payment for the hearing.

[74] Cf. the letter of January 3, No. 7, "To his Friends in Constance."

[75] Novotný, *Korespondence*, No. 124; Palacký, No. 63.

[76] Sigismund's messengers were princes Ludwig of the Palatinate and Frederick of Nuremberg, who delivered to the Council three treatises of Hus. Cf. Part I, Chap. III, pp. 165–66.

larly Michael de Causis, whom I heard, shouted "Let it be burned!" I am not aware of having a single friend in the whole multitude of the clergy except "Pater"[77] and one Polish doctor[78] whom I know. I am grateful to the bishop of Litomyšl[79] for his valuable aid, although he said no more than "And what have I done for you?"[80]

I am very grateful that you have arranged the articles[81] in such a form. It would be well to publish and recopy them in that form, etc.

The presidents said that I should have another public hearing. They did not want to hear the distinctions about the Church. Greet our faithful nobles and friends of the truth, and pray God for me, for there is need of it. I suppose that they will not allow me [to defend myself with] the opinion of St. Augustine about the Church and about its predestined and foreknown members, and about evil prelates. If only I could be granted a hearing that I might reply to the arguments of those who wish to impugn the articles stated in the treatises! I imagine that many who shout would turn dumb! But be it according to the will of heaven!

11. To His Friends in Constance.[82]

[In the Franciscan prison, June 7, 1415]

I am very glad that the *Hidden* remains hidden,[83] and the same about the other matters. I have eaten more good food these days than since the Feast of Easter to the last Sunday.[84]

I supposed that there would be greater discipline and courtesy at the Council.[85]

May my Lord John[86] be blessed for ever!

Would that I knew how the bearded Jerome,[87] who refused to obey the counsel of friends, is faring!

---

[77] It is not known who this mysterious friend was; he is mentioned elsewhere as well.

[78] The name of this Polish doctor is unknown.

[79] Bishop John "the Iron" of Litomyšl.

[80] These words are in Czech: "*A co sem tobě učinil?*" Perhaps the bishop urged the granting of the hearing.

[81] The articles which Hus answered in prison.

[82] Novotný, *Korespondence,* No. 125; Palacký, No. 66.

[83] This refers to Hus's treatise, "Contra occultum adversarium" (*Historia et Monumenta,* I, 168–79), which was given to the Council on June 5, but was not used against him.

[84] From March 31 to June 3.

[85] Hus made the statement at the second hearing on June 7.

[86] John of Chlum.

[87] Jerome of Prague.

Since they have my book, I no longer need this paper. Save the copy of the first articles with the proofs. Should there be need of proving some of the articles, note it there. Among them it will most likely be the article, "A virtuous man, whatever he does, does virtuously."

I am now sufering with toothache and at the castle[88] I suffered with vomiting of blood, headache, and the stone. These are the punishments due for sins as well as the signs of God's love toward me.

12. To Lord John of Chlum.[89]

[After June 8 (10?), 1415]

Dearly beloved Friend in Christ!

Please arrange for all the lords to go to the king and the Council and have them do what they agreed, namely: "At a future hearing you will receive a brief written statement and will make a reply to it." They can urge the king and the Council to that [action] by urging their own statement.[90] For with God's help I will tell the truth plainly. I desire that my body be consumed by fire rather than that I should be so iniquitously kept out of sight by them, in order that all Christendom might know what I have said in the end. I beg my lords for God's sake that they do so, showing to the last their earnestness and constancy. My hope in the Lord is ever firm.

Lord John, most gracious and most faithful supporter, may God be your reward! I beg you, do not leave until you see the end consummated. Surely you would rather see me led to the fire than to be so craftily stifled! I still cherish the hope that the Almighty God may snatch me from their hands on account of the merits of the saints. If I am to be brought to a hearing tomorrow, let me know. Greet all our friends in the kingdom, requesting them to pray God for me that if I am to remain in prison, I may humbly expect death without apprehension. Exhort the masters to stand in the truth, as well as our circle— the virgin Petra[91] with her household. Tell Master Jesenic to marry a wife. Ask my Jiřík and the Pastor[92] to be content, even though I did not reward them sufficiently for their services; for I could not. Let them greet my friends in Christ of both sexes, and pray to God for me.

---

[88] Gottlieben.

[89] Novotný, *Korespondence,* No. 128; Palacký, No. 60.

[90] It was promised Hus by Sigismund through Cardinal Zabarella.

[91] Petra of Říčany, a noblewoman, one of Hus's supporters; she lived near the Bethlehem Chapel. Several other pious women lived in the neighborhood.

[92] They were Hus's pupils and servants.

I know not who will repay those who advanced me money,[93] except the Lord Jesus Christ for Whose sake they advanced it. Nevertheless, I wish that some of the richer would collect among themselves to pay the poorer. But I fear lest that proverb "Out of sight, out of mind,"[94] be fulfilled in some of them.

13. To His Friends in Bohemia.[95]

[In the Franciscan prison, June 10, 1415]

Master John Hus, in hope a servant of God, to all the faithful Czechs who love the Lord God and will love Him, sends his wish that the Lord may grant them to dwell and die in His grace and to live forever in the joy of heaven. Amen.

Faithful lords and ladies,[96] dear to God, both rich and poor! I beseech and admonish you that you obey the Lord God, extol His Word, and gladly hear and follow it. I pray that you hold that truth of God which I have drawn from the law of God, and have preached and written from the teachings of the saints. I also beseech you that if anyone has heard at my preaching or in private anything against the truth of God, or if I have written it anywhere—which, I trust God, there is none of it—that he does not hold it. I also beseech you that if anyone saw in me any levity of morals in speaking or actions, that he does not hold them, but that he pray God for me that He may be pleased to forgive me. I beseech the priests, particularly those who labor in the Word of God, that they love good morals and extol and honor them. I beseech them to beware of deceitful men, and particularly of unworthy priests, of whom the Savior says that they are clad in sheep's clothing but inwardly are ravenous wolves.[97]

I beseech the lords that they deal mercifully with their poor and rule them justly. I beseech the burghers that they carry on their commerce justly. I beseech the craftsmen that they do their work faithfully and have their living from it. I beseech the servants that they serve their masters and mistresses faithfully. I beseech the masters that they, living worthily, teach their pupils faithfully: first of all to love God, and

[93] We thus learn that Hus had to borrow money for the trip to Constance.

[94] This is in Czech: "*Co s oči to s mysli.*"

[95] Novotný, *Korespondence*, No. 129; Palacký, pp. 117–18. Written in Czech. As is evident from it, Hus expected to be put to death on the next day.

[96] The address may be understood as including nobles; otherwise it should be rendered "masters and mistresses."

[97] Matt. 7:15.

to study for the sake of His praise and the benefit of the community, as well as for the sake of their salvation—but not for the sake of avarice or of wordly prosperity. I beseech the students and other pupils that they obey and follow their masters in the good, and that they study diligently for the sake of God's praise and their own and other people's salvation.

I beseech all together that they give thanks and be grateful for the diligence of the [following] lords: Lord Wenceslas of Dubá otherwise of Leštno, Lord John of Chlum, Lord George of Plumlov, Lord William Zajíc, Lord Myška,[98] and the other lords from Bohemia and Moravia, as well as the faithful lords of the Polish kingdom; for they, as God's brave defenders and supporters of the truth, have many times risen up against the whole Council and have brought proofs and arguments in order to secure my liberation. Especially believe what Lord Wenceslas of Dubá and Lord John of Chlum say, for they were present at the Council when for several days I defended myself. They know who the Czechs were who brought many unworthy accusations against me, and how the whole Council shouted at me, and how I answered to what they demanded of me.

I also beseech you to pray the Lord God in behalf of his royal grace, the Roman and Bohemian king and of his queen,[99] and the nobles, that the dear Lord God may dwell with them as well as with you in grace now and in the eternal joy afterward. Amen.

I wrote this letter to you in prison, in chains, expecting tomorrow the sentence of death, in full hope in God that I swerve not from His truth nor recant the errors that the false witnesses have witnessed against me. How the Lord God has dealt graciously with me and has remained with me in strange temptations you shall learn when with God's help we shall meet in His joy.

Of Master Jerome,[100] my beloved fellow worker, I hear nothing except that he is in a cruel prison, expecting death, even as I do, on account of his faith, which he showed so valiantly to the Czechs. And the Czechs, our fiercest enemies, gave us into the power of other enemies and into prison. I beseech you that you pray God for them.

I also beseech you, particularly the Praguers, to be kind toward

[98] George of Plumlov was the principal Moravian noble; both Zajíc and Myška were members of Sigismund's entourage.
[99] King Wenceslas and Queen Sophie.
[100] Jerome of Prague.

Bethlehem as long as the Lord God will be pleased that the Word of God be preached there. For the devil has become enraged at that place and has incited pastors and canons against it, perceiving that his kingdom was being ruined there. I trust the Lord God that He will preserve that place according to His will and increase its benefits through others more than He had done through my unworthy self.

Also I beseech you that you love one another, permit not the good to be oppressed by violence, and desire that every one learns the truth.

The letter was written on Monday night before St. Vitus, [and sent] by a good angel.[101]

14. To His Friends in Constance.[102]

[In the Franciscan prison, June 13, 1415]

In regard to Peter,[103] I am well pleased. I do not preserve his letters, but destroy them immediately. Do not send me the six-page folders [sexterni][104] for I fear a great danger to the messenger and to other persons. I still beseech you for God's sake that all the nobles together request the king[105] for a final hearing, because he himself said in the Council[106] that in the near future a hearing will be granted me, to which I am to write a brief reply. His shame will be great if he will disregard that word. But I suppose that his word is only as reliable as his safe-conduct, of which I was told to beware by someone in Bohemia. Others said: "He will surrender you to the enemies!" Lord Mikeš Divoký[107] told me before Master Jesenic: "Master, you may take it for certain that you will be condemned." I suppose he knew the king's intention. I thought that the king had a disposition toward the law of God and the truth: now I perceive in a way that he does not savor it much. He condemned me sooner than did my enemies. If at least he had adhered to the manner of Pilate, the gentile, who, having heard the accusations, said: "I find no fault in this man."[108] Or at least if he had

[101] Presumably the messenger who delivered it to the friends in Constance for transmission to Bohemia.

[102] Novotný, *Korespondence,* No. 131; Palacký, No. 70.

[103] Peter of Mladoňovice; naturally, no letter of Peter's from that period survives.

[104] Refers to some minor treatise of Hus, which he does not name, perhaps as a precaution.

[105] Sigismund.

[106] Cf. letter No. 12 and note 90.

[107] Mikeš Divoký, alias Divůček of Jemniště.

[108] John 18:38.

said: "I gave him a safe-conduct; if, therefore, he will not submit to the decision of the Council, I will send him back to the king of Bohemia with your sentence and testimonies so that he, along with his clergy, would judge him." Indeed, he[109] so informed me by Henry Lefl and by others, that he wished to procure for me an adequate hearing; and if I did not submit to the judgment, that he would send me back in safety.

15. The Last Reply of Hus to the Final Formulation of the Charges against Him (June 18–20).[110]

A

[Articles of John Hus, drawn from the book *De ecclesia* and certain other smaller treatises.]

1. There is only one holy universal Church [*said in the most essential sense according to Augustine*], which is the totality of the predestined. Subsequently it follows: the universal holy Church, [*said in the most essential sense*] is only one [*which is not part of another, properly speaking*], as there is only one number of the predestinate.

2. Paul was never a member of the devil [*foreknown as to the ultimate adherence*], although he committed some acts similar to those of the evilly-disposed toward the Church.

3. The foreknown are not part of the Church [*catholic in the most essential sense*], for no part finally falls away from it, since the predestinating love which binds them does not fail.

4. The two natures, divine and human, constitute one Christ [*concretely, by union*]. Subsequently in Chap. 10: Every man is a spirit [*that is often declared by the blessed Augustine in dealing with "On John"*], since he is composed of both natures.

5. The foreknown, although sometimes in grace according to present righteousness, nevertheless is never part of the holy Church [*catholic, said in the most essential sense*]; and the predestinate always remains a member of the Church, even though he sometimes falls away from

---

[109] Sigismund.

[110] Palacký, pp. 225–34. Hus's replies, written between the lines of the charges, are placed within square brackets and printed in italics. In comparison with the articles on which he was examined at the hearing of June 7 (Part I, Chap. IV), it will be seen that ten articles were deleted and two new ones, 4 and 30, were added. Moreover, in Palacký's version articles 20 and 21 were combined so that the total amounted to 29, not 30. I followed the division of the articles into 30.

the prevenient [*adventitia*] grace, but not from the grace of predestination.

6. Regarding the Church as the congregation of the predestinate, whether or not in grace according to present righteousness, the Church in that sense is an article of faith. [*That is the opinion of the blessed Augustine "On John"; further "On the Enchiridion"; further "On the Psalms"; further "On the Christian Doctrine" in the book* About the Sheep.]

7. Peter was not nor is the head of the holy catholic Church [*universal, said in the most essential sense*].

8. Priests living criminally in any manner whatever pollute the priestly power, and as faithless sons [*in Deut. 12: the perverse generation and faithless sons*] they think faithlessly concerning the seven sacraments of the Church, the keys, the offices, and the sacred things of the Church, the ceremonies, censures, morals, the veneration of relics, indulgences, and orders. [*This is stated in Psalm 77: "They loved him with their mouths but lied to him with their tongues; for their heart was not upright, nor were they faithful in their testimony."*].[111]

9. The papal dignity arose from Caesar and the papal preeminence and institution emanated from the Caesar's power. [*As to the temporal rule and the imperial insignia and the supremacy over the four churches.*[112] *It appears in dist. 96 and 63.*]

10. No one may reasonably assert without revelation [*special, as said in Eccles. 9: "No one knows whether he is worthy of grace or of hate"*][113] about himself or another that he is the head of a particular holy Church; nor the Roman pontiff that he is the head of the Roman Church.

11. It should not be believed that every Roman pontiff whatever is the head [*persevering in the merits of life*] of whatever particular holy Church, unless God predestined him.

12. No one occupies the place of Christ or Peter [*by office and merit*] unless he follows Him in morals; for in no other respect is it more appropriate to follow, nor has he otherwise [*under another condition*] received the procuratorial power from God; because for that

[111] Ps. 78:36–37.
[112] This refers to the four Eastern patriarchates.
[113] Eccles. 9:1.

vicarial office [*an agreement of*] both the conformity of morals and of the instituting authority are required.

13. The pope is not the manifest or true successor [*by office and merit*] of the prince of the apostles, Peter, if he lives in a manner contrary to Peter. And if he is avaricious, then he is the vicar of Judas Iscariot by living avariciously. For the same reason the cardinals are not the manifest and true successors of the college of Christ's other apostles unless they live after the manner of the apostles, observing the commands and counsels of the Lord Jesus Christ.

14. The doctors who state that anyone subjected to ecclesiastical censure, if he refuses to be corrected, is to be turned over to the secular judgment, actually follow therein the bishops, scribes, and Pharisees who, when Christ refused to obey them in everything, saying "It is not lawful for us to put anyone to death," turned Him over to the secular judgment [*the account there refers to those who turned Christ over to Pilate, as is evident therein*], are greater murderers than Pilate. [*I spoke there about the eight Prague doctors who wrote that whoever would not obey their dictates is to be turned over to the secular arm.*]

15. Ecclesiastical obedience is obedience according to the inventions of the priests of the Church aside from the express command of Scripture. [*That description deals with the obedience which is distinguished from the explicit obedience of the law of Christ, as is evident from the article from which it was taken; but God forbid that all obedience of the law of God were of that kind, which is also called in a manner obedience of the Church.*]

16. The obvious distinction between human acts is that they are either virtuous or wicked. For if a man is wicked, whatever he does, he does wickedly; and if he is virtuous, whatever he does, he does virtuously. For as wickedness which is called crime or mortal sin infects all man's acts totally, so virtue vivifies all man's acts efficaciously.

17. The priest of Christ living in accordance with His law, having knowledge of Scripture and a desire to edify the people, ought to preach, an alleged excommunication [*injurious and unlawful, fulminated out of malice*] notwithstanding; and subsequently, that if the pope or another orders a priest so disposed not to preach, the inferior ought not to obey.

18. Whoever has accepted the office of preacher in accordance with a mandate [*that is the saying of many saints—Augustine, Gregory,*

Isidore, etc.] and has entered upon the priesthood, ought to execute that mandate, an alleged excommunication [*injurious and unlawful, fulminated out of malice*] notwithstanding.

19. By ecclesiastical censures of excommunications, suspensions, interdicts [*alas! often done by the abuse of those censures, which can be, and often are, imposed legally*], the clergy subject the lay people to themselves for their own exaltation and the increase of avarice, and by malice protect and prepare Antichrist's way. It is, however, an evident sign that such censures, which in their trials they call fulminations, proceed from Antichrist. The clergy thereby proceed especially against those who make plain Antichrists's iniquity, for he has usurped the clergy mostly for himself.

20. The grace of predestination is the bond whereby the body of the Church and every member of it is linked indissolubly with the head.[114]

21. If the pope is wicked, and particularly if he is foreknown, then like the apostle Judas he is a devil, a thief, and son of perdition, and not the head of the holy Church militant [*acording to perseverance in meritorious life to the end*]; for he is not [even] its member, since the grace of predestination is the bond whereby the body of the Church and every member of it is linked indissolubly with the head.

22. A wicked or foreknown pope or prelate is putatively a shepherd, but actually a thief and a robber [*because he is not such according to office and meritorious life, but solely according to office*].

23. The pope ought not to be called the most holy even according to office [*for God alone is the most holy*], for otherwise a king ought also to be called the most holy according to office, and executioners and public criers ought to be called saints; indeed, even the devil should be called holy as being an official of God.

24. If the pope lives in a manner contrary to Christ, even if he has ascended by a rightful and legitimate election according to the established human constitution, he has nevertheless ascended otherwise than through Christ [*for he has elevated himself above Christ by pride*], even granted that he has entered by an election principally ordained by God. For Judas Iscariot was elected to the episcopacy rightfully and legitimately by Jesus Christ who is God; nevertheless, he entered by another way into the sheepfold of the sheep [*for he did not enter by the lowly door, namely Christ, who said: "I am the door; whoever en-*

[114] This article is divided into two, thus making the total of thirty.

ters through me shall be saved." That I said as a hypothesis, expecting better information].

25. The condemnation of the forty-five articles of Wyclif decreed by the doctors is irrational and unjust, and the reason alleged for it is wrongly conceived; that is, that none of them is catholic, but every one is either heretical, erroneous, or scandalous.

26. Not because the electors, or the greater part of them, have agreed *viva voce*, in acordance with human custom, upon some person [*as appears in the case of Agnes, who was esteemed by the Church to be a legitimate pope*] is that person *ipso facto* legitimately elected, or is *ipso facto* the true and manifest successor or vicar [*by office and meritorious life*] of Apostle Peter or of another apostle in an ecclesiastical office. Hence, whether the electors elected well or badly, we should believe the works of the elected. For that reason the more abundantly or meritoriously one labors for the benefit of the Church, the more abundant power therefor one has from God.

27. There is not a spark of apparent evidence that there should be one head ruling the Church in spiritual matters that should always abide with the Church militant; that is evident, since it is known that the Church has been without a pope for a long time, and now after the condemnation of John XXIII it so stands.

28. Christ without such monstrous heads [*as without Agnes and John XXIII and others who were heretics or otherwise criminal*] through his true disciples scattered over the circumference of the earth would rule His Church better.

29. The apostles and the faithful priests of the Lord had firmly ruled the Church in things necessary to salvation before the papal office [*as regards the temporal domination and rule*] was instituted. They would do so if there were no pope—as is highly possible—until the Day of Judgment.

30. No one is secular lord, no one is prelate, no one is bishop while he is in mortal sin [*according to office and meritorious life, as the saints have affirmed: Hosea 8, "They reigned, but not through me; they set up princes but I did not know them." That is adduced in common by saints Gregory, Bernard, etc.*].

B

[Here now they have placed the articles abstracted from the trial proceedings; and where the Scriptures or reason are stated as opposed

(to Hus), or rather are false and unjust, the witnesses, said to be trust-worthy, but who nevertheless were his enemies, ascribed it to him, al-though they themselves were strongly suspected.]

Articles abstracted from the trial proceedings against John Hus, ade-quately deduced and proved by trustworthy witnesses.

First, articles 4 and 8, which hold that John Hus stubbornly preached and defended the erroneous articles of Wyclif in the city of Prague, in schools, and in public preaching. *[It is not true that I ever advanced such things, but under protestation I argued in behalf of some of the articles that seemed true to me.]*

Further, article 9, which holds that on account of the above-men-tioned matters there followed a great sedition in the city of Prague, caused by the deceit and fault of John Hus to such a degree that no-table men and God-fearing Catholics were forced to leave and to hide outside the aforementioned city; and slaughter, condemnations, sacri-lege, and other horrible and execrable occurrences arose and followed with the aid and procurement of the forementioned John Hus along with his accomplies. *[It is not true that I have ever procured such things.]*

Further, article 10, which holds that John Hus in the said city of Prague had been and continued to be a follower, promoter, teacher, and defender of the errors of the *quondam* heresiarch, John Wyclif, and was regarded, designated, and reputed as such and for such in the said city and the neighboring parts. *[It is not true, although some enemies regarded me as such.]*

Further, articles 15 and 16, which hold that the lord archbishop of Prague, executing the mandate of the Lord Pope Alexander V of happy memory, who commanded and commissioned him that from then henceforth no one should dare to preach to the people in private places in the said city save in the cathedral, collegiate, parochial, and monastery churches and their cemeteries. The aforesaid archbishop, proceeding with the execution of the apostolic letter, prohibited acts of that kind in the general synod held at that time in Prague. John Hus, however, was actively opposed not only to the execution of the said letter and that kind of forbiddance and prohibition, but subsequently to that prohibition, in the month of June, and especially on the twenty-second day of that month, and thereafter on many and different occasions, he preached to the people in a certain chapel called Bethlehem and there convoked and caused the convocation of many people contrary to the aforesaid prohibition. [*It is true, because I appealed to that Alexander for his better information, as is evident from the trial proceedings.*]

Further, article 17, which holds that the aforesaid John Hus, both in the said month of June in the year of the Lord 1410, and also before and after, preaching to the people congregated on various occasions in the said chapel as well as in various other places of the city of Prague, composed, taught, disputed about, and as far as he could defended many errors and heresies both from the said books of the said *quondam* John Wyclif and from his own impudence and deceit; and above all the following, namely, that after the consecration of the host there remains on the altar the material bread or the substance of the bread. [*It is not true.*]

Further, article 18, which holds that a priest in mortal sin does not consecrate the body of Christ, does not minister nor baptize. [*It is not true; for I have preached the opposite.*]

Further, article 19, which holds that indulgences granted by the pope or bishops avail nothing. [*It is not true; however, I did reject the indulgences (granted) for money, accompanied by a tax, and the raising of the cross against Christians; and I wrote about indulgences that the priests of Christ can grant remission of sins and from punishment and guilt in a declaratory manner (ministerialiter) to the truly contrite confessors.*]

Further, article 21, which holds that the Roman Church is the synagogue of Satan. [*It is not true; for I state in the book* De ecclesia *that the Roman Church is holy, to which belong, according to the saints, all the faithful Christians pertaining to the obedience of the Roman pontiff according to the law of Christ.*]

Further, article 24, which holds that no heresy ought to be exterminated by force, but by disputations in schools. [*It is not true; but I said that the heretic should first be convinced by Scripture or reason, as Saints Augustine and Bernard say.*]

Further, article 26, which holds that the said John Hus, in order to seduce the people, particularly the simple ones, rashly dared to say that in England many monks and other masters, having convened in the Church of St. Paul against Master John Wyclif, were not able to convict him. For at once lightning and thunderbolt had struck from heaven and had split the door of the church, so that the masters and monks had hardly escaped into the city of London. And this he said in order to bolster the authority of the said John Wyclif. Thereupon, bursting into words, he exclaimed to the people: "Would that my soul were where the soul of John Wyclif is!" Later he frequently made public a certain forged letter, with the false seal of the University of Oxford, which stated, although falsely, that John Wyclif had been a true, catholic, and evangelical doctor of good report and of laudable conduct from the time of his youth to the day of his passing. [*That article is not true in many points and is full of contorted lies.*]

Further, article 29, which holds that seculars should take away the temporal possessions [of the clergy], that it is meritorious. [*It is not true.*]

Further, articles 32 and 37, which hold that John Hus, while excommunicated—later in aggravated excommunication—intruded into divine services, preached to the people, and publicly said that he disregarded the excommunication because one cannot be excommunicated by men unless he were first excommunicated by God. [*It is not true; but I said that I can preach under an appeal, and that an unjust excommunication does not harm a just man while he humbly bears it for God's sake.*]

Further, article 38, which holds that John Hus preached various errors, from which arose offenses among the prelates and the people of the kingdom of Bohemia and the masters and pupils of the Prague schools. [*It is not true.*]

Further, article VII, in part, charged and offered against John Hus in an inquisitorial investigation before the archbishop of Prague, which held that John Hus said to the people: "Look! the pope lately deceased, namely Pope Alexander V, recently wrote to the archbishop of Prague concerning the extirpation of the errors of John Wyclif in Bohemia and Moravia, and that there are many men holding Wyclif's opinions and errors against the faith, whose hearts are infected with heresy. I say, however, and give thanks to God, that I have not known any Czech to be a heretic." And that to the aforesaid words the people shouted: "He lies! he lies;" [*It is not true as regards the end, that the people shouted thus: for they shouted, saying: "They lie who call us heretics." But the article is true as regards the beginning.*]

Further, article IX, which holds that the same John Hus said in the vernacular to the people: "Look! the prophecy which James of Theramo[115] foretold is fulfilled: that in the year of the Lord 1409 one shall arise who shall persecute the Gospel and the Epistles and the faith of

[115] James de Teramo (1349–1417) was the author of the *Consolatio peccatorum*.

Christ," denoting thereby the Lord Alexander, who in his bulls ordered Wyclif's books to be burned. [*It is not true in that form; but I said some things (like that). Nor did Alexander himself command in the bull that Wyclif's books be burned.*]

Further, article XI, which holds that John Hus said about Pope Alexander, recently deceased, "Although I know not whether he be in heaven or in hell, he wrote on his skins of asses that the archbishop should burn the books of John Wyclif, in which many good things are contained." [*As to the first, it is true that I said it; but that he commanded them to be burned I did not say, since he did not write that in the bulls.*]

Further, another article about his reply, which holds that the said John Hus after he had left Bohemia sent a letter to be read to the people, which states that having in mind his earnest care, that he had of them ... [*They have not written more about that article to which, I think, you have the reply in the copy of the first articles copied in the first prison.*]

At the end it is written: The articles read against the teaching and person of John Hus, on Tuesday, i.e., the third day after Vitus, June 18, in the public session and turned over to the notary.

[*I, John Hus, ever in hope the servant of Jesus Christ, have written replies to the copies of the articles, as in this one, according to my conscience, concerning which I must render account to omnipotent God.*

To the articles abstracted from my books I could not write my conclusions both on account of the shortness of time, of the lack of paper, and of danger, etc. I think that in the copies of the first articles are stated the citations from the saints in explanation and proof of some of them.

Now it remains that I either recant and abjure and undergo an appalling penance, or that I be burned. May the Father, the Son, and the Holy Spirit, one God, in Whom I believe and trust, grant me, on account of the intercessions of all the saints and just men, the spirit of counsel and fortitude, that I may escape the snares of Satan and remain in His grace to the end. Amen.]

All the articles from the books and the trial proceedings so annotated in the reply to the Council, as are here briefly annotated, were presented on the Wednesday after St. Vitus.

Given on Thursday immediately after the feast of St. Vitus the Martyr from the prison of the Brethren called Minor or Barefoot.[116]

16. Hus's Answer to an Unknown Friend in the Council Whom He calls "Father."[117]

[c. June 20, 1415]

May the Almighty God, the most wise and most kind, grant to my Father, well disposed to me for the sake of Jesus Christ, eternal life in glory! Reverend Father! I am most grateful for your kind and fatherly grace. Nevertheless, I dare not submit to the Council in accordance with the terms proposed,[118] because I should thus either have to condemn many truths they call scandalous, as I have heard from themselves; or I should thus fall into perjury, if I recanted and confessed that I had held the errors. I should thereby scandalize a great many of God's people who have heard me preach the contrary.

If, therefore, St. Eleazar, a man of the Old Law, about whom is written in the Maccabees[119] that he refused to lie by saying that he had eaten flesh prohibited by law lest he acted contrary to God and left to posterity a bad example; how could I, a priest of the New Law, although unworthy, through the fear of transitory punishment, wish to transgress God's law by sinning more gravely; first, by retreating from the truth; secondly, by committing perjury; and thirdly, by causing offense to my fellows? Indeed, it were more advantageous for me to die than, to avoid momentary punishment, thus fall into the hand of the Lord, and afterward perhaps into eternal fire and dishonor.

---

[116] June 18 and June 20.

[117] Novotný, *Korespondence,* No. 136; Palacký, No. 78.

[118] The promised short formula of recantation was at last submitted to Hus, but he found that he could not accept it. The Council would have preferred to secure Hus's recantation rather than to condemn him. The present letter is one of the attempts, made by an unknown, but apparently highly placed member of the Council, to secure Hus's submission. The text of the recantation formula reads as follows:

"I, X.Y., besides the declaration I made at another time and which I here desire to be considered as repeated, declare again that although many things are ascribed to me which I never thought, nevertheless, in all that has been ascribed to me or has been objected to me, or has been abstracted from my books, or deposed by witnesses, I humbly submit to the merciful ordering, decision, and correction of the sacrosanct Council, that I abjure and recant it, undergo a merciful penance, and do all in its entirety and in every part that the said sacrosanct Council shall be pleased and gracious to command for my salvation; for which I commend myself most devotedly to that Council."

[119] II Mac. 6:18–28; the "prohibited flesh" was that of swine

Because I appealed to Christ Jesus, the mightiest and most just Judge, committing my cause to Him; therefore, I stand by His most holy decision and sentence, knowing that He judges and rewards every man not according to false testimony or according to erroneous counsels, but according to truth and merit.

17. The Answer of "the Father" to John Hus.[120]

[c. June 20, 1415]

As to the first, dearest, and most beloved brother, let it not disturb you as if you condemned the truth, because not you but they condemn it who are at present your as well as our superiors. Take heed of this word: "Do not depend on your wisdom." There are many knowledgeable and conscientious men at the Council. "My son, hear the law of your mother!" So much for the first point.

Likewise as to the second, dealing with perjury. Even if it were perjury, it would not redound upon you, but on those who exact it. Likewise, as far as you are concerned, no heresies exist if you cease from obstinacy. Augustine, Origen, and the Master of Sentences, etc. erred, but gladly returned. I had many times believed that I well understood something in which I erred; but having been corrected, I returned rejoicing.

Further, I write briefly because I write to an intelligent man. You will not retreat from the truth but yield to the truth. Nor will you have done worse but better. You will not cause offense but edification. Eleazar was a famous Jew, but Judas[121] with seven sons and eight martyrs was even more famous. Nevertheless, Paul was lowered "in a basket down a wall"[122] in order to procure better ends. The Judge, to Whom you appealed, the Lord Jesus Christ, gives you the [advice of the] apostles, which is this: even greater struggles for the faith in Christ will be granted you!

18. Hus's Answer to This Letter of "the Father."[123]

[c. June 20, 1415]

All these things the Council has often requested of me. But because it implies that I revoke, abjure, and undergo penance, in which I should

---

[120] Novotný, *Korespondence*, No. 137; Palacký, No. 76.
[121] I.e., Maccabeus.
[122] Acts 9:25.
[123] Novotný, *Korespondence*, No. 138; Palacký, No. 77.

have to retreat from many truths which the Council calls scandalous; and secondly, that I should have to abjure and thus to acknowledge as mine the errors that the Council falsely ascribes to me, and consequently be a perjurer; thirdly, that I should cause offense to many people of God to whom I have preached, for which cause it were better than "an ass' millstone be hanged about my neck and I were flung into the depth of the sea";[124] and fourthly, that if I did that, wishing to escape a brief disgrace and punishment, I should fall into the greatest disgrace and punishment, unless I repented most profoundly before death.

Hence, for my encouragement [the story of] the seven martyrs, the sons of the widow of Maccabeus, occurs to me. They desired rather to be cut in pieces than to eat flesh contrary to the law of the Lord. Also am I reminded of St. Eleazar, who, as is written there, refused even to say that he had eaten flesh prohibited by law, lest he afford a bad example to posterity, but rather endured martyrdom.[125] How, therefore, having these examples before my eyes, and of the many saints of both sexes of the New Law, who offered themselves to be martyred rather than to consent to sin; how could I, who have for so many years preached about patience and constancy, fall into many lies and perjury and give offense to many sons of God? Be it far, far from me! For Christ the Lord will abundantly reward me, granting me at present the aid of patience.

19. To Lords Wenceslas of Dubá and John of Chlum.[126]

[c. June 18–21, 1415]

Most gracious lords and most faithful lovers of truth and my comforters in the truth, appointed by God for me like angels!

I cannot fully describe my gratitude for your constancy and the kindly benefits which you have shown me, a sinner, although in hope a servant of the Lord Jesus Christ. I desire that He, Jesus Christ, our most kind Creator, Redeemer, and Savior, may reward you in the present time, giving you Himself as the best reward in the future. Hence, I exhort you by His mercy that you direct yourselves by His law, and particularly by His most holy commandments.

You, noble Lord Wenceslas, marry a wife and, abandoning the worldly vanities, live holily in matrimony. And you, Lord John, leave

[124] Matt. 18:6.
[125] II Mac. 6:18–31; 7:1–42.
[126] Novotný, *Korespondence,* No. 139; Palacký, No. 78.

already the service of mortal kings and stay at home with your wife and boys in the service of God. For you see how the wheel of worldly vanity spins, now lifting one, then plunging down another, granting very brief pleasure to the man it lifts up, after which follows eternal torment in fire and darkness.

You already know now the behavior of the spirituals, who call themselves the true and manifest vicars of Christ and His apostles, and proclaim themselves the holy Church and the most sacred Council that cannot err. It nonetheless did err: first, by adoring John XXIII on bended knees, kissing his feet, and calling him the most holy, although they knew that he was a base murderer, a sodomite, a simoniac, and a heretic, as they declared later in their condemnation of him.[127] They have already cut off the head of the Church, have torn out the heart of the Church, have exhausted the never-drying fountain of the Church, and have made utterly deficient the all-sufficient and unfailing refuge of the Church to which every Christian should flee for refuge.

What, therefore, becomes of the statement of the late Master Stanislav[128]—may God have mercy on him!—and of Páleč and his other fellow-doctors,[129] which they delivered through Stanislav, that the pope is the head of the Church, ruling it all-sufficiently, the heart of the Church vivifying it, the unfailing fountain full of authority, the channel through which all power flows to the inferiors, and the unfailing refuge all-sufficient for every Christian, to which every Christian should flee for refuge? Now faithful Christendom exists without a pope, a mere man, having Christ Jesus for its head, who directs it the best; for its heart, which vivifies it, granting the life of grace; for the fountain which irrigates it by the seven gifts of the Holy Spirit; for the channel in which flow all the streams of graces; for the all-sufficient and unfailing refuge to which I, a wretch, run, firmly hoping that it will not fail me in directing, vivifying, and aiding me; but will liberate me from the sins of the present miserable life, and reward me with infinite joy.

The Council has also erred three or more times by wrongly ab-

---

[127] Cf. the text of the charges in Hefele-Leclercq, VII/I, 234–39, 245. John XXIII was sentenced to life imprisonment, but was freed in 1419.

[128] Stanislav of Znojmo, who died before the opening of the Council.

[129] Hus refers to their definition of the pope and the Church written in 1413, in their treatises against him, such as Stanislav's *Tractatus de Romana ecclesia* and Páleč's *Antihus*. The text quoted is in "Responsio Joannis Hus ad scripta M. Stanislai," *Historia et Monumenta*, I, 341–42.

stracting the articles from my books, rejecting some of them by corrupting and confusing [their meaning]; and even in the latest copy of the articles[130] by abbreviating some, as will be evident to those who compare the books with those articles. From this I have plainly learned, along with you, that not everything the Council does, says, or defines is approved by the most true judge, Christ Jesus. Blessed are those, therefore, who, observing the law of Christ, recognize, abandon, and repudiate the pomp, avarice, hypocrisy, and deceit of Antichrist and of his ministers, while they patiently await the advent of the most just Judge.

I beseech you by the bowels of Jesus Christ that you flee evil priests but love the good according to their works; and as much as in you lies, along with other faithful barons and lords, that you do not suffer them to be oppressed. For on that account has God placed you over others. I think that there will be a great persecution in the kingdom of Bohemia of those who serve God faithfully, unless the Lord oppose His hand through the secular lords, whom He has enlightened in His law more than the spirituals.

O, how great madness it is to condemn as error the Gospel of Christ and the Epistle of St. Paul, which he received, as he says,[131] not from men, but from Christ; and to condemn as error the act of Christ along with the acts of His apostles and other saints—namely, about the communion of the sacrament of the cup of the Lord, instituted for all adult believers! Alas! they call it an error that believing laity should be allowed to drink of the cup of the Lord, and if a priest should give them thus to drink, that he be then regarded as in error, and unless he desist, be condemned as a heretic![132] O Saint Paul! You say to all the faithful: "As often as you eat this bread and drink this cup, you proclaim the Lord's death until He comes;"[133] that is, until the Day of Judgment, when He shall come. And lo! it is even now said that the custom of the Roman Church is in opposition to it!

---

[130] Probably the last revision of his articles presented to him on June 18. Cf. No. 15.

[131] I Cor. 11:23.

[132] The decree, adopted on June 15, is to be found in Hefele-Leclercq, VII/I, 283–86.

[133] I Cor. 11:26. The communion of the cup was forbidden by the Council on the ground that it was contrary to the Roman custom. Jean Gerson formulated the decree.

20. *John Hus to His Friends in Constance.*[134]

[June 21, 1415]

This is my final intention in the name of Jesus Christ: that I refuse to confess as erroneous the articles which have been truthfully abstracted, and to abjure the articles ascribed to me by false witnesses. For to abjure means to confess that I have held errors or error, and to abandon them and to hold the opposite. For God knows that I have never preached those errors which they have concocted, leaving out many truths and adding falsehoods. For if I knew that my articles were contrary to the truth, I would most gladly amend and revoke them and teach and preach the opposite. But I think that none is contrary to the law of Christ and the teachings of the holy doctors, although they are called by those whom they displease to be scandalous and erroneous. Hence, whatever false meaning is contained in any article by my intention, that I reject and subject myself to the correction of the omnipotent and best Master, confident that in His infinite mercy He will most kindly cleanse me from my secret sins.

I thank all the barons, knights, and squires of the kingdom of Bohemia, and particularly King Wenceslas and the queen,[135] my gracious lady, that they have dealt affectionately with me, have treated me kindly, and have striven diligently for my liberation. I thank also King Sigismund for all the good he has shown me. I thank all the Czech and Polish lords who steadfastly and firmly strove for the truth and for my liberation; I desire salvation for all of them, now in grace and afterward in everlasting glory. May the God of all grace guide your life in the health of soul and body to Bohemia, that serving there the King Christ, you may attain the life of glory!

Greet all our friends whom I cannot mention, for if I mentioned some and not others, it might seem to them that I am a respector of persons; and those whom I would not mention might suppose that I do not remember them, or that I do not love them as I ought.

Written in prison, in chains, the Friday before the Feast of St. John the Baptist.[136]   John Hus,

> in hope a servant of Jesus Christ, from which hope the devil could never separate nor will ever separate me, with the help of the Father, the Son, and the Holy Spirit, blessed for ever and ever. Amen.

[134] Novotný, *Korespondence,* No. 140; Palacký, No. 83.
[135] Queen Sophie.
[136] Friday, June 21, 1415.

21. *John Hus to His Friends in Constance.*[137]

[Constance, June 22, 1415]

There have already been a great many exhorters, persuading me by many words that I ought and lawfully can recant, subjecting my will to the holy Church which the sacred Council represents. But none of them knows how to evade satisfactorily [the objection], if I put him in my place, that, knowing he had never preached, held, or asserted the heresy which was ascribed to him, and wishing to save his conscience, he would by recanting confess that he falsely held that heresy! Some said that to abjure does not mean that, but is only a renunciation of heresy either held or not held. Others, that to abjure means a denial of the attested charges, whether they be true or false. To them I said: "Very well! I will swear that I have never preached, held, or asserted those attested errors, and that I will never preach, hold, or assert them." Immediately they draw back.

Some argue that a man, even assuming that he is innocent, by submitting to the Church, confesses himself guilty out of humility and thus obtains merit. To prove it, one doctor adduced the case of a certain saint from the *Lives of the Fathers,* in whose bed someone had placed a book; and being admonished and inculpated on its account, the saint denied it. But they said: "Look! you stole it and put it in your bed!" Then when the book was found there, he acknowledged himself guilty. Another man proved his point by a certain saintly woman[138] who lived in a cloister wearing man's clothing. She was accused of having fathered a boy by a certain woman. She acknowledged it and cared for the boy. Later it became manifest that she was an innocent woman. And many other such cases were adduced.

A certain Englishman said: "If I were in your place, I would willingly and conscientiously recant; for in England all the masters, very good men, who were suspected of Wyclif's opinion, all in order recanted at the command of the archbishop." In the end they agreed yesterday upon my throwing myself entirely on the grace of the Council.

Páleč visited me at my request, for I wished to make my confession to him. I had petitioned the commissioners or exhorters that he or someone else be assigned me. I said: "Páleč is my principal adversary; I want to confess to him; or give me, I beg you for God's sake, another

---

[137] Novotný, *Korespondence,* No. 143; Palacký, No. 84.
[138] This legend is told about St. Marina.

suitable man." And it was done. I made my confession to a certain doctor, a monk, who heard me kindly and very graciously [*pulchre*], gave me an absolution and counsel, but not a command, as the others also had counseled me.

Páleč came and wept much along with me, when I asked him to forgive me if I had said any reproachful word, and especially that I had called him a deceiver [*fictor*] in writing.[139] I also said that he was a "pointer dog" for all others,[140] and he did not deny it. Also that when I denied at the hearing the articles of the witnesses, he arose, saying: "This man does not fear God!"[141] This he denied; but he surely said it. Perhaps you heard him. I also told him that he had said in the prison before the commissioners that "since the birth of Christ no heretic except Wyclif had written more dangerously against the Church than you."[142] He had also said that "all who have attended your sermons are infected by the error concerning the sacrament of the altar." He denied it, saying: "I did not say all, but many." But he certainly had said it, because I then reproved him, saying: "O master, how grave a wrong you are committing, calling all my hearers erroneous!" Later he had counseled me the same way as the others. Furthermore, he has kept on constantly asserting how much evil has been done by me and my adherents. He also said to me that they have a letter that was written to Bohemia, in which it is mentioned that I had sung two verses about the chains at the castle to the tune of "God almighty."[143]

For God's sake, save the letters; do not let them be carried by any clerk. Let the lords save them carefully among some secular documents. Let me know if the lords are to ride with the king.[144] Christ Jesus ever keeps me by His grace in my former resolve.[145]

---

[139] Hus calls Páleč "*fictor*" in the treatise "Contra Paletz."

[140] This word in Czech is "*slednik*," a pointer dog.

[141] This scene is not mentioned in Peter's *Account*. It must have occurred on June 5, before the Czech lords with Peter arrived at the hearing. In that case Hus forgot that Peter had not been present.

[142] Páleč's statement is mentioned by Hus in his letter written in January. He states it definitely in his letter of June 9. Cf. No. 7.

[143] Why it was regarded as an offense that he had sung the song at Gottlieben is not clear. The tune of the hymn "Buoh wšemohúcí" was regularly used at the Bethlehem Chapel.

[144] Perhaps this refers to the trip to the Richtenthal estates.

[145] This refers to Hus's resolve not to recant.

22. *John Hus to Preacher Havlík.*[146]

[June 21, 1415]

Dearly beloved brother Havlík, preacher of the Word of God!

Do not oppose the sacrament of the cup of the Lord[147] which the Lord instituted through Himself and through His apostle, and to which no Scripture is opposed, but only custom, which I suppose has grown up by negligence. We ought not follow custom, but Christ's example and truth. Now[148] the Council, giving "custom" as the reason, has condemned the lay participation in the cup as an error. Whoever should practice it, unless he recover his senses, shall be punished as a heretic. Alas! now malice condemns Christ's institution as an error!

I beseech you for God's sake to attack Master Jakoubek no longer, lest a schism occurs among the faithful that would delight the devil. Also, dearly beloved, prepare yourself for suffering on account of the eating [of the bread] and the communion of the cup. Stand valiantly in the truth of Christ, putting behind unlawful fear, comforting the other brethren in the gospel of the Lord Jesus Christ. You will find the reasons for the communion of the cup, I think, in what I wrote in Constance.[149] Greet the faithful in Christ.

Written in bonds on the vigil of the Ten Thousand Knights.[150]

23. *John Hus to Lord John of Chlum.*[151]

[June 23, 1415]

Dearly beloved Friend!

You should know that Páleč, in his attempt to persuade me, said that I should not care about the shame of recanting, but should consider the good that would come of it. I said to him: "It is a greater shame to be condemned and burned than to recant. In what way, therefore, do I fear shame? Counsel me as to what you would do if you

[146] Novotný, *Korespondence,* No. 141; Palacký, No. 80.

[147] The granting of the cup to lay people was introduced by Jakoubek of Stříbro, but was opposed by Havlík, Hus's substitute at the Bethlehem Chapel. This letter proves that, although Hus did not introduce the practice, he approved it.

[148] June 15, when the decree forbidding the practice was passed by the Council.

[149] Hus refers to his treatise, "Utrum expediat laicis fidelibus sumere sanguinem Christi sub specie vini," written before he was imprisoned.

[150] June 21. The Feast of the Ten Thousand Knights was held in commemoration of the soldiers said to have been crucified on Mount Ararat in the days of Marcus Aurelius. Cf. *Acta sanctorum,* V, 151–62.

[151] Novotný, *Korespondence,* No. 145; Palacký, No. 82.

knew with certainty that you did not hold the errors ascribed to you. Would you be willing to recant?" He replied: "That is difficult," and began to weep. We talked about many things that I held against him. Michael,[152] poor man, stood several times before the prison with the deputies. While I was with the deputies, he said to the jailers that "by the grace of God we will soon burn that heretic on whose account I have expended many a florin!" Understand that in writing this I do not desire vengeance upon him; for I committed it to God, and I earnestly pray God for him.

I exhort you again to be cautious with the letters. Michael has arranged that no one be now admitted before the prison, not even the jailers' wives. O Holy God! how widely has Antichrist extended his power and cruelty! But I hope that his power will be curtailed, and more, that his iniquity will be bared before the faithful people.

God Almighty will strengthen the hearts of His faithful whom He has chosen before the foundation of the world that they may receive the unfading crown of glory![153] Let Antichrist rage as he will, he shall not prevail against Christ, who "shall slay him with the breath of his mouth," as the Apostle says.[154] And then "the creation will be liberated from its bondage of decay to the glorious liberty of the sons of God," as the Apostle says, adding: "We ourselves groan inwardly for the adoption of the children of God, expecting the redemption of our bodies."[155]

I am greatly consoled by the word of our Savior: "You shall be blessed when men shall hate you and when they exclude and revile you and cast out your name as evil on account of the Son of Man. Rejoice and exult: for behold! great is your reward in heaven."[156] It is good, indeed the best, consolation, but difficult, not in respect of being understood, but to be fully sustained; that is, to rejoice in these tribulations. James held that rule along with the other apostles; he said: "Count it all joy, my brethren, when you fall into various temptations, knowing that the testing of your faith works patience, and patience then has perfect effect."[157] Surely it is difficult to rejoice without perturbation, and to esteem it all joy in various temptations. It is easy to talk about

[152] Michael de Causis.
[153] I Peter 5:4.
[154] II Thes. 2:8.
[155] Rom. 8:21, 23.
[156] Luke 6:22–23.
[157] I James 1:2–4.

it and to expound it, but difficult to fulfill it. Even the most patient and most valiant soldier, knowing that on the third day He would rise, conquering by His death the enemies and redeeming the elect from damnation, after the Last Supper was troubled in spirit and said: "My soul is sorrowful even unto death."[158] The Gospel says of Him that He began to tremble, to be sorrowful and in dread, indeed in agony, but was comforted by an angel. "His sweat became like drops of blood falling down on the ground."[159] Nevertheless He, being troubled, said to His faithful: "Let not your heart be troubled, neither let it be afraid."[160] Be not troubled on account of my brief absence, nor fear the cruelty of those who rage; for you will have me eternally, and the cruelty of the raging you will conquer.

Hence, looking upon that leader and king of glory, His soldiers have fought a great fight. They pased through fire and water, yet were saved and received the crown from the Lord God. James, referring to it in the canonical, says: "Blessed is the man that endures temptation, for when he has been tested, he will receive the crown of life which God has promised to those that love him."[161]

That crown, I firmly hope, the Lord will allow me to share along with you, most fervent lovers of the truth, and along with all who firmly and steadfastly love the Lord Jesus Christ, Who suffered for us, leaving us an example that we should follow in His steps. He had to suffer, as He Himself says;[162] and it behooves us to suffer, that the members would suffer along with the head. He says: "If anyone would come after me, let him deny himself and take up his cross and follow me." [163] O most kind Christ, draw us weaklings after Thyself, for unless Thou draw us, we cannot follow Thee! Give us a courageous spirit that it may be ready; and if the flesh is weak,[164] may Thy grace go before, now as well as subsequently. For without Thee we can do nothing, and particularly not go to a cruel death for Thy sake. Give us a valiant spirit, a fearless heart, the right faith, a firm hope, and perfect love, that we may offer our lives for Thy sake with the greatest patience and joy. Amen.

---

[158] Matt. 26:38.
[159] Luke 22:43–44.
[160] John 14:1.
[161] James 1:12.
[162] Mark 8:31.
[163] Matt. 16:24.
[164] Matt. 26:41.

Written in prison in bonds, on the vigil of St. John the Baptist,[165] who was beheaded in prison and in bonds because he had rebuked wickeness. May he be pleased to pray the Lord Jesus Christ for us. Amen.

24. *John Hus to His Friends in Bohemia.*[166]

[June 24, 1415]

Master John Hus, in hope a servant of God, to all the faithful who love and will continue to love God and His law, sends his wish that they would dwell in the truth, grow in God's grace, and courageously persevere unto death!

Dearly beloved! I exhort you not to fear or to allow yourselves to be terrified because they [the Council] had condemned my books to be burned. Remember that they burned the prophecies of St. Jeremiah, which God had commanded to be written, but did not escape that which he had prophesied. For after they had been burned, the Lord God commanded him to write the same words, having added some others; and it was done. He dictated them, sitting in prison, and St. Baruch, who was his scribe, wrote them. Thus it stands written in Jeremiah 36.[167] Also in the books of the Maccabees it is written that they burned the law of God and tortured those who possessed it.[168] Then in the New Law they burned the saints along with the books of God's law. The cardinals moreover condemned and burned the books of St. Gregory and would have burned them all had not the Lord preserved them through Peter, one of his [Gregory's] disciples.[169] Also St. John Chrysostom had been twice condemned as a heretic by a priestly council,[170] but the Lord God revealed their lie after St. John's death.

Having these things before your eyes, do not allow yourselves to be terrified into giving up the reading of what I have written or into surrendering your books to be burned by them. Remember what our merciful Savior told us as a warning in Matthew 24, that prior to the

---

[165] June 26.

[166] Novotný, *Korespondence*, No. 147; Palacký, pp. 134–35. This letter is in Czech.

[167] Jer. 36:4.

[168] I Mac. 1:56–57.

[169] Cf. John the Deacon's *Vita Gregorii Magni*, IV, 69. Migne, *Patrologia latina*, Vol. 75, Cols. 221–22.

[170] The synods of "the Oaks" and of Constantinople, in 403 and 404.

Day of Judgment "there will be so great a tribulation as has not been from the beginning of the world and never will be afterward."[171] It will be so great that it may happen that even the elect would be led into error; but these days shall be shortened for the elects' sake.

Remembering that, dearly beloved, stand firm! For I hope in God that the Antichrist's school will be afraid of you and will leave you in peace. The Council will not come from Constance to Bohemia! I think that many of that Council will die before they wrest the books from you. They will scatter from that Council over the world like storks; and when winter comes, they will recognize what they perpetrated during the summer.

Take notice that they condemned their head[172] as a heretic. Answer now, you preachers,[173] who preach that the pope is the earthly god, that he cannot sin, and cannot commit simony! The jurists say that the pope is the head of the entire holy Church, which he governs very well; that he is the heart of the holy Church, which he nourishes spiritually; that he is the fountain from which flows all power and goodness; that he is the sun of the holy Church; that he is the unfailing refuge to which every Christian must flee. Well! that head is already cut off, the god of this world is bound, and his sins are already made manifest; the fountain has already dried up, the sun is darkened, the heart is torn out, and the refuge is fled from Constance and is imprisoned so that no one would flee to it.[174] The Council condemned him as a heretic because he had sold indulgences, bishoprics, and other benefices; and many of those who condemned him had bought them from him, while others had trafficked in them. Among them was John, bishop of Litomyšl, who had twice attempted to buy the archbishopric of Prague,[175] but others exceeded his offer. O why did they not first take out the beam from their own eye?[176] For their own law[177] says: "If anyone

---

[171] Matt. 24:21.

[172] Pope John XXIII.

[173] This is a reference to Stanislav of Znojmo and Stephen Páleč. The same assertions had been made by Augustino Triumfo of Ancona in his book, *De potestate ecclesie*, dedicated to Pope John XXII, and by other extreme papal partisans.

[174] The deposed pope was imprisoned at the castle of Gottlieben only a few days after Hus had left it.

[175] Bishop John of Litomyšl tried to secure the archbishopric after the death of Zbyněk in 1411, and previously after the death of Puchník in 1402. Cf. "On Simony" in my translation in *Advocates of Reform*, XIV, 213, n. 56.

[176] Matt. 7:5.

[177] Gratian's *Decretum*, pars II, c. I, qu. 3, cap. 15. Friedberg, I, 449.

should obtain any dignity by purchase, let him be deprived of it; and the seller and the buyer, the go-between or middleman, be openly condemned." St. Peter condemned and anathematized Simon because he had wanted to buy the gift of the Holy Spirit.[178] These men have condemned and anathematized the seller, while they themselves remained buyers and middlemen and continue to sell at home. There is a bishop in Constance who bought and another who sold [a benefice], and the pope accepted money for consenting to it. The same has happened in Bohemia, as you know.

O that the Lord Jesus would have said to the Council: "He that is among you without the sin of simony, let him condemn Pope John!" It seems to me that they would have all run out one after another! And why did they kneel before him, kiss his feet, and call him the most holy Father, when they knew that he was a heretic, a murderer, and a sodomite,[179] the sins which they themselves made public later? Why did the cardinals elect him to the papacy when they knew that he was such a cruel murderer as to have murdered the most holy father?[180] Why did they allow him to practice simony while he was pope, having been appointed his advisers for the purpose of counseling him well? Are they not guilty who have themselves committed simony along with him? Why, before his flight from Constance, could no one address him otherwise than as "the most holy father?" They were still afraid of him. But when the secular arm had seized him by God's permission or will, then they conspired among themselves, agreeing not to let him free.

Surely now the wickedness and abomination and shame of Antichrist has manifested itself in the pope as well as in others of the Council! The faithful servants of God can now understand the meaning of the Savior's words when He said: "When you see the abomination in a desolate place of which Daniel prophesied, let him who reads under-

---

[178] Acts 8:20–23.

[179] The text has "*němý hříšník*," literally "a dumb sinner," i.e., one whose sin should not even be mentioned.

[180] Pope John was commonly regarded as having poisoned his predecessor, Alexander V; but this charge was not included in the official verdict. But the papal secretary, Cerretano, reports in his *Journal* that the charges against John were "very ugly and provocative of scandal" and were omitted not because they were untrue but because they would be offensive to the papacy and the Church universally, particularly "if witnesses should be heard and their testimony published later." Loomis, *op. cit.*, pp. 496–97.

stand!"[181] "The abomination" is the great pride, avarice, and simony; and "the desolate place" is the dignity that is void of humility and of other virtues, as we clearly see in those who hold office and dignity.

Would that it were possible to describe the wickednesses so that the faithful servants of God might beware of them! I would like to do it; but I trust God that after me He will raise up braver men, and that they exist even now, who will better declare Antichrist's wickedness and will risk their lives to death for the truth of the Lord Jesus Christ, Who will grant you and me eternal joy. Amen.

This letter is written on [the feast of] John the Baptist, in prison and in bonds, remembering that John also was beheaded in prison and in bonds for God's truth.

25. Hus to Peter of Mladoňovice
and to John "Cardinal" of Rejnštejn.[182]

[June 24, 1415]

Because they [the Council] had condemned only the treatises,[183] I pray, amend the last Czech letter that I sent today,[184] lest the people of God suppose that all my books had been condemned, as I had supposed according to yesterday's letter.[185] I would be glad to see that no letter written in this prison be shown to anyone, for it is yet not definitely certain how God will deal with me. I fear having any letter of mine sent by Ulrich.[186] I still pray for God's sake, preserve cautiously your letters, words, and actions. O how consoled I have been by your letters which, along with mine, will, I hope, by the grace of God, benefit the people!

As long as I am aware that you and the lords[187] are in Constance, so long it is a consolation to me, assuming that I should already be led to death. I take it for certain that God has given you as angels to me, comforting me, weak and wretched, in greatest trials. Of what kind they have been, still are, and will be, God Almighty knows! He is

---

[181] Matt. 24:15.

[182] Novotný, *Korespondence*, No. 149; Palacký, No. 66.

[183] Hus supposed at the time that only some of his treatises had been condemned, not all his works.

[184] The letter of June 24, given above as No. 23.

[185] This refers to a letter of June 23, which is lost.

[186] Perhaps one of the servants of the Czech lords; it may be the same man who informed Peter of Mladoňovice of the Council's intention to condemn Hus in his absence at the session on June 5. Why Hus warns against him is not clear.

[187] Wenceslas of Dubá and John of Chlum.

"my mercy and my refuge, my upholder and my liberator; in Him have I trusted."[188]

I have been questioned by two [emissaries] who had been sent to me to the prison to inquire if I had more books of my own composition. I said that I had. They said: "Where?" I said: "In Bohemia." They inquired whether I had them here. I said that I did not have any, although I had brought the *Super Sentenciarum*,[189] a Bible, and others.

And now I heard that my cleric, John,[190] went away.

They said: "Have you come to any conclusions?" I said: "No," for that is true. They said: "Do you wish to recant or revoke?" I said: "Come to the Council and there you will hear; for I must stand before the Council and reply to it. Why do you tempt me? Have you come to console a prisoner or to harass him?" Hearing that, they interposed a few words and went away.

Take care of the books, if you have any—I do not know. Tell Master Jesenic that the notary wrongly changed my testimony regarding the comments about the bull,[191] as you have heard, since I said it publicly in the Council.

26. *Hus to His Friends in Constance.*[192]

[June 25, 1415]

I still exhort you, for God's sake, not to show the letters to anyone, or to make them public, for I fear a danger to some persons.[193] Be cautious in words and deeds. Vitus,[194] if he will remain, should be very cautious. I am also very glad to hear that my gracious lord has come.[195] Our Savior restored Lazarus to life four days after his decomposition; He preserved Jonah for three days in the fish and then sent him to preach; He drew up Daniel from the den of lions to write prophecies;

---

[188] Ps. 144:2.

[189] I.e., Flajšhans, *Super IV Sententiarum.*

[190] He is not known otherwise.

[191] This refers to Hus's statement that he supposed the comments about the "crusading bull" of John XXIII had been made by John of Jesenice (cf. the hearing of June 8), which the notary stated as a fact.

[192] Novotný, *Korespondence,* No. 150; Palacký, No. 61.

[193] It would be dangerous to those who were named or addressed in his letters, who would thus be denounced as his friends if the letters were intercepted, as they sometimes were.

[194] He is not known with certainty, but may be identified with Vitus, a servant of John of Chlum, who made himself suspect by his contacts with Jerome of Prague.

[195] It is uncertain whether this refers to a visit of John of Chlum.

He saved the three youths from the flames in the oven of fire; He freed Susanna, already condemned and going to her death.[196] Why could He not still liberate me, a miserable wretch, from prison and death, in the same manner, if it were for His glory, for the benefit of the faithful, and for my better? His power, Who led Peter out of prison by an angel, and from whose hands the fetters fell when he should already have been led to death in Jerusalem, is not weakened.[197] Let His will ever be done, however, for I desire that it be fulfilled in me for His glory and on account of my sins.

A certain doctor told me that whatever I did in submitting to the Council would be good and lawful for me; and he added that "if the Council said that you had only one eye, even if you had two, you should confess with the Council that it was so." To whom I replied: "Even if the whole world said that to me, I, having reason which I am now using, could not without harm to conscience say that!" Thereupon, expatiating at great length about it, he retreated from that statement and said: "It is true I have not given a very good example."

"The Lord is with me as a valiant warrior."[198] "The Lord is my light and my salvation; whom shall I fear?" "The Lord is the protector of my life; before whom shall I tremble?"[199] To Him in these times I frequently repeat the antiphon: "Lord I suffer oppression, reply on my behalf: I know not what to say to my enemies." The Lord be with you!

27. Hus to John of Chlum and Wenceslas of Dubá.[200]

[c. June 26, 1415]

My most gracious benefactors and protectors of the truth! I exhort you by the bowels of Jesus Christ that you, laying aside the vanities of this age, fight for the eternal King, the Lord Christ. "Do not have confidence in princes, in the sons of men, in whom there is no salvation,"[201] because the lying and deceiving sons of men today are and tomorrow perish; but God abides for ever. He has servants not because of His need, but for their well-being. What He promises to give them, He fulfills; what He pledges them, He fulfills. He deceives no man by a

---

[196] John 11:39; Jonah 2:11; Dan. 6:6 ff.; Dan. 3:23; Apocrypha, "The History of Sussana," *passim.*

[197] Acts 12:7.

[198] Jer. 20:11.

[199] Ps. 27:1.

[200] Novotný, *Korespondence,* No. 152; Palacký, No. 88.

[201] Ps. 146:3.

safe-conduct, drives from Himself no one faithfully serving Him; for He says: "Where I am, there shall my servant be also."[202] That Lord makes every servant of His the lord of all His possessions,[203] giving Himself to him and all things with Himself, that he may possess all things without worry and fear, nay, without any lack, rejoicing with all the saints with infinite joy. O, "blessed is that servant whom, when that Lord comes, He shall find watching!"[204] Blessed is that servant who shall receive that King of glory with joy! Serve, therefore, that King in fear, dearest lords, and He will, I hope, now conduct you to Bohemia in His grace and in health, and later to the everlasting life of glory. Farewell!

I suppose that this is my last letter to you, because tomorrow, I think, I shall be purged of sins, in the hope in Jesus Christ, by a dreadful death. I cannot describe what I have passed through this night. Sigismund has acted deceitfully in all things—may God forgive him, and that solely for your sake. You yourselves heard the sentence which he has decreed.[205]

I pray, have no suspicion of the faithful Vitus.

28. *John Hus to All the Faithful Czechs.*[206]

[June 26, 1415]

Master John Hus, in hope a servant of God, to all the faithful Czechs who love God and will love Him, sends his wish and unworthy prayer that they would live in God's grace, die in it, and dwell with God for ever!

Faithful and beloved in God! I have yet in mind to call to your attention that the proud and avaricious Council, full of all abomination, condemned my Czech books, having neither heard nor seen them; even if it had heard them, it would not have understood them. For there were Italians, French, English, Spaniards, Germans, and others of other languages in that Council—unless perhaps Bishop John of

---

[202] John 12:26.

[203] Ps. 105:21.

[204] Luke 12:43.

[205] This refers to the conversation of Sigismund with the cardinals after the session on June 8, overheard by the Czech lords, in which he asserted that even a fraction of the charges against Hus would suffice for his being sentenced to death.

[206] Novotný, *Korespondence,* No. 153; Palacký, *op cit.,* No. 85. The letter is in Czech.

Litomyšl might have understood them somewhat. For he was there along with other Czechs, the provocators, with the Prague and Vyšehrad chapters from whom had originated the calumny against the truth of God and of our Bohemian land. I hold that land, in the hope of God, as the land of the best faith, knowing of her desire for the Word of God and for morals.

O, had you seen that Council which calls itself the most holy, that cannot err, you would surely have seen the greatest abomination! For I have heard it commonly said by the Swabians that Constance or Kostnice,[207] their city, would not for thirty years rid itself of the sins which that Council had committed in their city. They say, furthermore, that all have been scandalized by that Council, and others spat when they saw the abominable things.

I say to you that when I stood before that Council the first day, seeing that there was no order in it whatever, I said aloud, when they were all quiet: "I had supposed that there would be greater honesty, goodness, and better order in this Council than there is!" At that time the presiding cardinal[208] said: "What do you say? You spoke more humbly at the castle!"[209] And I answered, saying: "Because at the castle nobody shouted at me, and here all are shouting!"

Because that Council conducted itself in such a disorderly way, it has done more harm than good. Therefore, faithful and in God dear Christians, do not allow yourselves to be terrified by their decrees, which, I hope in God, will profit them nothing. They will fly away like butterflies, and their decrees will turn into a spiderweb. They wanted to frighten me, but could not overcome God's power in me. They did not dare to oppose me with Scripture, as those gracious lords heard, who, despite all shame, stood bravely by the truth—the Czechs, Moravians, and the Poles; but especially Lord Wenceslas of Dubá and Lord John of Chlum. For they were present there, since King Sigismund himself permitted them to be in the Council. They heard it when I said: "I ask for instruction; and if I have written anything wrong, I wish to be instructed therein." Then the presiding cardinal said: "As you wish to be instructed, here is your instruction: you must recant, as fifty masters of the Holy Scriptures have so concluded!"

---

[207] The Czech form of the name.
[208] Pierre d'Ailly, who presided.
[209] Gottlieben.

Yea! what a fine instruction! So St. Catherine,[210] a young maiden, should have retreated from the truth and faith of the Lord Jesus Christ because fifty masters stood up against her! Nevertheless, that dear maiden remained steadfast unto death and brought the masters to the Lord God, whom I, a sinner, am unable to bring!

I am writing this to you that you may know that they did not defeat me by any Scripture or any proof, but that they sought to seduce me by deceit and threats to recant and abjure. But the merciful Lord God, Whose law I have extolled, has been and is with me, and I hope that He will be with me to the end and will preserve me in His grace until death.

The letter was written on Wednesday after St. John the Baptist,[211] in prison and in chains, in the expectation of death; but by reason of God's secret counsels I cannot say whether it is my last letter. For the Almighty God can yet set me free.

29. *John Hus to His Friends in Bohemia.*[212]

[June 27, 1415]

God be with you! Having had many reasons for the strong supposition, I wrote you as if I were to die tomorrow. But since I again learned of the postponment of my death, I am writing you once more, gracious and faithful friends in God, to show my gratitude for as long as I can, ever taking pleasure in being able to converse with you by letter. I say to you that the Lord God knows why He postpones my death as well as that of my dear brother, Master Jerome, of whom I have hopes that he will die holily, without guilt, and that he will conduct himself and suffer more bravely than I, a fainthearted sinner. The Lord God has granted us a long time that we may better recollect our sins and forthrightly regret them. He has granted us time so that the long-drawn-out and great testing may divest us of great sins and bring us consolation. He has granted us time to remember our King, the merciful Lord God Jesus' terrible disgrace, and to meditate on His cruel death and, for that reason, to suffer more gladly. Also that we may remember that we are not to pass from the feasts of this world to the

---

[210] This refers to the story of St. Catherine of Alexandria. Emperor Maximin promised a great reward to any philosopher who would convert her to paganism. She withstood them all. Hus probably had the story from the breviary for November 25.

[211] June 26.

[212] Novotný, *Korespondence,* No. 156; Palacký, pp. 140–42. The letter is in Czech.

feasts of that other world, that we may remember that the saints entered the heavenly kingdom through many sufferings; for some were cut up piece by piece, others impaled, others boiled, others roasted, others flayed alive, buried alive, stoned, crucified, crushed between millstones, dragged, drowned, burned, hanged, torn in pieces, having been first vilified, imprisoned, beaten and chained. Who can describe all the tortures by which the saints of the New and the Old Testaments suffered for God's truth, particularly those who rebuked the priestly wickedness and preached against it! It would be a strange thing if now one would not suffer on account of a brave stand against wickedness, especially that of the priests, which does not allow itself to be touched! I am glad that they were obliged to read my small books, which openly reveal their wickedness. I know that they have read them more diligently than the sacred Scriptures, desiring to find errors in them.

The letter was given on Thursday,[213] before the vigil of St. Peter, in the evening. Amen.

30. John Hus to the Members of the University of Prague.[214]

[June 27, 1415]

Honorable and in Christ Jesus dearly beloved masters, bachelors, and students of the University of Prague! I exhort you for the sake of the most kind Jesus Himself, that you love one another, root out schisms, and promote the honor of God before all else, keeping me in memory that I always sought the advancement of the university to the honor of God, that I grieved over your discords and excesses, and wished to unite our illustrious nation into one. And see how some of my dearest friends,[215] for whom I would have risked my life, turned exceedingly bitter against me, afflicting me with calumnious vilifications and finally with a bitter death! May the omnipotent God forgive them, for they know not what they have done. I pray for them with a sincere heart that He may spare them.

Moreover, dearly beloved in Christ Jesus, stand in the truth you have learned, for it conquers all and is mighty to eternity. You should also know that I have neither revoked nor abjured a single article. The

---

[213] June 27.

[214] Novotný, *Korespondence*, No. 155; Palacký, No. 87.

[215] Stephen Páleč and Stanislav of Znojmo, as well as the rest of the Prague theological faculty.

Council desired that I declare that all and every article drawn from
my books is false. I refused unless they should show its falsity by
Scripture. I said that I detest whatever false sense exists in any of the
articles, and commit it to the correction of the Lord Jesus Christ, Who
knows my sincere intention and does not interpret it in a wrong sense
which I do not intend. I exhort you also in the Lord that whatever
false sense you may be able to discern in any of those articles, that you
relinquish them, but always preserve the truth that is intended. Pray
God for me, and greet one another in holy peace.

Master John Hus,

> in chains and in prison, already standing on the
> shore of the present life, expecting tomorrow a
> terrible death which will, I hope, purge my sins,
> by the grace of God find no heresy in me; for
> I confess with all my heart whatever truth is
> worthy of belief.
> Written on Thursday[216] before the vigil of
> St. Peter.
>   I pray you, love Bethlehem and appoint
> Havlík[217] in my place; for I hope that the
> Lord is with him. Amen.
>   I commend Peter of Mladoňovice to you, my
> most faithful and most constant comforter and
> upholder.

31. John Hus to Peter of Mladoňovice.[218]

[c. June 29, 1415]

I dare not have the temerity to say with St. Peter—for I have in-
comparably less fervor and fortitude than he—that I will never be
offended in Christ, even if all should be offended.[219] For Christ so far
has never expressly called me blessed as He did Peter,[220] nor did He
promise me such great gifts;[221] and a mightier, more intense struggle is

---

[216] June 27.
[217] He was Hus's pupil and served as his substitute at Bethlehem. Actually,
it was Jakoubek of Stříbro, who succeeded to the post soon after.
[218] Novotný, Korespondence, No. 160; Palacký, No. 62. I hesitate to oppose
my judgment against those of Novotný, Palacký, and others, but from the context I should assume that this letter was written much earlier, soon after the
formula of abjuration had been offered to Hus.
[219] Mark 14:29.
[220] Matt. 16:17.
[221] Matt. 16:18–19.

beginning, and by a greater number of people. I say, therefore, that having hope in Christ Jesus, when I shall hear the formula,[222] I intend with the help of the saints to adhere to the truth unto death.

If Lord John[223] has incurred a loss by expecting a payment from me,[224] secure it, dear Peter, when you come home, from the mintmaster and his wife,[225] both of whom bravely promised a contribution, and from other friends known to my pupil, the Pastor.[226] If a horse with a wagon is still available, it should be kept by Lord John.

As for you, Master Martin,[227] if he is alive, or Master Christian,[228] on whom I depend, will provide four, and I wish it were rather ten, *sexagenae* of *grossi*. Be assured that there is not enough money with which I should like to recompense you for your most fervent, most firm, and most faithful love which you have for the truth, and for your services and consolations which you have shown me in my tribulations. May God be your great reward, for I have not whence to reward you! Should it happen that I live in Prague—for by the Lord's grace my return to Prague is not impossible—I would wish then to share everything with you as with my own brother, and even to a greater extent. I do not long for it, however, unless it be according to the will of the Lord Who is in heaven.

I do not know who will receive the breviary[229] which I bequeathed to Master Martin. I still have it. Dispose of the books in accordance with what I wrote to Master Martin, and choose from the few Wyclif's works whatever pleases you. I have now the greatest concern about our brethren who, I suppose, will be persecuted, unless God interposes His hand! And I fear that many will be scandalized.

I pray you, as always, to greet all the Czech and Polish lords with much love and with giving of thanks; and particularly Lords Wenceslas of Dubá and John of Chlum. I wish they would be at the hearing. Farewell in Christ Jesus.

John Hus

---

[222] For the formula of abjuration, cf. n. 118.

[223] John of Chlum.

[224] This refers to a loan made to Hus by Lord John.

[225] The mintmaster was Peter Zmrzlík of Svojšín, and his wife was Anna of Frimburk.

[226] He is mentioned in Part I, p. 96.

[227] Master Martin of Volyně.

[228] Master Christian of Prachatice.

[229] Incidentally, Master Martin did not get the breviary.

32. Hus's Last Declaration to the Council.[230]

[July 1, 1415]

I, John Hus, in hope a priest of Jesus Christ, fearing to offend God and to fall into perjury, am not willing to recant all or any of the articles produced against me in the testimonies of false witnesses. For God is my witness that I neither preached, asserted, nor defended them, as they said that I had defended, preached, and asserted them, etc.

Furthermore, concerning the articles drawn from my books, at least those drawn correctly, I declare, if any of them contains a false sense, that I repudiate. But fearing to offend against the truth and to speak against the opinions of the saints, I am not willing to recant any of them. If it were posible that my voice could now be heard in the whole world, as at the Day of Judgment every lie and all my sins shall be revealed, I would most gladly recant before all the world every falsehood and every error I ever have thought of saying or have said.

This I say and write freely and voluntarily. Written with my own hand on the first day of July.

33. To His Friends in Constance.[231]

[July 5, 1415]

Tomorrow at the sixth hour I must respond; first, whether I am willing to declare that every article drawn from my books is erroneous, and whether I will recant it and will preach the opposite. Second, whether I am willing to confess that I have preached those articles that have been proved by the witnesses. Third, that I recant them. If only God in His grace would bring the king to the hearing! I should like to see him hear the words that the most kind Savior will put in my mouth!

If they would give me a pen and paper, I hope with God's help to reply in writing as follows:

"I, John Hus, in hope a servant of Jesus Christ, am not willing to declare that every article drawn from my books is erroneous, lest I condemn the opinions of the holy doctors, particularly of the blessed Augustine. Secondly, concerning the articles ascribed to me by false witnesses, I am not willing to confess that I have asserted, preached, and held them. Thirdly, I am not willing to recant, lest I commit perjury."

For God's sake, carefully preserve the letters, and send them to

---

[230] Novotný, *Korespondence,* No. 162.
[231] Novotný, *Korespondence,* No. 163; Palacký, No. 64.

Bohemia with similar caution, lest great danger to persons ensue. Should I not write to your love on account of some contingency, I implore you along with my friends that you keep my memory, and pray that I be given constancy along with my beloved brother in Christ, Master Jerome; [232] for I suppose that he also will suffer death, as I understood from the delegates of the Council.

34. John Hus to the Entire Christian World.[233]

[July 5, 1415]

I, Master John Hus, in hope a servant of Jesus Christ, heartily desiring that Christ's faithful after my decease should have no occasion to be offended on account of my death by judging me as if I were an obstinate heretic; and taking Christ Jesus as witness, for Whose law I desire to die, write this as a memorial to the friends of truth.

First, that in the very many private hearings and later in the public hearings of the Council I protested my willingness to submit to instruction and direction, revocation and punishment, were I taught that anything I had written, taught, or said in reply was contrary to the truth. And fifty doctors, delegates of the Council, as they said, often rebuked by me even in the public hearing of the Council because of their false abstracting of the articles, were not willing to give me any private instruction; yea, they were not willing even to confer with me, saying: "You must stand by the decision of the Council." As for the Council, when I adduced in the public hearing Christ's Scripture or [the opinion] of the holy doctors, they either mocked me or said that I understood it wrongly, while the doctors said that I adduced it inappropriately. Also a certain cardinal, the highest in the Council[234] and delegated by the Council, taking out a paper, said at a public hearing: "Look, a certain master of sacred theology presented me this argument: answer it!" It was an argument about the common essence which I had conceded to exist in divine things. Afterward, when he floundered, although he is reputed to be a most eminent doctor of theology, I spoke to him about the common created essence which is the first created being and is communicated to every individual creature. From this he wished to prove the remanence of the material bread. But being ob-

[232] Jerome of Prague.

[233] Novotný, *Korespondence*, No. 165; Palacký, No. 65. I follow Novotný's decision in placing it as Hus's last letter, although some think that it should be dated June 7.

[234] Pierre d'Ailly.

viously reduced to the utmost lack of knowledge of the argument, he became silent.

Immediately thereafter an English doctor began to argue, but he similarly floundered, and another English doctor, who at a private hearing said to me that Wyclif had wished to destroy all knowledge and that in every one of his books and his treatises of logic he had committed errors; he, rising, began to argue about the multiplication of the body of Christ in the host. Failing in the argument, when they told him to keep still, he said: "Look! he [Hus] astutely deceives the Council! Beware, lest the Council be deceived as it was deceived by Berengar!"[235] When he became silent, someone began to argue noisily about the common created essence; but he was shouted down by the crowd. I, however, standing up, asked to be accorded a hearing, saying to him: "Argue boldly; I shall gladly answer you." But he likewise gave up and ill-temperedly added: "It is a heresy!"

What clamor then, what mocking, jeering, and reviling arose against me in that assembly is known to lords Wenceslas of Dubá and John of Chlum and his notary Peter, the most steadfast knights and lovers of God's truth. Hence even I, being often overwhelmed by such clamor, spoke these words: "I had supposed that in this Council would be greater reverence, piety, and discipline." Then they all listened because the king ordered silence. The cardinal presiding over the Council[236] said: "You spoke more humbly in the castle!"[237] I said: "Because then nobody shouted at me; while now all are shouting against me." And he added: "Look! the Council requests whether you are willing to submit to instruction." I said: "Most gladly am I willing, in accordance with my declaration." And he said: "Yea, this constitutes your instruction, that the doctors declare the articles drawn from your books to be erroneous. You must revoke them and abjure those which were deposed against you by the witnesses." The king then said: "They will be shortly written for you, and you will reply." And the cardinal said: "This will be done at the next hearing." And immediately the Council rose up. God knows what great temptings I suffered afterward!

[235] The whole scene is described by Peter in his *Account,* Chap. III, at the hearing of June 5, although Hus makes some significant additions. For instance, nothing is said by Peter about Berengar (d. 1088).

[236] Pierre d'Ailly.

[237] At Gottlieben.

35. The Council's Definitive Sentence against John Hus.[238]

The sacrosanct general Council of Constance, divinely convened and representing the catholic Church, to the eternal memory of the act. Because by the witness of the Truth a bad tree customarily bears bad fruit,[239] for that reason the man of damned memory, John Wyclif, like a poisoned root, by means of his death-bearing doctrine bore many pestiferous sons, whom he left as successors of his perverse dogmas. He bore them not in Christ Jesus through His gospel, as formerly the holy fathers who bore faithful sons, but contrary to Christ's saving faith. Against them this sacred Synod of Constance, as against spurious and illegitimate sons, purposed to rise and to uproot their errors as noxious brambles from the Lord's field by the most watchful care and the knife of ecclesiastical authority, lest the cancer spread to the destruction of others.

Thus when at the general Council recently held in Rome[240] it was decreed that the teaching of John Wyclif of damned memory be condemned, and his books, containing that kind of teaching, be burned as heretical; and the teaching itself was [actually] condemned and his books comprising such insane and pestiferous doctrines were burned; all these decrees were approved by the authority of this sacred Council. Nonetheless, a certain John Hus in this sacred Council here personally present, a disciple not of Christ but rather of the heresiarch John Wyclif, with temerity dared to oppose himself to it thereafter and contrary to the condemnation and the decree, by having taught, asserted, and preached his [Wyclif's] many errors and heresies, condemned both by the Church of God and also by certain former fathers in Christ, lord archbishops, bishops of various realms, and masters of theology of many schools; and particularly by the scholastic condemnations of those articles of Wyclif proclaimed many times by the University of Prague. He, however, with his accomplices, publicly resisting them in schools and in preaching, declared him, John Wycliff, before the multitude of the clergy and the people in support of his teaching a Catholic man and an evangelical doctor. He also asserted and publicly declared that certain articles, hereafter described and many others meriting con-

---

[238] Novotný, *Fontes,* VIII, 501–3. Also in two versions, both of them preliminary, in Sedlák, *Studie,* I, No. 4, 353–61.
[239] Matt. 7:17.
[240] Held in 1412.

demnation, are catholic, which are notoriously contained in the books and minor works of that John Hus.

On that account, having first been fully informed of the said matters, and after a diligent deliberation by the most reverend fathers in Christ of the holy Roman Church, lord cardinals, patriarchs, archbishops, bishops, and of other prelates and doctors of the Holy Writ and of both laws in large numbers, this sacrosanct Synod of Constance declares and defines that the articles hereafter described are not catholic, nor are to be taught as such, but many of them are erroneous, others scandalous, others offensive to pious ears, and many of them are rash and seditious, and several of them are notoriously heretical. They had been collected by many masters of the Holy Writ and found to be contained in those books and minor works written by his own hand; which likewise that same John Hus in a public hearing before the fathers and prelates of this sacred Council had confessed to be contained in his books and minor works. They have been already long ago reprobated and condemned by the holy fathers and general Councils, and strictly prohibited to be preached, taught, or approved in any manner. But because the hereafter described articles are expressly contained in his books and his treatises, namely, in the book entitled *De ecclesia* and others of his minor works; therefore, the above-named books and his teachings and every other treatise and minor work, in Latin or in vernacular Czech published by him, as well as in any other language by others or another translated, this sacrosanct Synod reprobates and condemns, and decrees and defines that they be solemnly and publicly burned in the presence of the clergy and the people of the city of Constance and others, adjudging on account of the said matters all his teaching to be and should be suspect as to the faith and to be shunned by all faithful of Christ. Further, in order that the pernicious teaching be eliminated from the midst of the Church, this sacred Synod absolutely orders that the local ordinaries diligently search for those treatises and minor works of every sort, and by ecclesiastical censure, and also, if need be, by adding punishment for promoting heresy, procure their public burning by fire. If, however, anyone should be found to violate or contemn this sentence or decree, this sacred Synod orders the local ordinaries or the inquisitors of heretical pravity to proceed against such a one or such ones suspected or as ones suspected of heresy.

Considering the above proceedings as an act or acts in the cause of inquiry of and about heresy held and conducted against the said John

Hus, we first received from the commissioners appointed for this cause and of other masters in theology and doctors of both laws a faithful and complete account in, of, and concerning the act or acts. We also received the testimonies of trustworthy and numerous witnesses, which testimonies were openly and publicly read to him, John Hus, before the fathers and prelates of this sacred Council. By these testimonies of the witnesses it is most plainly evident that he, John Hus, had taught many evil, offensive, seditious, and dangerous heresies and had publicly preached them during the course of many years. Therefore, invoking the name of Christ, this sacrosanct Synod of Constance, having God alone before its eyes and being legitimately assembled by the Holy Spirit, by this definitive sentence set forth in these presents pronounces, decrees, and declares the said John Hus to have been and still to be a veritable and manifest heretic and that his errors and heresies have long ago been condemned by the Church of God, and are now condemned, and that he had taught and publicly preached many things scandalous, offensive to pious ears, rash and seditious, to the unmitigated offense of the divine Majesty and of the universal Church, to the detriment of the catholic faith. He had also despised the keys of the Church and ecclesiastical censures, in which he had persisted for many years in an obdurate spirit, offending Christ's faithful by his excessive obstinacy, contemning the due ecclesiastical process by resorting to an appeal to the Lord Jesus Christ as to the supreme judge, and stating in it many false, injurious, and offensive things in contempt even of the Apostolic See as well as of ecclesiastical censures and keys. Therefore, on account of the said matters and many others, this sacred Synod declares that the said John Hus is a heretic, and as a heretic should be adjudged and condemned; and it judges and condemns him by these presents, reprobating by ecclesiastical jurisdiction the said appeal as injurious, scandalous, and illusory. And [judges] him, John Hus, as having seduced the Christian people, most of all in the kingdom of Bohemia, in his public preaching and writing compiled by him, and was not a true preacher of the gospel of Christ to that people in accordance with the expositions of the holy doctors, but was in truth their seducer.

Truly, on account of these things that this sacred Synod has seen and heard, it recognizes that John Hus is obstinate and incorrigible, and as such does not desire to return into the bosom of the holy mother Church, nor is willing to recant the heresies and errors publicly defended and preached by him, but even now defends and preaches them. For that reason, this sacred Council declares and decrees that John Hus be deposed and degraded from the priestly order and from the other orders by which he has been esteemed to be distinguished. Moreover, it commits him to the reverend fathers in Christ, the lord archbishops of Milan, Feltre, Asti, Alessandria, Bangor, the bishop of Lavour, the suffragan of the bishop of Constance, and the bishop of Bangor,[241] to carry out the said degradation in the presence of this sacrosanct Council according to the order required by law.

This sacrosanct Synod of Constance, seeing that the Church of God has nothing more it can do with John Hus, relinquishes him to the secular judgment and decrees that he be relinquished to the secular court.

---

[241] This scene is described by Peter in his *Account*, Chap. V. He speaks, however, of only seven bishops without naming them.

BIBLIOGRAPHY

I. PRIMARY SOURCES

Works about John Hus

Císařová-Kolářová, Anna, ed. and trans. M. Jan Hus, Betlemské poselství. 2 vols. Praha, Jan Laichter, 1947.

Erben, K. J., ed. Mistra Jana Husi Sebrané spisy české z nejstarších pramenů. 3 vols. Praha, 1865–68.

Flajšhans, V., and M. Komínková, eds. Opera omnia. 6 vols. Praha, J. R. Vilímek, 1903–07.

Flajšhans, V., ed. Mag. Io. Hus Sermones in Bethlehem, 1410–1411. 5 vols. Praha, Královská česká společnost nauk, 1938–42.

Mathias Flacius Illyricus, ed. Historia et Monumenta Joannis Hus atque Hieronymi Pragensis confessorum Christi. 2 vols. Nuremberg, J. Montanus et U. Neuber, 1715. New ed. of the work of 1558.

Jeschke, J. B., ed. Mistr Jan Hus, Postilla. Praha, Komenského ev. fakulta bohoslovecká, 1952.

Mareš, B., trans. Listy Husovy. 2d ed. Praha, "Samostatnost," 1901.

Novotný, Václav, ed. M. Jana Husi Korespondence a dokumenty. Praha, Komise pro vydávání pramenů náboženského hnutí českého, 1920.

Palacký, František, ed. Documenta Mag. Johannis Hus. Praha, F. Tempský, 1869.

Ryba, B., ed. Magistri Johannis Hus Quodlibet. Praha, Orbis, 1948.

———, Betlemské texty. Praha, Orbis, 1951.

———, Sto listů M. Jana Husi. Praha, Jan Laichter, 1949.

Schaff, David S., trans. John Hus, The Church. New York, Charles Scribner's Sons, 1915.

Schmidtová, Anežka, ed. Magistri Joannis Hus, Sermones de tempore qui Collecta dicuntur. Praha, Československá akademie věd, 1959.

Sedlák, Jan. Articles from Hlídka. Brno, 1911–12; contains treatises of Stanislav of Znojmo, "Sermo contra 5 art. Wiclef," "Tractatus de Romana ecclesia"; and Stephen Páleč's "Sermo contra aliquos art. Wiclef," "De equivocatione nominis ecclesia," and "Antihus."

———, M. Jan Hus. Praha, Dědictví sv. Prokopa, 1915. The second part contains some sources pertaining to Hus and his times, particularly Stephen Páleč's "Tractatus de ecclesia," partes selectae.

Šimek, F., ed. Mistr Jan Hus, Česká kázání sváteční. Praha, Blahoslav, n.d.

Spinka, Matthew, ed. and trans. "Hus on Simony," in Advocates of Reform, Library of Christian Classics, Philadelphia, The Westminster Press, 1953. Vol. XIV, pp. 199–278.

Stein, Evžen, ed. and trans. M. Jan Hus jako universitní rektor a profesor. Praha, Jan Laichter, 1948.

Thomson, S. Harrison, ed. Magistri Joannis Hus Tractatus de Ecclesia. Boulder, Colo., University of Colorado Press, 1956.

Workman, H. B., and R. M. Pope, trans. The Letters of John Hus. London, Hodder and Stoughton, 1904.

Žilka, F., ed. Vybrané Spisy Mistra Jana Husi. 2 vols. Jilemnice, n.d.

Primary Works on the Conciliar Leaders and Hussiana

D'Ailly, Pierre. Tractatus Petri de Alliaco de potestate pape et auctoritate cardinalium, factus per eum in concilio Constantiensi, post depositum Johannis pape vicesimi tertii. n.d., n.p.

Cameron, James Kerr, "Conciliarism in Theory and Practice, 1378–1418." 2 vols. An unpublished doctoral dissertation at the Hartford Seminary Foundation, Hartford, Conn., 1953, Vol. II comprises translations of selected works of Henry of Langenstein, Jean Gerson, Pierre d'Ailly, and Dietrich of Niem.

Finke, Heinrich, et al., eds. Acta Concilii Constantiensis. 4 vols. Münster, Regensburg, 1896–1928.

Finke, Heinrich. Forschungen und Quellen zur Geschichte des Konstanzer Konzils. Paderborn, Schöningh, 1889.

Friedberg, E., ed. Corpus juris canonici. 2 vols. Leipzig, Taubnitz, 1879. Vol. I comprises Gratian's Decretum.

Gerson, Jean. Opera omnia. Edited by E. du Pin. 4 vols. Antwerp, sumptibus Societatis, 1706.

———, Epistola tripartita de erroribus Hussitarum. Coloniae, 1484.

———, "De auctoritate concilii," in Revue d'Histoire Ecclesiastique. Edited by Z. Rüger. 1958, pp. 775–95.

Hardt, Hermann van der, ed. Magni et universalis Constantiensis Concilii tomi VI. Frankfurt and Leipzig, Gensius, 1697–1700. Completed by a seventh volume of indices by C. Ch. Bohnstedt, Berlin, Henningius, 1742.

Hefele, C. J., and H. Leclercq, Histoire des conciles. 10 Vols. in 20. Paris, Letouzey, 1907–38.

Loomis, Louise R., trans. The Council of Constance: the Unification of the Church. Edited by John H. Mundy and Kennerly M. Woody. New York and London, Columbia University Press, 1961.

Novotný, V., ed. Fontes rerum Bohemicarum. Praha, Nadání Františka

Palackého, 1932. Vol. VIII. Contains the "Relatio de Magistro Johanne Hus" of Peter of Mladoňovice and many other pertinent documents.

Ockham, W. Dialogus de potestate papae et imperatoris. Torino, Bottega d'Erasmo, 1959.

Pez, B., ed. Thesaurus anecdotorum novissimus. 6 vols. Augsburg, 1721–29. Contains treatises of Stephen of Dolany: "Medulla tritici, seu Antiwickliffus;" "Antihussus;" "Dialogus volatilis inter Aucam et Passerem adversus Hussum;" "Liber epistolaris ad Hussitas."

Richental, Ulrich von. Chronik des Constanzer Conzils. Edited by Michael Richard Buck. Hildesheim, 1962.

Sedlák, Jan. Studie a texty k náboženským dějinám českým. 2 vols. Olomouc,Matice Cyrilo-Methodějská, 1913–19.

Sikes, J. G., et al., eds. Guillaume Occami Opera politica. 3 vols. University of Manchester Press, 1940–56.

Šimek, F., ed. Jakoubek ze Stříbra, Výklad na zjevenie sv. Jana. Praha, 1933.

II. SECONDARY WORKS

Bartoš, F. M. Literární činnost M. Jakoubka ze Stříbra. Praha, Česká akademie věd a umění, 1925.

——, Husitství a cizina. Praha, Čin, 1931.

——, Co víme o Husovi nového. Praha, Pokrok, 1946.

——, Čechy v době Husově, 1378–1415. Praha, Jan Laichter, 1947.

——, Knihy a zápasy. Praha, Husova ev. fakulta bohoslovecká, 1948.

——, Literární činnost M. Jana Husi. Praha, Česká akademie věd a umění, 1948.

——, "Osud Husova evangelisty Petra Mladoňovice," Křestanská Revue, Praha, 1963, supplement, pp. 78–85.

Boehner, Philotheus. Collected articles on Ockham. Edited by E. M. Buytaert. Bonaventure, N.Y., The Franciscan Institute, 1958.

Boulier, Abbé J. Jean Hus. Paris, Club français du livre, 1958.

Bliemetzrieder, F. Das Generalkonzil im grössen abendländischen Schisma. Paderborn, 1904.

Combes, André. Jean Gerson: commentateur dionysien. Paris, 1940.

Dress, Walter. Die Theologie Gersons. Gütersloh, 1931.

Hauck, Albert. Kirchengeschichte Deutschlands. 5th ed. Berlin, Akademie-Verlag, 1953. Vol. V/II.

Heimpel, T. Dietrich von Niem. Münster, Regensberg, 1932.

Jacob, E. F. Essays in the Conciliar Epoch. 2d ed. Manchester, University Press, 1953.

Krofta, K. Listy z náboženských dějin českých. Praha, Historický klub, 1936.

Kybal, V. M. Matěj z Janova, jeho život, spisy a učení. Praha, Královská česká společnost nauk, 1905.

Lenfant, Jacques. Histoire du Concile de Constance. 2 vols. Amsterdam, 1714.

Loomis, Louise R. "The Organization by Nations at Constance," Church History, I, pp. 191 ff.

Lützow, F. The Life and Times of Master John Hus. New York, E. P. Dutton & Co., n.d.

McGowan, John T. Pierre d'Ailly and the Council of Constance. Washington, Catholic University, 1936.

McNeill, John T. "The Emergence of Conciliarism," in Medieval and Historical Essays in honor of James Westfall Thompson. Chicago, University of Chicago Press, 1938, pp. 269 ff.

Masson, L. Jean Gerson. Lyons, 1899.

Meller, B. Studien zur Erkenntnislehre des Peter von Ailly. Freiburg, 1954.

Morrall, John B. Gerson and the Great Schism. Manchester, University Press, 1960.

Mourin, Louis. Jean Gerson, predicateur français. Brugge, 1952.

Neander, Aug. General History of the Christian Religion and Church. Translated by Joseph Torrey. Boston, Houghton, Mifflin & Co., 1871. Vol. V.

Novotný, V., and V. Kybal. M. Jan Hus, život a učení. Praha, Jan Laichter, 1921–31. Vols. I, i–ii, Vol. II, i–iii.

Novotný, V. Náboženské hnutí české v 14. a 15. století. Praha, J. Otto, n.d.

Oberman, Heiko A. The Harvest of Medieval Theology. Cambridge, Mass., Harvard University Press, 1963.

Odložilík, Otakar. Jan Milíč z Kroměříže. Kroměříž, Kostnická Jednota, 1924.

———, M. Štepán z Kolína. Praha, Společnost Husova musea, 1924.

———, Wyclif and Bohemia. Praha, 1937.

———, Jan Hus. Chicago, Národní Jednota Československých Protestantů, 1953.

Roberts, Agnes E. "Peter d'Ailly and the Council of Constance," Transactions of the Royal Historical Society, 4th ser., XVIII. London, 1935.

Salembrier, L. Le grand Schisme d'Occident. 5th ed. Paris, 1921.

Schaff, David S. John Hus, His Life, Teachings and Death after Five Hundred Years. New York, Charles Scribner's Sons, 1915.

Scholtz, R. Unbekannte kirchenpolitische Streitschriften aus der Zeit Ludwigs des Bayern, 1327–1354. 2 vols. Rom, Loescher & Co., 1914.

Schwab, J. B. Johannes Gerson, Professor der Theologie und Kanzler der Universität. Würzburg, 1858.

Spinka, Matthew. John Hus and the Czech Reform. Chicago, University of Chicago Press, 1941.

Stacey, John. John Wyclif and Reform. Philadelphia, The Westminster Press, 1914.

Thomson, S. Harrison. "Philosophical Basis of Wyclif's Theology," *Journal of Religion,* 1931, pp. 86–116.

Tierney, Brian. "Ockham, the Conciliar Theory, and the Canonists," *Journal of the History of Ideas,* 1954, pp. 40–70.

———, Foundations of the Conciliar Theory. Cambridge, University Press, 1955.

Tschackert, P. Peter von Ailly. Gotha, Perthes, 1877.

Vischer, Melchior. Jan Hus, sein Leben und seine Zeit. 2 vols. Frankfurt, 1940.

Valois, Noel. La France et le grand Schisme. 4 vols. Paris, Picard, 1900–02.

Vooght, Paul de. L'hérésie de Jean Huss. Louvain, Publications universitaires de Louvain, 1960.

———, Hussiana. Louvain, Publications universitaires de Louvain, 1960.

Workman, H. B. John Wyclif. 2 vols. Oxford, Clarendon Press, 1926.

Wylie, J. H. The Council of Constance to the Death of John Hus. London, 1900.

INDEX

318   INDEX

Mallard, William, cited, 28*n*
Mansi, J. D., cited, 14*n*, 65*n*
Marcus Aurelius, 277*n*
Marina, Saint, 275*n*
Mark, Book of, 243, 253*n*, 279*n*, 290*n*
Mark of Hradec, Rector of Prague University, 42, 228*n*
Marriage, 29
Marriage (Hus treatise on), 120
Marsilius of Padua, 3, 5-7, 10, 21
Marsilius of Padua, The Defender of Peace (Gewirth, trans.), 5-7*nn*, 10*n*
Martin V, pope: election of, 65, 66, 72, 75, 121*n*; Hussite wars and, 71; on conciliarism, 76; Conrad of Vechta and, 93*n*
Martin Luther, Selections from his Writings (Dillenberger, ed.), 59*n*
Martinmas, 106
Martin of Volyně, 30, 94-96, 291
Matthew, Book of, 107*nn*, 108*n*, 147*nn*, 201, 248*n*, 257*n*, 283*n*, 295*n*; on Peter, 6, 52, 290*nn*; on alms, 172, 200; on the Church militant, 183*n*; on heresy, 194; on preaching, 198, 206, 210, 245; on love, 200-201; on communion, 253*n*; on the death of Christ, 279*nn*; on the Last Judgment, 280-81
Matthew of Chlumčany, 150
Matthew of Janov, 24-26, 29
Mauroux, Jean, patriarch of Antioch, 141*n*, 142, 163-64
Medici, Cosimo di, 65, 121*n*
Meisterman, Ludolf, 34
Mělník, 34
Mendicancy, 16, 22
Merseburg, bishop of (Nicolas Lubich), 137, 226*n*
Meziříčí, Moravia, 136*n*, 154
Michael de Causis, 38, 85, 239, 240, 244; John of Jesenice and, 39, 228*n*, 241*n*; Páleč and, 101, 111, 114, 249*n*, 254, 278; proceedings posted against Hus, 102-3, 105; trial of Hus, 118, 221, 255
Michael de Cesena, 7
Michael of Prachatice, 144, 150
Michael de Prziest, 90
Mikulov, Moravia, 40, 106*n*

Milan, archbishop of (Bartolomeo de la Capra), 229*n*, 298
Milíč of Kroměříž, 23-24, 25, 26
Minorites, *see* Franciscan order
Miracles, 37, 59*n*
Mistra Jana Husi Sebrané spisy české z nejstaršich pramenů (Erben, ed.), 46*n*
Mistr Jan Hus, Česká kázání sváteční (Šimek, ed.), 31*nn*
Mistr Jan Hus, Postilla (Jeschke, ed.), 46*n*, 242*n*, 245*n*, 246 *nn*
M. Jana Husi Korespondence a dokumenty (Novotný, ed.), 45*n*, 89*n*, 91*n*; Hus's appeal to Wenceslas, 92*n*; letter to Martin of Volyně, 95*n*; letter to the people upon departure for Constance, 96*n*; notice posted on churches on the way to Constance, 98*n*; letter from Nuremberg, 99*n*; letters from Constance to Prague, 102*n*, 107*n*; John of Rejnštejn letters, 104*nn*, 106*n*; Gerson opinion on Hus, 171*n*; Hus's appeal to Christ, 237*n*; Hus's letter to Bohemian Supreme Court, 240*n*; Hus's acceptance of safe conduct, 247-48; Hus's letters to John of Chlum, 249*n*, 252*n*, 256*n*, 271*n*, 277*n*; letters to friends in Constance, 254*n*, 255*n*, 259*n*, 274*n*, 275*n*, 284*n*, 292*n*; letters to friends in Bohemia, 259*n*, 280*n*, 288*n*; letters to 'Father', 269*n*, 270*nn*; letters to Wenceslas of Dubá and John of Chlum, 271*n*, 285*n*; letter to Havlík, 277; letter to Peter Mladoňovice and John of Rejnštejn, 283-84; Hus's letter to all the faithful Czechs, 286*n*; letter to the University of Prague, 289*n*; letter to Peter of Mladoňovice, 290*n*; last declaration to the Council, 292*n*; letter to the entire Christian world, 293*n*
M. Jan Hus (Sedlák), 51*nn*, 52*n*, 53*nn*, 54*nn*, 164*n*
M. Jan Hus, Betlemské poselství (Císařová-Kolářová, ed.), 37*n*, 196*n*
M. Jan Hus, Obrany v Kostnici (Flajšhans), 60*n*, 117*n*
M. Jan Hus, život a učení (Novotný and Kybal), 43*n*, 47*n*, 51*n*95, 53*n*,

RL

N/33BLC

John...

KV-106-791

WITHDRAWN
MAGDALEN COLLEGE LIBRARY
SHELF No. 172.1
FEI
COL

305069286$

For several decades the work of Joel Feinberg has been the most influential in legal, political, and social philosophy in the English-speaking world. This volume honors that body of work by presenting fifteen original essays, many of them by leading legal and political philosophers, that explore the problems that have engaged Feinberg over the years. Among the topics covered are issues of autonomy, responsibility, and liability. It will be a collection of interest to anyone working in moral, legal, or political philosophy.

IN HARM'S WAY

Cambridge Studies in Philosophy and Law

GENERAL EDITOR: JULES L. COLEMAN (YALE LAW SCHOOL)

ADVISORY BOARD

David Gauthier (University of Pittsburgh)
David Lyons (Cornell University)
Richard Posner (Judge in the Seventh Circuit Court of Appeals, Chicago)
Martin Shapiro (University of California, Berkeley)

This series reflects and fosters the most original research currently taking place in the study of law and legal theory by publishing the most adventurous monographs in the field as well as rigorously edited collections of essays. It is a specific aim of the series to traverse the boundaries between disciplines and to form bridges between traditional studies of law and many other areas of the human sciences. Books in the series will be of interest not only to philosophers and legal theorists but also to political scientists, sociologists, economists, psychologists, and criminologists.

Other books in the series

Jeffrie G. Murphy and Jean Hampton: *Forgiveness and mercy*
Stephen R. Munzer: *A theory of property*
R.G. Frey and Christopher W. Morris (eds.): *Liability and responsibility: Essays in law and morals*
Robert F. Schopp: *Automatism, insanity, and the psychology of criminal responsibility*
Steven J. Burton: *Judging in good faith*
Jules L. Coleman: *Risks and wrongs*

In harm's way
Essays in honor of Joel Feinberg

Edited by

JULES L. COLEMAN   ALLEN BUCHANAN
Garver Professor of Jurisprudence   *University of Wisconsin, Madison*
Yale Law School

CAMBRIDGE
UNIVERSITY PRESS

MAGDALEN COLLEGE LIBRARY

Published by the Press Syndicate of the University of Cambridge
The Pitt Building, Trumpington Street, Cambridge CB2 1RP
40 West 20th Street, New York, NY 10011-4211, USA
10 Stamford Road, Oakleigh, Melbourne 3166, Australia

© Cambridge University Press 1994

First published 1994

Printed in the United States of America

Library of Congress Cataloging-in-Publication Data
In harm's way : essays in honor of Joel Feinberg / edited by Jules L.
Coleman, Allen Buchanan.
    p. cm. – (Cambridge studies in philosophy and law)
Includes bibliographical references
ISBN 0-521-45410-7 (hard)
1. Law–Philosophy. 2. Law and Ethics. 3. Liberalism.
4. Feinberg, Joel. I. Feinberg, Joel. II. Coleman, Jules L.
III. Buchanan, Allen E., 1948–   . IV. Series.
K235.I5   1994
340'.1—dc20   93-45339
                       CIP

A catalog record for this book is available from the British Library

ISBN 0-521-45410-7 hardback

Contents

Preface

Given how far-ranging and subtle Joel Feinberg's work is, and how eloquently it speaks for itself, no brief overview could possibly do it justice. Instead, we will limit ourselves here to a few unsystematic remarks about what we take to be some of the most distinctive features of his approach to philosophy, knowing full well that we will not succeed in indicating its richness. Our attempt to convey something of the man's character will be even less satisfactory.

It is no secret that Feinberg's writings achieve an unparalleled combination of rigor, sensitivity, and clarity. No other contemporary philosopher writing in English is as able to deal with complex and nuanced issues without lapsing into the false security of jargon. That Feinberg's books and essays represent much of what is best in liberal, legal, and moral philosophy is also widely recognized. What is less often appreciated is the fact that Feinberg's work achieves something that some of the most vociferous contemporary critics of Liberalism assume to be incompatible with Liberalism: a highly contextualized, concrete rendition of the liberal point of view, rooted in the actual practices and culture of a distinctive society, rather than in an abstract and ahistorical conception of the moral agent.

It is interesting (some less charitable might say suspicious) that "communitarians" and "contextualists" such as MacIntyre and Sandel, who excoriate Liberalism for its abstractness and sterility, almost uniformly fail to engage Feinberg's work. Yet here, if anywhere, we find Liberalism, or one interpretation of it, as a living doctrine built on the common values of a certain type of society and political culture, within a definite historical context.

Feinberg draws upon patterns of legal reasoning (especially in the common law), public and scholarly constitutional debates, common sense moral thinking, and the best, most systematic thought of Western Judeo-Christian secular and religious ethical theory. In this sense Feinberg actually does what these critics advocate but do not themselves attain. He articulates, refines, and sometimes challenges the shared values of a community – what we might call the liberal community of principle – in the right context of the historically evolving, particularistic conflicts of values which that community now faces. What is more, the substantive views he puts forward are unmistakably liberal

– just the sorts of views which these critics of Liberalism mistakenly think are necessarily rooted in a noncontextualist, abstract approach to values.

In other words, Feinberg not only talks about the importance of rooting moral philosophy in a community of values, he actually participates in that community by deftly negotiating the practices, discourses, and institutions in which those values are embodied. To say that Feinberg always treats these wellsprings of liberal values critically is true, but fails to capture his more important accomplishment: In his own thinking, he shows quite convincingly that the liberal culture which nourishes him and which he in turn nourishes contains concepts and styles of argumentation that make its own self-criticism possible. And in doing so, he gives us a special reason to give our allegiance to this community.

There is something highly artificial about dividing our comments between Feinberg the philosopher and Feinberg the man. Joel Feinberg is a good man, writing and speaking well, about things that matter. Sympathy without sentimentality, a sensitivity which does not sacrifice strength, rectitude without rigidity, seriousness of purpose leavened by a wit that is sharp but never malicious – these rare virtues are equally well expressed in his life as well as his writings.*

For those who have not had the good fortune to know him personally, we take the liberty of mentioning two anecdotes which do something to convey a sense of wholeness of the person and the thinker. Both incidents occurred when Feinberg was a young soldier in World War II. In the first, he was reprimanded while he was an officer candidate because he was too polite towards the troops under his command in a trial exercise ("Bill, would you please move that machine gun forward a bit?" was thought to lack command presence). In the second, Joel was sentenced to thirty days in the guard house for having allowed the prisoners he was guarding to come into a boiler room out of the bitter cold. These vignettes are of course endearing and indicate Joel's kindness and generosity. But what is equally significant is what he did with the experiences – reflection on them helped generate his interest in the relationship between law and morality. It is no doubt because Feinberg the thinker and Feinberg the person are one that his work provides not only knowledge but wisdom.

Allen Buchanan
Jules L. Coleman

*A complete bibliography of Joel Feinberg's works appears at the end of this volume.

Contributors

RICHARD J. ARNESON is Professor of Philosophy at the University of California, San Diego.

ALLEN BUCHANAN is Professor of Business and Philosophy at the University of Wisconsin-Madison.

JULES L. COLEMAN is Garver Professor of Jurisprudence and Philosophy at Yale Law School.

JOHN MARTIN FISCHER is Professor of Philosophy at the University of California, Riverside.

HYMAN GROSS is Fellow in Law at Cambridge University.

JEAN HAMPTON is Professor of Philosophy at the University of Arizona.

SANFORD H. KADISH is Professor of Law Emeritus at the University of California, Berkeley.

SHELLY KAGAN is Professor of Philosophy at the University of Illinois, Chicago.

DAVID LYONS is Sage Professor of Philosophy and Law at Cornell University.

JOAN MCGREGOR is Associate Professor of Philosophy at Arizona State University.

THOMAS MORAWETZ is Professor of Law at the University of Connecticut.

JEFFRIE G. MURPHY is Professor of Law and Philosophy at Arizona State University.

MARK RAVIZZA is Assistant Professor of Philosophy at the University of California, Riverside.

DAVID A. J. RICHARDS is Professor of Law at New York University.

ROBERT F. SCHOPP is Professor of Law at the University of Nebraska.

HOLLY M. SMITH is Professor of Philosophy and Associate Provost at the University of Arizona.

1

Liberalism and group rights

ALLEN BUCHANAN

I. Challenges to Liberalism

Two recent developments, one theoretical, the other practical, appear to challenge liberal political philosophy at its core. The first is the vigorous, impassioned, and often eloquent critique of Liberalism advanced by communitarian thinkers. The second is a twofold political transformation: the growing spate of secessionist movements from Croatia to Lithuania to Quebec, which highlights the disturbing silence of liberal theorists on the question of secession; and the emergence of the indigenous peoples' rights movement in various contexts of international law, including the United Nations, a movement whose members often claim that liberal theory cannot adequately express their fundamental aspirations.

Communitarians complain that Liberalism fails to take seriously the centrality in human life of participation in groups, and that the liberal preoccupation with justice, understood largely as respect for individual rights, both results from and reinforces this neglect. Advocates of indigenous peoples' rights contend that the individual rights Liberalism champions, including their international expression in the United Nations' Declaration of Human Rights, do not address the special concerns of North, Central, and South American Indians, Southeast Asian Hill Tribes, Saamis (Lappes), and other indigenous peoples who find themselves embedded in existing states. Those who raise the banner of secession typically do so in the name of their group's right of self-determination, not by appealing to individual rights. The communitarians' theoretical onslaught and the political practice of the advocates of secession and of rights for indigenous peoples strike at what is supposed to be the core of Liberalism: an exclusive preoccupation with individual rights and an assumption that the liberal framework of individual rights can accommodate the legitimate interests of all groups.

I have argued in detail elsewhere that Liberalism can and should recognize a limited right to secede.[1] To attempt to summarize briefly those complex arguments here would be to hazard oversimplification. Furthermore, I also believe that a number of its defenders have already shown that Liberalism properly understood can meet most communitarian objections.[2] Consequently, I will concentrate here on the charge, frequently voiced by those who purport to speak for indigenous peoples, that Liberalism not only has failed to recognize *group rights,* but also is morally or conceptually barred from doing so.[3] Focusing on the question of whether Liberalism can accommodate group rights will enable us to see whether Liberalism can respond adequately to the challenge of the indigenous peoples' rights movement. At the same time it will allow us to frame the usually purely negative communitarian challenge to Liberalism in a more constructive way by exploring the hypothesis that a proper appreciation for the good of community requires group rights. For after all, if the complaint is that Liberalism devalues the individual's identification with and participation in the group and that the liberal preoccupation with individual rights both expresses and contributes to this error, then a natural alternative is the idea of group rights. This strategy will not only help us to move beyond the now predictable thrusts and counterthrusts in the war of words between liberals and communitarians and recast the theoretical issues in a fresh way; it will also lend needed concreteness to that suspiciously academic debate by connecting it with matters of great political urgency.

My aim in this investigation is to make a case for three related theses:

1. that Liberalism can and should recognize group rights, including special rights for indigenous peoples and other vulnerable minorities, under certain conditions;
2. that nevertheless Liberalism ought to preserve a strong presumption in favor of individual, rather than group rights, even for purposes of protecting the goods individuals can only attain from participation in groups; and
3. that individual rights are normatively prior to at least one important class of group rights – those with regard to which individuals as such do not have standing but which must instead be exercised collectively by the group or its putative agents. In general such group rights ought to be recognized only when certain individual rights are in place; while in general individual rights ought to be recognized even in the absence of group rights.

II. The compatibility of Liberalism and group rights

The first step in showing that Liberalism can accommodate group rights is to fix on relatively uncontroversial conceptions of what Liberalism is and what group rights are. The second is to dispel the erroneous preconception that Liberalism is wedded to certain discredited ontological, motivational, or valuetheoretic assumptions. The third is to provide positive liberal arguments in favor of certain group rights that do not rely upon the discredited ontological, motivational, or value-theoretic assumptions.

For our purposes Liberalism may be given a rather lean definition: It is a normative thesis, a thesis about what the proper role of the state is, namely, first and foremost to uphold the fundamental civil and political individual rights, including the rights to freedom of expression, freedom of religion, of association and assembly, as well as various due process rights, including the right to freedom from arbitrary arrest and seizure, the right to a fair trial.[4] To repeat: Liberalism is the view that the state is to uphold the priority of these individual civil and political rights. It is neither a world view nor a theory of society or of social relations; nor does it purport to be a comprehensive moral view, much less a complete theory of value.

We can fix a working conception of group rights by contrasting them with individual rights as follows. Individual rights are ascribed to an individual, who can in principle *wield* the right – that is, exercise the right (as with the right to free speech) or invoke it to make a claim (when one's right is interfered with) or waive (as with the right to legal counsel) – independently, in her own name, on her own authority. In addition, except in cases in which the possessor of an individual right is not competent to wield it (as with minors, for example) the right can only be wielded by the possessor.

In contrast, a right is a group right, if it can be wielded – that is, invoked, exercised, or waived – in either of two ways. First, the right can *only* be wielded *nonindividually.* Individuals, as such, have no standing with regard to the right – no individual as such and acting in his own name, can invoke, exercise, or waive the right. Instead, the right can only be wielded (a) by the group through some collective procedure (e.g., majority decision making) or (b) by some agent (or agents) that wields it for the group. Group rights in this first sense may be called nonindividual group rights. Examples of nonindividual group rights are the various rights of internal self-government possessed by American Indian tribes. Such rights of internal self-government may only be wielded nonindividually, either collectively, through some sort of direct majoritarian voting process, or by agents of the group (for example, hereditary or elected leaders). No individual in the group, as an individual, can wield these rights.

Second, some group rights have what may be called *dual standing:* Any individual who is a member of the group can wield the right, either on his own behalf or on that of any other members of the group, or the right may be wielded nonindividually by some collective mechanism or by some agent or agents on behalf of the group. An example of a dual standing group right might include the right to engage in cultural or religious ceremonies or rituals. An individual who is a member of the group might invoke the right if his participation in cultural or religious ceremonies or that of others in the group was being interfered with, or official representatives of the group (say, members of the priesthood) might invoke it on behalf of the group.

Among the rights sometimes classified as group rights are language rights. Two types are often distinguished: negative rights not to be interfered with in speaking one's language; and positive rights to subsidies for the teaching of the language. The former can be classified as individual (negative) rights, since individuals have standing with regard to them. (For example, if local government interferes with my speaking the language of the ethnic minority of which I am a member, then I can invoke the right to claim state protection of my speaking the language if there is a right to speak one's language.) However, even though it is true that from the perspective of *standing* (who can wield the right) negative language rights are individual rights, there is perhaps still some point in calling them group rights. The point is that even if the individual has standing as an individual and can invoke the right independently, the interests served by recognizing the right, and hence the ultimate justification for the right, are not his alone. Rather, it is because of the importance of the use of the language for the group, for many individuals, that the negative right to use the language is recognized. Nevertheless, as I shall argue presently, the question of who has standing with regard to a right turns out to be extremely important, and for that reason, I will concentrate more on the distinction between nonindividual standing rights, on the one hand, and individual or dual standing rights on the other.

Positive language rights – rights to subsidies for preserving the language – are usually group rights in the first sense: They are not wielded individually, the subsidies not being granted to individuals as such, but rather to groups, which then exercise some control over how they are used, either by some collective decision process or through agents purporting to act for the group.

To summarize: Individual rights are those with regard to which the individual as such has standing – she can exercise, invoke, or waive the right on her own authority, in her own name. Group rights are those which have either nonindividual standing (as with rights of internal self-government for ethnic minorities), in which case they can only be wielded collectively or by agents of the group, but not by individuals as such; or they have dual standing, in which case they can be wielded either nonindividually or individually (as with rights to participate in cultural ceremonies).

The chief sorts of group rights whose compatibility with Liberalism I shall now explore are these.

1. Group language rights, including rights to government subsidies for teaching the language in question (positive language rights), as well as rights of groups to restrict the use of competing languages (prescriptive language rights, e.g., Bill 101, which prohibits the display of signs in English or any language other than French in public places in Quebec).

2. Group property rights, which empower a group (or its putative agents) to place restrictions on property transactions by individuals (e.g., rights

granted by the Federal governments of Canada and the United States to prohibit the sale of lands occupied by Indians to non-Indians).

3. Various limited self-government or political autonomy rights for groups within states. (There is a range of alternatives here, from rights of self-government concerning the group's internal affairs, to the right to control over a portion of the central government revenues, to rights to participate in decision making concerning natural resources and development in the region, to participate in various economic relationships with foreign states).

Limited political autonomy rights confer varying forms and degrees of independence on a group short of the *right to secede,* understood as the right of a group to renounce entirely the jurisdiction of the state in which it now exists and to appropriate a portion of that state's territory. In this essay I shall concentrate mainly on (1) positive group language rights and (2) group property rights, while acknowledging that the distinction between them and limited political autonomy rights is somewhat artificial. (Both group property rights and limited political autonomy rights can serve to further the group's self-determination).

All three of these types of rights are nonindividual standing rights: In all three cases the right is wielded not by individuals, but either collectively or by putative agents of the group. It is precisely because they are characterized by the nonindividual standing feature which makes them dubious candidates for inclusion within a liberal political philosophy. For both the proponents of Liberalism and its detractors have tended to assume that because Liberalism bases its normative conclusions ultimately upon the importance of individuals, it is individuals and only they who should have standing with regard to rights. Consequently, if I can show that Liberalism can accommodate such nonindividual group rights, I will have established a more interesting conclusion than if I limited the claim to dual-standing group rights, which give standing to individuals and are therefore much closer to the individual rights which are the stock and trade of Liberalism.

Now that we have working definitions of 'Liberalism' and of 'group rights' before us, we can address and refute the charge that Liberalism is committed to ontological and/or motivational assumptions, or assumptions about the nature of value, which are implausible in their own right and which preclude it from embracing group rights. Although there may be some who call themselves liberals who espouse these assumptions, the most plausible versions of Liberalism are not committed to them.

First, Liberalism is individualistic in a *moral,* not an ontological sense. As suggested above, liberals hold that what matters ultimately, morally speaking, is individuals. It is true that different thinkers develop different lines of justification for the liberal normative thesis concerning the priority of individual rights, in part because they start with different understandings of what exactly it is about individuals that is of such ultimate moral significance. But generally speaking they locate the ultimate source of value in the individual as a choosing being capable of developing and fulfilling herself through her choices.

In order to develop plausible lines of justification from the starting point of the moral significance of individuals to the liberal normative thesis about individual rights, one need not deny the existence of groups. Nor need one assert that all putative properties of groups can be reduced to properties of individuals. Moreover, there is nothing in Liberalism that requires us to deny that in order to describe the interest that individuals have in participating in groups it is necessary to make reference to institutions and practices, not just to features of individuals. Liberalism can also cheerfully admit that the institutional or social concepts used to describe the interests that individuals have in belonging to groups and pursuing shared ends are not reducible to preinstitutional or presocial concepts. Liberalism, as a normative thesis about the priority of individual civil and political rights, does not entail any such views, nor do the more plausible lines of justification invoked to support that thesis include any such views among their premises.[5]

Similarly, opponents of Liberalism often assume that it is committed to some rather unsavory motivational assumptions: that individuals generate their preferences without benefit of social influences, that persons are by nature exclusively concerned with their own interests, that their interests are exclusively self-regarding and private, and so on. Again, none of these extreme motivational assumptions is entailed by the liberal thesis about the priority of individual civil and political rights, and none need figure in the various strands of argument that can be invoked to support it. Liberalism can and should recognize the fact that our most fundamental preferences are socially shaped, that most human beings take an intrinsic interest in the interest of others, that many have genuine common, as opposed to purely private interests, and that they regard the goods of community as intrinsically good, not merely as instrumentally valuable in pursuit of private, individual goods. In particular, Liberalism can and should acknowledge and accommodate the fact that for most if not all people participation in a community of some sort – and the cooperative pursuit of genuinely shared ends that this involves – is of vital importance, both in their conception of themselves and their conception of the good life.

Finally, there is nothing to prevent a liberal from espousing a value theory that affirms the objectivity of value, nothing to preclude her from acknowledging not only that most, if not all, people do in fact desire the goods of community, but also that these are in fact among the most important elements of the good life.[6] It is another matter, however, as to whether liberal theories have adequately reflected the importance of the goods of community, and in particular, whether their doing so requires the recognition of group rights in addition to the familiar liberal individual rights. And that is the question to which we must turn our attention.

But before we do so it is worth emphasizing a point which several recent defenders of Liberalism have made, but which its detractors still fail to appreciate.[7] Some of the most important liberal individual rights are valulable in great part because they protect *groups* and allow them to flourish, and it is the "communitarian" value of these rights which provides one of the chief justifications for recognizing them. Historically, the legal and constitutional recognition of the rights to freedom of expression, of religion, of association and assembly was at first the result of compromises of tolerance in the aftermath of the wars of religion of the sixteenth and seventeenth centuries; and these individual rights continue to play a crucial role in preserving not only religious but political and "life style" communities today.

The point is that the core of Liberalism – the fundamental individual civil and political rights – can be seen as an affirmation of the importance of the goods of community, not a denial of them in the name of an implausible, hyper-individualist view, whether moral, ontological, or value-theoretic. Liberalism can and should rest its case for some of the most fundamental individual civil and political rights on their value in protecting groups. Such "communitarian" justifications for individual rights are perfectly consistent with Liberalism's insistence that what matters ultimately, morally speaking, is individuals. All that is required to render Liberalism's moral individual consistent with a "communitarian" justification for individual rights is the quite plausible view that the value of groups is the value that membership in groups has *for individuals*.[8] The question, then, is whether Liberalism, in order to reflect an appropriate appreciation of the significance of community in human life, ought to supplement the individual rights with group rights, and if so, what sorts of group rights and under what conditions?

III. The liberal case for group rights

No attempt can be made here to develop a comprehensive liberal theory of group rights. My aim is more modest: to show that a strong case can be made from a liberal perspective for recognizing some group rights under certain conditions. I begin with group language rights.

As noted earlier, it is important to distinguish between negative and positive language rights. A negative language right is simply a right not to be interfered with in using one's preferred language. This right, I have suggested, is best understood as an individual, not a group right, just as the right to freedom of expression (of which it may be a specification) is generally understood to be an individual right. A positive language right – a right to public subsidies for the preservation of a language – is more plausibly construed as a group right. And in most cases it will be a group right of the nonindividual standing sort. However, even if the form the public subsidy took was an individual allowance (say for tuition to a French language school for Walloons living in the Flemish part of Belgium), the basic entitlement would be understood as an entitlement of the members of the language community in question *as members of that group,* and the interests (in preserving the language and the associated culture) which justify the ascription of the positive right would be the interests that individuals have in the preservation of the language group and its culture. The entitlement to public subsidies is an entitlement of the group to resources needed to enable its members to continue to enjoy the goods of community which the existence of that group provides.

A third type of language right may also be distinguished: A *prescriptive* language right. A prescriptive language right is the right of a group to restrict the use of competing languages within a certain territory. (An example is Bill 101, which legally prohibits the display of signs in English or any language other than French in public places in Quebec). A prescriptive language right is even more clearly a group right: It is the right of a group – acting through its political mechanisms for collective or delegated decisions – to impose restrictions on the use of competing languages within a specified jurisdiction. The right to prohibit signs in English in Quebec is clearly not an individual right, nor is it a group right of the dual-standing sort.

From a liberal standpoint prescriptive group language rights are obviously more problematic than positive group language rights because in exercising its right to restrict the use of a competing language the members of a group restrict the liberties of others to speak that language. So there is at least an apparent conflict between this group right and the individual right to freedom of expression, if we assume that the right to freedom of expression generally includes the right to use the language of one's choice. The mere fact of such a conflict does not show that Liberalism cannot supplement the individual rights with some group rights, however, since there can be conflicts among individual rights as well. For example, the right to freedom of expression can conflict with the right to a fair trial when media coverage of alleged crimes prejudices prospective jurors.

When such conflicts occur, Liberal theorists develop various strategies for balancing the competing interests which the rights in question protect, sometimes by invoking priority principles, sometimes by pruning back the scope of one or both of the conflicting rights. To make a case for recognizing group rights, then, the liberal need not show that individual and group rights can never conflict. Instead she must show that the case for the group rights in question is sufficiently strong to warrant the kind of complex balancing strategies that are invoked to sort out conflicts among individual rights.

Perhaps the strongest case for recognizing both positive and prescriptive language rights, from a liberal standpoint, is that such rights may, under certain conditions, prove indispensable for preserving minority cultures that are threatened as a result of a long history of unjust treatment at the hands of the majority. Will Kymlicka has argued, quite persuasively in my opinion, that the need to preserve the cultures of Native Americans and other indigenous groups can, under certain circumstances, justify not only positive and prescriptive group language rights but group property rights as well. The argument, which can be strengthened and extended to cover both positive and prescriptive language rights as well,[9] has two stages.

The first explains the importance of membership in a cultural group for the individual; the second shows how recognizing the group right in question can, under certain circumstances, make an indispensable contribution to the preservation of the culture. Kymlicka notes that cultural membership provides the individual with a *context for meaningful choice*. This point is extremely important and deserves elaboration. The culture not only makes salient a manageably limited range of alternative goals, rescuing the individual from the paralysis of infinite possibilities; it also does so in such a way as to invest certain options with *meanings* that allow the individual to *identify with* and be *motivated* by those options. The culture also *connects* what otherwise would be fragmented goals in a coherent, mutually supporting way, offering ideals of wholeness and continuity, not only across the stages of an individual human life but over generations as well. Without the context for meaningful choice supplied by a culture, the individual may feel either that nothing is worth doing because everything is equally possible or that life is a series of discrete episodes of choice, each of which is impoverished because of its utter unconnectedness with the others. The landscape of choice may seem so flattened and featureless that movement seems pointless, and the sense that one's life is a journey in which milestones can be reached may evaporate.[10] With some simplification we can say that the first source of the value of a culture for the individual who belongs to it, its being a meaningful context for choice, is that the culture provides an appropriate *structure* for the individual's pursuit of the good life. And it is worth emphasizing that there is nothing here that assumes that the content of the individual's goals is egoistic or purely self-regarding. On the contrary, it is characteristic of the value structure provided by a culture that it encourages identification with the cultural group and hence fosters the pursuit of common goals.

A second and equally important source of value for the individual of cultural membership is the fact that for most if not all individuals participation in community is itself an important ingredient in the *content* of the good life, not just a part of its structure. Participation in community is a fundamental intrinsic good, not merely a structural condition for the successful pursuit of other goods or a means toward procuring them. And in many cases the community that is most important in the individual's life will be a cultural (rather than a political, professional, or aesthetic) community. Nothing in Liberalism or its understanding of human good bars it from embracing this basic truth. Given its importance, then, both as a structure for the individual's choices and in supplying some of the main ingredients of the content of her conception of the good, cultural membership warrants protection.

The second stage of the argument is to show how group rights can sometimes provide the needed protection – protection that the traditional liberal individual rights alone may not adequately provide. The case of positive group language rights is relatively straightforward: under certain conditions, public financial support for the teaching of a minority language (e.g., Hopi in the state of Arizona) may be necessary for the preservation of a culture. The group in question may lack the resources, and, in the case of indigenous peoples, the need for special arrangements for sustaining the language and the lack of resources for doing so may have the same source: a history of unjust treatment at the hands of the majority.

The case for prescriptive language rights and group property rights is somewhat more complex. These group rights can be justified as mechanisms for overcoming *collective action problems* that would otherwise prevent the groups in question from doing what is necessary to preserve their cultures. Even though French Canadians understood that the preservation of their culture depends upon the continued use of French, individual members of that group were under strong incentives to use the majority language (English). A prescriptive language right (established by Bill 101) allowed this group, through the agency of the government, to counterbalance these incentives for using English by penalizing the use of English on signs in public places. Similarly, American and Canadian Indian tribes (or bands) may benefit from laws that prescribe the teaching of their languages in tribal schools, as well as the use of those languages in tribal meetings, on tribal ballot forms, and in certain other contexts.

The liberal argument for group property rights has the same structure. If the preservation intact of a minimal contiguous area of territory occupied and controlled exclusively by members of an indigenous group is in fact a necessary condition for the preservation of that group's culture, group property rights can be justified, if it can be shown that they will help prevent incursions into the territory by nonindigenous peoples. Such group property rights can contain any of several elements, including the right of the tribe (or band) to prohibit nonmembers from settling permanently in the territory or the right to prevent individual members or families in the group from selling land to nonmembers. These are property rights in that they are legally recognized forms of (limited) control over the disposition of land. They are group property rights because the control is vested in the group not in individuals as such.

Whether or not the recognition of either group language rights or group property rights or both is the best means for preserving the culture in question is a complex contingent matter. The point is that these options cannot be ruled out *a priori* and that there will surely be some circumstances in which they may be vitally needed.

Group language rights fall under the heading of what are sometimes called *minority culture rights,* which include the right to wear traditional cultural dress and to engage in traditional cultural ceremonies. Today indigenous peoples – from Central American Indians to Lapps, Aleuts, and native Hawaiians – not only are demanding minority cultural rights but *political autonomy rights* as well. Political autonomy rights accord groups varying degrees and forms of independence as political entities. As group property rights increase in scope they come to approximate the jurisdictional authority that states enjoy. Thus group property rights occupy a range of positions between mere minority cultural rights and political autonomy rights.

As the political autonomy rights of a minority group within a state increase, the sovereignty of that state with respect to that group and the territory and resources over which the group exercises some control suffers successive limitations. The most extreme right of political autonomy for a group is the right to secede: the right to free itself and a certain portion of the territory entirely from the jurisdiction of the state. Thus we can envision a range of group rights, from minority culture rights to political autonomy rights of varying scope and strength, with the right to secede at the extreme end of a rough continuum.

IV. The primacy of individual rights

Thus far I have argued (1) that Liberalism can accommodate the legitimate concerns about groups and their role in the good life which communitarians and advocates of group rights for indigenous peoples rightly emphasize; (2) that the strongest case for the liberal individual civil and political rights rests in part upon the protection those rights provide for groups; and (3) that Liberalism can acknowledge group rights under certain circumstances without repudiating its commitment to the moral priority of individuals. I wish to conclude by making a case for the thesis that there is an important sense in which individual rights are primary: In general group rights – at least those of the nonindividual standing variety – should be recognized only if there exists an appropriate backdrop of effective individual rights capable of reducing some of the moral risks which the recognition of group rights entails. I will also suggest that there can be and indeed are circumstances in which individual rights alone, without supplementation by group rights, can provide adequate protection for individuals as individuals and as beings whose membership in groups is essential to their identity and their well-being. Although I will not attempt a systematic demonstration of this thesis of the primacy of individual rights, I will provide enough support to make it plausible.

Group rights of the nonindividual standing type cannot be wielded by the individual group member as an individual. They must be exercised, invoked, or waived either (1) by the group as a whole through some majoritarian decision procedure or (2) by some individual or subset of the group putatively acting as the agent of the group. It is crucial to understand that both methods carry serious risks – risks that can best be reduced by embedding group rights in a framework of individual rights.

If a majoritarian decision procedure must be used before the right can be exercised, invoked, or waived, collective action problems may occur. (For example, even if invoking the right is in the interest of all or most members of the group, it may be rational for the individual member not to participate in the collective effort necessary for invoking it, as in standard free-rider problems for voter participation generally). Or, at the very least, collective exercise of the right may involve significant delays and logistical costs. (This is one reason why ascribing rights to individuals has certain advantages. For example, if it is the individual who has the right to freedom of religion, then all it takes to invoke the protection the right provides is *one* individual stepping forward, because it is individuals as such who have standing with regard to the right.) In contrast, if the right is to be wielded by an individual or a minority on behalf of the group, this requires not only an organizational structure for the group but a hierarchy. Those who have the authority to wield the right for the group will thereby have powers which others in the group lack. And wherever hierarchy (and hence inequality) exists, there is the danger that those who have greater powers will use them for their own benefits or for what they believe to be the benefit of the group, rather than in ways that actually benefit the group. Indeed, the minority that wields the right may, in part because of its special powers, develop its own special corporate interests and pursue them to the detriment of some or all members of the group.

It is important to note that abuses of the power to wield the group right need not arise exclusively from self-interested motives. The elite who wield the right may attempt to act in the group's interest but may be mistaken about what it is.

One usually think of rights as barriers against paternalistic interference, and when they are individual rights they often function in just this way. But if others must decide for us whether to exercise, invoke, or waive our rights, then there is the possibility of paternalism being practiced upon us *in the name of our rights.*

In terms of principal/agent theory, we can say that the person or subgroup who wields the right (allegedly for the group) is the agent of the group (the principal) and that here, as in all principal/agent relationships, there are agency-risks – opportunities and incentives for the agent to act in ways that are contrary to the interests of the principal, regardless of whether the agent is motivated by self-interest or by his perception of the principal's interests.

The great advantage of individual rights – rights which accord to the individual the independent authority to wield the right – is that they eliminate the agency risks associated with depending upon *others* to wield the right on our behalf, while at the same time also avoiding the collective action problems and costs of majoritarian procedures for wielding the right. Moreover, even if the collective action problems involved in wielding nonindividual standing group rights by majoritarian procedures can be surmounted and the costs of majoritarian procedures can be kept within tolerable limits, there are still agency-risks, since, in effect, the majority, in wielding the right, will be acting for the minority as well as itself. The majority may vote to wield the right in ways that serve its own distinct interest rather than the interest of the group as a whole. Or the majority may be mistaken about what is best for the group. So regardless of whether they are wielded by an elite or through majoritarian procedures, they are inherently risky devices.

Yet as we saw earlier, in certain circumstances individual rights may not be sufficient. Indigenous peoples may require special protections that can only be provided by group language rights of the positive or prescriptive sort, group property rights, and perhaps a range of political autonomy rights (short of complete sovereignty) as well. How can we gain the benefits of group rights in those special circumstances in which they are valuable, while reducing to a tolerable level the dangers and costs they involve?

My suggestion is that the problems endemic to group rights (at least those of the nonindividual standing variety) can be ameliorated (though not eliminated) only if they are embedded in a framework of appropriate individual rights. A few examples will illustrate. If empowering an elite to wield a right for the group is to be tolerable there must be mechanisms for increasing the likelihood that the elite will be well-informed about the interests and preferences of the rank and file and for holding the elite accountable for its conduct in wielding the right. Individual rights to freedom of expression, of assembly, and of association are important elements of such mechanisms. These individual rights are significant in any case, but they are especially crucial if individuals lack the right to participate as equals in a process of selecting those who will wield the right for the group because they may provide the only means for criticizing and influencing the elite.

In contrast, if the elite who are to wield the right are selected through a democratic process, then these same rights can contribute to the quality of the selection process by reducing the risk that people will be selected who will not wield the right appropriately for the group. So regardless of whether ordinary members of the group have a say in choosing those who are to wield the right for the group, individual rights can play a valuable role in reducing the risks associated with group rights.

If the right is to be wielded not by an elite, but rather through a majoritarian procedure, then individual rights are again essential. Among the most important are not just the individual right to participate in the decision procedure by having an equal vote, but also supporting rights, including the right to freedom of expression and to freedom of association and assembly, which are needed to ensure that political equality is more than formal.

Similarly, if group property rights of the sort described earlier are to be tolerable, individuals, as individuals, will require certain rights: in particular, the right to own property outside the area the group controls and the right to exit from the group's territory without unacceptable costs. In U.S. and Canadian Indian law individual tribal and band members enjoy these rights. The ability to leave the group and to participate in a system of individual private property rights in land in the larger society, along with the right to leave and to return to the group without losing one's rights as a member of the group, go a long way toward offsetting the liabilities of group property rights. Without these individual rights, group property rights would make individuals and minority subgroups extremely vulnerable. If all major resources were subject to group property rights, individuals and subgroups would lack any independent access to or control over them. Those who disagreed with the majority or the elite who wield the rights might be out of luck.

So far I have argued that nonindividual standing group rights are likely to be tolerable only if they are embedded in a framework of appropriate individual rights. I will conclude by suggesting that the reverse is not generally true. The strongest case for group rights is that they are needed as special protections for the distinctive interests of indigenous peoples and other minorities who are especially vulnerable – typically as a result of historical injustices perpetrated against them. Where such special problems do not exist, there may well be no need for group rights, and no justification for courting the risks they can entail. Individual rights may serve quite well, both for our protection as individuals and as beings who identify with and flourish within groups. In general, group rights, including those of the nonindividual standing type, are special remedies for circumstances in which serious conflicts of interest between groups exist or in which certain minority groups require special protections. Even where these problems do not exist, individual rights will generally still be valuable, and not just for "individualists" but for those who identify closely with the community and whose good includes shared ends.[11]

Notes

1 This is a main theme of my book *Secession: The Morality of Political Divorce From Fort Sumter to Lithuania and Quebec* (Boulder, Colorado: Westview Press, 1990).

2 Allen Buchanan, "Assessing the Communitarian Critique of Liberalism," *Ethics,* 99, no. 4 (July 1989): 852–82. Joel Feinberg, *Harmless Wrongdoing* (Volume Four of *The Moral Limits of the Criminal Law*), (New York: Oxford University Press, 1988), 81–123. Will Kymlicka, *Liberalism, Culture, and Community* (Oxford: Oxford University Press, 1989).

3 The emphasis on these individual rights is the core of Liberalism. On the question of positive rights (e.g., to health care or to a decent minimum of income) liberals divide into libertarians, who reject them, and welfare liberals, who embrace them.

4 This discussion of what Liberalism is not committed to is borrowed from *Secession,* chapter 1, 79–81.

5 There are a number of possible justifications for the liberal emphasis on individual civil and political rights. Among them are utilitarian arguments, arguments that take individual autonomy as the fundamental value, and arguments that recognize both welfare and autonomy as fundamental.

6 Buchanan, "Assessing the Communitarian Critique of Liberalism," 856–82.

7 *Ibid.,* 858–59; Joel Feinberg, *Harmless Wrongdoing,* Chapter 29; and Joseph Raz, *The Morality of Freedom* (Oxford: Oxford University Press, 1986), 253–4.

8 Allen Buchanan, *Secession,* 52–74, 79–80; and Will Kymlicka, *Liberalism, Community, and Culture,* chapter 10.

9 Allen Buchanan, *Secession,* 52–80; and Will Kymlicka, *Liberalism, Community, and Culture,* chapter 10.

10 The description of the importance of culture in providing a structure for choice is drawn from *Secession,* 53–4.

11 I am greatly indebted to Gerald Postema for his acute comments on a draft of this paper.

2

The argument from liberty

SHELLY KAGAN

I

Libertarianism is often said to be the moral system which most purely reflects or expresses the value of individual liberty and freedom. If this is so, at the very least it indicates an attractive feature of libertarianism – and this much is frequently conceded even by libertarianism's critics. But it is natural to take this thought further, and see it as pointing to and providing the basis for what I take to be an intuitively plausible and widely held *argument* for libertarianism: the argument from liberty. Liberty is obviously a significant value, and libertarianism is the system that most fully incorporates or captures that value; libertarianism is thus to be defended by appeal to the very fact that it is the moral system which gives greatest expression to individual liberty and freedom.

There are, of course, other possible arguments for libertarianism,[1] but in this essay it is only the argument from liberty with which I am concerned. It is, I think, an argument whose force we can easily feel: The libertarian leaves us free to do as we see fit – both in matters of personal life-style, and in the economic sphere – provided only that we refrain from interfering with the like freedom of others. Accordingly, if we place sufficient value on freedom, a powerful case for libertarianism appears to emerge.

This initial statement of the argument from liberty is admittedly somewhat vague, and in what follows I shall try to state it more precisely. But even without moving beyond this rough formulation, there are two familiar objections to the argument that can immediately be raised.

The first complains that although liberty or freedom is indeed a significant value, it is not the only moral value which commands our attention. For example, it might be suggested that welfare or equality (whether of welfare, or of resources) are themselves important values which merit expression in any adequate moral system of rights, duties, and permissions. Libertarianism may well be what emerges if we set ourselves the goal of designing a moral system that reflects the value of liberty alone, but such a narrow focus is unjustified. Once we aim instead to reflect the value of welfare and equality as well as that of liberty, the system that emerges will significantly diverge from that of libertarianism. It will at least sometimes limit individual liberty when this is necessary to promote or protect equality or well-being. (The details of the objection will of course depend on the specific additional values being endorsed.)

The success of this first objection is conditional upon the critic's ability to establish the validity and significance of the values being proposed to supplement the concern with liberty. Justifiably or not, the libertarian can thus resist the objection by denying the existence of these other values, or by insisting that, although real, these other values can never outweigh the value of liberty (and so departures from libertarianism can never be justified by appeal to these values). It should be noted, in particular, that nothing in this first objection calls into question the claim that libertarianism is indeed the system that most fully reflects or expresses the value of liberty.

The second objection does call this claim into question. It holds that even if we agree with the libertarian to restrict our attention to expressing the value of liberty or freedom, the argument from liberty unjustifiably restricts itself to one *kind* of freedom – freedom from interference. For it is only freedom from interference which is protected by the system of rights and permissions endorsed by the libertarian: We are free – that is, free from interference – to do as we see fit, provided that we do not interfere with others. Yet such "negative freedom," as it is sometimes called, is not only the kind of freedom with legitimate moral significance. An adequate moral system should also express the value of "positive freedom," or the ability to accomplish one's various goals.[2] If we set ourselves the aim of designing a moral system that reflects the value of "freedom to" and not merely that of "freedom from," the system that emerges will once again diverge significantly from libertarianism. In at least some cases it will condone interfering with individual freedom when this is necessary to guarantee that all have certain minimal abilities to pursue their goals. (As before, the details of the objection will obviously depend upon the specific characterization of the other forms of freedom being endorsed.)

As with the first, the libertarian can resist this new objection by denying the significance of these other kinds of freedom, either by denying that positive freedom is a genuine value, or by insisting that, although real, it can never outweigh negative freedom. And armed with this denial, the argument from liberty still goes through, since nothing in this second objection challenges the claim that libertarianism is indeed the moral system that emerges if we do set ourselves the goal of expressing the value of negative freedom, and negative freedom alone.

Now I do not mean to be endorsing the libertarian's answer to either of these objections. In point of fact, I take both objections to be well-founded. But it is striking for all that that these two familiar objections leave the major

MAGDALEN COLLEGE LIBRARY

premise of the argument from liberty untouched. As I have noted, both objections concede that the argument from liberty might well succeed if only it were granted that individual negative freedom, or negative liberty, is the only fundamental value to be reflected. Nonlibertarians may well find it implausible to claim that negative liberty is the only fundamental value. But critics and friends of libertarianism alike apparently find it plausible to hold that it is indeed libertarianism that emerges once we agree that it is individual negative liberty – freedom from interference – whose value is to be reflected.

It is this claim that I want to challenge in this paper. It is not that I find the claim implausible. On the contrary, it strikes me as quite plausible on the face of it, and I think that it explains a great deal of the intuitive appeal of libertarianism. Yet it seems to me that when looked at more carefully, this central claim of the argument from liberty can be seen to be either false, or at least rather dubious. Failure to appreciate this is due to a nearly universal failure to bring the claim sharply into focus.

II

To defend the argument from liberty, one would need a reasonably precise formulation of libertarianism. After all, the claim is that it is libertarianism that emerges from a concern with individual liberty, construed as freedom from interference. It would be impossible to establish this claim definitively without having a specification of all the essential features of libertarian systems. However, it may be possible to give adequate grounds for *rejecting* this claim without a full account of libertarianism before us. Provided that we can identify a few core features of libertarianism – so that any system that failed to incorporate those features would be rejected by all libertarians – it may be possible to show that the argument from liberty fails as a defense of libertarianism, if it can be shown that the system that emerges from a concern with individual liberty will fail to possess one or more of these core libertarian features.

There are two core features of libertarian systems upon which my argument will rely. The first is the libertarian's endorsement of wide-ranging and potent negative rights: The libertarian holds that each of us has negative rights against the use of force and coercion, a right not to be harmed or killed, and more generally, a right not to be interfered with. The second core feature identifies an important exception or limitation on these general negative rights: We have a right not to be interfered with – *except* when we are interfering with others, violating *their* negative rights. When we are in the process of violating the rights of others then it *is* permissible to use force against us.

These two features do seem to me to be core features of libertarianism, in the sense that I have explained. I am not claiming that they are the only such core features. It would certainly be plausible to suggest, for example, that a duty to keep one's promises (and a corresponding right to have promises made to one kept) would also figure as an essential component of all libertarian systems. But for my purposes, so far as I can see, it will not be necessary to take a stand on this matter. We can put aside the question of what other core features of libertarianism there may be, provided that we are in agreement about the two that I have identified.

I have deliberately kept my characterizations of certain aspects of the two features rather minimal. This is particularly true of the first. I have said that the libertarian believes in negative rights that are wide-ranging and potent. In calling them "potent," I mean to call attention to the libertarian's belief that these negative rights are forceful and at best rarely overridden. But I do not mean to be saying that the rights are *absolute*. On this matter I take it that libertarians can disagree. Similarly, although all libertarians would certainly agree that the negative rights are "wide-ranging," I will not try to define this range here. So, for example, although I believe that virtually all libertarians would think that my negative rights extend to rights over *private property*, and not merely to rights over my labor and my body, I do not mean to build this into the account of the core feature either.

As far as the second core feature goes, the idea is that libertarians do believe that the use of force is justified in the enforcement of, or protection of, rights. Once again, various questions can be left unresolved, for example, whether force can be used preemptively, or whether punishment after the fact can be justified in this way. Furthermore, if the libertarian goes on to recognize certain positive rights, such as the right to have promises made to one kept, then presumably the second core feature will have to be understood to permit the use of force not merely to stop violations of negative rights, but also to enforce positive rights. But here too we need not pursue these matters.

Armed with this minimal account of libertarianism, we can return to the argument from liberty. If we concede that individual liberty, construed as freedom from interference, is the fundamental moral value, is it a libertarian system that best reflects or captures this value? If the system that emerges contains wide-ranging and potent negative rights, protecting individuals from interference except when they themselves have violated the rights of others, then at least these two core features of libertarianism will have received a defense of sorts. But if the system that emerges does not incorporate these two core features then I think we can safely conclude that as a defense of libertarianism the argument from liberty is a failure.

We are not yet in a position to evaluate the argument from liberty. Up to this point I have spoken of the importance of "reflecting" the value of individual liberty, of having a moral system that "captures" or "expresses" the value of freedom from interference. Such metaphors are certainly evocative, and I

would not want to claim that they are without content. I think we have
sufficient grasp of them to feel the intuitive force of the claim that the moral
system that best protects individual liberty or reflects its value is libertarianism. Nonetheless, if we are to evaluate this claim carefully I think we need to
find a somewhat more explicit formulation.

What I take to be the most plausible suggestion is itself perfectly familiar,
and as often as not the argument from liberty is presented in these terms from
the start: Given that individual liberty is the supreme moral value, morality
should grant the most extensive liberty – the most extensive freedom from
interference – possible, compatible with the same liberty being granted to all.
The central claim of the argument from liberty, therefore, is that libertarianism is the moral system that grants the most extensive freedom from interference with like freedom for all. It is this claim that I aim to dispute.

III

Before turning to see whether or not it is indeed libertarianism that grants the
most extensive freedom, it may be of some interest to consider the basis of the
significant qualification that the moral system we are looking for must be one
that grants *like freedom for all*. That is, the aim is not that of finding the moral
system that grants the greatest personal liberty possible (say, to some particular individual); it is, rather, that of finding the system that grants the greatest
personal liberty with the *same* liberties being granted to everyone. We are
looking, not for the system with the greatest liberty, but only for the one with
the greatest *equal* liberty. The importance of this "equality constraint" is
evident. Without it, for example, it might well turn out that the system that
grants the greatest individual liberty is one in which someone – let us say,
Josiah S. Carberry – is moral dictator, able to do absolutely whatever he
wishes, with all others morally required to obey his commands. Arguably,
Carberry's freedom under such a system is greater than that to be had under
any alternative system, libertarianism included. But even if this is so, it will
hardly give the libertarian grounds for dismay: what we are after is the most
extensive system of liberties with the same liberties being granted to *everyone*. It is *this* criterion which the libertarian claims to meet.

Well and good, but just where does the equality constraint come from? We
are working from the assumption that the only fundamental moral value is
liberty – how now do we suddenly start insisting upon the importance of
equality as well?[3] Doubtless, it is tempting for the libertarian to say that the
equality constraint is merely a "formal" constraint. But if this means a constraint imposed by logic, a constraint that will eliminate only incoherent moral
systems, then I think such a claim is mistaken. (The system with the moral
dictator, however implausible, does not seem to be an incoherent one.)

The realization that the equality constraint is not formal in this sense makes it tempting in turn for the critic of libertarianism to insist that the libertarian has appealed to a second substantive value – equality – along with that of liberty. What's more, the equality constraint seems to reveal that even the libertarian recognizes that equality has priority over liberty, and if that is so here, why not elsewhere? Thus the libertarian seems to have opened the door for a return of the first of the two objections mentioned in section I.

I suspect, however, that this second interpretation of the origin of the equality constraint is mistaken as well. The equality constraint should not be viewed as the importation of a second, substantive value. It is indeed a formal constraint – but in the sense that it gives a determinate *form* to the appeal to liberty. Of course, other possible formal constraints are available as well. Thus one could search instead for the system that gives the greatest *total* liberty, or the system that gives the greatest *average* liberty, and similarly for other, more complex functions. The choice between these is not dictated by logic, so it is not merely formal in that sense. But the constraint is formal in that *one* or another of these various possible functions must be chosen if the argument from liberty is to have a determinate form. What the equality constraint provides is a particular "shape" for the appeal to liberty, a "form" that can be filled, rather than a second, substantive value. And this form, like the others, could in principle be filled by alternative contents, provided by alternative substantive values. (Thus we could aim at finding the system with the greatest equal liberty, or the greatest equal utility, or the greatest equal moral virtue, and so on.)

If something like this is correct, then the truth lies somewhere between the first two accounts of the equality constraint. Acceptance of the equality constraint does not introduce a second, substantive value – one that can be promoted independently, and that can in principle conflict with the value of liberty. But it is nonetheless true that acceptance of the equality constraint rather than one of the alternatives is indeed a further choice in need of justification. In particular, recognition of liberty as the fundamental value does not in and of itself dictate acceptance of the equality constraint rather than one of the others.

In thinking about possible justifications for the equality constraint, it is important not to confuse two distinct claims. The first claim is relatively modest, and holds that the liberty of all individuals is to count, and to count equally, toward the assessment of the various possible moral systems. Many will think that this first claim is self-evident, or guaranteed by certain elementary conceptual truths. What is important for our purposes is to see that this first claim – however it is to be defended – must be distinguished from a second, bolder claim, which holds that the liberties of all individuals must *be* equal under an acceptable moral system. (As an analogy, consider the difference between the modest claim accepted by utilitarians that the welfare of all is to be counted equally, and the bold claim insisted upon by egalitarians that the welfare of all should *be* equal.) The second claim goes beyond the first, and so a defense of the first will not necessarily constitute a defense of the second. But it is only the second claim that yields the equality constraint that is at work in the argument from liberty. It is the second, bold claim that must be defended by an advocate of that argument.

How, then, is the imposition of the equality constraint to be justified? I will not attempt to answer this question here; I certainly do not think the answer is obvious. But it must be admitted that the equality constraint does seem plausible for all that. So let us simply grant the libertarian the legitimacy of imposing the equality constraint. And let us add this to our earlier concession – also made for the sake of argument – that freedom from interference is the sole fundamental value. Given these premises, it does seem plausible for the libertarian to hold that the most acceptable moral system will be the one that grants the most extensive liberty, subject only to the qualification that the same liberty is to be granted to all. The question still facing us, and to which we can now return, is whether the libertarian is in fact correct in her claim that it is libertarianism that best meets this standard.

IV

There remains one further interpretive matter that must be addressed before we can evaluate the central claim of the argument from liberty. We are to look for the system that provides the most extensive individual liberty, with equal liberty for all. But what, exactly, is the nature of the liberty that is to be provided?

It is natural to think that we have already answered this question. The liberty in question is negative liberty, freedom from interference. But in point of fact I think that this is still subject to different possible interpretations, and depending upon what precise interpretation we take, the argument from liberty will lead us to strikingly different conclusions. Which system grants the most extensive freedom from interference will depend crucially upon what we take the relevant freedom to be.

One possibility is this. The relevant sort of freedom from interference includes, and is perhaps even limited to, freedom from interference by *morality*. On this conception, when morality imposes a requirement upon an agent that he perform a given act, or refrain from performing a given act, this interferes with the agent's freedom. Although this conception of freedom from interference may not be the one that most readily comes to mind, it is, I think, one that many people endorse. It is certainly a common objective to moral systems (such as utilitarianism) that impose pervasive and severe demands that such systems radically restrict the agent's freedom. Each time a moral system imposes an obligation, it forces the agent to act in the way specified: Moral requirements thus interfere with and limit the agent's freedom.

I am not myself convinced that such talk of morality "forcing" an individual to act in a given way, or "interfering" with an agent's freedom, is legitimate. As I see it, the existence of a moral requirement simply consists in the existence of morally decisive reasons for acting in the given manner. And reasons do not by themselves coerce, or force, or interfere. Or so it seems to me. But many people seem to feel rather differently about the matter, and it is plausible to think that libertarians may well be among this group.

After all, in the course of defending libertarianism by appeal to the argument from liberty, libertarians are apt to point out that under libertarianism the agent is free to do as he sees fit, so long as he does not interfere with the similar freedom of others. A straightforward interpretation of this remark is that the agent is *morally free* to do as he sees fit – that is, he is free from moral requirement. But why is such a remark even relevant for supporting the claim that libertarianism is the system that grants the most extensive individual freedom (with similar freedom for all)? Obviously enough, it will be directly relevant if such freedom from moral requirement is to be counted as part of the individual freedom with which the argument from liberty is concerned. Thus it is reasonable to think that in looking for the moral system that provides the most extensive individual freedom (with equal freedom for all), the libertarian intends to include freedom from moral interference.

Let us consider the possibility that this is in fact the only freedom from interference with which the argument from liberty is concerned. I am not suggesting that this is the most natural interpretation of the argument from liberty, but it will be helpful if we can first consider several "pure" versions of the argument, where it is only a particular sort of freedom from interference that is at issue. The possibility of more pluralistic, or "mixed" arguments can be considered later.

On this interpretation of the argument, then, we are looking for the moral system that grants the most extensive individual liberty – construed as freedom from moral requirement – subject only to the condition that similar liberty is to be granted to all. Since freedom from moral requirement with regard to any given act is the same thing as being morally permitted to either perform the act or not perform the act, under the current interpretation of the argument from liberty we are looking for the moral system that provides the most extensive set of moral permissions, with similar permissions being granted to all. But the system that does this will not be libertarian at all; it will rather be a system with no moral requirements whatsoever, a system in which each agent is morally permitted to do absolutely anything.

A system in which everything is permitted is obviously not a libertarian one. It lacks the first core libertarian feature that I identified in section II. Libertarians believe in wide-ranging and potent negative rights; but the effect of such rights is to require everyone to refrain from interfering with others, to refrain from using coercion and force. Since libertarians believe we are all required to respect these negative rights, they certainly believe in the existence of moral requirements. But the system in which everything is permitted is one in which there are no moral requirements at all. So if I am right in claiming that this is the system that grants the greatest individual liberty – construed as freedom from moral interference – then it is certainly not libertarianism that is supported by the argument from liberty, at least under our first pure interpretation of that argument.

Can the claim that it is this system of unlimited permission which grants the most extensive freedom from moral requirements be resisted? It is difficult to see how. Since this system has no requirements whatsoever, it seems clear that no alternative system could possibly offer *more* extensive freedom from moral requirement. And it is obvious, at any rate, that in comparison libertarianism offers far *less* freedom from moral interference.

It might be objected, however, that the system of unlimited permission fails to satisfy the equality constraint. (And if this is so, it might still be the case that libertarianism is the system that offers the most extensive freedom with equal freedom for all.) A hasty critic might reason as follows: Under the system of unlimited permission, an agent is permitted to interfere with the freedom of others, harming them, or even killing them; yet if this happens the victims will hardly possess the same freedom as that had by the agent; so this system does not yield equal liberty for all. But this objection loses sight of the fact that under this first interpretation of the argument from liberty it is only freedom from moral interference that is relevant. It is *this* freedom that must be extended equally to all. And under the system of unlimited permission it *is* extended equally to all: *Everyone* is equally permitted to do any act whatsoever.

I conclude, therefore, that if the argument from liberty is understood as being concerned solely with freedom from moral interference, it is in fact a system of unlimited permission which is supported. As a defense of libertarianism, the argument fails.

V

The natural response to the argument of the previous section is to point out the obvious fact that libertarians are also concerned with interference by flesh and blood human beings, and not merely, if at all, with the possibility of moral interference. If freedom from interference is of value, what is of value must certainly include freedom from *acts* of interference, that is, interference by embodied human agents.

This suggests a second possible interpretation of the argument from liberty. We are interested in finding the moral system that grants the most extensive freedom from interference. And we are taking this to include, or perhaps even to be limited to, acts of interference by other agents. So we are looking for the moral system that grants the most extensive freedom from acts of interference. Perhaps, then, we should understand this as saying that we are looking for the system that provides the most extensive *protection* from the interference of others.

But what kind of protection is it that can be offered by moral systems per se? The straightforward answer seems to be: *moral* protection. That is, a moral system can protect us from a given kind of act, in a given situation, by morally ruling out acts of that kind in that particular situation. Thus, for a moral system to grant us freedom from acts of interference is for that system to *forbid* acts of interference. (In this way it protects those who could otherwise be permissibly interfered with.)

So let us consider a second pure interpretation of the argument from liberty. Let us suppose that the argument from liberty is concerned with the provision of such moral protection from acts of interference, and that its sole concern is with the provision of such protection. On this second interpretation, then, the argument's concern with providing freedom from interference is understood solely in terms of providing *moral* freedom from *acts* of interference. (In contrast, on the first interpretation, the concern with providing freedom from interference was understood solely in terms of providing freedom from *moral* interference. Thus the first interpretation aimed at the *absence* of moral requirements, while the second aims at the *presence* of certain moral requirements – namely, those prohibiting interference.) Once again, I am making no particular claim as to whether this new construal of the argument from liberty is the most plausible one, but as before, I think it helpful to consider the various pure versions of the argument first.

On this second construal of the argument from liberty, we are looking for the moral system that provides the most extensive moral protection from acts of interference, subject only to the qualification that equal protection is to be provided to all. Now as already noted, a moral system provides protection from a given kind of act by ruling it out in some situation or the other – and the more widespread the circumstances under which the act is forbidden, the more extensive the protection. Thus if we are looking for the system that provides the most extensive possible protection from acts of interference, it seems that we will be led to a system that prohibits acts of interference in all, or virtually all, circumstances. It seems plausible to take this to mean that the system that emerges will be one that includes wide-ranging and quite powerful negative rights.

At first glance, this result will give comfort to the libertarian. Unlike the first interpretation, this second interpretation of the argument from liberty leads us to moral systems that incorporate the first core feature of libertarianism: wide-ranging and potent negative rights. But this does not mean that it is indeed libertarian systems that provide the most extensive moral protection from interference. Unfortunately for the libertarian, the systems that emerge from this second version of the argument will still fail to be libertarian, for they will fail to incorporate the *second* core feature of libertarianism.

This second feature, it will be recalled, permitted the use of force against those who were in the process of violating the rights of others. It provided a significant *exception* to the general rule that under libertarianism we are forbidden to use force against, or otherwise interfere with, other individuals. According to libertarianism, we are permitted to interfere with those who are unjustifiably interfering with others.

But no such exception will be included in the moral systems that emerge from the current version of the argument from liberty. The more extensive the prohibitions against interference, the more extensive the moral protection from acts of that sort. Thus the systems that provide the *most* extensive moral protection from interference will be those that simply *forbid* the use of force – even against those who are in the process of violating the rights of others. That is, the systems that emerge will be versions of *pacifism,* not libertarianism. And it should be noted that it will be pacifism of a rather extreme sort: not only will it be impermissible to kill, or to use physical violence, to defend oneself from unprovoked attack; it will even be impermissible to jail or otherwise constrain aggressors. (Just how extreme the pacifism is will depend on how widely we construe "interference." This is a matter I put aside in section II; but presumably jailing someone will count.)

Once again, a hasty critic might object to this argument on the grounds that it fails to take into account the equality constraint: If a victim of unprovoked attack cannot use force to fend off the attacker, then her freedom from interference will obviously be diminished. So if we are restricting our attention to systems that grant equal freedom to all, we must permit interference with those who unjustifiably interfere. But as with the similar objection raised in the previous section, this criticism fails to bear in mind the particular sense of freedom from interference that is relevant to the present interpretation of the argument from liberty.

As we are currently understanding that argument, it is concerned solely with the provision of moral protection against acts of interference. The equality constraint demands in turn that this protection must be given equally to everyone. But the system of extreme pacifism we are considering *does* give the same moral protection to everyone: Absolutely everyone is protected by the same set of negative rights. This is true even for the victim of aggression. She is interfered with, to be sure; but even though they are violated, the negative rights protecting her are the same as those protecting everyone else. The equality constraint is indeed met.

It seems, then, that if we interpret the argument from liberty as being concerned to find the moral system that provides the most extensive moral protection from acts of interference, with equal protection for all, the system that best meets this standard will be a system of extreme pacifism. Since such a system prohibits interference even against those who are violating the rights of others, it lacks the second core feature essential to libertarian systems. And what this means, of course, is that as a defense of libertarianism, the argument from liberty is still a failure.

VI

Reflection on the argument of the previous section suggests, once more, a natural response. Freedom from interference should indeed be construed as freedom from acts of interference. But what is fundamentally of value in such freedom is not the presence of moral protection against such acts; it is, simply, the *absence* of the acts of interference. If we value negative rights it is primarily, or perhaps even solely, because they typically secure for us what is genuinely of value – lives free from acts of interference, that is, lives in which others simply do not interfere with us. But as the example of the victim of aggression shows, one can have the former without the latter, one can have the moral protection without the "tranquility." Yet it is the actual tranquility – the concrete, historical fact about a person's life that others have not interfered with that person – that is of fundamental value. The libertarian might suggest that recognizing this explains the importance and legitimacy of a right to self-defense. Permitting the use of force against those who are violating the rights of others helps to secure the tranquility that would otherwise be taken from the victim.

This points to a third possible interpretation of the argument from liberty, according to which the possession of tranquility is the argument's sole concern. On this approach to the argument – our last pure interpretation – finding the moral system that provides the most extensive freedom from interference is to be understood as being a matter of finding the system that actually produces the most tranquility. That is to say, we are looking for the moral system under which the smallest amount of human interference will occur.[4]

It should be noted that understanding the argument in this way introduces a significant change from the first two interpretations. When talk of "free-

dom from interference" was understood in terms of morality's lacking requirements (the first interpretation) or morality's forbidding interference (the
second), perfect freedom was, as it were, available at the stroke of a pen.
Since possession of the relevant sort of freedom was directly constituted by
morality's having or lacking the relevant requirements, it was an easy matter
to describe moral systems that logically guaranteed complete and perfect
freedom of the relevant sort. But once freedom from interference is understood in terms of tranquility, provision of the relevant freedom is no longer
directly constituted by the various requirements and permissions of morality.
It is not morality that directly provides tranquility; it is, rather, human agents,
who refrain from interfering with one another. Of course, since morality can
influence human action, it can have an impact on the extent to which tranquility is in fact provided. Thus provision of tranquility can indeed be a goal
to be kept in mind as we design and evaluate alternative moral systems. But
what design will provide the most extensive tranquility is an empirical rather
than a logical question.

On this third interpretation, then, the argument from liberty instructs us to
find the moral system that, as a matter of empirical fact, is most conductive to
tranquility. That is, we are to find the particular system of permissions and
requirements that maximizes tranquility. When the argument is understood
in this way, libertarianism certainly emerges as one possible outcome. The
existence of wide-ranging and powerful negative rights under libertarianism
would presumably elicit respect from many people on many occasions, and so
would significantly reduce acts of interference; and those tempted to violate
these negative rights might well be deterred, either by the thought that under
libertarianism force could be permissibly used against them, or else by the
actual use of such force. And so, it might be suggested, under a libertarian
regime tranquility would be extensive and widespread.

The difficulty with this argument, of course, is that it seems possible that
some alternative moral systems might do even better in terms of promoting
tranquility. This is of course an empirical question, but it is not too hard to
think of cases in which it seems that tranquility might well be better promoted
by allowing departures from libertarianism. For example, it seems plausible
that many acts of interference – crimes of sundry sorts – are caused by people
who lack alternative means of providing for themselves. It seems possible that
various welfare programs – minimum income, guaranteed education, job
training, job provision, and so on – might significantly reduce such criminal
acts of interference. But effectively providing for such welfare policies might
well require coercing the better-off members of society, even though they
themselves have not violated anyone's negative rights, or interfered with
anyone. To be sure, such interference with the better off would itself constitute a reduction in tranquility, but it might be amply compensated for by the

increase in tranquility constituted by the reduction in crime. In short, such a welfare state might provide more extensive tranquility overall.

Of course even if this empirical claim is correct, this is only an objection to the argument from liberty if such a welfare state is incompatible with libertarianism. Most libertarians would presumably think so; I imagine that most libertarians would claim that the coercion of the better off that I have described would violate the negative rights which comprise the first core feature of libertarianism. But whether this is actually so or not depends on how the welfare state is maintained, and even more importantly details concerning the range of the negative rights. Obviously enough, if the libertarian's negative rights include property rights, then it seems quite likely indeed that the welfare state will be incompatible with libertarianism. But in section II the possibility was left open that, although extensive, the negative rights embraced by the libertarian are limited to rights over one's labor and one's body. And it is at the very least not obvious that maintaining welfare programs will require violating *these* rights.

So let us consider one more example, even more schematic. Suppose that by killing one innocent person I can save the lives of two other innocent people who would otherwise be murdered. Imagine that there is no other way to save the two, and all other things are equal. I take it that under any libertarian system at all, it would be impermissible to kill the one: however narrowly we construe the libertarian's negative rights, they are presumably wide enough to cover cases of this sort; and since the one has not violated anyone's rights, this is *not* a case in which force can be justifiably used against him. And yet it seems plausible to claim that killing the one would nevertheless maximize tranquility: *Two* lives would be free from horrendous acts of interference, rather than only *one*. Therefore, a system that permitted killing the one, in at least some cases of this sort, would better promote tranquility. But such a system would most certainly not be a libertarian one. And so libertarianism still fails to find support, even under this third interpretation of the argument from liberty.

Again one might object that this argument fails to consider the implications of the equality constraint. Our habitually hasty critic might complain that our aim is not, strictly speaking, that of finding the system that maximizes tranquility; it is, rather, that of finding the system that maximizes tranquility subject to the constraint that equal tranquility is to be provided to *all*. Yet if the one is killed to save the two, the one obviously suffers a loss of tranquility unmatched by any of the rest of us! Thus a moral system that would permit killing in such cases does not satisfy the equality constraint, and so cannot claim to be the system that best meets the standard put forward by the argument from liberty.

Both times previously when the comparable objection was raised, the equality constraint had in fact been perfectly satisfied. This time, however, I must concede that it has not been. If we kill the one to save the two, this certainly imposes upon the one a loss of tranquility unmatched by an equivalent loss on the part of, say, the two. But this admission can bring no comfort to the libertarian, for it seems clear that in cases of the kind I am describing, the equality constraint simply cannot be met. If we kill the one to save the two, the one possesses less tranquility than the two. Yet if we forbid killing the one – as the libertarian would have us do – then the two will be murdered, and so *they* will possess less tranquility than the *one*. Strict equality of tranquility is simply unavailable. So if this third version of the argument from liberty is going to keep anything like the equality constraint at all, it will have to be satisfied with something like equalizing tranquility so far as this is possible.

This modified constraint is, admittedly, vague, but there is no obvious reason to believe that a system that permits killing the one will fail to satisfy it. And whatever the merits of this particular case, it still seems quite likely that in at least some cases, interfering with certain individuals who have not themselves interfered with others may better promote the goal of maximizing tranquility, even when this is subject to the constraint that tranquility is to be equalized as far as this is possible. There is at any rate, no reason to think that it is libertarianism that best meets this standard.

VII

We have so far considered three different versions of the argument from liberty, each with its own interpretation of the central notion of freedom from interference. None of these arguments succeeded as a defense of libertarianism. However, a plausible explanation of this fact is not hard to find. For all of the arguments we have examined up to this point have been pure, in that each was concerned solely with a single kind of freedom. Perhaps, then, the libertarian would do better with a mixed or pluralistic interpretation of the argument – one in which all three conceptions of freedom from interference were taken into account. On such a mixed interpretation of the argument from liberty, freedom from interference would be a complex matter, with three "components": the absence of moral requirements, the presence of moral prohibitions against interference, and the nonoccurrence of acts of interference. Our concern would be to find the moral system that provides the most extensive freedom – where freedom was understood to have this complex character – subject to the constraint that this freedom had to be distributed in as close to equal a manner as possible.

Such a pluralistic approach to the concept of freedom from interference has an undeniable attractiveness. We might well wonder, after all, what the true value would be of having any one of the three components, if it is not combined with the others. For example, what would be the point of having freedom from *moral* interference (i.e., absence of moral requirements), if other people were nonetheless morally permitted to interfere with you (i.e., lack of moral protection)? Or what would be the point of having tranquility (freedom from acts of interference) if you were nonetheless morally obligated to make the relevant sacrifices anyway (lack of freedom from moral interference)? Questions like these do not so much undermine the claim that freedom from interference is a value; rather, they reinforce the thought that freedom from interference is a complex matter, and that it has its full value only when its several components are all present.

So it seems plausible for the libertarian to suggest that the argument from liberty is to be understood in terms of such a mixed interpretation. We want to find the moral system that grants the most extensive freedom from interference (subject to the modified equality constraint), recognizing that freedom from interference involves all three of the components we have identified.

In fact, however, recognizing that freedom from interference is a function of all three components does not make it easier to argue for libertarianism – it makes it harder. The difficulty of course is that the three elements can conflict. One system may provide more tranquility, but include more moral requirements. Another system may include more freedom from moral requirements, but less moral protection from acts of interference. How are we to choose between them?

Now if there were a single system such that for each of the three elements that system provided more of that particular element than did any alternative system, we could of course safely conclude that it was this system that provided the most extensive freedom from interference. But there can in fact be no such system, maximally effective in all three categories. (And, at any rate, libertarianism is certainly not such a system.) So we are forced to choose between "imperfect" systems, systems that do better in terms of one component while doing worse in terms of another. But what is to guide our choice? How are we to decide which systems provide more extensive freedom from interference taking *all three* components into account? Lacking some reasonably specific proposal about how the various components trade off against one another, it is difficult to see how we are to judge that a given system does better in this regard than another. But then what grounds do we have for accepting the claim that it is indeed libertarianism that provides the most extensive freedom from interference?

The libertarian might hope that despite our lack of a theory concerning how the three components are to be weighed against one another, we might nonetheless find ourselves capable of making intuitive judgments on these matters. If these intuitive judgments supported the claim that it was indeed libertarianism that provided the most extensive freedom from interference overall, and if these intuitive judgments were ones in which we had a high degree of confidence, then they might suffice for the purposes of the argument from liberty, even though we lacked an adequate account of their theoretical basis.

Unfortunately, for the libertarian, however, it does not seem to me that we find ourselves in possession of the requisite intuitions. In my own case, at least, when I try to muster intuitive judgments comparing different moral systems with regard to freedom from interference, explicitly bearing in mind its complex character – often no judgments are forthcoming at all, and I have no great confidence in those that I can evoke. Many initial intuitions disappear altogether once I remind myself that all three components are to be given weight; others become shaky and uncertain. At times, of course, I do share the intuition that it is libertarianism that grants the greatest freedom from interference; but at other times this claim seems just as plainly false. In short, once we realized the complex nature of freedom from interference, I doubt that our intuitions by themselves provide any kind of reliable support for libertarianism.

This leaves the libertarian in need of some more specific proposal concerning how the three components of freedom from interference are to be combined. One suggestion I find particularly intriguing starts with the observation that two of the components – moral protection and lack of moral requirements – are in a certain kind of logical balance: Each time we add moral protection against some further type of human interference, we necessarily reduce the freedom from moral interference. For each extra bit of protection against a given kind of act consists of a new prohibition, which is to say a new moral requirement, constraining the behavior of others. And given the equality constraint, we cannot protect one person without offering the same protection to everyone. So any increase in moral protection against human interference necessarily triggers a corresponding reduction in freedom from moral interference. Similarly, any reduction in moral protection against human interference necessarily triggers a corresponding increase in freedom from moral interference.

To put the same point the other way around, increasing moral requirements can increase the amount of moral protection from acts of interference – in those cases where the extra requirement is a requirement not to interfere. But not *all* extra moral requirements increase the protection from interference. One could, for example, add a moral requirement that we aid the needy; this would increase moral interference without adding any extra moral protection against *acts of interference*. Accordingly, *eliminating* such moral requirements – that is, eliminating moral requirements that do not have the function of creating moral protection against interference – would reduce moral interference, without reducing moral protection against interference. Putting aside for the moment questions of tranquility, such a change would necessarily be superior in terms of the mixed interpretation of freedom from interference as it would increase the extent of one of the components, without reducing the second.

Suppose then that we restrict our attention to moral systems that are optimal in this way in terms of these two components. That is, suppose we restrict our attention to systems for which there could be no further increase in freedom from moral requirements without thereby reducing moral protection from interference. This will certainly eliminate some of the moral systems that compete with libertarianism since, as we have just seen, it will rule out systems that require you to aid others, rather than merely requiring you to refrain from interfering with them.

On the other hand, it is still true that a large number of alternative systems will provide a balance of permission and protection that is optimal in the present sense. At one extreme, we have the system of unlimited permission discussed in section IV; at the other extreme, we have the system of extreme pacifism discussed in section V. Libertarianism will be optimal as well,[5] and will lie somewhere in between these two. (There are of course many other optimal systems beyond these three.) Since all three of these systems are optimal, and since all satisfy the equality constraint, there is still no ground for preferring libertarianism.

But now we can reintroduce tranquility. As we noted in section VI, libertarianism can plausibly argue that it does a fair job of promoting tranquility. It seems plausible to hold that it will do better on this score than either of the two extreme positions – unlimited permission or extreme pacifism. So the conjecture might be made that libertarianism is the moral system that best promotes tranquility while remaining optimal in terms of permission and protection.

Offering this conjecture is compatible with admitting that there are other systems that may do better than libertarianism in terms of tranquility alone. Consider, for example, a moral system that consists simply of a requirement that one perform the act that best promotes tranquility (distributed as equally as possible). Such a consequentialism of tranquility would presumably do better with regard to tranquility than would libertarianism. But it would certainly not be optimal with regard to permission and protection; in many cases requirements to do particular acts could be eliminated without thereby reducing moral protection from interference (the level of *tranquility* might go down, but not the level of moral protection).

Accordingly, the libertarian might propose that the argument from liberty should be understood as instructing us to find the moral system that best promotes tranquility while remaining optimal in terms of freedom from moral interference and moral protection from human interference. If the three components of freedom from interference are ordered in this way, then perhaps we have at last found the standard according to which libertarianism does best.

Although I do find this proposal intriguing, it faces two obvious difficulties. The first question is why permission and protection should be given this kind of lexical priority over tranquility. Why should our concern for promoting tranquility be restricted to choosing among systems that are optimal in terms of moral interference and moral protection? Why rule out systems that might do significantly better in terms of tranquility even if somewhat less well in terms of the balance of permission and protection? Nothing in the realization that freedom from interference has a complex character entails that one of the components should take a back seat to the other two. Nor can I think of any plausible way for the libertarian to motivate this strong ordering.

But there is a further objection. Even if the specified ordering of the three components is granted to the libertarian, there remains the empirical question of whether libertarianism is indeed the optimal moral system that best promotes tranquility. For reasons similar to those given in section VI, I find this empirical conjecture implausible. Recall the schematic example in which I can save two innocent people from being murdered, but only if I kill a third innocent person. Admittedly, a moral system that *required* me to kill the one in cases like this would not be optimal (eliminating the requirement would reduce moral interference, without reducing moral protection); so such a system poses no threat to libertarianism under the current interpretation of the argument from liberty. However, a moral system that merely *permitted* me to kill the one *could* be optimal (eliminating such a permission would increase moral interference). And it seems that it would better promote tranquility as well (if I killed the one, two would be free from horrendous acts of interference, rather than only one). Yet as we have seen, such a system would not be libertarian; it would permit interfering with those who have not themselves interfered with others or violated their rights.

So libertarianism is not in fact the optimal system that best promotes tranquility. Even given the current interpretation of the argument from liberty, the defense of libertarianism fails.

VIII

One possible response to the argument I have given in sections VI and VII is this. In both cases, my objection to libertarianism has been on the grounds that greater tranquility can sometimes be achieved by deliberately sacrificing the tranquility of some innocent person. I have claimed that once we recognize the value of tranquility, we have to be open to the possibility that interfering with someone who has not interfered with anyone else might nonetheless reduce the amount of interference overall. In short, I have assumed that the proper approach to take with regard to tranquility is *maximization*. It might be suggested, however, that there are actually two possible approaches one can take to any given value: The first is to maximize (instances of) the value; the second, incompatible, approach is to *respect* the value. By assuming that it is maximization of tranquility rather than respect for tranquility that is called for, I may have begged the question against the libertarian.

For our purposes, the salient difference between these two approaches is that with maximization the aim is to produce as great an amount of the given value as possible; accordingly, one is prepared to make smaller, local sacrifices of the value when necessary for the sake of overall, global gains. In contrast, when a value is respected, one is never prepared to go "against" it, or to "violate" it, even for the sake of greater gains overall; promotion of the value – or indeed of any other goal – is limited to means that do not themselves constitute violations of that value.

The argument from liberty is grounded on the assumption that freedom from interference is the fundamental value. Given this assumption, we are led to try to find the moral system in which this value is best reflected. And if freedom from interference is to be understood at least in part in terms of tranquility, we are led to try to find the moral system in which the value of tranquility is best reflected. But which systems count as best reflecting the value of tranquility will obviously depend on whether that particular value is to be maximized or respected. If tranquility is to be maximized, I have argued, we will be led to systems that differ from libertarianism in that they sometimes permit interfering with individuals who have not themselves interfered with others. But if it is rather respect for tranquility which is the appropriate approach, then this result is blocked; in looking for the moral system in which the most extensive tranquility is granted, we will have to restrict our attention to systems that *respect* the value of tranquility.

Now I have been arguing that there are various systems that do better in terms of promoting tranquility than libertarianism does. This is true, however, only by virtue of the fact that – unlike libertarianism – each is sometimes willing to sacrifice someone's tranquility for the sake of greater tranquility for others. But this means that these systems fail to respect tranquility; and so, if tranquility is to be respected rather than maximized, they can be ruled out. Thus it remains possible that it is indeed libertarianism that best expresses the value of freedom from interference, where this includes tranquility.

I will not here undertake the task of determining how the libertarian might try to defend the claim that tranquility is indeed to be respected rather than maximized. Along with the various other foundational assumptions of the argument from liberty, I propose to simply grant it for the sake of argument. For even when this further assumption is granted, it still does not seem to me that it is libertarianism that emerges from the argument from liberty. On the contrary, we are led, once again, to a system of extreme pacifism, of the sort described in section V. After all, the current suggestion is that if I use force against someone, or otherwise interfere with them, then I am sacrificing or violating the value of tranquility, in a way that is ruled out by the respect approach. But if this is so, then it seems to me that it must remain true even if the person I am interfering with was herself in the process of unjustifiably interfering with another. If we are always to respect tranquility, if tranquility can never be sacrificed, then I cannot permissibly defend myself or others by interfering with the would-be aggressor, actively sacrificing *her* tranquility. Yet libertarianism holds that it is permissible to interfere with those who are violating the rights of others; this was the second core feature of libertarian systems. Apparently, then, taking a respect approach to tranquility rules out libertarianism.

One possible response to this argument would be to claim that the use of force against an agent who is herself unjustifiably interfering with others does not actually constitute interference. But this claim seems false on the face of it. Even if we are justified in interfering with an aggressor, it is not any the less interference for that fact. (Interference should not be confused with unjustified interference.)

A more plausible response would concede that using force against an aggressor is of course interference, but would hold that the use of interference in such a case is nonetheless legitimate. Since we are assuming a respect approach to tranquility, a person taking this line would have to hold that interfering with someone for the sake of stopping them from interfering with someone else does not actually show disrespect for the value of tranquility.

There are two difficulties facing this reply. First, of course, it is unclear how it is to be defended. Is it a general truth about value and respect that "infringing" a given value to stop someone from violating that value is itself compatible with respecting that value? Or is this true only in the special case where the particular value being respected is tranquility? And at any event, why should we believe that it is true at all? Second, if it is compatible with respect to infringe a value so as to stop someone from violating that value, why is this so only when your infringement of the value is directed at the very person who is trying to violate the value? Why wouldn't it also be compatible with respect to infringe the value with regard to innocent bystanders, if this is indeed the only way to stop the person who is trying to violate the value? Less abstractly, if it is compatible with respect for tranquility to kill the would-be murderers in order to save their two innocent victims, why wouldn't it also be compatible with respect for tranquility to kill an innocent third person, if this were the only way to save the two?

Lots of rhetoric gets produced in response to these questions, but little by way of convincing argument. For example, it is sometimes suggested that using force against violators of a given value actually *affirms* the significance of the value that the person was trying to violate; thus, interfering with those who would violate the tranquility of others actually affirms the value of tranquility, rather than showing it disrespect. I find this response uncompelling, at least within the general framework of the respect approach. But if it did succeed, it would seem equally successful as a defense of killing the one to save the two from being murdered: Rather than showing disrespect for the value of tranquility, killing the one would actually *affirm* the significance of tranquility. But this result is itself incompatible with libertarianism. In short, arguments that try to show the compatibility of the respect approach with the second core feature of libertarianism simultaneously threaten to undermine the first core feature.

I must admit that these worries do not constitute a proof that no adequate defense can be provided. That is, it might be that adequate analyses of respect and tranquility would support the legitimacy of using force against those who interfere with others, but not against those who do not. So the libertarian might suggest that if we grant this one final assumption we have – at last – an argument for libertarianism.

But what we have at this point is actually no longer an argument; it is simply the promise of an argument. Yes, it is true that if we assume that freedom from interference is the only fundamental value, and we assume that respect for this value is the correct approach, and we assume that what respect yields in this case is the permissibility of interfering with those who are themselves interfering, but the impermissibility of interfering otherwise, then we arrive at libertarianism. But this is no argument at all. It really just asks us to assume that libertarianism is the system that best expresses the value of freedom from interference. But this assumption is the central claim of the argument from liberty, and I have argued that there is no good reason to believe it true, and considerable reason to think it false. To ask that this claim nonetheless be granted as well is to abandon any pretense of *arguing* for libertarianism via the argument from liberty.

IX

It remains tempting to think that the equality constraint must somehow explain why it is permissible to use force against those who interfere. If this were so, then the libertarian could resist my claim that once we adopt a respect approach to freedom from interference, we are led to a system of extreme pacifism.

The tempting thought, I take it, is something like this: Everyone is entitled to some minimum amount of freedom; so it must be permissible to curtail someone's freedom – even by force if necessary – to protect others from having their freedom *destroyed* by that person. If it is not permissible to use force against aggressors, then some people – the aggressor's victims – will *lack* liberty, and so the equality constraint will be violated. However, if it *is* permissible to use force against aggressors, then although this restricts liberty somewhat (since aggressors are no longer totally free from interference), it does so *equally* (since the same restrictions apply to all). What's more, it still leaves a considerable *amount* of liberty (since one is free to do what one wants, except to interfere), and *that* liberty is equally provided to all. There are of course other moral systems that are even *more* restrictive in terms of liberty, although they too satisfy the equality constraint. But what we want is the system that grants the *greatest* liberty while satisfying the equality constraint. And it is libertarianism – with its permission to interfere with those who interfere, but only with those who interfere – that is least restrictive. That is, it is libertarianism that provides the greatest liberty while providing equal liberty to all.

But this argument confuses the three distinct components of freedom from interference. The key step in the argument is the claim that if the use of force against the aggressor is not permissible, then the liberty of the victims will be destroyed, and so the equality constraint will not be met. But with regard to freedom from moral interference or moral protection against human interference, this is simply false. An act of aggression does not make it any less permissible for the victim to do what he was previously permitted to do or make it any less forbidden for the act of aggression to have occurred. Neither freedom from moral interference nor moral protection is diminished at all by aggression; thus the permissibility of using force against the aggressor cannot be motivated by appeal to some need to make sure that these freedoms are not destroyed.

On the other hand, it is certainly true that an act of interference can reduce the victim's *tranquility*,[6] and so the victim may well end up with less tranquility than the aggressor, which seems to violate the equality constraint. But as noted previously, in some cases the strict equality constraint simply cannot be met, and this is such a case. Equality of tranquility is impossible here: If we use force to stop the attacker, then *she* will end up with less tranquility than her intended victims. We simply cannot guarantee strict equality of tranquility. And if, accordingly, we move to a modified equality constraint, there is still no reason to assume that what will emerge will be the general permissibility of using force to stop others from interfering. (Perhaps, instead, we can keep tranquility most nearly equal by permitting would-be interferers to succeed a certain percentage of the time.)

It is possible that our intuitions here are misled by a misguided analogy with more familiar aspects of corrective justice. If you and I start out with equal amounts of property, for example, and I take some of your property, then I end up with more and you end up with less. Using force to stop me from taking your property, or to make me return it, simply maintains or returns us to the original position of equality. But things are quite different if it is tranquility that is our concern. You and I may both start out with perfect tranquility, but if I interfere with you, this diminishes your tranquility without thereby increasing my own. Using force to stop me does not maintain (or return us to) a position of perfect equality; it simply yields the result that it is now my tranquility that is diminished, rather than yours. Commitment to the equality constraint – whether in its strict or modified form – provides no reason to think that it is the aggressor's tranquility that is to be sacrificed, rather than that of the victim.

Now nothing at all that I am saying should be taken as an argument against the permissibility of using force to stop someone from unjustifiably interfering with others. I am not claiming that a right to self-defense cannot be defended. I am only denying that the argument from liberty has the resources to generate such a right (at least without simultaneously generating other features incompatible with libertarianism).

For example, we might well try to defend the right to self-defense by appealing to considerations of justice, or desert, or any of a variety of other values. Obviously enough, however, if the libertarian starts appealing to such additional, substantive values, she undermines her claims that freedom from interference is the sole fundamental value. But then we no longer have reason to seek the moral system that best expresses the value of liberty, and liberty alone. The libertarian cannot appeal to such values without abandoning the argument from liberty altogether.

X

I cannot claim to have surveyed here all possible forms of the argument from liberty. The notion that we are to seek the moral system that best captures or expresses the value of liberty is sufficiently amorphous that it remains susceptible to a variety of interpretations. In fact, as we have seen, even if we move to the more determinate suggestion that we are to seek the moral system that grants the greatest freedom from interference with equal freedom for all, the argument from liberty can still be given a surprising number of distinct, and incompatible, interpretations. Perhaps then there is some further interpretation of the argument that I have overlooked, which can succeed in underwriting libertarianism. I cannot prove that this is not so. But each time the argument from liberty has been given sufficiently determinate form to evaluate it with care, it has failed as a defense of libertarianism. And this gives us reason to be sceptical of the libertarian's hope that some other version may yet succeed.

What then explains the intuition that it is indeed libertarianism that most fully expresses the value of liberty, construed as freedom from interference? I am not sure, but I think it may well be that when we are not paying careful attention, we easily conflate the three different elements of freedom from interference that I have tried to distinguish.

Under libertarianism I am free to do as I see fit, except for reducing someone else's freedom. When described in such terms, it does seem plausible to view libertarianism as giving complete freedom to everyone, subject only to the requirement that everyone is to be given the same freedom. But thinking of libertarianism in this way disguises the fact that it is only a very specific mixture of the three elements that is provided by libertarianism. Other mixtures are possible, and there is really nothing in the concept of freedom from interference itself to guide us in libertarianism's direction. Indeed, each time we start out with an account of freedom from interference that has some independent motivation, we are led in the direction of nonlibertarian systems.

The question still remains: What *is* the moral system that best expresses the value of freedom from interference? As I have pointed out, the answer will depend on our views concerning a number of logically prior matters, including respect versus maximization, and the relative value of the three elements. For myself, I think that if we make the assumption that freedom from interference is the sole fundamental value, the moral system to which we are led is in fact a consequentialism of tranquility. But I hasten to add that I do not think that freedom from interference *is* the sole value, nor is it even the most important one. I would not want to endorse the argument from liberty in any of its forms.

Under libertarianism, I am left free so long as I leave others free. I have not tried to deny that this thought can often seem an attractive one. What I have tried to show is that – attractive or not – it will not lead to a successful defense of a libertarian system. Libertarianism finds no support in an argument from liberty.

Notes

1 An extremely helpful critical survey can be found in Will Kymlicka, *Contemporary Political Philosophy* (Oxford University Press, 1990), chapter 4. Kymlicka discusses the argument from liberty as well; his criticisms complement, but are largely distinct from, my own.

2 For a valuable discussion of various concepts of freedom, see chapter one of Joel Feinberg's *Social Philosophy* (Englewood Cliffs, N.J.: Prentice-Hall, 1973). Since this essay is being written as part of a volume in Feinberg's honor, a personal recollection may be in order. When I was first preparing to go on the job market from graduate school, I wondered whether I could legitimately list social philosophy as one of my areas of competence – I had written a thesis in moral philosophy, but

had no idea what *social* philosophy was. So I read Feinberg's classic to find out. And history repeats itself: recently one of my own graduate students told me that he had just read Feinberg's *Social Philosophy* in order to find out if *he* could list social philosophy as an area of competence!

3 Cf. Kymlicka, 136.

4 There are of course problems with an approach like this. For example, it is hardly clear how to enumerate acts of interference, or how to measure the "amount" of interference in a given act; nor is it plausible to disvalue all "comparably sized" acts of interference equally. (See Feinberg, 18–19; and Kymlicka, 139–41.) However, even if we put these, and related difficulties aside, and allow intuitive judgments about when we have increased tranquility overall, there remains the question of whether it is indeed libertarianism that is the moral system that does best in this regard.

5 Strictly, this will only be true for *minimal* libertarianism, which denies the existence of any moral requirements beyond those requiring one not to interfere. *Standard* libertarianism, which recognizes special obligations generated by voluntary acts of the agent – such as promising – will only be optimal in the "natural" state, prior to the generation of special obligations. I should also note the possibility of *modest* libertarianism, which would recognize the existence of general moral requirements to provide aid, but would hold that such requirements cannot be coercively enforced (only requirements not to interfere can be enforced); such a version of libertarianism would not be optimal at all, and so could not be defended in terms of the present argument.

6 It can also reduce the victim's *ability* (i.e., to promote his goals). But the libertarian cannot consistently appeal to this fact; ability per se is irrelevant if, as the libertarian insists, the sole fundamental value is freedom from interference.

3

Autonomy and preference formation

RICHARD J. ARNESON

In its simplest formulation, *subjectivism* as I shall understand it holds that a person lives a good life (attains well-being) to the extent that her basic self-interested preferences are satisfied, weighted by their relative importance as rated by that very person.[1] One may prefer something for its own sake or as a means to some further end; the former sort of preference is *basic*. *Self-interested* preferences are those that register what a person wants insofar as she aims to benefit herself, and sets aside what she wants in order to satisfy moral requirements, benefit other persons altruistically, or achieve a nonmoral good that is deemed to be valuable from an impersonal standpoint, though not advantageous to her. Roughly, the idea is that the good life consists in getting what you want from life.[2] Subjectivism is a thesis about what is nonmorally valuable and implies nothing at all about what is moral, right, or just. Subjectivism competes not with deontology but with hedonism and perfectionism and other views about the nature of the human good.

But the simplest formulation of subjectivism is not persuasive. Even if my preferences form a consistent set, they might be based on misinformation, ignorance, or confused reasoning. Fulfilling such preferences is not achieving a good life. This thought has stimulated many to advance a revised formulation of subjectivism: A person lives a good life to the extent that her basic self-interested preferences (a) conform to her hypothetically rational preferences and (b) are satisfied, with the value of satisfying a preference weighted by its relative importance as it would be rated by her after ideal deliberation.[3] Hypothetically rational preferences are stipulated to be those the person would have if she were to deliberate about them in an ideally extended way, with full pertinent information, while reasoning clearly, and in a calm mood. This revised formulation of subjectivism is subject to difficulties that stem from the idea that an idealized counterfactual situation determines what is actually good for an agent. For example, suppose that in my unenlightened state I prefer checkers to chess, but that if I were to deliberate about this preference while making no reasoning errors, I would be a person who is far more intelligent than I actually am, and if I were that intelligent, I would prefer chess to checkers, since chess is more intellectually complex. The possibility that my preference would change in this way in a counterfactual situation does not seem to impugn the claim that what is best for me is playing checkers, not chess. Problems of this short should not be underestimated, but for purposes of this essay I assume that with appropriate tinkering they can be solved. This essay focuses on another and to my mind more troublesome objection to which any preference satisfaction view of human good appears to be vulnerable.

A familiar objection to taking the degree to which an individual's preferences are satisfied as the measure of the extent to which she leads a good life is that those preferences may have been formed by an unhealthy or stunting process. Amartya Sen writes, "The battered slave, the broken unemployed, the hopeless destitute, the tamed housewife, may have the courage to desire little, but the fulfillment of those disciplined desires is not a sign of great success and cannot be treated in the same way as the fulfillment of the confident and demanding desires of the better placed."[4] The objection is that subjectivism, even revised subjectivism, goes badly astray by ignoring the formation of wants. Oppression might injure its victims by blocking or distorting their capacity to identify themselves with ambitious desires rather than by denying them fulfillment of the squalid and broken-spirited desires that they do come to develop. Jon Elster's commentary on the fable of the fox and the grapes makes a somewhat related point.[5] In deciding how to increase the fox's welfare, we cannot take at face value the fact that he has no desire for the grapes that are hanging just out of his reach if that lack of desire is caused by his perception that he cannot get the grapes. And in judging retrospectively the degree to which the fox succeeded in living a good life, we cannot simply add up the extent to which his preferences, as weighted by the importance he attached to each of them, are satisfied, because unfavorable circumstances may have crimped his preferences, so their satisfaction should count for less than the satisfaction of uncrimped preferences.

Shifting allegiance from the simplest to the revised version of welfarism does not suffice to meet this objection. Suppose that an individual suffers a repressive upbringing that distorts the formation of her preferences. For example, suppose a person of color grows up under a regime of apartheid and as a result she is disposed to want to occupy the lowest rungs on whatever status hierarchy impinges on her. If the person has been psychologically damaged in some way by apartheid, so that her self-esteem is low and her wants meager, to imagine the individual with these preferences in place engaging in ideal fully informed rational deliberation about her preferences is not necessarily to imagine that the causal impact of unfair socialization on her preferences disappears. Ideal rational deliberation operating on a stunted set of preferences might well generate a set of hypothetically rational preferences that bears the scars of its earliest formation, and that is in any case very different from the outcome of ideal rational deliberation operating on a more robust initial set of preferences. It would be counterintuitive to hold that the person who undergoes a repressive childhood that malforms his preferences lives a good life or not depending only on the degree to which his hypothetical rational preferences (that are determined by ideal deliberation operating on his actual preferences) are satisfied.[6]

It is less clear that Elster's puzzle of the fox and the grapes poses a difficulty for the revised version of subjectivism. The interesting possibility that might be thought problematic would be the case in which the person who lacks access to the grapes would continue to have no desire for them even after ideal rational deliberation, whereas the person given access to the grapes would continue to desire them even after ideal rational deliberation. If hypothetical rational preferences are sensitive to changes in circumstances in this way, I am not sure that adaptive preference formation as Elster conceives of it could consistently yield the opposed preferences we are considering. Elster observes that adaptive preference formation is "a causal process taking place 'behind my back'." This strongly suggests that if the individual becomes fully informed of the nature of the causal process, it ceases to operate 'before my face.'

I wish to explore the question of whether the examples mentioned above show that it is best to abandon subjectivism or to retreat from it. And if retreat is warranted, how much ground should the subjectivist concede?

The Sen and Elster examples can push judgment in different directions. To some philosophers the examples have suggested that only the satisfaction of autonomous preferences truly enhances one's well-being; the more autonomous one's preferences, the more their satisfaction increases one's well-being, other things being equal.[7] Another conclusion to which one might be led is that preference satisfaction is simply an inadequate measure of true well-being, because preferences adjust to circumstances, so that to judge a person's well-being one must gauge the objective goodness of her life circumstances and of what she succeeds in making of her life from these circumstances. In this latter view autonomy figures insofar as it is taken to be a crucial component of an objectively good human life.

I wish to resist these antisubjectivist responses but straightaway I acknowledge that a preference satisfaction conception of welfare must be supplemented by a conception of desirable ways of forming preferences. But this supplement significantly changes the character of an otherwise subjectivist view. The view under consideration now is that a person leads a good life to the extent that her preferences (as these would be if corrected by ideal deliberation) are satisfied and to the extent that her preferences are formed in a healthy way. But the healthy preference formation component of this conception of the human good is not itself subjectivist: The fact that an individual's preferences were formed in conformity with her preferences about how her preferences would be formed is neither necessary nor sufficient for judging whether the individual's preferences were formed in a healthy way. The view of human good that I espouse in this paper is subjectivist with respect to the content of people's preferences but perfectionist with respect to the issue of how (at least initially) preferences should be formed.

It is hard to imagine how a strictly subjectivist view of healthy preference formation could be plausible. A newborn infant has a very limited repertoire of simple desires and lacks the cognitive prerequisites for having second-order preferences – preferences about how one's preferences should be formed. If we assume that only Smith's present preferences (actual or corrected) can determine what is good for Smith, and if infant Smith's preferences only concern getting simple pleasures and avoiding simple pains, then a preference formation process applied to Smith is good for him to the extent that it maximizes his net pleasure. This illustrates that an individuals' preferences at birth are too thin to provide a reasonable standard of assessment of the processes by which his preferences are formed. The "maximize pleasure" standard implied by infant preferences will strike us as plausible only if we adhere to hedonism rather than preference satisfaction as the measure of individual good. Another possibility is to judge the goodness of the preference formation processes applied to an individual by the extent to which they conduce to maximal satisfaction of his preferences over his life span (including whatever preferences the processes themselves induce). But this perspective on preference formation is committed to regarding individuals as "bare persons," who can be made best off if they are caused to have a maximal number of preferences that are maximally easy to satisfy. To avoid this absurdity, I am led to affirm that subjectivism about the nature of human good is bounded by a nonsubjectivist account of desirable preference formation.

Does this qualification of a subjectivist analysis of human good initiate a slide towards the position that preference satisfaction has value only to the extent that the person who has the preference is autonomous with respect to it or toward the more extreme position that rejects subjectivism on the good altogether? I doubt it. To investigate this issue, I begin by explicating the notion of autonomy that is often used as a battering ram in attacks on subjectivism.

One preliminary clarification: The autonomous person is not correctly conceived as one who successfully pursues her maximal self-interest. She might, or she might not. The autonomous person is self-governing; she lives her life according to a self-chosen or self-ratified plan. Such a plan might include conformity to moral principles and action to satisfy altruistic or other non-self-interested aims, so that living autonomously might well involve deliberately foregoing benefits to herself in order to respect the moral principles she accepts or in order to benefit other persons at her expense. But since my concern in this essay is the relationship between achieving autonomy and attaining a good life for oneself, I ignore all conflict between self-interest and autonomously chosen aims. Throughout this essay we deal with decision contexts in which it is understood that the agent can only benefit herself by her actions, and so conflicts between prudence and morality or prudence and altruism cannot arise. This allows a focus on the issue of whether subjectivism is an inadequate account of the good because it fails to register the value of autonomy.

Autonomy and the Real Self condition

My starting point is Joel Feinberg's observation that "I am autonomous if I rule me, and no one else rules I." This comment immediately calls attention to one reason that autonomy is an elusive notion: If I issue a command to me, how can we distinguish me's insubordination (if the command is resisted) from I's changing its mind? It would seem that we have to distinguish a part of the self that is the Real Self – the "I" that ought to govern the self's behavior – from another part of the self that might have a will of its own that might take charge of the self's behavior but which (we judge) should be subordinate to the commands of the "I." Nor can we count on "I" and "me" to agree among themselves as to which is the rightful ruler. In addition to this Real Self requirement, the concept of autonomy, as explicated by Feinberg's quip, also includes what we might call an Independence requirement ("no one else rules I"). Competing conceptions of autonomy will differ in their interpretations of one or both of these requirements. Deferring discussion of the Independence requirement until the next section, I turn first to the Real Self ideal.

At least since Plato, most philosophical writers who have made use of a notion of autonomy have identified the idea with "critically reflective, rational self-governance."[8] On this view the Real Self is linked to the agent's capacity for rational critical reflection, and the Real Self component of autonomy is fulfilled insofar as the agent effectively exercises this capacity, so that the outcome of critical reflection determines the behavior of the agent.

To refine the critical reflection construal of the Real Self requirement I will pose and attempt to answer five questions regarding it:

1. How rational must an agent's critical reflection be to qualify her as autonomous?

A process of critical reflection must be responsive to reasons to some degree if it is to count as a process of critical reflection at all. A mentally deranged or severely retarded person who tries to subject his plan of life to critical reflection, but succeeds only in entertaining before his mind a random sequence of unconnected thoughts, has not critically reflected. A person who completely misunderstands every reason that comes to his mind that supposedly has a bearing on the rationality of his current life plan, on which he is trying to reflect critically, has only tried and not succeeded in engaging in critical reflection. There would appear to be a minimal threshold level of rationality in deliberation below which the deliberative process should not count as genuine deliberation for purposes of deciding whether the person is autonomous. But the idea of critical reflection looks to be a "range" concept. Above the minimal threshold, the greater or lesser rationality of an agent's critical reflection does not affect the correctness of the claim that she is engaging in critical reflection.

Suppose an agent deliberates long and hard about the direction he wants his life to take and about what goals are worthy of pursuit. The person's deliberations, let us say, are inept, so that the conclusions he reaches as to what would make his life go best are utterly unsupported by his deliberations. Nonetheless, the agent has exercised faculties of critical deliberation and if the conclusions of that deliberation effectively shape his values, desires, and conduct, the fact that a fully rational agent would have reached different conclusions seems insufficient to disqualify this agent as nonautonomous. Being autonomous does not guarantee that one is rationally autonomous, one might think.

This issue is delicate, however. We might identify the idea of an autonomous life with the idea of a life that is voluntarily chosen. In whatever circumstances the agent finds herself, she does the best she can according to her own standards. But if her choices are determined by ignorance, misinformation, confused reasoning, failure to ponder possible consequences carefully, distracting emotion, or the like, these choices will be less than fully voluntary.[9] If a perfectly autonomous choice must be fully voluntary, then to the degree that one's choice fails to be reasonable and based on correct information, one fails to be fully autonomous.

For some readers this last claim might seem a fit target of Isaiah Berlin's scathing warning against the political implications of the notion of positive liberty: "The immature and untutored must be made to say to themselves: 'only the truth liberates, and the only way in which I can learn the truth is by doing blindly today what you, who know it, order, or coerce, me, to do, in the certain knowledge that only thus will I arrive at your clear vision, and be free like you.'"[10] But from the stipulation that the fully autonomous choice is the rationally self-made choice it does not of course follow that forcing the individual to conform to the rational choice made by others counts as a greater degree of autonomy than would be achieved if the individual were let alone to determine her conduct by irrationally self-made choice.

Purely for terminological convenience and without intending to prejudge any issue of substance I will stipulate that *autonomy* can be fully attained by an agent who critically deliberates at or above the threshold level of rationality and *rational autonomy* can be fully attained only by an individual who critically deliberates with full information and perfect rationality.

2. For an agent to count as autonomous, must he form his plan of life by critical reflection and then critically review it periodically (or frequently), or does it suffice for autonomy that one initially decides on a plan of life by critical reflection?

Consider a person who follows an authority uncritically. Whatever my priest, guru, mayor, or other chosen authority asserts, that I believe. Could uncritical conformity to authority be anything other than extreme forfeiture of autonomy?[11] One response is to distinguish two types of conformist. The conformist of the first type at some time in the past decided through critical reflection that uncritical conformity to authority is the best path to take in life. The conformist of the second type is not following a policy that was ever selected after critical reflection. For example, the revolutionary comrades in Bertolt Brecht's play *The Measures Taken* declare their willing subservience, body and soul, to the authority of the revolutionary party. The control chorus exhorts the comrades to make themselves into "blank pages on which the revolution writes its instructions."[12] We may presume that joining a communist party in this manner was itself a carefully considered and reflective decision. Considering the great urgency of the situation, the imperative of unified collective action, the evident wisdom and virtue of party authorities, and one's tendency to overvalue the merits of one's own opinion in a crisis, one judges that the best strategy for reaching one's top-priority goal is to resolve to obey the commands of party authority come what may. Clearly a steadfast resolution to conform is more autonomous if this resolution is the product of critical reflection than if it is arrived at thoughtlessly.

Besides the issue of whether the pattern of conduct the agent follows was ever decided upon through critical reflection, there is also the issue of whether the agent's failure ever to subject this initial decision to further critical review just happens or is itself the product of that initial critical reflection. The more it is the case that what the agent does was intentionally decided upon in a critically reflective manner, the more autonomous we judge the agent to have been.

It would be mistaken to insist that the autonomous person must exercise critical reason continuously, or even frequently. Continuous review of one's decisions would in many settings prevent one from implementing them. In some settings frequent review would likewise block success. But it also sounds implausible to suggest that a single reflective decision renders autonomous an entire life that unreflectively conforms to it. Imagine that the comrades in the Brechtian story decide that their resolution to follow authority will be threatened by their proclivity for critical reflection, so to protect their resolution they take steps to uproot their capacity for dangerous critical reflection by such means as undergoing psychosurgery or consuming alcohol to excess over an extended period. Even if the decision to take such drastic measures is as autonomous as you please, the individual who acts on this decision transforms herself into a zombie, incapable of autonomy.[13]

To reconcile seemingly conflicting intuitions here it helps to think of autonomy as including a disposition. The autonomous person's behavior is controlled by what she has decided are good reasons. To live an autonomous life an agent must decide on a plan of life through critical reflection and in the process of carrying it out, remain disposed to subject the plan to critical review if disturbing or unanticipated evidence indicates the need for such review. The level of counterevidence that would trigger a critical review is set by the agent. Finally, the autonomous agent must remain disposed to undertake critical review of the decision that set the level of counterevidence that would trigger review, if surprising evidence becomes available that calls into question that trigger-setting decision.[14] If all goes well, the autonomous agent might sail through life without ever encountering evidence that indicates a need for critical review of her values and plans. But she is disposed to reflect if that course seems advisable. Conceivably an agent might autonomously decide to undertake a commitment that will not be subject to critical review (the trigger levels are set so high that they will never be reached). But the autonomous agent on this construal always is disposed to reflect should the trigger levels be reached and never destroys her rational capacities to engage in such reflection (so the zombie is nonautonomous).

In the Brechtian example we have been considering, the worry is that individuals resolve to hold fast to present values come what may, even to the point of insulating these values from further critical reflection. A related problematic instance of forfeiture of autonomy involves resolving to bring about or permit change in one's present values by way of insulating the anticipated process of change from the control of one's critical reflection. Suppose that someone moves from the Midwest to New York City, becomes a taxi cab driver, and over time thoughtlessly and gradually imbibes sophisticated urban tastes and values that would have appalled the individual had she ever put these incipient changes in her values under critical scrutiny. Had the individual reflected, she would have resisted these changes successfully, let us assume. To this story add the further detail that the individual moved from the Midwest to New York City either (a) deliberately for the purpose of bringing about changes in her values which she wanted, but knew she would resist if she allowed critical reflection to monitor the process of value change, or (b) foreseeing but not intending that this move to New York City, valued for other reasons, might likely cause undesired changes in her values in just the way that change actually occurred.

In case (a) as described the individual sets her trigger level high, so that the processes of preference drift that she undergoes fail to set off critical review. The description is then compatible with the supposition that she has decided on a plan of life by critical reflection and executes it while remaining disposed to reassess her plan should evidence indicate the need for such reassessment. In case (b) the process of preference drift is not voluntarily chosen (though it is accepted as an unwanted element in a package that is desired all things considered), so to that extent the preference change that occurs is less autonomous. In both cases we can regard the agent as seeking a plan of life that copes in a sensible way with the self-acknowledged limits of her own rational deliberating ability.

If we are attempting to determine to what extent an individual is autonomous over the course of her life, we should notice two different ways of measuring autonomy which we might label the "global method" and the "aggregative method" of measurement. The difference corresponds to two different ways of construing the notion that an agent's behavior is controlled by reasons that the agent herself accepts. According to the global method, an agent is autonomous to the degree that her behavior conforms to a plan of life selected through her critical reflection. The selection need not be close in time to the behavior. In contrast, according to the aggregative method, an agent is autonomous to the degree that her behavior at each moment conforms to a plan of life selected through her critical reflection and monitored (dispositionally ratified) by the agent's reason at that moment. If the agent is disposed at a given time to review her plan of life if she detects appropriate signals, then her plan is monitored (or dispositionally ratified) by her reason at that time. The global but not the aggregative way of measurement allows that an agent could be autonomous at this moment even though she is incapable of subjecting her plan of life to critical review at this moment, provided she is executing a plan decided upon in a critically reflective manner. Subsequent discussion in this essay presupposes the "aggregative method" of measurement.

3. To what extent must an agent's values, preferences, and conduct be influenceable, and actually influenced, by critical reflection, for the agent to qualify as autonomous? The autonomous person's critical reflection is not an idle wheel spinning aimlessly. Her critical reflection has a shaping power over her values, preferences, and conduct. At the extreme, a person who chooses a plan of life by a process of critical reflection but is utterly unable to bring her conduct into conformity with the plan's requirements is not autonomous. One's critical reflection must be effective.[15]

Two quite different pictures of the autonomous person spring to mind in this connection. On one view, the autonomous person has desires and dispositions to conduct that are completely malleable by her critical reflection. No part of the self would be resistant to any change dictated by the voice of critical reflection. On an alternate view, an aspect of autonomy is the achievement of self-knowledge, including knowledge of one's resistance to critical reflection. This conception of autonomy supposes that it is fully achieved if the agent reflectively decides upon a plan of life and implements it even if the agent's choice of plan is constrained by entrenched desires impervious to rational criticism, weakness of will, and related defects of motivation. On the first view, constraints on planning due to one's motivational defects lessen the degree of autonomy one can attain; on the second view, these motivational defects fix the context in which reflective choice of a life plan occurs and do not per se lessen the extent to which the agent can become autonomous.

4. In order to qualify as autonomous, is more required than that a person must critically reflect upon what plan of life to follow, her basic values and preferences being taken for granted? Or must the autonomous person also subject these values and desires to critical reflection? This is a question about the scope of the critical reflection that a person qua autonomous undertakes.

It will be useful to distinguish three stipulations of what autonomy requires in terms of its scope that I will call "narrow," "wide," and "restricted" autonomy.

A person is *narrowly* autonomous insofar as she subjects her basic preferences and values to effective critical deliberation. Critical deliberation on preferences and values is *effective* insofar as (1) the preferences and values supported by critical reflection become the preferences and values of the agent and (2) these preferences and values shaped by critical reflection determine the conduct of the agent. In other words, narrow autonomy is achieved by someone who has thought critically about what is best to value and prefer and adopts the conclusions of that thought as her own values and preferences, which she strives to achieve in her actions.

Broad autonomy includes narrow autonomy plus more. A person is *broadly* autonomous insofar as she (a) is narrowly autonomous and (b) follows a plan of life selected by critical deliberation about how to fulfill her values and preferences. In other words, a narrowly autonomous person is autonomous with respect to her basic life goals and a broadly autonomous person is also autonomous with respect to the means chosen in order to achieve those goals.

Restricted autonomy is broad autonomy minus its narrow autonomy component. A person achieves *restricted* autonomy to the extent that she follows a plan of life chosen by a process of critical deliberation that takes her basic values and preferences for granted and reflects about how best to fulfill them.

Does restricted autonomy deserve the name "autonomy"? Arguments about the proper names of concepts are usually pointless, but it is worth noting that in everyday life worries about autonomy often go deeper than concerns about whether our plans are instrumentally rational, given our aims. Much of our talk about efforts to achieve autonomy appears to refer to subjecting one's basic aims and desires to critical scrutiny, sometimes at great personal cost. The desires that move me to action might not be the desires that I would have if I could subject these desires to rational critical scrutiny. What emerges, when all goes well, from the self-turmoil that is provoked by that alienating thought is what we usually have in mind by "autonomy." The fact that we talk in this way does not ensure that we are making sense, but prima facie there is reason not to characterize as "fully autonomous" a person who never subjects her basic aims and preferences to critical scrutiny.

So far in this section I have been analyzing the critical reflection conception of the Real Self requirement for autonomy. There are rival conceptions of the Real Self requirement.

The ideal of autonomy is salient when there is, at least potentially, psychic conflict. The art of self-governance consists in the skillful successful management or avoidance of psychic conflict. A conception of autonomy among other things provides instructions for identifying in cases of intrapersonal conflict a part of the self that is to be considered the Real Self for purposes of deciding whether or not the person is self-governing.

The Real Self aspect of autonomy is an ideal that pertains to us in virtue of our limited capacity to decide rationally what goals to seek and what means to take in order to have the best shot at attaining those goals (as well as limited capacity to identify rationally compelling limits on acceptable pursuit of goals). If we were always perfectly rational in thought and wholeheartedly inclined to put rational thought into action then psychic conflict would not exist and the problem of deciding which contender in these conflicts is the Real Self fit to rule would not arise.

Autonomy is salient for us given our limited rationality. It would be wrong to leap to the conclusion that the ideal of autonomy must identify the Real Self of an individual with her reasoning or deliberative faculties. Just because human reasoning ability is limited, it is possible that following the dictates of some rival intrapersonal "agency" might yield better results, results more in line with the outcomes that perfectly rational and wholehearted creatures would reach. "The heart has its reasons, whereof reason knows nothing": The term "reason" in the second clause of this saying must be read with scare quotes, for it connotes a blinkered, partial viewpoint that ignores considerations that would be taken into account by a fully rational agent. For a similar example, untutored instinct might predictably do better than tutored reason by reason's own standards. Something like this appears to have been a characteristic Romantic viewpoint. Consider Tony Tanner's evocation of the attitudes of Samuel Clemens exhibited in the musings of the central character in his *Huck Finn*:

We have said that Huck is forcibly involved with society from time to time, but his most dangerous involvement is an internal affair. Certain social mores have invaded, pervaded his mind; have corrupted his conscience to use Clemens's own formulation. Whenever he stops to think rationally, *socially,* he feels the only goodness lies in betraying Jim. This is a most dramatic metaphor which highlights Huck's midway position between two worlds: the world of men (the shore) and the world of nature (the river – and Jim), and his dilemma of being torn between inculcated morality and instinctive humanity.

Huck's heart has picked up the rhythm of the river, he is attuned to the pulses of nature which he so intimately understands. That is to say that a presocial order of being is feeling through him which melts and dissolves all rational obstructions, asserting instead echoes of a harmonious ideal world which is not based on degree (white man superior to negro) and property (man owning negro, *selling* negro), but on pre-individualistic harmony in which people and days flow into each other in peace and concord. [Huck's] speech with its wistful or joyous cadences, its haunting evocative rhythms, cannot owe anything to the syntax and categories of society – indeed owes everything to its apparent ability to recall a more primitive manner of speech when man's capacity for wonder was more marked. It is the naive vision which enables Clemens to achieve this. A response not founded on reflection but nourished by natural impulse, a naivety which testifies to an unimpaired heart. [16]

Any thinking, calculating decision-making procedure available to Huck will assuredly lead him astray, in the world of the novel. An individual does better following his natural impulses. Because these impulses are overlain by artificial education and socialization, an individual might have to attend carefully in order to feel them, or place himself in the right setting for natural impulse detection, as Huck happens to do when he floats on a raft down the river. This is Samuel Clemens's message, deciphered by Tanner. Presumably some variety of Romantic theory would be invoked to explain why natural impulses are inherently trustworthy.

Clemens might be thought to be repudiating the ideal of autonomy. I think it is more perspicuous to say that the conception of autonomy that he implicitly affirms identifies the Real Self with natural impulse rather than the reflective, deliberative part of the self. In contrast, a writer like Edmund Burke, suspicious of calculating reason and spontaneous impulse alike, appears to locate the Real Self in the inclination to loyalty to the uncritically accepted conventions and traditions of one's society. [17]

The existence of competing conceptions of autonomy proposing something other than critical reflection for the role of the Real Self raises the question how to choose which is best. Obviously, a given conception of autonomy will likely be embedded in a larger complex of empirical, metaphysical, and normative theories, and the evaluation of these enveloping theories will have implications for the acceptability of their associated notions of autonomy. So, for example, the Romantic affirmation of spontaneously unreflective self-governance invites the challenge that we have no warrant for thinking that what a person is spontaneously inclined to think when attending to "nature" is less tainted by social learning and indoctrination than what a person is inclined to think after extended critical deliberation.[18]

But even if there are errors in the social theories associated with a particular conception of autonomy, in many cases at least it will be feasible to decouple the conception from any such errors. I suppose that the conception of autonomy as spontaneously or instinctively nonreflective self-governance can be prized apart from Romantic illusions. Once this is done for a set of rival conceptions, how might we decide among them? Choosing one among rival conceptions of autonomy requires a judgment as to which conception coheres better with the value we mean to affirm in affirming the ideal of autonomy.

The possibility I want to suggest is that we can and should appeal to instrumental considerations. From a revised welfarist standpoint, conceptions of the Real Self are assessed according to their welfare productivity: The best conception of the Real Self component of autonomy is the one such that if people guided their choice of values and preferences and life plans by it, would best enable people to adopt and fulfill the values and preferences that they would affirm in an ideally considered manner. Notice first of all that from this subjectivist standpoint, the ideal conception of autonomy very likely will vary from cultural setting to cultural setting and also from person to person. Whether a conception of the Real Self that identifies it with (for example) critical reflection, unreflective spontaneous impulse, or steadfast allegiance to the traditions and conventions of one's society is best will depend on the character of the traditions and conventions of one's society, on the degree to which one possesses the ability to engage constructively in reflective deliberation, on the content of what one is likely to identify as one's spontaneous impulses, and so on. Which conception of the Real Self is best cannot be determined a priori.

Does independence suffice for autonomy?

My provisional assumption has been that two requirements must be satisfied if a person is to qualify as autonomous: the Real Self condition ("I rule me") and the Independence condition ("no one else rules I"). Against this assumption the suspicion might arise that from the start I have packed into the concept of autonomy one requirement too many. If no other person than Madeline rules Madeline, isn't she self-governing? Perhaps the Independence condition, properly construed, suffices for autonomy. Perhaps the Real Self condition is otiose.

Consider the parallel case of political sovereignty. One might suppose that if no people other than the French are the rulers of the French, then France is a self-governing nation, whether its political constitution be monarchist, republican, or whatever you will. But a moment's reflection reminds us that there is at least one alternative besides home rule to foreign rule: perhaps no one is ruling at all. A land that is not ruled by outsiders might be a chaotic, disordered anarchy. And similarly a person not steered by any external agency might be just rudderless, rather than autonomous. If the Independence condition is satisfied, then the person is not ruled by any agency external to the self, but this does not suffice for autonomy. Some form of home rule must be operating.

Looked at in this light, the Real Self requirement can be reformulated as the condition that the life of an individual must meet some threshold standard of order. Once again, think of the political analogy that inspires the ideal of personal autonomy.[19] France might lack any political institutions or structured rule, yet conceivably she might be well-ordered by means of peaceful, cooperative anarchy. If France were a nation of individuals who acknowledge no crown or government but nonetheless contrive to manage their mutual affairs quite satisfactorily, we would still be right to hold that France is self-governing. To imagine a people as self-governing is to imagine them successfully coordinating their common affairs, making and executing collective decisions on common problems, and so on.

So perhaps we had better say that it is not strictly required for autonomy that the individual constitute herself as an "I" that rules and a "me" that is ruled. The Real Self interpretations that we have been canvassing identify some agency within the individual self as entitled to rule, therefore uniquely fit to become the "I" to which "me" – the rest of the self – is subject. Such partial interpretations of autonomy are like political doctrines that proclaim one form of political constitution to be best for a nation. The alternative view of the Real Self would hold that the parts of the self or intrapersonal subagencies that might contest for control of an individual person must fall into some at least minimally orderly working arrangement if the individual self is to be autonomous. Whatever is identified as "I" and "me" must compose a psychic harmony. Conformity by "me" to the dictates of "I" is one possible way of achieving inner harmony, but there are others. We could say that the Real Self requirement should be understood loosely, so that it would count as "I rule me" if "I" and "me" coordinate their activity above some threshold level of order, even if there is no hierarchical domination of one part of the self over the others. "We jointly monitor each other" counts as a limit case of "I rule me" on the view I am suggesting.

Interpreting the Real Self condition as a minimal psychic order requirement appears to change its meaning from the interpretations discussed in the previous section. Notice that satisfaction of the Real Self requirement along the lines suggested in the preceding section does not guarantee the presence of minimal psychic order. Suppose that the Real Self condition is read as requiring that critical reflection should govern the individual. But critical reflection can run amok. Consider a person whose life is dominated by an obsession for critical reasoning. He fails to carry out any decision that he reaches because any decision tentatively reached is always shortly thereafter countermanded by doubts engendered by critical reason. The person is always deciding and never in a position of having decided that is sufficiently stable to be the basis for forming a rational plan of life. Here the agent's critical reasoning proclivity is a tyrant that oppresses a disordered self.

The argument just made in effect challenges the idea that the conceptions of the Real Self condition canvassed in this essay are properly regarded as necessary for autonomy. Rather they are better regarded as partial ideals of the good life, conceptions of what sort of life is choiceworthy. What is required to be autonomous is one question, what choice of values an autonomous person should make, in order to lead the best possible life, is a quite different question. But in keeping with the dialectical purpose of this essay, I will ignore this point in the arguments to come. My arguments aim to engage critics of revised subjectivism who generally conceive of autonomy as a life controlled by critical reflection and who posit autonomy so conceived as a crucial component of the good life, radically misunderstood and undervalued by blinkered subjectivisms. So in the balance of the essay I follow the critics of subjectivism in supposing that the critical reflection interpretation of the Real Self figures essentially in the ideal of autonomy.

According to the argument of this section, the Real Self condition, suitably interpreted (as psychic order), is a necessary condition for autonomy, so satisfaction of the Independence condition alone cannot suffice. The question then arises whether satisfaction of the Independence condition is anyway necessary for autonomy, even if not sufficient.

Independence and autonomy

The autonomous person chooses a plan of life (perhaps a very loose plan that allows ample room for deferred decision and spontaneity) and amends it as seems appropriate in the light of her values. This by itself does not seem sufficient to guarantee autonomy, for it could be that the values in the light of which the individual chooses are not themselves authentically related to the person. The values that are foundational for the agent's practical deliberation might be imposed through a repressive upbringing, indoctrination, or even direct stimulation of the agent's brain by some other person who is able to manipulate the agent's brain states using some device that entirely bypasses the normal human preference formation process. In these and other ways the individual who freely chooses her plan of life may yet be a puppet controlled by others. In these examples the strings through which outside control is exercised are the preferences and values of the agent. So we are led to posit that preferences and values must themselves be autonomous if the agent is to qualify as truly autonomous. But now we seem close to positing an impossible ideal of self-creation ex nihilo. The ideal of autonomy as a life voluntarily chosen appears to evaporate on inspection.

Two strategies for preserving a viable notion of autonomy against the threat of evaporation are worth considering. Harry Frankfurt has suggested one strategy: that a desire or preference is to be regarded as truly the agent's own for the purpose of deciding whether or not she is autonomous just in case she identifies with it. Identification is construed to be a decision to endorse a motivating impulse in such a way that it counts as partially constituting her self rather than an alien influence on her behavior.[20] According to this proposal, whether or not an agent is autonomous with respect to a given desire depends on her present relation to it and not on the causal history of how she came to have the desire. Perhaps as a matter of contingent fact agents will not identify with desires that have bizarre or otherwise dubious causal histories. In principle, however, there is no conceptual bar to identifying with any desire whatsoever that one has, and autonomy consists in action in accordance with desires and preferences with which one identifies.

The other strategy insists that a value or preference of an agent must have the right sort of causal history if it is to count as truly the agent's own for purposes of deciding her autonomy status. The task of specifying what sort of causal history is the right sort has proven elusive. But the identification strategy is plagued by a difficulty that suggests the causal-history strategy must be on the right track, even though its outline is not yet clear. The difficulty is that the same sort of behind-the-back manipulation that vitiates the autonomy of the agent when it generates his preferences can just as readily be imagined to issue in the act of identification that is supposed to certify the agent's autonomy.[21] Suppose a merchant manipulates Smith into forming a desire for pickles. The psychological process that forms this desire is such as to render it nonautonomous, let us assume. Now suppose that by an act of will Smith decides to identify with the desire for pickles. This characterization is compatible with the further stipulation that this act of identification is produced in Smith by the same type of manipulative psychological process that initially generated the inauthentic desire for pickles. But in this case our reasons for doubting that Smith's pickle desire is autonomous (or that Smith is autonomous with respect to this desire) are doubled, not removed. Positing acts of identification with suspect desires just kicks the problem up a level and need not eliminate our initial grounds for suspicion.

An advocate of the identification strategy might reply that an act of identification brought about by psychological manipulation is not a genuine act of identification. However, this reply either does not engage the worry that prompts it or smuggles in a causal history constraint. Notice that the psychological manipulation that produces the questionable act of identification need not be contemporaneous with it. The manipulation might give rise to a chain of reflection that might equally have been stimulated by nonsuspected causes, so that the culmination of this reflection in a present act of identification could be identical in every respect to an hypothetical nonproblematic act of identification proceeding from nonsuspect causes except for the past causal history. If causal history can taint present acts of identification, the identification strategy looks doomed.

Consider next a hybrid suggestion asserted by Gerald Dworkin. Dworkin's proposal is that our capacity for autonomy is our capacity (1) to subject our desires and values to critical reflection, from which emerge higher-order desires that affirm or reject the desires that have been reflected upon, and (2) to take effective steps to bring our lower-order desires in line with our higher-order evaluations (acts of identification and rejection). So far this is like the view drawn from Frankfurt, with an emphasis on critical reflection as the appropriate pathway to true acts of identification and rejection. Regarding this conceptual proposal, Dworkin comments, "Second-order reflection cannot be the whole story of autonomy. For these reflections, the choice of the kind of person one wants to become, may be influenced by other persons or circumstances in such a fashion that we do not view these evaluations as being the person's own."[22] So another condition is required for autonomy: The agent's higher-order reflection on her desires and aims issuing in acts of identification and rejection must be "procedurally independent," which means it must not be brought about by "influences such as hypnotic suggestion, manipulation, coercive persuasion, subliminal influence, and so forth." It would be desirable to have a more illuminating characterization of the notion of procedural independence, but I forbear criticism, because I do not know how to improve on Dworkin's characterization by means of a list of examples. What bothers me is something else.

Why is it only the causal history of the agent's acts of reflection that is relevant to the question of her autonomy status, and not also the causal history of the desires themselves about which the agent is reflecting? Suppose that the agent has undergone a harsh and repressive upbringing, the result of which is that the agent's desires are centered on catering to authority and attaining the lowest rung on whatever status hierarchy impinges on her. The agent's cognitive faculties are intact, and she is motivated to undertake critical reflection on her desires and values, but the outcome is meager: The agent identifies wholeheartedly after deliberation with her catering and bottom-rung desires. If following Dworkin we insist on the "procedural independence" – the right sort of causal history – of the agent's autonomy-establishing reflection, why not go further and insist on this condition or some analogue of it for the formation of the desires and aims that are the object of this reflection? Invoking a causal history condition at the level of the agent's prereflective desires and values would permit the judgment that in the example just above the agent's repressive upbringing has diminished the level of autonomy which she can now attain, no matter how thoughtful her reflection and no matter how successful her efforts to mold her desires to the outcome of that reflection.

The proposal now to be considered interprets the Independence condition as ruling out alien influences on the processes by which the agent's values and preferences are formed and her decision making shaped. The problem is to distinguish the alien influences that distort preference formation from influences we would wish to deem nonproblematic. Many ordinary life events that have an impact on our values and aims are not voluntarily chosen or under our control yet can hardly count as alien unless autonomy is to become a pie-in-the-sky ideal. An individual is spurned by his lover, suffers bouts of unemployment, attracts praise for his athletic prowess, is moved by news media reports of current events, and so on. Life events that are as ordinary as changes in the weather and just as difficult to predict or control exert causal influence on preference change. An ideal of autonomy that precluded such influences would be utterly beyond human attainment. In keeping with the core idea that an autonomous life is one freely chosen, we might entertain the suggestion that preference change factors reduce autonomy to the extent that they exert their impact against the (procedurally independent) will of the agent.

In this connection we should distinguish preference change factors that work their effects (1) before the individual has much experience of the world and a fully formed set of preferences in response to it and (2) afterward. The line between childhood and adulthood roughly coincides with this distinction. Evidently the Independence requirement must differ for the two stages of an individual's life.

We are led to this interpretation of the Independence requirement for autonomy: An agent attains independence to the degree that (1) her upbringing or initial socialization is nonrepressive and (2) from then on, the causal influences that shape further preference change are either voluntarily chosen by her or voluntarily accepted as foreseen concomitants of her chosen plan of life.

The notion of a nonrepressive upbringing should not flout the common sense understanding that children need to be tamed for their own good and for the good of society. The young child is conceived as containing innate propensities that in the course of ordinary interaction with her environment would develop into basic preferences unless blocked by effective repression. An upbringing is nonrepressive to the extent that these propensities are actively encouraged by persons who interact with the young child, or tolerated by them, or at least not successfully squelched, except insofar as discouragement of these propensities is required in order to instill in the child a disposition to be moral, to safeguard the child's predictable vital interests, or to develop in the child traits and skills that are needed so that at maturity the child will have the ability successfully to pursue a reasonable range of significantly different plans of life in a modern society. To the degree that the child's initial propensities conflict either in the sense that developing one impedes the development of others or that the satisfaction of the preference that develops from a given propensity would require frustration of other preferences that develop from other propensities, selective parental encouragement of some but not other propensities is nonrestrictive, provided the child is gradually given increasing freedom to choose for herself which propensities to develop.[23] Notice that the definition allows the possibility that a child might endure an upbringing intended to be repressive but be unfazed by it and win through to autonomy despite it. A childrearing regimen that would psychologically cripple one child might merely pose a small surmountable obstacle to another child's search for her own path in life.

The second condition required for Independence – for having a set of preferences and values that is truly the agent's own – is that once the agent has reached maturity, further preference change should not occur against her will. This condition must be understood as a counsel of perfection, an ideal rather than a minimal threshold condition. A clear case of voluntarily chosen preference change would be the deliberate choice by an agent to undergo a self-transforming experience just in order to be transformed. In some circumstances joining a monastery would be an example of such a choice. In another range of cases the agent accepts causal influences on her preferences that are unwanted, taken by themselves, but which are components of arrangements that are attractive overall and chosen over alternatives. For example, a woman might choose on balance to marry a certain man even though she understands that such a marriage will have some tendency to change her into a prig, against her wishes. In such a case, whether or not it is right to say that the woman has undergone voluntary preference change depends on the extent to which she made her choice from a large and significantly diverse set of options.

Suppose that an agent chooses an option that is on balance attractive but harbors a small risk that unwanted preference change will occur and that in the event this unwanted change does occur, against the odds. The agent might wish to take a vacation that offers great swimming along with a chance that she will be kidnapped by local guerrillas and subjected to fiercely efficient indoctrination and brainwashing. Reflecting carefully, she chooses to take the vacation, but unfortunately the kidnapping occurs and she is subjected to psychological manipulation that drastically changes her desires in an unwanted direction. The agent voluntarily chose to undergo a risk of unwanted preference change, but the change itself occurs against her will. Here the agent has voluntarily chosen to risk loss of Independence.

It should be reiterated that the willing done by the agent that renders processes that change her desires more or less voluntary must satisfy the condition that Dworkin calls procedural independence. The willing that renders desire change more or less autonomous must not itself be manipulated or coerced (or the like) by another agent.

Summary

So far I have tried to decompose the ideal of personal autonomy into two components, the Real Self condition and the Independence condition.

I have focussed on the critical reflection interpretation of the Real Self condition. According to this interpretation, the Real Self component of autonomy is satisfied by a person to the extent that the conduct of her life is controlled by what she takes to be good reasons, picked out by her in the light of her fundamental values and preferences, which have been ratified by her activity of critical reflection. The control that critical reflection exerts over the life of the autonomous individual is mainly dispositional: Having chosen a plan of life in the light of values that have survived her own engagement in critical reflection, the autonomous agent thereafter remains able and disposed to rethink her plan or reconsider the values on which it is based if new evidence indicates the need for such reflection by exceeding trigger levels set by the agent (provided she is also disposed to reset the trigger levels if new evidence indicates that is appropriate). Moreover, the control that critical reflection exerts on the autonomous agent's life is not unduly limited by entrenched desires impervious to critical reason, weakness of will, and related character defects. The ideally autonomous agent's character, desires, and conduct are all fully receptive to whatever dictates her critical reason might issue. Finally the critical reflection, engagement in which renders a person autonomous, must at least attain a minimal threshold level of rationality or it does not count as critical reflection at all.

Satisfaction of the Real Self condition does not suffice for autonomy, for it could be that the values of the individual even though subjected at some point to critical scrutiny are not authentically "her own." These values might have been imposed initially through a repressive upbringing, indoctrination, or direct manipulation of her brain states. The individual who chooses a plan of life in the light of critical reflection and acts to carry out that self-chosen plan may yet be a puppet controlled by others.

The Independence condition for autonomy is met by a given agent to the degree that (a) her upbringing or initial socialization is nonrepressive and (b) from then on, the causal influences that shape her further preference change are either voluntarily chosen by her or voluntarily accepted as foreseen concomitants of her chosen plan of life. An upbringing is deemed nonrepressive to the extent that the innate propensities of the child are actively encouraged by persons who interact with the young child, or tolerated by them, or at least not successfully squelched, except insofar as discouragement of these propensities is required in order to instill in the child a disposition to be moral, to safeguard the child's vital interests, or to develop in the child traits and skills that are needed so that at maturity the child will have the ability successfully to pursue any of a reasonable range of significantly different plans of life in a modern society.

The value of rational autonomy

On a subjectivist view, the instrumental value of autonomy is apparent. If the good consists in rational preference satisfaction, then other things being equal, a person is more likely to attain the good if she subjects her present preferences to rational deliberation and gathers information that is pertinent to such deliberation. Actual preferences are more likely to coincide with hypothetically rational preferences if actual preferences have emerged from the agent's critical deliberation. This is particularly so in modern pluralist societies. Confronted with competing conceptions of the good embraced by fellow members of society, the individual has little choice but to exercise the ability to choose reasonably among them. Joseph Raz observes, "The value of autonomy is a fact of life. Since we live in a society whose social forms are to a considerable extent based on individual choice, and since our options are limited by what is available in our society, we can prosper in it only if we can be successfully autonomous."[24]

Besides noting this instrumental role for autonomy, we should note that many persons desire to be rationally autonomous. Moreover, at least for many of these persons, there is no reason to doubt that this desire would survive extended rational scrutiny. For these persons rational autonomy is intrinsically desirable, a component of their good.

On a subjectivist view, the connection between autonomy and the good, though tight, is not watertight. This should be obvious. I might subject a naively held preference to extended critical scrutiny, thus enhancing the degree to which I am autonomous with respect to this preference. Yet my critical scrutiny might be thoroughly inept, even though it lies above any plausible minimal threshold of rationality that is required if deliberation is to qualify the deliberator as autonomous. How I evaluate a preference when I am confused and making errors cannot determine the contribution that the satisfaction of the preference under review would make to my welfare. The value that I autonomously affirm after deliberation might be a worse value, according to the subjectivist standard, than what I had affirmed prior to deliberation.

Nor is it always the case that the more rationally autonomous one becomes, the better are the values and preferences that one pursues. In making this negative claim I do not invoke the possibility that in virtue of becoming more rationally autonomous, one might decide to pursue moral aims or act from altruistic concern for others to the detriment of one's own welfare. As mentioned previously, I am excluding this matter from the scope of this discussion.

A simple example will illustrate what I do have in mind. Assume that naively, thoughtlessly, Smith would affirm wine, men, and song as her final aims. If she engaged in sophisticated rational scrutiny, she would change her mind and affirm mystical contemplation as her final aim. But if she were to engage in hypersophisticated rational scrutiny, that relentlessly evaluates every relevant argument in an ideally well considered way, in the presence of full relevant information, she would (let us suppose) revert to affirmation of wine, men, and song as her final aims. In this example Smith becomes more rationally autonomous when she shifts from naive, thoughtless affirmation to sophisticated affirmation following rational scrutiny. But as it happens her sophisticated judgment is worse – even though better reasoned – than her naive judgment. To avoid irrelevant complications, let us further assume that naive Smith would achieve exactly the same degree of satisfaction of her final aims as would sophisticated Smith. On these assumptions, naive Smith achieves a higher degree of rational preference satisfaction than sophisticated Smith. The judgment of revised subjectivism is that it would have been better for Smith had she not become rationally autonomous. One might say that the unexamined life can be worth living, if the life happens to be such that it could withstand ideal rational examination.

A similar conflict between rational autonomy and rational preference satisfaction can occur whenever someone happens by good fortune to stumble upon a set of rational final ends while failing spectacularly to attain rational autonomy. Imagine that Jones happens to want close friendship, loving intense family relations, and scientific achievement, and achieves all of these, but has never subjected her aims to any scrutiny. Jones is a naive evaluator but it is her good luck, let us assume, that her ends would be affirmed if she were to engage in ideal rational scrutiny. The description supplied so far leaves open the possibility that Jones might also desire to be a rationally autonomous person or to be a person of a sort that presupposes attainment of rational autonomy. But it just so happens that she has no such desires. Jones could nonetheless devote some personal resources toward becoming more rationally autonomous, at some cost in terms of her expected level of satisfaction of her final ends. But from her own standpoint there is no reason to devote resources to the project of becoming rationally autonomous. That is, there is nothing in her current preferences, even as they would be after correction by ideal rational scrutiny, that gives her any intrinsic reason to want to become rationally autonomous. This attainment is simply not part of her good.

According to subjectivism there are strong instrumental reasons for seeking rational autonomy, particularly in modern pluralist societies. But on this view rational autonomy is not necessarily an intrinsic element of everyone's good. Is this an implausible position?

Recall the two antisubjectivist responses to preference formation worries: (1) Rational autonomy is desirable for its own sake, an important component of the good life for any person, whatever her own tastes, values, and preferences might be, and (2) satisfaction of preferences genuinely contributes to an individual's welfare (the degree to which her life goes well) only to the extent that she is rationally autonomous with respect to these preferences.

The case of Jones is a counterexample to claim (2). According to subjectivism, engagement in critical reflection does not automatically increase the value of the preferences that critical reflection affirms. Critical reflection is at most a way of discovering what is valuable, not a way of constituting what is valuable in the life of the reflector.

To see this point it may be useful to focus attention on simple, ordinary preferences or on otherwise attractive preferences that we are very inclined to suppose would pass the counterfactual test with flying colors. I like the taste of sweet desserts and the feeling of solving intellectual puzzles and have never given a moment's thought to the issue of whether these preferences would survive ideally extended critical deliberation. I would have scarcely any idea how to begin thinking about the issue. So with respect to these preferences I spectacularly fail to satisfy the ideal of rational autonomy. Assume that these preferences would survive ideally conducted critical deliberation. If so, why suppose that satisfying these preferences now adds less to my welfare than their satisfaction would bring if I had critically deliberated about them? It is possible that critical deliberation would change the character of these preferences. Perhaps the reflective taste for desserts would differ from the nonreflective preference; perhaps desserts would taste different in subtle ways, and better, if I deliberated about my sweet tooth. But if so, then the revised subjectivist view would itself accord greater value to the satisfaction of the reflective than of the nonreflective taste, all else being equal. The person who holds that the more autonomous one is with respect to one's preferences, the more their satisfaction increases one's welfare, must hold that reflection per se renders preferences more valuable, quite apart from possible effects like those just considered. I submit that once we get the issue clearly in focus, the idea that critical reflection is inherently value-conferring has no appeal.

The claim that the satisfaction of a preference is good for a person only to the extent that the preference is autonomously held is hard to reconcile with a reasonable attitude toward the likely goodness of the mode of life of isolated hunter-gatherers. As described by anthropologists, the lives of hunter-gatherers often appear attractive and worthwhile. It is extremely unlikely that isolated hunter-gatherers, who after all must have been ignorant of the kinds of lives prevalent in other groups, engaged in critical reflection regarding the true value of their way of life. The skills and concepts needed for effective critical reflection would not be within the repertoire of such cultures, nor would the need for such skills and concepts be salient. Any critical reflection that did occur within such cultures must have been extremely rudimentary and crude. But surely to imagine a primitive culture whose members are completely nonautonomous with respect to their traditional mode of life is not per se to show that the mode of life is valueless. According to revised subjectivism, it is not the extent to which hunter-gatherers actually affirmed their values after ideal deliberation that determines their worth but rather the extent to which they would have affirmed their values had they subjected them to ideal deliberation. Revised subjectivism leaves room for the thought that one might be naive and uncritical in affirming one's values, yet those values are nonetheless worth affirming and not rendered intrinsically less worthwhile by one's failure to confirm their worth by critical reflection.

Laurence Haworth argues explicitly for the claim that satisfaction of a preference enhances a person's welfare only to the extent that the person is autonomous with respect to that preference.[25] He considers the example of a preference for hula hoop consumption induced by manipulative advertising. Suppose that I come to want to own a hula hoop because I have watched television ads that associate hula hoops with pleasant images of fun at the beach, physically attractive men and women and women in skimpy bathing suits, and so on. I do not actually believe that ownership of a hula hoop would increase my enjoyment of leisure-time outings or increase the sex appeal of the friends I am likely to meet at such gatherings. Nonetheless the pleasant scenario depicted in the advertisement causes me to want a hula hoop for its own sake. If we agree with Haworth that my subsequent purchase of a hula hoop satisfies a strong basic preference but probably contributes little or nothing to my welfare, are we then committed to the further conclusion that, other things being equal, well-being varies directly with the autonomy of the preferences one succeeds in satisfying?

No. Haworth appears to have described a case in which an individual's preferences are manipulated or malformed in such a way that (a) they would not withstand rational scrutiny and (b) the individual is not rationally autonomous with respect to them. This is the wrong sort of case for joining the issue whether (b) alone severs the link between satisfaction of one's preference and increase in one's welfare. Haworth implicitly assumes away the possibility that preferences might be (a) but not (b). Once the possibility is recognized, I see no rationale for claim (2) in his discussion.

If claim (2) is rejected, what of claim (1)? No doubt it is perfectly coherent to hold that preference satisfaction is one component of the good and that rational autonomy is another, independent component – perhaps one among several. On this view, someone who is striving to make prudent life choices should strive to maximize an appropriately weighted sum of all the various components deemed elements of the good human life. Hence rational preference satisfaction should sometimes be sacrificed for more than compensating gains on the score of rational autonomy. Call this position the "mixed view."

Though the mixed view is coherent, some arguments for it are inconclusive. Jon Elster speculates that in the transition from feudalism to capitalism workers might have undergone release from adaptive preferences, thus achieving lesser preference satisfaction and greater autonomy. The judgment that the release from adaptive preferences in these circumstances was good for these workers implies a rejection of the view that the good is identical with utility, according to Elster. He writes, "It cannot be true that the smallest loss in welfare always counts for more than the largest increase in autonomy. There must be cases in which the autonomy of wants overrides the satisfaction of wants."[26]

This argument proceeds too swiftly. From a revised subjectivist standpoint, the relevant question is whether the workers with adaptive preferences achieved a higher level of rational preference satisfaction than they achieved once freed from adaptive preferences. My understanding of Elster's conception of an *adaptive preference* is that an adaptive preference is formed by a causal process that occurs behind the back of the agent, hence would not likely survive rational scrutiny. If so, then release from adaptive preferences might improve the rationality of one's preferences according to the counterfactual test and so one might secure a higher level of rational preference satisfaction even though one's straight preference satisfaction level is deteriorating.

Consider then the case in which release from adaptive preferences leads to a lower level of rational preference satisfaction along with an increase in rational autonomy. Initially I wanted only potatoes. My wants were constricted owing to my poverty. Contact with the wider world has liberated me from this poverty-induced want; I now want meat and fish. Neither is readily available, so although my new preferences are slightly superior to my old ones according to the counterfactual reflection test, superiority on this score is outweighed by the greater satisfiability of my old wants. Regarding this sort of case, it is plausible to hold that release from adaptive preferences renders me worse off in welfare (rational preference satisfaction) but better off in rational autonomy hence better off overall?

I have no persuasive argument for the negative answer to this question to which I am inclined. The most I can do is point out a cost of assent to the mixed view. We are asked to judge that the agent is better off undergoing a "liberating" preference change even though from the agent's own standpoint his life is thereby rendered worse. Moreover, nothing in the agent's own standpoint even as it would be if corrected by fully rational deliberation with full pertinent information provides a ground for the judgment that liberation has rendered him better off. The value of rational autonomy has so to speak been counted once in the agent's own hypothetical deliberation about his good, and given its full value from the agent's own (corrected) standpoint. The mixed view overrides the agent's own deliberate standpoint on his good. The mixed view requires us to judge the agent's life as better or worse according to the degree to which it attains a value, rational autonomy, the importance of which is set by a standard that is completely independent of the agent's own values, tastes, and perceptions, even as they would be after ideal rational scrutiny. In this sense the mixed view in assigning objective value to rational autonomy is a perfectionist doctrine.

Anyone with minimally liberal political instincts would be skeptical of the claim that an individual's good consists in spiritual salvation as defined by a sectarian religious doctrine – regardless of the judgment of this matter that would be rendered by the person herself after ideal rational deliberation. I submit that anyone should be equally skeptical of the claim that an individual's good consists in rational autonomy – regardless of the judgment on this matter that would be reached in ideally rational fashion from that very individual's standpoint. In each case perfectionism involves an overriding of the agent's own judgment in a strong sense.

The value of independence

So far I have argued against the idea that rational autonomy either conditions the value of rational preference satisfaction or is an element of the good life independent of rational preference satisfaction. The focus has been entirely on the critical reflection element in rational autonomy: Is critical reflection good for an agent independently of its consequences? And secondly: Must preferences be subjected to the agent's critical reflection if their satisfaction is to count fully toward the agent's welfare?

This way of posing the issue leaves it open whether the Independence component of autonomy must be satisfied if one's preferences are to count as authentically one's own, so that their satisfaction should count fully toward increasing one's welfare.

The Independence component of autonomy addresses the worry that a person might fail to be autonomous even though she engages in reflection about her values and preferences which is effective in shaping them and they in turn shape her conduct. This failure might come about in either of two ways. The person may have acquired an initial set of preferences (on which her further reflection operates) by some process that is manipulative or oppressive or otherwise defective. Or it might be the case that the person who has acquired an initial set of preferences in a healthy way is subject to subsequent change of preference against her will, even though she engages in effective critical deliberation throughout her life. Change of preference comes about owing to the operation of causes whose influence she would prefer to avoid. In such a case the person's preferences may not be authentically her own even though she satisfies the critical deliberation interpretation of the Real Self condition for autonomy. An extreme example would be a person who is placed against her will in a prison or concentration camp, and whose preferences and values are altered over time by the traumatic experiences she undergoes while in confinement, even though she is able effectively to deliberate critically about her values and preferences throughout the ordeal.

These considerations suggest this Independence condition for autonomy: An agent is autonomous to the degree that (1) her upbringing or initial socialization is nonrepressive and (2) from then on, the causal influences that shape further preference change are either voluntarily chosen by her or voluntarily accepted as foreseen concomitants of her chosen plan of life. We can call (1) the nonrepression condition and (2) the authenticity condition for Independence.

Any plan of life that is available to an individual will include the likelihood of being buffeted by events which will powerfully influence one's values but which one would prefer not to undergo and which one specifically wishes would not mold one's values. That is just the human condition. One could avoid it only by becoming entirely indifferent to the question of what causes will influence one's values. But one can be subject to such influences to greater or lesser degree. Roughly, the greater the range of significantly different life plans, involving significantly different causal influences on one's desires and values, among which one is free to choose over the course of one's life, the greater the extent to which one attains authenticity.

I suggest that the nonrepression component of Independence conditions the value of rational preference satisfaction and is an independent component of the human good, distinct from rational preference satisfaction. This is the minimal retreat from subjectivism which is required by a reasonable position on autonomy.

Once a person who is fortunate enough to have enjoyed a nonrepressive upbringing enters maturity, however, her hypothetically rational preferences – including her hypothetically rational preferences about how her preferences might be changed – determine the value of the preferences and aims she comes to have. In some cases these ideally considered preferences will imply agreement with an authentic preference standard for weighing the value of the satisfaction of an individual's actual preferences. But in other cases they will not. The authenticity component of the Independence condition for autonomy does not determine the value of the actual preference satisfaction attained by the person. At least, this is what I shall now urge.

My claim is that whether preferences are authentic or inauthentic does not ipso facto render their satisfaction more or less worthwhile. But I am also claiming that the inauthenticity component of Independence is genuinely a requirement of autonomy: Other things being equal, a person is less autonomous if she undergoes preference change against her will. Both claims are disputable. Consider the second claim. Imagine that a person greatly values contemporary rock music and is strongly disinclined to pursue informed critical deliberation about its merits for fear that she might change her mind. One day she is tricked or coerced into a critical argument about contemporary music and her view does change in just the way she had feared. Her new musical desires, being the result of involuntary preference change, are inauthentic. But how can engagement in critical discussion leading to better informed, more reflective opinion involve a loss of autonomy? My answer is simply that the two components of autonomy that I have distinguished are independent of one another and do not necessarily rise and fall together. In the example as described, the agent becomes more critically reflective about her values, so her score on the Real Self component of autonomy rises, but because she undergoes preference change against her will, her Independence score drops. Whether she becomes more autonomous on balance depends on the relative weight that should attach to the two components of autonomy. The claim that engagement in critical reflection must always boost autonomy thus amounts to the proposal that the slightest gain or loss on the Real Self condition should count for more than any gain or loss of any size on the Independence condition. I see no reason to adopt such an extreme lexical priority ranking.

The objection to the claim that the value of satisfying a preference need not be greater or lesser depending on the degree to which it is inauthentic is essentially that the tainted genesis of a preference must lower its value. The revised subjectivist position that I defend must hold that in principle we could help a person's life go better by kidnapping him and brainwashing him in such a way that he achieves such a high level of satisfaction of his newly coercively instilled preferences that his lifetime welfare is higher than it would have been had we left him alone. I agree that revised subjectivism has this implication but I deny it is objectionable.[27]

When considering whether revised subjectivism is objectionably reductionist, there are easy and hard cases to ponder. In the easy cases, the values to which the individual is loyal are ill-considered and the individual irrationally rejects a preference change mechanism that would alter his values toward those he would now affirm if his preferences had been subjected to ideal deliberation. I now loathe art exhibits, but if dragged kicking and screaming to a museum by a friend, my values would shift and I would become a loyal patron of the arts. It is implausible to assert on a priori grounds that any such change of preference against my will must worsen my life. But revised subjectivism can yield the judgment that change of preference against the agent's will, when the agent's preferences including her aversion to this preference change would withstand ideal rational scrutiny, need not make her life go worse. And if the agent does undergo unwanted preference change in such a case, and if the new preferences would themselves withstand ideal rational scrutiny, their satisfaction is not to be discounted on account of their tainted origin – according to revised subjectivism.

Consider the following case. An independent-minded heterosexual woman is choosing whether to cohabit with a man or live alone – let us stipulate that these are the only options that are both feasible and reasonably attractive to her. Cohabiting with a man carries the advantage of an increased expectation of material prosperity and the disadvantage of an increased risk of unwanted preference change. For simplicity, suppose the woman now has just two first-order desires, a desire for material prosperity and a desire for rewarding personal achievement. If she lives alone, she can expect a low level of material prosperity and a moderate level of rewarding achievement. If she cohabits with a man, she can expect a high level of material prosperity, and an undesired change in her desires. Her desire for rewarding material achievement will gradually be replaced by the desire, which she now finds repulsive, to flatter and serve men. (So in addition to her first-order desires, the woman now is assumed to have a third desire to the effect that her present desire for rewarding achievement not give way to the alternative self-abnegating desire.) The woman understands that the desire to flatter and serve would be more easily satisfiable than the desire for rewarding personal achievement, and that the two desires are similar in the importance each would have for her, so there is a net expected utility gain if the personal achievement desire is supplanted by the self-abnegating desire. Moreover, the woman understands that both the personal achievement desire, if she keeps it, and the flatter-and-serve desire, if she acquires it, would pass the hypothetical rationality test. Once one has either desire, the rationality of keeping it would be affirmed by fully rational deliberation with full information. Suppose further that there are no other differences between the choice of living alone and the choice of living with a man that should affect the rationality of choosing either course.

Let us distinguish two significantly different ways in which the description given so far could be completed. (1) In the first variant, the woman from her present standpoint reasonably judges that she would be better off cohabiting with a man, even though this choice would bring about unwanted preference change. The disvalue to her of this unwanted preference change is outweighed by the gain she expects, and presently values, from the increased material prosperity that cohabiting will bring about. (2) In the second variant of the example, the woman from her present standpoint reasonably judges that she would be worse off cohabiting with a man, because the disvalue to her of unwanted preference change outweighs the advantages of cohabitation. This variant in turn has two subvariants worth mention: (2A) If the woman were to undergo the situation of cohabiting with a man against her will, her values would change as she expected and from this revised standpoint she reasonably would judge herself to be worse off than if she had avoided cohabitation. (2B) If the woman were to undergo the situation of cohabiting with a man against her will, her values would change as she expected and from this revised standpoint she would reasonably judge herself to be better off than if she had avoided cohabitation.

I take it that the first variant of the example is nonproblematic from the standpoint of affirming that the nonmoral value or goodness of a person's life is solely a function of the rational preference satisfaction she obtains after a nonrepressive upbringing. Some people, perhaps including me, would deny that the desire to flatter and serve men as a major aim of one's life could ever be rational. Certainly there are ways of acquiring such a desire (for example, via the belief that men are inherently superior to women or that woman's true nature is to serve) that would collapse under rational deliberation with full information. Others would affirm that the desire to flatter and serve men as a major aim of one's life could be rational.[28] But all that my position requires is agreement to a claim that is less controversial – that if a certain course of action involves fundamental preference change and if the person, judging with full deliberative rationality in the light of all pertinent knowledge, judges that this course of action is best for her both prior to the change and afterward, then this change-inducing course of action really is best for her.

Case 2A is not problematic either. If unwanted preference change renders a person worse off as she would reasonably judge the matter both before and after the change, then she is worse off, period. Here the revised subjectivist position yields the judgment that unwanted preference change can lessen the value of satisfying the changed preference. The hard case is 2B.

In this case unwanted preference change occurs, and the supplanting preference would withstand ideal rational scrutiny. Notice that this means that the knowledge of how one's preference was formed does not lessen one's commitment to it, after ideal deliberation about the preference. Given the discontinuity between what the person wants from life now (and would want if fully rational) and what she wanted earlier (and would want if fully rational), what constitutes a good life for the person? My inclination here is to let all times of the person's life count the same. At each moment of her life the person has a set of preferences (which ex hypothesi are hypothetically rational). The preferences may concern what happens to her at other times of her life. To determine how well the person lived, at the end of her days, one adds up the extent to which each moment's preferences are satisfied or frustrated. Nothing rules out the possibility that preference change against one's will might induce preferences that one will later affirm with as much reason as one now rejects them. On this view, the fact that a preference was acquired against one's will only lessens its value insofar as that fact lessens its capacity to withstand ideal well-informed rational scrutiny. Autonomy only matters insofar as we care about it (provided that caring would not dissipate with ideal reflection).

Conclusion

My tentative conclusion is that the revised subjectivist account which identifies human welfare with rational preference satisfaction is not shown to be inadequate by its failure to register the value of autonomy. The value of autonomy like the value of anything else is determined from the standpoint of each person for that person. However, the correct standard for evaluating the initial preference formation of an individual must be nonsubjectivist. But it is not true in general that autonomy conditions the value of utility. Preference satisfaction may prove not to be the entire story of human welfare, but a separate chapter for autonomy is not needed.

Notes

1 I borrow this use of the term "subjectivism" from T. M. Scanlon, "Preference and Urgency," *Journal of Philosophy* 72 (1975): 655–69. Scanlon defends the use of objective criteria of well-being in deciding issues of distributive justice.

2 My conception of wants or preferences may be idiosyncratic. I view preferences as normally involving agreement among choice behavior, felt desires, and judgments of what is nonmorally valuable for oneself. Normally when I prefer x to y it is true of me that (a) I am disposed to choose x over y, all else being equal, when presented with a choice between them, (b) when the issue is on my mind I feel that I want x more than y, other things being equal, and (c) I judge that x would be more valuable for me than y. When (a), (b), and (c) come apart, we are often unsure what preference to impute to the person who is sending conflicting signals. I stipulate

that (c), sincere judgment or verbal avowal, has priority in deciding what a person's preferences are. See my "Liberalism, Distributive Subjectivism, and Equal Opportunity for Welfare," *Philosophy and Public Affairs* 19 (1990): 158–94. See also David Lewis's discussion of "besire" in his "Dispositional Theories of Value," *Proceedings of the Aristotelian Society,* supp. vol. 63 (1989): 113–37.

3 The idea that the good for a person is constituted by the outcome of hypothetical ideal practical deliberation appears in John Rawls, *A Theory of Justice* (Cambridge, Mass.: Harvard University Press, 1971), 416–24. See also Richard B. Brandt, *A Theory of the Good and the Right* (Oxford: Oxford University Press, 1979), 110–29; also the criticisms of Brandt's notion of cognitive psychotherapy in Allan Gibbard, *Wise Choices, Apt Feelings* (Cambridge, Mass.: Harvard University Press, 1990).

4 Amartya Sen, "The Standard of Living: Lecture I, Concepts and Critiques," in Amartya Sen, John Muellbauer, Ravi Kanbur, Keith Hart, Bernard Williams, and (ed.) Geoffrey Hawthorn, *The Standard of Living* (Cambridge University Press, 1987), 11.

5 Jon Elster, "Sour Grapes," in his *Sour Grapes* (Cambridge University Press, 1983), 109–40; see 109–11.

6 To clarify: If I have undergone an unhealthy or otherwise undesirable preference formation process, my hypothetically rational preferences still provide the right measure of my welfare. Given that my life has already gone badly in this respect, the best I can hope for is satisfaction of my hypothetically rational preferences. But in this case we should be unwilling to equate satisfaction of these ideally considered preferences with attainment of a good life.

7 Lawrence Haworth, *Autonomy: An Essay in Philosophical Psychology and Ethics* (New Haven and London: Yale University Press, 1986), 169–82.

8 The quoted phrase is from T. M. Scanlon, Jr., "The Significance of Choice," in Sterling M. McMurrin (ed.), *The Tanner Lectures on Human Values,* vol. 8 (Salt Lake City: University of Utah Press, and Cambridge: Cambridge University Press, 1988), 174. See also Stanley I. Benn, *A Theory of Freedom* (Cambridge University Press, 1988), 176–83.

9 See the excellent discussion of "substantially voluntary choice" in Joel Feinberg, *Harm to Self,* vol. 2 of *The Moral Limits of the Criminal Law* (Oxford: Oxford University Press, 1986), 106–24.

10 Isaiah Berlin, "Two Concepts of Liberty," in his *Four Essays on Liberty* (Oxford: Oxford University Press, 1969), 151–52, cited after John Christman, "Introduction" to his collection *The Inner Citadel: Essays on Individual Autonomy* (Oxford: Oxford University Press, 1989), 12.

11 For an interesting discussion of this and related questions, see Gerald Dworkin, *The Theory and Practice of Autonomy* (Cambridge University Press, 1988), 21–3. See also Benn's distinctions between autonomy, autarchy, and heteronomy, in *A Theory of Freedom,* 152–83.

12 Bertolt Brecht, *The Measures Taken,* in Martin Esslin (ed. and trans.), *The Jewish Wife and other Short Plays* (New York: Grove Press, 1965), 75–108.

13 Here we should distinguish the deliberate intention to destroy one's rational faculties (as in the example in the text) from the mere countenancing of the loss of one's

rational faculties as a foreseen but unwanted byproduct of the pursuit of other goals. It is arguable that the latter need not constitute loss of autonomy.

14 Some readers may detect the threat of an infinite regress here. I disagree. In principle, the autonomous agent is disposed to undertake review of any trigger-setting decision of any higher order that comes under challenge. In practice, challenges do not emerge at any level beyond one or two iterations, and anyway the ordinary agent's capacity to hold in mind higher-order challenges and subject the object of the challenge to critical review is limited.

15 On this issue, see Robert Young, *Personal Autonomy: Beyond Negative and Positive Liberty* (London and Sydney: Croom Helm, Ltd., 1986), 46–62; also G. Dworkin, *The Theory and Practice of Autonomy*, 15–17.

16 Tony Tanner, *The Reign of Wonder: Naivety and Reality in American Fiction* (Cambridge University Press, 1965). The first quotation in the text is from page 165, the second from page 166, the third from page 168.

17 "We are afraid to put men to live and trade each on his own private stock of reason; because we suspect that the stock in each man is small, and that individuals would do better to avail themselves of the general bank and capital of nations and of ages," writes Edmund Burke in *Reflections on the Revolution in France*, cited after Jeremy Waldron, "Theoretical Foundations of Liberalism," *Philosophical Quarterly* 37 (1987): 127–50; see 149.

18 Jonathan Glover gives a succinct statement of this defense of critical reason in the context of moral judgment in his *Causing Death and Saving Lives* (Harmondsworth, Middlesex, England: Penguin Books, 1977), 29–31. The issue here is delicate, as is indicated by Philippa Foot's remarks: "For what tells us that the correct moral intuitions may not be those we think of first but later abandon ('first thoughts are best')? What tells us that primitive peoples do not have a faculty of correct moral intuition that civilization tends to destroy?" See Foot's "Introduction" to her edited collection, *Theories of Ethics* (Oxford: Oxford University Press, 1967), 3.

19 Joel Feinberg has an illuminating comparison of political autonomy and personal autonomy in *Harm to Self* (Oxford: Oxford University Press, 1987), 47–51.

20 Harry G. Frankfurt, "Identification and Wholeheartedness," in his *The Importance of What We Care About: Philosophical Essays* (Cambridge University Press, 1988), 159–76; see 171.

21 I borrow this point from John Christman, "Introduction," in his edited collection *The Inner Citadel: Essays on Individual Autonomy* (Oxford: Oxford University Press, 1989), 10.

22 G. Dworkin, *The Theory and Practice of Autonomy*, 18.

23 See the fine discussion in Feinberg, *Harm to Self*, 33–5.

24 Joseph Raz, *The Morality of Freedom* (Oxford: Oxford University Press, 1986), 394.

25 Haworth, *Autonomy*, 170–82.

26 Elster, "Sour Grapes," 135.

27 I emphasize that the issue under consideration is not whether coercive interference in people's lives with a view toward altering their values is morally objectionable and should be sanctioned. The question is whether or not in principle it could be

the case that undergoing preference change against one's will can improve one's life all things considered. For an interesting attempt in a slightly different context to argue for a negative answer to this question, see Ronald Dworkin on the "priority of ethical integrity" in his "Foundations of Liberal Equality," in Grethe B. Peterson, ed., *The Tanner Lectures on Human Values,* vol. 11 (Salt Lake City: University of Utah Press, 1990), 1–119. I discuss Dworkin's position in my "Liberal Democratic Community," forthcoming in *NOMOS XXXV: Democratic Community,* John Chapman and Ian Shapiro, eds. (New York: New York University Press).

28 George Sher might be one who would make this affirmation. See his "Our Preferences, Ourselves," *Philosophy and Public Affairs* 12,n. 1 (1983): 34–50.

4

Critical analysis and constructive interpretation

DAVID LYONS

This essay concerns two problems of legal practice – interpretation and the justification of judicial decisions. Largely because of Ronald Dworkin's work, legal theory now addresses without skeptical presumptions the issue of interpretation, and his "constructive interpretation" is the most important entrant in that field.[1] But legal interpretation (in the relevant sense of discovering the determinate meaning or implications of existing law) is not an end in itself but serves adjudication, which impinges on important human interests. For our purposes, judicial decisions should be viewed not as propositions of law but as things that are done to people in the name of the law.[2] And the things that judicial decisions do[3] to people, such as depriving them of life, liberty, or valued goods, require moral justification.

Many of those who come before courts do so under duress and have lacked a reasonable opportunity to affect the political process. We cannot assume that they would approve of the law that determines their fate or that they are committed in any way to the law that is applied against them. What is done to them in the name of the law requires substantive moral justification. And the fact that something is required by law does not itself provide such a justification.[4] So interpretive legal theory is, or should be, concerned with the justification of judicial decisions. The issues to be addressed include not only logical support for legal propositions but also the moral defensibility of their practical implications.

Constructive theory is important in part because it aims to provide guidance for interpretations that promote the moral justifiability of judicial decisions. Because what counts as law is not automatically limited by moral criteria, the achievement of that ambition encounters serious obstacles. Statutes can be morally indefensible and common law doctrines can suffer grave moral defects, so the soundest interpretive theory may be incapable of ensuring that each legal requirement enjoys some measure of moral justification.

The theory that I call "critical analysis" appears in prominent writings associated with the critical legal studies movement (CLS).[5] The features that it shares with constructive interpretation suggest the possibility that critical analysis might provide the foundation for a distinctive approach to legal interpretation, despite the fact that CLS has been linked with the notion that indeterminacy pervades the law, a view that precludes interpretation.

Section I explains the need for interpretive legal theory. Section II examines constructive interpretation and argues that it fails to justify a crucial class of decisions, including some that may not be justifiable. Section III considers critical analysis as a possible basis for legal interpretation, with constructive interpretation as a point of reference.[6]

I. The need for interpretive theory

Many theorists seem skeptical about the possibility of legal interpretation. This is not limited to those who regard the law as pervasively indeterminate, for many theorists who accept that there are legal rules with clear enough meaning hold that such meaning is more limited than the scope of the rules. They hold, in effect, that when interpretation is needed it is impossible, and courts can then decide cases only by changing the law.

A. Open texture

If law's determinate meaning is limited to what is clear and uncontroversial among competent lawyers, that stems from something distinctive about law. For the general idea that a subject matter is determinate only where experts confidently agree about it implies that facts of all kinds are creatures of confident consensus, unmade by dissensus or uncertainty which is simply implausible.

The most widely accepted basis for such an idea about law is H. L. A. Hart's theory that law is "open textured."[7] From the fact that competent language users are uncertain or disagree about some applications of a word (e.g., whether a wheelchair counts as a vehicle), Hart infers that corresponding legal propositions (e.g., whether bringing a wheelchair into a park violates the park's prohibition against vehicles) are neither true nor false. Hart speaks only of law, and he could not plausibly generalize to other subjects. For we do not generally assume, nor would it seem true, that where linguistic conventions are imprecise (where competent language users are uncertain or disagree about the applications of terms) the corresponding states of affairs are indeterminate. But Hart fails to explain why disagreement and uncertainty render law indeterminate.

So this theory about law requires justification. And there is reason to doubt it. Suppose the government uses its power of eminent domain and condemns my home to make way for a public highway. The constitution of my state says that "private property shall not be taken for public use without just compensation."[8] In the absence of strong reason to the contrary, we must suppose that this requires what it says – just compensation. The constitution does not define just compensation, and we may be uncertain or disagree about it.[9] According to open texture theory, if uncertainty or disagreement is widespread among competent language users, the provision lacks determinate meaning until a court confers such meaning on it. But that does not seem right.

Suppose a judge has to decide whether I have received just compensation. If she were interpreting the clause without aid of interpretive precedent or if she questioned past interpretations, she might reasonably believe that the answer to the legal question (How to interpret the just-compensation requirement for this sort of case?) depends on the answer to a moral question (What constitutes just compensation?). Uncertainty or disagreement about the moral question does not mean that it has no right answer. And we have as yet no other reason for concluding that there is no sound answer to the legal question.

When judges are uncertain about the law, they seem to reason about its meaning. Their interpretive arguments are subjected to appraisal by others. Unclear law is treated not as indeterminate but as subject to analysis. Disagreement does not discourage but rather spurs interpretive reasoning. These facts suggest that lawyers and judges try to interpret law and believe that interpretation is possible even when there is disagreement or uncertainty. Their practice might be misleading; they might be deceiving others or even themselves. But we lack reason to believe this. We cannot dismiss the possibility of legal interpretation, and theory is needed.

B. Original intent[10]

The most familiar interpretive legal theory is that courts should read statutory and constitutional texts in terms of what the lawmakers had in mind. Original-intent theorists believe that interpreting law by reference to that historical state of affairs respects the separation of powers that is required by both democratic principles and our constitutions. These theorists equate lawmaking with the exercise of moral judgment, which they assume need not be exercised in the process of legal interpretation.

The standard theory of original intent is misconceived. First, the intention of one who drafts or votes for a law is not an initially promising criterion of meaning. The words we use have meanings determined by social conventions. Original-intent theorists fail to explain why the meaning of written law is determined by lawmakers' purposes and the applications that they contemplate instead.

Second, the just compensation example seems to show that the desire for value-free interpretation is unrealizable.

Third, the theory is ambiguous. A drafter or adopter may intend a law to serve an identifiable purpose and intend it to have certain specific applications because he assumes that they would serve that purpose. But he may be mistaken, so his two intentions may clash. Original intent would then offer inconsistent guidance for interpretation.[11]

Fourth, original-intent theory presumably implies that a law which is drafted or adopted by several persons has determinate meaning only if there was an intentional consensus. But law makers can and often do have differing intentions. Now, it would be implausible to attribute an intention to a legislature or one of its enactments when, for example, most members intended the enactment to serve a different purpose or to apply differently. Reflection on such considerations would lead one to conclude that an intent can be attributed to a legislature only when a substantial proportion of the legislators[12] have the same intentions about its content. That condition does not always obtain.

The standard *theory* of interpretation based on original intent seems overwhelmed by such difficulties. But legal *practice* may fare better. Judicial opinions and legal commentaries often reason from framers' or legislators' intent. But these arguments often do not square with the standard theory. Because that theory regards original intent as an historical state of affairs, it requires there to have been an intentional consensus. Evidence is rarely offered to show that there was probably an intentional consensus on the point at issue. And we know that those who enact law often have differing intentions and that some who vote for a bill give it little thought. We have good reason to doubt that enactments are generally accompanied by an intentional consensus regarding the full meaningful content of the written law. But if original-intent arguments were purely historical, strong evidence that there was a relevant consensus would be needed. This crucial element is almost always missing from original-intent arguments without, however, weakening their persuasive force.

There are two possible explanations for this gap between original intent theory and practice. Either judicial references to original intent are unsubstantiated or they must be understood differently. I suggest the latter. What an original-intent argument often seems to do is identify a *plausible justifying rationale* for the legislative or constitutional provision in question.[13] Given that, we can often decide the specific interpretive issue. I believe that is how original-intent arguments often work.

Construed in this way, original-intent arguments make sense and have some hope of being sound. But then they are neither purely historical nor value free; they involve judgments of political morality. And they approximate constructive interpretation.

II. Constructive interpretation[14]

Legal interpretation is presented by Dworkin as a special case of a widely applicable approach: To interpret a social practice, we must view it in the best light. A practice is seen, if possible, as serving values that make it worthwhile. The rules of the practice are reinterpreted as needed to more effectively serve those justifying values.

Dworkin suggests "that the most abstract and fundamental point of legal practice is to guide and constrain the power of government" by reference to prior legislative, judicial, and other authoritative decisions.[15] This mode of deciding cases promotes procedural fairness and predictability. Dworkin also believes that, when past decisions are understood as committing the government to acting even-handedly, on principle, legal practice promotes "political integrity" and true political community for a heterogeneous population. Past decisions are interpreted by reference to the moral principles that provide their best justification.[16]

Dworkin's theory is meant to be both normative and descriptive: It is supposed to give *guidance* for interpretation so that judges will be able to decide cases in the way that existing law *requires* them to be decided. An interpretation must closely fit the legal facts. But Dworkin's theory is not purely descriptive. He wishes to explain how law can provide some genuine moral justification for judicial decisions. The question I shall raise is whether constructive interpretation succeeds – whether it ensures that all of the decisions it authorizes enjoy, as a consequence, some measure of justification, however slight.

Value-guided interpretation, such as Dworkin's theory requires, offers some promise of respecting this moral imperative. The constructive approach interprets law in terms of principles that are capable of providing moral justification for what is done to people. Within the constraints imposed by the descriptive aspect of genuine interpretation, this would seem to maximize the capacity of interpreted law for justifying current decisions. That improves the likelihood that applications of law will be justifiable.

Still, the normative ambition of constructive interpretation is difficult to achieve, and several features of Dworkin's theory render it more manageable. First, Dworkin holds that law enjoys a measure of justification whenever, but only when, constructive interpretation is possible. As he appreciates, a community's law can be so outrageously immoral as to provide not even the slightest justification for its application.[17] In that extreme case, constructive interpretation is inapplicable.

Second, Dworkin does not claim that the relevant law is always justifiably enforced. There can be good justification both for and against enforcement. All things considered, a legally required decision might be morally unjustifiable.[18] His theory aims only to account for defeasible justification.

Third, Dworkin believes that law can have moral force even when it is morally deficient. This corresponds to the notion that citizens can have an obligation to obey such a law. If the specific law being applied is morally deficient, some special justification is required for enforcing it. Constructive interpretation must therefore have recourse to indirect justification of what is done in particular cases.

According to Dworkin, common law decisions can be justified only by invoking moral principles. He does not assume that the common law is morally perfect. Rather, he assumes, crucially, that *nonideal* principles are capable of justifying decisions. This enables him to believe that judicial decisions can be justified under morally deficient common law doctrines.

That assumption is not implausible. In a parallel way, we may assume that we have a genuine right to compensation for economic losses that others have culpably caused us, without supposing that the system of property under which we owned what was lost is morally perfect. Even so, I am skeptical.

Here is the sort of legal situation that constructive interpretation seems clearly intended to cover. Suppose that prevailing precedent in personal injury law firmly embraces the doctrine of contributory negligence. The victim of another's negligence is entitled to compensation, but only if she has not contributed to the loss by her own negligence. This may be regarded as a plausible principle, for it requires compensation justly in many cases.

Suppose, however, that Alice was very careless and as a result Barbara suffered greatly; but Barbara was slightly careless and would otherwise have suffered slightly less. Then Barbara has no valid legal claim to any compensation from Alice. Dworkin's theory implies that a judgment denying Barbara compensation enjoys some measure of justification. Its moral force has two possible sources. One is the doctrine of contributory negligence itself. But I do not see how the fact that this principle justly requires compensation in *other* cases[19] confers some measure of justification on its application in this case. For this case is just the sort of situation that led jurists to reject the doctrine.

Nonideal principles such as contributory negligence have implications that are morally unproblematic in some cases. But these applications do not seem to confer any measure of justification upon the problematic applications. The problem for constructive interpretation is to explain how justification is conferred on applications that embody the *defects* of nonideal principles.

If nonideal principles cannot do the required work, can the principle of political integrity fill the moral gap? I do not see how. "Political integrity" is a name for the special virtue of a system in which courts view past authoritative decisions as commitments to principle. Widespread acceptance of this value is supposed to promote the most desirable form of political community, in which each member accepts a responsibility of equal concern for all other members, and the constitutional foundation of such a community is regarded as most likely to generate a genuine obligation to obey the law.[20] Suppose these claims are sound, and general acceptance of political integrity would have those desirable consequences.[21] I do not see how *that* helps to justify decisions representing the morally deficient aspects of the law. Those consequences do not seem *relevant* to the problem of justifying (say) the judgment denying Barbara compensation.

Now consider the statutory context. Dworkin seems to hold that unjustifiable statutes can justifiably be enforced. He does not explain how, but he suggests that a decision which cannot be justified directly, on its merits, may still be justifiable indirectly.

Here is an example.[22] Half a century ago, Mr. Daniels was a street trader and Mrs. Tarbard operated a pub in the South London neighborhood of Battersea. Mr. Daniels purchased a bottle of R. White's lemonade from Mrs. Tarbard at her pub. Carbolic acid was in the lemonade, and Mr. and Mrs. Daniels suffered accordingly. Carbolic acid must have combined with the lemonade in R. White's bottling plant, for the bottle remained sealed until used by Mr. and Mrs. Daniels. They sued the manufacturer of the lemonade as well as Mrs. Tarbard.

Judge Lewis applied the negligence test for manufacturer's liability, found that the evidence had not established negligence, and held the manufacturer free of legal liability. But the Sale of Goods Act made Mrs. Tarbard liable to Mr. Daniels because she sold him "goods of unmerchantable quality." Judge Lewis acknowledged that Mrs. Tarbard was "entirely innocent and blameless in the matter," but he held her liable for Mr. Daniels's loss.

We may assume that Judge Lewis believed not only that his judgment against Mrs. Tarbard was required by law but also that his rendering it was morally defensible. The latter belief bears scrutiny. He might have believed that the decision against Mrs. Tarbard was fair to her though regrettable. But his remarks suggest that it was unfair to Mrs. Tarbard, and our analytic purpose is served by considering this possibility. If he believed that his judgment was morally defensible although unfair to Mrs. Tarbard, then he must have believed it could be justified indirectly. He might have believed that imposing strict liability on retailers was justifiable despite regrettable applications. For present purposes, however, let us suppose that he had strong reservations about strict liability and regarded the statute as unfair. If so, he must have believed that unfair statutes can (sometimes) justifiably be enforced. A justification of his judgment against Mrs. Tarbard would then rest on some broader claim about, say, the virtues of that legal system or of respecting law.

In his discussion of *Daniels,* Neil MacCormick suggests some such arguments:

1. "it is good that judicial decisions be predictable and contribute to certainty of law, which they are and do when they apply known rules

identified in accordance with commonly shared and understood criteria of recognition";

2. "it is good that judges stay within their assigned place in the constitutional order, applying established law rather than inventing new law";
3. "it is good that law-making be entrusted to the elected representatives of the people, not usurped by non-elected and non-removable judges";
4. "the existing and accepted constitutional order is a fair and just system, and accordingly the criteria of recognition of laws which it institutes are good and just criteria which ought to be observed."[23]

Considerations like these are often advanced for compliance with law, especially when the relevant laws or their applications are morally problematic. They might be used to argue that the judgment against Mrs. Tarbard is justifiable; but I am skeptical.

Dworkin once presented the most important element of such arguments as follows:

The constitution sets out a general political scheme that is sufficiently just to be taken as settled for reasons of fairness. Citizens take the benefit of living in a society whose institutions are arranged and governed in accordance with that scheme, and they must take the burdens as well, at least until a new scheme is put into force either by discrete amendment or general revolution.[24]

This conventional picture of political obligation is plausible if we assume conditions such as the following: The objectionable laws are aberrations, and the objectionable applications are otherwise randomly distributed results of honest error or of the unavoidable characteristics of rules, such as under- and overinclusiveness.

But such an argument cannot be applied widely enough to serve its purpose. Such an argument is implausible when applied, for example, to someone who suffers injustice systematically under the law. The fact that benefits and political rights are enjoyed by others would not seem to justify enforcement of unjust law against its usual victims.

In some cases, justification seems quite problematic. Consider *Thomas Sims's Case.*[25] Under the Fugitive Slave Act of 1850, Sims was taken prisoner and held for a hearing before a federal commissioner. The Act provided for summary hearings in which alleged fugitive slaves could not testify. Upon hearing a claimant's evidence, a commissioner was empowered to authorize him to transport the prisoner to the slave owner's locale.

Petitioners sought a writ of *habeas corpus* for Sims on the ground that conferring judicial authority on commissioners violated the federal Constitution. The Massachusetts court rejected this argument. Chief Justice Shaw explained that he was bound by precedents validating the Act, and he defended the Fugitive Slave Clause, which was implemented by the Act, as necessary for the constitutional settlement and as proper because it served the interests of the states.

Dworkin has suggested that decisions for slave owners under the Fugitive Slave Act might enjoy some measure of justifiability.[26] The problem is how any plausible expansion of revision of Shaw's reasoning could justify the court's sending Thomas Sims to slavery.[27] As an African-American (slave or free), Sims was not a beneficiary of the constitutional accommodation. He was barred from the political processes that led to and followed from the Constitution. Neither benefits for others nor their political rights tend to confer any measure of justification for enforcement of the Fugitive Slave Act.[28]

I am not arguing against the possibility of indirect moral justification of judicial decisions. I do not assume, for example, that the *Daniels* judgment was morally indefensible. But neither do I assume the contrary. The burden of proof falls on those who wish to claim that what is done to people in the name of the law enjoys some measure of moral justification. Dworkin's arguments do not seem to sustain this burden.

III. Critical legal analysis

CLS appears to embrace a less favorable view of our law. One might therefore suppose that its approach to interpretation – if it has one – would be more sensitive to the problem of justifying what is done to people in the name of the law.

Critical scholars perceive a definite deep structure in the law. They hold that law contains some reasonably determinate rules that represent reasonably determinate underlying values. They regard those values as pregnant with further implications. This suggests that the values might provide the basis for further interpretation.

The underlying values are held to have a certain character. In any branch of law, such as contracts, property, or torts, some established rules are seen as reflecting one particular moral position, usually called "individualism," and other rules as reflecting a rival view, called "altruism."[29] It is claimed, for example, that rules holding people to contracts reflect individualism whereas rules relaxing contractual rigors reflect altruism.[30]

The opposing views have parallel structures. Each holds that we as individuals have a certain degree of responsibility for what happens to others[31] and rights to others' consideration, perhaps even to their positive help. They differ about the extent of those rights and responsibilities. Individualism maintains that it is legitimate to pursue one's own interests with less regard for others than altruism requires, and it accordingly holds that one has a narrower right to others' aid or concern.[32] Altruism maintains that we have a greater responsibility for what happens to others, a greater obligation to share one's resources and to make sacrifices for others' sake, and thus a greater right to others' consideration and positive assistance.

According to critical analysis, the law is in tension between these views. Individualism is dominant in our society, but an altruistic tendency is ineradicable. Thus law has a deep bipolar structure.

Can critical analysis ground a normative approach to legal interpretation? That possibility is suggested by the fact that individualism and altruism are seen as providing rationales for rules of law. Interpretation might be based on those values – extrapolating further from them – as in constructive theory.

There are several obstacles to developing a theory of interpretation from critical analysis. (1) It is unclear that the underlying moral positions have the requisite relation to rules – that they account for rules by *justifying* them. (2) If those values are to ground interpretations of the law, conflicts between them (or their respective rules) must be resolved in particular cases. For this to be possible, we must reinterpret the values, for they are defined in contradictory terms. But by specifically identifying the underlying values, critical analysis resists such a move. Furthermore, it seems to maintain that we lack the means for effecting a principled resolution of the conflict. (3) It is doubtful that critical scholars *want* their analysis to serve as the foundation for legal interpretation. It seems intended for a different purpose.

1. Critical analysis presents us with a puzzle: What is the relation supposed to be between either of the polar moral views and the rules it is said to explain? Compare critical analysis with constructive interpretation, which tells us that the relevant values provide the best systematic, coherent justification of past authoritative decisions. Now, one may be unhappy with this prescription; for it provides no litmus test. Different well-informed, reflective judges might reasonably reach different conclusions when attempting constructive interpretation. But at least the theory gives us a clear idea of the relation that principles must have to past political decisions in order to qualify for an interpretive role. Critical analysis, by contrast, does not clearly tell us what relation is supposed to obtain between legal rules and the underlying moral positions. We need to know this in order to understand and test its analytic claims. And if the underlying values do not account for rules and particular decisions by justifying them but have a different relation to rules, it is unclear that we should wish to or could use them as the basis for further interpretation.

One reason to suspect that the underlying values do not necessarily justify their respective rules is that critical scholars suggest more serious reservations about individualism than about altruism. They might well regard it as incapable of truly justifying rules and decisions under them. In addition, individualism and altruism may be meant to play a role within the law different from that of justifying rules. Critical scholars suggest that acceptance of the underlying values has causally contributed to the development of the law. The law serves as a repository of past political decisions, and we should expect to find within it rules representing the moral views that helped to shape them. It is plausible to suppose that law has been shaped by differing views about the rights and responsibilities that may legitimately be enforced, views that might well differ as individualism and altruism do.[33] In that case, critical analysis offers a *genetic* theory of law – an historical, causal account of legal development. And a theory that explains why decisions have been made neither promises to justify them nor clearly offers guidance for interpretation.

2. There is another bar to finding interpretive guidance in critical analysis. The conflict between individualism and altruism is supposed to be irresolvable, which explains why, according to critical analysis, judges cannot simply apply the law. Whenever judges reach for law, they find conflicting rules, alternative grounds of decision, some reflecting a wider conception of other-regarding obligations, others a narrower conception. Critical scholars maintain that those conflicts cannot be resolved without a "meta-principle."[34] And they hold that no meta-principle is available, so a judge must simply *decide* which way to go, which is why, according to critical analysis, judges cannot neutrally apply the law and why adjudication is said to lack legitimacy.

This does not mean that judicial practice is totally unpredictable. Individualism is regarded by critical scholars as the dominant view in our society, one that most judges can be expected to share. A judge who is uncertain about the law can be expected to interpret narrowly its requirements of assistance for others and to interpret broadly its recognition of a right to be free from legal intervention.

Ironically, this suggests a resolution of the conflict that critical analysis finds within the law. If individualism is the dominant tendency, one might imagine that a faithful interpretation of the law would systematically favor individualist interpretations. But I think that this would be unacceptable to critical scholars. I cannot imagine their endorsing an approach to adjudication that would reinforce individualism. Besides, as I mentioned earlier, critical scholars might well regard individualism as incapable of truly justifying rules and decisions under them. In Dworkin's terms, individualism "fits" well but fails adequately to justify the relevant decisions and rules.

The reverse applies to the opposite strategy, resolving such conflicts in favor of altruism. Critical scholars may favor altruism and may believe that it more adequately justifies the decisions and rules it has engendered. But, precisely because they hold that individualism dominates the law, critical scholars are committed to holding that altruism does not fit enough of the law to provide overall guidance for genuine interpretation.

Can one escape between the horns of this dilemma? Part of the problem is that critical scholars understand law as filled with clashing rules reflecting moral views that are *logically* incompatible. Individualism and altruism are defined so as to represent contradictory positions on issues such as the extent of one's responsibility for what happens to others. This aspect of the conflict seems avoidable. An alternative interpretation of the same body of law might depict the value conflict as a clash between, say, the principle that one may legitimately be held accountable in law for what happens to others and the principle that coercive state action should be minimized. These clash in practice, but they are not logically incompatible. Individualism and altruism could then be seen, not as the values underlying law, but as differing conceptions of the appropriate resolution of the conflict. To interpret the law, one would seek the most reasonable resolution (in general, in the branch of law, or in the particular case).

Critical scholars are mistaken if they assume that conflicting principles must necessarily be contradictories. Consider a conflict between one's obligations as a teacher and as a parent. It may be impossible for me both to stay with my sick child and to teach my scheduled class. What I should do will depend on the facts, such as whether my child requires personal attention and, if so, whether anyone else is available to provide it. It will also depend on what inconvenience my students will suffer if I do not appear. If my child is either an infant with a life-threatening condition or a capable teenager with a minor illness, the right decision may be clear. Other decisions will be more difficult. But we have no reason to assume that conflicts between obligations (or principles generally) necessarily resist rational resolution. Nor need we assume that their resolution requires recourse to "meta-principles."[35]

If we had adequate reason to analyze law in bipolar terms, with principles like the ones suggested substituting for individualism and altruism, we might have the basis for a distinctive approach to legal interpretation. The result, however, would not clearly be distinguishable from constructive interpretation.

3. Critical scholars can be expected to resist my suggested reinterpretation of the underlying values. For one thing, they specifically identify individualism and altruism as those values. Furthermore, the rhetoric of critical scholarship does not seem to encourage interpretation beyond bipolar analysis. Why should that be?

One possible reason is this. Critical scholars wish to liberate the bench and the bar from what they regard as a deeply entrenched assumption that law must continue to develop largely along individualistic lines. They emphasize the availability of alternative directions in decision making. They wish to persuade judges that they have opportunities to reform the law as they decide cases. It would seem as if they wish judges to try, where feasible, to do justice *directly* in the cases that come before them, rather than rely on law to work justice indirectly. They suggest, for example, that adjudication should favor the less advantaged, because it is reasonable to assume that their disadvantages cannot be justified and will otherwise be intensified.

Conventional wisdom counsels otherwise. It says that courts should assume that justice will be done, if not directly then indirectly, when courts apply the law as it stands. This assumes not only that law is by and large determinate (which critical scholars may mean to deny) but also that justice can effectively be done indirectly, and thus that the law merits respect. But our discussion of constructive interpretation suggests how difficult indirect justification may be.

The problem facing judges is not merely to apply the law but to render decisions that are morally defensible. Suppose, as commonly happens, the law requires interpretation. Theories of interpretation tell one how to apply it. But interpretation is problematic; one cannot be confident of success. One might reasonably have even less confidence in the moral claims that are conventionally made on behalf of adherence to existing law. Critical analysis can be understood to suggest that one often has much stronger reason to expect success if one tries to do justice directly than by trying to interpret and apply existing law.

Thus, critical scholars avoid the issue that is addressed, in effect, by constructive justification – how to show that there is at least some measure of justification (however slight) for every judicial decision that is required by law. They do so either by maintaining (perhaps unsoundly) that deep value conflicts prevent law from requiring decisions one way rather than another in particular cases; or else by advocating that judges use their opportunities to do justice directly as they decide cases (perhaps on the ground that differing decisions are unlikely to be justifiable anyway).

Neither position is adequately defended or even articulated. But our examination of these two theories about adjudication suggests that the *moral* problem facing interpretive theory is more important than the literature implies. It is in fact almost totally neglected. The simple reason, I believe, is that legal theorists generally assume (as Dworkin quite clearly does) that judicial decisions that are required by law, and thus the things that are done to people in the name of the law, normally enjoy some measure of moral justification. That assumption seems to me unwarranted. It is quite possibly wrong and demands very careful scrutiny.[36]

Notes

1 Ronald Dworkin, *Law's Empire* (Cambridge, Mass.: Harvard University Press, 1986). "Constructive" is the generic name Dworkin gives to interpretation of social practices; he calls its legal application "law as integrity." I ignore that detail here.

2 For simplicity's sake, I assume that judicial judgments are implemented. Joel Feinberg has reminded us, moreover, that legal judgments themselves have important expressive functions.

3 Or cause to be done.

4 See my "Derivability, Defensibility, and the Justification of Judicial Decisions," *Monist* 68 (1985): 325.

5 See, e.g., Duncan Kennedy, "Form and Substance in Private Law Adjudication," 89 *Harvard Law Review* 1685 (1976), and Roberto Unger, *The Critical Legal Studies Movement* (Cambridge, Mass.: Harvard University Press, 1986). For a broader sample of important CLS writings, see *Critical Legal Studies,* ed. Allan C. Hutchinson (Totowa, N.J.: Rowman & Littlefield, 1989); another CLS collection is *The Politics of Law,* Rev. Ed., ed. David Kairys (New York: Pantheon, 1990).

6 I consider these as approaches to interpretation, not as theories about the nature of law.

7 H. L. A. Hart, *The Concept of Law* (Oxford: Clarendon Press, 1961), pp. 121–32.

8 New York State Constitution, Art. 1, § 7. Compare the U.S. Constitution, Amendment V.

9 Does it depend on whether one's ownership is just, as well as lawful? If so, one must determine when ownership is just. If it doesn't (or if my ownership is just) we must determine the value of my house for the purpose. Should it be based on market price or replacement cost? How would the former be determined without a sale in a competitive market? How would replacement cost be determined? And so on.

10 I criticize original-intent theory in "Constitutional Interpretation and Original Meaning," *Social Philosophy & Policy* 4 (1986) 75, and suggest a reconstruction of original-intent practice in "Basic Rights and Constitutional Interpretation," *Social Theory and Practice* 16 (1990) 337.

11 As the disjunction "drafter or adopter" may suggest, the theory is ambiguous in other ways, too.

12 Perhaps a number sufficient to enact the legislation, counting only those who voted for it, wishing it to be enacted.

13 Note how often the *Federalist Papers* are relied upon for guidance, when no evidence is offered that they reflect a consensus among constitutional framers or ratifiers.

14 I consider Dworkin's theory (and other problems for it than those discussed here) in "Reconstructing Legal Theory," *Philosophy & Public Affairs* 16 (1987) 379.

15 Dworkin, *Law's Empire,* 93.

16 These rationales need not be laid down in written law or endorsed explicitly by courts.

17 Dworkin, *Law's Empire,* 101–8.

18 Dworkin, *Law's Empire,* 108–13 (on the "grounds" and "force" of law).

19 This is the main if not the only basis that it has for being considered the sort of principle that can be included in the constructive interpretation of a body of law.

20 Dworkin, *Law's Empire,* 190–1.

21 I see no reason to suppose that any community has ever satisfied those conditions.

22 *Daniels and Daniels v. R. White & Sons, Ltd., and Tarbard* ([1938] 4 All E. R. 258).

23 Neil MacCormick, *Legal Reasoning and Legal Theory* (Oxford: Clarendon Press, 1978), 63–4.

24 Dworkin, *Taking Rights Seriously,* 106 ("Hard Cases").

25 61 Mass. (7 Cush.) 285 (1851).

26 In Dworkin's "'Natural' Law Revisited," 34 *University of Florida Law Review* 186 (1982).

27 It has been suggested that the arrangements could be justified as mere extradition hearings, to be followed by regular trials in the claimants' locales (see Allen Johnson, "The Constitutionality of the Fugitive Slave Acts," 31 *Yale Law Journal* 161 [1921–2]). It is unclear how this warrants excluding testimony from prisoners or how realistic it was to suggest that alleged fugitives would receive fair hearings in slave owners' courts.

28 I do not consider the possibility that political integrity might justify the application of unjust statutes because it is unclear how it might help in a statutory context. In *Law's Empire,* Dworkin suggests that indirect justification in a statutory context relies upon fairness in the distribution of political power. My point is that such fairness as could have been found in the contemporary system is irrelevant to justifying what was done to Sims in the name of the law.

29 The terms vary. Individualism is sometimes opposed by "communitarianism." In a constitutional context the poles may be seen as "liberalism" and "civic republicanism."

30 As both enforcement of and refusal to enforce a contract are advantageous to one party and disadvantageous to another, this analysis needs justification. Enforcement requires one party to serve another's interests, so it could be thought to reflect altruism instead of individualism; nonenforcement benefits one party at some cost to the other, so it could be thought to reflect individualism instead of altruism. If a given rule is to be associated with one position to the exclusion of the other, that must depend on other factors. Thus Kennedy suggests that individualism embodies the ideal of "self-reliance," whereas altruism represents a notion of interdependence.

31 And that we may justifiably *be held accountable by law* for what happens to others. The descriptions offered of the polar positions typically ignore the possibility that some moral rights and obligations should not be enforced by law.

32 As noted above, critical analysis associates "self-reliance" with this view. I focus on the relevant moral principles, but that may not do justice to the analytic theories.

33 This represents only part of the explanation for the bipolar analysis of law as is found in CLS writings. Critical analysis has other sources, such as a predilection for Hegelian dialectics and the idea that humans are torn between social and antisocial dispositions reflecting our simultaneous need for and vulnerability to others.

34 See, e.g., J. M. Balkin, "Taking Ideology Seriously," 55 *University of Missouri-Kansas City Law Review* 421 (1987), and Clare Dalton, "An Essay In the Deconstruction of Contract Doctrine," 94 *Yale Law Journal* 1025–6 (1985).

35 My impression, however, is that philosophers have not addressed sufficiently the question whether the rational resolution of a conflict between principles requires appeal to a further principle.

36 Early versions of this paper were presented at Brooklyn Law School, Cornell University, the Graduate Center of the City University of New York, the University of Kansas, McGill Law School, Tulane Law School, and a joint symposium of the Canadian Philosophical Association and the Canadian Society for Social Philosophy. I am grateful to Greg Alexander, David Dyzenhaus, Stephen Massey, and Roger Shiner for comments.

5

Liberalism, free speech, and justice for minorities

DAVID A. J. RICHARDS

Joel Feinberg's political philosophy is to twentieth century thought what John Stuart Mill's was to that of the nineteenth century, the classic contemporary articulation of the moral demands of liberal conscience.[1] Feinberg, like Mill, has focussed on that subclass of demands imposing limits on the criminal law as a distinctive form of political power requiring justification. Those demands are of two sorts: the specially stringent limits on the criminalization of expressions of conscience and speech, and the general limiting principles on the criminalization of acts in general. Feinberg, like Mill, has sought to articulate common principles governing both areas, for example, principles requiring some showing of harm or offense to others as a necessary condition of criminal liability. Presumably, such principles would, if plausible, explain the special burden of justification required to justify abridgement of expressions of conscience or speech in contrast to acts in general. For example, the criminalization of conscience might, on grounds of the harm principle, more often illegitimately fail to satisfy this principle than criminalization of acts in general. That fact, if it is a fact, might explain why the abridgement of conscience more often fails to satisfy the demands of liberal principle than the criminalization of acts as such, and thus the special stringency of the political principles limiting the abridgement of speech.

The idea of a unified liberal theory of this sort is subject, however, to two kinds of objections, one internal to the project, the other external. The internal objection queries whether anything so simple as the harm principle can explain the special protection liberalism extends to conscience and speech. For example, much speech harms people, and many self-regarding acts harm no one, so the special protection of speech in contrast to action seems misplaced on grounds of the harm principle. Something more by way of principle is apparently required to justify the characteristically liberal concern for protection of conscience and speech.[2]

The external objection does not infer from such consequences of the reasonable interpretation of the harm principle that the principle is itself questionable, but on the ground of the harm principle questions the liberal project itself, in particular, the protection liberalism accords forms of conscience and speech that apparently work injustice on minorities. The classic example of such harmful speech has been blatantly racist and anti-Semitic speech, speech that libels a group by falsely attributing to members of the group morally degrading characteristics[3]; a more recent example to similar effect is pornography that allegedly libels women as such by falsely attributing to them a morally degrading sexual availability, including desires to be raped.[4] If the harm principle limits criminalization to speech or action that on balance inflicts harms on persons, group libel, so the external objection goes, inflicts such harms; and thus the liberal protection of such speech is misplaced. Sometimes, this external objection is expressed as a more general critique of liberal individualism and neutrality on the ground that its intrinsically atomist and abstract modes of argument fail to capture, indeed render invisible and inarticulate, the distinctive forms of injustice that racism and sexism inflict on minorities.[5] Liberalism and these claims of injustice work, as it were, at cross purposes; and liberalism, because it cannot give these claims the weight they deserve, must yield place to political theories less wedded to its internal ideals of individualism and neutrality.

I want to offer here a critical response to the external objection that addresses its central concern, the nature and weight of the distinctive injustices inflicted by racism and sexism and the remedies appropriate to such injustices. The two questions – the nature of the substantive injustice and its remedy – are fundamentally integrated, as the external objection itself makes clear. It is precisely because the external objection interprets the injustice of racism and sexism in a certain substantive way that it takes the prohibition of the harm inflicted by group libel as a remedy appropriate to ending that injustice. My argument will be, to the contrary, that the proper analysis of the injustice of both racism and sexism necessarily makes reference to rights-based liberal political theory and that the appropriate remedies for such evils must reasonably respect the basic rights (including free speech) on which their critical analysis stands. I begin with the analysis of the evil of racism and examine the constitutionality of group libel laws from that perspective, and then offer a similar discussion of sexism and corresponding constitutional doubts about antipornography laws.[6]

I. The injustice of racism

We need to ask initially how we should properly understand what the injustice of racism is. A useful starting point is the criticism of John Hart Ely's theory of judicial review.[7]

Ely stands out among contemporary constitutional theorists by virtue of his serious attention to both good arguments of critical historiography and his honesty in acknowledging the normative arguments central to that history, in particular, arguments protective of both enumerated and unenumerated basic human rights.[8] An interpretivist theory of the Constitution would, Ely argues, fully protect rights, including an unenumerated right like the constitutional right to privacy extended to a woman's right to an abortion in *Roe v. Wade.*[9] However, Ely argues that the historically based interpretivist theory of the Constitution must be critically assessed in light of the best political theory of democratic constitutionalism, a theory Ely associates with the Reconstruction Amendments in general and the Equal Protection Clause of the Fourteenth Amendment in particular. If the interpretivist theory yields a result inconsistent with the political theory, that result is wrong; *Roe v. Wade,* though having a sound interpretivist basis in American constitutional history, is wrong because the judicial decision cannot be supported by what Ely takes to be the best democratic political theory.

The two parts of Ely's theory work at critical cross purposes in this way because of the nature of the political theory that he takes to be the best democratic political theory of equal protection. That theory is skeptical about arguments of human rights because Ely finds contemporary theories of rights to be so controversial.[10] In the past, such forms of rights-skepticism have been advocated by constitutional theorists, like Learned Hand, as a consequence of Bentham's utilitarian skepticism about rights (as, famously, "nonsense on stilts").[11] The utilitarian requirement of maximizing the net balance of pleasure over pain of all sentient beings may often, on this view, require that some minority's interests be sacrificed to the extent required to secure a greater aggregate over all; arguments of human rights, that often protect certain interests from such sacrifice, are invalid because they frustrate the utilitarian imperative; they are nonsense on stilts because they have no foundation in the only solid basis ethics can have, namely, utilitarianism. Ely does not expressly avow utilitarianism as the basis for his skepticism about rights, including it (with rights-based ethical theories) as one among the unacceptably controversial political theories now in the field.[12] Ely's version of the best democratic political theory is presented as an appropriately noncontroversial, because nonsubstantive, political theory, namely, fair representation.

Fair representation interprets the values of political democracy in terms of whether the persons in the relevant political community affected by the state's actions have been fairly represented in the political process leading to these actions. The theory is strongly supportive of political democracy because it clearly calls for equal political rights as one way of insuring the required fair representation; it supports the institutions of constitutional democracy because it requires judicial intervention in a political process of equal voting rights when that process expresses prejudices that fail to give fair representation to the interests of a minority victimized by such prejudices. Ely identifies two relevant kinds of such prejudice: first-order prejudice, like blind racial hatred, that is aggressively hostile to the interests of a racial minority; and second-order prejudice that expresses itself in the use of stereotypes – "those involving a generalization whose incidence of counterexample is significantly higher than the legislative authority appears to have thought it was."[13] *Roe v. Wade,* however well rooted in interpretivist constitutional history, is illegitimate because it does not, in the required way, rectify unfair representation; indeed, on some views, it itself unfairly fails to give weight to relevant interests (those of fetuses).[14]

The appeal of Ely's version of democratic political theory is its putatively nonsubstantive, procedural character. But its proceduralism is a sham, resting on some substantive normative metric that delegitimates the frustration of certain human interests (those of victimized minority groups) by certain kinds of motivated political action by dominant majorities. Why these interests and those motivations? One natural explanation would be that some appropriately defined utilitarian principle forbids such actions by the state in order to realize the higher net aggregate of pleasure over pain produced by the prohibition of the infliction of the severe frustration of human interests for no correspondingly weighty gain in the pursuit of welfare. If so, Ely's rights-skepticism rests on an unexamined commitment to utilitarianism at its foundations. Or, it rests on some form of value comparison or even rights-based metric (weighing certain interests as more weighty than others) that is clearly substantive in nature. Ely's proceduralism, allegedly attractive because of its nonsubstantive character, assumes a substantive political theory. Ely's repudiation of substantive moral theory rests on a substantive theory, one that substitutes labels for the kind of careful weighing of substantive moral arguments that the issue surely deserves if it is to be the Archimedean point from which interpretive history is to be criticized and sometimes rejected.

The theoretical incoherence of Ely's argument undermines the interpretive cogency of his affirmative case for judicial intervention. Such intervention rests on the alleged political unfairness of two kinds of prejudice. But the first kind of prejudice, overt racial hostility, captures only the most blatantly obvious evils of racial discrimination; it fails clearly to articulate the nature of the political evil even in so clearly unconstitutional a practice as state-sponsored racial segregation,[15] which has certainly been justified (the doctrine of separate but equal) as the best way of assuring the interests of all alike.[16] And the second kind of prejudice, resting on factually inaccurate stereotypes, fails to take seriously the powerful constitutional objections to be made to factually accurate stereotypes that rest on and therefore legitimate a prior history of unjust subjugation.[17] Ely's quasi-utilitarian account of prejudice is aspect blind to the nature of the political evil central to much equal protection jurisprudence, a jurisprudence that it was surely Ely's purpose to defend in contrast to the substantive due process jurisprudence that he meant to condemn. He has neither well defended the one, nor fairly attacked the other.

Ely's political theory of equal protection, precisely because it is not well defended as the substantive political theory it is, gives no compelling reason to interpret the Constitution in one way or not interpret it in another. Certainly, Ely's attempt to edit and revise an interpretivist reading of American constitutional history (that takes seriously its commitment to the protection of human rights both enumerated and unenumerated) wholly fails. He has offered a freestanding political theory, against which interpretivist history is found wanting, but he has given us neither a well argued political theory nor a good reason for subverting interpretivism. The challenge must be, in the wake of Ely's incoherence, to investigate whether we may construct both a better political theory and, at the same time, a better interpretation of our tradition.

To understand racism and sexism as injustices condemned by American constitutional principles of equal protection, we must take seriously, in a way Ely does not, the kind of class-based deprivation of basic human rights fundamental to our understanding of these prejudices as distinctive constitutional evils. The constitutional concern for racism as a political evil arose from antebellum abolitionist rights-based analysis.[18]

The key to the abolitionist position was their very unpopular attack on the colonization movement, the idea, advocated by Jefferson among others,[19] that abolition of slavery would be followed by colonization of freedmen abroad. Garrison prominently attacked colonization because it expressed and reenforced "those unchristian prejudices which have so long been cherished against a sable complexion" taking blacks to be "a distinct and inferior case"[20] – what Lowell called "a depraved and unchristian public opinion".[21] The gravamen of the accusation was that American conscience had assuaged its guilt about the evil of slavery by advocating a policy, abolition and colonization, which rested on the more fundamental evil of racism, the evil on which both the injustice of slavery and of discrimination against free blacks rested.

The most remarkably perceptive and probing abolitionist analysis of the moral evil of racial prejudice and its role in American politics was L. Maria Child's *An Appeal in Favor of Americans Called Africans*.[22] Basing her argument on Montesquieu's theories, Child offered the most elaborate abolitionist criticism of the common American racist assumption of the inferiority of blacks and urged "that the present degraded condition of that unfortunate race is produced by artificial causes, not by the laws of nature."[23] The evil of racial prejudice was to make of the product of unjust institutions, subject to criticism and reform, "a fixed and unalterable law of our nature, which cannot possibly be changed".[24] In truth, "[w]e made slavery, and slavery makes the prejudice".[25] Correspondingly, the alleged inferior capacities of blacks are themselves the product of unjust cultural patterns, and cannot, without vicious circularity, justify unequal treatment; for, by virtue of that policy,

. . . the wrongs of the oppressed have been converted into an argument against them. We first debase the nature of man by making him a slave, and then very coolly tell him that he must always remain a slave because he does not know how to use freedom. We first crush people to the earth, and then claim the right of trampling on them for ever, because they are prostrate.[26]

The abolition of slavery in the North did not, Child argued, exempt the North from her criticism, since the North practiced a range of discriminations against blacks (including laws requiring segregation and forbidding intermarriage, schooling, voting, travel, and the like) resting on unjust racial prejudice; her cogent criticism of the antimiscegenation laws (on the ground that "the government ought not to be invested with power to control the affections, any more than the consciences of citizens"[27]) was, in her historical context, especially remarkable. And, anticipating de Tocqueville,[28] Child argued:

Our prejudice against colored people is even more inveterate than it is at the South. The planter is often attached to his negroes, and lavishes caresses and kind words upon them, as he would on a favorite hound: but our cold-hearted, ignoble prejudice admits of no exception – no intermission.[29]

Comparing the strength of racial prejudice in America with that in other countries (including countries that retain slavery), Child concluded: "no other people on earth indulge so strong a prejudice with regard to color, as we do".[30]

The abolitionists' quite modern critical insight into the cultural roots of racism (its essential confusion of culture with nature[31]) was integrally connected to the centrality to their criticism of slavery of the argument of toleration. The abolitionists were committed to the right of radical Protestant moral conscience, and they made central to their criticism of slavery the way in which it depended on the abridgement of the right to conscience, both of slaves and of anyone who would criticize the institution. They understood, in a way in which no other Americans of their generation did, the extent to which the political legitimation of slavery in Protestant America depended on, *indeed compelled* the assumption that blacks were, in their nature, what Augustinian intolerance supposed could be only the product of a culpable defect in will, namely, blind heretics, what in 1834 the Synod of South Carolina called "that heathen of this country . . . [who] will bear comparison with the heathen of any part of the world".[32] On the abolitionist view, racism is, as it were, toleration's evil genius of unreason, arising and sometimes flourishing in reaction to what appear to be the greatest achievements of political reason (for example, a constitution committed to universal toleration).

The abolitionist insight captured an important truth about the origins of slavery in colonial America and perhaps a deeper truth about the enduring cultural roots of American racism and its modern European analogue, anti-Semitism. The point about origins was the early historical justification of slavery on the ground that blacks were heathen non-Christians,[33] perhaps an outgrowth of the Spanish and Portuguese association of blacks with the dangerous infidelity of the moor[34] and the putative legitimacy of enslavement of infidels.[35] Shakespeare's *Othello* certainly supports an English conflation of blacks and moors, and suggests corresponding anxieties and fears centering on race and sex.[36] Desdemona's father, Brabantio, who had welcomed Othello into his house, is easily persuaded by Iago that the marriage was "against all rules of nature"[37], which suggests prejudice easily rationalized as natural group boundaries not to be breached. Such a "folk bias"[38] against blacks thus probably antedated slavery in Britain's American colonies, and hardened into racism under the impact of the special harshness of American slavery. Colonial Americans found it all too natural to legitimate the permanent enslavement of blacks, even after their religious conversion, on the racist assumption that blacks so lacked moral capacity that they were, so to speak, heathens permanently and thus exiled from a political community whose condition of unity was the moral powers fundamental to the principal of toleration.

The abolitionist theory of racism offers a cultural analysis both of how this was done and how it was sustained. American racism arose reactively as a way of justifying cultural boundaries of moral and political community – ostensibly universalistic in their terms – that had already excluded a class of persons from the community. Slavery was such an excluding institution, and it was historically based on a folk bias against Africans that centered on their unfamiliar culture for which color became a kind of proxy. A public culture, based on the principle of toleration, is and should be open to all persons on fair terms of freedom of conscience and moral and cultural pluralism. American slavery not only violently disrupted and intolerantly degraded the culture of African slaves; but the peculiarly onerous nature of American slavery (prohibitions on reading and writing, on religious self-organization, and on marriage, and limitations and eventual prohibitions on manumission)[39] deprived black slaves of any of the rights and opportunities that the public culture made available to others, including respect for their creative moral powers of rational and reasonable freedom in public and private life. The nature of American slavery and the associated forms of racial discrimination against free blacks both in the South and North had socially produced the image of black incapacity that ostensibly justified their permanent heathen status (outside the community capable of Christian moral freedom). For the abolitionists, consistent with the argument for toleration, slavery and discrimination were forms of religious, social, economic, and political persecution motivated by a politically entrenched conception of black incapacity that enforced its own conception of truth against both the standards of reasonable inquiry and the reasonable capacities of both blacks and whites that might challenge the conception. A conception of political unity, subject to reasonable doubt as to its basis and merits, had unreasonably resolved its doubts in the irrationalist racist certitudes of group solidarity on the basis of unjust group subjugation. Frederick Douglass, the leading black abolitionist, stated the abolitionist analysis with a classical clarity:

Ignorance and depravity, and the inability to rise from degradation to civilization and respectability, are the most usual allegations against the oppressed. The evils most fostered by slavery and oppression are precisely those which slaveholders and oppressors would transfer from their system to the inherent character of their victims. Thus the very crimes of slavery become slavery's best defence. By making the enslaved a character fit only for slavery, they excuse themselves for refusing to make the slave a freeman.[40]

The abolitionists thought of the political evil of racism in America as more fundamental an evil than slavery itself. It was the political evil in terms of which Americans justified slavery, and its evils could, if unrecognized and unremedied, corrupt abolition by means of the illegitimate construction of the boundaries of moral and political community on terms that excluded blacks (as colonization had).

The cultural construction of racism accordingly required exclusion from the competence for the rights that were central to the moral identity of the culture: conscience, free speech, intimate personal and family life, free labor, and the like. These rights are, in their nature, culture-creating rights, forms of moral creativity through which people authenticate themselves, the larger meaning of their lives, and the culture of public reason that affords the resources of critical reflection, testing, imagination, and scientific and humane learning required for exercise of our moral powers as persons. The systematic denial of these rights to any group is, at least from the perspective of the dominant culture, a kind of condemnation of that group to cultural death and deformed marginality, a form of denationalization.[41]

The condition of the national identity of dominant white America was the effective construction of its negative identity (what an American is not) by means of a culturally defined image of a race-defined people whom it must give lower moral status on the familiar grounds that various rights were not in order because of underlying incapacity. Under slavery, the image of blacks as subhuman was constructed on the basis of alleged incapacities disqualifying them from basic rights: for example, incapacity for moral reflection and deliberation (no right to conscience), lack of reasoning skills including incapacity for literacy (no right of free speech), incapacity for responsible sexual intimacy and moral education of the young (lack of privacy rights of sexual autonomy and family integrity), and lack of rational powers for many forms of work calling for independent exercise of rational powers (no right to free labor).[42] The underlying image of incapacity, itself constructed on the basis of the abridgement of such rights, was then used as the allegedly reasonable basis, grounded in natural race differences, for the subjugation of blacks by means of the forms of rather total control that American slavery – in contrast, for example, to that in Latin America – peculiarly involved (including abridgements of legal rights to religious liberty, free speech, and family life, and restrictions on manumission).[43] A group, thus supposedly by nature not entitled to the basic rights constitutive of American nationality, could not, by definition, be part of American nationality.

The depth of the abolitionist criticism of American racism was to observe that the same definition of national identity that had justified slavery in the South also justified racial discrimination against free blacks both in the South and the North.[44] The alleged inferior capacities of blacks as a class (itself constructed on the basis of abridgement of rights) was then invoked as the reasonable ground on which one might exclude blacks from the extent of the protection of rights accorded whites. The alleged inferiority of blacks could not, on this view, justify slavery, but it could justify deprivations of rights aimed to exclude blacks from the political community, including constitutional provisions in several states forbidding blacks to enter[45] and various discriminatory measures in voting rights, education, and the like that would encourage free blacks to leave.[46] The natural expression of this view, as some abolitionists clearly saw, was the advocacy of abolition on terms of colonization abroad, confirming the basic racist image of the terms of American national identity – a view defended in the antebellum period even by Lincoln.[47] The abolitionist analysis of the evil of racism (the unjust construction of a national identity on the basis of the abridgement of human rights) thus applied to both slavery and racial discrimination, and the theorists of radical antislavery drew the required inference that blacks must be fully included in the terms of a national citizenship that extended equal protection of basic rights to all.

The transformation of religious persecution into racial degradation is the key to this analysis. The racist subjugation of blacks took root in America under the circumstances of the American institution of slavery combined with the denial that blacks, as "heathens," were within the ambit of the argument for toleration.[48] Religious persecution here took the form of enforcement at large of a politically entrenched view of religious truth that condemned "heathen" forms of cultural life as not reasonably entitled to respect; in effect, a political orthodoxy (concerned to maintain slavery as an institution) both imposed on the "heathen" sectarian standards of what counted as reasonable thought and inquiry and, on that ground, degraded them from the status of persons capable of exercising moral powers reasonably. Religious persecution became racist subjugation when the sectarian enforcement of the political orthodoxy unreasonably interpreted the "heathens" as not merely wilfully blind to religious truth (as Augustine supposed the Donatists to be[49]), but constitutionally incapable of the moral powers that entitle one to be regarded as a bearer of rights at all. The central mechanism of the cultural construction of racism was the radical isolation (through the institution of slavery and practices of racial discrimination) of a race-defined people from the public culture of equal rights extended to all others, and, on the basis of that unjust exclusion, then unreasonably to condemn their culture and, ultimately, them as irrationally subhuman. The mechanism of such isolation was, as we have seen, the abridgement of the culture-creating rights central to the public culture of equal rights; deprived of those rights (to conscience, free speech, education, family life, labor), blacks were supposed to be an inferior people not entitled to membership in the moral community. Accordingly, the idea of racist degradation must be interpreted in terms of these deprivations, and its operative constitutional meaning understood accordingly.

Racism as a constitutional evil thus rests on a history and culture of the moral subjugation of a race-defined group based on that group's unjust exclusion from the inalienable rights of the public culture of the nation; the analysis of this evil is, *pace* Ely, ineliminably rights-based. If the underlying substantive injustice of racism is to be thus understood, the appropriate remedies must be understood in terms of it; guaranteeing access to the basic rights of the public culture on fair terms must be fundamental. Both desegregation and affirmative action make remedial sense in these terms, reasonably advancing the goal of the just inclusion of black Americans in the public culture that unjustly excluded them.[50] These are legitimate exercises of state power (extending basic rights) required by aims of justice (defined by rectifying exclusion from such rights).

But the legitimacy of putative remedies for the injustice of racism (defined as the deprivation of culture-creating rights) cannot reasonably extend to measures that themselves violate the very respect for such rights that motivates the remedial project. The political evil of racism crucially rests on the enforcement on society at large of sectarian political epistemologies of racial inferiority that unreasonably excluded black Americans from equal respect for basic rights like conscience and speech. The wrong of abridgement of such basic rights is the state's interposition of its view of the worth or value of conscience or speech in place of the exercise of the moral powers of rational and reasonable judgment regarding such matters. If racism is in part rooted in such abridgements of basic rights, it cannot be a reasonable remedy for racism as such for the state to abridge such rights even when its ostensible purposes are to combat racist attitudes. The roots of racism, that lie in the deprivation of such rights, require the fair empowerment of the subjugated people themselves to assert, exercise, demand, and cultivate such rights on their own terms as free people.

The interposition of the state in these matters enlists state power in the support and legitimation of what counts as a group identity and the proper respect owed that identity as the measure of what can count as reasonable public debate about such matters. But, the state's judgments in this domain are no more impartially reasonable than they are in the area of religion or politics; the state here enforces inevitably crude majoritarian stereotypes of group identity on a par with similarly illegitimate enforceable state judgments about true religion and good politics. The relationship between individual and group identity must, in a free society, be open to the fullest range of reasonable discussion and debate on terms that allows persons to question, debate, and renegotiate their evaluative understanding of value in living on their own terms, including the relationship between their sense of themselves as individuals and as self-identified members of various groups. The terms of individual and group identity must, in a free society, be open to broad and robust discussion and debate to allow the fullest range of public intelligence and imagination reasonably to be available to all on terms that respect moral autonomy and individuality. Otherwise, essential issues of public debate about value in living – the very terms of one's moral integrity – will be truncated to the measure of unreflective and oppressive majoritarian stereotypes. It cannot be a reasonable remedy for racism to legitimate a power in the state that perpetuates racism's stereotypical evils.

Group libel laws are for these reasons constitutionally suspect under current American law.[51] Such laws, making it a criminal and/or civil wrong to engage in defamation of racial, ethnic, or religious groups, require a demonstration that claims about certain groups subject its members to false disparagement of social esteem, like the harm inflicted on a person by a libel of him as an individual. But the analogy to individual libel is defective in ways of grave constitutional concern. Individual libel actions have two distinctive features: They require the publication of false facts, often known to be false or easily thus ascertainable; and belief in such false facts by the audience, which naturally disparages the reputation of the individual expressly written or spoken about. But the communications, restricted by group libel, express general conscientious views of speakers and audiences, whose nature and effect both depend on evaluative conceptions. Group libel actions, in contrast to individual libel actions, require the state to make abstract evaluative judgments about the value of what is said and about the legitimacy of the objection taken to the assertions. These state judgments about the nature and effect of communicative utterances place group libel laws at the heart of the values of free speech.

In effect, a broad range of personal grievances at hearing conscientious views opposed to one's own (and rebuttable as such) triggers state prohibitions. Inevitably, such laws impose state restrictions in the core area of evaluative conceptions appealing to the moral powers of speakers and audiences on the basis of state judgments of the worth of such conceptions, thus usurping the sovereign moral judgment of free people.

The point is not that state judgments about the worthlessness or viciousness of such speech are necessarily false. Indeed, because the speech may be uncontroversially false to the central conscientious conceptions of democratic majorities (and thus rebuttable by them), it is all the more urgent that equal respect forbids *state* prohibition of such speech. Persons, consistent with principles of equal respect, must themselves deliberatively express their disagreements with others on the terms of civility that affirm and express the moralizing experience of a moral community of equal respect for the sovereign moral judgment of free people. Group libel laws are inconsistent with this conception of equal respect.

It is, of course, true that racist attitudes and practices are themselves inconsistent with equal respect, indeed that they socially degrade persons from the recognition and respect due them as equal moral persons. It is facile, however, to suppose that it is a reasonable remedy for such unjust degradation for the state to forbid the verbal utterance of speech expressive of such unjust degradation in the absence of any clear understanding of the nature of the underlying injustice. If, as I have argued, the nerve of the underlying injustice is the abridgement of basic culture-creating rights, the reasonable remedy is the forceful guarantee of such rights – exercised, claimed, articulated, demanded in the public culture in the voice and in terms of the vision of those heretofore culturally marginalized, silenced, excluded, ignored. Such forceful recognition of basic rights is advanced, not retarded, by a regime of free speech, like that of the United States, that regards group libel laws as constitutionally suspect.[52] We need surely an explanation of why this has been so in the historical experience of the United States, and the underlying theory of the injustice and remedy of racism, here proposed, offers such a theory. The unconstitutionality of group libel laws has not retarded the struggle of racial justice through law because it has affirmed the forceful respect for basic rights that has empowered and energized black Americans to demonstrate their moral powers as free people in their own terms as persons worthy of equal respect.[53]

II. The injustice of sexism

A comparably forceful argument can and should be made against the similar claim that antipornography laws are reasonable ways to secure women their just claims to equal respect. The antipornography claim, like that in support of group libel laws, focusses on the remedy of widespread unjust degrading attitudes, in this case, sexist attitudes that reduce the moral personality of women solely to their sexuality, allegedly ascribing to them sexual interests (for example, enjoying rape) that they lack. But, again, it is facile to suppose that it is a reasonable remedy for such unjust degradation for the state to forbid the verbal utterance of speech allegedly expressive of such unjust degradation in the absence of any clear understanding of the nature of the underlying injustice. In the case of pornography, unlike group libel, the very judgment that the speech in question degrades is a highly controversial interpretive claim, and we urgently need, to make sense of its merits, as in the case of racism, an understanding of the underlying substantive injustice of sexism.

That injustice crucially turns on the required ethical analysis of the history and culture of gender hierarchy. Contractualist ethical analysis requires us to ask whether this politically enforceable conception of gender hierarchy could be reasonably justifiable to all subject to political power in terms of respect for inalienable human rights and the public interest. The argument for toleration was so profoundly important in the abolitionist ethical analysis of the wrongness of racism because it powerfully articulated a demanding perspective of ethical impartiality for the critical analysis of patterns of political degradation (including both slavery and racial discrimination) that deprived persons of inalienable human rights on the basis of political epistemologies themselves hostage to the political degradation in question and immunized from wider reasonable public criticism by the abridgement of such rights of both the oppressed class of persons and others critical of such institutionalized degradation. The pattern of analysis clarifies as well the fundamental political evil in the history and culture of gender hierarchy.

By gender hierarchy, I understand the distribution of the basic goods of life (including rights and responsibilities) associated with social and political life in terms of dominant and often exclusive control of the most culturally valued goods by and at the discretion of men; the hierarchy of power and privilege is the consequence of masculine control over these goods, to which women have access only at the discretion of men.

The nature and defects of the justifications offered for the history and culture of gender hierarchy may be usefully examined in the arguments of presumptive public reason offered by philosophers of the Western tradition who, as philosophers, professed a commitment to press critical and abstract public argument as far as it could reasonably be pressed. If there is a notable gap between their professions and their performance that can be analyzed, its analysis affords constitutionally relevant insight into the nature and extent of the political corruption of public reason required to support gender hierarchy that may have been pervasively influential on thought and practice.[54] No one would ever suppose than an ancient political philosopher as communitarian as Aristotle or a modern philosopher as rights-based as Rousseau would have much in common on any question, but their structurally similar defenses of gender hierarchy, within political philosophies otherwise so radically different, suggest a pervasive rationalization for gender hierarchy throughout the Western political tradition. Aristotle offered a functionalist account of women's nature inferred from the conventional roles as wife and mother defined for them in his society, concluding, on that basis, that women have a moral nature inferior to men but superior to that of natural slaves[55] (persons, for Aristotle, so lacking moral capacity that they may be justly enslaved[56]); Rousseau, who demanded of men full commitment to both the equal rights of citizens and of mankind, exempted women from both these rights and responsibilities on grounds of a romantic nature, as wife and mother, incapable of these demands.[57] In both Aristotle and Rousseau, public reason was interpreted in terms of a functionalist account of women's conventional social roles to yield a view of woman's nature on the basis of which women's place in the gender hierarchy was ethically and politically justified.

What makes the comparison between Aristotle and Rousseau so striking is that they use the same basic functionalist analysis of women's nature to the same political effect although they offer such divergent general views of how justification in politics should be ethically understood. Aristotle's basic ethical theory is perfectionist with a corresponding greater ethical weight accorded certain excellences of thought and action that are to be fostered by those incapable of such excellences, including (for Aristotle) those classes of persons justly deprived of rights by institutions of slavery and the subjection of women[58]; but Rousseau's basic ethical theory is contractualist and egalitarian, with slavery ruled out as, in principle, inconsistent with respect for inalienable human rights.[59] How has contractualist political theory, understood by a rights-based interpreter like Rousseau as antislavery, been rendered consistent with the legitimation of gender hierarchy?

The question is not unique to the contractualism of Rousseau though it was given there much the most extravagant romantic expression it was to receive. Leading other expositors of contractualist political theory – whose use of it diversely included Hobbes's defense of political absolutism[60] and Locke's[61] and Kant's[62] defenses of rights-based constitutionalism – also ultimately legitimated gender hierarchy. How has contractualist political theory (particularly, the rights-based interpretation of it in Locke, Rousseau, and Kant) been, at once, so critical of slavery, yet so legitimating of gender hierarchy?

Rousseau's political theory gave such an arresting expression to this ethical paradox because he so sharply distinguished what he regarded as the premoral relationships of the state of nature from the ethical reconstruction and transformation of the abstract moral powers of human nature in a political society organized on proper contractualist lines (in accord with his conception of the General Will).[63] Rousseau exempted women as a class from the ethical demands of contractualist political transformation because he took it to be a fact of their natures, qua women, that they were not only incapable of the transformation, but their inclusion in it would imperil the only ethical transformation that was practicable, namely, that of men.

It is, in my judgment, a pivotally important feature of what motivated Rousseau's highly personal way of interpreting rights-based contractualism that he took violent personal objection, very much in the spirit of Molière's "Les Femmes Savantes"[64] earlier, to women's participation in the explosive intellectual life of prerevolutionary France. No one during this period had a more trenchant and searing moral contempt for the illegitimacy of French monarchical absolutism and the way in which intellectuals of the French Enlightenment like Voltaire often pandered to it or its companion absolutisms elsewhere[65]; and Rousseau's contempt apparently embraced, as one of the causes of the intellectual degeneracy about him, what he regarded as the effeminization of French culture from the participation of women (especially Parisian women) in it.[66]

It is from the perspective of this analysis that Rousseau wholly excluded women from the ethical transformation of the General Will. The critical mistake of prerevolutionary France had been to include them in public culture, and the lesson to be learned was that their moral incapacities for public life required them to be forever kept in a private sphere of husband and family that would keep public life free of their corrupting taint. On this view, women's moral nature was exclusively suited to the private romantic attachments of family life and incapable of the impartial ethical demands of public life from which, for this reason of incapacity, they may and indeed must be totally excluded.

Rousseau's argument is remarkable not for its substance (other rights-based contractualists shared the view) but for the highly original and naive transparency of the revelatory way he expressed the argument.[67] If the legitimation of gender hierarchy on rights-based contractualist grounds was as tenuous as I believe it was, we need to understand the force of the assumptions (summarized in the idea of women's nature) that validated it for so many. Rousseau's way of expressing the point revealed its essentially reactionary motivations. In the mode of a defense of the demands of an apparently severely abstract ethical argument, the abstract ethical demands of public life must be protected and indeed immunized from the preethical realm of personal romantic spontaneity and attachment. In effect, the demands of abstract ethical argument – motivated by an emancipatory conception of public reason – required men, the bearers of public reason, sharply to divide their public lives as men with men from their private lives with wives and mothers, and sharply to maintain the distinction as necessary to both personal and ethical integrity.

Rousseau's arguments about the morally inferior nature of women, like the comparable arguments of antebellum proslavery thought and of European racist anti-Semitism, arose in the context of a long history and culture of patterns of hierarchy and subjugation some of which (slavery and the subjection of women) had been philosophically justified by Aristotle, among others.[68] These patterns of political hierarchy and their philosophical supports were now, in light of the argument for toleration, subject to criticism in terms of ideas of human rights and to political action in terms of the revolutionary constitutionalism to which such ideas gave rise. Rousseau was one prominent advocate of such ethical criticism and revolutionary constitutionalism in many areas, but not in the area of gender hierarchy. Rousseau put his argument in the non-Aristotelian terms of protecting human rights, but, to do so, he assumed, without reasonable contractualist justification, the good sense of Aristotle's functionalist account of women's moral nature. That is the reason why, in my judgment, the comparison of Aristotle and Rousseau is so revealing. Aristotle, the great classical defender of natural hierarchies, while rejected in other areas (for example, slavery) on rights-based grounds, is uncritically accepted by Rousseau in the area of gender. In effect, women's traditional roles in the history and culture of gender hierarchy are taken to be the measure of their inferior moral capacities as persons, and that view of women's nature is then used as a pivotal assumption in the general contractualist analysis.

The interest of Rousseau's way of expressing the argument is its rather obvious reactionary motivations centered in special worries about the emancipatory consequences that the argument for toleration, so central to contractualist political theory, might be interpreted to have for women, a point Mary Wollstonecraft (an acute critic of Rousseau) clearly saw when she centrally criticized Rousseau's insistence that men must control women's religious conscience.[69] Rousseau did not, of course, object to the argument for toleration itself; it was as central to his rights-based contractualism as it was for Locke or Kant.[70] Indeed, he paid tribute to the argument by the very way in which he defended his exclusion of women from public culture; the exclusion was necessary in order to protect a political community of human rights from its subversion by the improper generalization of the argument for toleration to women, subversive consequences Rousseau thought he saw in prerevolutionary France. But, Rousseau's interpretation of the argument illustrates both the effects and motivations yet again of the forms of intolerance that comparably arose as a reactionary response to the American abolition of slavery and the European emancipation of the Jews. The context of Rousseau's argument was what he saw as the French Enlightenment's wrongheaded tendencies to emancipate women; and Rousseau's reactionary response was, like that of American racism and European anti-Semitism, to offer a conception of the political community of human rights as necessarily masculine and to defend it on the basis of, if anything, a more thoroughgoing deprivation of the culture-creating rights of women that would confirm the image of their degraded moral incapacity.

The key to such intolerance is the decadent uses to which it must, in order to rationalize intolerance, put the idea of public reason. The argument for toleration is in its proper nature emancipatory of public reason because it subjects political power that abridges basic rights to the test of impartial justification to all in terms not hostage to the entrenched political epistemology of the political power under scrutiny. Corrupt political arguments for natural hierarchies of power and privilege are, on the basis of this analysis, shown to rest on stunting the capacity of persons to know and claim their human rights, and the consequence of the argument is that political power must be tested in light of the emancipation of persons' moral powers to claim their rights, an emancipation which the argument for toleration thus fosters. In contrast, such forms of intolerance, based on truncating the force that the argument of toleration should have, must unreasonably deny that whole classes of persons have the moral powers to originate and deliberate about claims of public reason.

The motivation of the intolerance, in effect, subverts the ethical purposes of the argument it is interpreting, depriving public reason of precisely the discourse it most clearly demands and requires. As in the case of American racism, this form of political argument must, in order to sustain its self-image of commitment to the argument for toleration, resort to forms of political irrationalism (cultivating bad arguments based on circularities or forms of allegiance antagonistic to free public reason) to construct an apparently reasonable image of the subhuman capacities of those excluded from the ambit of toleration; thus, its gargantuan appetite for bad science. Such irrationalism must in its nature both distort the very standards of reasonable argument and debate appropriate to the issues under discussion (the nature and role of blacks, or women) and correlatively deny that the persons excluded have the reasonable moral powers to originate claims and arguments relevant to that discussion. Both features mark the contractualist rationalization of gender hierarchy.

The argument for toleration rests not on ultimate epistemological and moral skepticism, but on a skepticism about the reliability of politically entrenched sectarian epistemologies that sustain dominant religious and political orthodoxies by making themselves the exclusive measure of reasonable discussion and debate and repressing all other views. Essentially sectarian views of fact and value thus immunize themselves from wider criticism in terms of independent reasonable standards of thought and inquiry, and indeed unreasonably make themselves the measure of what counts as reasonable inquiry and debate.

The political epistemology supportive of gender hierarchy familiarly rested its substantive claims about women's nature on such sectarian views of fact and value, largely inferred, as we have seen, functionally from women's traditional roles as wives and mothers in the family. The inference was, of course, epistemologically and morally flawed, as was the comparable circular inference in the case of race, because it took the consequences of unjust moral degradation as the measure of natural moral capacity. A political epistemology, thus wedded to the insular defense of a historically entrenched political orthodoxy, decisively shaped as well an alleged science of gender that was at least as epistemically unreliable as the comparable science of race; indeed, the science of gender and race differences flourished together, used quite similar crude physical measures of moral capacity, and served precisely similar ideological functions in the cultural construction of images of racist and sexist moral inferiority.[71] Such distortions of the alleged human sciences by the self-rationalizing requirements of a dominant politically entrenched epistemology were, of course, quite ancient; they took new forms under the impact of the growing public respect for the physical sciences in the nineteenth century, but, in the area of sexuality and gender (as of race), they were, if anything, more powerfully wedded than ever to reinforcing a politically dominant cultural image of the basic moral incapacity of women.[72] These views were not held on the basis of impartial standards of critical reason that could be publicly justified to all at large, but were polemically entrenched modes of legitimating the established practices of gender hierarchy.

Distortions of fact and value were here motivated by the normative models of family roles at the heart of the dominant political epistemology, taking the form, in nineteenth century America and Europe, of images of women as asexual, passive, essentially limited by their natures to their roles as wives and mothers, as caretakers of children and men.[73] The most profound resulting distortion of value was the incomplete and truncated interpretation of contractualist political theory required to rationalize this political epistemology. Contractualist political theory that had, in the hands of Locke,[74] been used fundamentally to criticize Filmer's appeal to patriarchalism as the justification for political absolutism among men,[75] was inhibited in its reasonable application to the family in general and to the political relations between men and women in particular that derived from roles in the family. As Carol Pateman has quite properly put the point, the social contract ideologically obfuscated the illegitimacy of the underlying sexual contract.[76] This truncation of contractualist analysis left the family essentially immune from scrutiny in light of arguments of political legitimacy; and the idea of women's nature – functionally interpreted in terms of uncritically accepted private family roles – pivotally reflected and rationalized this failure of ethical and political analysis. Plato's argument in *The Republic* had shown that such a view of women's nature was not philosophically inevitable,[77] but the very context of his analysis (abolition of the private nuclear family) confirmed, if anything, the close links of the two questions, the family and women, as if the retention of the one required the inferior moral status of the other.[78] Even John Stuart Mill, who argued eloquently in *The Subjection of Women* for the rights of women in public life,[79] largely immunized the family itself from his analysis.[80]

The consequence of this truncated interpretation of democratic political theory in general and contractualist theory in particular was an impoverishment of its analysis of the scope and meaning of human rights, a result clearly seen in Rousseau's unusually revealing statement of the view. Rousseau sharply separated the abstract human rights required for the public political life of men from the romantic absorption and partiality of private life, the world of women. But this gave not only a falsely hypermasculinized image of the rights of public political life, but equally falsely failed to articulate the many issues of justice and human rights that arose in the context of the family, including justice between spouses, between parents and children, and between children and the political community at large.[81] The ethics of care, nurturance, and education in child-rearing, for example, itself calls upon the exercise of the moral powers of both parents and children, at least some of which require sensitive concern for rights-based issues of fair respect for developmental independence and autonomy.[82] It distorts both the ethics of human rights and the ethics of care to isolate them in hermetically sealed political compartments called, respectively, public and private life; and women's moral experience, as many abolitionists certainly believed,[83] may have much to teach political contractualism about the nature and weight of human rights and how, in light of such rights, both private and public life may be critically disencumbered of the vicious sexist significance Rousseau's contractualism accorded them.[84] Rousseau's truncated interpretation of contractualism neither made sense of many of these claims of rights for the same reason that he made no sense of women as bearers of rights; he failed reasonably to apply contractualist analysis to the family and to women. In consequence, his contractualism gave a false picture of what rights were and, derivatively, of women's nature as bearers of human rights.

Such an unreasonable interpretation of human rights, based on an insular and parochial political epistemology enforced on society at large, further rationalized and was rationalized by the unreasonable exclusion of women from the political community of culture-creating rights, including the rights of conscience, free speech, and associational liberty, including their right to make decisions bearing on intimate personal life. The political epistemology, that rationalized gender hierarchy, was in its nature ascriptive; certain roles were mandatorily ascribed to women. It is a pivotally important feature of the reasonable contractualist assessment of such gender hierarchy that such hierarchy reflected a history and culture of sexist degradation of the moral powers of women, *i.e.,* that it was a cultural construction of men during a period that unjustly excluded women from the culture-creating rights of conscience, free speech, and associational liberty that respect their constructive moral powers as free persons. Mary Wollstonecraft's eloquent query was thus much to the point:

Absolute, uncontroverted authority, it seems, must subsist somewhere: but is not this a direct and exclusive appropriation of reason?

The public culture of human rights and reason had been defined, in Rousseau's understanding of political community, as in its nature masculine, and, on that basis, given rise to a sexist political epistemology that legitimated a cultural construction of gender hierarchy immunized from serious criticism in terms of a reasonable understanding of basic human rights.

Simone de Beauvoir was thus quite precisely correct when she called for a common analysis of the characteristics "ascribed to woman, the Jew, or the Negro."[86] In the terms of my analysis, a common pattern of cultural intolerance and marginalization, based on intolerance, was the unjust basis of a sense of community based on the moral degradation of Jews, or blacks, or women, as the case may be. A sense of political community – based on Aryan or white or male supremacy – rested on an irrationalist corruption of the political ethics of human rights, feeding on unreasonable stereotypes themselves based on the abridgement of human rights. De Beauvoir's characterization of men as transcendent and women as immanent[87] does not endorse, but describes this corruption of ethics in which men originate creative moral projects and women are its opposite, the Other[88] – inert and passive; the importance of her analysis is not her own view of appropriate remedies (which has been questioned as itself hypermasculinized[89]), but her critical articulation of the depth and extent of the ethical corruption and the way in which it has rested and rests, like the comparable evils of anti-Semitism and racism, on systematic historical exclusion from the public culture of human rights.

A constitutional community committed to the protection of the inalienable human rights of all persons, like that of the United States, has a preeminent obligation to extend to all persons the fair basis of social respect that makes available to all a secure public culture of respect for their claims of human rights. The forms of intolerance underlying racism and sexism are, in their nature, breaches of this obligation, in which the constitutional order has itself been complicitous with the unjust and constitutionally illegitimate construction of forms of moral subjugation and contempt that deny whole classes of persons the fair basis of social respect that is their right. Anti-Semitism, racism, and sexism all rest on such cultural intolerance, marginalization, and colonization: the deepest insult a culture ostensibly committed to human rights can inflict on the human rights of its citizens, namely, the denial of the very moral powers by which they could give authentic voice to the just claims of their creative moral powers of personality on their political community. Such deadening of ethical sensibility is, in its nature, an incommensurable ethical wrong. In a constitutional community committed to human rights, it is a constitutional wrong as well, one at the heart of suspect classification analysis. In the United States, a defective understanding of the political community of equal rights had, as in the case of race, legitimated the political construction of gender hierarchy that unjustly subjugated women as bearers of human rights; and the political and constitutional community, as in the case of race, was unjustly complicitous with this cultural construction of gender hierarchy.[90]

The political and constitutional evil of sexism, thus understood, requires as its correlative remedy measures that reasonably rectify women's unjust exclusion from the basic rights of American public culture. The essential political evil of sexism is keyed to the unjust cultural construction of gender hierarchy that limited women to mandatory roles in family life and, on that basis, excluded them from the political community of inalienable human rights. Accordingly, reasonable remedies for sexism must focus on any law or policy that, by act or omission, reinforces the culturally constructed incapacity of women keyed to the sexist interpretation of private life, for example, one that depends on the cultural idea that women's access to culturally valued public goods, in contrast to men's, turns on their dependent relations on the opposite gender, not their own independent and responsible origination of claims as free and rational persons.

From the perspective of this analysis, obscenity prosecutions would raise issues of constitutional principle if these prosecutions are based, as they appear to be, on paternalistic state-enforced judgments about the disrespectful character of the putatively obscene materials and of the thoughts and experiences to which use of such materials leads. It does not dispel but only aggravates the issue of free speech principles to redescribe the putative evils, as some American feminists[91] and the Canadian Supreme Court now do,[92] in terms of the degradation of women as such. That argument clearly places obscenity prosecutions in the framework of group libel[93] and, for that reason, renders them altogether more constitutionally problematic.[94] Why are certain pornographic images of women (as opposed to others) or pornographic versus nonpornographic images of women taken to express disrespect for women as such? The idea must be that these images (as opposed to others) morally degrade women as such from their status as full persons and as bearers of

equal rights. But even to state the claim is reasonably to contest it. Pornographic images (in contrast to conventional group libel claims) make no such
express claims as such. The claim that they do is a controversial interpretive
claim, ascribing to producers and users of these materials condemned moral
attitudes (a kind of corrupt conscience), quite like the motivation for group
libel laws. In fact, such materials may be, as some feminists argue they are,
emancipatory of the unjustly stunted and starved sexual interests of women as
well as men, an emancipation of interests that many persons of conscience
(profoundly concerned with traditional injustices in the area of gender and
sexuality) take now to be central to a life well and humanely lived.[95] Indeed, nonpornographic material (not only advertising, but traditional religious
views of women's nature and role) may be more degrading, more debilitating
of the integrity and autonomy of women as creative moral agents. In the midst
of such increasingly free and reasonable debate about the sources of the unjust
subjugation of women, enforceable state judgments of the worthlessness or
disvalue of certain thought and speech enforce intrinsically controversial *interpretive* judgments based on the dominant sexually repressive and now
highly questionable political orthodoxy about issues of sexuality and gender.
They do so precisely in the way (on the putative ground of a corruption of
conscience) that, on grounds of free speech, we have good reason to suspect
unreasonably to limit discussion and debate on these matters and deprive
persons of their inalienable rights of thought, experience, and discussion. To
deny that such laws abridge rights of conscience circumscribes unreasonably
the scope of protected conscience to the measure of majoritarian views of the
good life. Human rights, trimmed to the measure of such majoritarian judgments, lack their proper force precisely in the area where, as a matter of
constitutional principle, they are most exigently required (namely, protection
of the human rights of minorities).

Such majority judgments, if enforced through law in the domain of speech,
mandate a kind of orthodoxy of appropriate tribalization in the terms of public
discourse. Public claims disrespectful of groups are subject to state prohibition. But, as we have seen, this empowers the state to determine not only what
discourse is properly respectful and what not, but what groups are entitled to
such protection and what are not. But such state-enforced judgments introduce stereotypical political orthodoxies as the measure of human identity, thus
removing from public discourse precisely the contest of such stereotypical
boundaries that a free people often most reasonably requires. The identity of
no moral person can be exhaustively defined by their ethnicity, race, gender,
sexual preference, or any of the other terms of common group identification
familiar today. The social force such group identifications often have today
unreasonably diminishes both the range of diversity and individuality that
exists within such groups and the similarities between members of such
groups and the groups with which they are contrasted. To enforce such identi-

fications through law censors from public discourse precisely the kind of discourse that best challenges them. Such state censorship of a range of discourse stifles, in turn, the empowering protests of individuals to that discourse through which they express, demand, and define their individuality as persons against such stereotypical classifications. Paradoxically, it is precisely the groups that the state may regard itself as most reasonably protecting from group libel (the most historically stigmatized groups, like blacks in the United States, or women and sexual minorities generally) that should, as a matter of free speech principle, most reasonably be constitutionally immunized from such protective state power. Ralph Ellison's *Invisible Man* pleaded for racial justice in America in these eloquent terms: "Our task is that of making ourselves individuals. The conscience of a race is the gift of its individuals."[96] If the struggle against the stereotypical indignities of racism or sexism or homophobia is essentially a struggle for individuality, free speech rightly requires that the terms of emancipation must be the empowering responsibility of individuals, including the voluntary organizations through which they define themselves and their struggle.

III. Conclusion

The full inclusion of women, like blacks, in the community of human rights requires not the abridgement of such rights, but the full protection of such rights on the uncompromising terms of principle that recognize the inalienable right of all persons to take charge of their own moral lives. The issues of human rights raised by both group libel laws and by the forms of unjust prejudice they putatively remedy cannot reasonably be analyzed in isolation from one another. Indeed, once we understand both racism and sexism as the injuries to moral autonomy that they are, we correlatively understand why the reasonable remedy of such injustices urgently calls not for the dilution of guarantees of conscience and speech, but for their fuller protection. If the unjust cultural construction of racism and sexism is to be remedied, it must be on the terms and in the authentic voice of the moral powers of free people who understand their ultimate and inalienable moral responsibility reasonably to define the moral meaning of their lives and struggles against a culture so traditionally hostile to such claims. Liberalism is the doctrine that requires both such strenuous moral freedoms and such demanding moral responsibilities.

Notes

1 See, in particular, Joel Feinberg, *The Moral Limits of the Criminal Law* (New York: Oxford University Press, vol. 1, 1984, vol. 2, 1985, vol. 3, 1986, vol. 4, 1988). Cf. John Stuart Mill, *On Liberty,* Alburey Castell, ed. (New York: Appleton-Century-Crofts, 1947).

2 See, for example, Frederick Schauer, "Must Speech Be Special?", 78 *Northwestern U.L. Rev.* 1284 (1983).
3 For a defense of such laws, see David Riesman, "Democracy and Defamation: Control of Group Libel," 42 *Colum. L. Rev.* 727 (1942).
4 For argument to this effect, see Catharine A. MacKinnon, *Feminism Unmodified: Discourses on Life and Law* (Cambridge: Harvard University Press, 1987); *Toward A Feminist Theory of the State* (Cambridge: Harvard University Press, 1989).
5 See, for example, Elizabeth Fox-Genovese, *Feminism Without Illusions: A Critique of Individualism* (Chapel Hill: University of North Carolina Press, 1991).
6 The general framework of my analysis of racism and sexism is developed at much greater length in *Conscience and the Constitution: History, Theory, and Law of the Reconstruction Amendments* (Princeton University Press, 1993). A fuller analysis of the unconstitutionality of group libel laws appears in my "Free Speech as Toleration," in a volume edited by Wil Waluchow (forthcoming, Clarendon Press: Oxford, 1993).
7 See John Hart Ely, *Democracy and Distrust: A Theory of Judicial Review* (Cambridge: Harvard University Press, 1980).
8 See Ely, *Democracy and Distrust*.
9 410 U.S. 113 (1973).
10 See Ely, *Democracy and Distrust,* 56–60.
11 See Learned Hand, *The Bill of Rights* (New York: Atheneum, 1968); for Bentham's classic criticism of rights, see Jeremy Bentham, "Anarchical Fallacies," *The Works of Jeremy Bentham,* book II (published under the superintendence of Bentham's executor John Bowring, Edinburgh, 1843), 491–529.
12 See Ely, *Democracy and Distrust,* 58.
13 Ibid., 157.
14 See John Hart Ely, "The Wages of Crying Wolf: A Comment on *Roe v. Wade,"* 82 *Yale L.J.* 920 (1974).
15 See *Brown v. Board of Education,* 347 U.S. 483 (1954).
16 For a good recent history of the doctrine, see Charles A. Lofgren, *The Plessy Case: A Legal-Historical Interpretation* (New York: Oxford University Press, 1987).
17 See *Craig v. Boren,* 429 U.S. 190 (1976).
18 For much fuller analysis and argument, see Richards, *Conscience and the Constitution* cited in note 6.
19 See Thomas Jefferson, *Notes on the State of Virginia,* William Peden, ed. (Chapel Hill: University of North Carolina Press, 1955), 135–6.
20 William Lloyd Garrison, *Thoughts on African Colonization* (New York: Arno Press and The New York Times, 1968; originally published, 1832), 21. See also William Jay, *Inquiry into the Character and Tendency of the American Colonization, and American Anti-Slavery Societies* (originally published, 1835), reprinted in William Jay, *Miscellaneous Writings on Slavery* (New York: Negro Universities Press, 1968), 7–206; James G. Birney, *Letter on Colonization Addressed to the Rev. Thornton J. Mills, Corresponding Secretary of the Kentucky Colonization Society* (New York, 1834).
21 James Russell Lowell, "The Prejudice of Color," in *The Anti-slavery Papers of James Russell Lowell,* vol. I. (Boston: Houghton Mifflin, 1902), 19.

22 L. Maria Child, *An Appeal in Favor of Americans Called Africans* (New York: Arno Press and The New York Times, 1968; originally published, 1833).

23 Ibid., 148.

24 Ibid., 133.

25 Ibid., 134.

26 Ibid., 169; see also p11, 66, 133–4.

27 Ibid., 196.

28 See Alexis de Tocqueville, *Democracy in America*, vol. 1, Phillips Bradley, ed. (New York: Vintage, 1945), 373, 390–1.

29 Ibid., 195.

30 Ibid., 208.

31 See, for example, Pierre L. van den Berghe, *Race and Racism* (New York: John Wiley & Sons, 1967), 11.

32 Cited in Theodore Parker, "A Letter on Slavery," reprinted in Theodore Parker, *The Slave Power*, ed. James K. Hosmer (Boston: American Unitarian Association, 1916), 75.

33 See Winthrop D. Jordan, *White over Black: American Attitudes Toward the Negro, 1550–1812* (New York: W. W. Norton, 1977), 56, 65, 91–8; Edmund S. Morgan, *American Slavery American Freedom: The Ordeal of Colonial Virginia* (New York: W. W. Norton, 1975), 328–32.

34 See David Brion Davis, *The Problem of Slavery in Western Culture* (Ithaca: Cornell University Press, 1966), 170, 195, 207–8, 214, 281.

35 Ibid., 246–7, 473.

36 See Jordan, *White over Black*, 37–8.

37 See William Shakespeare, *Othello*, Act I, scene III, I. 101, in W. J. Craig, ed., *Shakespeare: Complete Works* (London: Oxford University Press, 1966), 947.

38 See Carl N. Degler, *Out of Our Past: The Forces That Shaped Modern America*, 3rd ed. (New York: Harper and Row, 1984), 30.

39 On the special features of American slavery in contrast to slavery elsewhere see Stanley M. Elkins, *Slavery: A Problem in American Institutional and Intellectual Life*, 3rd ed. revised, (Chicago: University of Chicago Press, 1976); Kenneth M. Stampp, *The Peculiar Institution: Slavery in the Ante-Bellum South* (New York: Vintage, 1956); Eugene D. Genovese, *The World the Slaveholders Made: Two Essays in Interpretation* (Middletown, Conn.: Wesleyan University Press, 1988); John W. Blassingame, *The Slave Community: Plantation Life in the Antebellum South* rev. ed. (New York: Oxford University Press, 1979); Carl N. Degler, *Neither Black Nor White* (Madison, Wis.: University of Wisconsin Press, 1986); Peter Kolchin, *Unfree Labor: American Slavery and Russian Serfdom* (Cambridge, Mass.: Harvard University Press, 1987).

40 See Frederick Douglass, "The Claims of the Negro Ethnologically Considered," in Philip S. Foner, ed., *The Life and Writings of Frederick Douglass*, vol. 2 (New York: International Publishers, 1975), 295.

41 For a related mode of analysis, see Orlando Patterson, *Slavery and Social Death* (Cambridge, Mass.: Harvard University Press, 1982).

42 On these features of American slavery, see Elkins, *Slavery*; Stampp, *The Peculiar Institution*; Eugene D. Genovese, *Roll, Jordan, Roll: The World the Slaves Made*

(New York: Vintage Books, 1974); Eugene D. Genovese, *The World the Slave-holders Made;* Blassingame, *The Slave Community;* Herbert G. Gutman, *The Black Family in Slavery and Freedom 1750–1925* (New York: Vintage Books, 1976). For a leading proslavery justification of many of these features of the institution, see Thomans R. R. Cobb, *An Inquiry into the Law of Negro Slavery in the United States of America* (New York: Negro Universities Press, 1968) (originally published, 1858).

43 See works cited in previous note, especially Elkins, *Slavery;* see also Herbert S. Klein, *Slavery in the Americas: A Comparative Study of Virginia and Cuba* (Chicago: Elephant Paperbacks, 1989). It remains controversial, however, whether on balance slaves were treated worse in the British colonies of North America than in the non-British colonies of Latin America. See, for example, David Brion Davis, "The Continuing Contradiction of Slavery: A Comparison of British America and Latin America," in Ann J. Lane, ed., *The Debate Over Slavery: Stanley Elkins and His Critics* (Urbana: University of Illinois Press, 1971), 111–36; Herbert S. Klein, "Anglicanism, Catholicism, and the Negro Slave", *id.,* 137–90. For an important general study, see Carl N. Degler, *Neither Black Nor White.*

44 On the South, see Ira Berlin, *Slaves Without Masters: The Free Negro in the Antebellum South* (New York: Pantheon Books, 1974). On the North, see Leon F. Litwack, *North of Slavery: The Negro in the Free States 1790–1860* (Chicago: University of Chicago Press, 1961); V. Jacque Voegeli, *Free but Not Equal: The Midwest and the Negro During the Civil War* (Chicago: University of Chicago Press, 1967).

45 Three states – Illinois, Indiana, and Oregon – incorporated such anti-immigration provisions in their state constitutions, which were overwhelmingly approved by white state electorates. See Litwack, *North of Slavery,* 70–4.

46 By 1840, some 93 percent of northern free blacks lived in states which either completely or as a practical matter excluded them from the right to vote. See Litwack, *North of Slavery,* 74–5. Although some white schools admitted blacks especially before 1820, most northern states either excluded them from schools altogether or established racially separate and unequal schools for them. Id., 114.

47 See Abraham Lincoln, "Speech on Kansas-Nebraska Act", delivered October 16, 1854, reprinted in Done E. Fehrenbacher, ed., *Abraham Lincoln* (New York: The Library of America, 1989), vol. 1, 316.

48 See, for example, Jordan, *White over Black,* 91–8; Morgan, *American Slavery American Freedom,* 77; Davis, *The Problem of Slavery in Western Culture,* 170, 195, 207–8, 214, 246–7, 281, 473.

49 See David A. J. Richards, *Toleration and the Constitution* (New York: Oxford University Press, 1986), 86–8.

50 For fuller defense, see Richards, *Conscience and the Constitution,* cited at note 6, ch. 5.

51 See further argument to this effect, see Richards, *Toleration,* 190–3.

52 See Richards, *Toleration,* 190–3.

53 See Harry Kalven, Jr., *The Negro and the First Amendment* (Chicago: University of Chicago Press, 1965).

54 A comparable analysis to similar effect might be extended to other arguments

influential on the cultural construction of gender hierarchy, for example, those based on the interpretation of the Bible. See, for example, Elaine Pagels, *Adam, Eve, and the Serpent* (New York: Random House, 1988); Rosemary Radford Ruether, *Womanguides: Readings Toward a Feminist Theology* (Boston: Beacon Press, 1985); Rosemary Radford Ruether, *New Woman New Earth: Sexist Ideologies and Human Liberation* (San Francisco: Harper & Row, 1975); Mary Daly, *Beyond God the Father: Towards a Philosophy of Women's Liberation* (London: The Women's Press, 1973); Daphne Hampson, *Theology and Feminism* (Oxford: Basil Blackwell, 1990); Uta Ranke-Heinemann, *Eunuchs for Heaven: The Catholic Church and Sexuality,* John Brownjohn trans. (London: Andre Deutsch, 1988); Susanne Heine, *Women and Early Christianity: Are the feminist scholars right?,* John Bowden trans. (London: SCM Press, 1987). On social background, see Gerda Lerner, *The Creation of Patriarchy* (New York: Oxford University Press, 1986).

55 See Aristotle, *Politics,* Ernest Barker trans. (New York: Oxford University Press, 1962), 35–6; for probing commentary, see Susan Moller Okin, *Women in Western Political Thought* (Princeton: Princeton University Press, 1979), 73–96. See also Jean Ethke Elshtain, *Public Man, Private Woman: Women in Social and Political Thought* (Princeton: Princeton University Press, 1981), 19–54.

56 See Aristotle, *Politics,* 13.

57 See, for example, Jean-Jacques Rousseau, *Emile,* Barbara Foxley trans. (London: J. M. Dent, 1961), 321–56. For incisive commentary, see Okin, *Women in Western Political Thought,* 140–94; see also Elshtain, *Public Man,* 148–70; Carole Pateman, *The Sexual Contract* (Cambridge: Polity Press, 1988), 96–9. For a general treatment, see Joel Schwartz, *The Sexual Politics of Jean-Jacques Rousseau* (Chicago: University of Chicago Press, 1984).

58 See, in general, Aristotle, *Nicomachean Ethics,* Martin Ostwald trans. (Indianapolis: Bobbs-Merrill, 1961); for discussion of perfectionism and its normative implications, see David A. J. Richards, *A Theory of Reasons for Action* (Oxford: Clarendon Press, 1971), 116–17.

59 See Jean-Jacques Rousseau, *The Social Contract,* in *The Social Contract and Discourses* (New York: E. P. Dutton, 1950), 11.

60 See, in general, Thomas Hobbes, *Leviathan,* Michael Oakeshott ed. (Oxford: Basil Blackwell, 1960). For illuminating commentary on Hobbes's acknowledgement of the equality of women and yet his justification for gender hierarchy, see Elshtain, *Public Man,* 106–27; Carole Pateman, *The Sexual Contract,* 43–50; Susan Moller Okin, *Women in Western Political Thought,* 197–9.

61 See, in general, John Locke, *Two Treatises of Government,* Peter Laslett ed (Cambridge University Press, 1960). For illuminating commentary on Locke's defense of gender hierarchy, see Susan Moller Okin, *Women in Western Political Thought,* 199–201; Elshtain, *Public Man,* 108–27; Carole Pateman, *The Sexual Contract,* 52–3.

62 See, in general, Immanuel Kant, "On the Common Saying: 'This May be True in Theory, but it does not Apply in Practice,'" in Hans Reiss, ed., *Kant's Political Writings* (Cambridge University Press, 1977), 61–92. For commentary on Kant's defense of gender hierarchy, see Pateman, *The Sexual Contract,* 168–71; Okin, *Women in Western Political Thought,* 6.

63 For illuminating general discussion, see Judith N. Shklar, *Men and Citizens: A Study of Rousseau's Social Theory* (Cambridge University Press, 1985); for comparable discussion focussing on Rousseau's treatment of gender, see Okin, *Women in Western Political Thought,* 99–194.

64 See Molière, "The Learned Women," in Molière, *The Misanthrope and Other Plays,* Donald M. Frame trans. (New York: New American Library, 1981), 357–428.

65 See Shklar, *Men and Citizens,* 101–4, 108–10, 114, 116, 117, 123–4, 221–2, 229.

66 Ibid., 144–5. For a related argument, albeit certainly not in the defense of gender hierarchy, about nineteenth-century American culture, see Ann Douglas, *The Feminization of American Culture* (New York: Alfred A. Knopf, 1977).

67 For the importance of transparency in Rousseau's thought, see, in general, Jean Starobinski, *Jean-Jacques Rousseau: Transparency and Obstruction,* Arthur Goldhammer trans. (Chicago: University of Chicago Press, 1988).

68 See, in general, Davis, *The Problem of Slavery.* On historical background, see Lerner, *The Creation of Patriarchy.*

69 See Mary Wollstonecraft, *A Vindication of the Rights of Woman* (New York: W. W. Norton, 1967; first published 1792), 141, 147, 161, 281–2.

70 See, for example, Jean-Jacques Rousseau, *Emile,* 228–78; cf. *The Social Contract,* 129–41.

71 See, in general, Stephen Jay Gould, *The Mismeasure of Man;* Cynthia Eagle Russett, *Sexual Science: The Victorian Construction of Womanhood* (Cambridge: Harvard University Press, 1989); Londa Schiebinger, *The Mind Has No Sex?: Women in the Origins of Modern Science* (Cambridge: Harvard University Press, 1989). For the continuing force of these political epistemologies today, see Anne Fausto-Sterling, *Myths of Gender: Biological Theories About Women and Men* (New York: Basic Books, 1985); Cynthia Fuchs Epstein, *Deceptive Distinctions: Sex, Gender, and the Social Order* (New Haven: Yale University Press, 1988).

72 For a brilliant recent development of this theme of a continuity and even worsening of sexism through changing models of female sexuality, see Thomas Laqueur, *Making Sex: Body and Gender from the Greeks to Freud* (Cambridge: Harvard University Press, 1990).

73 See, in general, Russett, *Sexual Science.*

74 See, in general, John Locke, *Two Treatises of Government.*

75 See, in general, Sir Robert Filmer, *Patriarcha and Other Writings,* Johann P. Sommerville, ed. (Cambridge University Press, 1991).

76 See, in general, Pateman, *The Sexual Contract.*

77 For Plato's argument that women were qualified to be guardians of his ideal state and for the abolition of the private family, see Plato, *Republic,* Book V, in Edith Hamilton and Huntington Cairns, eds., *Plato: The Collected Dialogues* (New York: Pantheon, 1961), 688–720. For probing commentary, see Okin, *Women in Western Political Thought,* 15–50.

78 For incisive commentary on this point, see Elshtain, *Public Man,* 19–41.

79 See John Stuart Mill, *The Subjection of Women,* in John Stuart Mill and Harriet

Taylor Mill, *Essays on Sex Equality,* Alice S. Rossi, ed. (Chicago: University of
Chicago Press, 1970), 125–242.

80 For incisive commentary along these lines, see Okin, *Women in Western Political
    Thought,* 197–230.

81 For a recent attempt to raise these issues within the context of a contractualist
    theory of justice, see Susan Moller Okin, *Justice, Gender, and the Family* (New
    York: Basic Books, 1989); cf. David A. J. Richards, "The Individual, the Family,
    and the Constitution," 55 *N.Y.U. L. Rev.* 1 (1980).

82 Cf. Sara Ruddick, *Maternal Thinking: Toward a Politics of Peace* (Boston: Beacon
    Press, 1989).

83 For a powerful example of the systematic appeal to women's experience as a way
    of giving expression to an articulate sense of the moral evils of slavery, see, in
    general, Harriet Beecher Stowe, *Uncle Tom's Cabin or, Life Among the Lowly*
    (New York: Penguin, 1981, originally published 1852). On the importance of
    women and the woman question in antebellum abolitionist thought and practice,
    see Aileen S. Kraditor, *Means and Ends in American Abolitionism: Garrison and
    His Critics on Strategy and Tactics, 1834–1850* (1967; reprint, Chicago: Elephant
    Paperbacks, 1987), 39–77. For commentary and primary sources reflecting the
    impact of women on abolitionist thought and the emergence therefrom of an
    independent feminist movement, see Alice S. Rossi, ed., *The Feminist Papers:
    From Adams to de Beauvoir* (Boston: Northeastern University Press, 1973), 241–
    322, 378–470. For commentary, see Ellen Carol DuBois, *Feminism and Suffrage:
    The Emergence of an Independent Women's Movement in America 1848–1869*
    (Ithaca: Cornell University Press, 1978).

84 See, for illustrations of this point, Okin, *Justice, Gender, and the Family* and
    Elshtain, *Public Man.* For studies of the distinctive nature of women's moral
    experience, see Carol Gilligan, *In a Different Voice: Psychological Theory and
    Women's Development* (Cambridge: Harvard University Press, 1982); Eva Feder
    Kittay and Diana T. Meyers, eds., *Women and Moral Theory* (Totowa, N.J.:
    Rowman & Littlefield, 1987).

85 See Mary Wollstonecraft, *A Vindication of the Rights of Woman,* 141.

86 See Simone de Beauvoir, *The Second Sex,* H. M. Parshley trans. (New York:
    Vintage Books, 1952), xvi. De Beauvoir expressly invokes, as useful analogies,
    Myrdal on American blacks and Sartre on European anti-Semitism, 144. See
    Gunnar Myrdal, *An American Dilemma: The Negro Problem and Modern Democ-
    racy,* 2 vols. (1944; reprint, New York: Pantheon Books, 1972); Jean-Paul Sartre,
    Anti-Semite and Jew, George J. Becker trans. (New York: Grove Press, 1948).

87 See, in general, de Beauvoir, *The Second Sex.*

88 Ibid., xix.

89 See, for example, Elshtain, *Public Man,* 306–10.

90 See, for example, *Bradwell v. The State,* 83 U.S. (16 Wall.) 130 (1872) (woman
    denied admission to state bar held consistent with equal protection).

91 See, in general, Catharine A. MacKinnon, *Feminism Unmodified: Discourses on
    Life and Law* and *Toward a Feminist Theory of the State.*

92 See *Donald Victor Buter v. Her Majesty the Queen,* decided February 27, 1992
    (slip opinion). The Supreme Court of Canada also cites alleged arguments of harm

from such material, largely depending on the highly controversial fact-finding of the Meese Commission in the United States. On the complete unreliability of this study from the perspective of the principle of free speech (its question-begging distortion by ideological motives of censorship), see David A. J. Richards, "Pornography Commissions and the First Amendment: On Constitutional Values and Constitutional Facts", 39 *Maine L. Rev.* 275 (1987).

93 MacKinnon quite clearly sees and espouses this analogy; see *Feminism Unmodified,* 156–7.

94 This argument assumes that group libel laws are or should be constitutionally problematic for the reasons already discussed in the text. The constitutionalism of nations like Canada, which accept the legitimacy of group libel laws, has at least been consistent in extending the analogy to obscene materials. The same cannot be said of the United States, whose constitutionalism rejects group libel laws but accepts anti-obscenity laws.

95 See, in general, Varda Burstyn, ed., *Women Against Censorship* (Vancouver: Douglas & McIntyre, 1985).

96 Ralph Ellison, *Invisible Man* (New York: Vintage, 1989), 354.

6

Liberalism and the new skeptics

THOMAS MORAWETZ[1]

The concept of autonomy is the bulwark of liberal theory in politics and law. Accordingly, contemporary debates between liberal and communitarian theorists frequently concern the role, nature, and scope of individual rights implementing autonomy. Joel Feinberg has been as persuasive as anyone in explaining and defending the liberal theory of rights. Notwithstanding his powerful analysis,[2] liberalism and the concept of rights remain controversial among legal and political theorists who reject some of the presuppositions of his approach. The contemporary forms of critical jurisprudence – critical legal studies, feminism, critical race theory, neopragmatism, modern civic republicanism – incorporate skeptical forms of antifoundational arguments. The picture of law and society generated by these antifoundational arguments is, according to critical theory, incompatible with the liberal account of rights.

I begin by summarizing Feinberg's interpretation and defense of a liberal account of rights. In part II, I explain the skeptical version of antifoundationalism and show how it constitutes a strong thread that ties together various forms of critical jurisprudence. Then in part III, I discuss a different version of the antifoundational argument, a version that does not incorporate skepticism. I argue that the skeptical form of antifoundationalism is flawed because it involves a paradox about theory and practice, a paradox that implicates the metaphor of (the scholar-observer) being inside/outside a practice or conceptual scheme. In part IV, I defend the second version of antifoundationalism, purged of its skeptical basis and the accompanying paradox. Finally, in part V, I reassess the liberal account of rights in the light of this revised antifoundational critique and, more generally, relate liberalism to individualism.

I. Liberalism, communitarianism, and rights

The liberal conception of rights rests on a principle of limited government. It presumes that government prevents and mediates conflicts among persons through rules that define and safeguard personal autonomy. Government, according to this principle, may not use law to restrict autonomy to shape and condition persons' preferences. It may not, in other words, tell persons what they may say and do or place conditions on what they say and do, unless such limitations are justified in terms of autonomy. "Autonomy" embraces both liberty and equality: Legal interventions may be justified in terms of autonomy when they protect the liberty of persons *and* when they are consistent with rights of action being distributed in an egalitarian way.

The catechism of legal rights spells out, in part at least, the dimensions of autonomy protected by the state through law. The history of the Supreme Court's interpretation of the Bill of Rights offers up countless examples of the protection of autonomy *and* of its costs. The enforcement of civil rights and liberties characteristically has social costs and is therefore controversial. For example, the exclusionary rule, derived form the Fourth and Fifth Amendment rights of criminal defendants, restricts the use of evidence even when such evidence is indisputably probative and reliable. The protection of First Amendment rights allows the dissemination, largely without regard to content, of newspapers, magazines, television programs, and other media that shape our shared environment. No one would argue that what is offered is for the most part edifying.

Feinberg's characteristically careful and open-minded defense of liberalism responds to such controversies. First, he clarifies the scope and intent of liberal theory. For Feinberg, liberalism is neither a theory about human nature nor a theory about social interaction.[3] In particular, it does not rest on an individualistic claim that "each person is an atom, or island, whose essential character is formed independently of the influences of social groups and who is in principle self-sufficient."[4] Autonomy characterizes neither human essence nor actual social conditions but describes a fundamental norm under which persons, whatever their nature and whatever their mutual dependence, are able to experience respect and exercise choice.

Having addressed the scope of liberalism, Feinberg answers the first of two substantial communitarian challenges. So-called communitarian theorists argue that some account of the common good is an essential ingredient of political justification and that liberal theory is flawed because it precludes any justification of governmental acts by reference to the common good. Feinberg responds that some conceptions of the common good, for example a conception of loyalties based on "mutual respect" and "devotion to the ideal of a national community in which an unrestricted myriad of social groups prosper and flourish,"[5] are in fact *implicit* in liberalism and in the idea of a community of autonomous persons. On the other hand, Feinberg points out, critics who argue that more controversial characterizations of the common good should play a justificatory role tend in fact to demand that legal interventions be justified by the common good *even when* they do not comport with social justice and respect for the rights of persons. In other words, either appeals to the common good are innocuous from the liberal standpoint because they reinforce respect for the rights of autonomous persons or they are to be unacceptable precisely because they fly in the face of such rights.[6] Note that this response does not rule out in principle the common good as an *independent* justification, but it emphasizes the cost of doing so. For the liberal the cost of choosing the common good over justice and rights is always too high.

Feinberg also addresses the second substantial communitarian challenge, that the liberal ignores the value of tradition and the role of law as a repository of traditional values.[7] Again, Feinberg poses two circumstances. Liberals can accommodate traditions when preserving them comports with respect for persons' autonomy, but when tradition is not compatible with such respect for the rights of persons, preserving tradition is too costly.

Feinberg points out that liberals are wary of using tradition as the repository of shared ideals when doing so frustrates pluralism. A society embraces many subcommunities and many traditions. "When each person is a member of many groups, the phenomenon of overlapping membership is greatly magnified. The naturally diverse needs and attitudes of the people will unite some in one context and separate them in another."[8] For liberals, communitarian appeals to tradition often disguise contests between the will of the majority and the non-conforming preferences of individuals. Accordingly, nontraditional choices that neither harm nor offend other discrete individuals in significant ways deserve protection from majority coercion.[9]

Liberalism, in the view that underlies Feinberg's analysis, holds that rights and autonomy are related conceptually and instrumentally. Conceptually, the realm of autonomy is defined by the scope of rights. But the ongoing articulation of rights through legal and political decision making is also the instrument or vehicle by which autonomy is secured. The difference between liberals and communitarians is a difference between two forms or styles of justification. For liberals, the first question regarding any legal intervention is its effect upon relevant rights; rights trump justifications based on appeal to the common good. For communitarians, the scope of rights is limited by *prior* delineation of the common good. Liberals and communitarians thus invert each other's justificatory priorities.[10]

II. Critical theory

A premise of the liberal debate with communitarians is that conflicts between autonomy rights and the common good will be exceptional. In general the common good can be pursued in harmony with the rights of persons. The disagreement between liberals and communitarians focuses on whether rights trump the common good or whether the common good trumps rights in the relatively narrow domain of conflict.

Duncan Kennedy, as a proponent of critical legal studies, questions the possibility of valid and neutral criteria for deciding such questions and offers what may be regarded as an antifoundational critique of liberalism. Both liberalism *and* communitarianism can be seen as foundational theories at least to the extent that they rest on the possibility of justifying policies by appeal to neutral criteria, the possibility of evaluating political arrangements and legal decisions objectively. (In part IV, I discuss antifoundational forms of liberalism.) Kennedy challenges the possibility of having and using such criteria. He argues that "there are two opposed modes for dealing with substantive [legal] issues . . . individualism and altruism. . . . [W]e are divided, among ourselves and also within ourselves, between irreconcilable visions of humanity and society, and between radically different aspirations for our common future."[11] Nonetheless, "the rhetoric of individualism so thoroughly dominates legal discourse at present that it is difficult even to identify a counterethic."[12] Liberalism, with its focus on autonomy and rights as a trump, expresses that individualist ideal.

Altruism, on the other hand, "enjoins us to make sacrifices, to share, and to be merciful. It has its roots in culture, in religion, ethics and art, that are as deep as those of individualism."[13] Altruism underlies the communitarian regard for tradition and the common good. It denies both the "arbitrariness" and the "subjectivity" of values. "Ends are collective and in process of development."[14]

Even though Kennedy stresses that "the 'freedom' of individualism is negative, alienated, and arbitrary" and "has no moral content whatsoever,"[15] he does not defend altruism over individualism. He is concerned instead with the epistemological significance of both modes and of their inevitable clash within our debates. "We cannot 'balance' individualist and altruist values. . . . The only kind of imagery that conveys the process by which we act . . . is that of existential philosophy. We make commitments and pursue them."[16]

Kennedy echoes liberals in rejecting the communitarian assumption that rights must be balanced against the common good. But he does so for altogether different reasons. Liberals hold that rights have priority over interests (or the common good) while Kennedy suggests that decision makers opt "existentially" for some notion of the common good and circumscribe their accounts of rights accordingly. In this sense, Kennedy is sympathetic to communitarians. Nonetheless he distinguishes himself from "altruists" because his references to "existentialist" commitment imply that values used by decision makers are arbitrary and subjective.

Kennedy's tale is essentially one of reciprocal delusion. Liberals are deluded in thinking that individualist values provide a neutral standpoint for decision making, neutral among conflicting conceptions of the common good. Altruists are deluded in thinking that the conceptions of the common good that they deploy are anything but arbitrary or subjective. Liberals and communitarians, for better or worse, simply make commitments with regard to ends and the shared goals of community and implement those commitments.

In light of this analysis, critical theorists such as Kennedy characterize law in terms of power, domination, conceptual relativity, and legitimating ideologies. If law is the arena of conflicting and arbitrary values or value-compromises, and if power is unevenly distributed, then law is bound to embody the choices of those with power. So-called neutral justifications of the legal system through foundational arguments, the kind of arguments that he sees as the core of liberalism, mask systems of domination. The true nature of the system may *also* be masked from the dominators. "The ruling class itself is taken in by legal ideology; it believes that it's acting justly when it acts according to law, that everyone is getting approximately the best possible deal, and that change would make everyone worse off."[17] The prevailing political and social rhetoric becomes a legitimating conceptual and ideological scheme for maintaining "hegemony."

Many feminist theorists and critical race theorists draw on this fund of ideas. Feminists have two characteristic analytic postures. Some argue that the experiential differences between men and women give women a dis-tinctive "voice" and orientation. The conception of rights embodied in individualism, based on separateness and on the distinctiveness of each per-son, is a so-called masculinist position. Unlike men, women gain access by virtue of their "hedonic" experience to a distinctive way of regarding what is important personally and socially. They may express that view with different concepts.[18] The importance of the concept of rights in liberalism and of a neutral, foundational argument for rights is thus tied to male conceptual demands.

Radical feminists, representing a different feminist position, embrace the paradox that women, having been dominated and subjected to male categories over history, are alienated from their distinctive voice. "Feminism criticizes this male totality without an account of our capacity to do so or to imagine or realize a more whole truth. Feminism affirms women's point of view by revealing, criticizing, and explaining its impossibility."[19] The fissure that entails an antifoundational form of argument is not, as it is for Kennedy, between irreconcilable values or political choices. It is deeper, a division grounded in epistemology and language. Domination has deprived women, on this view, of the tools to express their experience and their dignity.

"Different voice" feminists and radical feminists agree in regarding the liberal language of rights, insofar as it has pretensions of neutrality and objectivity, as a "legitimating ideology" for a male conceptual perspective. According to Robin West, the "total subjective experience of masculinity" entails the fundamental value of autonomy as separateness. Only the male ideal is reflected by the concern that "[t]he individual must be treated by his government (and by others) in a way that respects his equality and his freedom"[20] through the definition and protection of autonomy by a system of rights.

The antifoundational position shared by critical legal theorists like Kennedy and feminist theorists is elaborated by Roberto Unger. He says critically that the role of rights within liberalism, with its claim to be based in an atemporal, nonideological, nongender-based view of autonomy, dissolves into a discredited doctrine asserting "a canonical form of social life and personality that could never be fundamentally remade and reimagined. . . . [The history of liberalism] consists in the attempt to deflect the critique of objectivism and formalism by accepting some of its points while saving increasingly less of the original view."[21]

Feminism's critique of objective foundations is echoed in critical race theory, which attempts "to identify and emphasize . . . what *distinguishes* the 'voices' of minority men and women from the voices of other persons."[22] Many race theorists reject the so-called homogenization of persons implicit in arguments for autonomy and the implication that the liberal conception of rights of autonomy embodies objective values rather than the preferences of a dominant race.

The antifoundational arguments of critical legal theory, from critical legal studies through feminism and critical race theory, have their philosophical ground in the work of Richard Rorty. His highly influential contemporary version of pragmatism concludes that the assumption and pursuit of "objectivity" is an illusion. He argues that "it is useless to hope that objects will constrain us to believe the truth about them, if only they are approached with an unclouded mental eye, or a rigorous method, or a perspicuous language."[23] The liberal account of autonomy and rights aspires to be objective in this sense, to explain the importance of personal respect and dignity by a rigorous method and with an unclouded eye. It presupposes the possibility of a posture of neutrality with regard to political agendas and personal goals. For Rorty, what is crucially in error is "the tradition in Western culture which centers around the notion of the search for Truth. . . . [This tradition] is the clearest example of the attempt to find a sense in one's existence by turning away from solidarity to objectivity."[24]

Rorty concludes that only solidarity as "the idea of Truth as something to be pursued . . . because it will be good for oneself, or for one's real or imaginary community"[25] adequately justifies political and social ends. The most we can do is to offer competing conceptual schemes and remain mutually engaged in endless "conversations"[26] – the conversations between the genders, between the races, and between the empowered and the powerless.

III. Inside and outside: skepticism

Kennedy's critical attack on objectivity and the liberal account of rights rests on the metaphor of inside/outsideness. Insiders characteristically entertain the illusion of objectivity. Liberals/individualists and altruists suffer reciprocal illusions. Liberals are self-deluded in regarding their account of autonomy as more or less objective and independent of any particular scheme of social preferences or political order. Altruists, who frankly embrace a conception of the common good, are self-deluded in thinking that the scheme is neither arbitrary nor subjective. Kennedy claims to unmask such illusions. In this crucial sense, he posits himself as an outsider to the process of choice and decision making, an outsider describing the inevitable illusions of insiders.

The theme of delusion and an appeal to the inside/outside metaphor run pervasively through feminism and critical race theory. For feminists, the alienation of women from power is said to give a privileged perspective, an outsider's perspective, for seeing that what is thought to be universal is in fact partial, power-based, and gender-based. "Different voice" feminists condemn the assumption of separateness at the root of ideas about autonomy and rights and speak metaphorically about the equally gender-based ideas of connectedness. Radical feminists condemn *any and all* received concepts and terms that emanate from a system of sexual domination because their use perpetuates that system. Using a parallel argument, some minority critics attack the vocabulary of autonomy and individualism as manifesting the "voice" and therefore the preferences of the dominant race. In all these arguments, being "inside" is equated with having delusions about objectivity and about the availability of neutral foundations.

Kennedy exposes the paradox inherent in the inside/outside metaphor when he remarks that our concepts are thoroughly determined by the individualist framework of autonomy, rights and objectivity. When we step outside that framework to criticize it as partial and subjective we have no alternative conceptual scheme. We can speak only negatively and identify delusions and mistakes.

From the standpoint of critical scholars, the separation between insider and outsider is total. Any insider must believe in her preferences as objective in order to justify imposing them on society at large; any outsider must see such a belief in objectivity as misguided. To observe with Rorty that solidarity with like-minded persons must replace belief in objectivity and universality and that discourse (the "search for truth") is no more than a conversation among groups with different preferences and agendas, is necessarily to associate oneself with the outsider's perspective. The outsider's analysis indicts insiders with the charge of objectifying an arbitrary conceptual scheme.

Feminist and race theorists struggle with this paradox. How can one participate in decision making with commitment, if any agenda of rights, any claim of neutrality or objectivity, is tainted with partiality? Their attempt at an end-run consists of displacing substantive theory with biographical narrative. They embrace subjectivity and the notion of conversation. Chastened by outsiders that claims to objectivity in developing a theory of rights and an explication of autonomy are *necessarily* ill-founded, they narrow their account-from-the-inside to that which is personal and relative.

If there is a central flaw in the critical argument, it can be uncovered by questioning the polarity between the perspectives of the insider and the out-sider, the polarity between what the insider believes and what the outsider knows to be the case. As long as the theorist can speak as outsider, she can disable the insider from claiming objectivity and, among other things, from aspiring to give a neutral account of autonomy and its associated rights. Thus, she can assault liberalism conceptually and epistemologically. The critical argument succeeds *if* it gives, in turn, a correct account of the insider's use of objectivity claims about autonomy and rights. But *is* the account correct?

The critic's disabling argument has a much longer pedigree than its modern incarnation in legal theory and in the Rortian revival of pragmatism. It repli-cates traditional skeptical arguments of the form, "You cannot claim *x* unless you can show *y*." In its most banal and familiar guise the argument is that you cannot claim to know that you are awake now unless you can show that you are not now merely dreaming and merely imagining you are awake. You cannot claim that other persons have minds unless you can show what differ-ence it would make in your experience for others to offer all the *external* manifestations of mind but lack subjective cognitive experience.

P. F. Strawson's seminal diagnosis of skepticism is that such skeptical arguments are viciously and fatally self-defeating. "[W]ith many skeptical problems[,] their statement involves the pretended acceptance of a conceptual scheme and at the same time the silent repudiation of one of the conditions of its existence. That is why they are, in the terms in which they are stated, insoluble."[27] Or, in other words, "[skepticism] allows us the alternatives of meaning something different from what we do mean, or of being forever unsure; because the standard for being sure while meaning what we do mean is set self-contradictorily high."[28]

Drawing on this insight one can ask whether critical theorists set the stan-dard for objectivity so high that *in principal* it cannot be met. In particular, how can one ever make the defense that an analysis of autonomy is not gender-relative, race-relative, or determined by the preferences of the class with power? Is it sufficient for the critical theorist to demonstrate subjectivity by showing that the analysis is controversial, that opinions differ? Is it suffi-cient for the critic to show that a different and internally consistent agenda can be produced?

Questions can be raised about the partiality that critical theory associates with an individualist account of autonomy and rights. Is individualism, as Kennedy argues, systematically at odds with altruism because the two notions express irreconcilable conceptual perspectives on human nature and society? Or are individualism/autonomy and altruism reconcilable, with the former a precondition of the latter? Do care, concern, and identification with others not *presuppose* respect for their choices and decisions, for their freedom?

One may question other critical assumptions about autonomy. Is autonomy an expression of the characteristic separateness of male experience; or, on the contrary, is autonomy a condition of women's freedom and self-regard just as it is for men? Such questions are linked by asking whether critical theory's assumptions about partiality rest on the self-defeating skeptical paradox and whether critics have raised the stakes for legitimating talk of objectivity, neutrality, autonomy, and rights so high that they can never be satisfied.

A second philosophical tool for examining critical theory, closely related to Strawson's analysis of skepticism, is Donald Davidson's critique of the idea of a conceptual scheme. Whether or not they use the term explicitly, feminists, critical race theorists, and critical legal theorists often write as if they commend seeing legal discourse as a contest among competing conceptual schemes. On this view, as the domination of the powerless by the empowered is ameliorated, these conceptual schemes move toward engagement in what Rorty terms "conversation."

Davidson says that "[c]onceptual relativism is a heady and exotic doctrine, or would be if we could make good sense of it."[29] He argues that "[t]he dominant metaphor of conceptual relativism, that of differing points of view, seems to betray an underlying paradox. Different points of view make sense, but only if there is a common coordinate system on which to plot them; yet the existence of the common system belies the claim of dramatic incomparability."[30] Critical theorists are on the horns of a dilemma, implicitly presupposing a conceptual scheme that they explicitly reject as untenable.

They may attempt to salvage talk of conceptual schemes by contending that the language of theorists as outsiders provides the common coordinate system by which to plot the different "insider" points of view. But this attempt is open to two serious objections. First, the critical theorist assumes rather than argues that the language of objectivity, autonomy, and rights belongs to particular subjective points of view and not to the common coordinate scheme. Secondly, the kind of empirical challenge that the critical theorist offers to *particular* claims about rights and autonomy, for example that they reinforce power and/or are self-defeating, implies that the *language* of rights and autonomy is inescapably the common scheme for debate. It is the language needed and used by the critical theorist herself to make her points.

These two objections suggest that the implicit use by critical theory of inside/outside metaphors begs serious questions. For one thing, the argument from skepticism puts in question whether critical theory uses the terms, "objectivity," "autonomy," "rights," in a way that conforms to normal use. Davidson's analysis implies that such terms and points of view can and perhaps must be seen as belonging to a bridging vocabulary or array of concepts, one that binds the powerless and the powerful, men and women, minorities and majorities as much as it distinguishes them. One cannot assign concepts and arguments by fiat to the realm of partiality rather than the realm of mutuality.

Some critical theorists themselves anticipate these objections. Unger draws attention to a distinction between what he calls ordinary skepticism and true skepticism. "The only true skepticism about knowledge is the radical one – as irrefutable as it is empty – that denies that controversies over particular truths could ever reveal anything about the world other than the stratagems of our self-deception or that they could even allow us to pursue our practical interests more successfully."[31] Distinguishable from such true skepticism is "ordinary" or "normative" skepticism which "represents an attack upon one form of normative argument by the proponents of another. Behind such attacks we are likely to find disagreements over what personality and society are really like and how we may live in society."[32]

Unger denies that he is a "true skeptic." Thus, unlike Kennedy, West, MacKinnon, and others who concern themselves primarily with strategies of self-deception, he employs a conceptual apparatus for positive normative argument. Unlike most critical theorists, he does not raise the stakes for normative argument about truth beyond the possibility of realization. Rather, he engages liberals and others in intelligible disagreements over the nature of personhood and society.

Rorty's remarks about "outsideness" also convey insight into the problem of changing meaning by speaking from "outside" a conceptual scheme. Rorty concerns himself with outsideness in trying to refute foundationalism. As a pragmatist, he seeks to show (as we have already seen) "that it is useless to hope that objects will constrain us to believe the truth about them, if only they are approached with an unclouded mental eye, or a rigorous method, or a perspicuous language."[33] No method, no language lets us go *outside* our methods and languages to find out how "things really are." That sort of aspiration is a quixotic quest.

In this form, Rorty's critique of foundationalism harmonizes with the Strawsonian critique of skepticism. Both foundationalism and skepticism ratchet up the stakes for objectivity and truth and do so by changing the use of terms. But Rorty's account of the argument is flawed in a way that makes him in fact speak in the voice of an outsider *malgré lui*. If the foundationalist's notions of objectivity and truth carry unacceptable baggage, *so too* does Rorty's claim that all opinions are subjective and that the notion of truth must yield to the notion of solidarity. To make the latter claim is to digest only half of the rejection of foundationalism because it is to deploy the notions of subjectivity and falsity *as the foundationalist would use it*. A fully consistent antifoundationalist account would say, by contrast, that the criteria for using objectivity, subjectivity, truth, and falsity descriptively must be the criteria used by insiders, but insiders who are not hostage to foundationalist assumptions. Thus, Rorty, in commending subjectivity and solidarity, stands foundationalism on its head but continues to use terms as a foundationalist, an outsider, would use them. This instantiates the skeptical paradox by employing untenable criteria for objectivity/subjectivity and truth.

IV. Antifoundationalism without skepticism

I have argued that some critical theorists assume that political and legal disagreements are produced by rival conceptual schemes, each scheme harboring its own illusions about truth and objectivity. This picture generates skeptical paradoxes and embodies incoherent assumptions. It must therefore yield to a more complex picture of agreement and disagreement than one positing rival conceptual schemes. The task is to accommodate the best insights of antifoundationalism without stumbling over this misleading picture and its skeptical implications.

Links between (a) the epistemological alternatives of foundationalism and antifoundationalism and (b) the debate between liberals and communitarians need to be clarified. As portrayed by its critics, liberalism rests on a limited notion of the common good based on respect for persons' autonomy and on a shared conception of the rights ingredient to such autonomy. Such critics of liberalism argue that the notion of the common good is not thin but empty because autonomy is itself an altogether indeterminable value, because the political and legal rights of autonomy cannot be specified without favoring one or another controversial system of ideas and power.

What forms of foundationalism are associated with liberalism? Liberal legal philosophers such as Ronald Dworkin sometimes argue that over time a legal system "works itself pure."[34] Others, for example Owen Fiss, argue that objectivity is secured by the disciplining rules that govern judicial interpretation.[35] This idea of an objective consensus achieved through collective articulation of shared goals and values is an example of what Rorty criticizes as the search for truth with a privileged method and an unclouded eye, the search for foundations.

Even if the foundational version of liberalism must be given up, the project of liberalism can be construed and defended on alternative (antifoundational) grounds. Let's distinguish two antifoundational perspectives. The first, as we have seen, is distinguished by an assault on truth and objectivity as masks for bias and coercion. It is harnessed, as in Rorty's analysis, to a social picture in which society is divided into subcommunities each with a distinctive conceptual scheme and in which law is the legitimating ideology of those with power.

A different kind of antifoundationalism focuses on individuals rather than groups. This approach, like the first, rejects the notion of a privileged method to "truth" (foundations) and affirms a plurality of conceptual strategies, ways of understanding and interpreting experience and ascribing value. But this second kind of antifoundationalism attends to those aspects of consciousness and language that bind an individual, conceptually and experientially, to the rest of society as well as to those aspects that separate and distinguish one person from another.

The second kind of antifoundationalism rests on the following observations. In legal and political debate, as in other kinds of deliberation, persons characteristically understand and anticipate the arguments and responses of others. They share language, not only rules governing reference but also shared communicative techniques of irony, nuance, implication, and so on. They share a sense of what is and what is not relevant to debates. Their disagreements – whether about civil rights, or abortion, or the general scope of liberty or privacy – generally have a predictable shape even when they have an unpredictable resolution. In such debates, disagreement reflects not merely different value orientations. For example, debates about abortion rights or privacy inevitably reflect differences about many kinds of belief – about human nature, about the course of history, about the ideals at the heart of our culture, and about the nature of human suffering. Fact and value are bound inextricably, and each person's mode of understanding reflects her personal history, the evolution of her personal strategies for understanding.

If all this is correct, then in any debate it is an open rather than a closed question whether the conceptual strategies of individuals are bridged or not by shared beliefs regarding respect for persons and basic rights. Neither agreement nor disagreement on such fundamental issues can be presupposed in general. Agreement on these issues depends on the pervasiveness of underlying beliefs about such matters as the efficacy of self-awareness and action, the circumstances of human flourishing, the role of government and law, and the meaning of history. When agreement on these relevant beliefs extends across the disparate groups of society – across groups in and out of power, across the races, across genders – then the ideals of autonomy will also be shared and generally serve as the parameters of debate. In these circumstances liberalism correctly mirrors and articulates a shared heritage of value and shared projections of goals.

If it is possible to harmonize liberalism (holding autonomy and rights provisionally to be bridge concepts) with an antifoundational epistemology in this way, then liberals may claim that their descriptions of social value and legal rights are true and objective in the important but limited sense of being deeply embedded in shared belief systems. Each individual has some beliefs or convictions that are readily overturned by evidence: a belief in the quality of a restaurant may be unseated by one bad meal, and a belief in the life dates of Flaubert may be revised upon inspection of an encyclopedia. She has other beliefs and convictions that are so basic to her interpretive and justificatory strategies that they serve as the measure for other beliefs; religious beliefs, beliefs about human nature (human capacities, vulnerabilities, etc.), and beliefs about politics or economy often have this character. The latter kind of belief, one by which the individual organizes and judges experience, is what that person holds true, what one who is necessarily "inside" her way of understanding means by "truth." When such beliefs have the same deep role for persons generally in the society, their status as truths is widely shared. Liberals can be said to claim that their observations about autonomy and the rights of autonomy are true in this sense.

Similarly, reasoning about rights is objective *not* when it involves a privileged insight into eternal verities but when it follows justificatory patterns that are generally recognized as part of the shared practice. Judges who disagree can nonetheless be said to be objective when they justify their decisions by using understandable beliefs about human nature, the role of government, deference to history, and so on. Judgments not grounded in these ways are appropriately called subjective preferences, arbitrary conclusions even in relation to what their author is presumed to believe.

These accounts of truth and objectivity reflect the way these concepts are understood by "insiders" and yet are compatible with an antifoundational account of reasoning. This account does not imply that insiders are deluded about the truth or objectivity of their claims because it does not describe the claimants as appealing to timeless verities. Moreover, antifoundationalism of this (second) kind does not imply that individuals as insiders are trapped within irreconcilable and discrete conceptual schemes.

The second and preferable kind of antifoundationalism does not generate skeptical paradoxes because it does not involve distorted criteria for truth and objectivity in political and legal discourse. It does not claim to find foundational assumptions at the heart of "insider" reasoning and therefore does not discredit such reasoning from an "outsider's" perspective. Rather, this second kind of antifoundational analysis is committed to a univocal sense of truth and objectivity, terms that characterize judgments made by participants who follow divergent justificatory strategies that are, nonetheless, mutually understood to have a certain epistemological precedence within a shared practice. Given this epistemological basis, liberalism as a theory asserts that autonomy and a particular account of the rights of autonomy are widely and deeply presupposed.

V. Liberalism and critical theory reassessed

We have seen that liberalism may be challenged in two altogether different ways. The first kind of challenge, characteristically offered by conservatives but also by left-oriented communitarians, is framed as an attack on liberal *policy*. Liberalism, from this standpoint, lacks a coherent and well-formed sense of the common good as well as respect for the values implicit in tradition. Because the role of government is to define and pursue the common good and to perpetuate the traditional norms and bonds of the community, liberalism subverts that role insofar as it emphasizes minority rights or individual rights as a trump over government policy.

This first (communitarian) challenge is intuitive and is an appeal to what John Rawls, in defending liberalism, calls "reflective equilibrium." "It is an equilibrium because at last our principles and judgments coincide; and it is reflective since we know to what principles our judgments conform and the premises of their derivation. At the moment everything is in order. But the equilibrium is not necessarily stable."[36] The method of reflective equilibrium is one of testing intuitions about the justice and fairness of particular decisions against more general (tentative) principles which order and explain them. To what extent do various ways of elaborating the notion of autonomy through the articulation of rights fit our intuitions of justice? The method of reflective equilibrium tends to yield agreement on abstract and general principles rather than on more specific ones. The persuasiveness of liberalism over communitarianism depends on acceptance of quite general principles, principles giving priority to rights of autonomy in the face of the claims of tradition and of a richer notion of the common good.

Critical theory's challenge to liberalism is altogether different. We have seen that communitarians agree with liberals that intuitions about justice and fairness are shared and are to be regarded as objective. These intuitions can therefore serve as parameters of discourse in pursuit of reflective equilibrium. But communitarians believe that these intuitions yield communitarian and not liberal principles. Critical theory makes no such methodological concession. Indeed, it condemns appeals to justice and fairness just as it condemns appeals to autonomy and rights as masking preferential agendas with the legitimating rhetoric of neutrality. It condemns, in other words, the idea of a bridging set of concepts that transcends conceptual schemes. On this analysis, liberalism is not bad (or counterintuitive) policy but incoherent epistemology. Competing agendas are all there can be.

My point in parts III and IV was not to defend liberalism in general but rather to identify the flawed and paradoxical character of the critical challenge. Not all writers identified (or self-identified) with critical theory speak of irreconcilably diverse conceptual schemes. My diagnosis of critical theory as flawed by skepticism and its paradoxes applies only to this one form of argument found within critical theory, not to critical theory in general. Critical writers in fact offer both kinds of criticisms of liberalism, that it has counterintuitive policy implications *and* that it is based on an incoherent epistemology. Having considered the second of these criticisms, I turn once more to the first.

In part critical theory confronts liberalism with a series of admonitions rather than counterarguments. One admonition is unexceptionable and is the common denominator of all forms of hermeneutics, the proposition that theoretical discourse reflects the perspective of the theorist. Among other things, this means that the way in which an issue is formulated, the purpose served in addressing the issue, the tools used in addressing it, and the criteria of successful analysis or resolution of the issue are all affected by the personal history of the theorist and the culture to which she belongs. To concede this is not to concede that all theorizing is biased and subjective. It is, however, to concede that one's practical assumptions about neutrality and objectivity must be tested continually in discourse with diverse fellow discussants. Claims of neutrality and objectivity are always provisional and always made relative to the shared tests for bias and partiality within a particular shared deliberative practice.

A second admonition is that debates about liberalism, autonomy, and rights can be general and abstract in a way that conceals genuine disagreement. Liberals who try to show that there is broad and deep agreement about important aspects of autonomy – self-awareness, self-respect, and the capacity to make and implement choices – *may* camouflage disagreement about the political, social, and economic circumstances that make autonomy possible. Disagreement about concrete instances of these rights may and will exist within the context of adherence to a more general framework. The success of an argument for liberalism depends essentially on how well this array of general insights solves concrete problems.

The most destructive charge made by critical theory is that liberals cannot solve problems because agreement even on basic terms and commitments is illusory. I have tried to show why this charge fails insofar as it rests on a skeptical form of antifoundationalism. On the other hand, the challenge of communitarianism to liberalism is that at the most abstract level the ideal of autonomy cannot adequately express and serve the ends of society. On this point, debate must remain open.

This essay is about individualism in two different but complementary senses. First it identifies respect for individuals as a defining characteristic of liberalism. The story that guides liberals is one in which individuals are doubly threatened, by other persons who may harm or offend them and by government. The power of government may not only harm persons but may impose on them a particular version of the common good, the version held by the majority or by those who are otherwise in control. For liberals, government and law function justifiably and well whenever they show sensitivity to these threats and act to minimize them. Critical theorists tend to regard this view of government and law as naive about power and domination – physical and conceptual – in social arrangements. Communitarians, on the other hand, are less concerned with power and domination than liberals *or* critical theorists and argue that government and law must shape and limit individual choices in the light of a larger conception of the common good.

This essay is also individualistic in its methodology. It questions and rejects the implication of critical theorists that individuals merely instantiate groups with which they share conceptual schemes and values, groups that they represent by virtue of race, gender, or a history of powerlessness (or of power). My methodological assumption, which draws on the liberal notion of autonomy, is that individuals have unique justificatory strategies and ways of understanding, and yet are bound to deliberative practices that bridge their several unique perspectives. They recognize each other's ways of thinking as belonging to a shared practice and, while maintaining a stake in their own ways of thinking, recognize that others have a corresponding stake in theirs. A model of deliberative practices that takes account of these features is different from a model in which individuals inhabit discrete and separate conceptual domains. Such a mistaken model can explain neither the bridging concepts through which discourse occurs nor the self-awareness of individuals engaged in such discourse.

Individualism and liberalism are sometimes attacked as tools of cultural and ideological imperialism. To think of them, as I have suggested, as bridging theories rather than as ingredients of a parochial conceptual framework is, it is said, to mask and rationalize the cannibalization of one framework by another. But those who make this kind of critical argument may themselves perpetrate a kind of imperialism and abuse of power. They may rule out the possibility of communication by suggesting that all political discourse is legitimating and none is legitimate.

Notes

1 I wish to acknowledge the care and insight which my research assistants of the University of Connecticut School of Law, Melinda Westbrook and Marcella Hourihane, brought to this project.

2 See, for example, J. Feinberg, *Harmless Wrongdoing* (New York: Oxford University Press, 1988), 81–121.

3 Ibid., 83–6.

4 Ibid., 84.

5 Ibid., 88.

6 Ibid., 87–90.

7 Ibid., 90–8.

8 Ibid., 107.

9 These themes are explored and defended in the first three volumes of Feinberg's

The Moral Limits of the Criminal Law, of which *Harmless Wrongdoing* is the last. The others are *Harm to Others* (1984), *Offense to Others* (1985), and *Harm to Self* (1986).

10 Compare, for example, Ronald Dworkin's defense of liberalism in *Taking Rights Seriously* (Cambridge: Harvard University Press, 1977), 82–90, with Michael Sandel's discussion of the self as moral subject in *Liberalism and the Limits of Justice* (Cambridge University Press, 1982), 15–65.

11 D. Kennedy, "Form and Substance in Private Law Adjudication," 89 *Harvard Law Review* 1685 (1976).

12 Ibid., 1717.

13 Ibid.

14 Ibid., 1772.

15 Ibid., 1771.

16 Ibid., 1775.

17 R. Gordon, "Critical Legal Histories," 36 *Stanford Law Review* 57, 94 (1984).

18 This view is associated with the work and influence of Carol Gilligan. See especially *In a Different Voice: Psychological Theory and Women's Development* (Cambridge: Harvard University Press, 1982). Among legal scholars Robin West has drawn heavily and provocatively on Gilligan's work.

19 C. MacKinnon, "Feminism, Marxism, Method and the State," 7 *Signs* (1982): 515, 516.

20 R. West, "Jurisprudence and Gender," 55 *University of Chicago Law Review* 1, 5–6 (1988).

21 R. Unger, *The Critical Legal Studies Movement* (Cambridge: Harvard University Press, 1986) 12.

22 S. Brewer, "Choosing Sides in the *Radical Critiques* Debate," 103 *Harvard Law Review* 1844, 1851 (1990).

23 R. Rorty, *Consequences of Pragmatism* (Minneapolis: University of Minnesota Press, 1982), 165.

24 R. Rorty, *Objectivity, Relativism, and Truth* (Cambridge University Press, 1991), 21.

25 Ibid.

26 See R. Rorty, *Philosophy and the Mirror of Nature* (Princeton University Press, 1979), 389–95.

27 P. F. Strawson, *Individuals: an Essay in Descriptive Metaphysics* (London: Methuen, 1959), 106.

28 Ibid., 34.

29 D. Davidson, "On the Very Idea of a Conceptual Scheme," in *Inquiries into Truth and Interpretation* (Oxford: Clarendon Press, 1984), 183.

30 Ibid., 184.

31 Unger, *Critical Legal Studies Movement*, 96.

32 Ibid.

33 Rorty, *Consequences of Pragmatism*, 165.

34 See R. Dworkin, "'Natural' Law Revisited," 34 *University of Florida Law Review* 165 (1982).

35 See O. Fiss, "Objectivity and Interpretation," 34 *Stanford Law Review* 739 (1982).

36 J. Rawls, *A Theory of Justice* (Cambridge: Harvard University Press, 1971), 20.

7

Tort liability and the limits of corrective justice

JULES L. COLEMAN

Oliver Wendell Holmes held the view that a loss should remain where it has fallen (naturally) unless a good reason exists for shifting (by law) its incidence. Among the losses Holmes had in mind were those resulting from accidents. What are the good reasons for shifting the costs of accidents? Rules specifying the conditions for shifting a loss are "tort liability rules." The core liability rule is the fault rule according to which a loss may be shifted from a victim to someone else only if the party who is being asked to shoulder the loss is *at fault* in having caused it, only if, in other words, the victim's loss is the party's fault.

The fault rule invites two kinds of distinct philosophic inquiries, one analytic or conceptual, the other normative. The analytic questions concern its meaning or truth conditions. Under what conditions are sentences of the form, "such-and-such loss is so-and-so's fault," true? The normative questions concern its defensibility. Why, and under what conditions, is imposing liability on the basis of fault justifiable?

In his "Sua Culpa,"[1] Joel Feinberg provides both an account of the meaning of "his-fault" judgments and a defense of the practice of imposing liability on the basis of fault. On behalf of the claim that liability is justly imposed on those who are at fault in causing another's loss, Feinberg notes that otherwise the innocent victim will have to bear his own costs and that would constitute an injustice to him, a penalty against his "innocence." As between a faulty injurer and a faultless victim, the loss should be imposed on the faulty injurer in order to protect the innocence of the faultless victim. Thus, liability is not imposed on those at fault in order to punish or otherwise to penalize them, as it would be under a more conventional retributive account. Rather, imposing liability on the faulty is a way of protecting the faultless. According to Feinberg, the principle at work is the "weak retributive" principle.

The weak retributive principle has a limited scope at best. In fact it provides no reason for imposing a loss on those who are at fault in harming others. Instead, it provides a reason for imposing a liability on the faulty if the choice is between imposing it either on the faulty or the faultless. Were there another way of protecting the innocent – perhaps by distributing accident costs throughout the population as a whole, or through a voluntary no-fault insurance pool – the weak retributive principle would provide no reason for imposing the victim's loss on the faulty. Indeed, the weak retributive principle would simply not apply.

No one who is at fault is innocent in the appropriate sense. This is as true of those whose fault is "harmless" as it is of those whose faulty conduct harms the interests and rights of others. Imposing the losses of innocent victims on faulty agents will have the effect of protecting the victim's innocence, whether or not the faulty agent's conduct harms anyone. Therefore, to the extent Feinberg's argument is sound, it does not distinguish among those whose faulty conduct harms others and those whose faulty doings are harmless. In short, the weak retributive principle does not provide a reason for imposing liability on those at fault in harming others. It does not give adequate weight to the causal connection between fault and harm, and it applies only if there are no other ways of protecting the victim's innocence.

In some of my work, most recently in *Risks and Wrongs*, I have taken up the problems first addressed by Feinberg. Instead of grounding the fault rule in the weak retributive principle, I have advanced the claim that the best moral reason for allocating accident costs on the basis of fault derives from the principle of corrective justice.[2] A person who suffers a loss as a consequence of another's fault incurs a wrongful loss. Corrective justice brings faulty agents together with wrongful losses by providing agent-relative reasons for acting in the form of duty to repair. Imposing the victim's loss on the injurer who is at fault in causing the harm is one way of discharging through law the injurer's duty in morality under corrective justice. Thus, I have tried to provide a reason in justice for imposing liability upon those who are at fault in causing harm to others that is not based on protecting the innocence of victims, but is instead grounded in the duties of injurers to their victims.

Sometimes an individual can incur a duty to repair a loss that he is responsible for but not at fault in having created. The best example is of permissible conduct that is nevertheless invasive of the rights of others. Conduct invasive of the rights of others, whether justified or not, can create wrongful losses within the meaning of corrective justice.[3] This is one way in which rights have normative significance. Let me explain. Grant me that rights protect or secure legitimate interests. Not every legitimate interest, however, reaches the level of a right. I have a legitimate interest in the success of my scholarly endeavors, but no right to their success. One way of cashing out the moral significance of the difference is this: Not every harming of a legitimate interest grounds a claim to repair in justice; only faulty or wrongful harmings do. On the other hand, every harming of a right (at least potentially) grounds a claim to repair in justice, whether the harming is permissible or wrongful. In torts, cases like *Vincent v. Lake Erie* are examples of permissible, yet tortious invasions of rights, in which liability is thought appropriate.[4] In morality, a good example of a permissible invasion of a right is given by Feinberg's famous backpacker.[5]

In sum, I hold that there are at least two ways in which an agent's conduct can create wrongful losses within the meaning of corrective justice. Wrongful losses can result from conduct that is at fault in harming a legitimate interest. The loss is wrongful because the conduct that causes it is. Alternatively, wrongful losses can result from conduct that harms or invades a right, whether or not that conduct is itself wrongful. Here the loss is wrongful because it results from the invasion of a right. I refer to invasions of rights as wrongs, and to wrongful conduct as wrongdoing. Thus, in my view, wrongful losses can arise from wrongdoing or wrongs.

Many of the cases governed by lability rules in torts, both strict and fault based, can be understood as reflecting the social decision to implement in law the moral principle of corrective justice – or so I have argued. Indeed, the core of tort law, in my view, expresses just such a commitment to corrective justice. On the other hand, many of the claims to repair and the duties to provide it that are sustained by tort law are not best understood in these terms. Though important, corrective justice is only part of the story. More importantly, the relationship between law and corrective justice is much more complicated than we have so far suggested. For it is not simply a question of whether and to what extent the law implements corrective justice. Instead, the extent to which corrective justice itself imposes *moral* duties and reasons for acting within a particular community is a function of the nature and scope of legal and other practices, including those governing the allocation of accident costs.

This essay tries to make sense of and defend both of the following claims, then: (1) Many of the important rights and duties sustained in tort law are justifiable departures from tort law's corrective justice core; and (2) the extent to which corrective justice (as a moral principle) creates reasons for acting in a community depends on the nature and scope of nonmoral, including legal, practices. So it is a mistake to think of law only in terms of the extent to which it implements or is otherwise influenced by morality. The scope of morality can itself be determined in part by legal practice; or so I will argue.

Four kinds of cases [1]

With regard to the claim that many of the duties sustained in tort law do not implement corrective justice, it will be helpful to distinguish among four different kinds of cases.

1. The victim has suffered a loss owing to the fault of the injurer or as a result of a right of his being invaded. The victim's loss is imposed on the injurer whose fault or conduct is responsible for it.
2. The victim has suffered a loss owing to the fault of the injurer or as a

result of a right of his being invaded. The victim's loss is imposed on someone other than his injurer, someone who is not responsible for its occurence.

3. The victim has suffered a loss that is no one's fault and which does not involve a right of his being invaded. (For example, he loses out to another in a competitive business context.) The victim's loss is imposed on the party whose conduct is causally responsible for the loss, but who is otherwise faultless.

4. The victim has suffered a loss that is no one's fault and which does not involve a right of his being invaded. But instead of the loss being imposed on the party whose conduct is causally responsible for the loss (as in case 3), it is imposed on someone else altogether.

Whereas tort law provides us with examples of all four kinds of cases, only cases of the first sort implicate corrective justice. If I am right that corrective justice represents the core of tort law, then these other cases must be departures from corrective justice. The question is whether, and under what conditions, these departures are justifiable or defensible.

Suppose a manufacturer provides an ineffective (or inefficient) warning. It is inefficient because it fails fully or adequately to warn and, therefore, to deter. Someone uses the product and injures himself as a result. In order for his loss to be wrongful under corrective justice, the warning would have had to be ineffective; the victim would have had to have read it; had the warning been adequate it would have deterred him from using the product; he would have had to use the product believing that it was safe for him and so on. An optimal warning would have deterred him from using the product had he read it. The warning on the product would not have. In fact, the victim never read the warning. The warning is not optimal, but it does not in fact contribute to the victim's loss. Though there is no denying that the manufacturer is at fault, the victim's loss is not the manufacturer's fault. The victim has suffered a loss, but not one for which he has a claim in corrective justice to repair. One might even say that the loss is his own fault.

Nevertheless, a court might well impose liability on the product manufacturer for the purpose of encouraging more efficient warnings. Though he has no right to it, compensation provides the victim with an incentive to litigate. By litigating, he acts as a private regulator. The manufacturer has a defective warning that needs to be improved. If part of the goal of the law is to encourage product manufacturers to provide optimal warnings, why should a court wait until a victim comes along who has a valid claim to repair in justice? The goal of encouraging efficient warnings does not discriminate between those victims who have suffered wrongful losses and those who have not.

Presumably few would object if the state fined the manufacturer an amount equal to the damage that results from a defective warning. Suppose the money from that fine were to go toward funding the relevant public regulatory scheme. In private litigation, the victim is acting as a private prosecutor. The liability judgment works like a fine. Instead of funding the public regulatory scheme, it funds a private regulatory scheme. On what grounds could one object to holding the product manufacturer liable to the "victim"? He is being paid to "prosecute."

The plausibility or desirability of the private prosecutor approach does not depend on the legitimacy of the underlying claim. Whether or not the victim has a right in corrective justice to repair, imposing his loss on the manufacturer can be defended on the grounds that it creates an attractive system of incentives to litigate and to invest in safety.

Here, then, is a case in which the plaintiff recovers against a defendant, though they are not brought together by considerations of corrective justice. The defendant has acted wrongfully, but his wrongdoing is not responsible for the plaintiff's loss. The plaintiff has no right to repair in justice; the defendant has no duty either.

This sort of case differs, therefore, from others in which the plaintiff has a right to repair in justice, but liability for his loss is imposed on someone other than the wrongdoer or injurer. Let's now consider such cases.

Liability and the cheapest cost-avoider

In the case I am imagining, the victim has a claim in justice to repair, but the defendant does not have a duty in justice to him. The interesting feature of this case is that someone other than the defendant owes a duty of repair to the victim. Thus, there are the victim who has the sort of claim that would be valid under the principle of corrective justice, as well as an agent who has the duty to the victim because he is responsible for having created the loss, and some third party who the court is prepared to hold liable to the victim because he is the cheapest cost-avoider, though he is in no way responsible for the harm. (For example, suppose you wrongfully injure me causing substantial damage, but instead of me suing you, I sue your Dean who is not responsible for my loss or your conduct, but who, I believe, might be a good person to sue for a variety of reasons. Perhaps he has "deeper" pockets, or he is the cheapest cost-avoider, that is, he can optimally reduce (in the future) the probability of harm at the lowest cost.)

Were the court to impose liability on the cheapest cost-avoider, it would be enforcing a claim valid in corrective justice, but it would not otherwise be implementing corrective justice (it would not be imposing the loss on someone who has the duty to repair it). The question here is whether in imposing the victim's loss on the third party tort law violates corrective justice.

One reason for thinking that imposing the victim's loss on someone other than the individual who has the moral duty to repair it is wrong is that the third party does not volunteer to have the loss imposed upon him; another is that the third party is innocent of wrongdoing. Suppose Donald Trump volunteers to pay all my debts of repair. If he pays them off, all claims against me are extinguished thereby; no injustice is done. The example suggests that someone other than the injurer can shoulder the victim's loss without violating corrective justice. In that example, however, Trump volunteers to bear my costs, and it is for that reason, one might say, that no violation of corrective justice occurs. Had my costs been imposed on him without his consent, our moral assessment of the situation would have been very different. This suggests that corrective justice is violated when the costs of accidents are imposed on someone who does not agree so to bind herself.

Involuntariness is not an adequate criterion of wrongfulness, however. There is no corrective injustice in imposing the victim's loss on the *wrongdoer*, though the wrongdoer does not agree to bear those costs. Similarly, a victim may sometimes be asked to bear his own costs (e.g., when no one else has an obligation in justice to shoulder them), though there is no reason to suppose that he agrees so to bind himself. Though it may sometimes be unjust to impose a loss on someone who has not agreed so to bind herself, the mere fact that someone does not volunteer to be liable is not sufficient to make imposing a loss on her wrongful and a violation of corrective justice.

Neither the cheapest cost-avoider nor the wrongdoer agrees to bear the victim's costs. Though neither agrees to shoulder the relevant costs, there is an obvious difference between them; the cheapest cost-avoider is, ex hypothesi, innocent of mischief, the wrongdoer is not. This suggests that the reason that it is permissible to impose the victim's loss upon the wrongdoer, but not on the cheapest cost-avoider (if he is not the wrongdoer), is that the latter is innocent of wrongdoing, whereas the former is not. The reason that imposing the victim's loss on the cheapest cost-avoider violates corrective justice, then, is that corrective justice prohibits imposing losses on innocent persons. Thus, imposing the loss on the wrongdoer is compatible with corrective justice (even required by it perhaps), but imposing the same loss on the cheapest cost-avoider violates justice.

In fact, imposing liability on someone innocent of wrongdoing need not constitute a corrective injustice. Innocent individuals can sometimes have a duty in corrective justice to repair. Far from being an offense to justice, imposing liability on them may be required by it. An individual who justifiably infringes the right of another may have a duty in justice to repair, a duty grounded in the fact that his conduct constitutes a wrong to the person injured. I discussed such cases earlier. Following Joel Feinberg and Judith Thomson, we can call these infringement cases. *Vincent v. Lake Erie* is a good example; so, too, is Feinberg's backpacker. In both cases, the injurer has a very good, indeed compelling, reason for acting contrary to the constraints imposed on him by the rights of others. We capture this by saying that his conduct is, all things considered, justifiable. On the other hand, it is still conduct invasive of the rights of others, that is, contrary to the demands those rights impose. We capture this feature of the conduct by saying that his conduct, though justifiable, constitutes a wrong to the victim. Justifiably invading the rights of others can constitute a wrong, and when it does, it can give rise to a duty to repair in justice. Being innocent of blame, therefore, indeed, being worthy of praise, is not a bar to having a duty in morality to make good another's loss.

Because it is sometimes permissible to impose liability on the innocent and the unwilling, does it follow that imposing the loss on anyone, whether he or she is responsible for a loss or otherwise at fault, can be compatible with the demands of corrective justice? If it is permissible to impose a loss on anyone regardless of innocence or unwillingness to shoulder the costs, then a fortiori it is permissible to impose the loss on the cheapest cost-avoider.

By showing that it is not always impermissible to impose a loss on an innocent and unwilling party, we have not shown that the state would always be justified in doing so. In the first case, we showed that it may be permissible to impose the loss on the wrongdoer even if he does not volunteer to bear the loss. But there is a reason for imposing it on him, even if he does not volunteer, and that is that he is the wrongdoer; he has done wrong; he is not innocent of mischief. Then we showed that it is sometimes permissible to impose the loss on someone who has not done wrong. But in our example, the loss was imposed on someone who, though he did no mischief, had a duty in corrective justice to make repair nevertheless. He was not at fault, but he still committed a wrong. For all we have shown, the state may have authority to impose liability on someone only if they have a duty in corrective justice to repair. It's just that innocence and voluntariness are not essential to determining whether a person has such a duty.

On the other hand, we could view these examples as illustrating a different point, namely that the state must have a good reason for imposing liability. If it does not, then it acts beyond the scope of its authority, and in doing so, it may impose its own corrective injustices. Imposing the loss on someone who has the duty in corrective justice to make repair, whether or not that person volunteers or is innocent of fault, falls within the scope of its authority. By the same token, as the manufacturer example from the previous section shows, imposing the loss on the person who is in the best position to reduce harm also falls within the scope of its authority. If the loss is imposed on someone for good reason, that is, for a reason that falls within the scope of the state's authority to enforce or implement, no corrective justice is done.

The manufacturing example shows that creating a system of effective incentives to reduce the incidence of accidents could count as a good reason for imposing liability. In that case imposing the victim's loss on the cheapest cost-avoider would not violate corrective justice.

If the state is free to impose liability on the wrongdoer (under the auspices of corrective justice) or on the cheapest cost-avoider (under the auspices of efficiency consistent with corrective justice), then, provided the costs of searching out the best risk reducer are low enough, why would the state ever choose to implement corrective justice?[6] If the state chooses to implement corrective justice, then it will miss an opportunity to create a scheme of accident-cost-minimizing incentives, and for no good reason. As long as the victim who has a claim in corrective justice is compensated, why should the state foolishly impose the loss on the person with the moral duty in corrective justice to make repair if imposing it on the cheapest cost-avoider promises to accomplish some good and does not itself violate corrective justice? And, remember, imposing the loss on the cheapest cost-avoider does not violate corrective justice because the state has a good reason for imposing the loss on him, and therefore does him (the cheapest cost-avoider) no wrong.

If this is a sound argument, then it is problematic that a state should ever concern itself with making sure that the victim's loss is imposed on the party who has the duty in corrective justice to repair it. As long as the victim is compensated and some good is accomplished by imposing the loss on some-one who can do something about such losses, why bother? But the argument may not be sound. Imposing the loss on an innocent cheapest cost-avoider may in fact violate corrective justice. What might the argument that it does look like?

Perhaps the problem with imposing liability on the cheapest cost-avoider in the kind of case we are imagining is that the loss is imposed on an innocent individual when there is someone else who is a wrongdoer. The problem with this suggestion is that there are wrongdoers everywhere, all the time, most of whom are completely unconnected to the harm and to the goals of tort law. Imposing the loss on them would serve no obvious social policy or goal, other than the diffuse and not obviously defensible one of imposing burdens, even random ones, on wrongdoers. At least imposing the loss on the cheapest cost-avoider has the effect of creating an attractive and valuable incentive.

We are getting closer, however. Perhaps the real problem with imposing the victim's loss on the cheapest cost-avoider is that it is unjust to do so *when there is someone else who has the duty in corrective justice to make repair*. It may be permissible to impose a loss on the cheapest cost-avoider, even if that person is free of mischief and unwilling to bear the costs voluntarily – pro-vided there is no individual who has a duty in justice to bear those costs. If there is such a person, as there is in our example, then imposing the loss on the cheapest cost-avoider is wrongful for exactly that reason.

We might want to distinguish between two kinds of cases. In one, there is a wrongful loss, but there is no one who has a duty in corrective justice to repair it. In the other, there is a loss that someone has a duty in corrective justice to repair. The claim, then, is that although it may be permissible to impose liability on someone who is neither a wrongdoer nor otherwise responsible for the loss in the first case, provided there exists some other justification for doing so, it is impermissible to impose liability on someone other than the individual who has the duty in corrective justice in the latter case, whether or not there exists some other good reason for doing so.

This objection amounts to the claim that if the state has the opportunity to implement corrective justice in a particular case, then it must do so. To put the loss on anyone else, for whatever reason, is wrongful. And it is wrongful just because there is someone who has a duty to make repair in corrective justice. The fact that an opportunity exists for imposing liability in accord with corrective justice is, in effect, all that makes the imposition of liability on other grounds, however strong, wrongful. This conclusion follows only if corrective justice demands an absolute priority with respect to all other goals the state may legitimately pursue within a tort system. This conclusion cannot be sustained, however.

We might distinguish between two different ways in which imposing liability on someone unconnected or otherwise not responsible for an accident's occurrence might be viewed as imposing a wrongful loss. In one case there are no good reasons whatsoever for imposing the loss on her. She did not cause the harm; she was not negligent or otherwise at fault in any way; nor is she in a good position to reduce or spread risk. In this sense, the loss is imposed on her for no good reason connected to any plausible account of the point or purpose of accident law; it is imposed entirely without justification, and is wrongful in that sense. Liability, therefore, imposes a wrongful loss and violates the constraint of corrective justice. There may have been nothing wrongful in imposing the loss had she been in an especially good position to reduce or spread risk, both legitimate goals of tort law that fall within the state's authority to implement. Thus, what makes the imposition of liability wrongful, and thus a violation of corrective justice in this sense, is that there exists no good reason or justification recognized within the relevant political morality for imposing the loss on her.

Suppose, instead, that there exist good reasons of the sort recognized as legitimate within the relevant political morality for imposing the loss on her. Perhaps, she is the optimal risk-reducer. In the sense of wrongful just characterized, imposing liability would not be wrongful. However, we can imagine another sense of the term or criterion for its application that makes it wrongful to impose liability (even if there are good reasons of the sort the state is authorized to implement for doing so) that is, whenever liability could have been imposed on someone else who has the duty in corrective justice to make repair. Because there are good reasons for imposing the loss in some way other than that dictated by corrective justice, the only ground for holding that doing so is wrongful is that any such liability judgment forgoes the opportunity to do corrective justice. And that in turn can be wrongful only if doing corrective justice has some kind of absolute priority over other legitimate goals the state may pursue through its tort system.

I accept the first and reject the second way in which imposing losses on third parties can constitute a corrective injustice. The state must allocate costs for a reason that is within its authority to implement, and it must do so in a way that falls within the constraints of the relevant principles of justice and political morality. If it has no good reason of the relevant sort for imposing liability, it violates corrective justice, and, very likely, other principles of justice as well. On the other hand, if it acts on the basis of good reasons within the scope of its authority, it does not violate corrective justice, even though it does not implement it. Imposing the loss on an innocent third party may not be a good idea on other grounds, but it is not wrongful just because in doing so the state misses a chance to impose the loss on that person who has the duty in corrective justice. On the other hand, imposing the loss on a third party who is not a good risk-reducer or -spreader may create a wrongful loss, whether or not there is someone who has the duty in corrective justice to make repair, simply because there exists no justification for imposing the loss on him. The fact that someone has a duty to make repair in corrective justice has little, if anything, to do with the wrongfulness of imposing liability without a good reason for doing so.

In this account, corrective justice does not invariably or absolutely cancel or override reasons for acting that the state may be otherwise authorized to implement. It has no absolute priority with respect to the state's other legitimate goals.

I have not demonstrated just yet that mine is the proper conception of the role of corrective justice in political argument. I have not shown, in other words, that it is not wrongful to miss the opportunity to implement corrective justice whenever the opportunity to do so presents itself. Such a view depends on a political theory about the way in which considerations of corrective justice constrain other legitimate reasons for acting. In what follows, however, I want to show that far from constraining legal practices that might otherwise ignore its dictates, corrective justice, as a moral principle, is itself constrained by legal and other social practices. In other words, I want to defend the odd-sounding position that whether or not corrective justice imposes *moral* reasons for acting will depend on prevailing legal and social practices. If anything, the proponent of the view that it is unjust to forgo opportunities to implement corrective justice in legal practice whenever the opportunity presents itself has matters absolutely backwards.

Limiting corrective justice

It is one thing for a body of law to seek to achieve a particular goal or principle as its overarching ambition or purpose. It is quite another to devise a set of rules, guidelines, policies, and practices capable of actually implementing that ambition in practice. If I am correct, pursuing corrective justice is the point of the core, if not all, of our current tort practice. Implementing corrective justice requires a set of substantive liability rules, for example, a rule of liability for negligence. In addition to substantive liability rules, implementing corrective justice requires administrative rules establishing burdens of proof and evidence. These rules are defensible because they provide the best chance of practically implementing corrective justice under less than ideal circumstances; and they do so within the relevant constraints of justice. One consequence of applying these rules in particular cases is that there will be times when the outcome will not conform to what corrective justice would, under ideal circumstances, have required. The results of applying these rules under conditions of uncertainty, in other words, will be less than ideal. Therefore, we will have to be careful not to infer too much about the substantive goals of tort law from an examination of the cases.

Two cases famous in torts case books help to illustrate the relationship between administrative rules and the principles they are designed to implement. Consider first *Ybarra v. Spangard*.[7] In *Ybarra*, the plaintiff undergoes surgery, and, while under general anesthetic, is apparently mistreated. The plaintiff can establish neither negligence nor responsibility. He can prove that he suffered an injury. The court holds that the most plausible explanation of his injury suggests negligence on someone's part. The court applies the doctrine of res ipsa loquitur in order to shift the burden of proof to the defendants to show that no negligence transpired. In effect, the court holds that under the circumstances, each of the named parties within the operating room should have the burden of showing that he or she was not the responsible party. A defendant who cannot show that he or she was not responsible will remain subject to liability. And this will be true even if that defendant is not someone who has the duty in corrective justice to repair; even if, moreover, that person is not in a good position to reduce or spread the relevant risk.

Nevertheless, it is easy to see how such a rule for shifting the burden of proof could be thought of as constituting a plausible way of implementing corrective justice. In *Ybarra*, the best way for a defendant to free herself of the burden of liability is to identify the party who is responsible for the plaintiff's misfortune. Presumably, at least some of the defendants know who that person is. Being excused from liability provides each defendant with the incentive to reveal that information. If the information is revealed, then that person who is in fact responsible for the loss will be solely liable for it, and corrective justice will have been served.[8]

Summers v. Tice[9] can be given a similar rationale. In that case, two hunters negligently fire in the direction of a third. The plaintiff is hit by one bullet, but there is no way he can determine whose bullet is responsible for his injury. If, in order to recover, he had to identify the responsible party, he would be out of luck. Instead, the court allows the burden to be shifted to the defendants, both of whom acted negligently. Either could free himself of liability by showing that his bullet was not the effective one. In that case the other party whose bullet is responsible for the damage would be solely liable and corrective justice done. As it happens, the defendants are in no better position to identify the responsible bullet than is the plaintiff. Neither can free himself of liability. Both are liable to the plaintiff, when in fact only one has the duty in corrective justice to repair. Still, it is a mistake to infer that *Summers* marks a departure from corrective justice simply because someone other than the person who has the relevant duty must bear some of the costs. Rather, the outcome in *Summers* is a predictable consequence of applying evidentiary rules designed to implement corrective justice under conditions of uncertainty.

It is tempting to extend the rationale of *Summers* to modern torts cases like *Sindell*[10] and *Hymowitz*.[11] If *Summers* can be understood as an effort to extend the ambit of corrective justice, then *Sindell* and *Hymowitz* might be subject to a similar analysis. In each case plaintiffs had been injured as the result of diethylstilbesterol (DES) administered to their mothers during pregnancy as a miscarriage preventive, and the defendants were the manufacturers and marketers of the drug. During the period the defendants marketed DES, they knew or should have known that it causes cancerous or precancerous vaginal and cervical growths in the daughters of mothers who took it, but they failed to test for efficacy and safety or to warn of its potential danger. Because of the passage of time between ingestion of the drug by the mother and harm to the daughter, and the large number of manufacturers using the same drug formula, the plaintiffs in DES cases usually are not able to identify which defendant manufactured the drug ingested by their respective mothers.

Although the court in *Sindell* found inapplicable theories of "alternate liability," "concert of action" liability, and industry-wide ("enterprise") liability, it adopted a "market share" theory in order to find for the plaintiffs. Under the court's market share formula, the plaintiff joins as defendant the manufacturers of a substantial share of the particular market of DES from which her mother might have taken. Damages are apportioned to each defendant's share of that particular market, and each defendant may cross-claim against other manufacturers or demonstrate that it, in fact, could not have produced the particular drug ingested by the plaintiff's mother.

While also adopting the market share theory, the *Hymowitz* court rejected the particular or appropriate market limitation, choosing instead to apportion damages based on each named defendant's share of the national market. Admitting that the national market share test fails to provide a reasonable link between liability and risk created by a particular defendant to a particular plaintiff, the court concluded that such apportionment corresponds to overall culpability of each defendant measured by the risk created to the public at large. Given this overarching rationale, the court also rejected the idea in *Sindell* that a particular defendant could free itself of liability by showing that it could not have produced the particular drug ingested by the plaintiff's mother.

In the ideal *Sindell*-type case, all the wrongdoers and all the victims of wrongdoing are brought together in a consolidated litigation. Each victim is able to establish that she has suffered a wrongful loss caused by one or another of the defendants. Each defendant has been shown, moreover, to have fallen below the relevant standard of behavior. All that is left, according to corrective justice, is to link particular wrongdoers with their victims. If that could be done, then corrective justice could be achieved. But that is precisely what is missing and, worse, practically unobtainable. The absence of the relevant information, and the practical impossibility of obtaining it, make it impossible to link particular wrongdoers with their victims in the way required by corrective justice.

Following the line of reasoning in *Ybarra* and *Summers*, one could argue that the burden can be shifted legitimately to each of the many defendants to show that he is not responsible for anyone's wrongdoing. Indeed, that is part of the holding in *Sindell*. In other words, if a particular defendant can show that none of the drugs he manufactures is responsible for any of the harms suffered by members of the plaintiff class, he can free himself of liability. Because there is no practical way of determining which harms are the responsibility of those manufacturers who are not able to free themselves of liability, the court adopts the principle that each should be liable for that percentage of the total damages that corresponds to its share of the market. This is the principle of market share liability. If market share is a reasonable proxy for causal responsibility, then one can view *Sindell* as an extension of *Summers* and *Ybarra*, which in turn can be understood as efforts to pursue the overarching goal of corrective justice when facing substantial epistemic obstacles.

The problem with this, the standard interpretation of *Sindell*, is revealed by the ruling in *Hymowitz*. In *Hymowitz*, one of the defendants in fact establishes that his product is not causally responsible for any of the harms suffered by members of the plaintiff class. Under the *Sindell* formula, any defendant who can establish his freedom from causal responsibility is able to free himself of liability. The *Hymowitz* court, however, rejects this option, and allows the defendant liability reflecting his share of the national market.

One response to *Hymowitz* is to treat it as a mistake that does not conform to the administration of corrective justice story we have been weaving. Another alternative is to contend that *Hymowitz* in fact fits within the corrective justice account of tort law. This is Richard Wright's view.[12] According to Wright, *Hymowitz* establishes that the relevant *harm* for which people can be justly held liable in torts (in cases of this sort) is the *wrongful imposition of risk*. The defendant in *Hymowitz* cannot show that he did not impose unjustifiable risks. Indeed, he did. All he can show is that the risks he imposed did not mature into full blown harms of the relevant sort. Therefore, he can be held liable in corrective justice for the risks he creates. The degree of his liability reflects the degree of risk he imposes; his liability is for the harm he causes under the principle of corrective justice where the relevant harm is the unjustifiable risk created.

The problem with Wright's argument is that it is unmotivated and ad hoc. It is not helpful to say that *Hymowitz* introduces another category of harms particularly appropriate to cases of a certain sort (market share cases). Either the imposition of unjustifiable risk is the relevant harm in all cases, both those in which the risk matures and those in which it does not, or it is not. One cannot claim that in the uncomplicated torts case, the relevant harm is the injury the victim suffers, whereas in other cases in which this conception of the harm is problematic – those like *Hymowitz* – the relevant harm is the risk imposed. This is simply an ad hoc solution to a difficult problem.

This is not to suggest that one could not defend the view that the morally relevant harm in all torts cases is the unjustifiable imposition of risk. My trouble with Wright's solution is that he treats the imposition of risk as morally relevant in some cases and not in others. His solution lacks consistency and integrity. Let's take a moment to outline how one might go about defending the view that in all torts cases, complicated or not, the morally relevant harm is the imposition of unreasonable or unjustifiable risks. In the typical case in which the risk matures into injury, victims do not sue until they have suffered an injury because actual injury provides them with the best evidence that the wrongdoer has imposed unjustifiable risks. Actual harm is evidentiarily connected to the underlying wrong, which is the wrongful imposition of risk. In other cases, perhaps those of the DES variety, it may be possible to obtain evidence that the wrongdoer has wrongfully imposed risks on the plaintiff without the benefit of actual injury. In any case, actual harm provides no additional evidence of unjustifiable risk taking than that which is already available. Allowing a defendant to defeat liability by showing in fact that he caused no harm to anyone would undermine the possibility of holding him liable for what is the real harm for which he is responsible, namely, the wrongful imposition of risk. No doubt there will be problems in pursuing such a reconstruction of tort law. Still, such a project is needed if one wants to pursue the general line of interpretation of *Hymowitz* that the Wright argument suggests.

The standard interpretation rejects *Hymowitz* as a mistake, an unjustifiable departure from tort law's preoccupation with implementing corrective justice under the conditions of uncertainty bound to obtain. To his credit, Wright rejects this interpretation. His mistake is in thinking that *Hymowitz* can be defended as a form of corrective justice in which the relevant harm is the wrongful imposition of risk. The best interpretation of *Hymowitz*, however, does not view it as a mistake or as an attempt to implement corrective justice for a distinct category of harms. To understand *Hymowitz* and *Sindell*, we have to consider the principle of corrective justice once again.

Suppose that we all lived in New Zealand or that our community, wherever it was, decided to implement a no-fault plan like New Zealand's. Let's now set aside all questions about whether doing so would be a smart or otherwise desirable thing to do. The question we need to address is in what way does this no-fault plan affect or otherwise relate to the principle of corrective justice? Suppose Carol negligently rams her automobile into Alan. Under corrective justice, Alan has a right to repair in corrective justice and Carol has a duty to provide it. In the world in which Carol, Alan, and the rest of us live, however, Alan recovers from the treasury, not from Carol. What do we want to say about this situation as regards its bearing on corrective justice? There are at least three alternatives.

The first thing we might say is that our New Zealand plan affronts corrective justice. Carol has the duty to compensate Alan, and any other scheme in which Alan secures compensation violates corrective justice. Note that this example simply generalizes the problem we began discussing in the last section when we asked whether imposing liability in a particular case on some third party would create a wrongful loss whenever there exists an individual who has the duty to repair in corrective justice. In that case, corrective justice is "ignored" on a case-by-case basis; here it is being ignored systematically. If it is wrong to impose liability on someone who is not responsible for a loss when there is someone who can be held liable and is responsible, then it is wrong to do so on a general basis. So one view we might hold about New Zealand plans is that they are impermissible departures from corrective justice. To ignore corrective justice, to decide on some other scheme for allocating accident costs, is, in effect to violate corrective justice.

The second thing we might say is that the New Zealand plan has no bearing on the relationship between Alan and Carol with regard to corrective justice.

Alan has a moral right to recover and Carol a moral duty to compensate, both derivable from corrective justice. That Alan has been compensated in some other way does not change that fact. The compensation scheme is a public or legal mechanism; the relationship between Alan and Carol under corrective justice is private and moral. The legal institution cannot affect the moral relationships. Thus, if Alan suffers a million dollars in damages as a result of Carol's mischief, Carol owes Alan a million dollars; and that does not change as a result of the existence of some public compensation scheme.

Both of these alternatives are implausible. The New Zealand plan neither affronts corrective justice, nor is its existence irrelevant to corrective justice. If Alan recovers from the treasury, he no longer has a moral right to recover from Carol. Some who accept this conclusion might argue that the reason he has no moral claim against Carol is that he forfeits or gives it up by accepting another form of compensation. Others might say that his claim against Carol is extinguished by the fact that he consents to some other compensation scheme, and so on. Whatever the underlying reason, the important point for our purposes is that in fact he has no claim in corrective justice to repair.

The reason he has no claim in corrective justice to repair is that there exists some other mechanism through which the costs of accidents are to be allocated. That means that whether or not corrective justice in fact imposes moral duties on particular individuals is *conditional* upon the existence of other institutions for making good victims' claims to repair. The capacity within a particular community of corrective justice to impose the relevant *moral* duties depends on the existence of certain *legal* or *political* institutions or social practices.

Even tort theorists like Ernest Weinrib, who deny that it is permissible to impose a loss on an innocent third party in a particular case, claim that it may be permissible to substitute a New Zealand no-fault plan for the tort system as a whole. The suggestion is that the state for a variety of presumably good reasons might choose to forgo implementing in law the demands of corrective justice. It can choose, for example, not to have a tort system, even if the tort system is itself the legal embodiment of the ideal of corrective justice. This claim is revealing in its own right, but does not go far enough.

The view I am suggesting is that whether or not corrective justice itself imposes moral duties on individuals in a community will depend on other practices that are in effect. The reason is this. Corrective justice links agents with losses. It provides individuals with agent-relative reasons for acting. These reasons for acting can be superseded by other practices that create reasons for acting, both agent-neutral and agent-relative. Such practices can sometimes sever the relationship between agents and losses. The victim's wrongful loss may give her a right to recover. That right is part of the normative basis for imposing a duty of repair. The nature and scope of the duty depend on the practices in place. The content of the duty and the reasons for acting to which it gives rise do not follow logically from the nature of the right to repair, but from the normative practices in place within the community, practices that, in conjunction with the victim's right, give rise to specific obligations.

My view is not that other social and legal practices sever all of the relationships between wrongdoer and victim. After all, the wrongdoer may be responsible for the victim's loss. The question is to which duties does this relationship give rise. And my argument is that the nature and scope of the duties depend on the prevailing practices. Moreover, even if no-fault practices exist for handling accident costs, the injurer, and no one else, may have the duty to apologize, or the like.

The question before the state is not whether to forgo corrective justice; instead, it is, what ought to be done about losses including those that result from wrongful conduct. If there is a comprehensive plan put into effect for dealing with those losses by imposing them on everyone or on all those individuals who are at fault, whether or not their fault results in harm to others, then corrective justice itself imposes no duties within that community.[13] Thus, although corrective justice is private justice – justice between the parties – whether or not it imposes obligations between the parties depends on other social, political and legal practices. This, I take it, is a controversial, but I think inescapable truth about corrective justice. It may be true of other moral principles as well.

If corrective justice is conditional in this sense, then the state may choose to allocate accident costs in any number of ways. It may do so through a tort system that implements corrective justice; it may do so through a New Zealand no-fault scheme; it may do so through a generalized at-fault plan; it may do so through a variety of localized or limited at-fault plans; it may do so through a tort system that seeks to spread or minimize risk; or it may seek to do so through a tort system that seeks to do a combination of these things.

Suppose that instead of a New Zealand plan, our community had decided to implement an at-fault pool for automobile accidents. The total costs of injuries suffered by the victims of car accidents over some period of time would be summed and then distributed among those drivers who are at fault in operating their vehicles whether or not their fault actually leads to any damage. If everyone were equally at fault and drove equally as often, then the likely solution would be to divide the costs among the class of drivers equally. If some drove more than others, then the division of the costs would likely reflect each driver's "market share."

Given the view of corrective justice I have just articulated, were such a scheme in place, Alan would have no claim in corrective justice against Carol, and she would have no duty to him. It would be a mistake, moreover, to view the at-fault pool itself as an effort to extend the ambit of corrective justice to the case of many injurers and victims. That argument would not be improved by claiming either that the at-fault pool merely shifts evidentiary or other burdens in an effort to implement corrective justice in a world of uncertainty or that it implements corrective justice in which the relevant harm for which one is entitled to recover is the unjustifiable imposition of risk. The at-fault pool cannot be reconstructed as an implementation or extension of corrective justice. It is simply an alternative means for allocating traffic accident costs, one that if implemented and compatible with other demands of justice and morality, simply extinguishes all rights and duties under corrective justice.[14]

With this discussion in mind, let's return to the troubling cases of *Sindell* and *Hymowitz*. My suggestion is that we read the DES cases not as an effort to implement corrective justice in an imperfect world but as an effort to implement localized or constrained at-fault pools to deal with injuries caused by certain kinds of defective products. The losses are spread among those individuals who are at fault in creating unjustifiable risks of the sort that lead to the kinds of injuries that the members of the plaintiff class have suffered. If we assume that each manufacturer is equally at fault in producing a defective drug, the best approximation of the amount each should pay to the plaintiffs is given by the share of the market each has garnered. (The tort suit is used as a forum for implementing this plan simply because it uses the plaintiff class as private prosecutors and is presumably desirable on those grounds.)

The problem comes from trying to reconcile *Sindell* with *Hymowitz*. According to *Sindell*, although at fault, a defendant who could establish that his fault was not responsible for anyone's damage would free himself of liability. In *Hymowitz*, the absence of responsibility is inadequate to free the defendant of liability. *Hymowitz* is, in fact, the correct interpretation of the basic principles set forth in *Sindell*. *Sindell* is not an extension of corrective justice. Instead, it involves a localized at-fault plan. Under such a plan, whether or not one causes harm is irrelevant. Moreover, allowing a defendant who can show the absence of causal responsibility to free himself of liability will defeat the very point of allocating costs according to the fault of the agents.

To see this, return to our at-fault plan for automobile accidents. The plan allocates accident costs among motorists according to the risks associated with their motoring. Now suppose that we add a wrinkle to our plan that allows each motorist to free himself of liability by showing that his negligence is harmless. That little wrinkle completely destroys the at-fault pool. That is precisely the point: One can have either a corrective justice scheme or an at-fault pool but not both at the same time. For that reason, *Sindell* does not fully comprehend the underlying principles of liability that it creates. It is caught between two paradigms: corrective justice and at-fault liability. Perhaps, the *Sindell* court fails to see that the two cannot be reconciled; perhaps the court believes that imposing liability on the basis of fault or market share is at the heart of corrective justice, and that because it is, any defendant who can in fact show that he did not cause any harm should be able to free himself of liability. Whatever the reason, *Sindell* is torn between two conflicting approaches to allocating the relevant costs: one that imposes the duty in corrective justice; the other that imposes losses according to a localized at-fault scheme. Therefore, rather than being an unjustifiable departure from the logic of *Sindell*, *Hymowitz* represents the correct understanding of *Sindell*'s underlying logic.

Notes

1 Joel Feinberg, "Sua Culpa," in *Doing and Deserving* (Princeton: Princeton University Press, 1970).
2 Jules L. Coleman, *Risks and Wrongs* (Cambridge University Press, 1992).
3 Coleman, Ibid., chapter 17.
4 Vincent v. Lake Erie, 109 Minn. 456, 124 N.W. 221 (1910).
5 "Voluntary euthanasia and the inalienable right to life," 7 *Philosophy and Public Affairs* 93 (1978).
6 For the sake of this argument we are assuming that the wrongdoer is not the cheapest cost-avoider, although there is no reason to think that the two will always be different individuals. We are concerned with that case in which they are different, however, because we want to know whether imposing the loss on the cheapest cost-avoider violates corrective justice, and it could only if the two were different individuals.
7 Ybarra v. Spangard, 25 Cal. 2d 486, 154 P.2d 687 (1944).
8 It is a further question whether such a burden shifting rule will actually prove effective. The point here is simply to illustrate how various rules can still be interpreted as part of a general plan to implement an ideal, say, of corrective justice, even if the results the rules generate in particular cases do not fully correspond to the results corrective justice would require.
9 Summers v. Tice, 33 Cal. 2d. 80, 199 P.2d 1 (1948).
10 Sindell v. Abbott Laboratories, 26 Cal. 3d 588, 607 P.2d 924, 163 Cal. Rptr. 132 (1980).
11 Hymowitz v. Eli Lilly and Co., 73 N.Y. 2d 487, 539 N.E. 2d 941 (1989), cert. denied sub nom. Rexall Drug Co. v. Tigue, 110 S. Ct. 350 (1989).
12 Richard W. Wright, "Responsibility, risk, probability, naked statistics, and proof: Pruning the bramble bush by clarifying the concepts" 73 *Iowa L. Rev.* 1001 (1988).
13 There are some conditions that must be satisfied before this is valid. First, the victims must be fully compensated under the alternative plan, or they must be as fully compensated under the alternative as they would be under a scheme that implements corrective justice. Second, the alternative must accomplish some additional goals not secured by a corrective justice plan. Third, the alternative must conform to the relevant demands of justice and morality.

In my earlier work, I claimed that the duties in corrective justice could be discharged by parties other than those who are responsible for creating wrongful losses. Thus, my claim was that no-fault plans were ways of discharging duties in corrective justice (provided other conditions like those mentioned above were met). I still accept the claim that it is possible for someone other than the wrongdoer to discharge the wrongdoer's obligations, otherwise insurance would be unthinkable, but I reject the idea that no-fault plans are ways of meeting the demands of corrective justice. Instead, certain practices simply mean that no duties in corrective justice arise in a particular community. Thus, it is not as if New Zealand has an unusual approach to meeting the demands of corrective justice with respect to accident-related losses. Rather, in New Zealand, there is no practice of corrective justice with respect to such losses. After all, in corrective justice, the faulty injurer has a duty to repair, and under the plans we are talking about, there simply is no agent-relative duty of any sort. The victim's right grounds a duty, but the duty it grounds depends on the practice. The practice of corrective justice imposes that duty on the faulty injurer. Other practices or social conventions might well impose different duties.

Whereas I used to say that other practices can *discharge* the wrongdoer's duty, I now say that such practices either *extinguish* duties in corrective justice that would otherwise arise or that duties in corrective justice simply do not arise. The difference between the latter two approaches is important. In one view, corrective justice is like a default rule. If no other practices of the appropriate sort exist, then corrective justice does, and it imposes duties of a certain agent-relative kind. In the other, if there is no practice of corrective justice, there are no duties of corrective justice, whatever other practices may exist. I have settled on a view about which of these alternatives is correct, but everything I have said so far is compatible with both interpretations.

14 It follows that even if the state is authorized to act on the basis of corrective justice, it is not required to do so. It may simply ignore corrective justice, though it may not be free to ignore the plight of the victims of wrongdoing altogether. See note 7 for a further development of this idea.

8

Liberalism, retribution and criminality

JEAN HAMPTON

When readers first confront Joel Feinberg's four volume work *The Moral Limits of the Criminal Law*,[1] they are struck both by the enormous philosophical labor that has gone into the project and by the philosophical vision that Feinberg shows, not only in formulating the principles that might be thought to provide good reasons for criminalizing certain conduct, but also in clarifying, arguing for and applying the principles that he eventually endorses. Feinberg claims that there are two principles implicit in our political system which are used to criminalize conduct: The first is the "Harm Principle," which maintains that "the need to prevent harm to persons other than the actor is always a morally relevant reason in support of proposed state coercion."[2] The second is the "Offense Principle," which says that "the need to prevent hurt or offense (as opposed to injury or harm) to others" is always a morally relevant reason in support of state coercion.[3] Each of these principles is understood to provide a relevant reason for criminalizing conduct, and not to provide either necessary or sufficient conditions for justified state coercion. Each fails to provide a sufficient condition because each might be outweighed by certain relevant moral or practical costs of criminalization. Each fails to provide a necessary condition because each, by itself, does not preclude the other from being valid. "In short, each liberty-limiting principle puts forth a kind of reason it claims always to be relevant – always to have some weight – in support of proposed legal coercion, even though in a given instance it might not weigh enough to be decisive, and even though it may not be the only kind of consideration to be relevant."[4] Feinberg takes great care to clarify and give meaning to his two principles such that they are alive and useful guides to legislators, and in the process he puts his enormous analytical abilities to effective use. Moreover, he argues, true to what might be called the tradition of liberalism in our society, that a liberal political regime can sanction only these two principles for criminalizing conduct – in particular, he argues that no principle that prescribes a more active moral role for the state can be justified.

The study of both these principles will be important for future work in philosophy of law. But what I have found particularly interesting is the methodology he uses to define and argue for these principles. Feinberg doesn't follow the standard method, exemplified, for example, by Jeremy Bentham's work *The Principles of Morals and Legislation*, in which a moral theory is developed and refined to provide one or more principles for legislators to use in determining why and how to criminalize conduct, and then defended by applying the principle(s) to easy and hard cases in a way that is supposed to harmonize with our intuitions, or, at any rate, not do too much violence to them. Instead, Feinberg starts from these practices themselves, in particular, certain paradigm cases of what we take to be criminal behavior in our society, and uses these to formulate the two principles that he takes to explain and justify why behavior of this sort is considered criminal.

Feinberg defends his departure from the standard method, and his emphasis on starting from practice rather than moral theory, as follows:

> It would be folly to speculate whether the moral theory implicit in this work is utilitarian, Kantian, Rawlsian, or whatever. I appeal at various places quite un-selfconsciously, to all the kinds of reasons normally produced in practical discourse, from efficiency and utility to fairness, coherence, and human rights. But I make no effort to derive some of these reasons from the others, or to rank them in terms of their degree of basicness. My omission is not due to any principled objections to "deep structure" theories (although I must confess to skeptical inclinations). I do not believe that such an approach is precluded, but only that it is unnecessary. Progress on the penultimate questions need not wait for solutions to the ultimate ones.[5]

So, on Feinberg's view, we don't need to have in hand the true moral theory to understand how and why to criminalize certain kinds of conduct, and the principles we use to construct the criminal law may turn out to be as deep as we can get in understanding the theoretical foundations of this aspect of our moral and legal life.

Feinberg's method has other advantages. Those who do not merely theorize about but also act within the institution of criminal justice will appreciate the fact that he does not subject his readers to an elaborate philosophical scheme that may not seem terribly relevant to their decision making. Moreover, if Feinberg is right about the coherence and moral strength of this part of the law, his practice-based approach to understanding it may be a promising way to generate new and viable (middle-level) theories of its appropriate operation.

Of course, others will find Feinberg's method philosophically dissatisfying both because it eschews the kind of abstract theorizing many of us love best, and because it involves taking what may seem an uncomfortably humble stance towards its subject matter. Still, his method may be right for all that. Feinberg's project challenges us to be more respectful of and answerable to the traditions around us, and less inclined to assume that the traditions and practices of our society are too infected with error to be relied upon or respected in our theorizing.

Nonetheless, despite its attractions, Feinberg's method has its dangers. First, if we use it, we must beware not to rely on practices for the formulation of principles if the practices are not morally "strong" enough to bear the strain of being the foundation for the theory. And second, we must eschew reliance on practices if the ideas animating those practices come into conflict with one another. If a practice is informed by theory, it may be informed by more than one, with inconsistent results. And if a practice is informed by bad theory, or informed by no theory at all, it may not be morally respectable.

Feinberg is convinced that our criminal justice system is, on the whole, morally respectable, and I shall not dispute this here. But does it really give us *one* set of principles, or are there conflicting tendencies in the practice of the criminal law that reflect the influence of more than one theory in its operation and structure? Rather than considering such a large question in this paper, I shall examine a particular instance of it in the context of Feinberg's work. Specifically, I shall ask whether Feinberg's commitment to liberalism and its effects on the development of the criminal law causes him to miss an aspect of our criminal justice system – its interest in retribution – that may be inconsistent not only with some formulations of liberalism, but also with the two principles that he claims animate our criminal justice system. However, I shall argue that Feinberg's theory is able to accommodate retribution better than some of his readers may think.

I. The criminal law and retribution

Feinberg is not merely concerned with understanding the criminal law; he is also interesting in understanding its role and place in a liberal political society. Now criminal law has a major impact on what liberals care about most: the liberty of the citizenry. Hence it is not surprising that, as a liberal, Feinberg concentrates his attention on how far the state's interference in personal liberty through the use of criminal sanctions can be justified. And of course the most natural justification for the state to use as it limits liberty is that it ought to do so whenever such interference deters socially undesirable behavior. So the reader is unsurprised to see Feinberg assert, "The whole purpose of the criminal prohibition is to discourage the particular antisocial behavior that is forbidden."[6]

But is this really the *whole* purpose? Consider that there are many methods of deterrence, only some of them involving punitive sanctions. As Feinberg himself notes, legislatures can deter conduct by "creating any of a range of civil disabilities, through such measures as withholding licenses, withdrawing professional certification, refusing to enforce certain kinds of contracts, job dismissals by public agencies, suspending governmental subsidies or financial support, child custody discontinuances, and so on."[7] So why should a society deter via punitive sanctions rather than via other nonpunitive methods?

In particular, why shouldn't it use tort remedies to do so? John Kleinig and Jeffrie Murphy have complained that there is little if any discussion by Feinberg in these volumes of the difference between criminal and tortious sanctions and the reasons that make one rather than the other the appropriate response to certain kinds of behavior.[8] Kleinig distinguishes two kinds of question regarding the criminal law: First, what is it about harms that makes *legal* action against them appropriate? And second, for what kinds of harm is *criminal* law the appropriate response? He goes on to contend that Feinberg's discussion really addresses the first and not the second question, so that the book, in Kleinig's view contains "something of a puzzling *lacuna . . .* puzzling because, in a treatise that purports to focus on the moral limits of the *criminal* law, one would expect to find *some* consideration of the factors that make criminal sanctions the appropriate response to some kinds of wrongfully produced harm, and only impositions of a noncriminal kind the appropriate response to others."[9]

Kleinig notes that Feinberg isn't completely silent on this issue. In *Harm to Others*, Feinberg believes he can make the distinction between the way that the state deters differently when it punishes as opposed to when it taxes, suspends or disables, by seeing the former as a more severe interference in the citizens' liberty than the latter:

the technique of direct prohibition through penal legislation, *on the whole* is a more drastic and serious thing than its main alternatives, if only because criminal punishment (usually imprisonment) is a more frightening evil than lost inducements, increased taxes, and various civil disabilities, and . . . more coercive.[10]

This emphasis on the difference in strength between the two kinds of coercive devices is repeated shortly afterward:

the legal coercion exerted by penal statutes is not only typically greater than the coercion of bills of taxation; there is also a difference in the mode of coercion so significant that it amounts to a difference in kind as well as degree. The typical criminal sanction is imprisonment, which is not only a severe deprivation of liberty in all its important dimensions, but also a brand of censure and condemnation that leaves one, in effect, in permanent disgrace. Punitive fines are less stigmatic, and therefore fall on a scale of coerciveness somewhere between punishment proper and taxation. Taxation, however, is a much more impersonal transaction than exacting fines. There is nothing pointed and condemnatory about it, no symbolic judgment of censure, no stigma of disgrace. These differences make plausible the view that criminal sanctions are special enough to require their own liberty-limiting principles, and among all the common techniques of official coercion, are opposed initially by the strongest presumptive case.[11]

The idea seems to be that behavior that ought to be criminalized is more seriously wrong than other sorts of behavior that we also want deterred, and that criminal sanctions are a more severe kind of deterrent response than responses such as taxing, fining or suspending, and so only warranted when the behavior in question is seriously wrong. In particular, they are more severe in the sense of being more "stigmatizing," "censoring," or "disgracing."

Granted that this condemnatory aspect of criminal punishment makes it different from noncriminal penalties, fines and damage assessments, the question that Feinberg needs to answer is "What is it that generates the condemnation?" Is it simply a byproduct of the *severity* of the criminal punishment? If so, the censoring of conduct which a criminal experiences would be an indirect result of the severe sanction he would be forced to undergo, and not something introduced independently of that sanction. Hence, the more severe the sanction inflicted, the more severe the condemnation.

But this can't be right. Consider that some punishments can be milder than civil penalties; for example, having to pay $500 for being convicted of tampering with a smoke detection device in an airplane lavatory is less severe than having to pay $1,000 in withholding penalty to the IRS in virtue of the fact that one was underwithheld during that tax year. The fact that the person convicted of tampering would experience condemnation as he paid the $500 fine, whereas the person paying the $1,000 penalty to the IRS would not, shows that the condemnation is a feature that is not a byproduct of the criminal sanction but something inflicted upon the criminal over and above whatever sentence he is made to serve, and perhaps introduced prior to any sentencing at the very time he is judged guilty of a certain criminal offense.

What is this condemnatory aspect of criminal punishment, involving, as Feinberg puts it "stigmatization"? And what is its purpose?

How one answers this question depends upon what theory of criminal punishment one embraces. Someone who advocates what is called the deterrence theory of punishment will likely see any stigmatization as a sullying of reputation which is normally perceived as unpleasant by the offender and by most other people, and which will therefore work to deter both the offender and other members of the population from engaging in this kind of conduct again. So on this view, we can distinguish criminal sanctions from other kinds of sanctions using the fact that only the former involve this reputation-sullying feature, consistent with the view that the sole purpose of punishment is deterrence, by interpreting that stigmatization as a special deterring device reserved only for the most severe harmful conduct. This distinction between tortious and criminal actions would therefore be drawn on the basis of severity of harm, and the stigmatic character of the response of criminal actions would be explained as a function of society's desire to create a severe deterrent for the severe harms belonging in the class of crimes.

However this theory does not fit the facts of the criminal law as it now operates. On this view, all criminal behavior ought to be more harmful, and thus more heavily stigmatized, than all tortious behavior. But as Murphy asks,

Is defamation treated as a tort and auto theft as a crime because the former is morally trivial (no serious harm, no major rights violations, nothing worthy of solemn moral condemnation) whereas the latter is morally important? Surely not. My life may be trashed utterly as the result of a believed defamation, and the cost to me of the theft of my auto is probably simply a bit of inconvenience while I wait for my insurance company to buy me another one. But it still strikes me as reasonable that the law deals with the former as a tort and the latter as a crime. [12]

Murphy's example shows that in this society there are torts that constitute worse harms, from a moral point of view, than some crimes. So in this society stigmatization cannot be taken to track the moral seriousness of harm in our legal system, and thus cannot be interpreted as a device used simply to enhance the deterrent consequences of performing what are called "criminal" behaviors.

Those theorists who are retributivists about punishment will argue that a better understanding of the source of this stigmatization is that it is largely – perhaps exclusively — a function of the retributive message implicit in the punishment, and thus not implicit in nonpunitive (hence nonretributive) responses to actions, for example, fines, penalties, discontinuances or dismissals. On this view what distinguishes the criminal law from other sorts of law (e.g., tort, contract, tax law), all of which involve limiting, circumscribing or defining the citizen's liberty, is that criminal law alone involves the threat of a sanction which is *deservedly* inflicted as retribution for the wrong done, and not merely or even primarily inflicted for purposes of deterrence.

It is intriguing that in the first three volumes of Feinberg's work there is no mention of the retributive function of criminal punishment, and only a brief discussion of it in volume IV, despite the fact that an influential previous paper of his accorded to punishment an "expressive role" that I have argued is strongly suggestive of a retributive understanding of the point of criminal sanctions. [13] Given that generations of legal theorists have defended this conception of criminal punishment, why didn't Feinberg emphasize it in his discussion of the role and purposes of criminal legislation?

Perhaps the explanation has to do with the perspective on the law that he takes. As a liberal, criminal sanctions appear liberty-limiting in their nature, and precisely for that reason problematic. Whatever other role or purpose they might have in a community might strike a liberal as less philosophically problematic than the very fact of their coercive interventionist nature. Indeed, when Feinberg responds to Kleinig's complaint that he says too little about the difference between torts and crimes, he admits that in his four-volume work he is worried, first and foremost, about how much power the state can have to interfere with our lives through criminal sanctions: "My primary concern in *Harm to Others*, however, was . . . with the more purely philosophical question: When is a coercive legislative purpose morally legitimate?" [14] Note that

Feinberg is understanding legislatures that criminalize certain behavior as having "a coercive legislative purpose," that is, a purpose that involves interfering with our lives in order to coerce us. And although he doesn't explicitly tell us what that coercive purpose is, in light of the passages such as those already quoted above, it is natural to interpret him as having in mind primarily, if not exclusively, a deterrent purpose. Thus his primary concern as he discusses the criminal law in these four volumes – namely, when can a liberal tolerate the coercive interference of the state in the lives of its citizenry – seems to be one that he has *in virtue of taking* a deterrent perspective on the *point* of the criminal sanction. The concern a retributivist would have in reflecting upon the legitimacy of criminal legislation would have to be very different because this theorist would describe such legislation as primarily condemnatory, and only secondarily (if at all) coercive in the pursuit of any desirable consequences. Hence, the retributivist would worry about the legitimacy of inflicting suffering aimed at morally condemning the wrongdoer's conduct just as much as, if not more than, the coercive, liberty-limiting aspects of that method of condemnation.

It is intriguing to note that Feinberg is not the first philosopher working in the liberal tradition to "forget" retribution when thinking about the nature and proper role of law. Immanuel Kant, a man notorious for his virulent retributivist sentiments, nonetheless sounds remarkably like a deterrent theorist when he describes the role of criminal legislation:

Any opposition that counteracts the hindrance of an effect promotes that effect and is consistent with it. Now, everything that is unjust is a hindrance to freedom according to universal laws. Coercion, however, is a hindrance or opposition to freedom. Consequently, if a certain use of freedom is itself a hindrance to freedom according to universal laws (that is, is unjust), then the use of coercion to counteract it, inasmuch as it is the prevention of a hindrance to freedom, is consistent with freedom according to universal laws; in other words, this use of coercion is just.[15]

Moreover, when distinguishing torts from crimes in the same work, Kant doesn't define the latter as those wrongs which require a retributive response and the former as those which do not; instead he defines the latter as those wrongs which are considered public "because through them the commonwealth and not just a single individual is exposed to danger."[16] But even if Kant is right about this, it is puzzling that his own commitments to retributive punishment do not surface in his explanation of the point of criminalization.

Why does it seem so easy to forget about a retributive role for criminal punishment when writing on the law? Jeffrie Murphy notes that anyone reflecting on what justifies the state will be adopting a perspective that makes the deterrence of wrongdoing the natural and primary reason for criminal legislation.[17] For example, the standard contractarian justification contends that in virtue of the chaos that would exist without the existence of an institution that is exclusively authorized to inflict negative sanctions on those who do not behave cooperatively, the creation of such an institution is justified. This argument seems to establish that the use of sanctions to coerce cooperative behavior from those who are normally not disposed to engage in it *is* indeed the natural and primary reason for such legislation, even if retributive ends may also be pursued through the infliction of criminal sanctions.

If Murphy is right, perhaps we have a way to adjudicate between deterrence theorists and retributivists who disagree about the primary justification of state punishment: It may be possible to argue that, as liberals, we can only justify the state by interpreting its power to inflict sanctions as primarily designed to deter wrongdoing. This would mean that deterrence must be the first aim of criminal punishment, and retribution, if it is a permissible goal for the state at all, can only be permissible if it is pursued subject to the limits defined by the state's deterrent goal. As Murphy says, "If we were forming a government and deciding to live under a rule of law, our primary concern would surely not be with the question of how to deal with persons who have already violated our rights but with the question of how to prevent persons from violating our rights in the first place. Thus it would seem that deterrence (or some form of crime prevention) will always be the dominant general justifying aim of punishment with retribution – even on a sophisticated theory of retribution – being at most a side constraint and a secondary aim."[18]

It is not clear that Murphy's argument dooming retribution to secondary status is correct, as I will discuss below. But suppose a retributivist were to urge Feinberg to embrace the idea that the state's goal in creating the criminal law is at least secondarily (within the constraints of the deterrent goal) retributive. The question Feinberg should consider before doing so is whether or not even the secondary introduction of retribution is inconsistent with his endorsement of liberalism. Indeed, might Feinberg's and Kant's omission of retribution when defining the purpose and limits of criminalizing conduct be a sign that they instinctively suspect that the limited role of a liberal state precludes it from engaging in retributive punishment?

If retribution is not within the mandate of a liberal state, then a liberal is committed by his theory of the state to a deterrent justification of criminal punishment (so that retributive aims could only be pursued in private realms). But it may also be that this commitment to deterrence is interestingly at odds with the present-day understanding of criminal law practices in contemporary political societies (which also happen to call themselves liberal) because the political rhetoric used within the criminal law and the condemnatory aspect of this branch of the law are best explained as retributive in nature. If that is so, Feinberg's project of attempting both to understand the principles underlying the practice of criminalization in our society and to defend criminalizing behavior only by reference to the only principles capable of being sanctioned by a liberal state, is inherently conflicted. This would mean that to the extent the state's punitive response in its criminal law is, fundamentally, a retributive response, then to that extent the state cannot be a liberal state, and so cannot be thought subject to the harm and offense principles appropriate for such a state. Indeed, if the only way of distinguishing a criminal response from a tortious response is to accord the former and not the latter a retributive aim, it would turn out that the very idea that there are "liberal" principles for criminalizing behavior is inherently contradictory, and any system of criminal law which claimed, as ours arguably does, to be both retributive and liberal, would be internally inconsistent.

In the remainder of this paper, I want to pursue whether or not a system of criminal law can have a retirbutive aim but still be part of a liberal state. Two sorts of outcomes can result from this pursuit:

1. Criminal sanctions in a liberal state can indeed be justified, either entirely or in part, for retributive reasons. (If these sanctions are also justified for other reasons, such as deterrent reasons, retribution would be either the primary or the secondary goal, and would predominate depending upon moral factors which the liberal theory would have to make explicit.)
2. Criminal sanctions in a liberal state can only be justified for deterrent reasons, and may not be used to pursue retributive ends.

Outcome 2 is bad news for those who think of themselves as retributive liberals. Outcome 1 would allow a liberal to give the criminal law some kind of retributive role, although depending on how the theorist formulated that role, it might be quite limited.

It may be that liberalism is sufficiently "flexible" as a political theory to allow for a formulation yielding either of these outcomes on the place of retribution in a liberal state. If so, this would mean, first, that the debate between retributivists and deterrence theorists could not be decided by appeal to what (the speaker wrongly took to be) a unitary conception of liberalism and what that conception requires; and second, that the criminal law may be informed by more than one of these "liberalisms," in which case it is a practice at least some of whose animating ideas are in conflict. We must therefore determine how theoretically flexible the notion of liberalism is, and, in particular, how Feinberg understands this notion.

II. Liberalism and morality

Would a state that carried out retributive punishment on what it called criminal lawbreakers act like a state that we would intuitively recognize as liberal? After all, if the criminal law has a retributive purpose, it would appear to be a body of law that plays a fundamentally moral function in the community. One of the central jobs of political society would be to inflict what is perceived as "deserved suffering" on certain people meeting certain criteria as a way of righting moral wrongs. The legal theorist's job would be to define the criteria by which such people would be selected, and this would largely involve distinguishing which moral wrongs should merit a retributive response by the state, and which need only be deterred via penalties, tort remedies and the like. If the criminal law has a retributive aim, the state is squarely in the business of, if not enforcing morality, then punishing in the name of it. Is this too moral a role for a liberal state?

In order to answer this question we need a clearer understanding of what retribution and liberalism are.

Understanding retribution is no easy task. There have been a variety of attempts to formulate what retribution is and what justifies it as a response to wrongdoers, none of which has proved fully satisfactory to the community of theorists who have considered them. At the very least, however, we should distinguish among three different kinds of retributive positions which a state might have:[19]

1. Only the guilty deserve to be punished.
2. All and only the guilty deserve to be punished.
3. It is morally required that all and only the guilty deserve to be punished.

Position 1 is the weakest; it is in fact a side-constraint on the infliction of punishment. Whatever one's purposes in inflicting suffering, this principle insists that it is only justifiable when it is visited upon the guilty. The second principle forbids the punishment of the innocent, but positively commands the punishment of the guilty. A retributivist who embraced it would feel called upon to inflict suffering upon any wrongdoer for no other reason than the fact that he "deserved" it. But while this principle obliges us to punish the guilty, it does not require such punishment. The third principle does require it, insisting that the obligation to inflict retributive punishment on a wrongdoer is never defeasible. So, for example, the third principle would not permit refraining from inflicting deserved suffering on a wrongdoer out of considerations of mercy.

Few theorists have been able to tolerate the severe demands of principle three.[20] And few theorists have been able to resist endorsing principle one, some deterrent theorists contending that at least this minimal retributivism is consistent with the idea that legal punishment is mainly concerned with deterrence. Principle two is the best statement of what has traditionally been understood as the retributivist position.

The justification of any of these positions is obscure. Some theorists have denied that retribution needs a justification, claiming that the idea that wrongdoers (but not innocents) deserve suffering is part of the "bedrock" of morality. Others have tried to locate the justification in the concept of rights (e.g., Kant, Hegel). In other places, I have argued that the moral source of retributive punishment justifying its infliction is the idea that human beings have a certain kind of value.[21]

So retributivist positions come in various forms. But so, for that matter, does liberalism. In contemporary discussions there are two fundamentally different conceptions of what this political position involves.

First, there is what I will call "metaphysical" liberalism, so named because such liberalism implicitly involves a certain kind of metaethical position. Consider liberal figures in our tradition, such as John Locke, Immanuel Kant, Jean-Jacques Rousseau and John Stuart Mill. Each of these figures argued that the liberal state is an institution which protects and enforces rights. Of course they disagreed about the source and nature of these rights, reflecting the fact that each had a very different moral theory on which he based his view of the state's role and function. But the point is that each thought the state had a moral role and function. Hence this form of liberalism has a strong metaphysical commitment to objective moral theory, whether it is a theory that starts (as Locke's does) with a divine conception of the nature and origin of rights, or (as Mill's does) with a consequentialist moral theory from which the notion of individual rights to liberties are derived. The historical impact of this position has been substantial; the present governments of many western democracies, for example France, Great Britain and the United States, are directly indebted to these figures for their conceptions of the rights of citizens and the corresponding duties of governments both to respect and protect those rights (consider, for example, the Bill of Rights in the United States Constitution). And as Feinberg notes, it is John Stuart Mill who first formulated the harm principle which forms the foundation of Feinberg's theory of the criminal law.[22]

Contemporary political philosophers who align themselves with this form of liberalism sometimes disagree violently with one another about what political prescriptions the liberal state ought to operate upon. Consider, for example, the enormous differences between the theories of Robert Nozick and Ronald Dworkin. Dworkin explains the divergence of views about justice among liberals as a function of the way liberalism involves commitment to two different moral ideals, liberty and equality, with liberal thinkers differing over which ideal is predominant and why.[23] But no matter how liberal thinkers align themselves on this issue, the point to note here is that each of them is articulating what he takes to be the correct moral foundations of the liberal state. Metaphysical liberalism therefore perceives the liberal state as an institution that receives its justification and its distinctive (albeit limited) role from a particular moral theory.

Members of this tradition have taken more than one position on the role of criminal punishment. Because many of them (including, as we saw from the quoted passage, Kant), understand protection of rights as accomplished via sanctions that deter transgressions of them, there is a lot of support for the idea that criminal sanctions play a deterrent role. But some of them, for example, Locke and Kant, also clearly articulate the idea that a state is justified in imposing retributive punishment on offenders "in the name of" the rights which these offenders have transgressed.

Contrast this traditional liberalism with a very different kind of liberal position, which I will call "neutrality liberalism." This position has recently received endorsement by John Rawls in his most recent writings, and has been discussed by Thomas Nagel.[24] On this view, the essence of a liberal state is its operation from the principle of toleration. Divergent lifestyles, and different religious, moral and metaphysical commitments are to be tolerated in a liberal state, and this diversity protected. Accordingly, the state must reject the idea of operating from any particular metaphysical (and potentially sectarian) moral or religious doctrine, and should instead operate from and seek to develop an "overlapping consensus" among the state's disparate groups on principles of justice, which would be the basis for legislation and for the adjudication of conflicts. Such a consensus in a pluralistic society will serve as the intellectual cement binding the community together and which each group in the community may have different reasons for supporting in virtue of their different moral, religious or metaphysical beliefs and practices. This consensus is, at the very least, a *modus vivendi* for a pluralist community, but Rawls argues that it is more than that, in virtue of the fact that its support from each group in the community derives from the fact that each thinks (albeit for different moral or religious reasons) that the consensus is *correct*, as well as useful. So on this view, the state which operates from an overlapping consensus and which strives in all its dealings with the many different groups composing it to respect their different views and lifestyles is properly called "liberal" precisely insofar as *that state eschews commitment to any particular moral or religious code*. Consequently, it must eschew any kind of moral role for itself, because such a role means aggregating to itself a moral theory which defines and justifies such a role. To be properly neutral, and thus tolerant of the variety of moral and religious beliefs of its members, the state cannot explicitly take on any role driven by a particular – and inevitably contestable – moral doctrine, nor can it take any metaethical position on the possibility of an objective moral theory which would be used to condemn criminal behavior as (objectively) wrong.

For this kind of liberal, the idea that the state ought to inflict retributive punishment in either the second or the third sense would seem to be a real problem. It is not merely that some members of the society may have moral views that oppose punishment so conceived. More fundamentally, if the state perceived itself as the institution which inflicted deserved suffering upon wrongdoers (where it was either obliged or required to do so) it would be invoking moral notions and undertaking a moral role as it punished. As it acted upon that role, it would be committed to the idea that those it punished had not only acted harmfully but also *wrongfully*, such that they were morally blameworthy for their actions, and it would be committed to the idea of moral desert, an idea which would guide the way in which it designed and imple-mented punishment sentences. So not only would its punishment activities be concerned to effect social order; more controversially the state would be aiming to secure a moral result, namely, the infliction of suffering upon all and only those who deserve it in view of their wrongful actions. If the state becomes such a "servant" of morality – which invariably makes that state a servant of a particular theory of what morality involves, then it is no longer neutral between competing moral and religious conceptions, not only because it categorically rejects as morally wrong those conceptions of the good or the right which generate conduct deserving of a retributive response, but also because it is committed both to the idea of retributive desert and the idea that there is a right moral answer to questions about acceptable conduct.

Is the first retributivist position, which requires only that the state refrain from punishing the innocent, one that a neutrality liberal could incorporate into her liberal state? Yes and no. It would not be difficult for her to develop an argument appealing to the requirements of security and order to justify the idea that the state should use its negative sanctions only against those who had violated one of the state's promulgated laws. But it would seem to be impossi-ble for her to incorporate the explicitly *retributivist* principle that the morally innocent do not "deserve" punishment. This latter idea is informed by a conception of what counts as morally right and wrong conduct, as well as by a notion of desert that is itself bound up with a conception of fairness which the state would require a moral theory to explain and defend. Any opponent of the idea that such moral desert exists, or of the idea that there is conduct that makes us guilty as opposed to innocent of moral wrongdoing, or of the idea that there is an objective conception of fairness banning punishment of the innocent (where the class of innocents is defined as those who have not performed actions that are morally blameworthy) will see their state not only as unacceptably partisan, but also as buying into a host of controversial metaethical positions that are simply not its business.

A proponent of neutrality liberalism could reply to these arguments that it is at least contingently possible that a morally neutral state could punish re-tributively if any of the forms of retribution were part of the overlapping consensus governing the operation of the state. If this were so, *all* (or nearly all) people in the society, no matter their moral, religious or metaphysical views, would agree on one or more of these retributivist principles, where that agreement would involve the endorsement of the retributivist's notions of (objectively) blameworthy action, (objectively) innocent behavior, and the concept of desert. There could be no strict utilitarian deterrence theorists, no moral skeptics and no strict rehabilitationists in this society. It would therefore be a society completely unlike any contemporary democratic state, and its claim to being pluralistic would have to be limited. And this society's endorsement of retribution could last as long as, and no longer than, its members continued to agree that retributive ideas should be part of the overlapping consensus. Because there is no modern pluralistic society that could sustain such an overlapping consensus on retribution either now or in the forseeable future, a neutrality liberal would certainly have to insist that it would be impossible to justify retributive punishment in any liberal society of our time.

In another place I have questioned both the coherence and the wisdom of the neutrality conception of the liberal state.[25] But regardless of its success as a political theory, any person with Feinberg's commitments to rights should reject it as the kind of liberalism he wants to support. In fact, both in the fourth volume and in a recent paper, "Some Unswept Debris from the Hart-Devlin Debate,"[26] Feinberg makes it very clear that the kind of liberalism he endorses is unafraid of incorporating explicit moral ideas in its foundation, and indeed welcomes the idea (just as Locke, Mill and Dworkin have done) that the liberal state has a certain kind of moral role to play in the community.

Feinberg does not elaborate on his brand of metaphysical liberalism by developing the abstract moral theory upon which it is supposed to rest. But he does make clear that the punishment inflicted by a liberal state has a moral purpose. Starting with the (by now) familiar distinction between the general justifying aim of an institution and the rules of fair procedure governing its actions, Feinberg maintains that when we apply this distinction to the criminal law we find that

it is a misrepresentation of the liberal position (at least as I have tried to formulate it) to say that it ascribes an entirely nonmoral justifying aim to the criminal law. There is a clear respect in which the liberal's liberty-limiting principle *is* a moral one. The justifying aim of the system of criminal law, on his view, is not merely to minimize harms, in the sense of setback interests, all round. If that is what he advocated, he would have no quarrel with the legal paternalist. In fact, his principle permits prohibitory statutes only when necessary to prevent those harms (and offenses) that are also *wrongs*: those that are unconsented to, involuntarily suffered, and neither justified nor excused. The criminal law, he insists, must serve a profoundly moral purpose, namely the protection of individual's [sic] moral rights."[27]

Whereas the neutrality liberal has to attribute to any modern pluralist liberal state a nonmoral understanding not only of its punishment actions but of the offenders' acts which warrant it, Feinberg appreciates that as a metaphysical liberal who renounces the idea that the state must be morally neutral, he is free to appropriate moral language to characterize criminal actions not merely as harms but as wrongs, insofar as these acts are violations of rights. Hence Feinberg's liberal state is unabashedly taking metaethical positions: Some conceptions of right and wrong are rejected out of hand, and individuals who perform actions that demonstrate they subscribe to what this state determines to be false moral views would be told, via punishment, that both their views and their actions following from these views are unacceptable. As Feinberg puts it, "even a penal code based exclusively on the harm principle (and any penal code will be largely based on that principle) is meant to do more than merely prevent harm. In so protecting people, it also means to vindicate the morality of preventing harm and respecting autonomy."[28]

Those attracted to neutrality liberalism will find such moral intolerance unacceptable in a liberal state. But whether or not this criticism is reasonable, the legal paternalist may wonder why Feinberg's metaphysical liberalism doesn't make the state morally paternalistic. Feinberg's liberal state not only preaches but also enforces a moral code, in just the way that parents do as they raise children. Once he attributes such a role to the state, hasn't he fatally compromised the idea that the state should be "liberal"?

Feinberg would deny that he has. What makes a state "liberal" for him is not its rejection of any moral ideas as the foundation for its criminal law, but its rejection of the idea that any enforcement of moral behavior should include punishment of immoral behavior which nonetheless has no victim other than the offender himself. Even though the liberal state is in the business of enforcing morality, according to Feinberg, it is not in the business of enforcing those aspects of morality which do not involve the rights of others. The term 'paternalistic' for him refers only to states that take on the latter role, not to states that take on the former role. As he explains:

The liberal does *not* urge that the legislators of criminal law be unconcerned with "a man's morals". Indeed, everything about a person that the criminal law should be concerned with is included in his morals. But not everything in a person's morals should be the concern of the law, only his disposition to violate the rights of other parties. He may be morally blameworthy for his beliefs and desires, his taboo infractions, his tastes, his harmless exploitations, and other free-floating evils, but *these* moral judgements are not the business of the criminal law.[29]

So Feinberg believes that those who participate in and theorize about the liberal state are involved up to their necks in morality. Liberal states cannot be morally neutral on Feinberg's view because for him the foundation of liberalism is the idea that individuals have rights. Moreover, I suspect he would maintain that the Rawlsian hallmark of liberalism, the principle of toleration, could not be justified as anything more than instrumentally valuable to a pluralistic community except by an argument that understood toleration as required by a state's respect for the rights of its citizens.

But having said this, Feinberg want to dissociate himself from the position that the moral role of liberal states includes enforcing victimless morality, or, as he puts it, "nongrievance" morality. So he tries to mark out a middle ground upon which to build his conception of liberalism, one which acknowledges that the state is in the business of enforcing morality – but only a "grievance" morality:

The liberal . . . can and must concede that the criminal *process* in its very conception is inherently moral (as opposed to non-moral) – a great moral machine, stamping stigmata on its products, painfully "rubbing in" moral judgments on the persons who had entered in one end as "suspects" and emerged from the other end as condemned prisoners. The question the liberal raises about this moral machine is: "which actions should cause their doers to be fed into it?", and his answer is "only those actions that violate the rights of others." There is no doubt in his mind that the law may "enforce morality." The question is "*which* morality (or which sector of morality) may it properly enforce?", and he restricts the criminal law to the enforcement of "grievance morality."[30]

Indeed, Feinberg notes in volume IV that it is even possible for a liberal state to take on the role of moral educator as it punishes. I have developed and commended a moral education theory of punishment, arguing that when they have objected to legal paternalism, liberals have rejected only a view that allows the state to restrict what an individual can do to himself; they have not objected to the view that when the state justifiably interferes with a person's life after he has broken a law (whose content is only concerned with harm or offense to others) that it should intend good rather than evil toward him.[31] In discussing my argument, Feinberg agrees, noting that moral education and legal paternalism are answers to two logically different questions. Whereas the legal paternalist answers the question, "What ought to be made law?", the moral education theorist answers the question, "What moral attitude should the state take toward someone who has violated its criminal code?" And given that the Feinberg liberal is happy to attribute to a liberal state a moral interest in its pursuit of criminals, he can embrace the idea that such an interest may be a morally educative one.[32]

Although he notes that his liberalism allows him to embrace moral education as a theory of punishment, in fact Feinberg refuses to do so, arguing that those of us who advocate moral education as at least one aspect of punishment have yet to explain satisfactorily how punishment could ever, by itself, carry an educative moral message. Feinberg is happiest attributing to his liberal state only an interest in morally *condemning* the criminal through its punishment, "expressing public reprobation and moral censure of the harm-causing wrongdoer."[33] But both in volume IV and in the "Hart-Devlin" paper he goes beyond a merely expressivist theory and is sympathetic to the idea that the liberal state may also have a retributive goal as it punishes.

His cautious support of retribution never involves denying that the liberal state also uses punishment for deterrent purposes. Indeed, he supports the idea that punishment in excess of that deserved as retribution for an offense is justifiable in certain circumstances, for example, if the excessive punishment would strengthen the deterrent threat in the face of a population's rising interest in performing the offensive act. So Feinberg does not believe that deterrent purposes can only be pursued subject to the constraints of retribution. But contra Murphy's argument discussed earlier, Feinberg also doesn't believe the reverse, that is, that retribution can only be pursued subject to the constraints of the community's deterrent goal. For example, given the fact that he insists punishment can only be inflicted on the morally blameworthy, he has to believe that considerations of deterrence must bow to the retributive requirement that negative (and potentially deterring) sanctions can only be inflicted on the guilty.

Indeed, the power of this retributive requirement (and its popularity even among those who embrace deterrence, such as Hart) suggest that Murphy's proposal that retribution can be, at best, a minor aim of the liberal state is incorrect. If we believe that the state can only punish the guilty, then we must think that punishment is important for reasons other than deterrence – reasons which make its infliction on the innocent grossly *unfair*. Feinberg's insistence that the liberal state must be interested in expressing public reprobation and moral censure as it punishes nicely explains why a moral innocent should never receive it. It is wrong to condemn someone who has done nothing contemptible. And there is no reason why the liberal state cannot have, as its *primary* aim, this kind of censoring of those who are rights-violators as long as liberalism is not understood as the position that the state is committed to moral neutrality. Nonetheless, Feinberg insists that retribution and public censorship cannot be the only aims the liberal state has as it punishes, because of the importance which deterring harm must have in a community. His discussion suggests that the ideal relationship between these aims of punishment is morally very complicated, one that liberals may find difficult to define and about which they can disagree. In the end Feinberg leaves the tensions between these aims of punishment unresolved.

The preceding discussion suggests that the plausibility of Murphy's argument that liberal states can have only deterrent goals as their primary or sole justification of punishment comes from an implicit endorsement of the idea that liberal states must be morally neutral. If this is right, the neutrality brand of liberalism is the chief enemy of those who would be retributive liberals. But in volume IV Feinberg approvingly cites Neil MacCormick's observation that the criminal law is "morally loaded and essentially contested,"[34] so that those who create or apply the criminal law are always making controversial moral decisions about which interest to protect. As an example, Feinberg gives the liberal state's interest in protecting property rights from theft, noting (as Ernest Nagel has argued), that in a statute against theft, a liberal state must settle rules of property, "which represent moral decisions about which possessory interests are worth protecting on moral grounds, decisions made in different ways in different societies with different moral commitments."[35] And Feinberg's entire first volume tries to give substantive moral content to the harm principle, a project which assumes the essentially normative foundations of any criminal code. Indeed his argument shows that a neutrality liberal who wanted to follow Feinberg is using the principle of harm to define what counts as criminal law in a liberal state is in a difficult position: Such a liberal must either find a way to invoke the concept of harm to structure a criminal code without having recourse to "legitimate interests" or any other contestable normative notions, or he must show how any references to such notions could be thought to come from an overlapping consensus which all members of the community endorse. This is an unenviable task, and one that those of us who are committed, as is Feinberg, to the classic moral ideals of liberalism – that is freedom, individual autonomy, and equality – have no interest in pursuing.

III. Crimes and torts

The fact that Feinberg's liberal can support retribution as at least one justifying aim of punishment means Feinberg's reliance on the practice of criminal law in our liberal society for the generation of principles of criminality is not a reliance that dooms him to an inconsistent theory. Those philosophers who prefer a different conception of liberalism will not like the consistent theory he develops out of that practice. Nonetheless, the fact that our criminal law is informed by the liberal ideology of our time and also shot through with retributive language and intention can be explained so that these elements harmonize. I will now propose that Feinberg's ability to accommodate retribution into his theory of criminality not only allows him to be responsive to our practice of criminal law, but also gives him some theoretical machinery to make the kind of tort/crime distinction that critics such as Kleinig and Murphy want him to make.

As we have seen, Feinberg insists that not merely harms but *wrongs* are the subject matter of the criminal law, and he uses the term 'grievance' to further distinguish the class of wrong which this part of the law addresses. But neither the term 'grievance' nor the term 'harm' allow him to make the tort/crime distinction; victims of torts have grievances against tortfeasors, just as victims of crimes have grievances against criminals. Each kind of victim can rightly be said to have been harmed. But they are not harmed in the same way, nor do they have the same kind of grievance. In particular, the victim of a tort does not have a grievance nor suffer a harm which is the appropriate subject of retributive punishment. The absent-minded driver who hit my car, the neighbor whose tree fell over in a storm and struck my roof, the doctor whose bad decision not to do a Ceasarian section left my daughter with a damaged hand, all these individuals owe compensation, but none of them deserves retributive punishment for these harms.

So Feinberg can maintain that in order for conduct to be *criminally* prohibited, it must be the sort of thing that merits a retributive response. Like Feinberg's harm and offense principles, this principle offers only a morally relevant reason, and not a sufficient condition, for criminalizing behavior (so, for example, slander merits such a response but we may not decide to give it because of our concern to protect free speech). Unlike those principles, however, it claims to offer a necessary condition for criminalization; it *must* be the case that criminal conduct be conduct for which retribution is required. So whereas all sorts of unsavory behavior may merit a deterrent response, and thus be the subject of tort laws or contract legislation, the retributivist's point would be that a necessary condition of any conduct's being not only deterred but the subject of *criminal* punishment is that the person responsible for it merits deserved suffering.

The retributive criterion tells us decisively when we don't have a crime. But does it tell us decisively when we do? As Feinberg's quotations above make clear, a "retributivist liberal" will want to insist that not all morally wrong conduct which warrants a retributive response ought to be criminalized. Although the class of morally wrong conduct is what the legislature consults in determining the content of the criminal law, a Feinberg liberal will insist that only a *subclass* of this conduct is the appropriate subject of a *governmental* retributive response – a subclass picked out by the harm and offense principles. So the fully fleshed out retributivist liberal principle of criminal law goes as follows: "In order for conduct to be the appropriate subject of criminal prohibition, it must be conduct that merits a retributive response *and also* conduct picked out either by the harm principle or the offense principle." But such an elaboration may actually be redundant, because as Feinberg notes, it only makes sense to talk of retributive punishment for wrongs that are part of the class of grievance wrongs supposedly defined by these principles. Suppose we try to imagine retributive punishment for a victimless wrong:

If no one has a grievance in consequence of another's evil thoughts or private vices, who then can demand his own "satisfaction" through the other's suffering? How could punishment be a "return in kind"? How much suffering would constitute "payment" for one's sins? Who could "get even" with the self-regarding sinner, even symbolically or vicariously?[36]

So without taking any explicit stand on the best way to understand precisely what retribution is, Feinberg contends that whatever the language or conceptual tools one uses to develop the notion, the idea that one could retributively punish someone who either wronged only himself or who committed a victim-less "free-floating" evil simply doesn't make sense.

Feinberg's position here is intuitively plausible, but it is difficult to be sure that it is right because the notion of retribution is itself so underanalyzed.[37] Without taking the time here to advance my own theory of its intelligibility, let me simply say that we can buttress the idea that the appropriateness of a retribution response is the decisive marker of criminal conduct by making use of Feinberg's discussion of the position of James Fitzjames Stephens, who advocated a paternalistic legal approach to the proper subject matter of the criminal law. Feinberg notes that retribution is associated with a certain kind of anger or hatred. But this is not the kind of anger or hatred animating Stephens as he calls for the punishment of sodomists and others whose con-duct Stephens takes to be inherently wrong:

It is not a hate together with a sense of grievance, not hate on behalf of a victim, self or other. Rather it is hate as the automatic response of right-thinking people to *inherently* odious conduct, harmful or not.[38]

If this is a different kind of hate, then the actions towards which it is directed are hateful in a different way than harmful or offensive actions. But they are not *retributively* hateful. So people such as Stephens or Devlin want to *add* a quite different class of conduct to the class of retributive grievances Feinberg advocates as the source of criminality.

The fact that the two classes of conduct are different shows that retribution may not only be a marker of criminal as opposed to tortious actions, but a marker of what a genuine *liberal* should consider to be criminal conduct. Again, to give a full-scale argument for this idea on Feinberg's behalf, I would have to outline my theory of retribution and explain why, on my view, certain conduct merits a retributive response. But in any case, on an *intuitive* level, retribution can be used to pick out the sort of wrongs that liberals such as Feinberg want to be the subject matter of criminal law, and I take that fact to be interesting and supportive of his project. Moreover, we are also able to appreciate once again that just because Feinberg wants the state to be in the business of enforcing morality doesn't mean that he want the state to be using sanctions against the class of moral wrongs that Stephens and Devlin identi-fy.[39]

However, even if Feinberg were to specifically incorporate retribution into his legal theory, I do not think he would have succeeded in fully specifying the distinction between torts and crimes, for two reasons: First, Feinberg will have trouble placing offensive acts into the class of crimes if the class of criminal actions is picked out solely by what actions it makes sense to punish retributively. Intuitively it is difficult to understand not only how it could make sense to retributively punish someone who hurt only himself, but also how it could make sense to retributively punish one whose violation consisted solely in being offensive. Do we really want to "repay," "get even with," get restitution from, the person who defecates in public, or engages in public nudity? I suspect not: I suspect we really only want to deter such behavior. If this is right, then offensive behavior falls outside the class of grievances for which retribution is appropriate. However, precisely because it does fall outside of it, we may wonder whether Feinberg is right to insist that such behavior be criminalized. If deterrence, and perhaps also compensation to the offended party, are the aims of the law regarding such conduct, why not pursue them via a system of (perhaps steep) fines or penalties, rather than criminal sanctions? This is a question which Feinberg never specifically answers.

Second, even assuming that the harm and offense principles, either in conjunction with or implicit within retribution, single out the subclass of grievance morality which a liberal, but not a legal paternalist, would insist is the only class appropriate as content for the criminal law, there is good reason to believe this subclass is not small enough. Granted that the criminal law can only concern itself with grievances, and granted that these must be grievances for which it makes sense to offer a retributive response (in a way that is not true of any tort-like grievance), should *all* such grievances be the concern of the criminal law? Clearly not. Lies I make to my friends in private, or gratuitous promises that I make to them and break before they rely on them, or disrespectful conduct toward my fellow workers – all of these actions are ones that generate a legitimate grievance, all of them can be understood to violate others' rights, and all of them merit some kind of retributive response – *but not, we think, by the state through its system of criminal law*. On what idea is this intuitive response based? It may be an idea that is generated by another aspect of liberalism, that is, its interest in maximizing the freedom of individuals in their private lives, freedom which would be abridged if the state interfered too often with punitive sanctions. But we need more discussion to make explicit the moral considerations limiting the state here in order to have a theory that explains *which kind* of grievance morality, punishable by retribution, is the content of law in a liberal state. Feinberg's concern to answer the legal paternalist distracts him from such theoretical labor, which is nonetheless necessary to perform in order to complete a fully liberal theory of criminal law.

IV. Conclusion

Feinberg's reliance on practice does not force him into the development of a conflicted theory of criminality. Instead it enables him to take seriously both the retributive and liberal ideas present in contemporary criminal law, ideas that he elaborates in a way that allows them to fit surprisingly well together.

Moreover, if Feinberg explicitly brings retribution into his theory, it may enable him to define a principle that at least goes a long way toward differentiating torts from crimes.

But the analysis in this paper still offers only a partial vindication of Feinberg's method of studying the criminal law. By reflecting on our criminal law practices, Feinberg has uncovered interesting and defensible principles that, at least arguably, animate and guide it. But he has yet to complete an argument (although he certainly begins it) that the liberalism he elaborates in order to understand this practice is either the liberalism that really does animate it, or the version of liberalism that is the most plausible and defensible. Moreover, if both the neutrality brand of liberalism and the moral brand of liberalism are implicit in the criminal law, it would still turn out to be a conflicted practice. Finally we should note that if we attempt to complete Feinberg's theory of the criminal law by striving to understand the nature of retribution and liberalism, and by attempting to determine which aspects of grievance morality are appropriate targets of legal retribution, we are of necessity doing abstract moral theorizing, which will probably require venturing into certain metaethical territory. So Feinberg's project does not allow us to escape the sort of "practice-independent" theorizing for which philosophers are notorious if that project is the pursuit of a genuine understanding of and justification for the theoretical foundations of the criminal law.

Nevertheless I believe that by starting from the legal practice itself and using that practice as a springboard for reflection, Feinberg has succeeded in focusing our attention on what our abstract theorizing should be about if we want to develop the resources necessary to fully understand, correct and defend this respected legal institution. He has thereby significantly advanced philosophical study not only of the criminal law, but also of the liberal society in which we live.

Notes

1 The four volumes are: Volume I, *Harm to Others* (1984); Volume II, *Offense to Others* (1985); Volume III, *Harm to Self* (1986); and Volume IV, *Harmless Wrongdoing* (1988). Each has been published by Oxford University Press. Hereafter references in the text will be to volume number (e.g., *Harm to Others* will appear as "I"), followed by page number.

2 III, ix.

3 III, ix.

4 I, 10.

5 I, 17–18.

6 I, 20.

7 I, 22.

8 John Kleinig, "Criminally Harming Others," *Criminal Justice Ethics* (Win-

ter/Spring 1986): 3–10; and Jeffrie Murphy, "Legal Moralism and Liberalism" [hereafter referred to as LML], unpublished manuscript.

9 Kleinig, 4.

10 I, 23.

11 I, 24.

12 Murphy, LML, 13.

13 "The Expressive Function of Punishment" *Doing and Deserving* (Princeton, N.J.: Princeton University Press, 1970), 95–118. The idea that retribution is a kind of expression is advanced by me in "The Idea of Retribution," chapter 4, *Forgiveness and Mercy*, J. Murphy and J. Hampton (Cambridge University Press: 1988), and in Hampton, "Correcting Harms Versus Righting Wrongs: The Goal of Retribution," *UCLA Law Review*, vol. 39, no. 6 (1992); 1659–1702.

14 II, 17.

15 From *Metaphysical Elements of Justice*, trans. John Ladd (Indianapolis: Bobbs-Merrill, 1965), 35–6.

16 Ibid., 100. In a paper that details the many passages in which Kant opts for a deterrent justification of punishment, Jeffrie Murphy interprets the passage distinguishing torts and crimes differently. He argues that Kant believes wrongdoings that are made crimes are those which are best controlled by "public" rather than "private" law – so that criminal sanctions are seen as a kind of public technique for deterring crimes that cannot be successfully deterred through civil, i.e., private, proceedings. See "Does Kant Have A Retributive Theory of Punishment?" in *Columbia Law Review* 87, no. 3 (April, 1987): 509–32.

17 See Murphy, "Retributivism, Moral Education, and the Liberal State," in *Criminal Justice Ethics* (Winter/Spring 1985): 3–11.

18 Ibid., 7.

19 Something like these three principles can be found in John Mackie, "Morality and the Retributive Emotions," *Criminal Justice Ethics* 1, no. 1 (1982).

20 Jeffrie Murphy, who thought he wanted to endorse it, finally decides it is indefensible; see his "Mercy," chapter 5 of *Forgiveness and Mercy*.

21 See Hampton, "Correcting Harms Versus Righting Wrongs: The Goal of Retribution" and Hampton, "The Idea of Retribution," in *Forgiveness and Mercy*. In the same book Jeffrie Murphy argues that the moral source of retribution can be found in certain inescapable and morally respectable emotions which are normally generated in us when a wrong is committed.

22 The Millian basis of Feinberg's harm principle is discussed by David A. J. Richards in "The Moral Foundations of Criminalization," *Criminal Justice Ethics* (Winter/Spring 1986): 11–16.

23 See Dworkin's "Liberalism" in *Public and Private Morality*, ed. S. Hampshire (Cambridge University Press, 1976); reprinted in *Liberalism and Its Critics*, ed. M. Sandel (Oxford: Blackwell, 1984).

24 See Rawls's "Justice as Fairness: Political Not Metaphysical," *Philosophy and Public Affairs* 14 (1985) and "The Idea of An Overlapping Consensus," *Oxford Journal of Legal Studies* 7 (1987): 1–25. See also Thomas Nagel, "Moral Conflict and Political Legitimacy," *Philosophy and Public Affairs* 16 (1987): 215–40.

25 See my "Should Political Philosophy Be Done Without Metaphysics?" in *Ethics* 99: 791–814.

26 in *Synthese* 72 (1987): 249–75. Hereafter it will be referred to as "H-D".

27 H-D, 257. See also IV, 11–14.

28 IV, 12.

29 H-D, 259.

30 H-D, 260.

31 See "The Moral Education Theory of Punishment," *Philosophy and Public Affairs*, 13 (1984): 208–38.

32 He even wonders whether the moral education view presupposes a denial of legal paternalism, given that the theory wants to make, as the point of punishment, the lesson that harm to others is wrong the *point* of the punishment, and it would not make sense to deliver this message if one had only engaged in conduct hurting oneself. Although rights-violations are bad for the agents who perform them, that kind of harm doesn't make such actions morally wrong – what makes them wrong is the fact that they harm other people. Hence this is what a retributive punishment would be expressing. See IV, 352.

33 IV, 12.

34 Quoted in IV, 11; from MacCormick, *Legal Right and Social Democracy* (Oxford: Oxford University Press, 1982), 29.

35 IV, 12.

36 H-D, 266. See also Feinberg's discussion of retribution in IV, 159–65.

37 It turns out that on my analysis of retribution Feinberg's contention is right. I understand retribution as an act that sends a message vindicating the value of the victim, and specifically asserting that his value is equal to the value of the person who wronged him; if there has been no victim of one's wrong, then there is no point in engaging in this practice of vindication. There may, however, be something to the idea of retributively punishing oneself: We may believe that at times there is something in us that causes us to act in ways that fail to respect our own worth. In such situations we can get very angry with ourselves – even punitively angry, desiring to "punish ourselves" for what we have done. We may be trying to strike back at whatever it is inside us that is denigrating what we believe is our true worth. Feinberg would surely be right, however, to insist that no state could legitimately inflict punishment upon us in such cases.

38 H-D, 272.

39 Feinberg goes on to claim that the resistance of a liberal to the legal paternalists' position shows "one of the moral presuppositions of his position," namely that "it is not appropriate to hate people except (at most) for their disposition to harm and wrong others." (H-D, 272) This principle ought to appeal to liberals, although interestingly, because it is a moral principle, it is not one that a Rawlsian liberal could allow into his morally neutral political theory. Feinberg concludes that the lesson that we ought not to engage in such hate is one "that most 'right-thinking people', liberal or not, do not have to learn," (H-D, 272; and see also IV, 165), a remark which his more cynical readers will interpret as showing that the class of right-thinking people is small.

9

Responsibility for consequences

JOHN MARTIN FISCHER AND MARK RAVIZZA

I

In his essay, "The Interest in Liberty on the Scales," Joel Feinberg says:

We can think of life as a kind of maze of railroad tracks connected and disjoined, here and there, by switches. Wherever there is an unlocked switch which can be pulled one way or the other, there is an 'open option'; wherever the switch is locked in one position the option is 'closed.' As we chug along our various tracks in the maze, other persons are busily locking and unlocking, opening and closing switches, thereby enlarging and restricting our various possibilities of movement. Some of these switch-men are part of a team of legislators, policemen, and judges; they claim *authority* for their switch positionings. Other switchmen operate illicitly at night, often undoing what was authoritatively arranged in the daylight. This model, of course, is simpler than the real world where the 'tracks' and 'switches' are not so clearly marked; but it does give us a sense for how some closed options can be more restrictive of liberty than others. When a switchman closes and locks a switch, he forces us to continue straight on, or stop, or back up. What we cannot do is move on to a different track heading off in a different direction from the one we are on.

. . . The 'open option' theory of liberty is to be preferred, I think, to its main rival, the theory of liberty as the absence of barriers to one's actual desires, whatever they should happen to be. Suppose that Martin Chuzzlewit finds himself on a trunk line with all of its switches closed and locked, and with other 'trains' moving in the same direction on the same track at his rear, so that he has no choice at all but to continue moving straight ahead to destination D. On the 'open option' theory of liberty, this is the clearest example of a total lack of liberty: all of his options are closed, there are not alternative possibilities, he is forced to move to D. But now let us suppose that getting to D is Chuzzlewit's highest ambition in life and his most intensely felt desire. In that case, he is sure to get the thing in life he want most. Does that affect the way the situation should be described in respect to liberty? According to the theory that one is at liberty to the extent that one can do what one wants, a theory held by the ancient Stoics and Epicureans and many modern writers too, Chuzzlewit enjoys perfect liberty in this situation because he can do what he wants, even though he can do nothing else. But since this theory blurs the distinction between liberty and compulsion, and in this one extreme hypothetical case actually identifies the two, it does not recommend itself to common sense. . . . If Chuzzlewit is allowed no alternative to D, it follows that he is forced willy-nilly to go to D.

What then is the basis of our interest in liberty? Why should it matter that we have few 'open-options' if we have everything else we want and our other interests are flourishing? Our welfare interest in having a tolerable bare minimum of liberty is perhaps the easiest to account for of the various kind of interest persons have in liberty. If human beings had no alternative possibilities at all, if all their actions at all times were the *only* actions permitted them, they might yet be contented provided their desires for alternative possibilities were all thoroughly repressed or extinguished, and they might even achieve things of value, provided that they were wisely programmed to do so. But they could take no credit or blame for any of their achievements, and they could no more be responsible for their lives, in prospect or retrospect, than are robots, or the trains in our fertile metaphor that must run on 'predestined grooves.' They could have dignity neither in their own eyes nor in the eyes of their fellows, and both esteem for others and self-esteem would dwindle. . . . The self-monitoring and self-critical capacities, so essential to human nature, might as well dry up and wither; they would no longer have any function. The contentment with which all of this might still be consistent would not be a recognizably human happiness.[1]

In this extended passage, Feinberg gives voice to what might be called the "traditional" picture of the relationship between such notions as moral responsibility, accountability, and dignity, on the one hand, and liberty in the sense of the existence of alternative possibilities, on the other. Simply put, the traditional view is that moral responsibility and the related notions *require* liberty in the sense of the existence of genuine alternative possibilities. Without such freedom, it is alleged, there is no responsibility.

We disagree with the traditional picture. We begin by presenting a pair of examples which helps to motivate the rejection of the traditional insistence on a tight connection between responsibility and alternative possibilities. We then return to examine the passage from Feinberg in light of the examples.

There are cases in which a person is morally responsible for an action, although he could not have done otherwise. Here is a rather graphic case of this sort.[2] Sam confides in his friend, Jack. Sam tells Jack of his plan to murder the mayor of the town in which they live. Sam is disturbed about the mayor's liberal policies, especially his progressive taxation scheme. Whereas Sam's reasons for proposing to kill the mayor are bad ones, they are *his* reasons: he has not been hypnotized, brainwashed, duped, coerced, and so forth. Sam had deliberated coolly, and he has settled on his murderous course of action.

Sam is bad, and Jack is no better. Jack is pleased with Sam's plan, but Jack is a rather anxious person. Because Jack worries that Sam might waver, Jack has secretly installed a device in Sam's brain which allows him to monitor all of Sam's brain activity and to intervene in it, if he desires. The device can be employed by Jack to ensure that Sam decides to kill the mayor and that he acts on this decision; the device works by electronic stimulation of the brain. Let us imagine that Jack is absolutely committed to activating the device to ensure that Sam kills the mayor, should Sam show any sign of not carrying out his original plan. Also, we can imagine that Sam can do nothing to prevent the device from being fully effective, if Jack employs it to cause Sam to kill the mayor.

Sam and Jack both go to a meeting at the town hall, and Sam methodically carries out his plan to kill the mayor. He does not waver in any way, and he shoots the mayor as a result of his original deliberations. Jack thus plays absolutely no role in Sam's decision and action; the electronic device monitors Sam's brain activity, but it does not have any causal influence on what actually happens. Sam acts exactly as he would have acted, had no device been implanted in his brain.

Evidently, Sam is morally responsible for what he has done. Indeed, Sam is blameworthy for deciding to kill the mayor and for killing the mayor. But whereas Sam is morally responsible for his action, he could not have done otherwise. Sam could not have done otherwise because of the existence of a "counterfactual intervener" (Jack) who would have caused him (in a certain manner) to behave as he actually did, had Sam been inclined to do otherwise. Sam acts freely and is morally responsible for what he does because no "responsibility-undermining factor" operates in the actual sequence leading to his action. Rather, such a factor – Jack's use of the electronic device to stimulate Sam's brain – operates in the *alternative* sequence. In cases in which a responsibility-undermining factor operates in the alternative sequence but not in the actual sequence, an agent can be held morally responsible for an action, although he could not have done otherwise. The case of Sam and Jack is such a case; let us call it "Assassin." Assassin is a "Frankfurt-type" case.[3]

Assassin is a case in which Sam is morally responsible for a bad action, although he could not have done otherwise. Here is a case in which an agent is morally responsible for a good action, although he could not have done otherwise. Matthew is walking along a beach, looking at the water. He sees a child struggling in the water, and he quickly jumps into the water and rescues the child. Matthew doesn't even consider not trying to rescue the child, but we can imagine that if he had considered refraining, he would have been overwhelmed by literally irresistible guilt feelings which would have caused him to jump into the water and save the child anyway. We simply stipulate that in the alternative sequence the urge to save the child would be genuinely irresistible.

Apparently, Matthew is morally responsible – indeed, praiseworthy — for his action, although he could not have done otherwise. Matthew acts freely in saving the child; he acts exactly as he would have acted, if he had lacked the propensity toward strong feelings of guilt. In this case no responsibility-undermining factor operates in the actual sequence, and thus Matthew is morally responsible for what he does. Whether a responsibility-undermining factor operates in the alternative sequence is controversial, but at least it seems clear that the nature of the alternative sequence renders it true that Matthew could not have done otherwise.[4] Call the case of Matthew, "Hero." In Hero, Matthew is morally responsible for performing a good action, although he could not have done otherwise.

The cases just presented appear to show that moral responsibility and dignity do not require the sort of liberty that involves alternative possibilities. Consider, again, a few sentences from Feinberg:

> . . . all of [Chuzzlewit's] options are closed, there are not alternative possibilities, he is forced to move to D. But now let us suppose that getting to D is Chuzzlewit's highest ambition in life and his most intensely felt desire. . . . According to the theory that one is at liberty to the extent that one can do what one wants . . . Chuzzlewit enjoys perfect liberty . . . But . . . this theory blurs the distinction between liberty and compulsion. . . .
> . . . If Chuzzlewit is allowed no alternative to D, it follows that he is forced willynilly to go to D.

Now we can see why these sentences are problematic. From the lack of alternative possibilities, it does *not* follow that the agent in question does what he does as a result of *force* or *compulsion*. The lack of the existence of alternative possibilities is a fact about the set of alternative scenarios, whereas being forced or compelled to perform an action is a fact about the actual sequence which issues in an action. As Assassin and Hero show, one can freely perform an action (and thus can perform it without being forced or compelled to do so) even though one has no option but to perform it. In other examples it may well be the case that some factor which actually operates both makes it the case that the agent has no genuine alternative possibilities and that the agent does not act freely. But the previous examples adduced show that certain factors can render it true that the agent has no alternative possibilities without playing any role in the actual sequence and thus without making it the case that the agent does what he does as a result of force or compulsion.

So we deny the claim that moral responsibility for action requires alternative possibilities. But rejecting this traditional view does *not* require one to accept the simple-minded Stoic and Epicurean theory according to which an agent acts freely insofar as he does what he wants to do. The dichotomy between the "open-options" theory and the Stoic/Epicurean theory is not exhaustive. Elsewhere, we have developed a sketch of a theory of moral responsibility for action which is more refined than the Stoic/Epicurean theory but which still rejects the traditional association of moral responsibility for action with the existence of genuine alternative possibilities.[5] This theory is an "actual-sequence" theory of responsibility for actions: It fixes upon the properties of the actual sequence of events issuing in the action, and it does not require the existence of genuine alternative possibilities. We limn the outlines of such a theory in the following section.

II

We have been focusing upon moral responsibility for *actions*. Now we turn to the issue of moral responsibility for *consequences* of what we do. Before proceeding, we should point out that the events and states of affairs which are consequences of what we do can be construed as either particulars or universals. For our purposes, the distinction between consequence-particulars and consequence-universals will be made in terms of criteria of individuation. We stipulate that a consequence-particular is individuated more finely than a consequence-universal. Specifically, the actual casual pathway to a consequence-particular is an essential feature of it, so that if a different causal pathway were to occur, then a different consequence-particular would occur. In contrast, the same consequence-universal can be brought about via different causal antecedents.

For example, in Assassin one can distinguish between the consequence-particular, *the mayor's being shot*, and the consequence-universal, *that the mayor is shot*. Had Sam shown some indication that he would not shoot the mayor, and had Jack's device played a casual role in producing the outcome, a different consequence-particular would have occurred. (A different consequence-particular would have been denoted by, "the mayor's being shot.") In contrast, even if Jack's device had played a causal role, then the same consequence-universal, *that the mayor is shot*, would have occurred. (Note that what is important in the distinction between consequence-particulars and consequence-universals is the issue of individuation, not the sort of phrase used to refer to the different sorts of consequences. In this paper we shall generally follow the convention of referring to consequence-universals with such phrases as, "that the mayor is shot.")

In the case of Assassin, Sam shoots the mayor without the intervention of Jack's electronic device. In this case, the state of affairs, *that the mayor is shot*, obtains. But this same state of affairs could have been caused to obtain in different ways; in particular, it would have obtained even if Jack had caused Sam to shoot the mayor. Now the question arises as to whether an agent can be morally responsible for a consequence-universal, if he could not have prevented the consequence-universal from obtaining. Are there cases in which an agent is morally responsible for the occurrence of a consequence which is inevitable (for him)? (In what follows, we shall be primarily concerned with consequence-universals.)

It appears as if there are such cases. Take, for example, Assassin. It is plausible to say that Sam is morally responsible not only for shooting the mayor, but also for the consequence-universal, *that the mayor is shot*. And note that Sam cannot prevent the mayor from being shot in one way or another.

Consider a similar case, "Missile 1." In Missile 1 an evil woman, Elizabeth, has obtained a missile and missile-launcher, and she has decided (for her own rather perverse reasons) to launch the missile toward Washington D.C. Suppose that Elizabeth's situation is like that of Sam; she has not been manipulated, brainwashed, and so forth. Further, imagine that she has had exactly the same sort of device implanted in her brain as had been put into Sam's and that there is a counterfactual intervener associated with her who would ensure that Elizabeth would launch the missile, if Elizabeth were to show any sign of wavering. We also suppose that, once the missile is launched toward the city, Elizabeth cannot prevent it from hitting Washington D.C.

Now when Elizabeth launches the missile toward Washington, she does so freely, and we believe that she is morally responsible for the occurrence of the consequence-universal, *that Washington D.C. is bombed*. She is morally accountable for this state of affairs, even though it is inevitable for her; there is nothing she can do to prevent the obtaining of the state of affairs, *that Washington D.C. is bombed*.

"Missile 2" is exactly like Missile 1, except that there is no counterfactual intervener who is poised to manipulate Elizabeth's brain. Rather, there is another woman, Carla, who would launch the missile, if Elizabeth were to refrain. Further, there is nothing that Elizabeth could do to prevent Carla from launching the missile or to prevent the missile from hitting Washington D.C., once launched. In Missile 2 Elizabeth can also be held morally responsible for the fact that Washington D.C. is bombed, although she cannot prevent this fact from obtaining.

Missile 1 and Missile 2 are cases in which an agent *is* morally responsible for a consequence of what she does, although she cannot prevent that state of affairs from occurring. But there are other cases in which an agent *is not* morally responsible for a consequence of what she does, and this judgment seems based on precisely on the fact that she *cannot* prevent that state of affairs. Consider, for example, "Missile 3."

In Missile 3 Joan knows that Elizabeth has already launched a missile toward Washington D.C. But Joan has a weapon which she could use to deflect the missile in such a way that it would hit a less populous area of the city. Unfortunately, Joan is located very close to Washington, and because of this fact, the bomb's trajectory, and the nature of her weapon, she knows that, whereas she can deflect the bomb onto a different part of the city, she cannot prevent the bomb from hitting the city at all.

Imagine that Joan uses her weapon to deflect the bomb. In so doing she may well be morally responsible for the fact that one section of Washington (rather than another) is bombed. But is Joan morally responsible for the consequence-universal, *that Washington D.C. is bombed*? It seems that she is not. And there is a strong tendency to say that she is not morally responsible for the state of affairs *that Washington D.C. is bombed* exactly because she cannot prevent this state of affairs from obtaining.

Here is a similar case. Ralph is the driver of a train whose brakes have failed. The train is hurtling down the tracks toward a fork in the tracks. Ralph knows that although he can cause the train to take the right fork or the left fork, he cannot stop the train. Ralph also knows that both forks lead to Syracuse. When Ralph turns the train onto the left fork, he can be held morally responsible for the consequence-universal, *that the train takes the left fork* (rather than the right fork). But it just seems obvious that Ralph is not morally responsible for the consequence-universal, *that the train ends up in Syracuse*, given that Ralph is not morally responsible for the fact that he is on this stretch of track in the first place. (Notice that even if Ralph did not know that both tracks lead to Syracuse, we would not hold him morally responsible for the consequence-universal, *that the train ends up in Syracuse*.) And what could explain Ralph's lack of moral responsibility for the consequence, *that the train ends up in Syracuse*, other than the fact that Ralph cannot prevent the train from going to Syracuse in one way or another?[6]

The consideration of these examples leaves us in the following situation. First, there are cases in which an agent is morally responsible for performing an action, although he cannot avoid performing that action. Further, there are cases in which it appears that an agent is morally responsible for a consequence of what he has done which he cannot prevent from occurring. But there are also cases in which an agent is not morally responsible for a consequence-universal and in which it is very tempting to say that it is precisely the fact that the agent cannot prevent the state of affairs from obtaining that makes it false that he is morally responsible for it. An adequate theory of moral responsibility for consequences should *fit naturally* with the theory of responsibility for actions. Further, it should explain the fact that, whereas in some cases in which an agent could not prevent a consequence from obtaining he is morally responsible for the consequence, in other cases in which an agent could not prevent a consequence from obtaining he is not morally responsible for the consequence.

In the next section we shall argue that the theories presented (or suggested) by other philosophers fail to generate an acceptable account of moral responsibility for consequences. Finally, in the following sections we shall adumbrate our own approach and show how it would sort through the various cases.

III

1. Van Inwagen/Feinberg

The analogue of the traditional approach to moral responsibility for actions would claim that moral responsibility for a consequence-universal requires the freedom to prevent the consequence from obtaining. To the extent that Feinberg's claims can be applied to consequences, he can be associated with this view. And Peter van Inwagen explicitly argues for this view.[7]

A very serious problem for this view is that it does not allow one to say what we take to be the plausible and natural thing about Assassin: that Sam is morally responsible for the consequence, *that the mayor is shot.* This result in itself seems to be a decisive refutation of the view. Another (obviously related) problem for this approach is that it forces one to say that Missile 1, Missile 2, Missile 3, and "Train" are on a par. But we believe that, whereas in Missile 3 Joan is not morally responsible for the consequence-universal, *that Washington D.C. is bombed*, in Missile 1 and Missile 2 Elizabeth *is* morally responsible for the consequence-universal, *that Washington D.C. is bombed*. (Also, whereas in the first two missile cases Elizabeth is morally responsible for the consequence-universal, in Train Ralph is *not* morally responsible for the consequence universal, *that the train ends up in Syracuse*.) We believe, then, that the van Inwagen/Feinberg approach – the "traditional approach" – implies an implausible assimilation of cases. We need a subtler theory of moral responsibility for consequences. (In section IV, we sketch a theory of responsibility for consequences and return to some considerations presented by van Inwagen.)

2. Heinaman

Next consider an account of moral responsibility for consequence-universals suggested by Robert Heinaman.[8] Heinaman's suggestion is that an agent is morally responsible for a consequence-universal insofar as he knowingly and intentionally performs some action which is causally sufficient for the occurrence of the consequence-universal.

There are various problems with this formulation of Heinaman's suggestion. First, one can do something "knowingly and intentionally" without doing it freely. If one is acting as a result of the irresistibility of some urge, one can, nevertheless, be acting "knowingly and intentionally." But if one does not act freely in bringing about a consequence-universal, one might not be morally responsible for it. So let us revise Heinaman's criterion: A person is morally responsible for a consequence-universal insofar as he freely performs some action which is causally sufficient for the occurrence of the consequence-universal.[9]

But the notion of "causal sufficiency" employed here is rather vague. Heinaman appears to think that, when an agent does something which is causally sufficient for the occurrence of a consequence-universal, he does something which at least in part explains why the consequence-universal occurs. So one way of formulating Heinaman's suggestions is as follows: An agent is morally responsible for the occurrence of a consequence-universal insofar as he freely does something which at least in part explains why the consequence-universal obtains.

Heinaman points out that one can do something which entails that a state of affairs obtains without doing something which at least in part explains *why* the state of affairs obtains. So, for example, when one drops a vase and breaks it, one has done something that entails that the vase is breakable, but one has not done something which in any way explains *why* the vase is breakable. Thus, on Heinaman's suggestion, one will not be morally responsible for the consequence-universal, *that the vase if breakable*, although one might be morally responsible for the consequence-universal, *that the vase is broken*.

Yet even with such revisions and qualifications, problems remain for Heinaman's account. One wants to say that in Assassin Sam is morally responsible for the consequence-universal, *that the mayor is killed*, and in Missile 1 and Missile 2 Elizabeth is morally responsible for the fact that Washington D.C. is bombed. But it is unclear that Heinaman's criterion yields these results. For instance, it is at best unclear that in Assassin Sam's free action in any way explains the occurrence of the state of affairs, *that the mayor is killed*. Given the presence of Jack and the existence of the electronic device, it appears that we *already* have a full explanation of the fact that the mayor will be killed in some way or another. Given that Jack and his device are *sufficient* for the occurrence of the consequence-universal, *that the mayor is killed*, it is dubious whether Sam's free action constitutes part of an explanation of the occurrence of the consequence-universal. Heinaman is relying on a notion of "explanatory factor" according to which such a factor need not be a necessary condition of the *explanandum*, and this is, at best, obscure.[10]

Perhaps Heinaman's suggestion can be defended against this criticism by making an important (although admittedly delicate) distinction: one might distinguish between a "modalized" consequence-universal and a "purely descriptive" consequence-universal. The modalized consequence-universal is something like the fact that it *has to occur* that the mayor is killed, or perhaps that if the mayor were not killed in one way, he would certainly be killed in another way. In contrast, the purely descriptive consequence-universal is simply the fact that the mayor is killed in one way or another.

Now it might be argued that the apparent plausibility of the above response to Heinaman's criterion issues from a conflation of the modalized and purely descriptive consequence-universals. That is, it is admittedly implausible to suppose that Sam's free action of pulling the trigger in any way explains the *modalized* consequence-universal. But this is irrelevant, because what is at issue is the appropriate explanation of the obtaining of the purely descriptive consequence-universal. And it *is* plausible to think that Sam's free action in part explains the obtaining of this consequence.

Even if this is correct, however, Heinaman's criterion now faces the following problem. Heinaman must say that in Missile 3 Joan is morally responsible for the (purely descriptive) state of affairs, *that Washington D.C. is bombed (somewhere or another)*. That is to say, *if* it is plausible to suppose that Sam's free act of pulling the trigger at least in part explains why the purely descriptive state of affairs, *that the mayor is killed (in some way or another)* obtains, then it is equally plausible to suppose that Joan's free act of deflecting the bomb at least in part explains why the purely descriptive state of affairs, *that Washington D.C. is bombed (somewhere or another)* obtains. But it is an implausible result that Joan must be deemed responsible for this consequence-universal – even the purely descriptive consequence-universal. Whereas it is plausible to think that Joan is morally responsible for the fact that Washington D.C. is bombed *in one area rather than another*, it is implausible to say that she is morally responsible for the fact that Washington D.C. is bombed somewhere or another.[11] (A similar analysis applies to Train.)

There is a way of supplementing Heinaman's criterion which might seem to allow him to avoid the implausible result in Missile 3 and Train. In both of these cases, there is "already in motion" a causal sequence which would lead to the occurrence of the consequence-universal, no matter what action the agent performs (among those which he can perform). So one might refine Heinaman's criterion further: An agent is morally responsible for a consequence-universal insofar as (1) the agent freely performs an action which at least in part explains why the universal is brought about in one way rather than another, and (2) there is no causal sequence already in motion which would lead to the occurrence of the consequence-universal, no matter what the agent does (among the set of things he *can* do).

Regrettably (for Heinaman), this will not do either. For suppose that in Missile 1 there is a timing device which has already been set. This device would cause the missile to be launched, if Elizabeth were to refrain from launching it herself. The revised Heinaman criterion implausibly entails that Elizabeth would *not* be morally responsible for Washington's being bombed in this version of Missile 1: "Timer." But Elizabeth freely launches the bomb in Timer, and it seems as if she *should* be considered morally responsible for the consequence-universal, *that Washington D.C. is bombed*; certainly, she should be held morally responsible for it in Timer, if she is in Missile 1. Thus, the refined Heinaman approach would lead to an implausible result: the differentiation of Timer and Missile 1. Finally, we do not see any way of further refining the suggestion of Heinaman so that it would yield adequate results.

3. A Frankfurt-type strategy

Harry Frankfurt has proposed the following principle regarding moral responsibility for actions: If a person acts only because he could not have done otherwise, then he is not morally responsible for his action. This principle applies to actions, rather than consequences, and it specifies only a necessary, and not a sufficient condition, for moral responsibility. We shall very briefly explain the possibility of extending Frankfurt's suggestion to apply to consequences; we should emphasize that Frankfurt himself is not committed to this sort of extension.

Suppose that an agent freely performs some action which has a certain consequence which she cannot prevent. Imagine, further, that the agent's inability to prevent this consequence plays no role in her decision and action. Under such circumstances, the agent still might be morally responsible for the consequence. This suggests a principle of responsibility for consequence-universals which is similar to Frankfurt's approach to responsibility for actions: If (1) an agent freely performs some action which has a consequence (which she foresees) and (2) the fact that this consequence is unavoidable plays no role in the agent's decision so to act, then the agent can be held morally responsible for the consequence-universal.

To see the problem with this approach, consider again Missile 3. In Missile 3, Joan knows that she cannot prevent the missile from hitting Washington D.C. Intuitively, she is not morally responsible for the fact that Washington D.C. is bombed in one place or another. And it seems to us that she would not be morally responsible for this fact, even if she mistakenly believed that she could prevent Washington D.C. from being bombed. So, in "Missile 4" the situation is exactly as it is in Missile 3, except that Joan falsely believes that she can deflect the missile so that it would not hit Washington. Still, we claim that, in Missile 4, Joan is not morally responsible for the consequence-universal, *that Washington D.C. is bombed*. But the two conditions of the extended Frankfurt approach are met: Joan freely does something (deflects the bomb in a certain way) which she foresees will result in Washington D.C.'s being bombed, and the fact that she cannot avoid this result plays no role in her decision and action. The fact that she cannot avoid this result plays no role in her decision and action in part because she (falsely) believes that she *can* avoid this result. (Similarly, in Train Ralph would not be morally responsible for the fact that the train goes to Syracuse, even if he did not know that all tracks go to Syracuse.) Thus, although the Frankfurt-type strategy would say the correct thing about Missile 1, Missile 2, and Missile 3, it would not say the correct thing about such cases as Missile 4.

4. Berofsky

A case very similar to Missile 4 shows the theory of moral responsibility for consequence-universals proposed by Bernard Berofsky to be inadequate. Berofsky says:

> Let us describe conditions in which an agent Walters is derivatively responsible for a state of affairs {S} he cannot help producing in virtue of a prior, free act A.
> (1) Walters performed A in order to bring {S} about.
> (2) Walters believed that the probability that A would lead to {S} is very high.
> (3) {S} is not causally remote from A.
> (4) Walters freely undertook as part of his responsibilities the avoidance of states of affairs of which {S} is an instance.
> (5) Walters believed that he would be unable to prevent {S} once he did A.
> (6) {S} is morally significant.[12]

Note that, in Missile 4, it is not the case that Joan deflects the bomb in order to bring it about that Washington is bombed. Thus, Berofsky's condition (1) is not satisfied, and Berofsky can say the correct thing about Missile 4. But imagine that in "Missile 5" Walters has freely undertaken to protect Washington D.C. from attack. Unhappily, Walters is a secret agent working for the Soviet Union. When he sees that a Soviet missile is proceeding toward the east coast of the United States, he falsely believes that it will miss its intended target, Washington D.C. In order to cause the missile to hit Washington, Walters deflects it with his deflecting weapon. The bomb hits Washington D.C., but, unbeknownst to Walters, it would have hit Washington, no matter what Walters did (including not employing his deflecting weapon at all). That is, the missile was proceeding in such a way that, given Walters' weapon and his location very close to Washington, the missile would have hit Washington, no matter what Walters did. Just as with Joan in Missile 4, we believe that Walters is not morally responsible for the fact that Washington D.C. is bombed (in one area or another). He might well be morally responsible for his action of employing his deflecting gun, and also for the fact that Washington D.C. is bombed in one area rather than another. But it really is implausible to say that Walters is morally responsible for the consequence-universal, *that Washington D.C. is hit by a bomb*. Berofsky's account is problematic insofar as it appears to yield this unsettling result. Thus, although Berofsky's account adequately handles all of the other "Missile" cases, it does not say the correct thing about Missile 5.[13]

5. Rowe

In a recent article William Rowe has discussed a number of examples which are related in interesting ways to the examples we have developed above.[14] Further, he has suggested a theory of responsibility for consequence-universals. Here we shall lay out some of the examples and the theory which was developed in order to systematize the examples. Finally, we shall show how the theory cannot be adequately generalized to apply to examples similar to the Missile examples. Here is Rowe's Case A:

> There is a train approaching a fork in the track controlled by a switch. The left fork (#1) leads on to where a dog has been tied to the track. If the train proceeds on #1 it will hit the dog. Track #2, however, leads to a safe stopping point for the train. The switch is set for #2. You throw the switch to #1 with the result that the train proceeds on #1, hitting the dog.[15]

In Case A, Rowe says that you can be held (at least *prima facie*) morally responsible for the consequence-universal, *that the dog is hit*. We agree. Now here is Rowe's Case B:

> Let us again suppose that there is a speeding train approaching a fork in the track controlled by a switch. As in Case A, the switch is set for track #2. It is again in your power to switch the train to track #1 by throwing the switch. It is also in your power not to throw the switch. Unfortunately, unlike Case A, both tracks (#1 and #2) converge later at the point where the dog is tied to the track. It is inevitable, therefore, that the train will hit the dog. Nevertheless, you throw the switch so that the train proceeds on track #1.[16]

In Case B Rowe believes that you are not morally responsible for the fact that the dog is hit. Again, we agree. Rowe's Case B is relevantly similar to our Train, van Inwagen's and our Missile 3. Next here is Rowe's Case C:

> In case C we find a curious mixture of features in one or the other of the first two cases. As in Case A, track #2 does not converge with track #1. Instead, it leads to a safe stopping point for the train. Only track #1 leads to the spot where the dog is tied to the track. Unlike Case A, however, some other person, Peter, is so situated that he most certainly will throw the switch if, but only if, you do not. If you throw the switch, the train will be routed to track #1 and hit the dog. If you do not throw the switch, Peter will, with the result that the train will be routed to track #1 and hit the dog. Moreover, it is not in your power to prevent Peter's throwing the switch, should you not throw it yourself. As in our other two cases, you throw the switch, the train is routed to tract #1 and hits the dog.[17]

In case C, Rowe thinks that you can be held (at least *prima facie*) morally responsible for the consequence-universal, *that the dog is hit*. And, again, we agree. Rowe's Case C is relevantly similar to our Missile 2.

Let us now consider a case which is exactly like A except that a powerful being is poised to bend track #2 around if but only if you do not switch the train to track #1. (Call this Case "D.") In D – as in Case A – you actually switch the train to track #1. Whereas in Case B you are intuitively *not* morally responsible for the fact that the dog is hit, in Case D you are so responsible. Thus, a difference in conditions which are actualized can make a difference to moral responsibility, even if the difference is not causally efficacious. Rowe wishes to distinguish D from another case, "E." Case E is the same as D except that the powerful being is programmed to bend track #2 to the place where the dog is tied *whether or not you throw the switch*. Rowe claims that in case E you are not morally responsible for the fact that the dog is hit. He explains the difference in our intuitions concerning Cases D and E by pointing to the fact that in D your action prevents the relevant "ensuring condition" from being actualized, whereas in E your action does not prevent this condition from being actualized – it just prevents it from being efficacious.[18]

According to Rowe, the above examples suggest the following theory: S is responsible for E by doing X if and only if

1) S does X prior to or at the same time as E's occurrence.
2) S's doing X is a part of a sufficient causal condition of E, and
3) Either S's doing X is necessary for E's occurrence or any other condition that is sufficient (in the circumstances) for E has a part that is actualized only if S does not do X.[19]

To see the problem with Rowe's proposal, start with Missile 3. This is the case presented above in which Elizabeth has launched a missile toward Washington D.C. Joan has a deflecting ray which can deflect the missile away from the center of the city and toward a less populated area, but unfortunately the ray is not strong enough to deflect the missile away from the city entirely. In order to save the most people, Joan deflects the missile. Our intuition here is that Joan is *not* morally responsible for the consequence-universal, *that Washington D.C. is bombed*. (Of course, she may well be responsible for the fact that D.C. is bombed in one place rather than another.)

Consider now "Missile 6." This is like Missile 3 except for the fact that Elizabeth's missile has misfired and is now heading away from Washington D.C. Elizabeth realizes the situation and prepares to use her own deflecting ray to redirect the missile toward the center of the city. Joan learns of Elizabeth's plan, but fortunately realizes that she can redirect the missile to a less populated area of Washington D.C. before Elizabeth can fire her ray. In this case, Joan deflects the missile to a less populated area only because she knows that if she does not do so, Elizabeth will use her ray to deflect it to the most populated part of the city.

Clearly, if Joan is not morally responsible for the consequence-universal, *that Washington D.C. is bombed*, in Missile 3, then she is not morally responsible for this consequence-universal in Missile 6. Rowe, however, must say that Joan *is* morally responsible for the relevant consequence-universal in Missile 6. He must say this because Missile 6 is analogous to case D. Just as Rowe claims that you are morally responsible for the fact that the dog is hit in D because your action prevents the relevant ensuring condition from being actualized (i.e., your act prevents the powerful being from bending the track), so he should claim that in Missile 6 Joan is responsible for the fact that Washington is bombed because her action prevents Elizabeth from "bending" the missile back to the city. (This is analogous to bending the track in case D, since one can imagine that the "smart" missile is being guided on a "laser track.") Thus, Rowe's theory is not suitably generalizable.

IV

1. Responsibility for actions

We shall here present just the barest sketch of a theory of moral responsibility for actions. This theory has been elaborated elsewhere in greater detail, and it must be further refined and developed in future work.[20] But it is useful here to see how our theory of moral responsibility for consequences builds upon and fits together with the theory of responsibility for actions.

The basic idea is that (given that the relevant epistemic conditions are met[21]) an agent is morally responsible for performing an action insofar as (1) it is not the case that the agent does what he does solely because he could not have done otherwise, and (2) the bodily movement identical to the action issues from a weakly reasons-responsive mechanism. We shall here give a very brief sketch of weak reasons-responsiveness. To say whether an action issues from a weakly reasons-responsive mechanism, we first need to identify the kind of mechanism that actually issues in action. It is important to see that, in some cases, intuitively different kinds of mechanisms operate in the actual sequence and the alternative sequence. So, for instance, in Assassin the ordinary process of practical reasoning issues in Sam's act of squeezing the trigger, but a different type of mechanism (involving direct electronic stimulation of Sam's brain) would have operated, had Sam shown any sign of wavering. We cannot here develop an explicit account of mechanism-individuation. It suffices, for our purposes, to note that Sam's actual-sequence mechanism is intuitively of a different sort from the alternative-sequence mechanism. Similarly, we would want to say that in Hero, Matthew's actual-sequence mechanism is of a different sort from his alternative-sequence mechanism; in the actual sequence, he quickly deliberates and decides to save the struggling child, and his reasoning is uninfluenced by any overwhelming urge. However, in the alternative sequence, his deliberations are influenced by an overwhelming and irresistible urge to save the swimmer. Whereas it is difficult to produce an explicit criterion of mechanism-individuation, we believe that it is natural to say that in cases such as Assassin and Hero different sorts of mechanisms issue in the actions in the actual and alternative sequences.

In order to determine whether an actual-sequence mechanism of a certain type is weakly reasons-responsive, one asks whether there exists some possible scenario (with the same natural laws as the actual world) in which that type of mechanism operates, the agent has reason to do otherwise, and the agent does otherwise (for that reason). That is, we hold fixed the actual type of mechanism, and we ask whether the agent would respond to *some* possible incentive to do otherwise. If so, then the actually operative mechanism is weakly reasons-responsive. In contrast, strong reasons-responsiveness obtains when a certain kind K of mechanism actually issues in an action and if there were sufficient reason to do otherwise and K were to operate, the agent would recognize the sufficient reason to do otherwise and thus choose to do otherwise and do otherwise.

Under the requirement of strong reasons-responsiveness, we ask what would happen if there were a sufficient reason to do otherwise (holding fixed the actual kind of mechanism). Strong reasons-responsiveness points us to the alternative scenario in which there is a sufficient reason for the agent to do otherwise (and the actual mechanism operates) which is *most similar* to the actual situation. In contrast, under weak reasons-responsiveness, there must simply exist *some* possible scenario in which there is a sufficient reason to do otherwise, the agent's actual mechanism operates, and the agent does otherwise. This possible scenario need *not* be the one in which the agent has a sufficient reason to do otherwise (and the actual mechanism operates) which is *most similar* to the actual situation.

2. Responsibility for consequences

The account of moral responsibility for consequences is in certain respects parallel to (and also an extension of) the account of moral responsibility for actions. The leading idea is that (given that certain epistemic constraints are satisfied) an agent is morally responsible for a consequence insofar as (1) it is not the case that the agent brings about the consequence solely because he believes that he cannot prevent it from occurring (in some way or another), and (2) the consequence emanates from a responsive *sequence*. It is necessary to distinguish *two components* of the sequence leading to a consequence. The first component is the mechanism leading to action (bodily movement), and the second component is the process leading from the action to the event in the external world. We shall say that, in order for the sequence leading to a consequence to be responsive, both the mechanism leading to the action must be weakly reasons-responsive and the process leading from the action to the consequence must be "sensitive to action."

Before proceeding to the account, it is important to note that the counterfactual intervener in a Frankfurt-type case need not be another agent (whose action in the alternative sequence would bring about the consequence in question). As Frankfurt points out, the role of counterfactual intervener may be played "by natural forces involving no will or design at all".[22] Thus, in Missile 2 we could eliminate Carla and suppose instead that had Elizabeth not freely launched the missile, natural forces would have caused the missile's triggering mechanism to malfunction and fire the rocket at Washington D.C. (Perhaps a stray bird would have flown into the missile's launching apparatus, and this would have triggered the firing.) Given these types of examples, it seems that in evaluating the sensitivity of a process one wants to hold fixed not only the actions of other agents in the actual sequence, but also any natural events which play no role in the actual sequence but which would, in the alternative sequence, *trigger* causal chains leading to the consequence in question. For convenience we can group *both* other actions that would trigger causal chains leading to the consequence (e.g., Carla's firing the missile in the alternative sequence) *and* natural events that would do so (e.g., the bird triggering the missile's firing in the alternative sequence) under the heading "triggering events."

Let us think of a triggering event (relative to some consequence C) as an event which is such that if it were to occur, it would *initiate* a causal sequence leading to C. Such events as Carla's firing the missile and the bird's flying into the missile's launching apparatus are triggering events (relative to the relevant consequences) in the examples above.

Suppose that in the actual world an agent S performs an action A via a type of mechanism M, and S's A-ing causes some consequence C via a type of process P.[23] We shall say that the sequence leading to the consequence C is responsive if and only if there exists some action A^* (other than A) such that (1) there exists some possible scenario in which an M-type mechanism operates, the agent has reason to do A^*, and the agent does A^*; and (2) if S were to do A^* all triggering events which do not actually occur were not to occur, and a P-type process were to occur, the C would not occur.[24]

Before proceeding to show how this principle can be applied to explain our intuitive judgements about the cases discussed above, let us take a moment to discuss a few points which should help both to clarify and to illustrate our principle. (1) In formulating the definition of a responsive sequence, we make use of the intuitive notion of a "type of process" leading from the action to the event in the external world. This is parallel to the notion of a kind of mechanism issuing in action. As above, we concede both that process-individuation might be problematic and that we do not have an explicit theory of process-individuation. But, as we stated previously, we believe that there is a relatively clear intuitive distinction between different types of processes.

We do not deny that there will be difficult questions about process-individuation. Nevertheless, all that is required for our purposes is that there be agreement about some fairly clear cases. If we are unsure about an agent's moral responsibility for a consequence in precisely those cases in which we are unsure about process-individuation, then at least the vagueness in our theory will match the vagueness of the phenomena it purports to analyze.

(2) In ascertaining the responsiveness of a particular sequence involving a mechanism issuing in action, an action, and a process leading from the action to a consequence, we "hold fixed" the type of mechanism and the type of process. If it is the case that a different mechanism or process would have taken place if things had been different (i.e., if the case is a Frankfurt-type case), this is irrelevant to the responsiveness of the *actual* sequence. Further, imagine that we are testing the sensitivity of a particular process leading from an action to a consequence. Suppose that the agent actually performs a certain action thus causing some consequence, and that no one else actually performs that type of action. Under these conditions, we "hold fixed" others' behavior when we test for the sensitivity of the process leading from action to consequence. The point is that, when we are interested in the sensitivity of the process to action, we are interested in whether there would have been a different outcome, if the agent had not performed a certain sort of action *and all nonoccurring triggering events were not to occur.*

The theory claims that the sequence leading to a consequence includes more than just the mechanism issuing in action. Thus, it is not surprising that both components – i.e., the mechanism leading to the action and the process leading from the action to the event – are relevant to responsibility for a consequence, whereas only the first component is relevant to responsibility for an action. Thus, the theory of responsibility for a consequence involves two stages. It will be seen below that this two-stage approach helps us appropriately to distinguish different cases of responsibility for consequences which are inevitable. Further, it is important to note that when considering responsibility for consequences the second component should not be considered in isolation from the first. Our definition of the responsiveness of the sequence leading to a consequence requires a certain *linkage* of the two components of the sequence.

(3) The notion of a triggering event is – like the notions of mechanism and process – fuzzy around the edges. But, again, we believe that it is tolerably clear for the present purposes. Note that a triggering event is an event which would initiate a causal chain leading to a certain consequence. Although the concept of "initiation" is difficult to articulate crisply, we rely on the fact that there are some fairly uncontroversial instances of the concept. So, for exam-

ple, if a lightning bolt hits a house and there is a resulting fire, the event of the lightning's hitting the house could be said to initiate the sequence leading to the destruction of the house. And this is so even if there were certain atmospheric events which antedated the lightning bolt and which lead to it. Of course, the notion of initiation is highly context-dependent, and the truth of claims about purported initiations will depend on the purposes and goals of the individuals making (and considering) the claims. But we believe that the notion of initiation issues in tolerably clear intuitive judgments about the cases relevant to our purposes. So, for example, such events as Sam's (or Carla's) pulling the trigger, the bird's flying into the launching mechanism, and the timing device activating the bomb (in Timer) are all intuitively events which initiate the sequences leading to the relevant consequences. In contrast, consider the event of the train's proceeding in a certain direction in the example, Train. Given the set-up of the example, if this event were to occur, the train would (still) end up in Syracuse. But note that this event is not plausibly thought to *initiate* the sequence leading to the consequence in question. (The initiating event here would be Ralph's turning the train one way or another — or perhaps his choice to do so.)[25]

With the principle of moral responsibility for consequences in hand, we can explain the intuitive judgments about cases we have described. In Assassin, Sam is morally responsible for the consequence-universal, *that the mayor is killed*. In this case, the actual-sequence mechanism (ordinary practical deliberation) is weakly reasons-responsive, and the process leading from action to consequence (ordinary physical laws, no "abnormal circumstances") is sensitive to action: Had Sam not squeezed the trigger (either as a result of his own deliberation or because of Jack's intervention) and others' relevant behavior were held fixed, the mayor would not have been killed. Thus, the two components necessary for responsiveness are present, and Sam can be held morally responsible for the fact that the mayor is killed, although he could not have prevented it.

Exactly the same considerations apply to Missile 1: Elizabeth is morally responsible for the consequence-universal, *that Washington D.C. is bombed*: both components of the actual sequence issuing in the consequence-universal are suitably responsive and thus the total sequence is responsive. (Further, the same analysis applies to Rowe's Case A.)

We have claimed that if Elizabeth is morally responsible for the consequence-universal, *that Washington D.C. is bombed*, in Missile 1, she should also be considered morally responsible for this consequence-universal in Timer. (Timer is just like Missile 1 except that a timing mechanism has been set which would activate the bomb, if Elizabeth were to refrain from doing so.) The timing mechanism operates in the actual sequence, but it does not actually activate the bomb. Thus the triggering event of the timing mechanism's activating the bomb (relative to the consequence-universal, *that Washington D.C. is bombed*) is a non-occurring triggering mechanism. As such, its non-occurrence is held fixed, on our approach to ascertaining responsiveness: on our theory, the actual sequence issuing in the consequence-universal is responsive, and thus Elizabeth is deemed morally responsible for it.

Note that Elizabeth is also deemed morally responsible for the consequence-universal, *that Washington D.C. is bombed*, in Missile 2. Again, the actual sequence issuing in the consequence in responsive. When ascertaining whether the actual sequence leading to the bomb's hitting Washington is responsive, we hold fixed the inaction of Carla. (The same analysis applied to Rowe's Case C.)

But in Missile 3 Joan is not morally responsible for the consequence-universal, *that Washington D.C. is bombed*. This is because the sequence including Joan's action and the process leading from her action to the event of Washington's being bombed is not responsive. Of course, the first component *is* weakly reasons-responsive (and thus Joan can be held morally responsible for her *action* of deflecting the bomb). But the sequence is not responsive, because the second component – the process leading from action to event in the world – is *not* sensitive to action. That is, the world is such that, no matter how Joan acts, the bomb will hit Washington D.C. (Exactly parallel remarks apply to Train.)

Our principle of moral responsibility for consequences, then, explains the intuitive judgments about the various examples presented. (We do not here explicitly apply the theory to all the cases, but our claim is that our theory handles the cases in a felicitous manner.) Further, the theory explains why there is an important difference between such cases as Missile 1 and Missile 2, on the one hand, and Missile 3 and Train, on the other. The agent could have prevented the relevant consequence-universal in *none* of these cases. But, whereas in the first two cases the relevant consequence-universal issues from a responsive sequence, in the last two cases the consequence-universal does *not* issue from a responsive sequence.

Once it becomes evident that responsiveness of a sequence leading to a consequence requires the second component – sensitivity to action – as well as the first component, it becomes clear that the latter two states of affairs are interestingly different from the former two. In Missile 1 and Missile 2 the responsibility-undermining factor occurs in the *alternative* to the first component of the actual sequence. In Missile 3 and Train, the factor that rules out responsibility for the consequence-universal is part of the second component of the *actual* sequence. If one did not recognize that the actual sequence leading to a consequence contains two components, one could mistakenly think that the only way to explain the agents' lack of responsibility in Missile 3 and Train is to say that the agent could not have prevented the consequence-universal from obtaining. But our theory allows us to avoid using this sort of explanation, which in any case would lead to the wrong result in such cases as Missile 1 and Missile 2.

The difference between Rowe's Cases A and B illustrates an important feature of our theory of moral responsibility. The only difference between Cases A and B consists in facts about the world which play no role in what actually happens: Whether or not track #2 "bends around" so as to converge with track #1 is irrelevant to what actually transpires in both cases. But it is relevant to the responsiveness of the sequences issuing in the consequences, and, thus, to your moral responsibility for them. What is relevant here is that certain conditions in the world are *actualized*, not that they are efficacious. Thus, there is a distinction between Case B and Case D presented above (Case D is exactly like A except that a powerful being is poised to bend track #2 around if but only if you do not switch the train to track #1). In Case D – as in Case A – you actually switch the train to track #1. Whereas in Case B you are *not* morally responsible for the fact that the dog is hit, in D you are so responsible. Thus, a difference in conditions which are actualized can make a difference to moral responsibility, even if the difference is not causally efficacious.

Note that there seems to be a difference between the first component of the sequence issuing in the consequence (the mechanism leading to action) and the second component (the process leading from the action to the consequence), as regards the relevance of inefficacious factors. If an agent actually has an irresistible desire to do something, but the irresistibility of the desire plays no role in his actual decision or action, then it seems that he can be morally responsible for *his action*. Further, under such conditions, it would seem that the agent could be morally responsible for a consequence-universal. Consider, for instance, Frankfurt's "willing addict." When he takes the drug, he might not even know that he has an irresistible desire to take it. He can be held morally responsible for his taking the drug, and also, seemingly, for the fact that the drug is taken. Because the irresistibility of the desire is inefficacious, it is not relevant to the actual-sequence mechanism issuing in the action, and thus it is not relevant to the responsiveness of the sequence issuing in the consequence.[26] But in a case such as B, the fact that track #2 actually bends around is relevant to the sensitivity to action of the process leading from the action to the consequence, and hence it is relevant to the responsiveness of the sequence issuing in the consequence. Thus, there is a difference between action-producing mechanisms and the processes which go from actions to consequences: Inefficacious factors are irrelevant to the responsiveness of the former, but relevant to the sensitivity of the latter.

Having sketched out our approach to moral responsibility for consequences, we are in a position to address an argument van Inwagen employs to defend his approach to moral responsibility for consequence-universals.[27] Consider again Assassin. We have said that it is plausible to consider Sam morally responsible for the consequence-universal, *that the mayor is killed*. Van Inwagen would deny this, because Sam cannot prevent the mayor from being killed in some way or another. And van Inwagen might argue for his position as follows. If Sam is morally responsible for the state of affairs, *that the mayor is killed*, then Sam is morally responsible for the state of affairs, *Sam kills the mayor on his own or Sam kills the mayor as a result of the intervention of Jack's device*. But there is no difference between being morally responsible for this disjunctive state of affairs and such states of affairs as *Sam kills the mayor on his own or grass is green* and *Sam kills the mayor on his own or two plus two equals four*. But for the latter two states of affairs Sam is clearly *not* morally responsible. Thus, Sam should not be considered morally responsible for the state of affairs, *that the mayor is killed*.

But we claim that there is a relevant difference between *Sam kills the mayor on his own or Sam kills the mayor as a result of the intervention of Jack's device* and such states of affairs as *Sam kills the mayor on his own or grass is green*. The latter state of affairs contains a disjunct which would obtain even if the first disjunct obtains and which does not result from a responsive sequence: *grass is green*. In contrast, the former state of affairs does *not* contain a disjunct of this kind. In killing the mayor on his own, Sam can make it false that he kills the mayor as a result of Jack's device, and because Sam's killing the mayor on his own issues from a responsive sequence, the state of affairs, *Sam kills the mayor on his own or Sam kills the mayor as a result of Jack's device*, issues from a responsive sequence. Thus, on our approach Sam can be held morally responsible for the fact that the mayor is killed, but we need not say that Sam is morally responsible for the states of affairs, *Sam kills the mayor on his own or grass is green* and *Sam kills the mayor on his own or two plus two equals four*.

V

Return to Chuzzlewit. He finds himself with but one open option. But his lack of open alternatives need not imply that he acts as a result of force or compulsion. Martin Chuzzlewit may be like Sam (in Assassin) and Matthew (in Hero) and Elizabeth (in Missile 1 and Missile 2). He may act freely, even though he cannot do otherwise. And his acting freely is not explained by his acting in conformity with his desire (as in the simple-minded Stoic/Epicurean theory). Martin Chuzzlewit acts freely insofar as he acts as the result of a certain sort of weakly reasons-responsive mechanism.[28] Thus, we believe that it is *false* that

If human beings had no alternative possibilities at all, if all their actions at all times were the *only* actions permitted them, they . . . could take no credit or blame for any of their achievements, and they could no more be responsible for their lives, in prospect or retrospect, than are robots, or the trains in our fertile metaphor that must run of 'predestined grooves.' They could have dignity neither in their own eyes nor in the eyes of their fellows, and both esteem for others and self-esteem would dwindle.[29]

Further, in certain cases in which an agent cannot prevent a consequence-universal from occurring, the agent can nevertheless be responsible for it. Within the class of consequences which are inevitable for an agent, there is a proper subclass which emanate from certain sorts of responsive sequences. An agent may be morally responsible for the members of this subclass. The partitioning of the larger class into the two pertinent subclasses issues from a theory which builds upon the theory of responsibility for actions.

It is natural to think of the future as a "garden of forking paths" in Borges' phrase. Similarly, we might think of life as the "maze of railroad tracks" with at least some unlocked switches envisaged by Feinberg. But if it turned out that there were just one path into the future, it would *not* follow that we could not sometimes be morally accountable and that we could not have pride, indignation, or dignity. We could take pride in the way in which we take the path into the future.

Notes

1 Joel Feinberg, "The Interest in Liberty on the Scales," in *Rights, Justice and the Bounds of Liberty* (Princeton: Princeton University Press, 1980), 30–44, esp. 36–40.

2 We introduce this (and some of the other examples presented below) in John Martin Fischer and Mark Ravizza, "Responsibility and Inevitability", *Ethics* 101 (1991): 258–78.

3 Harry G. Frankfurt, "Alternate Possibilities and Moral Responsibility," *Journal of Philosophy* 66 (1969): 828–39; and "Freedom of the Will and the Concept of a Person," *Journal of Philosophy* 68 (1971): 5–20.

4 Of course, the case could be altered so that there would be a "counterfactual intervener" associated with Matthew. The case would then be precisely parallel to Assassin.

5 John Martin Fischer, "Responsiveness and Moral Responsibility," in Ferdinand Schoeman (ed.), *Responsibility, Character, and the Emotions* (Cambridge University Press, 1987), 81–106; and John Martin Fischer and Mark Ravizza, "Responsibility and Inevitability," *Ethics* 101 (1991): 258–78.

6 The Train case is related in an interesting way to Feinberg's railroad metaphor. In Feinberg's example of Martin Chuzzlewit, all of the switches leading onto alternative tracks are locked. Thus, Chuzzlewit has no open options with regard to the

particular tracks along which he proceeds. In contrast, in Train there are such alternatives, but all of the tracks lead to the same place. Thus, whereas Ralph has open options with regard to the tracks along which he proceeds, he has no option but to end up in Syracuse.

7 Peter van Inwagen, *An Essay on Free Will* (Oxford: Clarendon Press, 1983), esp. 171–80.

8 Robert Heinaman, "Incompatibilism Without the Principle of Alternative Possibilities," *Australasian Journal of Philosophy* 64 (1986): 266–76.

9 In the discussion of responsibility for consequence-universals, we shall assume that an agent can act freely, although he lacks the freedom to do otherwise. Further, in reformulating Heinaman's view, we assume (for simplicity's sake) that when an agent acts freely, he acts knowingly and intentionally.

10 We are indebted to correspondence with Carl Ginet for this point.

11 In response, one might begin with the (indisputable) claim that in Missile 3 Joan *is* morally responsible for the fact that the bomb hits the particular area it actually hits in Washington D.C. Allegedly, then, it would follow that Joan is responsible for the purely descriptive consequence-universal, *that Washington D.C. is hit somewhere or another*. But notice that whereas the first consequence-universal entails the second, it is *not* the case that the second entails the first. (The second is a disjunctive state of affairs of which the first is a component disjunct.) And notice further that the general principle (apparently required in order to underwrite the response to the criticism of Heinaman) that whenever an agent is morally responsible for *P* and *P* entails *O*, the agent is morally responsible for *O*, is invalid.

We conclude also that Missile 3 provides the material for a criticism of Heinaman's Principle (I) presented on page 274: (I) If *S* is responsible for a state of affairs, *A*, and if "F" is any false statement (other than "not-A"), then *S* is responsible for the state of affairs that *A* or *F*." But Joan is responsible for the fact that the missile hits a particular part of Washington D.C. Now form the disjunction of the true statement about where the missile hit and all the false statements about where the missile hit the city of Washington. Joan is *not* responsible for this state of affairs. After all, this disjunction is equivalent to the fact, *Washington D.C. is bombed in some place or other*, and Joan is not morally responsible for this fact.

12 Bernard Berofsky, *Freedom from Necessity* (New York and London: Routledge and Kegan Paul, 1987), 35.

13 For a different approach to such issues, see Berofsky's interesting discussion: Berofsky, 28–30.

14 William L. Rowe, "Causing and Being Responsible for What is Inevitable," *American Philosophical Quarterly* 26 (1989): 153–9.

15 *Ibid.*, 153.

16 *Ibid.*

17 *Ibid.*, 154.

18 *Ibid.*, 155–6.

19 *Ibid.* Rowe means to be giving an account of causal responsibility which, together with certain epistemic conditions, would give us the account of moral responsibility. Here we can assume that the epistemic conditions are met, and we can

scrutinize the theory as a theory of moral responsibility for consequence-universals.

20 Fischer, 1987. See also, Mark Ravizza, "Is Responsiveness Sufficient For Responsibility?" (typescript, University of California, Riverside).

21 Following Aristotle, one might distinguish between an epistemic and a freedom-relevant component of a theory of responsibility. Aristotle held that one acts voluntarily insofar as one is not in a relevant sense ignorant of what one is doing and one is not compelled to do what one does. We focus here primarily on the freedom-relevant component. For a useful discussion of issues pertinent to the epistemic component, see Joel Feinberg, *Harm to Self* (Oxford: Oxford University Press, 1986), 269–315.

22 Frankfurt, 1969, n. 4.

23 We should here assume that there is just one causal sequence leading to the consequence. We believe that our theory can be generalized so as to apply to cases in which more than one causal chain leads to a consequence. We shall not discuss such cases in this paper; thus, in this paper we are concerned with cases of preemptive overdetermination rather than simultaneous overdetermination. Further, the focus here is on what might be called "action-triggered" consequences. There might also be "omission-triggered" consequences for which an agent might be morally responsible. For example, in Assassin it seems as if the counterfactual intervener, Jack, might also be (fully) morally responsible for the fact that the mayor is assassinated, insofar as it is assumed that Jack could have prevented this consequence. We believe that omission-triggered consequences can be handled in a way parallel to the way suggested in the test in which action-triggered omissions can be handled.

24 It should be noted that the analysis of a responsive sequence given above is for cases of individual responsibility; it is not intended to address cases of simultaneous overdetermination in which several agents may be jointly responsible for the consequence produced. We believe that a similar analysis may work in these cases, but in evaluating the responsibility of any one agent it might be necessary to bracket the other triggering events that simultaneously produce the consequence, in order to ascertain if the agent's action was part of a responsive sequence that was sufficient to produce the consequence. The issues involved in such cases of joint responsibility are complex and we cannot fully pursue them in the present essay.

25 The notions of initiation and triggering need more discussion in future work. We believe that the lightning bolt could be said to "initiate" the sequence leading to the destruction of the house in the example in the text, even in a causally deterministic world. But the discussion of this point must await another occasion.

26 The happy addict is supposed to act on a desire which is in fact irresistible, but whose irresistibility plays no role in the outcome. Thus, there are scenarios in which the *same mechanism* (involving a desire for the drug with the intensity level *which is actually manifested*) issues in the agent's not taking the drug. Although the actual desire for the drug is irresistible, the level of intensity in virtue of which it is irresistible plays no role in the actual sequence; thus, this level of intensity is not preserved across the relevant possible worlds. This is precisely parallel to a

case in which a counterfactual intervener's presence ensures that an agent cannot choose or do otherwise, and yet the counterfactual intervener plays no role in what actually happens.

27 van Inwagen, 171–80.

28 We wish to assimilate Chuzzlewit to the other agents in regard to his *actions*. But of course we do not wish to suggest that he is in a similar situation in regard to the *consequences* of his actions, because the sequences issuing in certain of these consequences are not responsive.

29 Feinberg, *op. cit.*, 36.

10

Some ruminations on women, violence, and the criminal law

JEFFRIE G. MURPHY

I've decided that at bottom I'm just a sadist, and no damn good for any woman.
The reason – I can beat them up. Only with men do I act decently cause I'm scared
they'll whop me. Isn't human nature depressing?

Norman Mailer[1]

Introduction

Each one of us carries around his own personal demon, and mine has always
been boredom and the fear of boredom. I resonate in sympathy with the John
Berryman poem that begins "Life, friends, is boring" and have always understood – and see as more than mere wit – the suicide note of the actor George
Sanders who claimed that he simply could not stand being bored any more.[2]

To keep this demon at bay, I want life to be exciting, or at least interesting
and amusing. I want, among other things, for speech to be robust and open
even at the risk of being offensive or hurtful. I also want life to be erotically
charged – to challenge us with some level of ambiguity and uncertainty in the
relations between men and women, to electrify us with some undercurrent of
passion. Thus I fear an environment of safe, polite, inane discourse. I also
fear the desexualization of human interaction. I am thus initially ill-disposed
toward campus conduct codes that seek to curtail racially insensitive speech,
ill-disposed toward prohibitions against sexual harassment where the concept
of harassment is so vaguely defined as to inhibit all sexiness and flirtation, ill-
disposed toward modifications in the law of rape that make every seducer a
potential rapist, and ill-disposed toward that strand of grim feminism that
seems to have forgotten the beauty and ecstacy of abandon that can be (even if
it often is not) at the core of heterosexual intercourse.

Why am I sharing with you this small piece of my psychological auto-
biography? There are two reasons. First, as Susan Estrich has stressed in her
influential book on rape, people tend to bring their own very personal perspectives and passions to bear on what purport to be purely abstract discussions of intellectual topics, and it is productive of both clarity and honesty if
these perspectives are brought to consciousness and into the open forum.

(Estrich, for example, claims that most men come to the topic of rape being dominated by the nightmare of being falsely accused of rape, and most women come to the topic dominated by the nightmare of being raped. Thus it is not surprising that their discourse is often, at least initially, at cross purposes.[3])

A second reason for my personal confession is this: I suspect that the mental disposition to which I confess is widely shared by both men and women, although many would find it too politically incorrect to confess. I also suspect that what I call the fear of boredom and the corrective desire that life contain conversational and erotic excitement and uncertainty is simply a particular manifestation of that general moral and political sensibility often labeled *liberalism* (at least of the libertarian variety). For what is the libertarian nightmare if it is not the world of China under Chairman Mao – a world of uniformly (and *badly*) dressed drones all saying the same inoffensive things and all avoiding any conduct (even hand-holding) that might introduce passion and uncertainty and thus *danger* into the life presided over by the state? The nightmare world described is indeed a world of safety, but the liberal wants to hurl against it the famous taunt to timidity expressed by Benjamin Franklin: "They that can give up essential liberty to obtain a little . . . safety, deserve neither liberty nor safety." The liberal will admit that the exhilarating life of liberty is fraught with risks and dangers, but he will claim simply this: *it is worth it.* The benefits outweigh the costs.

Such, then, is my initial liberal bias. In recent years, however, and partly under the influence of certain aspects of feminism, I have come to see that this perspective cannot be the whole story and must be, not abandoned surely, but constrained or modified. It is one thing to say that liberty is worth risks and harms if these risks and harms are spread over all affected parties equally. It is quite another thing to say this, however, if these risks and harms are spread unequally and if some persons or classes of persons bear them to a considerably greater degree than others. If, for example, the burdens and harms associated with free speech fall mainly on members of racial minorities and if the dangers attendant to sexual liberty and excitement fall mainly on women, then white males should at least *pause* before glibly trotting out slogans about danger being the necessary price of liberty.[4] A liberty club in which all members pay equal dues for the benefits of membership could well take Franklin's slogan as its motto. A liberty club in which some members get the benefits while others pay the dues, however, is not really a liberty club at all and the cost/benefit rhetoric of "the necessary price of liberty" may here simply be an offensive mask to cover distributive injustice. I take it that one way of interpreting liberal feminism – on rape, on sexual harassment, on pornography – is as an attempt to exploit the tension between the liberal commitment to distributive justice (including a fair allocation of risks and harms) and the liberal commitment to a most extensive liberty principle. I have come to think, with some reluctance, that the feminist case, though frequently overstated, is on to something here.

Feminism and the substantive criminal law

I have thus far talked in large and general terms about such matters as liberty, liberalism, sexuality, and feminism. I now wish to move to a more specific topic: the philosophy of the substantive criminal law.[5] In my remaining (and somewhat free associational) remarks, I will try to address certain aspects of the feminist impact on criminal law theory – an impact that has mainly (but not exclusively) been addressed to two topics: the law of rape and the law of self-defense. Both areas involve women and violence, but the thrust in each area is interestingly different at least on the surface. The feminist impact on rape law has essentially been *anti*-violence – seeking to reform the law so as to provide women greater protection against this dangerous and degrading crime. The feminist impact on the law of self-defense, however, has in some sense been *pro*-violence – seeking to allow women (particularly so-called battered women) greater freedom to use violence, even deadly force, than the traditional law of self-defense allows. In both cases, however, a dominant concern is the desire to reduce the risks and harms that women face in those aspects of their dealings with men that are regulated by the criminal law – a desire to make the allocation of risks and harms between men and women more equal.

These feminist concerns have prompted me to rethink various aspects of the law of rape and the law of self-defense. In this essay, I present the fruits of these reflections and share them with my reader in full awareness that I enter the debate on feminism as an admitted late-comer and novice, raising questions and puzzles rather than presenting any systematic theories.

I shall not rehearse here the standard legal doctrines and philosophical literature on rape and self-defense; neither will I rehearse the various aspects of that movement of thought called "feminism."[6] I shall simply make some remarks on four puzzles raised by feminist criminal law theory: (1) *What is so special about rape?* Why, if at all, is a violent sexual assault worse (more evil? more harmful?) than any other physical assault? What is so special about sex? Some feminists like to say that the real issue is not sex but is rather dominance or power. If I provisionally concede this, I still have this question: Is using one's power to get sex worse than using one's power in other ways and for other ends? *Most* violent assaults surely involve (or at least attempt) dominance, humiliation, and degradation. When sex is involved, does this make it worse? (2) *What is the difference between rape and seduction?* How do we distinguish permissible threats and offers in the realm of sexuality from those threats and offers that merit treatment as serious felonies? We have all by now surely internalized the feminist slogan that "no" means "no," but we still have to grapple with the problem that "yes" does not always mean "yes." When does it not? When the "yes" is coerced. But what does *that* mean? (3) *When is sex obtained through fraud of such a nature as to merit treatment as a serious felony?* The traditional doctrine is that fraud in the act constitutes felony rape but that fraud in the inducement does not, for example, obtaining consent to sexual intercourse with a woman by deceiving her into believing that one is inserting a medical instrument is rape but obtaining consent to sexual intercourse by deceiving her into believing that the act, which she clearly recognizes as an act of sexual intercourse, will cure her of terminal cancer is not rape. Is this a morally coherent distinction? (4) *How can the "battered woman syndrome" or any other psychological pathology play a meaningful role in justifying, rather than excusing, conduct?* ("She is disturbed so she is not responsible for killing" has a kind of sense that seems to be lacking in "She is disturbed so she is justified, that is, acts rightly, when she kills.") Self-defense is normally conceptualized as a justification, so how, if at all, can the battered woman syndrome coherently fit – as many feminists want it to fit – under this doctrine?

Before chatting about these four perplexities, let me make three preliminary observations and qualifications. *First,* I am not at all confident that criminal law theory is the best lead-in to a profound discussion of women, sexuality, and violence. I subscribe to a very minimalist theory of law, particularly criminal law, seeing it as concerned to maintain through force the most basic rules required to make social cooperation and civilized life possible. It stands in defense of the *very least* we can demand of each other, and thus any discussion focusing on sexuality that is limited to a criminal law context will necessarily ignore many matters of great moral and psychological importance. I focus upon criminal law theory here simply because, since it is a topic on which I have thought and written extensively, I may have some chance of saying something about it that is at least informed.

Second, I have no illusion that subtle doctrinal changes in substantive criminal law will always have a profound effect in actually improving, in any practical sense, the treatment of women with respect to criminal violence. Recall, for example, the widely discussed 1976 English rape case *Regina v. Morgan.*[7] In that case, the House of Lords (interpreting common law rape and previous statutes) held that an honest mistake concerning a woman's consent is a defense to the charge of rape. An outraged English public, claiming that such a ruling in effect declared open season on women by inviting rape, campaigned for a *reasonable* belief standard on the element of consent. Parliament reacted by adopting a new rape statute that rejected the honest mistake defense and limited the defense of mistake of fact (on the issue of the woman's consent) to mistaken beliefs that were not reckless, that is, not consciously unreasonable beliefs.

Although I am willing to concede that this doctrinal change might add some slight additional protections for women, I would not be too optimistic. Recall that, in the law, "reasonable belief" does not mean what a philosopher might mean by the phrase, for example, it does not mean a belief arrived at by an unbiased person in ideal cognitive conditions. Rather it means simply this: a belief that an average member of the community (a jury member) thinks he would hold in the circumstances facing the defendant. If the average person is as filled with sexist biases as many feminists claim, such as the belief that women often say "no" when they really mean "yes," then we could expect an acquittal rate almost as high under a reasonable belief instruction as under an honest belief instruction.

Third, I should note that I come at the issues raised in this paper essentially from the perspective of one who takes seriously a *retributive* outlook on punishment: an outlook that at least seeks to constrain the pursuit of the utilitarian value of crime control by the demand that a criminal never be punished in excess of what, given his own responsible and blameworthy conduct, he *justly deserves.* (Criminal lawyers sometimes call this an emphasis on *subjective culpability* – an attempt to base culpability on not harm *simpliciter* but rather on harm intentionally brought about, foreseen, or at least such that a reasonable person would have foreseen it.) I have attempted to defend this perspective in numerous other writings and I do not intend to attempt another defense here; I mention it simply to make clear the perspective that I shall be bringing to bear in the discussion to follow.

What is so special about rape?

Before the practice was declared unconstitutional in *Coker v. Georgia,*[8] it was not uncommon for persons convicted of rape in many Southern states to be sentenced to death, a practice which placed rape on the small list of crimes (including first degree murder and kidnapping) regarded as sufficiently serious to merit the most severe punishment allowed by law. The reasoning of the court in *Coker* was very controversial, but it did raise a very important issue: Namely, if rape is to be punished as severely as murder, then either the harm of rape or the evil of the rapist (or both) should be comparable to the harm or evil we associate with murder. The court was not persuaded that the harm or evil is comparable, and thus the death penalty for rape was struck down as cruel and unusual because disproportionate.

The thought of the *Coker* court that society has overestimated the seriousness of rape by comparing it to murder and kidnapping could, of course, be the start of an argument that society has overestimated the seriousness of rape in ways more radical than anything contemplated in *Coker*. Although I cannot imagine anyone arguing that rape is not serious at all, I can imagine someone, someone who has perhaps internalized the sixties view that our society has overmoralized sexuality and sexual activity, arguing in this way: Perhaps it is wrong to regard rape as anything more than an assault or an unlawful touching and perhaps the gravity of rape, as with other assaults, should be assessed roughly in terms of the actual physical injury inflicted. The mere fact that sex, or sexual penetration, is involved would, on this view, be irrelevant as an aggravating factor. Most assaults, of course, do not involve the penetration of a bodily orifice. But that fact alone cannot be what makes rape the most grave of assault offenses. Imagine an individual who is motivated perhaps by contempt for the unwillingness of many people to try new foods and who assaults his victims in this way: He grabs them, holds them down, stuffs sushi into their mouths, and orders them to swallow it. Although such an individual should surely be punished for assault, we would not expect (nor, I assume, want) his sentence to be as severe as what would typically be given for forcible rape. But what is the difference except that forced sex is sex and forced sushi is not? Thus we cannot, I think, avoid reflection on the nature of sex itself in any theory of the crime of rape. What, then, is so special about sex?

The answer to this question is, I think, rather obvious: the importance of sex is essentially *cultural,* that is, there is nothing intrinsic about sexual assault that makes it objectively more serious than nonsexual assault. Our culture does in fact surround sexuality with complex symbolic and moral baggage, but it does not have to be this way, as the sexual revolutionaries of the sixties were fond of pointing out.

Sex is, of course, biologically tied to reproduction; and, because of this, evolutionary theory would teach us to expect that creatures would want to exercise control over their reproductive autonomy, which in part explains the origin of some of the symbols and taboos and may even once have partially justified them by linking them to a fundamental human concern. Sex as potentially reproductive, however, cannot *now* justify the symbolism and taboos in a world of easily available contraception and abortion.[9] Thus persons who want to continue conceptualizing rape as the most serious of all assaults cannot, I think, rest the main part of their case on issues concerning reproduction.[10] Rather the case will be based on sexuality itself: perhaps the idea, which is still quite pervasive in our culture, that a person's sexuality is sacred, mysterious, precious, and even fearful because it is deeply tied (in ways Freud helped us to understand) to love and to the essence of self and the meaningfulness of one's life (in a way that whether one's nose is bloodied, for example, typically is not).[11] *This* may be why sexual assaults are typically more serious than most others.

Because I think that many of the most important facts about us are cultural facts, I am generally sympathetic to defining harm partially in terms of those cultural facts. I am also sympathetic to the idea that a primary purpose of the criminal law is to protect people not merely from literal physical and psychological pain but also from acts that, given the cultural norms that define the symbolic meaning of their lives together, are regarded as deeply wrong or degrading and as, in that sense, harmful. In short, I do not think that the criminal law must always be stopped in its tracks by this question: "I know that most people regard this act as harmful, but can it be proven – independent of belief and cultural norm – that the act *really is* objectively harmful?" I suspect that the criminal law could not exist at all if all of its rules awaited a demonstration that the harms they seek to prevent really are harms in some culturally independent sense (whatever, if anything, that might mean).

Having explained my initial sympathy with the cultural approach, let me now explain some worries that I have about it that make me at least hesitant to adopt it as a final approach to the theory of criminal wrong or harm.

First, consider our present example of rape: the idea that rape is seriously wrong because it involves an invasion of the symbolic sanctity and mystery and fear with which our society, for better or worse, surrounds sexuality, particularly female sexuality. My worry is: What if it is for worse? Is it possible that the only theory of female sexuality that will retain rape as the most serious of all assault felonies is the very same theory that disadvantages women in other contexts? For example: One argument often given for not allowing female soldiers equal opportunity to serve in combat roles is the claim that they are, if captured, vulnerable to rape – a special kind of harm graver than any assault that a man is likely to suffer. Is it really in the interest of the total and long-range emancipation of women that their sexuality be regarded in this way?[12]

Second, those of us who think of ourselves as more enlightened than the general run of our fellow citizens know that the symbolic nature of evil and harm in our culture is sometimes skewed in ways that we find impossible to endorse. Suppose, for example, it just happens that most white women (or their male "protectors") regard it as a graver harm to be raped by a black man than by a white man. (Most of the states that formerly made rape a capital crime were southern, and some have speculated that racial fears may have played some part in the explanation for this.) Do we then want to make the race of the defendant an aggravating factor in the crime of rape? If we want to answer *no* to this question, then we must either admit that a theory of criminal harm that defines harm in a purely cultural way is not acceptable or find an appropriate way to state the relevant cultural norm so that it does not have this seemingly racist implication.

Third, there is the problem of the rape of a prostitute.[13] On the one hand, I want to regard the rape of a prostitute as equally serious with the rape of any other woman. On the other hand, it initially seems implausible to believe that a prostitute conceives of her sexuality in just the way that, as previously noted, would justify regarding rape as more serious than any other assault. The prostitute might seem to regard her sexuality, not as a sacred and mysterious aspect of her self-identity, but rather as a commodity to be traded on the market. Should we then agree with those sentencing judges who regard the rape of a prostitute as a crime to be punished less seriously than other rapes – perhaps because it is best regarded as, at least in part, a property crime?

How might one argue within the framework I am suggesting for punishing the rape of a prostitute just as severely as we punish any other rape? There are several routes one might go: (1) There might be psychological evidence that prostitutes cherish at least certain aspects of their sexuality in much the same way as non-prostitutes cherish theirs. The rape of a prostitute often consists in forcing her to perform sex acts other than the ones for which she has explicitly contracted; and perhaps she keeps these acts out of the market because she reserves them for her genuine love relationships. She may, in short, bifurcate her sexuality in complex ways – ways that do not become unworthy of protection simply because they are complex. (2) Even the fact that the prostitute sells her sexuality does not prove that it is not deeply tied to her most intimate sense of self. When I write books, for example, I sell (not for very much!) the contents of my mind. This does not mean that I do not regard the contents of my mind as intimately tied to myself and would not feel deeply wronged and degraded if someone, such as the inventor of a mind-reading machine, perhaps could gain access to the contents of my mind against my will. (3) Even if we assume that prostitutes do place lesser value on their sexuality than do other women, we still might want to punish the rape of a prostitute severely to reaffirm the value that *we* place on sexuality. We often punish to uphold *systems* of rights and values that we will sometimes maintain by punishing offenses even if a particular victim, because of idiosyncratic preferences and values, has less than a normal interest in the values at stake. We do this in part, of course, for efficiency reasons. It might simply be too costly as a practical matter to bother individuating and so we build our account of harm around the typical case. Efficiency may even promote fairness here, since the typical case will almost certainly be the reasonably forseeable case.

Fourth, and related to the efficiency problem, is a problem of evidence. If the gravity of rape is a function of how the woman regards her own sexuality, then evidence about her sexual past, which feminists want understandably and for a variety of reasons to bar from rape trials, would seem to be relevant after all and perhaps should be admitted either at trial or sentencing. The woman's career as a prostitute might, for example, be taken as evidence that she does not place the culturally normal kind of value on her sexuality and thus has been less harmed by an act of rape than a person whose sexual values correspond to the cultural norm. (As previously noted, it might, of course, be too costly to bother individuating in this way. My point is simply one of principle. Professor Uma Narayan, in an unpublished paper, has argued persuasively that criminal harm should not always be conceptualized around the standard or normal case but should sometimes include the special sensitivities and vulnerabilities of certain classes of people, for example, minorities. If nonstandard sensitivity can be an aggravating factor, then surely nonstandard insensitivity can in principle be a mitigating factor.)

Fifth is a problem raised by Michael Davis's well-known essay on rape.[14] As I interpret Davis, he is arguing that most people in fact do not regard rape as more serious than other aggravated assaults and thus that it is simply an illusion that there is a genuinely shared cultural norm that rape is of a seriousness next to murder. His test for this is not to find out the norms to which people pay lip-service but rather to conduct certain thought experiments wherein people are asked to imagine having a choice between evils that they will experience and then to see how most people would make the choice. Davis speculates that most people, faced (say) with a choice of being raped with a minimum of physical violence or being very badly beaten (an aggravated assault), would choose the rape – thus showing that we in fact do not regard rape as more serious than assault and that, therefore, we should not punish it more severely.

Davis has given us much to think about here, but I am not totally confident about his test for the seriousness of harms. If I had to choose between having my fingernail pulled out by a pair of pliers or having my character believably defamed and my reputation destroyed, I think I would choose the latter purely because of a physiological, reflexive response to the idea of intense physical pain. I still believe, however, that the actual harm to me in the defamation case would be greater, and I am not persuaded that it is inconsistent for me to believe this simply because of my psychological inability to endure the nail pulling.[15]

Sixth, there is a problem for those committed to retributivism as a theory of punishment. Retributivism depends, in some of its forms, on the idea that people deserve to suffer for the evil that they do. But does it make sense to say that people deserve to suffer, not for the genuine evil that they do, but simply for violating (perhaps irrational) cultural norms? As John Mackie once argued, retributivism is a test case for moral objectivity.[16] If all harm must be culturally defined, however, can the proper degree of moral objectivity be attained? Of course, people can feel pain and distress when they are forced to do things that run contrary to the norms of their culture, but should such pain and distress be conceptualized as genuine harm if the norms are themselves irrational? Was Crito really harmed by facing public shame for violating the cultural norm that taught that he should help his friend Socrates to escape? Socrates – given his own theory of harm – thought not.

Finally, it could be argued that rape should be punished more severely because of its pervasiveness, not because the act itself is more serious or evil or harmful than other assaults. (When train robbers were once given exemplary punishments it was because of an epidemic of train robberies, not because anyone believed that robbing trains was actually more evil than robbing, say, banks.) Such reasons are also sometimes given for punishing so-called hate crimes as aggravated offenses. If violence against women or blacks is epidemic and makes a whole class of people fearful, then one might argue for greater punishment purely on the utilitarian ground of the need for extra deterrence. The problem with this, of course, is that exemplary punishments, whatever their utilitarian merits, are clearly *unjust,* more than the wrongdoer deserves. It may be that rapes tend to make all women fearful and thus harm the entire class of women, but surely most rapists do not have such group harm as their intention when they act, nor are most of them even reckless about this. Will we then dispense with normal worries about *mens rea* when the interests of a whole group (women, blacks, etc.) are at stake?

Having explored some of the pros and cons of a cultural approach to the harm of rape, let me now move to the other puzzles I wanted to discuss.

What is the difference between rape and seduction?

I assume that we would all agree that it is sometimes permissible both morally and legally to obtain sex by the use of threats and offers. "Have sex with me or I will find another girlfriend" strikes me (assuming normal circumstances) as a morally permissible threat, and "Have sex with me and I will marry you" strikes me (assuming the offer is genuine) as a morally permissible offer. We negotiate our way through most of life with schemes of threats and offers – with a smile and a pocketful of change – and I see no reason why the realm of sexuality should be utterly insulated from this very normal way of being human.

What is often called seduction strikes me, at least in part, as a system of threats and offers. Some of these (e.g., the ones noted) may be morally innocent, but others may not be. And some seduction techniques should not be thought of as threats or offers at all. The common seduction technique of flattery, for example, may simply be an innocent way of evincing sexual desire; and being found desirable may be the very thing that causes sexual desire to arise in the person being seduced through flattery. This may be why flattery sometimes works, and I see nothing wrong with this.

Sometimes, however, flattery is a calculated attempt to play upon a person's vulnerabilities, for example, a tacit offer of ego support (or a tacit threat to withdraw such support) directed to a person with a fragile and limited self-esteem. Flattery used in this way strikes me as a kind of exploitation and is thus not utterly without moral taint. So too for the false presentation of self, for example, the presentation of oneself as an unusually sensitive and caring person (which I have been told turns some women on) when in fact one's actual self is – shall we say – more complex than this. This is not coercion but is a minor kind of fraudulent misrepresentation, and as such is not utterly without moral taint. However, because the immorality involved in both cases strikes me as no greater than that used by a car salesman to exploit my fragile male ego by trying to sell me a car that looks like a penis or by an advertisement that stresses only the good points about the car to which I am drawn, I find it hard to get *deeply* indignant about these cases. And I certainly would find it hard to imagine a good argument that seductive threats and offers of this nature should be *illegal*, as they currently and quite properly are not.

Let me, then, try out the following suggestion: The impermissible threats and offers that constitute rape (and distinguish it from even immoral seduction) are threats or offers to do things that are *illegal*.[17] If it is legally permissible for me to do X, then it is reasonable to assume, at least as a starting presumption, that it ought to be legally permissible for me to *threaten* or *offer* to do X.

This, of course, is only a start. "Have sex with me or I will not put my renewal tab on my license plate by the legally required date" is a threat to do something illegal, but it is a poor candidate for a rape threat since it (a) threatens only a civil wrong and (b) does not put the victim or anyone else at any particular risk. Thus perhaps the threats that constitute rape should be at least (seriously) criminal in nature.

Should it be a requirement for rape that the threat have the victim as its object? Consider this: Sex obtained by threat is felony rape if consent to the sex is secured by *a threat to commit an inherently dangerous felony of which the person refusing sex (or someone close to her) will be the victim.* So "Have sex with me or I will kill you (or your child)" is felony rape on this model, but "Have sex with me or I will embezzle your funds" or "Have sex with me or I will kill forty strangers" is not: the former because the threatened conduct, though felonious, is not inherently dangerous; the latter because the person refusing the sex is not the victim. The root of this idea is that the evil of rape through threat depends upon exploiting intense personal *fears* that are not normally attached to business transactions and to unknown third parties.[18]

Suppose, however, that one adopts a moral rather than a psychological theory of coercion that does not rely on the idea of fear making some decisions psychologically impossible but rather on the idea that some decisions, given a proper weighing of alternatives, are morally impossible for a morally sensitive agent – a sensitivity rendering such agents open to what might be called "moral blackmail." On this theory, one might regard the threat "Have sex with me or I will kill forty strangers" as (if resulting in sex) constituting rape – not because it was psychologically impossible (given her fears) for the woman to refuse but because it was morally impossible (given her moral convictions) to refuse.[19] Her inability to refuse is of the kind expressed by Luther when he said "Here I stand; I can do no other" – *not,* I take it, a remark whereby he tried to identify himself as a psychological compulsive.

I suppose that everyone would agree that sex obtained by an impermissible criminal threat of some sort is rape. But is such a threat necessary? Consider these cases: (1) "Have sex with me or I (your foster guardian) will send you back to that terrible state facility from which you came." (See *Commonwealth v. Mlinarich.*[20]) (2) "Have sex with me or I will fire you (or fail you in the course, or not promote you, etc.)." (3) "Have sex with me and I will pay for the chemotherapy for your dying child" (an example developed by Joel Feinberg[21]).

The problem is that the behavior in each of these three cases may seem morally dreadful, but what is threatened is not criminal and perhaps not even illegal. The guardian has a right to send his charge back; the employer has a right to fire (or the teacher to fail); and the sexually motivated philanthropist has no duty to pay for the medical care for another's child. Should any or all of these threats, if resulting in sexual intercourse, be rape?

With respect to the first two cases, we might argue that once the right is properly specified then the threatened conduct is *not* – initial appearances to the contrary – within the rights of the person doing the threatening. Perhaps a correct specification of the guardian's right is not that he has a right to return the child *simpliciter* but rather that he has a right to return the child for the *right sorts of reasons* (e.g., further delinquent conduct). Perhaps the employer's right is not that he has a right to fire *simpliciter* but rather that he has a right to fire (and the teacher to fail) for the *right sorts of reasons* (e.g., tardiness to work, or poor academic performance). Thus these threats (in no way germane to the values that define the context) may be illegal (or should be illegal) even if not criminal and thus may be good candidates, if not for felony rape, at least for some legal remedy, for example, sexual harassment charges in the second case. It does not seem to me absurd, however, to believe that the present civil remedy offered by sexual harassment law is inadequate and to suggest that these acts should be regarded as some degree of criminal rape.

I am much less inclined, however, to consider our sexually motivated philanthropist, who stands in no fiduciary or contractual relationship to the woman, as properly guilty of any legal wrong. For who is his victim? Because of his offer, the woman with the sick child has one more option in her life than she had previously; and thus I do not see how she would in any way be benefited from a system that prohibited (and thus deterred) the offer that has been made to her. Perhaps it is the only chance she will ever have to save her child, and if she values her sexuality more than her child she can simply refuse the offer. But why would she, as an autonomous person, not want the option of at least considering the offer?[22] It would, of course, be exceedingly nice for the man to pay for her child's therapy with no strings attached. He has neither a moral nor a legal obligation to do this, however, and I do not think that we want a system of criminal law that punishes people simply for failing to be exceedingly nice.

Suppose the demand in these three cases is not sexual but is of a totally different order, for example, "*Mow my lawn* or I will send you back (fire you, fail you, not pay for your child's therapy)." No doubt we find these threats much less shocking to our moral conscience and are considerably less inclined, even if we think they are in some way improper, to have them criminalized. Why is this? No doubt it is the cultural belief discussed in the previous section that sexual services are special, intrinsic to the person, in a way that lawn mowing services are not – special in ways that perhaps give rise to inalienable rights. The woman being offered a chance to save her child by trading sexual favors for medical payments is, we might say, simply being lured into *prostitution*. So too, perhaps, for the victims in the other two cases. The wrongness, then, is simply the wrongness of prostitution – a point obscured if we misleadingly try to conceptualize what is wrong here simply as coercion.

But *is* prostitution morally wrong, and can it be criminalized on an enlightened theory of feminist liberation?[23] I shall leave this question unanswered and shall pass to a discussion of my third puzzle.

When may sex be obtained through fraud?

More specifically: When is sex obtained through fraud of such a nature to merit treatment as a serious felony? When a man pretending to be a physician lures a woman into sexual intercourse by deceiving her into believing that the intercourse will cure her cancer, our moral sensibilities recoil; and we are shocked to discover that this is not felony rape. (See *Boro v. Superior Court*.[24]) The retributivist within us wants to protest that he is surely as evil and as deserving of punishment as if he had deceived her into believing that it was not his penis but rather a medical instrument that was being inserted into her vagina, which would be felony rape. We are thus, in this retributivist mode, inclined to argue that the legal distinction between sex obtained through fraud in the act (rape) and through fraud in the inducement (not rape) is absurd.

If there is any rationale for drawing and retaining this distinction, it must be to deal with this kind of case: the man who obtains a woman's sexual favors by falsely promising her a mink coat.[25] Tacky as it may be to get sex with such an inducement, I doubt that many of us would want to criminalize the sex so obtained as felony rape. Thus it is not surprising that, with these cases in mind, legislators have refused to conceptualize sex obtained by fraud in the inducement as rape.

If we want to conceptualize sex obtained by the false promise of a cancer cure as rape but not if obtained by the false promise of a mink coat, is there any consistent way to do this? Perhaps. Recall the earlier discussion of the symbolic significance of sexuality, the nearly sacred value placed upon it by many persons in our society. Perhaps we could coherently conceptualize as rape any sex obtained through fraudulent inducement *so long as the nature of the inducement itself does not provide strong evidence that the victim does not value sexuality in the way characteristic of the norms we seek to protect.* A woman trading sex for the promise of a mink coat would reveal such deviation (and thereby reveal an interest less worthy of protection), whereas a woman trading sex for life would not.

For those who like to think the basic issue in cases like this is power and not sex, consider this example: I persuade Polly (who believes she has terminal cancer) that my lawn contains a unique variety of grass – the pollen from which, if inhaled, will cure cancer. I thereby get her to mow my lawn (a small, easily mowed lawn) once a week. Is what I have done just as bad as the case above where sex is fraudulently put forward as the cure?

There will, of course, be hard cases here, but perhaps the distinction based on what the inducement tells us about the way in which the woman values her sexuality is at least a start toward an analysis that does not condemn us to retaining the counterintuitive claim that sex obtained by fraud in the induce-ment could *never* constitute rape.[26] This would be worth pursuing at greater length, but the shortness of space compels me to turn to the fourth and final puzzle.

When may battered women kill?

I do not wish to be a sucker for the latest trendy piece of psychobabble, but I am willing to concede that there is indeed a psychological pathology properly described as the "battered woman syndrome."[27] A woman is said to exhibit this syndrome when she continually returns to the husband who beats, rapes, and threatens her and her children with death even when she believes that the death threats are sincere and that she very likely will be killed. I have no idea what the underlying mechanism is that explains this behavior, and many of the psychological accounts I have read seem circular, that is, they are jargon-filled ways of simply repeating that she manifests the noted behavior. This does not worry me, however, for I do not think that we always need an underlying mechanism or theory properly to regard patterns of behavior as pathological or addictive. What better reason could we have for saying that a person is neurotic (or worse) than simply the fact that the person systematically acts contrary to what she perceives as in her most fundamental interest, fails to understand why she continues to do it, and views herself as unable to stop herself from doing it? I thus grant the existence of the battered woman syndrome and see no problem with its limited *evidential* use in criminal law, for example, to rebut the presumption that juries might otherwise adopt that the fact that the woman did not leave shows that the husband's abuse of her could not have been as bad as she claims. I can even see the syndrome playing some role in negating *mens rea* or as an *excuse,* perhaps functioning analogously to insanity or diminished capacity. In whatever sense of "can't help it" that operates to excuse in the criminal law, perhaps some battered women really can't help it when they kill their abusive husbands. They are more to be pitied than punished, more to be helped than further hurt.

Granting all of this, however, is not the same as accepting that such women act with justification.[28] For note that to which we are committed if we conceptualize their defense as a justification: (1) We, as a society, stand prepared to *encourage* such behavior, or at least to regard it as legitimate. (2) Because we regard the behavior as legitimate, it would be improper to have the acquittal of such persons followed up by other legal consequences, for example, hospitalization for psychiatric observation, loss of the right (even temporarily) to own a weapon, or loss (even temporarily) of the custody of one's children. (3) Because we regard the behavior as legitimate, third parties – hired assassins, perhaps? – ought to be allowed to assist the battered woman in attaining her legitimate objective. None of these (I think) absurd consequences, of course, would follow from accepting the battered woman syndrome as an excuse. Just because we sometimes excuse homicidal lunatics, for example, does not mean that we allow third parties to assist them in acting out their insane delusions.

It should be obvious that I am deeply skeptical concerning the use of the battered woman syndrome as a justification for homicide. Before rejecting it entirely, however, let us consider in more detail how some have suggested that it might be legitimately employed in this regard.[29]

The most frequently made suggestion for linking up the battered woman syndrome with justification is through the justification of self-defense. Very roughly, the law allows a person W to use deadly force against (i.e., kill) another person M if (1) M is an unlawful aggressor against W, (2) M poses an *immediate* threat to inflict death or grave bodily harm on W, and (3) the use of deadly force by W is *necessary* in order for W to escape M's threatened consequence, that is, there is no nonlethal way (e.g., retreating or running away) that will allow *W* to avoid the consequence. The law will typically allow this defense only if the defendant (*W*) acts in the *reasonable belief* that the threat is immediate and in the *reasonable belief* that the use of counter-deadly force was necessary in the specified sense.

It should now be obvious why the battered woman faces an uphill fight in attempting to argue self-defense. She typically will kill her batterer while he is asleep or drunk (and thus obviously poses no immediate threat to her), and she could avoid being hurt or killed simply by leaving the house (and thus it seems obvious that her use of deadly force is not really necessary).[30]

To overcome these problems, defenders of the use of the battered woman syndrome in the law of self-defense may argue for a radically *subjective* standard for the concept of reasonable belief in this justification, that is, argue that the standard should not be that of a reasonable man, nor even that of a reasonable woman, but rather that of a *reasonable battered woman*. Thus, according to this suggestion, jury members should vote to acquit (under self-defense) if they believe that if they were battered women then they would probably regard the threat as immediate and the use of deadly force as necessary in these circumstances.

This line of thought strikes me as deeply problematic, since it essentially destroys the entire distinction between excuse and justification. When a delusional psychotic says he kills in order to protect himself from the death rays emanating from the tongue of Mr. Brown (a dangerous assassin from Mars), we should – according to the logical progression of the above line of thought – regard his killing as justified self-defense. Why? Simply by applying the standard of the *reasonable psychotic,* a standard that invites each member of the jury to ask himself "If I were crazy as hell, might I believe that I was under immediate threat of death and that my use of deadly force was necessary to repel the attack against me?" The answer would surely be *yes,* and thus acquittal would surely be in order. Also, since the acquittal is based on a justification, we should give him his gun back, immediately restore him to the bosom of his family, and release (perhaps even pin medals on) any persons who assisted him in performing his justified act. This is, of course, utter nonsense.

But is the battered woman simply a kind of lunatic? I think it is too hasty to say this, because I cannot help feeling that she may be painfully and unfairly caught in an *objective bind* unlike that world of fantasy I sketched for the psychotic. Is there not some way of conceptualizing her conduct as justified that does not commit us to accepting the test of the reasonable psychotic and regarding his conduct as justified as well?

Let me try out the following: When the battered woman syndrome is described (see *State v. Kelly*[31]), the list of identifying marks is typically a very mixed bag of factors that belong in very different categories. The following two features, for example, have (along with many others) been said to be characteristic of the syndrome: (1) extremely low self-esteem that makes a woman dependent upon the pitifully small gestures of love she occasionally gets from her batterer[32] and (2) a history of attempting to leave the spouse and then being pursued and forced back.

Note how radically dissimilar these two traits are. The former is truly a psychological trait. It is the sort of thing that might well form part of the definition of what we would properly call a syndrome or even a pathology and seems naturally fitted to play a role in an excuse, not a justification. The second, however, is a trait of a totally different sort. It is not a fact about the woman's psychology at all – indeed it makes no reference to her psychology – and is not the sort of thing upon which we would want or need expert psychological testimony. It is simply an objective statement of what has *happened* to her when she has tried to leave – a statement, let us suppose, that she has called the police and they have not responded (or brushed off her complaint as merely a domestic dispute) or that she has gone to a friend's house or to a shelter for battered women and has been forcibly dragged back by her abusive husband, again with no interference from the police.

If facts of this second sort are present, then I begin to see the possibilities of a justification and not merely an excuse. Following the logic (though hope-fully with different results) of the prison escape cases,[33] I would be inclined to argue that some of these women should perhaps be acquitted – not on self-defense – but on the justification of *necessity* or *choice of lesser evils*. It strikes me as deeply unfair that an individual should be expected to obey the law that criminalizes escape from prison if such escape is his only way to avoid being the victim of repeated homosexual rape. If he chooses escape (an evil) over being the victim of rape (another evil), I am persuaded that he has chosen the lesser of these two evils and that his conduct should be regarded as justified. So too, I would argue, for the battered woman described above. If she has taken all possible legal means to escape her abuser and these have failed, she is then faced with a choice: to continue to be abused and perhaps killed (an evil) or to kill the husband (another evil). If she concludes that her innocent brutalization and death is a greater evil than the death of an abusive aggressor, I should be inclined to agree with her. Of course, as a practical matter, courts may not accept this justification, just as they have generally refused to accept it in the prison escape cases. They will no doubt be tempted to maintain the fiction that legal remedies are always available and thus that the unlawful remedy is never really necessary. I think this is a false and self-deceptive response for some of the escape cases, however, and am prepared to concede that it may also be the wrong response for some homicide cases where the defendant is a battered woman of the kind here discussed. Because the state either cannot or will not protect her, there is a sense in which the social contract is *off* in her case; and it is simply unfair to expect her to assume the level of risk that remaining with her husband imposes. I am inclined to see her killing of the husband as analogous to a slave killing an abusive slave-holder as his only means of escape – conduct I have no hesitation in regarding as justified.

In short: There are two kinds of battered women – each exhibiting a different sense of "cannot leave" in the sentence "She cannot leave her husband." If we are speaking of women who *psychologically cannot* leave their abusive spouses, then I am sympathetic to regarding their homicidal conduct as sometimes excused, but not as justified. If, however, we are speaking of women who *physically cannot* leave, then many of the objections to regarding their homicidal conduct as justified may, at least in some cases, disappear.[34]

Conclusion

Let me now bring to a close this somewhat random collection of ruminations on women, violence and the criminal law. I realize that I have raised far more questions than I have answered and that most of the suggestions I have made are very tentative and inconclusive. I assume, however, that one legitimate kind of philosophical endeavor is the mere raising of interesting questions and suggestions that provoke fruitful lines of further inquiry and discussion. But have my questions and suggestions been interesting and provocative in this way? That, of course, must be left for the reader to decide.[35]

Notes

1 Quoted in Martin Amis, *The Moronic Inferno and Other Visits to America* (New York: Viking Penguin, 1986), 72.

2 Number 14 in John Berryman, *77 Dream Songs* (New York: Farrar, Straus and Giroux, 1965). I think that somebody told me the George Sanders story at a cocktail party. Tracking it down and getting it just right would, of course, be too boring.

3 Susan Estrich, *Real Rape* (Cambridge, Mass.: Harvard University Press, 1987). Some feminists suggest that personal stories should not be dismissed as mere anecdotal sociology but should be accepted as legitimate devices for focusing the mind upon important intellectual issues. Traditionalists and men, of course, have their stories to tell as well, for example, that of my colleague who had to deal with a formal complaint filed by a racially sensitive student because she read in class a passage that contained the word "niggardly" and my own story of a female student who charged me with sexism because I have a print of Gustav Klimt's painting "The Kiss" hanging in my office. I fear that people are now being encouraged to conceptualize themselves as victims and to look for ways to be offended; and I fear that legions of the super-sensitive will bring again to the forefront of American life

those Puritan sensibilities that always lurk just beneath the surface and always pose a great threat to freedom.

4 I will not consider here if there may be some compensating benefits that might partially offset the increased risks and harms. Such a suggestion strikes me as implausible with respect to members of racial minorities but as more complex with respect to women.

5 By "substantive criminal law" I refer to the primary doctrines of criminal liability: the definition of criminal offenses (in terms of forbidden acts and *mens rea* culpability conditions), the grading of severity of criminal harms, and the nature and scope of excuses and justifications, and so on. Other important areas of criminal law where feminism has had an impact, such as on rules of evidence or matters of criminal procedure, are not my focus in the present essay.

6 For an excellent overview of the contemporary American doctrines governing the criminal law of rape and self-defense, see Joshua Dressler's *Understanding Criminal Law* (New York: Matthew Bender, 1987). For an excellent discussion and assessment of the impact of feminism on criminal law doctrine, see Stephen Schulhofer's "The Gender Question in Criminal Law" in *Crime, Culpability and Remedy,* edited by Ellen Frankel Paul, Fred. D. Miller, and Jeffrey Paul (Oxford: Basil Blackwell, 1990). I am, of course, aware that many men are victims of rape and that not all battered spouses (or domestic partners) are women. I focus on women as rape victims and women pleading self-defense simply because these cases have understandably been the focus of feminist concern. For a good general introduction to feminism and its role in legal and political theory, see the essays in *Feminism and Political Theory,* edited by Cass R. Sunstein (Chicago: University of Chicago Press, 1990).

7 House of Lords [1976] A.C. 182.

8 433 U.S. 584 (1977).

9 This applies, of course, only to rape victims who are not opposed on principle to contraception and abortion and assumes (a matter now of some doubt) that legal, safe, and reasonably inexpensive abortions will continue to be available. Consider, also, this grim thought: Sexuality is now, alas, more likely to be associated with disease and death than with reproduction. New symbolism and taboos may now be emerging to reflect this association. (Listen to the Leonard Cohen song "Everybody Knows.") In this new world, rape may be analogized with reckless endangerment or even with assault with intent to kill. I can even imagine a world in which rape victims die of AIDS acquired from rapists and I can imagine this world finding a way to conceptualize rape as a homicide offense.

10 I assume that most of us would want to regard as felony rape the forced genital penetration of a woman's anus or mouth or the forcing of an object (e.g., a broom handle) into her vagina. These acts, of course, carry no risk of pregnancy and thus "reproductive autonomy" does not strike me as the best slogan under which to protest them.

It is possible, of course, that women are psychologically traumatized by rape because of a psychological response that is deeply encoded in their natures because, at a time in evolutionary history when sexual intercourse and reproduction were strongly tied, such a response was adaptive (even if it now is not – at least to the same degree). The criminal law could take account of this response in assessing the degree of harm in rape but such an accounting would of course be based, not on a tie with reproduction, but on the existence of the response itself. In other words, what matters is the subjective pain felt by the woman, not the evolutionary explanation for why she feels the pain.

11 That this idea is still dominant in our culture shows, of course, that the sixties sexual revolution did not fully take. Most of us do not view sex as simply the pleasant scratching of an itch and do not view sex as strongly analogous to gourmet dining. If we did, we would accept my earlier sushi analogy. As my colleague Larry Winer has pointed out, a variant of my sushi example can be conceptualized as a grave harm once certain cultural norms are imagined, for example, the forcing of an orthodox Jew to eat pork.

12 My worry here is similar to my worry about the lengths to which some writers on rape will go to make us regard adult women as hopelessly vulnerable (bad at conflict, socialized to be agreeable, etc.) with respect to men in all sexual encounters. The rhetoric of woman as essentially victim sounds to me a great deal like the language used, for example, by senior male partners in a law firm to defend their view that women attorneys should not be litigators because they are by nature ill-suited for such a confrontational task. The whole area of power between men and women needs, of course, to be explored in much more depth than a criminal law context allows. The "woman as victim" crowd probably does not have the whole story, however. I think that the actress Natassja Kinski may have been on to something when (if I recall correctly) she responded in this way to a reporter's expectation that she cluck disapprovingly over the director Roman Polanski's use of his power to have sex with young girls: "You have it all wrong. It is beautiful young women who have all the power over middle-aged men."

13 Peter Arenella's comments on an earlier draft forced me to rethink this section on the rape of a prostitute. Whatever is now good in the section is more to his credit than to mine.

14 "Setting Penalties: What Does Rape Deserve?" in *Law and Philosophy* 3, N. 1 (April 1984).

15 In conversation with me, David Dolenko has raised this puzzle for Davis's analysis: Surely I would much rather be the victim of attempted murder than successful robbery. Does this mean that robbery is really a more serious crime than attempted murder and thus deserves more punishment?

16 "Retributivism: A Test Case for Ethical Objectivity" in *Philosophy of Law,* Fourth Edition, edited by Joel Feinberg and Hyman Gross (Belmont: Wadsworth Publishing Company, 1991).

17 On this theory it will not be legitimate to make blackmail a crime, because a blackmailer typically threatens to do things he has a full legal right to do, that is, circulate or publish true information. I accept this and have indeed argued elsewhere that, in principle, blackmail should *not* be a crime. See my "Blackmail: A Preliminary Inquiry" in *The Monist* 63, N. 2 (April 1980).

18 If one adopts this model, one might still want to make provision for protecting

persons possessed of pathologically idiosyncratic attachments and fears if the defendant knows of and exploits those attachments and fears.

19 I have explored moral and psychological accounts of coercion in my "Consent, Coercion and Hard Choices" in *Virginia Law Review* 67, N. 1 (1981).

20 498 A.2d 395 (Pa. Super. 1985).

21 See *Harm to Self,* Chapter 24, (Oxford: Oxford University Press, 1986).

22 I am here drawing on some points I made in an earlier essay about the difficulty of finding a victim for the crime of blackmail. See Murphy, *supra,* n. 17.

23 On this issue, see the essays by Laurie Shrage and Carole Pateman in *Feminism and Political Theory,* edited by Cass R. Sunstein (Chicago: University of Chicago Press, 1990).

24 163 Cal. App. 3d. 1224, 210 Cal. Rptr. 122 (1985).

25 "Where consent to intercourse is obtained by promises of travel, fame, celebrity, and the like – ought the liar and the seducer to be chargeable as a rapist? Where is the line to be drawn?" *Boro v. Superior Court* – defending the doctrine that sex obtained through fraud in the inducement is not rape.

26 The same cautions I discussed about efficiency, etc. apply here as well. My point here is simply one of principle.

27 The classic work on this syndrome has been done by Lenore E. Walker in her *The Battered Woman* (New York: Harper and Row, 1979) and *The Battered Woman Syndrome* (New York: Springer, 1984). For an overview and more recent bibliography on the issue of battered women and the law, see *Justifiable Homicide* by Cynthia K. Gillespie (Columbus: Ohio State University Press, 1989).

28 The critique I develop in the following pages may soon (I hope) be outdated and thus unnecessary. Some recent feminist writers on the battered woman syndrome are cautious in their development of a defense based on the syndrome and are inclined to conceptualize it more under the heading of an excuse than as a justification. See, for example, "The Excuse of Self-Defense: Correcting a Historical Accident on Behalf of Battered Women Who Kill," by Cathryn Jo Rosen in 36 *American University Law Review* 11 (1986). Even Lenore Walker in her second book on battered women develops an account of the syndrome that does not conceptualize it as a purely psychological pathology to the same degree as she did in her first book.

29 I suspect that some people favor acquittal for the woman who kills her batterer simply because they conceptualize her act as the administration of just punishment and therefore think that the man probably deserved what he got. Although I have no doubt that some of the killed batterers probably did indeed get their just deserts in some cosmic or moral sense, I do not think that a civilized society can allow vigilante activity to figure so blatantly in a justification for conduct that would otherwise be criminal. A civilized society must be committed not simply to the correct outcome but also to the use of the correct process for obtaining that outcome.

30 An extra complexity, which I shall not pursue here, is that in some jurisdictions the retreat requirement is not imposed when a person is in his or her own home. In these jurisdictions, the battered woman may have a better chance of arguing that

her use of deadly force was necessary – unless she lives in a jurisdiction that frees one from the retreat requirement in one's own home only if the aggressor is not also in his own home. In any event, it will still be hard to establish that the threat was immediate.

31 Supreme Court of New Jersey, 478 A.2d 364 (1984).

32 If this is really true, then one cannot help wondering what is going to reinforce her self-esteem after her batterer is dead.

33 See, for example, *People v. Unger,* Supreme Court of Illinois, 66 Ill. 2d 333, 362 N.E. 2d 319 (1977).

34 One might conceptualize this justification as self-defense if one follows the provision of the Model Penal Code (2.02) that seeks to define both recklessness and negligence in terms of what a law-abiding person (i.e., the legal notion of a reasonable person) would believe *in the actor's situation.* For reasons previously noted, I would not want the actor's situation understood in such a way that it includes the actor's psychological pathologies. I have no quarrel, however, with having it understood so as to include such objective facts as size and strength differential between the two spouses and past history of dealing with the abusive spouse. These objective factors surely are relevant to assessing whether the defendant was reasonable in believing that, for example, there was an immediate risk to her of death or grave bodily harm. A reasonable belief is a belief based on relevant evidence, and these facts are surely relevant evidence. See *State v. Wanrow,* Supreme Court of Washington, 88 Wash. 2d 221, 559 P.2d 548 (1977).

Even in many of these cases, it will not be clear that the woman is justified in killing if there is some action short of killing, for example, a crippling shot to each kneecap, that would keep the abusive spouse from tracking her down and forcing her to return.

35 An earlier version of this essay was presented as an invited address to a symposium on the philosophy of criminal law at the meetings of the American Philosophical Association (Pacific Division) in 1992. Other members of the symposium were David Dolenko, Donald Hubin, and Uma Narayan. I am very grateful for the helpful discussion they provided. I am also grateful to Peter Arenella, Larry Winer, and James Weinstein for their comments on an earlier draft. Whatever is good in the paper I dedicate to Joel Feinberg with esteem and affection.

11

Force, consent, and
the reasonable woman

JOAN MCGREGOR

Conservative estimates suggest that between 20 and 30 percent of females over the age of twelve experience a violent sexual assault outside of marriage at some point in their lives. Even though women are reporting rape in record numbers, recent studies suggest that rape is the most underreported of all violent crimes.[1] Moreover, the likelihood of a complaint actually ending in conviction is generally estimated at 2 to 5 percent. While most rapes are perpetrated by an acquaintance[2] of the victim these are precisely the type of offenses which criminal justice officials are most unwilling to prosecute.[3] The current laws of rape, based often upon stereotypes about women and female sexuality, do not adequately protect women from serious harms. Consider the following example: *State v. Rusk* (289 Md. 230, 424 A.2d 720 (1981)), the prosecutrix gave the defendant a ride home from a bar where they had met through a mutual friend. The defendant invited the prosecutrix up to his apartment; she declined, but after he took her car keys, she reluctantly accompanied him to his apartment. The defendant started to undress her. Before intercourse the prosecutrix said to the defendant: "If I do what you want will you let me go without killing me?" She started to cry and then the defendant, according to the victim, started lightly choking her. The Maryland Court of Special Appeals argued that she had not been raped as she had not been *forced* to have intercourse.[4] "Prohibited force" is defined in terms of the victim's resistance, and resistance is interpreted to mean physical resistance and not merely verbal protests. Failure to resist, according to many courts, must be based on a *reasonable* fear that if she (the victim) resisted, her attacker would visit great physical harm upon her. In *Rusk,* the victim's fear was based upon being isolated, in an unknown part of town, late at night, with a man she hardly knew who had taken her car keys, who intimidated her and whom she felt threatened by. These fears, according to the court, are not *reasonable.* "She may not simply say, 'I was really scared,' and thereby transform *consent* or *mere unwillingness* into submission by force. These words do not transform a seducer into a rapist (emphasis added)."

This opinion illustrates that inherent in the current rape laws are assumptions and standards about rape, consent, force, resistance, and reasonable belief which not only fail to account for the perspective of women but work to their detriment. Rape only occurs when there is "force," and it is only force when it is over a particular threshold with the victim physically resisting; the only excuse for not physically resisting is based upon "reasonable fear." One "consents" if one says nothing and/or one was afraid but it was not "reasonable" to be afraid. This paper will analyze what is the nature of the moral wrong of rape, supposing that the law should reflect whenever possible the moral proscription. Next we will examine some representative current rape laws and show how those fail to capture the variety of contexts in which women are wronged.[5] Finally, I will argue for specific changes which include requiring affirmative consent and relying upon the standard of the *reasonable woman* as evidence in rape cases. The proposed changes will advance the value of individuals' control over their own bodies and sexual self-determination.

A primary purpose of criminal law is to deter unconsented-to "border crossings"[6] of autonomous adults. The law, in a manner of speaking, backs up agents' rights to control their own "borders." One central aim of the criminal law, then, is to ensure that individuals have control over their "borders," which includes their bodies, and that there is protection against unconsented-to border crossings. Some theorists, most notably John Stuart Mill and more recently Joel Feinberg, claim that it is only the unconsented-to harms or "wrongs," as Feinberg calls them, that are the proper object of the criminal law.[7] We identify *wrongs* that we want to prevent, and we draw up rules specifying the conditions under which one agent perpetrates the harm to another. The rules need to be written in such a way that individuals can easily conform their behavior to them and know when they are running a risk of causing the wrong. Legal rules specify necessary elements for being morally incriminating. Criminal laws are intended to deter potential offenders, however, the rules should be written in such a way that if they fail to deter we can convict and punish wrongdoers.

With all criminals statutes, care must be taken when drawing up the rules that they are not overly vague or have other faults which might lead to convicting truly innocent persons. The effect of current rape laws, however, has been to place unjustifiable obstacles to prosecution. The result has been rules which fail to capture serious wrongs and rules which put incredible burden on the victims of these wrongs, including corroboration requirements, exposure of victim's past sexual history, special instructions to juries, and resistance requirements. These represent constraints over and above what is normally accorded to defendants in criminal cases. We should be concerned about protecting individuals against the coercive powers of the state. However, the point of having the state and the criminal law is to ensure that we can live our lives in relative security from attacks.[8] The same level of scrutiny that goes into concerns about miscarriages of justice from the application and enforcement of other criminal rules should be applied to the laws of rape. We have, of course, elaborate criminal procedural rules which are designed to ensure that in any criminal prosecution injustices do not occur.

What is the wrong of rape?

Rape conjures pictures of strangers wielding knifes or guns and threatening to use them if their victims[9] do not submit to sex. There are many variations on this scenario, but most commonly the attacker has no weapon. He forces himself on his victim with threats or superior strength. In a slightly different scenario, which turns out in fact to be the most prevalent form of rape, the victim knows the attacker, he is a date or boss or other acquaintance, and the victim has not agreed to have sexual relations with this person. The sex is against her will – unconsented-to sexual intercourse or sexual contact. All of the above scenarios seriously wrong their victims and strike terror and fear in potential victims. At the baseline what differentiates rape from other crimes is *sexual intercourse or contact without consent – nonconsensual sex is rape.* The guns, knives, threats, beating, intimidation, fear are various ways of having power over one's victim. They are additional wrongs to the victim and they help the attacker to perpetrate the wrong of rape. Many of the difficult issues in rape laws involve cases where there are no "weapons," such as knifes or guns or "excessive" physical force, and the victim was not physically abused beyond the rape itself. These are the kinds of cases where it is extremely difficult to get police and prosecutors to press charges against the aggressor. Yet, according to some surveys, a third of all rapes are documented to involve no weapon whatsoever; and excessive physical force is missing in over half of all rapes. In this paper, I will focus on nonaggravated rape, that is, rape that involves no weapons or excessive physical force.

Without weapons or "excessive" physical force what is the wrong of rape? The wrong of rape has been located by some theorists in the fact that the rape is nonconsensual. According to Shafer and Frye: "We would not want to say that there is anything morally wrong with sexual intercourse per se, we conclude that the wrongness of rape rests with the matter of the woman's *consent.*"[10] The fact that the rape victim's consent is overridden is central, yet we shouldn't stop there. In many instances one's consent may be overridden or circumvented and yet the injury is not a serious one. What explains the seriousness of the injury of rape is what the consent *ranges* over.

In general, the scope of one's power of consent ranges over one's "domain." Being a *person* is conceptually linked to having a domain which one controls through one's power of consent. Persons have particular traits and capacities which define personhood. Which exact traits and capacities an individual has to have to qualify as a person is controversial, yet it is generally accepted that a person has to be capable of identifying his/her own interests, making choices which fit into larger life plans based on one's interest, and have the ability to communicate those interests and choices to others. Persons, it is claimed, have autonomy rights over most issues within their domain. A sovereign nation has control over what happens within its country; analogously, an autonomous person has control over his/her borders. Personhood can, however, come in degrees; for example, children, incompetents, and the insane are not total persons in the sense described, that is, they do not have the power to consent over the range of issues which "full persons" have. Others act on their behalf and in their best interest.

Rights carve out a person's domain. The physical body is the physical locus of the person. Competent adults have an interest in what happens to their bodies and in controlling what happens to their bodies through their power of consent. That any unconsented-to touching violates a person's domain is reflected in the criminal laws through the assault laws. Modern liberal theory claims that we have an autonomy right over, among other things, what happens to our bodies. Following from that, even the most minor of unconsented-to touching of another's body violates that right. Just violating one's right to not have one's body touched may not be enough, some crossings may be too minor to warrant the coercive arm of the law.

Consider what makes some unconsented-to border crossings more *serious* than others. One way of thinking about the gravity or seriousness of an injury is to ask how close (metaphorically) to the personal and intimate aspects of ourselves is a particular offense; how "close" to the person does a particular offense come? Consider thinking about one's domain in terms of concentric circles with the ones closer to the center more central to one's personal integrity, identity, and dignity, to who one *really* is. Offenses to the inner circles then are more grave. Those wrongs constitute more serious crimes because they "touch" the person in a more profound way.[11] Those more serious wrongs have to do with loss of control, pain, humiliation, loss of personal integrity, loss of self-esteem. We have been assuming, which we must for establishing severity of crimes, that people are roughly the same in what they care about and thus how they assign levels of seriousness. These assignments depend on what people in fact care about and how they define their personhood. This, I think, may differ culturally. The fact that ordering of seriousness and even the offenses themselves may differ culturally is not an objection to this analysis since what we are proposing is a criminal code for this culture.

In the outer circles, on this model, we will have the level of offense associated with stealing one's newspaper or some other trivial theft. One's sense of personal space, one's dignity, and one's identity have not been affected at all with such trivial thefts. Next, consider car theft, which is a more serious offense. If one's car is stolen then the thief violated something within one's power of consent. Most of us don't have an extreme personal attachment to our cars, or even if we do, we do not feel violated in some private and personal way, that is, humiliated, degraded, physically hurt, and so on. If the car is insured then the injury will be very minor indeed, as the insurance company will simply replace the car. Other crimes move closer in to our personal, private, and intimate self, for example, breaking into one's house is a greater violation than car theft regardless of the value of the possessions which are stolen. Burglary involves a violation of one's personal space, one's privacy, and one's sense of security in one's home; the stealing of property is a distinct and separable injury. The uninvited or unconsented-to invasion of one's house is serious because it intrudes on our private area, the things which we choose to share only with people we are close to, with whom we would normally let down our guard.

Although there are some bodily invasions that are trivial, for example, patting another on the back when that person dislikes it, generally, the more "serious" offenses are ones where consent ranges over that part of our domain that concerns our bodies and our sexual lives. Much of our personal identity is tied to our gender and sexual expression and hence to our sexual self-determination. In our society, sexual interactions are regarded as personal, private, intimate relationships. Sexual relationships are not generally performed in public and are usually assumed to be performed by partners who have a close and caring relationship. Moreover, it is commonly believed that sexual relationships are imbued with significance and meaning beyond the physical act. Another reason for the seriousness of offenses that force a person to relinquish control over this aspect of one's life is that most individuals believe that they are most vulnerable and exposed in sexual interactions so in them, unlike in other interactions, it is even more important that we be able to control who we are intimate with, thereby controlling information about ourselves.

Taking away the power to consent to sexual relationships, to control this most personal part of our domain, is an extremely grave and serious injury.[12] All unconsented-to border crossings show disrespect for the victim, but some more than others. It is a function of how close to the center of one's domain the offense is. Rape not only denies the ability to control a central part of one's domain, but also in doing so makes the victim a mere object, an instrument of her attacker's gratification. Rape makes the victim feel dehumanized, denigrated, and humiliated. The victim is made to feel that she has an inferior status, sexually and morally. Furthermore, the terror of the experience of being violated in this way contributes to the gravity of the offense, as does the psychological trauma that lingers as a result. There is a surprising amount of consensus about how "serious" individuals take the crime of rape to be.[13] In a famous study carried out by Thorsten Sellin and Marvin Wolfgang, rape came in second to murder in a test that asked respondents to decide how serious a long list of crimes were.

The moral wrongness of rape consists in violating an individual's autonomy right to control one's own body and one's sexual self-determination and the seriousness of rape derives from the special importance we attach to sexual autonomy. The importance we attach to controlling our sexual lives should have a significant impact on the role of consent in sexual interactions and whether consent should be implied from the circumstances. The wrong and seriousness of rape is understood in terms of unconsented-to sexual relations, and not necessarily the "incidental" assaults that may accompany it. Whereas the law often, as we saw earlier, focuses on the *forceful* nature of the attack, this argument maintains that the focus should be on the nonconsensual aspect of sexual violation.[14] Nonconsensual sex constitutes a serious wrong to a person. The harm of rape may be secured with a weapon or threats of other assaults that compound the wrong done, but those are not required for non-consensual sex to be wrong.

The present criminal law of rape

Do present criminal rape laws protect against the harm of rape? In most jurisdictions, the law does not accept a simple "no" as satisfying the requirements for lack of consent which would establish the grounds for rape. Unlike other criminal statutes, where to rightfully cross an individual's border one needs consent, apparently a woman's verbal refusal is not sufficient to prevent the crossing of her border. Normally, unconsented-to border crossings are violations of a person's domain – violations of a person's rights. The standard for rape is quite different from other crimes, for example, those involving money. Most jurisdictions require a show of "force" for sexual assault. Consider the following cases with particular attention not only to the force requirement but also to how different the outcomes would have been if property were being secured through these means rather than sex.

In *State v. Alston* (310 N.C. 399, 312 S.E.2d 470 [1984]) the Supreme Court of North Carolina reversed Alston's rape conviction. The court said that the victim did not consent and the act of sexual intercourse was against her will, but it also claimed that there was no *force,* hence there was no rape. "Although (the victim's) general fear of the defendant may have been justified by conduct on prior occasions (he had beat her on previous occasions), absent evidence that the defendant used force or threats to overcome the will of the victim to resist the intercourse alleged to have been rape, such general fear was not sufficient to show that the defendant used the force required to support a conviction of rape." Moreover, the victim did not "resist," according to the court, meaning she did not physically resist.

In *Goldberg v. State* (41 Md. App. 58, 395 A.2d 1213 [1979]) a high school senior accompanied a man who told her he was a photographer and that she had an excellent prospect of becoming a model. She went with him to his "studio." Once there she engaged in sexual intercourse with the defendant because she was afraid of him. Her reasons for being afraid, were (1) she was alone with the appellant in a house with no buildings close by and no one to help her if she resisted, and (2) the appellant was much larger than she was. Appellate court said that "in the complete absence of any threatening words or actions by the appellant, these two factors, as a matter of law, are simply not enough to have created a reasonable fear of harm so as to preclude resistance and be the equivalent of force." The court said that she was "incredibly gullible." Even though the victim refused consent, she told the defendant that she "didn't want to do that [stuff]", the court said that her verbal refusal was not sufficient to make the intercourse rape.

In *People v. Mayberry* (15 Cal. 3d 143, 542 P. 2d 1337 [1975]) the California Supreme Court reversed the conviction of Mayberry saying that he "reasonably" and in "good faith" believed that the prosecutrix was consenting. Prior to intercourse, the defendant kicked, hit, knocked to the ground, threw a bottle and shouted obscenities at the victim, and threatened her with further assault. The victim was covered with bruises and swelling when the police arrived. Lack of consent is established not by verbal protest but by physical resistance. The attack perpetrated by the defendant is not considered "force" unless the victim physically resists. The attention shifts, in these cases, from the wrongful conduct of the transgressor to the conduct of the victim. Susan Estrich correctly argues that "[t]he prohibition of 'force' or 'forcible compulsion' ends up being defined in terms of a woman's resistance."[15] The victim is only permitted to withhold resistance if she can establish that she was "reasonably" afraid that if she resisted she was in danger of even greater physical harm. The victim in *Mayberry* claimed that she was too afraid to physically resist, the court rejected her fear as "unreasonable."[16]

In *Commonwealth v. Minarich* (498 A.2d 395 [Pa. Super. 1985]) the court claimed that "forcible compulsion" requires "physical compulsion or violence," but does not, according to the court, include "psychological duress." Minarich had threatened a fourteen-year-old girl living in his custody with return to a detention home if she refused to engage in intercourse.[17] The court said this was not rape; this was *seduction*.

Had the defendants in the above cases been seeking money instead of sex their actions would have been in plain violations of traditional state criminal prohibitions.[18] What is so different about sex or sexual interactions that makes the outcomes in these cases so at odds with other criminal rules? Indeed, the converse should be true, that is, if we suppose that sexual offenses are some of the most serious wrongs that can be perpetrated against a person then *any* sign of nonconsent should be sufficient to signal that the interaction is unwanted and thereby impermissible. We should, then, require *more care* about the existence of consent, because if one was mistaken about consent in this area it would constitute a very serious offense.

In most jurisdictions, the law requires a show of *force* by the assailant (physical or with explicit threats of physical assault) and physical resistance by the victim for the conviction of rape. What the law means by 'force,' what we will designate force$_L$, is sometimes described as "overwhelming physical force or violence"; it is only legally prohibited force$_L$ if it goes above a certain threshold. Exactly what that threshold is seems to be elastic. Where "normal" sexual behavior turns into unacceptable "force" is not clear; normal sexual relations, from the legal perspective, can include a lot of force. From whose standpoint should we be asking the question? Should we consider what the man thought was an acceptable level or what the victim thought? Glanville Williams's classic textbook on criminal law warns that women often welcome a "masterly advance" and "present a token of resistance."[19] This, of course, further complicates matters. Stereotypes such as Williams's make it virtually impossible for women to withhold consent because even attempts at resistance are taken as "tokens" that is, as signs of acceptance.

Furthermore, the threats which can stand in for the violence must be explicit, immediately given: their content must involve death or grievous bodily harm. Implicit threats are insufficient to establish force$_L$. Thus, if an assailant beat you at an earlier time, as in *Alston,* or is much larger than you, as in *Goldberg,* or if there is more than one aggressor, as in *Sherry*[20], none of these facts are sufficient to establish a threat to the victim thereby establishing force$_L$. Moreover, explicit threats that don't involve physical violence but do involve other harms, for instance, economic ones, are not sufficient to establish force$_L$.[21]

In all the previously mentioned cases there was question of force$_L$. Should the *actus reus* of rape include force$_L$ as a necessary element? What is the connection between the force and the absence of consent? Other criminal offenses have depended on the absence of consent, but those other offenses have not required physical force, nor have they required the victim to respond with physical resistance thereby demanding that the victim risk further harm in order to prove that she in fact is a victim.[22] What does the element of force add to the specification of the crime of rape? Are there some conceptual or normative reasons that necessitate "force" as opposed to mere nonconsent? Why not merely nonconsensual sexual intercourse? Some have argued that the offense of rape should be defined as "forcible sexual contact" or "sexual penetration with force," and that consent should bear on the culpability of the actor but need not be incorporated as an element of the offense.[23] The reason for this is that using force to gain sexual access is what is condemned in our society. George Fletcher takes this position and argues, then, that the defining elements of rape are "forcible" sexual contact, "with consent functioning as a ground for regarding the sexual act as a shared expression of love rather than as an invasion of bodily integrity."[24]

To use consent as a justification is not unproblematic, and even Fletcher is bothered by this classification, as it is unlike other justifications:

[T]here are some doubts that we ought to concede about classifying consent as a justification for sexual contact. First, if we take self-defense and lesser evils as the paradigmatic claims of justification, then a justification functions as an exception to a prohibitory norm; consent to sexual contact, however, is the normal case rather than the exception. Secondly, claims of justification usually represent good reasons for inflicting harm. In contrast, consent dissolves the harm and converts the act into one of mutual benefit.[25]

Consent in the sexual cases functions very differently from the other justifications. Consent as an element rather than a justification makes clear that persons possess rights over their bodies and their sexual experiences and that the wrong in the case of rape is the violation of those rights.

More troublesome for this analysis is that it assumes that *force*$_L$ is what makes rape wrongful. So that the moral prohibition embodied in the law of rape is against forcible sexual contact. This view is problematic since serious violations of one's rights to bodily and sexual self-determination occur whenever sexual penetration or touching is *nonconsensual*. For instance, if while unconscious a person was penetrated by another, that action would constitute a serious violation of the unconscious person's rights. Forcible sexual contact is wrongful but it is not exclusively wrongful. I am, however, a little uncomfortable about the claim that sexual penetration without consent does not itself involve "force." The courts have drawn a distinction between the "force" incidental to the act of intercourse and the "force" required to convict for rape.[26] This distinction is itself suspect, but for purposes of this paper we will not question the distinction.

Another reason that the moral proscription embodied in rape law is against *forcible* sexual interaction may rest on the assumption that no one would permit sexual penetration without their consent unless it was forcibly done.[27] Force and resistance thus become the *evidence* that in fact there was no consent to the sexual encounter. There is, however, a continuum of force: If we thought about force in the broadest of terms, including physical and nonphysical power, then the above assumption would be founded. The aggressor must have some power over his victim but it may not necessarily include, for instance, physically holding his victim down while accomplishing penetration. Because the law has adopted a narrower notion of force$_L$

(overwhelming physical force), we must ask if it is reasonable to assume force$_L$ is necessary for nonconsensual sexual relations. In other words, is it reasonable to suppose that one might submit to sexual relations without consent where there was no force$_L$? Most women are physically weaker and smaller than most men, and many women have been socialized away from using physical force or acting aggressively. Given the strength differential most women fear a physical confrontation with men. The added fact that law enforcement agencies have traditionally counseled women not to resist in order to avoid even greater harm makes it unlikely for women to physically resist a persistent, more powerful attacker. Recognizing all these facts makes it totally *reasonable* for women to be afraid when confronted with an aggressive and demanding man and to submit to sexual contact without consenting. Consider the "four big men" argument used in *People v. Flores* (145 P. 2d 318 [1944]): "If one were met in a lonely place by four big men and told to hold up his hands or do anything else, he would be doing the reasonable thing if he obeyed, even if they did not say what they would do to him if he refused." With a woman it may only take one big man. The notion that no one submits to sexual penetration against his/her will without force$_L$ assumes parity of physical strength and other assets which contribute to personal power in a situation. There are many circumstances where I would guess that many women would feel threatened and fearful, without displays of excessive physical force or explicit threats, and in which women would submit to a sexual relationship against their will.[28] A genuine violation or wrong would occur, one which the law ought to protect against.

Furthermore, the forceful aspect of any physical contact does not necessarily make it wrongful. Boxing, football, wrestling, surgical operations all involve forceful physical contact, yet where individuals have consented the acts are not wrongful.[29] Even some consented-to sexual relations are engaged in forcefully but we are not willing to assume that they are wrongful. What is objectionable about assaults is that the attacker intentionally "touches," sometimes with great severity, another *without the consent of that person.*

Another defense of the force$_L$ requirement is that we want to ensure that the defendant himself knew his victim was not consenting. This attempt to justify the force requirement rests on the assumption that in regard to rape "no" does not mean "no"; when women say "no" that it's reasonable to suppose that they mean "yes." In other words, it assumes that a woman's words are not worthy of respect and that men are not obliged to take care in determining whether in fact the woman is freely consenting. Otherwise we would establish what the defendant knew on the basis of what victim said or did not say. On the present standard, the level of force and amount of resistance must be sufficiently great that the aggressor realized he was forcing$_L$ her. Rape is only committed if the accused forces$_L$ the victim; the way he determines if his force is over the threshold, making what he is doing force$_L$, is if she *resists*. And the victim's resistance must be physical and aggressive enough so that he does not interpret the resistance along Williams's lines. This rationale cannot be accepted. The law must respect and protect the assertions of rational adults. Verbal protests and even failure to assent must be taken at face value. The additional requirement of force$_L$ puts the crime of rape at odds with other criminal statutes and puts an extra and unreasonable burden on the victims of rape.[30]

Though we all have interests in avoiding physical harm, we also have interests in determining our own sexual lives and in preserving the integrity and privacy of our own bodies. Moreover, we have a significant stake in avoiding psychological harm, which may also distinguish rape from other crimes. In general, adults are granted almost absolute control over the domain of their bodies, others can gain access only through the consent of the owner. Sexual contact without consent and without force violates those interests we have over our bodies, our privacy, our sexual self-determination, our psychological well-being. Physical force is not required to violate any of those interests. There are many ways of harming individuals and not all involve what Joel Feinberg has called "hurts."

Starting over: What should the rules look like?

The standard of rape's criminality centers on "excessive force," some level of force which the assailant thinks goes over what would be "normal" levels. It is only a crime when it goes above the excessive level, and what constitutes that is determined from the male point of view, including what the accused believes. Because rape is usually an offense which happens to women, women's perceptions about the harm should be determinative. The force requirement, as we have seen, does not necessary pick out all the offenses against a person's sexual self-determination. There are a variety of power relationships which compel women to submit to sex without freely consenting. Recognizing that the wrong of rape lies with undermining consent to sexual interaction and not with force$_L$ means that we need to refocus our attention to the conditions which undermine consent; and, positively, focus on criteria for when consent is expressed or when it is legitimate to infer the existence of consent. Given the circumstances under which the present criminal rape laws have inferred consent, it is absolutely unclear why consent is a morally significant notion. Traditionally, however, from the moral point of view, concern about personal autonomy and self-determination is represented by guaranteeing agents control over their domain through their power of consent. Consent cannot play this role if it is inferred from the mere fact of silence or submission through intimidation or implicit threats. In what follows, I will analyze the notion of consent.

Consent

There are a number of different ways of construing the nature and effect of consent. Consent is always given to the actions of other persons. One common understanding of consent is that one "authorizes" another to act in an area which is part of one's domain, for example, giving power of attorney to another. Another way of thinking about consent is that of giving "permission" to another to cross over a boundary of one's own. "Any act that crosses the boundaries of a sovereign person's zone of autonomy requires that person's 'permission,' otherwise it is wrongful."[31] Conceiving of consent in either of these ways has normative significance because it brings into existence new moral and legal relationships. In the case of rape, as in other areas, *consent* turns a criminal act into a noncriminal one. Consent must, then, be deliberate and voluntary since its "understood purpose is to change the structure of rights of the parties involved and to generate obligations for the consenters."[32]

Within the sovereign zone of our domain, all others have a duty to refrain from crossing over. Consent cancels that duty, at least in regard to the specific acts consented to, and for a specified time. Giving consent to someone does not mean that forever after that person rightfully has access to that part of the person's domain. If I let you use my car today, you are not violating my right by using it today. However, you have no claim over it tomorrow. Giving consent changes a wrongful act into a permissible one. In order for this change to take place, that is, in order for permission to exist, the person must consent. Consent is performative, it is something that an agent does.[33]

Consent can be given, however, in some cases, without explicitly saying "I consent." John Locke's famous discussion in the *Second Treatise on Government* on tacit consent has set the stage for later discussions. The argument is that silence or inaction, in some circumstances, expresses consent. A. John Simmons gives an example of a board meeting in which the chair announces: "We will meet again next Thursday unless there are any objections to that date. Does anyone have any objections?"[34] There is silence for a period and then the chair notes that everyone agreed (or consented) to the time. Consent to the proposal is given by the failure to speak up when one was given the opportunity. Silence can only be taken as a sign of consent under circumstances meeting very specific constraints. The actors must know that by not saying anything they are expressing consent, and they must know the substance of what they are consenting to, that is, they must not be deceived about what they are consenting to. They must intend to consent by their silence. They must be given a reasonable amount of time to respond and put forth their protests. They must not be acting under coercion, that is, they must be able to withhold consent without fear of reprisal. And finally, the means of dissent must be reasonably easy to perform. The following example shows when the means for indicating dissent are not reasonably easy to preform and the consequences of dissent are detrimental to the potential consenter. The Chairman in our previous example now says: "Anyone with an objection to my proposal will kindly so indicate by lopping off his arm at the elbow."[35] A more appropriate example for our topic would be that the consequence of not consenting to sex is a beating.

When the relevant constraints for tacit consent are met and hence when a person's behavior should be construed as consent can be problematic. David Hume raised concerns to Locke's argument that by remaining in residence in a country that persons tacitly consent to the government. Hume points out

Can we seriously say, that a poor peasant or partizan has a free choice to leave his country, when he knows no foreign language or manners, and lives from day to day, by the small wages which he acquires. We may as well assert that a man, by remaining in a vessel, freely consents to the dominion of the master; though he was carried on board while asleep, and must leap into the ocean, and perish, the moment he leaves her.[36]

Similar worries might be raised to tacit consent in other areas.

In discussing consent, Feinberg uses the notion of "symbolically appropriate" behavior as a sign of consent. "Symbolically appropriate" behavior suggests that certain behaviors in specified contexts are universally recognized as expressing consent. Feinberg views the following case as one where consent is clear.

A and B have sexual relations. . . . As preliminary caresses are exchanged A finds at each successive stage enthusiastic encouragement from B, who is all coos and smiles, though no words are exchanged, and no permission requested. After the fact he [A] would be rightly astonished at the suggestion that he had acted without B's consent. To fail to dissent when there is every opportunity to do so, while behaving in appropriately cooperative ways, is universally understood in such contexts to express consent.[37]

Though no explicit question was asked and no explicit answer given, Feinberg claims, consent in this circumstance was actually expressed, but not by "silence but by symbolically appropriate conduct in the circumstances." The notion of "symbolically appropriate" behavior as a sign of consent needs to be seriously questioned in sexual encounters, given the number of "misperceptions." Ellen Goodman, in a recent newspaper column discussing the alleged rape by Senator Kennedy's nephew, William Kennedy Smith, asks "How is it possible that there is such a perceptual gap about 'consent' for sex?" The woman in this case claimed that she was raped and the accused claimed they had consensual sex. One or the other might, of course, by lying. Nevertheless, what often happens is that there is a difference of perceptions about the same situation. Goodman claims "The man will portray steamy sexual intercourse in the grass with just a spicy soupcon of rough stuff. The woman will describe sexual assault and a piercing violation of her will." The man doesn't believe that he has used "force," nor does he believe that the woman resisted enough or more than what would be common with "normal seduction." He believes that she acted in "symbolically appropriate" ways. The problem, as Goodman points out, with this difference of perception (when it is that) is that the state is left with the burden of proof that the victim was *violated*. Just saying so is not sufficient.[38] The courts and public claim in many of the nonaggravated cases that the woman is lying or deceiving herself; there was no rape.[39]

So-called "symbolically appropriate" behavior can be radically redescribed in different circumstances. In Feinberg's example, B might be extremely afraid of A, concerned that if she doesn't "go along," A will hurt her. Perhaps on a previous occasion A hurt B or threatened her, as was true in *Alston,* where the defendant had beaten the victim on numerous previous occasions. It may well be doubted that B had "every opportunity" to dissent, every opportunity means an opportunity without fear of reprisals. If A and B had had a long-term caring relationship, then the scenario described in the excerpt from Feinberg could appropriately be one in which consent was expressed. On the other hand, if A and B had just met, and A had made frightening comments to B, then that same behavior would not necessarily express consent. Consent secured through behavior under one description cannot merely be transferred to that behavior under another description.[40] At least legally, in areas where it is known that misunderstandings are prevalent, it is not unfair to require that agents not rely upon "symbolically appropriate" behavior for consent. When the wrong committed if behavior were misinterpretated is serious – as in rape cases – it is proper to require agents to go beyond "symbolically appropriate" behavior to ensure that consent is given.[41]

This analysis of consent – granting permission to do that which would otherwise be impermissible – requires that the consent be given without the presence of coercion, force, or deception. "Consent" received through the later means does not entail permission to act. Consent is normatively significant since it is the method by which we grant others a right to cross our intimate borders. Only if the consent is *freely* given does the newly formed relationship secured through consent come into existence. The fact that "consent" was given is not a sufficient condition until the circumstances under which consent was allegedly given are scrutinized; in other words, a "yes" does not always mean "yes." Remember the *Minarich* case in which the fourteen-year-old girl "consented" to sex only because she was threatened with return to a detention home. Consent under those circumstances is not genuine, but counterfeit. Cooperative behavior should not, in all cases, be taken as expressing consent. A full account of the subtleties of coercion and deception will provide an accurate picture of the varieties of rape. This account, however, is beyond the scope of this paper.

Consent is vitiated by other factors which incapacitate a person. The fact that a victim was drunk or high on drugs should naturally lead to the conclusion that she was not consenting, as she was incapable of voluntary consent. Showing that the woman was incapacitated should establish the element of the *actus reus* 'without consent.' Consent is the vehicle through which individuals autonomously direct major parts of their lives, poor choices or choices which fail to conform to a person's good often result when choosing without one's full faculties. Hence consent granted at those times is not held as legitimate. It should be noted that we normally do not let others exploit an incapacitated person and use the incapacitated person's condition to their own advantage.

Rape statutes should spell out as essential elements of the offense that there was no freely given affirmative consent to the sexual acts. The statutes should specify exactly what is meant by 'consent,' thereby not leaving its interpretation to the discretion of judges and juries. The offense is knowingly committed, then, whenever the accused fails to secure affirmative consent. We considered earlier, *Alston, Rusk, Goldberg, Mayberry, Sherry,* all the defendants *knew* that the victim had never affirmatively expressed consent, *a fortiori* each defendant knew he was raping his victim. Explicitly stating in the statute what counts as consent, makes mistake defenses, which defeat the *mens rea* requirement, much more difficult to claim. Mistakes about consent, under the present system, are more readily accepted because of the way in which consent is construed; namely, that lack of physical resistance is a sign of consent, or passive submission or consent to previous relationships are signs of consent. Mistake defenses often, in practice, are resolved on the basis of what particular jurors believe it was reasonable for the defendant to believe. If a juror believes that "no" means "yes" then he/she will believe that it was reasonable for the defendant to believe that the prosecutrix was consenting hence the juror will vote to acquit on the ground of reasonable mistake. Or, if a juror believes that women often feign reluctance and disinterest, then again that juror will understand these as signs of consent. Leaving the question of mistake about consent up to juries will likely turn on the individual juror's perceptions, often based on outmoded and detrimental stereotypes, about women. However, with the analysis proposed here, how can the defendant claim that he was mistaken when he disregarded what the victim said or failed to take care and discover whether in fact she was consenting? How, indeed, can he claim to be mistaken when in fact she did not express affirmative consent?

Requiring affirmative consent to a sexual encounter marks a change in which value the law recognizes as more important and hence is going to protect. The current rules protect the value of maximal individual sexual freedom. In so doing, it should be apparent, that promoting that value leads to sacrificing other values, specifically ensuring individuals' control of their own bodies and sexual self-determination. The alternative, proposed here, is that we protect the value of individuals' discretionary control over their own bodies and decisions and choices concerning sexual matters. This alternative holds that it is a greater value to protect individuals' sexual self-determination and bodily integrity than to protect sexual liberty generally.[42] The greater care and caution that come with the change to affirmative consent may have a "chilling effect" on sexual liberty, and mean, for example, less casual sexual encounters. Individuals will need to be wary of circumstances in which the consent may be undermined. And when there are questions about the legitimacy of consent, engaging in sexual activity may involve risk of harm and liability for rape, thereby encouraging agents to take greater precautions about how they exercise their liberty.

Reasonable woman

The account of consent provided here is not in practice going to eliminate all disputed occasions of consent. Disputed claims about consent should be analyzed by asking whether in the circumstances it would be reasonable for a woman to consent. Would it be reasonable for a woman to be fearful or feel threatened in those circumstances? The fact that the "reasonable man" would not be afraid should not be relevant since what we want to know is when a woman has consented. When interpreting actions or behavior, that is, when it is being used as evidence of consent, the context in which it was preformed must be carefully analyzed. If the man had been abusive or violent, if he made intimidating remarks or gestures, if he had undue influence over her, if she hardly knew him,[43] if the woman was isolated and without transportation, these are factors which might make it reasonable for a woman to be fearful and/or that the circumstances were otherwise undesirable, thereby making it unlikely that consent was given. Genuine consent or permission is not secured by intimidation or attempts to frighten the consenter. Standards of consent are based upon what the choice of a reasonable person would be, because we are trying to determine whether the reasonable or average woman would consent, the relevant question should be what is reasonable from a woman's point of view.

In matters of sexual self-determination, one always has the option of withholding consent. The choice to engage in sexual activity is based upon the pleasure or other goods secured through the activity. In general, a person can consent without wanting to, something that one has reservations about, but it does not follow that consenting is just a matter of choosing amongst disagreeable alternatives, and picking the most "reasonable" choice. The latter view is consistent with coercion. Particularly in sexual matters, the reasons for consenting should be based on positive goods to be received from the encounter and not avoiding evils. Whether the reasonable woman or average woman would find the circumstances and/or the kind of sex attractive and enjoyable is the question that should be asked to determine whether a woman consented to a sexual relationship. This question is neglected in most jurisdictions, and women are held to have consented in circumstances and to acts which most women would be revolted by.

Consider the recent case in New York state involving a number of white male St. John's students and one black female student. If it had been asked whether the reasonable or average woman would have freely and knowingly consented to oral and anal sex with a group of men in the described circumstances then the answer would clearly have been no. Most women would not find the circumstances described in this case pleasurable, in fact, most would find them revolting. What reason could she have had to consent to this form of sexual contact? If she had received money for the sex then, at least, we would have *a* reason for her granting consent. Given the actual circumstances, however, there is no reason to suppose that the victim consented, so we should presume as a matter of evidence that she did not. The burden then, under this account, would shift to the defendant to show that the victim did in fact consent or that it was reasonable for the defendant to believe that she did. The law often utilizes presumptions to guide the fact finding process. When the facts given are best explained by a presumed fact, then the jury may presume that fact unless given some reason to the contrary. It operates thus: "If *B* is presumed from *A,* then on a showing of *A, B* must [may] be assumed by the trier in the absence of evidence of non-*B.*"[44] Once the prosecution has shown some facts essential to the crime, for example, (1) the defendant had sex with the prosecutrix; (2) that he did so under circumstances where the reasonable or average woman would not consent. Once these facts are established, then the jury may presume nonconsent and that the defendant knew that the victim was not consenting or knew it was possible that she was not consenting (that is, he was reckless about her consent). The burden, in a sense, shifts to the defendant to show that in fact she was consenting. This approach, using a presumption of evidence, retains the standard procedural guarantees for the defendant, most importantly, innocent until proven guilty. On the other hand, if the defendant claims that a woman did in fact freely consent in circumstances in which the reasonable woman or the average woman would not, he is going to be required to provide evidence supporting his account. When reason tells us that the reasonable woman would not consent, we need a positive argument to rebut that presumption. Instead of requiring the *victim* to prove that she did not in fact consent in circumstances in which the reasonable woman would not, we shift the burden of that argument to the defendant. Consider, *Alston* where the defendant threatened the victim and had physically abused her in past and engaged in sex that denied the victim sexual enjoyment. The reasonable woman would not consent to sex in those circumstances, and so the presumption would be that she was not freely consenting.

Showing that the victim was incapacitated establishes the *actus reus* – nonconsensual sex. The defendant might argue that he was unaware of the victim's incapacitation and hence believed that she was consenting. However, if the circumstances were ones in which the reasonable woman would not consent, then the burden would be on the defendant to show why it was reasonable for him to believe that she was consenting. Here the defendant would have to show why he didn't realize that she was incapacitated, and thus incapable of consenting, and why it was reasonable for him to believe she was freely consenting to acts or in circumstances where the reasonable woman would not consent.

Agents have a duty, before crossing the borders of others, not only to determine whether the other person is consenting but also they are accountable for having an awareness of the sorts of circumstances and actions which might prevent that other person from voluntarily consenting.[45] Clear cases are where, for example in *Alston,* he had on previous occasions beaten his victim and had only minutes earlier threatened to "Fix her face" if she refused his sexual advances. No one should be surprised that submission under those circumstances was less than fully voluntary. Because a person "went along" with the aggressor or acted cooperatively, if the circumstances were ones where it was reasonable for a woman to be fearful for her safety or otherwise threatened, or to find the circumstances undesirable for other reasons (having sex with a number of men), then the presumption in such contexts should be that there was no consent. This view is in line with other areas of the criminal law. If we find an event to which reasonable persons would not normally consent, whether it involves one's own death, transfer of one's money, or for example, a beating, we presume that it was done without one's consent. It is not that a person could not consent to another's doing these things, but rather that it is unlikely. Similar understanding is called for here, keeping in mind what average women are like and what they might find desirable to consent to, if the circumstances are not ones that the reasonable woman would consent to then we should presume that the victim did not.

Requiring that there be explicit affirmative consent to sexual intercourse grants women control over their own sexuality. If informed voluntary affirmative consent is spelled out in the substance of the statute, then assumptions or inferences from behavior will not be acceptable defenses to rape. Statutes which specify affirmative consent and rules of evidence which set out conditions making consent reasonable from a woman's point of view would nullify some of the effects of jury and judicial stereotypes and myths. Mistakes constitute a defense, but they defeat the *mens rea* requirement only if they are reasonable.[46] Mistakes, however, are much less likely when the statute requires freely given affirmative consent. This is particularly true when recklessness is sufficient for liability. If we assume (at least as a matter of law) that sexual relations are engaged in only once certain conditions are met, then the law should scrutinize the circumstances where consent was allegedly given. If we take sexual integrity and control of one's sexuality seriously we will require that the circumstances of consent to sex be similar to consent in other areas.

Sexual activity should be viewed as carrying considerable risks of very serious harm if engaged if in carelessly.[47] The consequences of misunderstandings are grave, so it is fair to demand of agents engaging in sexual activity that they proceed with utmost care and refrain whenever consent is in doubt, including circumstances where the legitimacy of consent may be questioned. It is proper for the law to hold agents accountable to a certain level of care in their behavior when serious harms could result.

Inevitably questions are raised about the benefits to be gained from changing the rape laws and the price that must be paid for the changes. Whenever the law prohibits behavior, there is a price to pay in terms of loss of liberty. Changing the criminal statute would mean that certain ambiguous situations, which at least some men and women find exciting and spontaneous, will have to be given up. But if what is meant by being exciting is that the man does not know whether the woman is consenting and thereby believes she may not be, then that kind of activity should be at one's own risk. Surely, women don't find it exciting when their own consent is unclear. If, as is often claimed, some women like to pretend not to consent when in fact they do want to have sex, then that will be a lost opportunity. Women will not be able to feign nonconsent, nor will men be able to infer consent from such behavior. If a man does not secure an uncoerced affirmative consent, then he is running an unreasonable risk of nonconsensual sex and hence liability for rape.

The benefits to be gained by changing the rape statutes are many. First, dropping the current force requirement and requiring affirmative consent would empower women with control over their sexual lives. Women's word would be taken at face value rather than being undermined by a system which takes away women's ability to choose and assumes that women don't know what they want or that they lie about their choices. In no other area of the criminal law are there such negative assumptions about the victims of crimes. Second, the law will protect against harms which women fear and describe the offense on the basis of women's violation. Thirdly, changing the standards of consent for rape will make it conform to other consensual arrangements. Fourth, establishing new rules should increase the safety of women against sexual assault because it should be much easier to prove rape and thereby to convict and punish more offenders. Ultimately, these changes will deter others from harmful behavior. And finally, these rules should have the effect of articulating the expectation that men have an awareness of women's preferences and respect their choices. This is done by requiring men to conform to standards of consent in sexual encounters that are "reasonable" from a woman's perspective.

Rape should be conceptualized as unconsented-to sexual intercourse or sexual contact – the force requirement should be dropped. Other changes include: (1) The law should assume that rational, competent adults express their desires through their power of consent; rape laws should be more in line with other areas of criminal law in requiring affirmative consent. (2) When disputes arise about whether in fact consent was given, the question that should be asked is whether the circumstances in question are ones in which it would be reasonable for a woman to consent, because the consent of the woman is at issue. (3) Mistakes about consent would be much less credible when the rules are changed. If the accused failed to take due care to secure explicit freely given affirmative consent, then he knew that she was not consenting, thus he knew he was raping her. When the harm that would be perpetrated is great – as unconsented-to sexual intercourse is – then we can fault individuals for failing to take great care.[48]

Notes

1 Deborah Rhode, *Justice and Gender* (Cambridge: Harvard University Press, 1989).
2 The term 'acquaintance' in this context means that the victim is in some way familiar with the rapist. This could mean very causally, e.g., were briefly introduced, all the way to a family member or "boyfriend." This is to be distinguished from the common assumption that rapists are always people that the victim does not know.
3 This paper is about rape when the victim is a woman. Men are also victims of rape, although the occurrence outside of prison is rare. Why it is so rare is the subject of conjecture only. A study of Philadelphia prisons claimed: "A primary goal of the sexual aggressor, it is clear, is the conquest and degradation of his victim." Alan Davis, "Sexual Assaults in the Philadelphia Prison System and Sheriff's Vans," *Studies in Human Sexual Behavior: The American Scene,* ed. Ailon Shiloh (Springfield, Ill.: Charles C. Thomas, Publisher, 1970), 340.
4 Rape statutes vary from state to state. The claims of this paper are meant to capture the doctrines that are incorporated into most state statutes. American rape statutes are based on common law which defined *rape* as "carnal knowledge [by a male] of a woman forcibly and against her will." Most American criminal statutes describe "rape" as sexual intercourse achieved "forcibly," "against the will" of the woman, and/or "without her consent."

It should be further mentioned that there was quite a bit of rape reform in the early 1980s. Those reforms included dropping the requirement of corroboration, changing the resistance requirement from "utmost resistance" to "physical resistance," and the so-called shield rules. These reforms, however, have not had the effect that was hoped for.

5 Some states, during the reforming of their criminal statutes, dropped "rape" as an offense. They have replaced the crime of rape with "sexual assault." Often these statutes are gender neutral. There are a number of reasons that these changes have not led to the desired reforms. See Susan Estrich, *Real Rape* (Cambridge: Harvard University Press, 1987), 80–ff.

6 Robert Nozick introduced this useful phrase "border-crossing" in *Anarchy, State, and Utopia* (New York: Basic Books, 1974), 71–ff.

7 Joel Feinberg, *Harm to Others* (Oxford: Oxford University Press, 1984), 33–4.

8 This is just not true of women in the United States where rape has increased to "epidemic proportions"; most women's daily activities are curtailed and controlled because of the specter of rape.

9 In this paper, I will use the term "victim" as opposed to much rape literature which uses the designation "survivor."

10 Shafer and Frye, "Rape and Respect" in Mary Vetterling-Braggin, Frederick Elliston, and Jane English, eds. *Feminism and Philosophy* (Totowa: Rowman and Littlefield, 1977), 337.

11 Feinberg, *Harm to Others*, 37.

12 One reason that criminalizing abortion is such an injury to women is that it also takes away control of one's body. Criminalizing abortion does not permit women to autonomously determine whether or not to become a parent.

13 See, for example, Thorsten Sellin and Marvin Wolfgang, *The Measurement of Delinquency* (New York: John Wiley & Sons, Inc., 1964). "Forcible rape" came in second to murder, well ahead of armed robbery and "aggravated assault."

14 Though I will not directly argue for it, I am assuming that part of the problem with rape laws is that there is often only one level of the offense, namely, aggravated rape, which carries a very stiff penalty. Since juries do not want to see individuals who are guilty of unaggravated offenses, that is, rapes without other serious physical injuries, go to jail for extended periods of time as the "rape" statutes often dictate, the juries will acquit the defendants thereby avoiding that outcome. The way to solve this problem is to have a number of levels of the offense, with penalties appropriate to the various levels.

15 Estrich, 60.

16 It should be noted that the requirement that the fear be reasonable if not without justification. Consider the case of a person who has irrational fears; even though, let us imagine, they were the basis for her consenting to sex if the accused didn't know about those fears then it might be unfair to hold him culpable for the offense. It is often the interpretation of the doctrine of "reasonable fear" which has been unfounded. Presumably, if the goal is to determine whether the victim's fear was reasonable or not, then it is appropriate for the court to focus on what the reasonable woman would fear.

17 This case has an additional complexity, namely, the question whether or not the threat posed by Minarich was sufficient for coercion given he had a right to return her to the detention home. I have argued elsewhere that threatening to do what one has a legal right to do can be coercive, but many theorists disagree. See literature

on coercion: Robert Nozick, "Coercion" in *Philosophy, Science and Method*, eds. Sidney Morgenbesser, Patrick Suppes, and Morton White (New York: St. Martin's, 1969), Michael Bayles, "A Concept of Coercion," in *Coercion*, ed. J. Roland Pennock and John W. Chapman (Chicago: Aldine, Atherton, Inc. 1972), Don Vandeveer, "Coercion, Seduction, and Rights," *The Personalist*, 58 (1977), David Zimmerman, "Coercive Wage Offers," *Philosophy and Public Affairs* 10 (1981), Joel Feinberg, *Harm to Self*.

18 Estrich, 70.

19 Other insidious examples of not taking women victims at their word is the famous special instructions derived from the words of Sir Matthew Hale cautioning jurors to be suspicious of the female accuser since rape is a charge easily made but difficult to defend against "be [the accused] ever so innocent."

20 *Commonwealth v. Sherry* 437 N.E. 2d 224 (Mass. 1982). In this case there were three men and one woman.

21 Interestingly, the crime extortion recognizes that threats other than threats to physically harm the person are instances of the crime. Extortion acknowledges that individuals may be intimidated by threats other than those foreboding bodily harm. There is no apparent reason why this is not also true in the sexual case.

22 See Rhode, 247.

23 George Fletcher, *Rethinking Criminal Law* (Boston: Little, Brown and Company, 1978).

24 Fletcher, 705.

25 Fletcher, 707.

26 Estrich, 60.

27 Most rape statutes have focused on penetration. See Catharine MacKinnon, *Toward a Feminist Theory of the State* (Cambridge: Harvard University Press, 1989), 172.

28 A couple of extreme cases where there was no force are: *R. v. Plummer* ((1975), 31 C.R.N.S. 220 (Ont. C.A.)) where the accused was charged with raping a girl after she had already been raped by another man. He found her naked and crying on the bed and had sexual relations with her. No threats were made but she submitted out of fear of bodily harm. In *R. v. Hallett* ((1841) 9 Car. P. 748) the victim was raped by eight men who attacked her. She did not resist after the initial attack so they were convicted of assault only.

29 See Feinberg's discussion of the legal maxim *Volenti non fit injuria* in *Harm to Self* (Oxford: Oxford University Press, 1986), 173–ff.

30 Another motivation for the force requirement might have come from concerns to protect women from the following kind of decisions. In *Regina v. Morgan* (1976 A.C. 182 [House of Lords]) the defendants were falsely told by the husband of the victim that she liked "kinky" sex and would feign lack of consent; in fact the victim did not consent to the forced sexual acts. The defendants argued that they lacked the *mens rea* for the crime of rape because they honestly believed that she was consenting. The prohibition against "forcible sexual contact" would have forestalled this defense.

31 Feinberg, *Harm to Self*, 177.

32 A. John Simmons, *Moral Principles and Political Obligations* (Princeton: Princeton University Press, 1979), 76.

33 Consent has sometimes been construed in the "attitudinal" sense of having an attitude of approval towards something. Even if this is a true sense of consent, it is not what we would want to say generates rights, that is, grants permission, to do what is otherwise impermissible.

34 Simmons, 77.

35 Simmons, 81.

36 David Hume, "Of the Original Contract" in A. MacIntyre, ed. *Hume's Ethical Writing,* (Collier-Macmillan, 1965).

37 Feinberg, *Self,* 184.

38 Catharine MacKinnon has commented on this same phenomenon, saying: "Reality is split – a woman is raped but not by a rapist? – the law tends to conclude that the rape *did not happen.*" *Toward a Feminist Theory of the State* (Cambridge: Harvard University Press, 1989).

39 There may be some cases in which the accuser lied (FBI estimate 2 to 4 percent), but that is true with other crimes as well.

40 At auctions certain gestures are taken to signify assent to particular prices. In many instances, individuals new to auctions have been misinterpreted as acting in these symbolically appropriate ways.

41 Something like this is done in contract law with the Statute of Frauds. The Statue of Frauds does not recognize certain agreements, e.g., verbal contracts for real estate exchanges because of the problems of misunderstanding that come out of those circumstances.

42 A good analogy, suggested to me by Peter Cervelli, is the rules pertaining to the possession and use of hand guns. Apparently, we believe that the value of permiting individuals to have access to and use hand guns is greater than the security of a society without them. Some harm will result from individuals having the liberty to possess and use guns. We are willing to take those risks and accept those costs because we believe that the value of owning and using hand guns is of greater importance.

43 Assume that sexual relationships are very personal and private and that they are not engaged in casually.

44 John Kaplan and Jon Waltz, *Evidence* (Mineola: The Foundation Press, 1984), 752.

45 This raises the issue of whether criminal liability should be based upon "objective" or "subjective" standards. This dispute often surfaces in determinations of whether a defendant intended to bring about a given result. According to "objectivists," a person intends the natural and probable consequences of his acts and his intention for purposes of imposing criminal liability is established by reference to the "reasonable person." If the reasonable person would have foreseen that a given consequence would follow from his conduct, then the defendant is held to have intended that result. "Subjectivists" contend that what a defendant intends depends only on what he in fact foresees. This debate is crucial in cases in which a reasonable person would have foreseen a given consequence, though the particular defendant did not.

46 If the defendant intentionally has sex without the consent of the woman that clearly leaves him culpable for the offense of rape. That the defendant have that intention, however, is not the only blameworthy condition. Recklessness about consent is also sufficient for culpability. Recklessness involves conscious choice of a risk of proscribed events occurring. If we grant that agents have a duty to secure consent before having sexual relations with another, then one can breach that duty without choosing to do so, that is by failing to secure consent. If the defendant claims that he was mistaken then the relevant question is whether the mistake is voluntary. A mistake is voluntary if the actor could have avoided the mistake. In the case of the reckless defendant, he was conscious of the risk and did nothing to ensure that the victim was consenting. Along with avoiding intentional harms, we want the criminal law to deter people from harming us through reckless attitudes to the inherent risks in their behavior. Since sexual relations without consent is a serious offense, the circumstances wherein sexual relationships take place should trigger heightened concern about consent. Consent to sexual relations is not a trivial matter, it is an arena where we now recognize communications are often misunderstood.

47 Christine Boyle, *Sexual Assault* (Toronto: The Carswell Company, 1984). She analogizes the benefits and the riskiness of sexual activity with the benefits and riskiness of driving.

48 A number of people have read this paper and provided me with useful comments. I would like to thank them all, with special thanks to my colleagues Jeffrie Murphy and Peter de Marneffe.

12

Self-defense*

ROBERT F. SCHOPP

I Introduction

Although the criminal law generally proscribes the use of force by one private citizen against another, most penal codes provide an exception for those who exercise force in self-defense. Standard cases of justified self-defense are relatively easy to identify. Suppose, for example, that a fully competent aggressor (A) purposely attacks an innocent victim (V) with intent to kill V for financial profit. V kills A in order to save her life in circumstances in which she can do so only by killing A.[1]

Although intuitions tend to converge regarding standard cases, theoretical accounts of self-defense encounter at least three types of difficulty. First, cases that vary from the standard form elicit ambivalent intuitive responses and raise substantial doubts regarding justification. Consider, for example, cases involving innocent aggressors (IA) who endanger the lives of innocent victims. Perhaps the innocent aggressor is a child who does not realize that the gun in his hand will actually harm the victim or a severely impaired person who attacks the victim out of delusional terror. Other intuitively problematic cases involve culpable aggressors who initiate attacks in circumstances that prevent their victims from taking preventive action without endangering innocent parties. Suppose that V can stop A only by ramming the car in which both A and an innocent bystander (IB) are sitting, or that A shoots at V while holding a hostage in front of him as an innocent shield (IS) such that V can protect herself only by shooting both A and IS.

Second, several controversial questions arise regarding the appropriate parameters of the use of force in self-defense. Must victims retreat from places they legitimately occupy in order to avoid inflicting injury on aggressors? Must they wait until the harm that justifies force is imminent, or can they injure aggressors in "preemptive strikes"? Can victims protect themselves by inflicting substantially more severe injuries than they are threatened with, or must they observe a rule of proportionality requiring that they accept less serious harm rather than inflicting severe injury? Suppose, for example, that the weaker V can escape blackened eyes only by fatally stabbing the strong A.[2]

Finally, the theoretical foundations of self-defense remain unsettled. Some writers have traced self-defense to historical roots in a public duty to prevent crimes, while others have justified the use of self-protective force through appeal to a lesser-evils rationale. Some theorists treat aggressors as central, arguing that they forfeit the right to life by engaging in aggression, while others emphasize the victim's role by appeal to a right to protect some interest such as personal autonomy. Each of the proffered rationales accommodates certain cases, but none provides a completely satisfactory theoretical foundation for all aspects of self-defense.[3]

This paper pursues two projects. First, it advances a substantive theory of self-defense addressing the important problematic concerns listed above. This account integrates the central features of current legal doctrine with justificatory principles found in liberal political philosophy. Second, this paper advances a methodological thesis in that it interprets the law of self-defense in light of the broader and more abstract principles of political philosophy represented by the legal rules. On this approach to legal analysis, the structure and content of the law reveal underlying principles of political morality. These principles inform a theory that addresses self-defense as morally justified individual action and as morally justified law. This method produces an analysis of the American law of self-defense as the law of self-defense in a liberal society.[4]

The argument proceeds in the following manner. Section II examines some current scholarship regarding self-defense in order to identify the central contributions of these theories and the remaining concerns. Section III advances an account of self-defense as individual action justified by the principles of liberal political morality reflected in contemporary American law. Section IV discusses self-defense as a legal defense, and it responds to potential criticisms. Finally, section V summarizes and concludes the argument.

II Current theories

A. Self-defense and autonomy

George Fletcher has developed the most complete contemporary theory of self-defense. Fletcher's theory reflects the historical roots of the defense in that it interprets self-defense as either a justification or an excuse according to the circumstances.[5] Consistent with contemporary law, Fletcher accommodates most cases under a justification rationale. Fletcher identifies two dominant theoretical approaches to self-defense law. The first interprets self-defense as a choice among evils in which victims must compare the harm caused by effective self-defense with the injury avoided and select the path that will minimize net harm. In making this determination, however, victims may discount to some unspecified degree the value of harm to the aggressor's interests. Fletcher represents this lesser-evils model as the currently dominant one in Anglo-American law.[6]

Fletcher endorses the second approach which justifies self-defense as a means of protecting and vindicating autonomy. Fletcher contends that this theory currently prevails in Germany and the Soviet Union and that it was widely accepted in early Anglo-American law. According to this theory, victims may exercise the defensive force necessary to protect autonomy. Although Fletcher does not offer a precise analysis of autonomy, he describes it as a prelegal concept that shapes and supports the law, and he contends that attacks upon legally protected rights and interests give rise to a right to use force in self-defense.[7] Fletcher advances the concept of *Right* (Recht) as morally sound law and contends that victims are justified in using force to defend against violations of any rights or interests protected by morally sound law. These rights and interests are part of the *Right,* and thus, attacks on them are violations of the entire social order. Victims are justified in using force to protect these rights and interests because by doing so they protect the *Right.* There is no requirement of proportion because maintaining the social order justifies any force necessary to defend a legally protected right or interest.[8]

Although Fletcher does not present a complete explication of his conception of autonomy, it appears to be inextricable from *Right,* and the two are apparently related in the following manner. Morally sound law creates a justifiable social order and protects certain individual rights and interests. Personal autonomy constitutes a broad general right on the part of individuals to exercise those specific rights and interests allocated to them within this justifiable social order. Aggressors who violate these rights and interests attack their victims and the social order. Victims or third parties may justifiably exercise the force necessary to protect specific rights or interests, the autonomy of the victims, and the larger social order.[9]

On Fletcher's view victims may exercise force in self-defense against innocent aggressors because the justification lies in the protection of victims and the social order, not in the aggressors' culpability. Victims may exercise all necessary force without regard for proportion because the justification for their action does not lie in the balance of harms. Defensive force protects the social order, and *Right* should never yield to wrong.[10] For the same reason, victims have no duty to retreat before exercising force in self-defense.[11] Compassion and concern for the humanity of aggressors may, however, temper the manner in which they should exercise defensive force.

Although Fletcher addresses most self-defense cases under the doctrine of justification outlined, he also recognizes a related excuse that applies under certain conditions. This excuse reflects the historical doctrine of *se defendendo* and applies only to defendants who have killed aggressors in order to save their own lives or those of their closely related family members. This defense is premised on the contention that threats to one's life elicit an involuntary response in self-protection. Under such circumstances, it is often said that the victims had no alternative or no real choice, and therefore, that we ought not punish them for doing what anyone would have done. In contrast to justified self-defense, *se defendendo* carries a duty to retreat before exercising deadly force because it applies only when victims have no alternative.[12]

Fletcher addresses two additional types of difficult cases through this excuse. First, if victims who kill innocent shields while protecting themselves from aggressors are appropriately exculpated, they should be excused rather than justified.[13] Second, putative self-defense may be excused but not justified. Putative self-defense occurs when victims exercise force against others under the reasonable but mistaken belief that the others are attacking. Fletcher denies that mistaken beliefs can justify action but contends that they may provide the basis for excuse.[14]

Fletcher provides the most comprehensive contemporary theory, and perhaps for this reason, it invites several criticisms. First, it generates intuitively problematic results in certain circumstances because it disregards almost entirely the culpability or interests of aggressors. Innocent aggressors, like culpable ones, are subject to any force necessary to protect victims' rights and the social order. In addition, Fletcher contends that justified conduct is right conduct, rather than merely tolerable.[15] Yet, it seems at least plausible to argue that injuring an innocent aggressor in order to prevent a similar injury to an innocent victim is tolerable rather than morally superior or mandated. It is not clear why it would be unacceptable for innocent victims to sacrifice their own interests to those of innocent aggressors or for third parties to refuse to injure innocent aggressors in order to prevent harm to innocent victims. In these circumstances, people must choose between innocent parties with no obvious grounds for preferring one over the other.[16]

Fletcher treats culpable and innocent aggressors alike insofar as he allows the victim to engage in justified self-defense against either, but the victim who kills an innocent shield is excused rather than justified. On this view, innocent aggressors are treated as if they are more similar to culpable aggressors than they are to innocent shields. Yet, it is difficult to find morally relevant reasons for differentiating in this manner among innocent aggressors and shields. Victims' interests are susceptible to similar injury by the acts or presence of culpable aggressors, innocent aggressors, or innocent shields. When attacked by culpable aggressors, however, victims must choose between innocent parties and culpable ones, while victims threatened by innocent aggressors or shields must choose among innocent parties.

These concerns are exacerbated because this theory imputes no duty of retreat or proportion. This approach would recommend grossly disproportionate injuries in certain circumstances because it grants no role to the consequentialist balancing of harms. Thus V can shoot a fleeing apple thief who is in the process of stealing a single apple from V's grove if that is the only means by which V can prevent the violation.[17] While Fletcher contends that compassion and concern for humanity should temper V's decision to exercise this right to engage in self-defense, it is not clear that this resolves the problem. If he intends this qualification to carry such force that V would not be justified in causing the disproportionate harm, then the theory subtly incorporates a proportionality requirement without providing a foundation for that provision in the broader theory. If, in contrast, he contends that V would be justified in exercising disproportionate force, then the intuitively problematic examples remain unaddressed.

Finally, the theoretical basis for this approach is not entirely clear. The central concepts are autonomy, *Right,* and the social order, but the precise relationship among these considerations remains troublesome. Concentration on autonomy suggests that individual rights and self-determination are of primary importance, while the social order emphasizes the larger system in which these individual rights are embedded. In many circumstances, one may reasonably expect these two levels of analysis to converge, but in certain situations, they might diverge. Suppose, for example, that V can prevent A from violating her rights only by shooting A in circumstances in which it is likely that doing so will precipitate a riot.

In summary, Fletcher's theory provides a comprehensive approach that addresses the historical roots of self-defense as both justification and excuse. In addition, the emphasis on victims' rights and the social order provides a plausible account of many standard cases and explains why innocent victims may justifiably inflict more severe injuries on aggressors rather than absorbing less serious harm from aggressors. It encounters difficulty when dealing with innocent aggressors and shields, however, particularly when victims can avoid injury only by inflicting markedly disproportionate harm on those persons. This concern arises from the failure of the theory to attribute any explicit force to the aggressors' culpability or to the consequentialist weighing of harms.

B. *Self-defense and distributive justice*

Recent work addressing self-defense as a problem in distributive justice explicitly addresses the balance of harms and aggressor culpability.[18] On the distributive theory of self-defense, an innocent victim can justify the exercise of force against a culpable aggressor as a decision to distribute unavoidable harm to the party who culpably created the situation in which someone must suffer the injury. This distributive theory is less comprehensive than Fletcher's in that it addresses only the standard cases in which an innocent victim can save her life only by killing the culpable aggressor. The core of this approach is the harm distribution principle (HD) which holds roughly that when harm is inevitable and will be of equal severity regardless of who suffers it, then distribute it to the party who culpably caused the harm to be inevitable.[19]

HD includes a proportionality principle in that it only authorizes defensive force when the severity of the harm will remain roughly equivalent regardless of who suffers it. It also includes an implicit duty to retreat before exercising force because it authorizes only the distribution of inevitable injury.[20] HD is grounded in the formal principle of justice which demands that one treat like cases alike and unlike cases differently in proportion to their morally relevant differences. When inevitable harm must be distributed, culpably causing that inevitable harm provides a morally relevant difference between victims and aggressors, justifying victims in distributing the injury to the aggressors.[21] Although culpability plays a central role in this theory, self-defense is not justified as a form of punishment. Rather, the culpable aggressor substantially worsened the victim's circumstances by creating conditions in which at least one of the parties must suffer some injury. The aggressor owes the victim restitution of this loss, and the victim is justified in rectifying her situation by directing the injury toward the aggressor.[22]

The distributive theory integrates a consequentialist concern for selecting the lesser harm with consideration of the culpability of the parties in that it allows one to allocate unavoidable harm to the culpable party but does not endorse infliction of disproportionate harms. In this manner, it avoids some of the intuitive difficulties encountered by either the lesser-harms approach or a culpability-based approach in their pure forms. The distributive theory is intuitively plausible in that it grants significance to proportion and treats innocent aggressors and shields differently than guilty aggressors. In addition, it is consistent with most law and applied morality in that it attributes weight both to consequences and to principles of responsibility.

Despite these assets, the distributive theory does not provide a fully satisfactory approach because it does not address nonstandard cases such as those involving innocent aggressors or shields. Neither does it address cases of culpable aggression in which the degree of injury caused will vary significantly according to which party suffers it. Thus it fails to accommodate cases in which it seems intuitively plausible that victims might be justified in inflicting disproportionate harm on culpable aggressors. Suppose, for example, that V can prevent A from breaking V's arm only by killing A. Reasonable people might differ regarding the justification of V's killing A, but the distributive theory simply fails to address cases that do not meet the condition of equivalent harms.

Although the distributive theory addresses both the balance of harms and culpability, it does not fully satisfy either consequentialist or desert-based concerns. The consequentialist theorist would compare the total amount of harm caused by available actions, but this theory compares the injury avoided by the victim to that inflicted on each culpable aggressor, thus allowing the victim to cause a much greater amount of harm than she avoids in cases involving multiple aggressors. Similarly, on a desert-based approach, it is not clear why an innocent victim is justified in distributing unavoidable harm to a culpable aggressor only when the amount of injury will be equal regardless of who suffers it. Thus, the distributive theory neither provides a priority ordering between consequentialism and culpability nor explains how to integrate these two principles in difficult cases.

Finally, the distributive theory addresses only self-defense as a justification, omitting the cases that arguably provide grounds for excuse. Fletcher's *se defendendo* excuse applies to cases in which it seems intuitively that the victims are not justified, yet should not be punished. Suppose, for example, that V can prevent her own murder only by killing A and two innocent bystanders. The distributive theory simply fails to address such cases.

Commentators have criticized each of the various principles proferred as the theoretical foundation for self-defense, rejecting each as insufficient to accommodate the practice.[23] We should not be surprised to learn that such a complex aspect of law and social morality cannot be explained by reference to a single principle or purpose. We need a complex theory that explains how various important principles and purposes of the legal system combine to support an integrated theory of self-defense. The following sections of this paper advance an approach to self-defense that conforms to the broad outline of contemporary American law and avoids the difficulties encountered by Fletcher and the distributive theory.

III Self-defense: A moral theory a liberal can live with

A fully satisfactory theory of self-defense must address the use of defensive force as individual action and as morally justified law. Section III examines hypothetical cases, current legal doctrine, and liberal principles of political philosophy in order to develop an account of self-defense as individual action justified by the liberal principles of political morality embodied in the law.[24] Section IV integrates this analysis with certain formal features of a system of law in order to derive an account of morally justified self-defense law from a liberal perspective.

A. *Legal defenses and individual interests*

The dominant approach to self-defense in contemporary American criminal law as represented by the Model Penal Code (MPC) allows one to exercise force against another person in self-defense when that force is immediately necessary for the purpose of protecting oneself from the use of unlawful force by that other person. The victim may exercise deadly force in self-defense, however, only when such force is necessary to protect herself against death, serious bodily injury, kidnapping, or compelled sexual intercourse. Any force that creates a substantial risk of death or serious bodily injury qualifies as deadly force.[25] Clear cases of justified self-defense under these provisions occur when the innocent victims kill aggressors in circumstances such that doing so was the only available means of preventing the aggressors from unlawfully killing them. Similarly, victims justifiably injure aggressors when doing so is necessary to prevent the aggressors from exercising unlawful but not deadly force against the victims. Consider the following example.

(SD1) V is walking home from work one night when an assailant steps from a doorway and grabs her arm and purse. V kicks A and hits him with her umbrella, running away when A releases his grip in order to protect himself from the umbrella.

The MPC also provides a general justification defense for innocent parties who encounter circumstances in which they must choose among harmful alternatives. The code provides this justificatory defense for actors who engage in behavior that would ordinarily constitute an offense when that conduct is necessary to avoid a greater harm or evil.[26] Known as the "lesser-evils" or "choice of evils" justification, this defense applies to cases such as the following one.

(LE1) A bicyclist suffers a fall on a lonely country road, disabling her bicycle and seriously injuring herself. As night falls and the temperature drops, she breaks into an empty farmhouse because doing so is necessary to call for help and prevent hypothermia.

The lesser-evils defense would exculpate the bicyclist because breaking into the house was necessary to prevent the potentially fatal hypothermia, although she would remain liable to the owner of the house for compensatory damages under civil law.[27] Although SD1 and LE1 present clear cases of the self-defense and lesser-evils justifications respectively, consider case SD2.

(SD2) V takes a book to a bench in the park, fully intending to sit there and read all afternoon; A approaches with a baseball bat, orders V to stay on the bench until 3:00 P.M., and threatens to hit V with the bat if but only if V tries to leave before 3:00.[28] When noise distracts A, V makes her escape by grabbing the bat and hitting A, breaking his leg.

In SD2, A threatened no injury to V's concrete interests.[29] V's hitting A was not necessary to avoid personal injury, property damage, or the loss of the opportunity to do anything that V actually wanted to do. V had planned to stay on the bench until after 3:00 P.M. independently of A's threat. The only injury V suffered from A's threat was the violation of her sovereignty over her own bodily movement.[30] A's threat injured V only insofar as it deprived V of the discretion to decide for herself either that she would stay on the bench until 3:00 P.M. or that she would change her mind and leave. LE1 provides a standard lesser-evils case in which the bicyclist suffers threat of injury to her concrete interests in avoiding illness and death, but she encounters no threat to her sovereignty because natural events can infringe upon concrete interests, but they cannot violate sovereignty. The farmhouse owners suffered temporary injury to their concrete property interests, but compensation cures this injury, and their right to compensation vindicates their sovereignty over their property. Had the owners never received compensation because the bicyclist was never found or died despite the break-in, the fact that they had a legal claim would vindicate their standing under the law as the parties who hold the right of sovereign control over their property.

In a standard self-defense case such as SD1, A threatens both concrete interests and sovereignty. The threat to or violation of each constitutes an independent injury, but the violation of sovereignty differentiates these clear cases of self-defense from many applications of the lesser-evils defense. A's culpable offense against V violates some aspect of V's sovereignty and subjugates V to A, imputing lesser standing to V. Norms requiring that V tolerate such an intrusion would effectively ratify that violation and the imputation of lesser standing, undermining V's equal status. Thus, the appropriate norm of self-defense for any particular legal system reflects not only the need to define the conditions under which private persons may protect their own concrete interests in the absence of immediate state assistance, but also the importance of personal sovereignty and equal standing to the political philosophy represented by that social system. A political philosophy vesting fundamental value only in maximizing the concrete well-being of the citizenry, for example, might collapse self-defense into the general justification defense, requiring that individuals always act in the manner expected to minimize the net harm to concrete interests. In contrast, a political system vesting significant value in individual self-determination must develop a set of defenses that grants corresponding weight to violations of sovereignty as well as to the balance of concrete harms.

B. *Liberal political philosophy and a legal system*

Respect for the individual's right to self-determination lies at the core of liberal political philosophy.[31] Contemporary liberals refine this basic principle. Joel Feinberg develops a conception of autonomy as a right that he describes as personal sovereignty analogous to the political sovereignty of nations. On this view, an autonomous individual enjoys a sphere of personal sovereignty within which he exercises discretionary authority. This right to self-determination extends to a domain of central self-regarding life decisions.

Respect for personal autonomy as sovereignty requires respect for the individual's unfettered choice in those matters that do not infringe on the legitimate interests of others.[32]

Sovereignty is a fundamental liberal value in that it is absolute, underivative, and noncompensable. It is absolute in the sense that any intrusion into the individual's sphere of self-determination constitutes a violation of sovereignty. Various matters may fall beyond the scope of the individual's sphere of personal sovereignty because, for example, they directly affect the legitimate interests of others. If a decision falls within the domain of individual sovereignty, however, respect for that person's right to self-determination precludes any intrusion by others.[33] It is underivative in that liberals value sovereignty independently of any instrumental purpose it may serve. Finally, it is noncompensable in that others cannot justify intruding into a clearly competent individual's sphere of sovereignty by providing other benefits, such as increased well-being in return.[34]

While Feinberg presents the fundamental nature of sovereignty as part of the very concept, John Rawls vests similar weight in self-determination by granting lexical priority over other benefits to a set of basic liberties. This set includes the political liberties to vote and be eligible for public office; freedom of speech, assembly, conscience and thought; freedom of the person and the right to hold personal property; and freedom from arbitrary arrest and seizure.[35]

Feinberg advocates a sphere of personal sovereignty that encompasses all primarily and directly self-regarding critical life decisions.[36] At this level of generality, the domain of sovereignty is identical for all competent adults. Similarly, Rawls contends that the basic liberties are the same for all members of society. He argues that the fundamental rights and liberties define the individual's standing in society and provide the basis for self-respect as well as for respect by others. On Rawls's view, self-respect is inextricable from respect within a community of shared interests that confirms one's endeavors and standing.[37] At this fundamental level, sovereignty and equality converge because government must treat persons with respect as beings capable of directing their own lives. It does so by according to each a sphere of personal sovereignty that equals that enjoyed by other members of the community and that identifies the person as a member in full standing of that community.[38]

In short, contemporary liberal political theory vests fundamental value in personal sovereignty as the right to self-determination. This requires a relationship between the individual and the government in which the government accords equal respect to all persons by recognizing a sphere of sovereignty within which each individual can direct his or her own life and develop self-respect as a member of a community of equal, sovereign citizens.[39]

The rule of law is central to this political philosophy in that law in a liberal society defines and protects each individual's right to self-determination. Constitutional law limits the scope of government power, preventing the government from directly intruding into the individual's domain of sovereignty and prohibiting the government from distributing social resources in a manner that imputes lesser status or worth to some persons than to others.[40] Criminal law protects personal sovereignty and equal status by proscribing, preventing, and punishing actions by some citizens that violate the rights and interests of others. Thus, the criminal law not only maintains the conventional social morality that we need for cooperative social interaction, it also articulates the contours of the individual's sphere of sovereignty by defining the intrusions that will be considered crimes.[41] When a liberal state enforces the criminal law, it not only maintains the public order and safety through deterrence and restraint, it also vindicates the sovereignty of the individual by punishing and condemning conduct that violates that person's right to self-determination.

Herbert Morris advances a theory justifying punishment by the criminal justice system as a method of redressing an imbalance of social burdens and benefits created by the criminal offense.[42] This theory is difficult to sustain when applied to the complete array of social benefits and burdens, and it remains difficult to defend when it is limited to the benefits and burdens specifically attributable to the criminal justice system. We punish those who attempt to commit crimes, for example, in cases in which the attempt had no apparent effect on the balance of benefits and burdens between the parties because no harm was done to the victim and no gain was realized by the criminal.

Consider, however, the contention that criminal punishment redresses an imbalance in the relative standing of the criminal and the victim. In addition to infringing on the concrete interests of victims, crimes violate the sovereignty of those victims, expressing disrespect for their right to self-determination. The crime places the victim and the aggressor in a relationship of relative inequality such that the aggressor violates the victim's sovereignty in order to promote his own interests, imputing lesser standing or importance to the victim. Even unsuccessful attempts express the offenders' disregard for their victims' standing. Criminal punishment, then, can be understood as vindicating the victim's sovereignty and rectifying an imbalance not in the concrete benefits and burdens of the parties, but in the relationship of equality under the law. The punishment represents a public repudiation of the aggressor's violation of the victim's right to self-determination and a public vindication of the victim's standing as a sovereign person.[43] In contrast, when the state fails to prosecute and punish violations against certain classes of citizens, such as prostitutes or transients, this failure effectively ratifies the imputation of inferior status to these parties.

On this view, the government can violate an individual's sovereignty either directly or indirectly. It can do so directly through state action that intrudes into the individual's domain of self-determination by violating political freedoms or that imputes inferior status to some through treatment that marks them as less important or worthy of respect than others. Constitutional law protects citizens from such direct violations. Second, the government can indirectly violate the individual's standing as an equal, sovereign person by acquiescing in criminal violations against her by another. Insofar as the criminal law defines and protects the contours of personal sovereignty, government derogates one person's standing indirectly when it subjects that person's sovereignty to violation by another by virtue of the manner in which it defines, enforces, or fails to enforce the criminal law.

C. Self-defense in the liberal society

When an innocent victim exercises force in self-defense against a fully responsible aggressor, the victim protects both her concrete interests and her right to self-determination, rejecting the imputation of inequality inherent in the unlawful aggression. Just as punishment for some attempted crimes can be justified at least partially as a vindication of the victim's sovereignty, self-defense can be justified as protection of sovereignty in cases such as SD2 that involve violations of the right to self-determination without apparent threat to concrete interests. The claim here is not that self-defense is a form of punishment or a down payment on punishment but rather that in a system of law representing a liberal political philosophy, both self-defense and punishment reflect a deeper value for the equal status of persons as autonomous individuals with their own spheres of personal sovereignty.[44]

On this view, any culpable criminal activity constitutes a serious transgression against the victim. An aggressor who commits even a minor crime not only threatens some minor concrete interests of the victim, he also violates the victim's sovereignty over some aspect of her life that is included in the sphere of self-determination that defines the standing of a citizen in that society. If the state did not defend the victim's right to self-determination against culpable violations by prosecuting and punishing those who committed offenses against her, it would indirectly violate her sovereignty by acquiescing in the offense and passively ratifying the imputation of lesser standing. Similarly, if the criminal law refused to recognize the victim's right to protect her own right to self-determination when state protection was unavailable, it would effectively require that she acquiesce in this violation of her sovereignty and imputation of lesser standing.

By initiating criminal activity in a manner such that the victim can prevent violation of her sovereignty only through the use of defensive force, the aggressor creates a situation in which either he or the victim must suffer some injury to interests that ordinarily merit legal protection. The victim's decision to protect her sovereignty through the exercise of force is not comparable, however, to a choice regarding which party will absorb equal and unavoidable injury.[45] By engaging in a criminal violation of the victim's sovereignty, the aggressor steps outside of the domain of central, self-regarding life decisions within which he can claim a right to freedom from interference. The victim's exercise of defensive force against the aggressor does not, therefore, violate his right to self-determination. In these circumstances, the victim must choose either to allow violation of her sovereignty or to inflict injury on the aggressor's concrete interests.

On the liberal theory, others cannot intrude into a competent person's right to self-determination for her own good because sovereignty is noncompensable. If a theory condemned paternalistic intrusions into a person's sovereignty but protected an aggressor's concrete interests at the expense of the victim's right to self-determination by forbidding her exercise of defensive force against that aggressor, it would effectively ratify the aggressor's imputation of lesser standing to the victim. It would do so by treating the aggressor's concrete interests but not the victim's as sufficient to limit the victim's right to self-determination. Thus the liberal theorist must allow the exercise of defensive force against an aggressor, even if the injury to that aggressor exceeds the setback to concrete interests the victim would have absorbed had she refrained from exercising force in self-defense.

The priority of the victim's sovereignty over the aggressor's concrete interests carries weight at the level of harm and at the level of risk. At the first level, the victim has no obligation to respect a requirement of proportion regarding concrete injuries; if she can protect herself from sustaining a black eye only by breaking her assailant's leg, for example, she has no obligation to absorb the black eye merely because a broken leg is disproportionate to a black eye. A victim may take any action against an aggressor necessary to prevent a culpable violation of her sovereignty by that aggressor because he steps outside his protected sphere when he attacks her. His sovereignty is not at stake, and her sovereignty takes priority over his concrete interests, just as it does over her own.

When a victim faces intrusion by an aggressor, she must decide how much force is necessary and sufficient to protect herself from that intrusion. As with any human decision, she might err, and the decision she makes reasonably includes a weighing of error preference. If the victim uses more force than necessary, she might harm the aggressor more than necessary to protect herself. If she uses less force than necessary, she might fail to dissuade the intrusion, possibly increasing the danger to her own interests. If, for example, V awakens during the night to find that A is climbing in through V's window,

V might hit A in the head with a baseball bat, or V might yell "stop or I'll brain you." If V does the former when the latter would have sufficed, V might severely injure A unnecessarily, but if V does the latter when the former was necessary, V might be severely injured (suppose A is armed and starts shooting). Just as A's culpable intrusion takes A beyond the bounds of his protected sphere and justifies V in protecting her sovereignty at the expense of harm to A's concrete interests, it also justifies V in granting priority to her right to self-determination regarding the error preference. Risk of intrusion into V's sovereignty takes priority over risk of unnecessary harm to A's concrete interests; thus V is justified in taking action necessary to repel the intrusion in a manner that places any risk of unnecessary injury on A.[46]

A similar analysis precludes a duty to retreat. A victim would have a moral duty to retreat from a place she legitimately occupied in order to avoid injuring an aggressor in self-defense only if that aggressor's concrete interests took priority over her sovereignty and concrete interests. In short, victims are constrained by the principle of necessity, but not by requirements of retreat or proportion regarding either harm or risk.

This interpretation justifies defensive force by appeal to considerations that differ markedly from those addressed by lesser-harms or forfeiture theories. In contrast to the lesser-harms position, this theory justifies victims in injuring aggressors by appeal both to the fundamental nature of the value for sovereignty in a liberal society and to the bounds of each individual's domain of protected choice. The noncompensable nature of the liberal right to self-determination gives priority to victims' sovereignty over aggressors' concrete interests, and culpable transgressions move aggressors beyond the boundaries of their protected domains, presenting victims with a choice between their sovereignty and the aggressors' concrete interests. When faced with this choice, victims may justifiably choose any necessary injury to the aggressors' concrete interests as the lesser sacrifice of important moral value. In doing so victims opt for the lesser evil although they inflict greater harm to aggressors' concrete interests than those aggressors would have inflicted on their victims' concrete interests.[47]

Some theorists contend that aggressors forfeit some right such as the right to life or bodily safety. Other writers reject forfeiture theories of self-defense because such theories seem to allow retaliation when the threat is over and to place the attacker outside the law's protection as an outlaw; yet we generally do not allow retaliation when the threat has terminated, and the law continues to protect the attacker from some conduct, including unnecessarily severe force.[48] On the account advanced here, defensive force is justified by the priority of the victim's sovereignty over the aggressor's concrete interests, not by forfeiture. Aggressors do not forfeit their sovereignty because their right to self-determination never extended to actions that intrude into victims' protected domains. Although victims may protect their sovereignty at the expense of aggressors' concrete interests, justified self-defense does not include unnecessarily severe defensive force because gratuitous injury would result in a net sacrifice of well-being without protecting the fundamental value for sovereignty.

The significance of sovereignty and equal standing in the liberal theory of self-defense differentiates self-defense from actions taken in response to threatening natural events. When natural events endanger two parties equally, neither has any obvious justification for shifting the loss to the other. Suppose, for example, that a flood is threatening two farms and that B can avoid the damage to his farm only by blasting the river bank in a manner that will redirect the flood entirely toward C's farm. B and C hold equal status, and neither is responsible for the natural event posing the danger to B. B has no grounds for violating C's interests or sovereignty to protect B's own. When the danger to B is much greater than the danger to C (for example, the bicyclist case LE1), B can choose to infringe on C's interests, but must compensate C because C retains equal standing with B. Under these circumstances, B can justifiably infringe on C's concrete interests without violating C's right to self-determination because B must choose between concrete injuries of disparate magnitude, and C's right to compensation vindicates C's sovereignty.

Sovereignty and equality of status under the law are properties of political relationships among persons. Natural events threaten concrete interests, but they do not threaten sovereignty or equality of status. Thus, two responsible but not culpable moral agents who encounter dangerous natural events must balance the respective harms to their concrete interests with no basis for weighing one party's interests over the other's. Contrast the clear self-defense case (SD1) in which culpable action by A threatens V's right to self-determination and concrete interests, providing a justificatory reason for V to favor her own sovereignty and interests over A's concrete interests.

Cases involving innocent aggressors resemble standard self-defense cases in that the threats to the victims' interests issue from human sources rather than from natural events. In the standard case, however, A's culpable violation against V justifies both V's use of defensive force against A, and the law's simultaneous condemnation of A's violation against V and ratification of V's use of force against A. Legal institutions justifiably differentiate between A's use of force and V's because A culpably creates the circumstances in which V must exercise force against A's concrete interests in order to protect her sovereignty. Innocent aggressors threaten their victims' concrete interests but they do not undermine sovereignty because they do not culpably deny the relationship of equal standing between the parties. The aggressor may be one who through no fault of his own does not realize that his conduct threatens the victim or one who believes that his harmful behavior is necessary and justified. The small child with the gun he thinks is a toy exemplifies the first type of innocent aggressor and the paranoid who shoots a policeman under the delusional belief that the policeman is a terrorist who is about to blow up the building exemplifies the second type.

Individual sovereignty plays a complex role in the relationships among aggressors, victims, and the social institutions within which they interact. By infringing on V's right to self-determination, A subjugates V's interests to his own and denies V's standing as a person who enjoys a sphere of sovereignty equal to that of all others in society, including A. In contrast, innocent aggressors threaten their victims' concrete interests, but they do not undermine their victims' sovereignty or their standing as equals. In order to understand why innocent aggressors do not erode their victims' sovereignty or standing, one must consider the relationship among sovereignty, equal standing, and self-respect. Each competent adult enjoys equal standing with all other competent adults in a liberal society by virtue of commanding a domain of personal sovereignty identical to that held by others.[49] Each such person participates in a community of equally sovereign persons and draws self-respect partially from this participation as an equal in a community of shared values.[50]

Innocent aggressors are not culpable for their transgressions because they suffer some disability or lack of information that prevents them from participating in the community as fully functioning members. For purposes of criminal liability, these innocent aggressors are excused by virtue of infancy, insanity, nonculpable mistake, or some similar excuse. When courts exculpate defendants by virtue of infancy or insanity, for example, they reaffirm the characterization of these defendants' conduct as offenses, but they exclude these defendants from the class of responsible persons who are appropriately held liable for criminal conduct.[51] By excluding these defendants from the class of responsible agents, the courts effectively remove them from the community of sovereign persons whose equal standing provides one source of self-respect for each. Thus, violations by these individuals do not impute lesser standing in the community to the victims because these aggressors have been excluded from the category of persons who participate in that community as equals.

Many agents from outside the community of equals, including natural events, animals, and innocent aggressors, can limit one's practical ability to choose within the domain usually protected by the right to self-determination. Legally sanctioned intrusions carry special significance, however, because law provides the official norms of the community. Direct legal intrusions impute lesser standing to the subject, and indirect legal intrusions ratify similar imputations by others. In contrast, legal rules that prohibit such intrusions and mark them as illegitimate repudiate the imputation of lesser status, reaffirming the standing of the victims and the bounds of their sovereignty. Thus, excused transgressions by innocent aggressors injure their victims' concrete interests, without undermining the victims' sovereignty or status as equals in the community.

The victims of these innocent aggressors encounter difficult choices among concrete interests with no grounds for disregarding those of the innocent aggressors. These victims may kill innocent aggressors rather than forfeit their own lives because they have no obligation to sacrifice their concrete interests for those of the innocent aggressors. They must retreat if they can do so safely, however, because the considerations of sovereignty and equal status that bar a duty to retreat from culpable aggressors do not apply. Victims who can avoid killing innocent aggressors by absorbing a less severe and compensable injury themselves ought to do so because this choice would produce the lesser concrete harm among innocent parties. Victims can claim subsequent compensation because they have no obligation to sacrifice their concrete interests to those of the innocent aggressor.

Cases involving innocent shields (IS) raise issues closely related to those involved in the IA cases. Consider the following examples.

(IS1): A stalks V for the clear purpose of killing V. Upon realizing that V has a gun and intends to kill A in self-defense, A grabs an innocent person (IS) and holds IS between V and himself for the purpose of discouraging V from shooting at A and for the purpose of using IS as a shield who will absorb the bullet if V fires. Can V fire at A, knowing that IS as well as A is highly likely to be killed?

(IS2): A stalks V for the purpose of killing her, and V can save herself only by grabbing IS and holding him in front of her while she reaches for her gun and shoots A. Here, as in IS1, V can save herself only by causing the death of both A and IS.

These two hypotheticals share the following common features: The culpable A initiates the danger; IS is entirely innocent; V can save herself only by causing the death of both A and IS. To many people, it seems intuitively clear that V may justifiably kill A but not that V can justifiably cause the death of IS. Although V can save herself only by causing the death of IS in either case, it is not at all clear that V is equally justified (or unjustified) in both cases. IS1 differs from IS2 only insofar as A holds IS while V shoots IS in IS1 and V holds IS while A shoots IS in IS2.

A simple lesser-harms calculation apparently precludes V from saving herself in either case, because she would be trading one culpable life and one innocent one for a single innocent life. If one disregards the life of A, then V must decide between innocent lives in both hypotheticals. If one frames the issues in this manner, there is no clearly superior action for V, but again, both cases appear to turn on the same choice. Yet, at least some readers will find intuitively that V seems more justified (or less unjustified) in IS1 than in IS2.

Consider IS1 first. A, V, and IS all stand to suffer the same concrete loss, in that each faces death. Under the approach advocated here, V can justifiably infringe A's concrete interests in order to protect her sovereignty from the threat that A culpably created. V and IS stand equally as two innocent lives. A culpably violates both of their spheres of sovereignty in order to threaten V's life, forcing V to choose between IS's life and her own. Although A's culpable aggression markedly distorts A's relationship with V and IS, it does not alter the relationship of equality between V and IS. Thus V has no justification for redirecting A's threat away from her and toward IS. As to the relationship between V and IS, A's threat resembles a natural event in that V has no grounds for favoring her own interests by shifting a comparable loss from either source to another innocent party. V would be justified, however, in saving her life at the cost of a compensable and significantly less severe injury to IS because by doing so she would choose the lesser of concrete harms and IS could claim compensation from either V or A. In short, the victim in IS1 encounters circumstances justifying self-defense against A but not justifying her in shifting comparable losses from herself to IS.

Although V can save herself only by causing the death of IS in either case, the interpretation advanced in this paper supports the intuitive inclination to say that IS1 and IS2 do not present morally equivalent circumstances. The explanation lies in the violation of IS's sovereignty. In IS1, A violates the sovereignty of both V and IS, forcing V to choose between the two innocent lives. In IS2, in contrast, it is V who violates IS's sovereignty, imputing a lesser status to IS than to herself. Although V is an innocent victim of A, V and IS do not stand as comparable parties in IS2 because V is a victim of A and a victimizer of IS, but IS is a victim of both A and V. V has an obligation not to violate IS's sovereignty for her own benefit in IS2.

In summary, self-defense must be construed in light of the broader political philosophy underlying the legal system. In a liberal society that respects the individual's right to self-determination and recognizes each sovereign person's equal standing, any culpable criminal conduct infringes on the victim's concrete interests and violates her sphere of self-determination. The aggressor creates an unfair imbalance of standing by culpably violating the victim's sovereignty, and according to a political philosophy that vests fundamental value in the individual's right to self-determination, any violation of sovereignty constitutes an injury to a fundamental interest. Liberal principles of political morality justify the victim in exercising any force necessary, therefore, to protect her sphere of self-determination against the culpable aggressor. She has no obligation to observe rules of proportion or retreat regarding the aggressor. She must not violate the sovereignty of an innocent party, however, and she must retreat rather than injure an innocent aggressor or shield. She has no obligation to allow an innocent aggressor to injure her and no justification for shifting the threat from herself to an innocent shield. Under certain circumstances, one can justify shifting lesser and compensable injuries.

IV Self-defense as morally justifiable law

Some critics might find this position wanting for at least two reasons. First, this theory apparently allows a victim to kill an apple thief.[52] By rejecting the principle of proportionality as a limit on the victim's exercise of force against culpable aggressors, this position allows severe violence when it is the only available means of preventing relatively minor transgressions. In addition to being intuitively questionable, this conflicts with predominant law which establishes a requirement of rough proportionality by establishing a series of rules for the use of deadly and nondeadly force in response to various types of threats to person or property.[53] Second, it may make unreasonable demands of impartiality in cases of innocent aggressors, shields, or bystanders. It may seem intuitively unreasonable to hold, for example, that victims are not justi-fied in protecting their lives at the expense of innocent parties. Can we realistically require such sacrifice to spare strangers?

A. Proportionality and the formal properties of law

Consider first the common intuitive response to the contention that one may justifiably kill an apple thief. Envision A stealing an apple from V and V shooting A because it is the only available means of preventing the theft. It seems likely that most people will imagine V as a farmer or vender and A as a child grabbing the apple and running away with it. If A is a child, however, the culpability condition is not met or, at least, it is in question. On the view advanced here, therefore, V should treat the case as one involving an innocent aggressor. If we replace the child with an adult, why would an adult engage in such activity? The most probable answer seems to be that this particular adult needs the apple very badly; that is, A is starving. If A is starving, however, the culpability condition again comes into question. When we fully describe the apparently counter-intuitive cases, A is likely to take on characteristics that render the transgression less than fully culpable due to incompetence or circumstantial pressure.[54]

Now complete the story carefully to establish a fully innocent victim, a fully culpable aggressor, and conditions that render the shooting necessary to stop the theft. Suppose V is an elderly farmer who grows apples in an orchard and sells them at the local market. A is the local bully who walks up to the farmer's stall at the market and takes the apple. When the farmer says "Stop, that is my apple," the bully responds "Tough, old lady, what are you going to do about it?" The farmer, who is old, frail, and less than arm's length away from the bully takes a gun from under her apron and shoots him.[55] Does this victim shooting this apple thief provide the intuitively clear case of an immoral act that we usually accept as an intuitive counterexample? When filled in with details that render A fully culpable and the shooting actually necessary to stop the culpable violation of V's sovereignty without submitting V to additional risk, it does not seem counterintuitive to me to say that V was justified.

Law, however, cannot adapt to each individual case and detailed hypothetical. The role of law requires that legal rules prohibit or justify relatively broad categories of conduct. The principle of legality mandates that "conduct is not criminal unless forbidden by law which gives advance warning that such conduct is criminal."[56] Fuller describes a set of requirements that he contends are necessary to qualify a set of norms as a system of law. He includes generality, constancy through time, and congruence between official action and declared rule. Fuller argues that these principles constitute a formal "inner morality of law" that must be satisfied in order to qualify an institution as a system of law.[57] Hart denies that these properties constitute a morality of law, but he agrees that such characteristics are necessary for an effective legal system.[58] Penal statutes must take the form of relatively broad proscriptions or exceptions that provide notice, address the variety of factual circumstances that actually occur, and allow relatively consistent application across time and circumstances. These rules are intended to state the conventional social morality of the society at a level of generality sufficient to reinforce that morality, guide individual conduct in conformity with the law, and guide decisions of officials in the enforcement of the law.

Officials who make and enforce the law must consider error preference, just as individual citizens must. A general rule of law allowing citizens to apply as much force as necessary to prevent culpable violations of their sovereignty would call upon individuals in highly stressful situations to make two complex determinations with little or no opportunity for evidence gathering or reflection. They would have to make instant appraisals of culpability and necessity. The rough rule of proportion represented by the dominant contemporary approach to the justified use of defensive force can be understood as an attempt to guide these decisions according to the moral principles presented in this paper with adjustments for practical limitations and defensible error preferences.

The MPC allows defensive force when it is immediately necessary to prevent an aggressor from using unlawful force. The code limits the use of deadly force, however, to situations in which the victim believes it necessary to protect herself from deadly force, kidnapping, or compelled sexual intercourse.[59] Although the code does not require retreat before using nondeadly force in self-defense, it does prohibit the use of deadly force when safe retreat is available. This retreat requirement does not apply, however, when the attack that justifies self-defense with deadly force occurs in the victim's dwelling or place of work.[60] The commentaries do not provide a comprehensive justification for these rules regarding proportionality and retreat, but they suggest that the rationale for both is primarily consequentialist in that they represent a decision to accept some relatively minor injuries and violations of rights in order to avoid loss of life. These comments assert that protecting human life enjoys a high priority among societal values, and they represent this value as the cornerstone of a lesser-harms rationale.[61]

A strictly consequentialist approach based on a preference for lesser concrete harms would apply proportionality and retreat requirements to all applications of force in self-defense unless there were good reasons to think that other considerations such as deterrence would support different rules as promoting lesser harm in the long run. Fletcher's theory, in contrast, would allow any force necessary to repel the aggression without regard for proportion or retreat because "right need never yield to wrong."[62]

The approach advanced in this paper explains these requirements in a more satisfactory manner than either Fletcher's theory or the lesser-harms rationale apparently advocated in the commentaries.[63] It does so by appealing to the primary importance of personal sovereignty adjusted for the necessary generalization of legal rules and a preference for nonfatal errors. The argument advanced in section III contends that the innocent victim is justified in exercising any force necessary to repel a culpable aggressor without regard for proportion or retreat. In order to avoid tragic errors, however, a law based on such a rationale could require safe retreat before exercising deadly force. Such a rule would qualify the practical priority of sovereignty in order to prevent fatal errors produced by inaccurate judgments of necessity or culpability.

This account does not endorse the high priority for protecting human life without regard for culpability that the MPC commentaries suggest. Rather, the priority accorded the protection of human life varies according to culpability, and an innocent person's right to self-determination takes priority in principle over the culpable aggressor's life when deadly force is necessary to protect the sovereignty of the innocent victim. It is not clear, however, that the code consistently endorses the priority for protection of life asserted in the commentaries. The MPC allows deadly force in self-defense when necessary to prevent kidnapping or compelled sexual intercourse. The code's authors may have considered these crimes to be among those that carried the most serious risk of deadly injury. It is at least as plausible to contend, however, that the severity of these crimes lies in the extreme degree to which they deprive the victims of the opportunity to exercise their right to self-determination. Offenders who commit these crimes exercise a degree of physical control over their victims that almost completely deprives them of personal discretion. By doing so, these crimes strike at the heart of the fundamental value for individual sovereignty.

Similarly, the dwelling place exception to the retreat rule can be understood as recognizing the importance of the sovereign person's ability to retain control of the single place in the world that is most clearly his or her own, not necessarily in the sense that the individual holds title to it, but rather in the sense that it is the place in which that person's decisions and actions are least susceptible to intrusion from the requirements of others.[64] In short, this analysis can accommodate the intuitively plausible proportionality and retreat requirements of the MPC without sacrificing the principled priority of individual sovereignty over the balancing of harms.[65] These requirements represent practical qualifications of the basic principles, and they are grounded in error preference, the formal properties of law, and hypotheses regarding human propensity to err. As such, they should remain open to modification in light of further empirical evidence.[66]

B. Innocent parties and se defendendo

The second set of problem cases involves the exercise of defensive force under circumstances that intuitively seem to justify neither the use of force nor punishment of the victim for exercising that force. These cases arise, for example, when A threatens V with severe harm in circumstances in which V can prevent that harm only by killing innocent parties. Suppose, for example, that A has taken two innocent hostages as shields and is about to kill V. V can prevent A from killing her only by taking action that will result in the deaths of A and both innocent hostages. On the analysis advanced in section III, V is justified in killing A but not in killing the two innocent hostages.[67] Yet, some people will find it unreasonable to hold V liable to criminal sanctions if she defends herself by causing the death of A and both hostages.

Fletcher's theory addresses such cases through the *se defendendo* excuse. This excuse applies when the threat is so severe and imminent that it elicits an involuntary reaction in self-protection. The victim responds reflexively to an imminent threat to life in a manner that leads many people to say that the victim had "no real choice." Thus, V is excused from liability although the action was not justified.[68]

Cases of this type, and the *se defendendo* defense generally, raise perplexing issues because excuses usually apply to defendants who suffer some disability that differentiates those defendants from the population in general and gives rise to an excusing condition that justifies exculpation.[69] The insanity defense, for example, exculpates defendants who suffer a serious psychological disorder (disability) that differentiates them from most people and prevents them from understanding that their conduct is wrongful (excusing condition). In the hypothetical described above, however, V suffers no disability differentiating her from most people. One might think of this case as appealing to two separate defenses. Suppose V raises the justificatory defense of self-defense regarding her killing A and the duress excuse regarding her killing the two innocent shields. Duress is usually classified as an excuse exculpating defendants who commit offenses in response to coercive pressure of such magnitude that a person of reasonable firmness would have been unable to resist. Duress is considered an excuse in that defendants who encounter such coercive circumstances are exculpated not because their conduct was justified, but because they were unable to control their conduct in the face of severe pressure.[70]

Consider the following hypothetical case which raises the duress defense. V runs a day-care center where he takes care of several preschool children. Mobsters enter the school, place a gun at the head of V's child, and threaten to kill the child unless V tells them which of the other children belong to a rival mobster on whom they plan to take revenge by killing his children. If V identifies the mobster's two children to save his own, V has traded two innocent lives for one, but V would have a plausible argument for the duress defense. This case of duress, like some of the problematic self-defense cases, involves unjustified conduct which is no worse than many reasonable, responsible people would probably perform under the circumstances. Although duress is usually categorized as an excuse, it includes a reasonable person standard usually thought more appropriate to a justification. Excuses usually exculpate those who suffer some impairment differentiating them from most people, yet the reasonable person clause appeals to the similarity between the defendant's action and that which most reasonable people would perform.

Although duress and *se defendendo* cases appear to be hybrid combinations of justification and excuse, they qualify as neither. They do not qualify as justification because they apply to conduct that society does not condone and wants to discourage. Both cases described above, for example, involve the sacrifice of two innocent lives to save one. The defendants in these two hypotheticals fail to meet the usual requirements for excuse because they do not suffer identifiable disabilities giving rise to excusing conditions. The usual formulations of duress and *se defendendo* ostensibly address actors who were unable to control their conduct. Intuitively, we tend to say that these actors "had no choice," "could not control themselves," or "were unable to resist the pressure." We are unable, however, to provide any satisfactory explication of these phrases. These actors do not suffer any impairment comparable to paralysis or convulsion that severs the usual association between directed physical movement and psychological processes such as deliberation and decision. They direct their conduct in a coordinated manner according to their decisions. These cases are exceptional due to the extremely difficult choices these defendants faced. Our intuitive judgment that we ought not punish them reflects neither justification nor disability-based excuse but rather the recognition that few people would have performed differently in these circumstances.

The criminal law ordinarily addresses wrongful conduct committed by responsible agents under difficult circumstances through mitigation in sentencing. By mitigating the degree of punishment, the law recognizes the defendant as less blameworthy for any of several reasons including unusually difficult circumstances.[71] If one interprets the *se defendendo* and duress defenses as claims of mitigation rather than excuse, then these defendants contend they deserve less punishment than most people who commit similar offenses because they are less blameworthy. Mitigation ordinarily reduces the severity of punishment, however, rendering it apparently inadequate for cases in which it seems intuitively unfair to submit the defendant to any punishment.

The criminal law constitutes a substantial component in the conventional morality adopted by a society as the framework required for cooperative social interaction. Mitigation's role in this framework differs significantly from that of excuse. Defendants who assert excuses contend that they did not act in the capacity of responsible agents who are accountable within the conventional morality, while those who assert mitigating conditions acknowledge their standing as accountable agents but contend that certain recognized conditions render them less blameworthy than those who commit similar offenses under ordinary circumstances. When compliance with the law would require exceptional discipline or fortitude, they contend, then the blameworthiness and appropriate punishment of those who fail to comply decreases just as the praise deserved by those who comply increases.

If the criminal law represents the conventional social morality we need for cooperative interaction, then one who is not blameworthy by the standards of the criminal law is not necessarily blameless by the most stringent moral standards, but rather one who displays the degree of moral discipline and fortitude that citizens must generally exercise in order to maintain the cooperative social process. Just as the criminal law does not forbid every type of wrongful conduct that critical morality would prohibit, it does not require the degree of moral discipline and fortitude that an ideal critical morality would demand. Rather, the criminal law proscribes those types of conduct which if generally engaged in would prevent effective social cooperation, and it requires the level of discipline and fortitude that citizens must generally exercise in order to maintain social cooperation. Individuals who encounter extraordinarily coercive circumstances might commit unjustified and unexcused offenses although they have exercised the degree of discipline and fortitude required by the conventional social morality.

The responsible defendant who kills the aggressor and two innocent shields in order to save herself, for example, commits an offense that is not justified under the moral theory of self-defense advanced in section III, and as stipulated, she suffers no disability that establishes an excuse. The degree of fortitude required to refrain from saving herself in those circumstances, however, may well exceed that which the criminal law generally requires in order to maintain cooperative interaction.

On this view, the criminal law defines and enforces the degree of individual discipline and fortitude required to maintain cooperative social interaction by punishing those who fall below this level while committing unjustified and unexcused offenses. Offenders who fail to exercise the required discipline and fortitude are blameworthy by the standard of the conventional social morality and subject to punishment. If the system allocates punishment to offenders in proportion to their blameworthiness for their offenses, then circumstances that demand unusual discipline and fortitude mitigate blameworthiness, reducing the appropriate punishment. Extraordinary circumstances may elevate the level of discipline and fortitude required for compliance beyond that which the conventional social morality demands for cooperative social interaction. Those who commit offenses in response to such extreme circumstances are not blameworthy by the standards of the conventional morality because they have not fallen below the level of discipline and fortitude required by those standards.

These offenders are neither justified nor excused, yet they are not appropriately subject to punishment. As usually understood, legal punishment involves harsh treatment of an offender, for an offense, administered by an authority in such a manner as to express moral condemnation.[72] The harsh treatment usually takes a form, such as incarceration, that expresses condemnation in that society, and the severity of the punishment is usually intended to reflect the degree of condemnation deserved by the offender. Individuals who commit offenses under extremely demanding circumstances merit conviction by the standards of the criminal justice system because they have fulfilled the offense elements without justification or excuse; yet they do not deserve punishment because they are not blameworthy by the standards of the conventional social morality which does not require heroic discipline and fortitude.

When extraordinary circumstances render the defendant inappropriate for blame and punishment by the standards of the system but do not provide any justification or excuse, then mitigation completely precludes the harsh treatment that expresses condemnation within the system, but it does not preclude conviction. This pattern of "systematically complete mitigation" leading to conviction without the harsh treatment that constitutes part of punishment would serve an important expressive purpose. These "purely vindicating convictions" would vindicate the law that proscribes acts of these types as defined at the level of generality available in the penal code and they would vindicate the standing of the victims by acknowledging that they were wronged. They would also recognize, however, that the defendant acted under conditions such that they were not blameworthy by the standards of the conventional morality represented by the criminal law.

C. Two potential criticisms

Critics might raise two objections to the proposed purely vindicating convictions. First, they might claim that it is inconsistent to contend both that criminal punishment inherently expresses condemnation and that some defendants should be convicted while they are not sufficiently blameworthy to merit the harsh treatment that constitutes part of legal punishment. These critics would argue that this practice implicitly asserts both that these defendants are appropriate subjects of condemnation and that they are not. Purely vindicating convictions vindicate just because they represent social condemnation of the defendant's conduct, they contend, yet we withhold the harsh treatment on the premise that these defendants are not sufficiently blameworthy to merit the condemnation represented by punishment. Second, some critics might contend that there is no difference between exculpation under excuse and this conception of mitigation to purely vindicating conviction. In either case, the verdict rejects the claim that the act is justified but exempts the actor from punishment.

Purely vindicating conviction avoids contradiction because the apparent inconsistency actually reflects the complexity of the institution of punishment. Any particular case of legal punishment involves the application of a complex social institution of punishment to a particular person for a particular offense. The institution must define both offenses and conditions of culpability in terms of relatively broad properties that do not capture every morally significant factor.[73]

Purely vindicating convictions reflect the separate functions of justification, excuse, and mitigation within the conventional morality represented by the criminal law, and they provide a legal devise through which officials can express the social judgment relevant to this conventional morality in a more precise manner. They ratify the systemic prohibition of acts of the type performed by the defendants as defined at the level of generality available to the system, and they recognize these defendants as accountable agents who have committed offenses as defined by the code. They withhold harsh treatment, however, in recognition of the specific factors that rendered conformity in these cases so difficult as to demand discipline and fortitude beyond that required by the conventional social morality.

In short, purely vindicating convictions reaffirm systemic condemnation of acts of the type performed by the defendant but withhold condemnation from this defendant for this particular act due to the extremely demanding circumstances. These convictions provide us with an official procedure for communicating to the defendant, "you are a responsible person, and acts of the type you performed are prohibited, but we realize both that under those conditions we probably would have done the same thing and that cooperative social interaction does not require heroism."

Although purely vindicating conviction and excuse both exempt the actor from harsh treatment without approving of the act as permissible, they are not interchangeable. Excuses exempt defendants who manifest excusing conditions due to disabilities that undermine their status as accountable agents who are appropriately subject to punishment. Excuses usually cite some impairment of the actors' capacities that deprived them of the functional abilities that we expect people to exercise in order to conform to the law, or they cite some source of ignorance or mistake that deprived the actor of the information needed to effectively exercise their capacities.[74] In contrast, purely vindicating conviction provides a method for explicitly recognizing those situations in which responsible actors fail to conform to the law for reasons that neither justify their acts nor undermine their status as responsible agents but which render punishment inappropriate in a system representing the conventional social morality required for cooperative social interaction. Categorizing these cases as excuses distorts them by directing attention away from the highly significant circumstances and toward nonexistent disabilities.

Some critics might contend that these actors suffered disabilities in that they lacked the capacities needed to conform in these circumstances. This interpretation distorts the relevant notions of responsibility and disability. The disability that grounds an excuse must differentiate excusable defendants from responsible agents and give rise to an accepted excusing condition.[75] Ordinarily, these disabilities deprive the offender of the capacities identified by Hart as capacity-responsibility.[76] On this understanding, "capacity-responsibility" refers to competence for a particular role; that is, the role of a citizen who can participate in the conventional social morality represented by the criminal law. Individuals possess the relevant capacities to greater or lesser degrees, and to say of persons that they are responsible in this sense is to say that they possess these capacities at least to the degree that we ordinarily require of persons before we hold them accountable under the law. Actors suffer disabilities relevant to these capacities when their level of ability falls below this norm defined by the minimally accountable citizen. Thus, to assert that an actor who possesses the capacities of ordinary citizens suffers a disability because he failed to successfully conform in unusually difficult circumstances is to distort this usual conception of capacity-responsibility by misrepresenting extraordinarily demanding circumstances as defective capacities.

In addition to distorting the relevant concepts, this interpretation of these cases as involving excuses denigrates the defendants and misleads concerned citizens. It denigrates the defendants because it misrepresents them as falling below a standard that most people meet, and it misleads the rest of us because it allows us to direct our attention toward the putative defects of these particular defendants without confronting the uncomfortable likelihood that they acted as they did not because they differ from us but rather because they are very much like us.

V Conclusions

The moral justification of self-defense reflects broad underlying principles of social morality. In a liberal society that vests fundamental value in the individual's right to self-determination and recognizes each sovereign person's equal standing, any culpable criminal conduct infringes on the victim's concrete interests and violates her sphere of sovereignty. The aggressor imputes inequality of standing by culpably violating the victim's protected domain, and in a liberal society any violation of sovereignty constitutes an injury to a fundamental interest. The victim may exercise any force necessary, therefore, to protect her sphere of self-determination against an aggressor whose culpable conduct extends beyond his own protected domain. She has no obligation to observe rules of proportion or retreat against an aggressor, but she must consider the interests of innocent aggressors or shields and must not violate the sovereignty of an innocent party.

Certain common legal provisions requiring retreat or rough proportionality may be justifiable as qualifications of the basic moral principles in light of the formal properties of law, defensible error preferences, and reasonable hypotheses regarding human propensity to err. These provisions should remain open to revision, however, if evidence undermines the empirical hypotheses that support them. In certain cases, actors exercise force in self-defense under circumstances that seem to justify neither their exercise of force nor their punishment. These cases reflect the complex nature of the institution of punishment and the relationship between ideal critical morality and the conventional social morality represented by the criminal law. These actors should be subject to purely vindicating convictions, reflecting systemically complete mitigation.

Although this paper advances an interpretation of justified self-defense in a liberal society, it does not endorse cultural relativism. The moral justification of self-defense and of the law of self-defense reflects the conventional social morality represented by the legal system, and that conventional social morality reflects underlying principles of political philosophy. It does not follow, however, that all political philosophies are equal. Evaluating competing theories of political philosophy remains an important task of critical moral theory. The moral justification of the theory of self-defense advanced in this paper depends ultimately on the justification of liberal political morality.

Notes

* I am grateful to Robert Audi and Stephen Kalish for helpful comments on an earlier draft of this paper and to Dennis Moynihan for capable research assistance. Joel Feinberg has contributed to this paper, as he has to so much of the contemporary work in legal and moral philosophy, through his writing and teaching. There is absolutely no admissable evidence, however, to support the rumors suggesting that it was purloined from the files of Josiah S. Carberry.

1 For the sake of convenience, I will employ the following conventions. Capitol letters such as "V" or "A" will represent specific parties in hypothetical cases. I will refer to general categories of actors in the text by spelling out the terms including "victims," "aggressors," and so on. Innocent aggressors will be identified as such in the text and represented by "IA" in hypotheticals. Thus, any aggressor represented as "A" is a culpable aggressor.

2 Perplexing questions also arise regarding the duties of third parties. I will not address these issues here, however, because they involve more general matters regarding the nature of justification defenses. George Fletcher, *Rethinking Criminal Law* 759–875 (Boston: Little, Brown and Co., 1978), [hereinafter *Rethinking*]; Joshua Dressler, *New Thoughts About the Concept of Justification in the Criminal Law,* 32 U.C.L.A. L. Rev. 61 (1984); Kent Greenawalt, *The Perplexing Borders of Justification and Excuse,* 84 Colum. L. Rev. 1897 (1984); Robert F. Schopp, *Justification Defenses and Just Convictions,* 24 Pac. L.J. 1233, 1282–1300 (1993).

3 *Rethinking, id.* at 855–75; Dressler, *id.* at 1163–5.

4 Courts frequently interpret statutes and common law rules by engaging in "policy analysis" of the legislative intent, social purposes, and legal principles supporting an interpretation of the specific rule. It may be more appropriate for courts to pursue this narrower form of policy analysis in order to restrain judicial latitude, but this paper pursues a scholarly inquiry rather than a judicial decision.

5 *Rethinking, supra* n. 2, at 759. Defendants who raise justification defenses concede that they fulfilled the offense elements but contend that their acts were not wrongful under the circumstances. Those who claim excuse concede that their acts fulfilled the offense elements and that these acts were wrongful but contend that they should not be held accountable for their conduct. Although various aspects of the theory of justification and excuse remain controversial, the broad distinction is widely accepted.

6 *Id.* at 857–60.

7 *Id.* at 860–8.

8 *Id.* at 862–4; George Fletcher, *The Right and the Reasonable*, 98 Harv. L. Rev. 949, 964–71 (1985) [hereinafter *Right and Reasonable*]; George Fletcher, *Punishment and Self-Defense*, 8 Law & Philosophy 200, 208–11 (1989) [hereinafter *Punishment*]. The theory attributed here to Fletcher is derived from several of his writings, some of which were not directed primarily toward self-defense. Although it is intended as an accurate representation of Fletcher's position, it may include some claims that he would not endorse.

9 A different conception of autonomy as personal sovereignty will be discussed later in section IIIB.

10 *Right and Reasonable, supra* n. 8, at 968–71; *Punishment, supra* n. 8, at 209–10.

11 *Rethinking, supra* n. 2, at 865–6.

12 *Id.* at 856–7.

13 George Fletcher, *The Right to Life*, 13 Ga. L. Rev. 1371, 1387–8 (1979) [hereinafter *Right to Life*].

14 *Rethinking, supra* n. 2, at 762–9; *Right and Reasonable, supra* n. 8, at 971–80. This issue, like third party duties, involves the nature of justification defenses generally and will not be addressed in this paper. *See* Schopp, *supra* n. 2, at 1267–82.

15 George Fletcher, *Should Intolerable Prison Conditions Generate A Justification Or An Excuse For Escape?*, 26 U.C.L.A. L. Rev. 1355, 1359–65 (1979) [hereinafter *Prison Conditions*]. By "right" Fletcher apparently means morally correct or superior rather than merely permissible.

16 Joshua Dressler, Understanding Criminal Law 84–5 (New York: Matthew Bender, 1987).

17 *Rethinking, supra* n. 2, at 871.

18 This discussion of the distributive approach draws primarily on the work of Phillip Montague and B. J. Smart. Montague explicitly designates his theory as a distributive one, while Smart presents his approach as rectificatory. I will draw primarily on Montague and secondarily on Smart.

19 Phillip Montague, *Self-Defense and Choosing Between Lives*, 40 Phil. Stud. 207, 216 (1981) [hereinafter *Choosing*]; Phillip Montague, *Punishment and Societal Defense*, 2 Crim. Just. Ethics 30, 32 (1983) [hereinafter *Societal Defense*]; Phillip Montague, *The Morality of Self-Defense: A Reply to Wasserman*, 17 Phil. & Pub. Aff. 81, 81–2 (1988) [hereinafter *Morality*].

20 *Choosing, id.* at 216; *Societal Defense, id.* at 31–2; *Morality, id.* at 81–8.

21 *Choosing, id.* at 215–16; *Morality, id.* at 82, 88.

22 B. J. Smart, *Understanding and Justifying Self-Defense*, 4 Int'l J. of Moral & Soc. Stud. 231, 237–42 (1989). Montague presents his theory as one of justified distribution rather than restitution.

23 *See supra*, n. 3 and accompanying text.

24 This paper will not attempt to defend liberal political philosophy. Rather, it will advance an account of morally justified self-defense within the liberal tradition.

25 American Law Institute, Model Penal Code and Commentaries §§ 3.04(1), (2)(b),

3.11(2) (Official Draft and Revised Comments, 1985). This paper will set aside the issue regarding the significance of necessity as opposed to the actor's beliefs about necessity because this controversy raises more general issues about the nature of justification defenses. *See* Schopp, *supra* n. 2 at 1267–82.

26 *Id.* at § 3.02.

27 *Id.* at § 3.01(2); The Law of Torts 147–8 (W. P. Keeton, ed.) (St. Paul, Minn.: West Pub. Co., 5th ed. 1984).

28 In specifying that he will injure V if but only if V moves, A may seem like an unusually precise thug. A is not uncommon, however, among the growing criminal subclass of unemployed-philosopher/mugger.

29 By "concrete" interests, I mean those involving one's material or physical concerns. In the current ordinary sense, "concrete" means "combined with or embodied in matter, actual practice, or a particular example; existing in a material form as an actual reality, or pertaining to that which so exists. Opposed to abstract." Oxford English Dictionary (Oxford: Oxford Univ. Press, compact ed. 1970). In this paper, concrete interests are those that involve the holders' physical, material, or financial well-being as opposed to their political standing or status. An earthquake or a declining market, for example, could severely impair the concrete interests of property holders without affecting their legitimate rights in their property. Conversely, zoning laws that prohibited members of certain racial groups from buying homes in certain neighborhoods would undermine the political standing of all members of that group, although these laws may have no effect on the concrete interests of the individual members of that group who lack the financial resources or desire to buy in that area.

30 By "sovereignty," I mean V's right to exercise discretion or authority over a specific domain. This concept will be developed further in the discussion of liberalism in section IIIB.

31 John Stuart Mill, On Liberty 68–69 (G. Himmelfarb, ed.) (New York: Penguin Press, 1974) (1859). "[T]he only purpose for which power can be rightfully exercised over any member of a civilized community, against his will, is to prevent harm to others. . . . Over himself, over his own body and mind, the individual is sovereign."

32 Joel Feinberg, Harm to Self 52–70 (New York: Oxford Univ. Press, 1986). Feinberg's conception of autonomy as sovereignty or a right to self-determination within a domain of personal control is similar to Fletcher's less completely articulated conception in that both can be understood as broad general rights to exercise discretion within a domain of recognized personal control. They differ, however, in that Feinberg vests fundamental value in personal sovereignty and develops political and legal structures designed to respect this underivative value. Fletcher's autonomy is apparently derivative in that it represents the individual's broad general right to exercise the specific rights and protected interests defined by the *Right*. Individual autonomy in this sense is derivative in that it depends upon some logically prior notion of morally sound law which defines the social order. On this view, the social order defined by morally sound law serves as the fundamental value. For this reason, it seems more appropriate to describe Fletcher's theory as

Right-based. In order to avoid confusion, however, I will continue to discuss this theory as the autonomy-based theory. I will refer to Feinberg's conception of autonomy as "sovereignty" or the "right to self-determination."

33 *Id.* at 54–5.
34 *Id.* at 57–62. Difficult issues arise regarding persons of questionable competence. Error preference becomes an important consideration in these cases. This paper will address error preference regarding self-defense in sections IIIC and IVA. For discussion of the role of error preference in paternalistic interventions, *see* Allen Buchanan & Dan Brock, Deciding For Others 41–7 (Cambridge Univ. Press, 1989); Robert F. Schopp, *Depression, the Insanity Defense, and Civil Commitment: Foundations in Autonomy and Responsibility,* 12 Int'l J. of Law & Psychiatry 81, 92–4 (1989).
35 John Rawls, A Theory of Justice 61, 243–51 (Cambridge, Mass.: Harv. Univ. Press, 1971).
36 Feinberg, *supra* n. 32, at 52–7.
37 Rawls, *supra* note 35, at 202, 440–6, 544–6.
38 *Id.;* Ronald Dworkin, Taking Rights Seriously 272–4 (Cambridge, Mass.: Harv. Univ. Press, 1968).
39 The purpose here is to describe a general principle of contemporary liberal theory. This paper does not defend or endorse any specific formulation.
40 Robert F. Schopp, *Education and Contraception Make Strange Bedfellows: Brown, Griswold, Lochner, and the Putative Dilemma of Liberalism,* 32 Ariz. L. Rev. 335 (1990).
41 Some types of activity might be criminalized for other reasons. Perjury, for example, is proscribed in order to promote the effectiveness of the legal system, and securities regulations are designed to promote effective functioning of the economy. Crimes such as those against person and property, however, help to define the individual's sphere of autonomy by forbidding others from intruding into those areas.
42 Herbert Morris, On Guilt and Innocence 31–58 (Berkeley: Univ. of Calif. Press, 1976).
43 Joel Feinberg, Doing and Deserving 104 (Princeton: Princeton Univ. Press, 1970). Feinberg discusses the role of punishment in vindicating the law.
44 *See generally, Punishment, supra* n. 8 (discussing the interpretation of self-defense as a down payment on punishment).
45 This liberal position differs in this regard from the distributive theory described in section IIB.
46 In some extended sense, any circumstances present some risk. On the account presented here, V is justified in sacrificing A's interests rather than subjecting herself to any realistic risk of harm created by A's culpable intrusion. Notice, however, that in most plausible cases, the principle of necessity provides substantial protection for A, because A can render the use of any force unnecessary simply by discontinuing the threat and acknowledging the wrong through surrender and compensation. Merely halting the attack may not suffice, particularly in contexts involving repeated aggression. I will not pursue this issue here.
47 Writers often use "lesser-evil" and "lesser-harm" interchangeably, but if "harm" is

understood as a setback to concrete interests, then the two must be distinguished because a lesser harm can constitute a greater evil. In a liberal society, a violation of sovereignty without substantial injury to concrete interests (e.g., SD2) may constitute a lesser harm but a greater evil as a greater violation of important moral value. The liberal who vests noncompensable value in personal sovereignty will hold that any violation of V's sovereignty by A constitutes a greater evil than does any necessary injury to A's concrete interests by V.

48 Hugo Bedau, *The Right to Life*, 1968 The Monist 550, 567–70; *Right to Life, supra* n. 13, at 1380–3.

49 The domains are equal at the abstract level of principle. They may differ, for example, in how much property the individual owns or controls. This paper discusses the significance of sovereignty and equal respect for self-defense by competent adults. Cases involving infants or incompetent adults as victims, bystanders, or shields raise additional issues that space limitations prevent me from examining here.

50 Rawls, *supra* n. 35, at 440–6; Joel Feinberg, Rights, Justice, and the Bounds of Liberty 151 (Princeton: Princeton Univ. Press, 1980).

51 Excuses exclude these defendants from the class of responsible agents for this particular act but not necessarily for all actions.

52 *Rethinking, supra* n. 2, at 871. Certain variations of the apple thief cases fall under self-defense or defense of property. Fletcher addresses these issues together as necessary defense, and the Model Penal Code addresses them in related provisions. *Supra* n. 25, at §§ 3.04, 06.

53 Model Penal Code, *supra* n. 25, at §§ 3.04–06.

54 Feinberg, *supra* n. 32, at 113–24. Feinberg argues for a variable standard of voluntariness according to which various degrees of coercion, ignorance, or impaired capacity can undermine voluntariness such that an act is not voluntary enough for a specific purpose.

55 The significance of the description of V as "frail and less than arm's length away" is not that V was afraid she would be attacked, but rather that she could not take out the gun and use it only as a threat because A could easily take it from her; that is, doing so would have put V at increased risk. Recall the discussion of the priority of sovereignty at the levels of harm and risk in section IIIC.

56 Wayne R. LaFave and Austin W. Scott, Jr., Substantive Criminal Law § 3.1 (St. Paul, Minn.: West Pub. Co., 1986).

57 Lon L. Fuller, The Morality of Law 33–94 (New Haven: Yale Univ. Press, revised ed. 1969).

58 H. L. A. Hart, The Concept of Law 61, 202 (Oxford: Oxford Univ. Press, 1961).

59 Model Penal Code, *supra* n. 25, at § 3.04.

60 *Id.* at § 3.04(2)(b).

61 *Id.* comments at 47–8, 52–7.

62 *Rethinking, supra* n. 2, at 865.

63 Fletcher does not intend to defend the code. He also recognizes, however, that most readers will find the pure autonomy theory counterintuitive in some cases. *Right to Life, supra* n. 13, at 1379.

64 This explanation does not address the workplace exception nearly as satisfactorily,

but the MPC is equivocal about the legitimacy of that exception. Model Penal Code, *supra* n. 25, at § 3.04 and comments at 55–7.

65 Some statutes limit self-defense (or deadly force) to cases in which V is threatened with imminent harm. The MPC does not require a threat of imminent harm, but it does require that the defensive force be immediately necessary to prevent the threatened harm. Model Penal Code, *supra* n. 25, at § 3.04(1). The MPC's position is consistent with the position advanced in this paper because force that is not immediately necessary may not be necessary at all, given V's fallibility in predicting future events. Recall, however, that V would not be required to postpone defensive force against A if doing so would increase the risk to V. It would not be consistent with the position advanced in this paper for the law to require imminence of harm because such a provision would preclude defensive force necessary to protect sovereignty merely because some delay would occur between the opportunity to exercise force and the unjustified injury. It is conceivable that an imminence requirement might be defensible as a concession to error preference similar to that which grounds the rough proportionality rules. It seems unlikely, however, that an imminence rule would serve this purpose more effectively than the "immediately necessary" clause.

66 The MPC's requirement that victims refrain from using deadly force when they can retreat in complete safety applies in relatively few cases if it is interpreted as written. Only rare circumstances will place a person in serious danger of unlawful attack, yet allow retreat with complete safety. Arguably, the law ought to be revised to remove these rough rules of proportionality from the substantive standards. On this view, it would be more consistent with the underlying moral principles to legalize any force necessary to defend oneself from culpable attack without exposing oneself to undue risk. Procedural devises such as the burden of persuasion could address these matters of error preference by requiring that the defendant carry that burden by showing that the force used was necessary in light of the risk in the circumstances. Addressing error preference procedurally would enhance the expressive function of the criminal law by allowing formulation of the substantive provisions in a manner that more nearly approximated the conventional social morality represented by the criminal law. A thorough analysis of procedural issues would extend well beyond the scope of this paper.

67 Readers persuaded by the argument in section III would conclude that V would not be justified in killing a single innocent hostage under these circumstances. I include two in this example in order to render it less controversial to those who think it calls for a balance of harms to innocent parties. *See* Schopp, *supra* n. 2 at 1300–21 for further development of the issues in section IVB.

68 *See supra,* section IIA.

69 Paul H. Robinson, Criminal Law Defenses § 161 (St. Paul, Minn.: West. Pub. Co., 1984).

70 Model Penal Code, *supra* n. 25, at § 2.09; Robinson, *id.* at § 177. Some jurisdictions do not allow this defense in homicide cases, but neither the MPC nor Robinson accept this limitation.

71 Model Penal Code, *supra* n. 25, at § 7.01(2); H. L. A. Hart, Punishment and Responsibility 14–16 (Oxford: Oxford Univ. Press, 1968).

72 Feinberg, *supra* n. 43, at 95–118; Hart, *id.* at 4–5.

73 *See, supra* section IVA; for a more complete discussion of the complex nature of the condemnation inherent in criminal punishment, *see* Schopp, *Wake Up and Die Right: The Rationale, Standard, and Jurisprudential Significance of Competency to Face Execution,* 51 La. L. Rev. 995, 1027–38 (1991); Schopp, *supra* n. 2 at 1258–67.

74 Robinson, *supra* n. 69, at § 161. Insanity and infancy excuse due to impaired capacity, and official misstatement of law or mistake regarding justification exculpate due to nonculpable ignorance.

75 *Id.* at § 161(a).

76 Hart, *supra* n. 71, at 227–30. Actors are responsible in this sense if they possess the capacities of understanding, reasoning, and control of their movement that enable most people to conform to the law.

13

Letting patients die: Legal and moral reflections[1]

SANFORD H. KADISH[2]

Since World War II dramatic advances in the power of medicine to sustain life have led to profound changes in the types of illness from which people die. At one time pneumonia, influenza, and other communicable diseases were the most common causes of death.[3] Today chronic, degenerative diseases such as cancer, heart disease and cerebrovascular disease have become predominant, accounting for approximately 70 percent of all deaths in the United States.[4] This in turn has shifted the locus of dying. Whereas at the turn of the century most patients died at home, today over 80 percent of deaths occur in hospitals. Patients with degenerative diseases can be kept biologically alive for long periods of time through the use of drugs and machines, though sensate and functional life has gone forever.[5] As a consequence, in the language of one court, "[q]uestions of fate have . . . become matters of choice raising profound 'moral, social, technological, philosophical and legal questions . . .' "[6] For example, does keeping people biologically alive in these circumstances make sense? Whose interests are served by sustaining a life so limited in scope? In what does the value of a life lie? What is the role of the patient's preferences in cases where he has made a competent current choice, where he has made an earlier choice, where he has made no choice? These questions, thrust upon us by advances in medical technology, raise doubts about the continued validity of some of our most deeply held moral beliefs about life and death.

Despite some paradoxes and inconsistencies (for example, in our attitudes toward war, capital punishment and risk), preservation of human life is generally seen as a supreme good in our culture.[7] Intentionally taking a life, at least an innocent life, is among the worst wrongs a person can commit. It is everywhere a crime, punishable by the severest penalties known to the law. Every innocent person, no matter the quality of his life, has a legal right that his life should not be taken.[8] Moreover, so great a value is put on life that a person may not waive his right to life; killing does not become nonculpable because the victim consented.[9] For similar reasons, suicide and attempted suicide were crimes at common law,[10] and helping another kill himself is still a crime in many American states.[11] Finally, although the law does not generally criminalize failure to save another, a physician who intentionally fails to save a patient's life when able to do so may be guilty of some form of culpable homicide. These norms constitute the moral tradition threatened by the remarkable power of medicine to prolong life. How can this tradition accommodate a deliberate decision not to use available medical power to save a life?

Departures from the official pieties usually occur first in our practices and only later in our professions.[12] So it has been with the issue of life-sustaining treatment. Doctors and hospitals have long engaged in or tolerated practices that contravene the moral tradition I have just described.[13] For decades doctors and hospitals have accepted what is called negative euthanasia. "Every day . . . respirators are turned off, life-perpetuating intravenous infusions stopped, proposed surgery canceled, and drugs countermanded. So-called Code 90 stickers are put on many record-jackets, indicating 'Give no intensive care or resuscitation.'"[14] And though medical killing on request (active euthanasia) is apparently not common, neither is it unknown in American hospitals.[15]

The public has come largely to accept these practices, principally through the impact of such dramatic and highly publicized cases as *In re Quinlan*.[16] In 1976, the New Jersey Supreme Court held that a parent of Karen Quinlan, a young woman in a permanent vegetative state, could authorize removal of a respirator which was keeping Karen biologically alive.[17] Since then public opinion polls have revealed an impressive shift of opinion in just one generation from a majority opposed to "pulling the plug" on permanently comatose patients to a large majority – sometimes nearly 90 percent – in favor of such measures.[18] Opinion as to whether doctors should be permitted actively to kill incurable and comatose patients has also changed. In 1947 a majority disapproved.[19] Since then majorities of up to 64 percent have favored such proposals.[20]

There appears to be even less dissent when the patient is not comatose and competently chooses to die. A recent national survey showed that 79 percent of adults support laws allowing terminally ill patients to refuse life-sustaining treatment or to order that it be stopped.[21] A recent California poll indicates that about 70 percent of Californians feel that assisted suicide of seriously ill patients who wish to die should be legalized.[22] In Washington state voters defeated a referendum proposing that doctors be permitted to kill terminally ill patients at their request by a vote of 56 percent to 44 percent.[23] But a month earlier a poll showed that of those likely to vote, 61 percent were in favor, 27 percent were opposed, and 12 percent were undecided.[24] The defeat of the referendum might have been a manifestation of the "cold feet" phenomenon that sometimes occurs when the voter enters the voting booth.[25] Despite this apparent setback, the marked increase in public acceptance of killing terminally ill patients, both in Washington and nationally, has been striking.

Equally striking are the changes in enacted laws. When Karen Quinlan became comatose in 1975 no state recognized a patient's right to set limits on life-prolonging medical efforts. Now over forty states have passed "living will" statutes,[26] giving effect to a person's choice of medical treatment in the event of incompetency.[27] Although these laws tend to be highly restrictive,[28] they nonetheless represent a radical departure from what could have been expected of a legislature a decade earlier. More significantly, many states have enacted statutes allowing a person to designate an agent, who, in the event of the patient's incompetence, could make those health care decisions which the patient himself could have made if competent.[29]

In light of this sea change in public, medical and legislative judgments, it was inevitable that American courts would be called upon to respond. Since the 1975 watershed opinion in the *Quinlan* case, there has been a rush of cases from the state and federal courts, with most decisions authorizing letting the patient die. These cases will figure prominently in this paper. Part I describes the courts' development of the right of autonomy, their use of it as the basis for changing the law, and the ways they sought to limit the scope of change portended by full application of that concept. Parts II and III deal with the problem of determining when patients may be left to die when the right of autonomy is not fully applicable, as in cases of advance directives, or not applicable at all, as in cases where the patient never made a choice during his competent life.

I. Autonomy and the competent patient

The fulcrum on which the courts moved the law away from its traditional hostility to forgoing treatment was the concept of consent. The requirement of consent goes back to the common law, which made it a battery to subject a person to any force to which he had not consented, including such force as might be involved in providing medical treatment.[30] In dealing with such issues as the constitutionality of laws prohibiting contraception and abortion, the United States Supreme Court gave new and powerful support to the common law concept of consent.[31] The Court developed a jurisprudence of autonomy (sometimes under the misleading label of privacy), finding in the Constitution a fundamental right of individuals to make choices with regard to their own bodies. The lesson of the new autonomy jurisprudence for refusals of medical treatment was plain, and the *Quinlan* case[32] was one of the first to draw it explicitly. In that case the New Jersey court found that just as the constitutional right of autonomy over one's body encompasses a woman's decision to have an abortion, so does it "encompass a patient's decision to decline medical treatment," at least under most circumstances.[33] Other courts soon followed the *Quinlan* lead.[34]

In *Cruzan v. Director, Missouri Department of Health*,[35] the United States Supreme Court, in an opinion by Chief Justice Rehnquist, went a good distance toward lending its authority to a constitutional right to refuse medical treatment. The case involved a Missouri statute requiring that before artificial nutrition and hydration could be withdrawn from a patient in a permanent vegetative state, it must be established by "clear and convincing" evidence that she had decided when competent not to be kept alive in these circumstances.[36] Although upholding the constitutionality of the Missouri standard, the opinion stated that the logic of the Court's prior opinions supported the existence of a patient's constitutionally protected interest in refusing life-sustaining medical treatment, including artificial nutrition and hydration.[37]

As the Court further noted in *Cruzan,* however, the existence of a constitutionally protected interest does not necessarily preclude state regulation, for a state might have sufficiently weighty interests to override that of the individual.[38] Indeed, state and lower federal courts have recognized four distinct state interests which weigh against the choice of a competent patient to decline treatment: (1) its interest in preserving life as such; (2) its interest in preventing suicide; (3) its interest in protecting the interests of innocent third parties; and (4) its interest in maintaining the ethical integrity of the medical profession.[39] Only the first two figure at all seriously in the decisions, however.[40] Though some courts have treated the interest in preserving life and the interest in preventing suicide separately,[41] they are obviously interrelated considerations.[42] It is noteworthy, however, that lower courts in virtually all cases have upheld the right of a patient to reject life-sustaining treatment as required by a constitutional right of autonomy, and as such outweighing these state interests.[43]

The problem that naturally arises concerning this right of autonomy is its extent. Does it come into play only in these medical contexts, or does it extend to all cases in which the person chooses to achieve his own death, including perhaps those in which he obtains the help of another to further his choice? Courts have declined to extend the right of autonomy to nonmedical contexts and have sought to avoid doing so by distinguishing these medical letting-die situations from conventional suicide and consensual euthanasia. Because such an extension would profoundly unsettle existing mores and might raise formidable problems for the law in preventing exploitation and abuse, it is not hard to understand the courts' motivation. Still, putting prudential considerations aside for the moment, can these distinctions withstand principled analysis?

One ground on which courts have sought to distinguish letting-die situations from conventional suicide is that the latter requires affirmative life-taking actions. On this view a patient refusing to be attached to an apparatus necessary for his survival is not taking his life, but is simply letting nature take its course. Hence death is caused by the disease, not by the person himself,[44] nor by the physician who respects his wishes. How persuasive is this distinction? Perhaps there is some support for it in the legal principle that imposes no duty to act to prevent a prohibited harm except in specified circumstances. After all, the traditional formulation of the ban on suicide is cast in terms of action,[45] so it is arguable that one who seeks death through inaction would not fall within the ban.[46] Yet it would be odd if that were so. The traditional disinclination of Anglo-American courts to interpret prohibitions on causing certain results as requiring action to prevent those results is based on the value of the freedom of the individual not to be constrained by the interests of others. But that value is not at stake in the prohibition of suicide for two reasons: First, because the interests of others are not necessarily involved, and second, because the ban on suicidal actions already constitutes a major inroad upon the person's freedom, so that excluding cases of passive choices to die out of concern for that very freedom would be eccentric at best.

In any event, if we view the issue in terms of moral principle rather than legal doctrine and take the traditional antisuicide position as a serious starting point, the distinction between intentionally killing oneself and intentionally submitting to an avoidable death is suspect. There is disagreement over the general moral significance of the distinction between doing and letting happen,[47] but the intuitive appeal of the distinction is less in some cases than in others, and its appeal seems particularly weak in cases of treatment refusal.[48]

Consider a patient who finds herself attached against her will to some life-sustaining apparatus she had earlier explicitly rejected. She removes it for the same reason she earlier rejected it – she prefers death to living attached to a machine – and dies moments later. Presumably this would constitute suicide, since she achieved her death by positive actions. But could we justifiably say that if the doctors had followed her instructions and she had died, this would not be suicide because her death would then not have been caused by her actions? Or consider an analogous case: A paralyzed person, sitting on a beach threatened by an incoming tide, deliberately, in order to end her life, declines to allow a lifeguard to move her out of harm's way, and drowns in consequence. (To make the analogy closer, assume she took no action to place herself in danger from the tide – say, for example, she was initially placed there against her will.) Would it not be correct to see this as a suicide? Yet the person dying of a disease who chooses not to permit some medical intervention which would save her is in no different situation.

We might have good reasons to think that in certain circumstances intentionally achieving one's death is justifiable, or that it is less blameworthy in some circumstances than in others. Moreover, we may for these reasons, or indeed for other reasons of a more practical and prudential character, want to call it something else. But as a matter of principle, that a person achieves her goal by refusing necessary medical intervention hardly seems a better reason to treat her action differently than that a person achieves her goal by letting the tide come to her rather than going to it.[49]

Another approach some courts have taken is to define suicide to require a purpose to take one's own life, sometimes called a specific intent. Those who reject treatment, it is reasoned, do not want to die; indeed, as one court put it, "they may fervently wish to live, but to do so free of unwanted medical technology, surgery, or drugs, and without protracted suffering."[50] When they reject treatment, therefore, they are not committing suicide.[51] Recently Ronald Dworkin has lent his considerable authority to this position.[52] In the course of criticizing Justice Scalia's argument in *Cruzan* that the venerability of the tradition of state condemnation of suicide establishes the state's equal entitlement to regulate treatment refusal,[53] Dworkin asserts that it is "bizarre to classify as suicide someone's decision to reject treatment that would keep him alive but at a cost he and many other people think too great."[54] He appears to be making two points: the first, that death is achieved by failing to act, I have already discussed; the second, that the person's decision is not suicide because his intention is not to achieve his death as such, but to avoid a life whose burdens are not worth the living, is an argument I take to be equivalent to the specific intent argument.

A case may be made for the specific intent argument in this context along the following lines. The purpose of the classic suicide in inflicting a mortal injury on himself, in the sense of purpose as the "conscious object" of an action,[55] is to cause his own death. The same cannot be said of all cases where the person refuses treatment he knows is necessary to keep him alive. In some of these cases his mental state with respect to his death is more properly characterized as knowledge rather than purpose;[56] that is, although he knows that his conduct will result in his death, his conscious object is not to die, but to be free of the medical treatment. That his object is not to die may be seen by noticing that if, contrary to the prediction of his doctors, he recovered without the treatment, it would not be the case that his purpose was frustrated. The same could not be said of the classic attempted suicide.

The trouble with this line of argument is that the distinction between purpose and knowledge in this context is without moral relevance. The cases where the refusal of treatment can be said not to reflect a specific intent to die are those in which the irremediable condition which makes living not worthwhile to the person is prospective rather than already existing. If it is in prospect, we are able to see his purpose as avoiding his affliction. But when the afflictive condition already exists, the ending of the person's afflicted life would presumably be seen as his purpose in refusing treatment. So, for example, if a patient refuses amputation of his gangrenous legs (because he doesn't want to live without them), his purpose is to avoid the amputation, not to die, so that his subsequent death would not be considered a suicide. He would have been pleased to live if his legs could be saved. But if a person whose legs have already been amputated refuses medical treatment necessary for his recovery (again because he doesn't want to live without his legs), his purpose is to die, so that his subsequent death *would* be counted a suicide. But except in the case where death is itself sought as an end (the insured who wants his beneficiary to recover on his life insurance, for example) all suicides are motivated by the desire to end experiencing something unbearable in the person's life. It is hard to see any point to treating choices to end one's life differently depending on whether the motivating condition is present or anticipated.

I suggest, therefore, that the efforts by courts to maintain the traditional authority of the state over suicide by distinguishing it from refusal of treatment do not withstand scrutiny. I do not mean to suggest that the law cannot justifiably make distinctions on pragmatic grounds; it frequently does so for all kinds of prudential considerations. I mean only to suggest that the distinctions under discussion cannot be defended *except* on pragmatic grounds.

Consider the basic argument courts and commentators make on behalf of the right to refuse treatment. The argument is that the choice between medical treatment and death is so fundamental that it is protected against state control by a constitutional right of autonomy. But that being the case, there is no principled basis for denying the same freedom of choice to those not dependent on medical treatment for survival. The failure of efforts to distinguish suicide from refusal of treatment is attributable not simply to usage and definition, but to the equivalence between the two. The moral case for autonomy extends to both if it extends to one.

It isn't hard to surmise why courts have drawn back from the conclusion that there is no difference between suicide and refusal of treatment. To accept it would be to acknowledge a radical break with the received tradition and open the door to positions the courts are not yet willing to adopt: for example, that the state may not act to prevent suicide (except perhaps temporarily to assure competent consent),[57] or to prevent a person from assisting another's suicide, or conceivably even to prevent one person from killing another who competently consents to being killed.[58] By "open the door" I do not mean that courts would be compelled by consistency to adopt these positions. There might well be compelling practical considerations for not doing so, such as fear of abuse and difficulties of administering controls to prevent such abuse.[59] I mean only that in not distinguishing suicide and consensual euthanasia the courts would by implication be endorsing these positions in principle. Yet this would be the greatest affront to the moral tradition. The courts, therefore, have chosen to improvise lines of distinction, even at the cost of some coherence, that permit the result they regard as right in the medical context, while giving at least the appearance of continuity with the established tradition and avoiding being pushed to positions that may be either impractical or premature. As I suggested, it is not unusual for common law courts to adopt lines of distinction out of unspoken considerations of strategy rather than of logic and principle. This is such a case.

Another way, besides distinguishing suicide, that courts have sought to confine the precedent of permitting patients to refuse life-sustaining treatment has been to stress the special circumstances of the particular case. Courts have emphasized that the patient was soon to die in any event,[60] or that he was in a permanently comatose condition,[61] or that the medical treatment was complicated and intrusive ("extraordinary").[62] The implication is that when the patient is not dying, but instead has some appreciable time to live, or when he is sensate, or when the treatment is not unusual and intrusive ("ordinary"), then the interests in preserving life as such and preventing suicide will prevail, and the patient will be compelled to submit to treatment.

It is hard to be sure whether the courts really mean this, or whether the qualifying language is meant as sugar coating to make the medicine go down. If the former, then much of the talk of autonomy in the cases is window dressing. After all, if what makes it proper to forgo treatment is the patient's inviolable right to choose, his choice can't be dependent on a court's willingness to let him have his way in some circumstances but not in others. Therefore, to the extent courts continue to insist that his choice *is* so dependent, they can no longer seriously defend permitting him to die on the ground that it is the patient's inviolable choice that they are enforcing and not their own. I expect that in the end these qualifying limitations are not likely to survive as part of the jurisprudence of forgoing medical treatment.[63]

II. Autonomy and the incompetent patient

The right of autonomy, then, is what ensures that a patient may refuse treatment. But autonomous choice requires a competent chooser. What of the cases (and most of the cases have been of this kind) where the patient is not competent? The response of the courts has been to rest on the intriguing argument that because incompetency cannot diminish a person's rights, denial of an incompetent's choice would constitute an unconstitutional discrimination on grounds of personal handicap.[64] At the outset, therefore, the cases of incompetents raise a formidable conceptual problem. How can the right of autonomy over one's own body have any application where the patient is incompetent to make a choice? Whatever rights an incompetent person may be said to possess, how can autonomous choice be one of them when incompetency means precisely the inability to exercise choice?[65]

First to summarize briefly what the courts have decided:[66] If the incompetent patient, at some time when he was competent, exercised his right to refuse medical treatment under circumstances like those now presented (possibly, but not necessarily, by a formal "advance directive" in a living will), the courts have been willing in most situations to give effect to that choice. So also where the patient, while competent, authorized another to make the choice in the event of his incompetence (by a so-called durable power of attorney). If, during his competency, he did not execute an advance directive, appoint an agent, or indicate a choice in some other way (which is the usual case),[67] the courts have invoked the concept of "substituted judgment" (sometimes called "surrogate decision making") under which the decider (the court, the family, or others – courts have disagreed on whether judicial intervention is necessary)[68] makes the choice on behalf of the incompetent.

A. Where the patient made a competent choice in the past: Advance directives

I will start with situations that seem to me to present the least difficulty, those where the patient has made an actual choice in the past. One set of such cases occurs when the patient is in a vegetative state that is known to be permanent. Lacking capacity now and forever for having experiences of any kind or for making a different choice, there is no basis for not respecting his earlier competent choice to die.

Cases at the other extreme also are easy; that is, those in which the person remains competent. If a competent patient decides to change his mind for some reason – perhaps because of new medical treatments, or because facing dying as a present reality is different than facing it as a future possibility, or perhaps because he has simply mellowed with age – the principle of autonomy requires, not just permits, that he may do so. There is, of course, the problem (to which I will return shortly) of determining whether a person is sufficiently competent to change his mind, which can be conceptually perplexing as well as practically difficult.[69] Assuming there is no question of his competence, however, the principle of autonomy requires the person's latest choice to govern.

The hard case is presented when a patient, plainly incompetent on traditional criteria, is still sentient. Consider this hypothetical. Composer Then is a famous musician whose whole life centers around music. She executes a durable power of attorney in favor of her son, instructing him that if she becomes permanently unable to experience music in any way, needs medical treatment to save her life, and is not competent to exercise choice, then no medical treatment should be administered to keep her alive. Assume that years later she is in precisely this condition, a victim of senile dementia, as well as of a life-threatening but readily curable disease. Call her Composer Now. But though disabled in the ways I have described and lacking competence as traditionally conceived, she still has some awareness and has the capacity for sensations. For example, suppose Composer Now smiles at the sight of her grandchildren, is apparently comforted by sitting in a garden or by being attended to and talked to, and shows preferences in foods and television programs. Assume further that she gives no sign of being uncomfortable, in pain, or unhappy. Finally, assume that when asked if she prefers to be left to die, she becomes agitated and says no, though how much she understands is unclear. (Shortly I will consider the hypothetical without this last circumstance.)

Should doctors be authorized (or required) not to treat the curable disease Composer Now has contracted because Composer Then would not have wanted her life to continue in these circumstances? Does vindication of Composer Then's autonomy require it? Or must Composer Then's earlier choice yield to Composer Now's present interest in continuing to experience the limited life available to her, as she now seems to want?[70]

Ronald Dworkin would apparently hold that Composer's right of autonomy requires that her earlier competent wish be respected:

A competent person's right to autonomy requires that his past decisions, about how he is to be treated if he becomes demented, be respected even if they do not represent, and even if they contradict, the desires he has when we respect them, provided he did not change his mind while he was still in charge of his own life.[71]

As he elsewhere emphasizes, he reaches this conclusion even in the harder case where the demented person "insists on and pleads for" medical treatment.[72] He argues that autonomy is the right to govern one's life, his life as a whole and not only part of it, so the right must extend throughout the life of the person – including the period of his incompetency, whether permanent or temporary (the "integrity" view of the person, as he calls it[73]). To fail to recognize the right of the person when competent to control his fate when incompetent violates what he calls the right of "precedent autonomy," whose point is to enable us "to lead our own lives rather than being led along them, so that each of us can be . . . what he has made himself."[74]

I do not dispute that the right of autonomy extends to having one's choices govern during periods of later incompetence – Ulysses' sailors would have been on solid ground in refusing to untie him as they passed the sirens, even if they could have heard his orders to do so. Nor do I hold that a person's right of autonomy may not be violated if he can never experience its violation, as is true of a person who will never regain his competence.[75] Rather I will argue, first, that in our Composer case (in contrast to Ulysses' case) precedent autonomy is not as compelling as an exercise of contemporary autonomy (i.e., a current choice) would be; and second, that such moral force as precedent autonomy has is morally overridden by considerations of human compassion.[76]

Dworkin tells us that he asked a number of people what they would prefer if they were suffering from senile dementia. He reports that they expressed a preference to be left to die.[77] I think he would have gotten a more mixed response if he had asked a different question – not what they would prefer for themselves if they were someone like Composer Now, but what they would do if they were responsible for deciding whether to treat Composer Now. A number of people to whom I have put both questions answer Dworkin's question the way he reports, but answer my question the opposite way. They themselves would prefer to be left to die rather than to hang on to a life so limited. They are not so ready, however, to inflict the same fate on another person on the basis of their own preference. But why not, if the patient indicated in her advance directive that that was her preference also? The reason, I suggest, is a lack of full confidence in the force of the earlier directive not to treat.

Some discounting of the advance directive in the Composer case is warranted on two grounds. First, the fact that advance directives are executed as future hypotheticals deprives them of the full moral force of contemporary choices. Unforeseen changes, such as new medical treatments, may substantially alter the person's interests. Moreover, the effect of severe, life-imperilling illness may well effect a marked revision in the attitudes and values of the person.[78] Indeed, even absent such traumas, it is common for people to reach very different conclusions depending on whether they are imagining a future hypothetical or confronting an immediate predicament – what they thought they would want often turns out very different from what they do want.[79] Finally, as Buchanan and Brock have pointed out, an advance decision to forgo life-preserving treatment is less likely than a contemporaneous choice to elicit protective and supportive responses from persons close to the patient; hence this informal safeguard against hasty and ill-considered action is not usually present in the case of advance directives.[80] In view of these considerations, disregard of the advance directive would not constitute as deep an inroad into the autonomy principle as would disregard of a contemporaneous choice.

This conclusion, of course, rests on the view that at least one major element in the rationale behind respecting autonomy is that people are normally the best judges of their own best interests – for the reasons just given this rationale is less well grounded in cases of judgments to die in future circumstances radically different from those experienced by the person at the time of decision. Dworkin rejects this view of autonomy, however, (the evidentiary view, he calls it)[81] in favor of the integrity view, which makes the decisive point of autonomy the right to govern the course of one's life, including one's incompetency, according to a "recognized and coherent scheme of value."[82] Certainly this is one of the virtues of autonomy, but it seems to me unduly limiting to give it the paramount place that Dworkin gives it, for reasons I will turn to in a moment.[83]

The second ground for discounting the advance directive is simply that Composer Now has now indicated that she prefers to live. Of course this would be determinative if she were competent. The question is whether to disregard her wish because she is not. I do not think we should. Competence is a matter of degree and depends upon the kinds of action at issue.[84] Impaired people have more or less capacity to think, reason and evaluate, and some actions will call for less of these capacities than others. A person may lack competence to choose his heirs, for example, but be perfectly competent to choose whether to watch television or go to the beach. It seems to me sound that an expression of a wish to live, even by a person incompetent for most other purposes, is entitled to carry weight, even if less than the full weight which a fully competent expression would command.

Why should we defer to a decision to continue living made by someone with the barest minimum of capacity for understanding and judgment? At bottom, I think the reason has to do with a general presumption favoring life over death. At least two factors seem to be involved. First, there is the universality of the struggle to survive we perceive in all living things, which makes it odd to justify disqualifying an expressed wish to live simply because of the person's cognitive limitations. Second, there is the seriousness and finality of what is at stake – the ending of a person's life. Buchanan and Brock have developed the case for taking into account the seriousness of the harmful consequences for the person in deciding whether he is competent.[85] I follow them here. Their approach is usually employed to justify overriding a person's choice to take a course that would greatly injure him or his interests (for example, a decision to refuse medical treatment necessary to sustain life). But I see no reason why it should not also justify complying with his choice to take a course that would avoid those serious and permanent consequences. Indeed, I am inclined to think that no person should be regarded as so incompetent that his expressed wish to live should be given no weight. I do not take issue with Professor Feinberg that greater harm may be done to a person by sustaining his life than by allowing it to expire.[86] But I do not believe that this is the case where the patient, even though generally incompetent, is asking to be kept alive.

Dworkin, to the contrary, believes that "autonomy, on the integrity view of that right, must be a *general* judgment about [the person's] overall capacity to seek integrity and authenticity, not a specific, task-sensitive judgment."[87] In his view, an autonomous person must have "the capacity to see and evaluate particular decisions in the structured context of an overall life organized around a coherent conception of character and conviction."[88] This seems to me too restrictive a limitation on the right of autonomy, for it would seem to deny the right to many ordinary people who, in virtue of qualities of tempera-ment or character, appear to lack an ability to make choices on the basis of consistent life-organizing conceptions. I think rather that a major point of autonomy is to enhance the freedom to decide for oneself, whether one decides with authenticity and a sense of coherence or just on the basis of immediate preferences and transient urges. An unwise, uninformed and ec-centric choice is still a choice. It may be that the ultimate value of autonomy is to permit people, to the extent they can, to make choices that create a coherent whole of their lives. But to deny a person his choices because he cannot choose in terms of a "structured context of an overall life organized around a coherent conception of character and conviction"[89] would deny choice to an unacceptably large segment of the population.

But while precedent autonomy (as Dworkin calls it) in our Composer's case falls short of the full moral force of contemporary autonomy, I have not argued that it has no force. What is there about the circumstances of Compos-er Now, which warrants overriding the force it has? For me and I expect, for many, it is compassion for the human being before us, living her limited life in apparent contentment and evidencing no wish to end it. Letting her die when cure is readily at hand requires a certain distancing of ourselves from our hu-man impulses, the suppression of a fundamental human empathy for another.

The choice to allow Composer Now to die is supported on the ground that earlier, when in full possession of her faculties, she stated that such a life for her would not be worth living. I do not mean to suggest that this is of slight moment. But neither does it have determinative significance. Without going so far as to regard Composer Now as a different person from Composer Then, I believe it is plain that there has occurred a great transformation in her capacities and perspectives. If we deny her the treatment that would save her, the harm we do is immediate and palpable – we end a life of sharply limited but still contented experiences, in stark violation of our humane sensibilities. If we grant her the treatment we also do harm, but the harm we do is remote and intangible – we violate an exercise of precedent autonomy that is so far separated and distant from her present circumstances that its entitlement to govern is severely compromised.

In the last analysis judgment turns on how much weight to give to the compassionate appeal of the person before us, as compared to the value of autonomy as a right to govern one's life according to a coherent normative structure. There is no algorithm for choosing. Still, those who choose, as I do, to give human compassion the greater weight have to confront whether the choice is a reflective, rational judgment or a reflexive, visceral response that should be the servant, not the master of our judgment. This raises the great question of the foundation of our moral judgments, which is quite beyond me. I offer just these passing observations.

First, if the ultimate value of autonomy is its intrinsic value, then one may without embarrassment make the equivalent claim for compassion. Second, insofar as the ultimate value of autonomy lies elsewhere – for example, in its being an essential ingredient of the good life, as Joseph Raz has argued[90] – it is relevant to observe that the sentiment of compassion for a fellow human being also serves a larger value, namely that it is an essential element in the very phenomenon of moral motivation and therefore of civilized society. Reflection, analysis and theory contribute importantly to our understanding of the phenomenon of moral experiences, but it is the direct human experience itself that is the ultimate source of any vital morality.[91]

Third, compassion is not another word for personal squeamishness of the person making the decision. If it were, it would have the status of just one more competing interest of another person, comparable to the interest of a relative in being relieved of the financial and psychological burdens attendant to the patient's continued life. But it is not just another's competing interest; it rises to the level of a moral concern. This is because morality has a dimension that has to do with the person doing the action as well as with the person being acted upon. The patient's right of autonomy is a moral concern of the latter kind; the actor's motivation stemming from the impulse of human compassion is a moral concern of the former kind. The well-known phenomenon of agent-centered restrictions on actions[92] – moral restraints that make it wrong for an agent to do an action that would produce the best available outcome overall (including the fewest actions of that same kind by others) – would not raise the profound problems for moral theory that they do were it not that morality has these separate dimensions.

One final comment on the Composer hypothetical. I have been addressing it on the assumption that Composer Now expressed a desire to be kept alive – an assumption that makes it harder to justify letting her die. I have done so to allow me to consider Dworkin's argument, which accepts the challenge of this harder case. It is apparent, however, that the argument from compassion I have made applies as well to a modified Composer hypothetical in which it is not possible for her to express a wish one way or the other. That she expresses a wish to live adds the appeal of autonomy to the appeal of compassion (as well as contributing to it), but I believe the appeal of compassion is enough without it.

B. *Where the patient never chose: Substituted judgment*

I turn now to what are called "substituted judgment" cases, those in which a person now incompetent never exercised a choice when competent. As I indicated, the courts try to deal with incompetents the same way they deal with competents, namely by seeking to determine the person's choice. But how do you find a choice when none was ever made? Courts have responded by looking for what the patient *would* have chosen: What would this patient choose if he were competent to appraise his situation, including his medical condition and prognosis, as well as his present and future incompetency?[93]

A puzzling feature of this standard is its implication that we are to ask what the permanently incompetent person would now choose if he were competent to choose and aware of his incompetency, as if this would tell us what an incompetent person would choose. But it cannot be known what an incompetent person would choose precisely because he cannot choose. We can try to imagine that he is temporarily competent and making a choice that takes into account his anticipated incompetency. But this would be a very different thing. Like an advance directive, it would be the choice of a competent patient anticipating, but not actually experiencing, his life as an incompetent; the choice, in short, of the person as he was, not as he now is, because he is now incapable of choosing.[94] This is, I think, all that courts can mean by the usual statement of the substituted judgment standard.

This distinction may seem like a cavil, but it serves to avoid the kind of error a Massachusetts court made in considering whether to forgo medical treatment for an elderly incompetent person who had been incompetent his entire life. The court stated:

In short, the decision in cases such as this should be that which would be made by the incompetent person, if that person were competent, but taking into account the present and future incompetency of the individual as one of the factors which would necessarily enter into the decision-making process of the competent person.[95]

The trouble with this approach is that it requires finding something which isn't there to be found, because the patient was never competent to make a choice.[96]

Another question raised by the substituted-judgment standard, even interpreted as I have argued it should be interpreted, is this: To what extent is it required by the patient's right of self-determination? In the Composer hypothetical, I considered that question in connection with advance choices generally, and concluded that while the right of autonomy was indeed involved (because the patient in fact exercised choice at some time in the past), the advance choice might in some circumstances lack the full moral force of a contemporaneous choice. The substituted-judgment standard entails the same difficulty since the evidence of what the patient would have chosen is in the patient's past. But this standard has an additional difficulty, namely that it is invoked where there has been no choice by the patient at all, either in the past or now. Courts applying this standard search for evidence of the patient's past life in order to determine how he would have chosen. But whatever the justification for this standard may be (I shall in a moment argue it is best understood as part of a best-interests assessment), it cannot be based on the autonomy principle. In these cases we cannot say that the patient has the right that his choice be respected, because he has made none.

The reason for this lies in the distinction between evidence of what a patient would choose and an actual choice.[97] The right of autonomy is the right to have one's own choices respected, not to have someone else make the choice he believes you would (or should) have made. The right protects the person's act of choosing. When someone else makes the choice, even if he chooses as he thinks you would, he is making the choice, not you. Since you made no actual choice, if he chooses to disregard evidence of what you would have chosen, he would not be violating your autonomous right to choose.

Why should an actual choice be that crucial? Aren't there many cases in which the past life of the patient allows us to conclude with reasonable assurance that, if competent, he would have chosen a certain way? Surely this is so. The reason why this is nonetheless not equivalent to an actual choice turns on a view of what an exercise of will entails. The view I am taking is that the will of a person stands apart from his character and dispositions; it is not one among other characteristics which, summed up, go to make the person what he is. Everything the person is and was may point to him doing X in some particular circumstance. But he is free to do not-X, and may do so, no matter how out of character it seems. The phenomenon of weakness of the will illustrates this point. Even when a person acknowledges that from the standpoint of every relevant criterion he accepts he should do X, he may still choose not to do X. Just as a baseball game, in a notable aphorism, is not over till it's over, so a choice is not made till it's made.[98]

Of course, it will sometimes be difficult to distinguish between an actual decision made in the past – and thus protected by the value of autonomy – and evidence of conduct pointing to what the patient would have decided. A written advance directive would be a paradigm case of the former, but less formal ways of choosing would also count, such as by orally declaring his decision to others. By contrast, examples of the latter would be the patient's general reflections on the subject of dying, positions he had taken in discussion with friends, religious commitments that would suggest one position or another, and so on. These may give us clues to what his decision would be had he made one, but they are not decisions. There may well be difficulties in applying this distinction, but that does not undermine the distinction in principle.

It does not follow from this distinction that evidence of the patient's preferences has no relevance. It plays a role in assessing his best interests, as I will argue. I only want to claim that cases of presumed preference are not morally equivalent to cases of actual choice, express or implied. This point is important because it allows us to see that, while in cases of contemporaneous choices (and, though to a lesser degree, in cases of advance choices as well) respect for autonomy requires doing as the patient directed, this is not so in substituted-judgment cases. Here, the deciding agent is obliged to make its own choice, the values and preferences of the patient in his competent state serving as guide to a best-interests judgment. Recall Composer Now and Composer Then. In order to make the case for treatment I had to justify compromising Composer Then's right of autonomy. But absent her directive not to treat, I would not have had to face that issue, because her autonomy would not have been involved.

The point has a further importance. So long as the ultimate issue is narrowly thought of as one of substituted judgment – that is, what the patient would choose if he could – there is some logic to courts insisting on a demonstration of that fact with a high degree of evidentiary certitude. This was the narrow issue in the *Cruzan* case, in which the Supreme Court upheld the Missouri law requiring "clear and convincing proof" that the patient would choose to terminate treatment.[99] Viewing the task more broadly, however, as involving a construction from all the circumstances of what treatment decision comports best with the life and character of the patient and therefore furthers his best interests, changes the focus of inquiry. It puts the issue of proof in a more appropriate and realistic framework: not, "unless it is demonstrated with a high level of certainty what the patient would have chosen, treatment must continue," but rather, "from the evidence that is available, including the character and attitudes of the patient, what decision – to continue or terminate treatment – will serve his best interests?"[100]

III. Best interests

The English courts of equity developed the best-interests standard in dealing with the estates of incompetent persons.[101] The standard makes the test of what is best for the incompetent, having regard to his own particular interests, determinative of whether to allow expenditures from the estate. But the standard has proved to be highly controversial in cases of incompetents who require medical treatment to stay alive.[102] There is concern over the appropriateness of the standard to determine whether a person should live or die and over how the concept should be interpreted and applied.

A fundamental objection arises from what is implicit in the standard, at least when understood apart from the setting of the patient's inferred preferences: that in certain circumstances the quality of a person's life may be so low that it is not worth living. This stands in stark opposition to the tradition that human life is always valuable. It is one thing for courts to defer to the patient's choice to die. This has proved difficult enough for some courts, as we saw, but at least the decision requires no judgment by the court or some other agent that the patient's life is no longer worth living – only that that is the judgment of the patient whose life it is. It is quite different when the best-interests standard is applied independently of the patient's inferred preferences, because this requires the deciding authority itself – the court or some other agent – to make the substantive judgment of whether what is left of the patient's life is worth the candle.

One concern animating this objection is that assessing the quality of the patient's life requires a judgment of its social worth. As one court put it, it is improper "to authorize decision-making based on assessments of the personal worth or social utility of another's life, or the value of that life to others" because to do so creates "an intolerable risk for socially isolated and defenseless people suffering from physical or mental handicaps."[103] Yet this concern seems misplaced, for there is nothing in the nature or history of the standard that requires judgments of the patient's worth to society generally or to particular others. Applied to the decision whether to treat, the accepted understanding of the best-interests standard is that it seeks to assess what would be best for the patient, not for his family, others, or the community as a whole.[104]

Even so, courts have found that judging whether a patient's future life is not worth living is a troubling decision for anyone to make. First, what makes a life not worth living anyway? Loss of the patient's cognitive powers, his ability to function independently, his ability to interact with others, his dependence on constant medical intervention? How much ability to sense and take comfort from experiences is required before we can say his life *is* worth living? At bottom the difficulty is that we have no way to make confident judgments about how far cognitive and physical deterioration must go before life ceases to be worth living, because the value judgments implicit in such a conclusion are in sharp contention in our society.[105] Second, there is the challenge of "don[ning] the mental mantle of the incompetent,"[106] understanding and judging his experiences as he lives and feels them, rather than from the biased perspective of a normally healthy person with unimpaired faculties. Finally, courts are often troubled by the specter of the slippery slope – the fear that once the precedent is established that a person may be left to die because someone judges his life not satisfying enough to be worth living, there will be nothing, or at least less, to stand in the way of that judgment being made of socially, mentally and physically handicapped people on the margins of society.[107]

Courts have tried in various ways to allay these concerns. The efforts of the

New Jersey Supreme Court in *Conroy*,[108] a case that attracted wide attention, are particularly instructive. In an effort to defeat the slippery slope, the court established the requirement of severe irremediable pain and suffering as a condition for any assessment of the quality of the person's life.[109] But medicine's considerable success in finding ways to suppress pain has largely eliminated it as a reason for letting a person die (in contrast to the impaired quality of life which pain suppression may entail).[110] Pain is one, but hardly the only, circumstance that might make a patient's life so burdensome that his best interests lie in extending it no further. Hence, requiring the presence of pain excludes many situations in which quality-of-life considerations may call for terminating treatment.[111]

Two other, more felicitous moves by the court to avoid the worst dangers of quality-of-life judgments were first, to preclude judgments based on the social utility of the patient's life or on its value to others,[112] and second, of more direct relevance to my argument, to require that enough be known about the patient to make a reasonable inference as to his likely preferences before a judgment of his best interests is permissible.[113] This constitutes a helpful reorientation of the substituted-judgment standard. It properly identifies the reason for consulting the patient's inferred preferences: it serves not his autonomy, but rather it furthers his best interests, on the view that making a treatment decision truest to the kind of person he was informs a best-interests judgment. Of course, if there were evidence that he made an actual choice when competent to reject treatment in the circumstances presented, his right of autonomy would require doing as he chose unless some powerful consideration required doing otherwise (as in the case of Composer Now). However, we are now considering cases where evidence of such a choice is insufficient, but where there is evidence of the kind of person he was. How should this evidence be appraised in making a best-interests judgment?

Certainly evidence of the values that guided his competent life (what Ronald Dworkin calls his "evaluative interests"[114]) bears directly on a best-interests judgment; for example, his character, how he led his life, his attitude toward medical treatment, what it was about life that he thought made it worthwhile, how much it mattered to him that he was burdening others, how sensitive he was to considerations of privacy and personal dignity. But there is another kind of consideration that needs consulting as well, namely his present experiences or lack of them (making up what Dworkin calls his "experiential interests"[115]). These include the patient's prognosis, the extent of his suffering, the degree of his mental and physical impairment, the kind of experiences he would be capable of if he survived. The question then becomes whether, on the basis of both kinds of evidence, we can conclude that a decision to forgo treatment would be consonant with the kind of life he led and the kind of person he was, as well as with the kind of person he is now. If so, we can conclude that it is in his best interests to deny treatment.

Some regard evidence of the first kind, his evaluative interests, as irrelevant, on the ground that one can have no interest in what is not and can never be experienced; under this view, only experiential interests count in cases of serious and permanent mental disability.[116] This argument has an attractive downright character, but as Joel Feinberg and others have shown, denying that a person's interests may be harmed when he does not and can never experience the harm takes too narrow a view of an interest.[117] Consider posthumous harms. There is a natural sense in which the interests of a person who is no longer alive may be harmed. Such harm occurs when that which he deeply cherished and to which he devoted his life suffers destruction, when his valued reputation as a person of honor and distinction is destroyed by malicious lies, or when significant promises he exacted to be performed after his death are foresworn. For like reasons, the evaluative interests of a living person (his sensibilities, his concerns for his own dignity and for not burdening others, his prized self-determination) may be harmed by how we deal with him after he has permanently lost capacity to be aware that these harms are being done to him. The Composer hypothetical would not have been so difficult were it not that Composer's interest in having her right of autonomy respected continued even though she could not (and could never) experience it. It is important to stress that this approach to ascertaining best interests offers some protection against the feared precedent of permitting someone else's judgment of the quality of a person's life to determine whether the patient should be permitted to die. It does so because it makes the patient's own value structure controlling of whether it is consistent with the patient's best interests to forgo treatment.

Ronald Dworkin, to the contrary, has proposed that except in cases where the patient has made a competent choice for treatment sufficient to invoke his right of autonomy (Dworkin agrees that evidence of preferences short of such choice are insufficient to involve this right),[118] the standard of evaluation of the worth of the patient's continued life (his evaluative interests) should be objective rather than subjective. In other words, the standard should not be necessarily what the patient himself would regard as in his best interests, but what *is* in his best interests, period. Referring to patients with permanent and severe dementia, he concludes that "a fiduciary should take over a person's responsibility to make his life as good a life as it can be when that person is no longer capable of this himself. . . . [I]t follows that the right to beneficence includes the right not to be given life-prolonging treatment when seriously and permanently demented."[119] This follows for Dworkin because a permanently and seriously demented person's life can contain nothing that would make his life better. Lacking a "sense of personality and agency," his experiences could not be rewarding.[120] And lacking "continuity of project and fulfillment," they could not be regarded as achievements.[121] On the other hand, a demented life can contain experiences that make the life of which it is a part worse – experiences of anxiety and pain, for example.

What I have given of Dworkin's argument for an objective best-interests judgment is the barest outline, which fails to convey its subtlety and complexity, but it is enough to allow me to say why I find it troubling. First, a basic premise of Dworkin's argument is that it is in the best interests of a patient that a decision makes of the patient's life as a whole as good a thing as it can be, one marked by a sensitivity to values of privacy and dignity, by respect for and deference to the interests of others, and so on. This evokes his theory of adjudication as interpretation, requiring the judge to make of the law as good a thing as it can be.[122] But there is an important difference, for I doubt that a person's life is made better by decisions that are not rooted in him as a person. If a person during the course of his competent life has been indifferent to matters of respect for his person and for the interests of others, it does not seem to me that it serves to make his whole life a better one that in the end someone has made decisions for him which manifest these virtues. They are, after all, imposed on him and hardly do him credit.

Moral luck plays some role in the living of a good life,[123] and on that basis an argument can be made that the patient's good fortune in being permitted to die after suffering serious and permanent dementia makes his whole life, on balance, a better one than it would be if he were kept alive. But this seems unconvincing. Luck may be a factor in permitting a person to lead a good life, but to say that his life is made a better one because a good thing luckily happens to him after he has finished leading his life yields too much to the authority of fortune. It is a bit like flowers on a grave: They make lots of things better, but scarcely the life of the person beneath them. Consider the example of being a burden to others, often given as one among a set of reasons for declining treatment: It is a virtue for a person to permit himself to die to save burdening others, and he makes his whole life a better one for doing so. But it hardly makes his life a better one that a third party decides to sacrifice it for the benefit of others.

My second reason for demurring to Dworkin's conclusion is practical: It invites the danger that many courts and commentators have seen in best-interests standards – the danger that those making the decision cannot be relied on to keep separate what is objectively best and what is best for them. It is often in the interest of those around the demented patient that he be permitted to die – he is a psychological burden to them, the ministrations required for his bodily functions often offend their sensibilities, he requires the use of valuable resources, and the positive qualities of his limited life seem slight compared to the negative influence on the lives of others. We may insist that it is in his best interest that he be allowed to die, but when that decision is one that serves the interests of others (who often are the ones making the decision) there is the ever-present danger that it is their interests, not his, that are motivating the decision.

Another problem with Dworkin's position is that it is, most uncharacteristically for him, paternalistic, at least in the sense that it makes the final act in a person's life turn on the normative standards of others rather than on those of the person himself. Dworkin accepts that a demented person's earlier competent choice for treatment must prevail even if it is against what Dworkin would regard as his best evaluative interests, considered from an objective perspective. But there are plainly going to be cases where the person's life has left evidence consistent with a preference for continued treatment, although he made no actual or implied choice which his right of autonomy would require deferring to. It seems to me we should want to say that such a person has an interest, that it is in *his* best interests, that the decision accord with his own values and preferences as best we can discern them. I agree that it would not violate his right to autonomy to disregard his inferred preferences (because he made no choice). Nonetheless, it would be inconsistent with his interest in having the end of his life governed by the kind of choices he made to govern his competent earlier life, and therefore in this sense paternalistic.

Nonetheless, there are situations where Dworkin's analysis has a strong appeal. These are the cases where we can make no reliable judgment based on the person's past values and commitments, either because the evidence is totally indeterminate or because he never was competent. Here it is not possible to tailor the choice to the character of the person. In this situation a decision that can be supported as better on impersonal, objective grounds is obviously preferable to a decision that cannot be so supported.

My final concern, which I suggested earlier in a related context, is that Dworkin's position unduly discounts the experiential interests of a demented person – the satisfactions that can come from sensory experiences and comforting feelings that do not require higher-order mentation. To paraphrase Bentham, the question is not whether demented people can reason, nor whether they can talk, but whether they can feel.[124]

IV. Conclusion

I conclude with a restatement of some of the positions I have tried to defend.

A constitutional right of autonomy has provided the foundation for judicial decisions to let patients die. In principle this right extends to suicide and assisted suicide, although the extension could be resisted on plausible, prudential grounds. The courts, however, have sought to distinguish cases of

letting patients die on such grounds as the doing/allowing and pur-
pose/knowledge distinctions, which have failed to carry the burden put on
them.

The principle of autonomy controls the decision whether to let a patient die
when there is a competent contemporary choice. In all other cases, it becomes
just one of several factors to consider.

For reasons I suggested in connection with the Composer hypothetical, an
advance competent choice has force, but not the conclusive moral force of a
contemporary choice and not so much force as to preclude consideration of
the possibly conflicting experiential interests of the patient.

Where the patient never made a choice during competency, the right of
autonomy is not implicated at all, contrary to what courts assume under the
substituted-judgment standard when they seek to discover what the patient
would have chosen. What we think the patient would have chosen is not what
the patient chose. A judgment based on a search of the patient's competent life
for preferences, values, and commitments is appropriate not because it is
required by the person's autonomy but because it is in his best interests.

The patient's interests include experiential interests – the quality of his
future life if kept alive – as well as evaluative ones, and if it is *his* best
interests that are to be furthered, any judgment upon them must be made with
reference to the values and commitments by which the patient chose to live.
For reasons I tried to suggest, this subjective approach to determining best
interests is preferable to an objective one, which would seek to make the
patient's life as a whole a better one in terms of some objective criteria of the
good life, but not those of the patient whose life we are deciding.

Notes

1 Copyright Sanford H. Kadish, 1992, Morrison Professor of Law, Emeritus, University of California at Berkeley.
2 I am indebted to Meir Dan-Cohen, Michael Flick, Mort Kadish, Yale Kamisar,
Eric Rakowski and Jeremy Waldron for their critical reading and helpful suggestions, and to Daniel Saunders for his faultless research assistance.
3 **President's Commission for the Study of Ethical Problems in Medicine and
Biomedical and Behavioral Research, Deciding to Forgo Life-Sustaining
Treatment** 16 (1983) [hereinafter **President's Commission**].
4 **Robert F. Weir, Abating Treatment with Critically Ill Patients: Ethical and
Legal Limits to the Medical Prolongation of Life** 18 (1989).
5 **President's Commission,** *supra* n. 3, at 17–18.
6 *In re* Farrell, 529 A.2d 404, 406 (N.J. 1987) (quoting *In re* Conroy, 486 A.2d 1209
(N.J. 1985)).
7 *See* Sanford H. Kadish, **Blame and Punishment** 109–32 (1987).
8 This is subject to the possible exception of a necessity defense, where the taking of

one life is the only way to avoid the death of several. There is moral authority for this defense, but its legal authority in cases of killing is doubtful. *Id.* at 123.

9 *See* **Glanville Williams, Textbook of Criminal Law** 579 (2d ed. 1983).

10 4 **William Blackstone, Commentaries on the Laws of England** 189 (U. Chi. Press 1979); *see also* Paul Marcus, *Suicide: Legal Aspects, in* 4 **Encyclopedia of Crime and Justice** 1526–7 (Sanford H. Kadish ed., 1983).

11 *See* George P. Smith, *All's Well That Ends Well: Toward a Policy of Assisted Rational Suicide or Merely Enlightened Self-Determination?*, 22 **U.C. Davis L. Rev.** 275, 290–1 and n.106 (1989).

12 Other examples of this lagtime can be found in the development of no-fault divorce, which came well after the widespread nullification of strict divorce requirements, *see* **Max Rhenstein, Marriage Stability, Divorce and the Law** 51–105 (1972); Lawrence M. Friedman, *Rights of Passage: Divorce Law in Historical Perspective,* 63 **Ore. L. Rev.** 649, 664–9 (1984); the legitimation of plea bargaining which followed decades of its widespread but officially denied practice, *see* Brady v. United States, 397 U.S. 742 (1970); **Mortimer R. Kadish and Sanford H. Kadish, Discretion to Disobey** 83–5 (1973); and the toleration of abortion under certain circumstances before Roe v. Wade, 410 U.S. 113 (1973), *see* Herbert L. Packer and Ralph J. Gampel, *Therapeutic Abortion: A Problem in Law and Medicine,* 11 **Stan. L. Rev** 417 (1959). There are situations, of course, in which pronouncements of moral principles precede and influence the practices themselves. One thinks of the Supreme Court's extension of the Bill of Rights and of its Civil Rights decisions, particularly in the Warren era. But these are cases where the change is from the low ground of practice to the high ground of principle, not where the change is the other way around.

13 Despite statues in over half the states making it criminal to help another commit suicide, several recent, widely publicized incidents of this kind have occurred. In one case a Rochester doctor described in the pages of the *New England Journal of Medicine* how he prescribed the barbiturates that a long-standing patient needed to kill herself, following her refusal of treatment for a severe form of leukemia. Timothy E. Quill, *Death and Dignity: A Case of Individualized Decision Making,* 324 **New Eng. J. Med.** 691 (1991); *see* Lawrence K. Altman, *Doctor Says He Gave Patient Drug to Help Her Commit Suicide,* **N.Y. Times,** March 7, 1991, at A1. An upstate New York prosecutor sought an indictment against the doctor for feloniously assisting another to commit suicide. Criticism of the prosecution was widespread, including that of the Officers and Members of the Council of the Society of General Internal Medicine, who wrote the District Attorney that Dr. Quill's actions "were consistent with the range of acceptable practice of compassionate physicians." **SGIM News** (Society of General Internal Medicine), Oct. 1991, at 5. Significantly, the grand jury declined to indict. Lawrence K. Altman, *Jury Declines to Indict a Doctor Who Said He Aided in a Suicide,* **N.Y. Times,** July 27, 1991, at A1.

Another recently publicized example is the case of Dr. Kevorkian. He connected an Alzheimer's victim to a suicide device he had made, and watched as she pushed a button to operate it and died. The victim had apparently traveled to Michigan in order to use the machine because Michigan law on assisting suicide was ambiguous, there being no statute explicitly making it criminal to help another commit suicide. Lisa Belkin, *Doctor Tells of First Death Using His Suicide Device*, **N.Y. Times,** June 6, 1990, at A1, B6. Dr. Kevorkian has since used his machine on other patients who have enlisted his services, and the final chapter on his activities has yet to be written. The "Dr. Strangelove" character of his death-promotional activities, however, has drawn considerable negative reaction. *See* Robert Carson, *Washington's I-119*, Hastings Center Rep., Mar.–Apr., 1992 at 7.

14 **Joseph Fletcher, Humanhood: Essays in Biomedical Ethics** 149 (1979).

15 *See It's Over Debbie*, 259 **JAMA** 272 (1988) (an anonymous letter describing the doctor-author's administration of a lethal dosage of morphine to a patient in great distress dying of incurable ovarian cancer who asked that death be advanced). Over 150 letters commenting on this publication were received by the editor of the journal. We are told that of those from physicians, 80 percent were unfavorable, implying that many, perhaps up to 20 percent, were supportive. George D. Lundberg, *'It's Over, Debbie' and the Euthanasia Debate*, 259 **JAMA** 2142 (1988) (editorial describing response to the letter).

16 *In re* Quinlan, 355 A.2d 647 (N.J.), *cert. denied sub nom* Garger v. New Jersey, 429 U.S. 922 (1976).

17 *Id.* at 671–2.

18 Maria Coyle, *How Americans View High Court*, **Nat'l. L.J.,** Feb. 26, 1990, at 1, 36 (citing National Law Journal/Lexis poll finding 88 percent in favor of letting the family decide whether to end life support); Andrew H. Malcolm, *A Judicial Sanction for Death by Assent*, **N.Y. Times,** June 28, 1987, § 4, at 26 (discussing shift in public opinion polls to a two-thirds majority in favor of giving patients the right to terminate treatment); Clay Richards and B. D. Colen, *Poll: Most Favor "Right to Die" Laws*, **Newsday,** June 10, 1990, at 15 (citing Times Mirror Center poll finding 80 percent supporting the right to terminate treatment). The rise of a book on how to commit suicide (Derek Humphrey's **Final Exit**) to the top of the best-seller list further reveals the shift in public attitudes towards death and dying. *See* Katherine Ames, *Last Rights*, **Newsweek,** Aug. 26, 1991, at 40.

19 *See* **D. Humphrey and A. Wickett, The Right to Die** 35–6 (1986).

20 Melinda Beck, *The Doctor's Suicide Van*, **Newsweek,** June 18, 1990, at 46, 47 (citing recent Hemlock Society poll reporting 64 percent approval); Andrew H. Malcolm, *Giving Death a Hand*, **N.Y. Times,** June 9, 1990, § 1, at 6 (N.Y. Times/CBS News Poll finding 53 percent approval).

21 Richards & Colen, *supra* note 18, at 15.

22 Lisa Belkin, *Doctors Debate Helping the Terminally Ill Die*, **N.Y. Times,** May 24, 1989, at A1, A25.

23 Jane Gross, *Voters Turn Down Mercy Killing Idea*, **N.Y. Times,** Nov. 7, 1991, at B16.

24 Peter Steinfels, *Beliefs*, **N.Y. Times,** Nov. 9, 1991, at 11; *cf. Euthanasia Favored in Poll*, **N.Y. Times,** Nov. 4, 1991, at A16 (results of an October national poll showing that "nearly two out of three Americans favor doctor-assisted suicide and euthanasia for terminally ill patients who request it").

25 The negative reaction to the exploits of Dr. Kevorkian and his suicide machine, to which wide publicity was given in the days before the vote, is thought by some to have been a contributing factor. *See* Carson, supra n. 13.

26 **Society for the Right to Die,** *Introduction* to **Refusal of Treatment Legislation** (1991). Living-will statutes had been introduced in state legislatures as early as 1906, but none was enacted until after the *Quinlan* decision. Part of the explanation is that the early proposals would have authorized active euthanasia, although the current crop of statutes excludes it. *See* 3 **Joel Feinberg, The Moral Limits of the Criminal Law: Harm to Self** 367–8 (1986). California passed the first living-will statute in 1976. See Natural Death Act, **Cal. Health & Safety Code** §§ 7185–95 (West Supp. 1992).

27 **Society for the Right to Die,** *supra* n. 26.

28 Typically, living-will statutes apply only to persons in permanent vegetative states, or where death is inevitable and imminent and the living will is executed after the person becomes terminally ill. They also typically exclude the withdrawal of artificial nutrition and hydration, as well as "affirmative euthanasia." *See, e.g.,* California's provision for durable power of attorney for health care, **Cal. Civ. Code** §§ 2430–44 (West Supp. 1992). For a comprehensive review of state legislation, see generally **Society for the Right to Die,** *supra* n. 26.

29 There have been a number of studies of judicial developments under these statutes. *See, e.g.,* **Mark A. Hall and Ira Mark Ellman, Health Care Law and Ethics in a Nutshell** 283–8 (1990); Rebecca Dresser, *Life, Death, and Incompetent Patients: Conceptual Infirmities and Hidden Values in the Law,* 28 **Ariz. L. Rev.** 373 (1986); Linda C. Fentiman, *Privacy and Personhood Revisited: A New Framework for Substitute Decisionmaking for the Incompetent Incurably Ill Adult,* 57 **Geo. Wash. L. Rev.** 801, 818–40 (1989); Nancy K. Rhoden, *Litigating Life and Death,* 102 **Harv. L. Rev.** 375 (1989); *Developments in the Law – Medical Technology and the Law,* 103 **Harv. L. Rev.** 1519, 1670–2 (1990) [hereinafter *Developments*]. The strength of public policy behind these laws is evident in the federal Patient Self-Determination Act, amending the Social Security Act, which seeks to assure wider publicity to state laws permitting patients to refuse treatment. Omnibus Budget Reconciliation Act of 1990, Pub. L. No. 101–508, § 4751, 103 Stat. 1388–204 to 206 (1990). Among other things, it requires medical institutions receiving Medicare or Medicaid funds to provide all patients with written information on their rights under state law to refuse medical care, including information on advance directives. It also requires the Secretary of Health and Human Services to develop and distribute informational materials on these subjects.

30 *See* Scholendorff v. Society of N.Y. Hosp., 105 N.E. 92, 93 (N.Y. 1914) (Cardozo, J.) ("Every human being of adult years and sound mind has a right to determine what shall be done with his own body; and a surgeon who performs an operation without his patient's consent commits an assault. . . .") (*overruled on other grounds by* Bing v. Thunig, 143 N.E.2d 3 [1957]).

31 *See* Griswold v. Connecticut, 381 U.S. 479 (1965) (right of access to contraception); Eisenstadt v. Baird, 405 U.S. 438 (1972) (same); Roe v. Wade, 410 U.S. 113 (1973) (right to abortion).

32 *In re* Quinlan, 355 A.2d 647 (N.J.), *cert. denied sub nom* Garger v. New Jersey, 429 U.S. 922 (1976).

33 *Id.* at 663.

34 *See Developments, supra* n. 29, at 1662–5. Since *Quinlan,* courts have upheld with substantial unanimity the right of competent patients (under state or federal

law) to reject life-sustaining treatment, at least in cases of terminal disease. *Id.* at 1645. Some have affirmed this right where competent patients were suffering painful and incurable ailments; and many have extended the right to include rejection of artificial nutrition and hydration. A review of the case law may be found in the material cited in n. 29, *supra.*

35   110 S. Ct. 2841 (1990).

36   *Id.* at 2854.

37   *Id.* at 2852.

38   *Id.*

39   *See In re* Conroy, 486 A.2d 1209, 1223 (N.J. 1985); Superintendent of Belchertown State Sch. v. Saikewicz, 370 N.E.2d 417, 425 (Mass. 1977).

40   *See* Martha A. Matthews, Comment, *Suicidal Competence and the Patient's Right to Refuse Lifesaving Treatment,* 75 **Calif. L. Rev.** 707, 729–43 (1987). In the early Jehovah's Witness blood transfusion cases, however, some courts gave as a further reason for compelling life-saving transfusion the interests of the patient's minor children. *Id.* at 732–3.

41   *See, e.g.,* Bartling v. Superior Court, 209 Cal. Rptr. 220, 225 (Cal. App. 1984); Brophy v. New England Sinai Hosp., 497 N.E.2d 626, 635–8 (Mass. 1986).

42   *See Conroy,* 486 A.2d at 1224 ("This state interest in protecting people from direct and purposeful self-destruction is motivated by, if not encompassed within, the state's more basic interest in preserving life. Thus, it is questionable whether it is a distinct state interest worthy of independent consideration.").

43   See n. 34, *supra.*

44   *See, e.g., Conroy,* 486 A.2d at 1224 ("Refusing medical intervention merely allows the disease to take its natural course; if death were eventually to occur, it would be the result, primarily of the underlying disease, and not the result of a self-inflicted injury."); *Saikewicz,* 370 N.E.2d at 426 n.11 ("[T]o the extent that the cause of death was from natural causes the patient did not set the death producing agent in motion . . ."); Satz v. Perlmutter, 362 So. 2d 160, 162–3 (Fla. Dist. App. Ct. 1978), *approved by* 379 So. 2d 359 (Fla. 1980). *See Cantor,* The Permanently Unconscious Patient, Non-Feeding and Euthanasia, 15 **Am. J. L. & Med.** 381, 433 (1989): "The assertion that rejection of life-saving medical treatment by competent patients constitutes suicide has been uniformly rejected – usually based on a distinction between letting nature take its course and initiating external death causing agents."

45   *See, e.g.,* 4 **Blackstone,** *supra* n. 10, at 189 ("A *felo de se* therefore is he that deliberately puts an end to his own existence . . .").

46   Deliberately starving oneself to death tends to strike people as suicide, although legal authority for that view seems limited to cases of force-feeding of prisoners, a very special situation involving the state's interest in the administration of the criminal justice system. The cases cited by Justice Scalia in his concurring opinion in the *Cruzan* case are of this kind. *See* Cruzan v. Director, Mo. Dep't. of Health, 110 S. Ct. 2841, 2861 (Scalia, J., concurring).

47   *See generally* **Jonathan Glover, Causing Death and Saving Lives** 92–112 (1977); Warren S. Quinn, *Actions, Intentions and Consequences: The Doctrine of Doing and Allowing,* 98 **Phil. Rev.** 287 (1989).

48 *Accord* **President's Commission,** *supra* n. 3, at 4, 65–72 (discussing the problem of overreliance on the act/omission distinction and the difficulty in evaluating the moral significance of acts and omissions causing death); *Conroy,* 486 A.2d at 1233–4 (rejecting "the distinction that some have made between actively hastening death by terminating treatment and passively allowing a person to die of a disease as one of limited use in a legal analysis of such a decision-making situation").

49 It would not make much sense to say that one may not kill oneself by walking into the sea, but may sit on the beach until submerged by the incoming tide; or that one may not intentionally lock oneself into a cold storage locker, but may refrain from coming indoors when the temperature drops below freezing." *Cruzan,* 110 S.Ct. at 2861 (Scalia, J., concurring).

50 *Conroy,* 486 A.2d at 1224; *see also Saikewicz,* 370 N.E. 2d at 426 n.11 ("in refusing treatment the patient may not have the specific intent to die").

51 *See, e.g., Conroy,* 486 A.2d at 1226 ("[R]ejecting her artificial means of feeding would not constitute attempted suicide, as the decision would probably be based on a wish to be free of medical intervention rather than a specific intent to die, and her death would result, if at all, from her underlying medical condition . . ."). For a discussion of the cases and a criticism of the distinction, see Matthews, *supra* n. 40, at 735–8.

52 *See* Ronald Dworkin, *The Right to Death,* **N.Y. Rev. of Books,** Jan. 31, 1991, at 14.

53 *Cruzan,* 110 S.Ct. at 2859 (Scalia, J., concurring).

54 Dworkin, *supra* n. 52, at 17. He goes on to say:
    Many people whose lives could be lengthened through severe amputations or incapacitating operations decide to die instead, and they are not thought to have taken their own lives for that reason. . . . People imagining themselves as permanently comatose are in the same position: their biological lives could then be prolonged only through medical treatment they would think degrading, and only in a form they would think worse than death. So it is a mistake, for that reason, to describe someone who signs a living will as committing hypothetical suicide.

55 *See* **Model Penal Code** § 2.02 (2) (a) (a person acts purposely with respect to a result of his conduct if "it is his conscious object to . . . cause that result").

56 *See id.* at § 2.02 (2) (b) ("A person acts knowingly with respect to . . . a result of his conduct [if] he is aware that it is practically certain that his conduct will cause such a result.").

57 *See* Matthews, *supra* n. 40, at 754–7 (suggesting that state interest should only be in preventing irrational suicides and proposing a test for determining competence).

58 *Cf.* **Feinberg,** *supra* n. 26, at 374 (arguing that the only possible justification for the state to continue prohibiting euthanasia is a "pragmatic" fear of mistake or abuse). *But cf.* Philippa Foot, *Commentary: Active Euthanasia with Parental Consent,* **Hastings Center Rep.,** Oct. 1979, at 20 (maintaining that it is easier to justify "passive" euthanasia than it is to justify "active" euthanasia); Allister Browne, *Assisted Suicide and Active Voluntary Euthanasia,* 2 **Can. J. of L. and Jurisp.** 35 (1989). Occasionally one finds a judge making the argument. *See, e.g.,* Bouvia v. Superior Court, 225 Cal. Rptr. 297, 308 (Cal. App. 1986). The court

authorized the removal of a nasogastric tube from a competent but permanently paralyzed young woman who preferred to starve herself to death rather than to continue living. A concurring judge criticized the majority for not admitting that

> [t]he right to die is an integral part of our right to control our own destinies so long as the rights of others are not affected. That right should, in my opinion, include the ability to enlist assistance from others, including the medical profession, in making death as painless and quick as possible. *Id.* at 307 (Compton, J., concurring).

It is interesting to note that some twenty years ago, before the *Quinlan* case launched the current rethinking of the right to die, Professor Glanville Williams advocated that proponents of euthanasia adopt as an interim strategy the distinctions to be found in Catholic doctrine between killing and letting die and between ordinary and extraordinary treatment. G. Williams, *Euthanasia*, 41 **Medico-Legal J.** 14, 18 (1973). He observed: "If this distinction between an act and an omission is thought to be artificial, its artificiality is imposed on us by our refusal to accord the same moral freedom for action as we do for inaction. Pending a change of thought, the concept of an omission is a useful way of freeing us from some of the consequences of overrigid moral attitudes." *Id.* at 21. For a fuller account of the story of the success of Professor Williams' proposal, see Yale Kamisar, *When is There a Constitutional "Right to Die"? When is There No Constitutional "Right to Live"?* 25 **Ga. L. Rev.** 1203, 1214, et seq. (1991).

59 *See* **Feinberg,** *supra* n. 26, at 374; **Laurence H. Tribe, American Constitutional Law** 1370–1 (2d ed. 1988). Recently, Professor Feinberg has challenged this pragmatic justification on the ground that it falsely assumes it's always a greater evil to let a patient die by mistake than to keep him alive by mistake. Joel Feinberg, *Overlooking the Merits of the Individual Case: An Unpromising Approach to the Right to Die,* 4 **Ratio Juris** 131 (1991).

60 *See, e.g.,* Tune v. Walter Reed Army Hosp. 602 F. Supp. 1452, 1455–6 (D.D.C. 1985); Satz v. Perlmutter, So.2d 160, 162 (Fla. Dist. Ct. App. 1978), *approved by,* 379 So.2d 359 (Fla. 1980).

61 *See In re* guardianship of Barry, 445 So.2d 365, 371 (Fla. Dist. Ct. App. 1984); *In re* Peter, 529 A.2d 419, 424 (N.J. 1987); *In re* Quinlan, 355 A.2d 647, 663–4 (N.J. 1976).

62 *See, e.g.,* Superintendent of Belchertown State Sch. v. Saikewicz, 370 N.E.2d 417, 424 (Mass. 1977) (extraordinary methods to prolong life not required); *Quinlan,* 355 A.2d at 667–8 (what is ordinary for the curable patient may be extraordinary for the terminal patient).

63 The extraordinary/ordinary distinction seems already defunct. *See, e.g., In re* Conroy, 486 A.2d 1209, 1234–6 (N.J. 1985) (decided nine years after *Quinlan* by the same court, rejecting any distinction between ordinary and extraordinary treatment, and between termination of artificial feedings and the termination of other forms of life-sustaining medical treatment); **President's Commission,** *supra* n. 3, at 82–90 (criticizing the distinction as hopelessly ambiguous). Professor Kamisar has concluded that, "The extraordinary/ordinary means distinction has been widely criticized and is now widely rejected." *See* Kamisar, *supra.* n. 58.

64 *See, e.g., Saikewicz,* 370 N.E.2d at 428 (failing to grant "the same panoply of rights and choices" to competent and incompetent persons downgrades "the status of the incompetent person by placing a lesser value on his intrinsic human worth and vitality").

65 For a definitive treatment of these issues see generally **Allen E. Buchanan and Dan W. Brock, Deciding for Others: The Ethics of Surrogate Decision Making** (1989).

66 For a discussion of the cases, see references cited *supra* n. 29.

67 The United States Senate's proposed "Patient Self Determination Act of 1989", *supra* n. 29, recites in its statement of purposes and findings that, "[e]stimates identify that 9 percent of the adult competent population have signed a living will; much less than 9 percent have designated a durable power of attorney for health care." S. 1766, 101st Cong., 1st Sess. § 2 (b) (5) (1989).

68 *Compare Quinlan,* 355 A.2d at 664 (decision by guardian and family), *with Saikewicz,* 370 N.E.2d at 435 (judicial resolution required) *and In re* Spring, 405 N.E.2d 115, 120–1 (Mass. 1980) (listing factors to be considered in determining whether prior judicial approval is required).

69 *See infra* text accompanying n. 85–88; *see also* Michael R. Flick, *The Due Process of Dying,* 79 **Calif. L. Rev.** 1121, 1142–3 (1991) (discussing Bartling v. Superior Court, 209 Cal. Rptr. 220 (1984), in which the patient vacillated between a desire to die and a desire to live).

70 Various positions in an ongoing philosophical debate over the nature of the self carry implications for how these questions should be answered. Some philosophers hold psychological continuity essential for determining the boundaries of the self. *See* **Derek Parfit, Reasons and Persons** 204–7 (1984); Donald Regan, *Paternalism, Freedom, Commitment, in* **Paternalism** 113, 126 (Rolfe Sartorius ed. 1983). On this view, Composer Now, totally lacking psychological continuity with Composer Then, would be a wholly different person for moral purposes, and therefore should not be governed by Composer Then's choices. *See* Dresser, *supra* n. 29, at 381. Others contest this theory of selfhood, instead stressing the moral importance of physical continuity. *See* Ronald Dworkin, *Autonomy and the Demented Self,* 64 **Milbank Q.** 4 (Supp. II 1986); Rhoden, *supra* n. 29, at 410–19. I will not here pursue the issue in these terms. *See generally* Allen E. Buchanan, *Advance Directives and the Personal Identity Problem,* 17 **Phil. & Pub. Aff.** 277 (1988).

71 Dworkin, supra n. 70, at 13.

72 **Ronald Dworkin, U.S. Congress, Office of Technology Assessment, Philosophical Issues Concerning the Rights of Patients Suffering Permanent Dementia** 49–50 (1987) *microformed on* Philosophical, Legal, and Social Aspects of Surrogate Decisionmaking for Elderly Individuals, OTA J952-30, CIS/MF.

73 Dworkin, *supra* n. 70, at 8–9.

74 *Id.* at 8.

75 *See infra* text at n. 117.

76 It is unclear whether Dworkin would agree. He recognizes that his conception of precedent autonomy has "austere consequences," but his discussion leaves uncertain whether he means by this that it might be morally correct to override autonomy

320   SANFORD H. KADISH

in such cases, or that it would be understandably difficult for people to resist being humane. Dworkin, *supra* n. 70 at 13.

77 **Dworkin**, *supra* n. 72, at 39, 46, 101.

78 Dresser, *supra* n. 29, at 381.

79 *See* Yale Kamisar, *Euthanasia Legislation: Some Non-Religious Objections*, 4 **Minn. L. Rev.** 4, 969, 989 (1958). This is one of the major arguments for not holding a surrogate mother to her agreement with the infertile couple who retained her. *See* **Martha A. Field, Surrogate Motherhood,** 69–70 (1988); *cf.* Stacey Okun, *Ruling Hailed by Opponents of Surrogacy,* **N.Y. Times,** Feb. 4, 1988, at B7 (surrogates may change their minds because at the time of the contract they are unable to project their feelings at the time of birth).

80 *See* **Buchanan & Brock,** *supra* n. 65, at 106–7. For a critique of living wills as advancing a patient's competent wishes over later, incompetent interests, see John Robertson, Hastings Center Rep., Nov.–Dec. 1991 at 6.

81 *See* Dworkin, *supra* n. 70, at 7.

82 *Id.* at 9.

83 *See infra* text at note 88.

84 *See* **Buchanan & Brock,** *supra* n. 65, at 60–5 (arguing that "competence is a *relational property* determined by a *variable standard.*" *Id.* at 60).

85 *Id.* at 51. *But see* Mark R. Wicclair, *Patient Decision-Making Capacity and Risk,* 5 **Bioethics** 91, 104 (1991) (arguing that although harmful consequences go to the necessity of deciding whether the patient is competent, they should not affect the standard used to determine competence).

86 *See* **Feinberg,** *supra* n. 59.

87 Dworkin, *supra* n. 70, at 10.

88 *Id.*

89 *Id.*

90 **Joseph Raz, The Morality of Freedom** 415 (1986).

91 *Compare* Mary Warnock, *The Artificial Family, in* **Moral Dilemmas in Modern Medicine** 138, (Michael Lockwood ed., 1985):

I disagree entirely with those philosophers who would claim . . . that feelings alone cannot amount to a moral view, and that morality has to be a matter of reason. . . . Indeed the whole notion of reason, on the one hand, and feeling or sentiment, on the other, essentially opposed to each other, seems to me to be a mistake – a hangover from an eighteenth-century way of looking at things. I don't see why a moral view cannot both be grounded in feelings and at the same time (in some suitably broad sense) be rational or at any rate not irrational. *Id.* at 154.

See also the discussion of the distinction between the cognitive sense or concept of justice ("Rechtsbewusstein") and its emotional component ("Rechtsgefühl"), in Wolfgang Fikentscher, *The Sense of Justice and the Concept of Cultural Justice – Views From Law and Anthropology,* 34 **Am. Behavioral Scientist** 314, 316 (1991).

92 *See* **Thomas Nagel, The View From Nowhere** 164–88 (1986); **Samuel Scheffler, The Rejection of Consequentialism** 80–114 (1982).

93 For discussion and criticism of the substituted-judgment standard, see **Buchanan**

and Brock, *supra* n. 65, at 112–17; **President's Commission,** *supra* n. 3, at 132; *Developments, supra* n. 29, at 1646–51.

94 *Cf.* Louise Harmon, *Falling Off the Vine: Legal Fictions and the Doctrine of Substituted Judgment,* 100 **Yale L.J.** 1, 58 (1990) (discussing substituted judgement, as developed in 19th century England, to dispose of lunatic's surplus income).

95 Superintendent of Belchertown State Sch. v. Saikewicz, 370 N.E.2d 417, 431 (Mass. 1977). The Massachusetts court continues to adhere to this analysis. See Guardianship of Jane Doe, 583 N.E. 2d, 1263 (1992).

96 *See* **Tribe,** *supra* n. 59, at 1369 (attempting to effectuate "patient's subjective wishes reaches almost Alice in Wonderland proportions"); **President's Commission** *supra* n. 3, at 133; Wikler, *Patient Interests: Clinical Implications of Philosophical Distinctions,* 36 **J. Am. Geriatric Soc'y.** 951, 956 (1988).

97 In support of this distinction *see* **Buchanan and Brock,** *supra* n. 65, at 116 (evidence of an individual's preference does not carry the same moral weight as an individual's deliberate choice); Dworkin, *supra* n. 70, at 13–14 (any appeal to precedent autonomy requires an actual choice by the patient in the past); Rhoden, *supra* n. 29, at 389 (right to autonomy is not violated absent an actual choice).

98 There is a political dimension to this view of autonomy: It defeats an attempted justification of unconsented-to authoritative actions based on the view that those affected *would* consent and therefore may be taken to have done so.

99 Cruzan v. Director, Missouri Dep't of Health, 110 S. Ct. 2841, 2846–55 (1990).

100 Nancy Rhoden makes a similar point in Rhoden, *supra* n. 29, at 390.

101 The history of the doctrine is told in Harmon, *supra* n. 94, at 16–55.

102 *See Developments, supra* n. 29, at 1651–3.

103 *In re* Conroy, 486 A.2d 1209, 1232–3 (N.J. 1985).

104 *See* Case Comment, *Natural Death: An Alternative in New Jersey,* 73 **Geo. L.J.** 1331, 1337 (1985) (arguing that decisions are to be made solely from the patient's perspective).

105 *See* **Tribe,** *supra* n. 59, at 1369.

106 Superintendent of Belchertown State School v. Saikewicz, 370 N.E.2d 417, 431 (Mass. 1977) (*quoting In re* Carson, 241 N.Y.S.2d 288, 289 (N.Y. Sup. Ct. 1962).

107 *See Conroy,* 486 A.2d 1233 ("More wide-ranging powers to make decisions about other people's lives . . . would create an intolerable risk for socially isolated and defenseless people suffering from physical or mental handicaps."); Cruzan v. Harmon, 760 S.W.2d 408, 420 (Mo. 1988) (*en banc*) ("Were quality of life at issue, persons with all manner of handicaps might find the state seeking to terminate their lives."); *see also Saikewicz,* 370 N.E.2d at 432 (the court bridled at the suggestion that the quality of life available to a retarded person should be considered).

108 *Conroy,* 486 A.2d 1209, 1232.

109 *Id.* at 1232. The court held that treatment may be forgone when the pain reaches the "point that the net burdens of [the patient's] prolonged life markedly outweighs any physical pleasure, emotional enjoyment, or intellectual satisfaction that the patient may still be able to derive from life." *Id.*

110 **President's Commission,** *supra* n. 3, at 19, 50–1. However, there are a variety of social and institutional restraints – for example, inadequate medical education in pain management and fears of addiction – that hinder the use of available knowledge. *See* Kathleen M. Foley, *The Relationship of Pain and Symptom Management to Patient Requests for Assisted Suicide,* **J. of Pain and Symptom Management** 289 (1991).

111 It is instructive that even the dissenting Justice in *Conroy,* while embracing a best interests or quality-of-life standard, qualified its application by requiring that it first be established that the patient be facing imminent death, be incurable, in a comatose state, and suffering the loss of at least one major bodily organ or system. *Id.* at 1244, 1249 (Handler, J., dissenting).

112 *Conroy,* 486 A.2d at 1232–3.

113 *Id.* at 1231–2.

114 **Dworkin,** *supra* n. 72, at 32.

115 *Id.*

116 *See, e.g.,* Dresser, *supra* n. 29, at 389:

> Legal decision-makers have accepted the dubious notion that what was vitally important to incompetent patients when they were competent remains vitally important to them in their incompetent states. But incompetent patients differ from competent patients in material ways that invalidate this notion. Incompetent patients are incapable of appreciating the values and preferences they once held dear. As a consequence, standards attempting to honor those values and preferences fail to advance the incompetent patient's present welfare.

See also John A. Robertson, Cruzan and the Constitutional Status of Nontreatment Decision for Incompetent Patients, 25 **Ga. L. Rev.** 1139, 1158–62 (1991).

117 **Feinberg,** *supra* n. 27, at 83–95 (1984) (arguing that people have interests that survive their death); *see also Conroy,* 486 A.2d at 1229:

> The right of an adult who . . . was once competent, to determine the course of her medical treatment remains intact even when she is no longer able to assert that right or to appreciate its effectuation. As one commentator has noted:
>> Even if the patient becomes too insensate to appreciate the honoring of his or her choice, self-determination is important. After all, law respects testamentary dispositions even if the testator never views his gift being bestowed. . . . Any other view would permit obliteration of an incompetent's panoply of rights merely because the patient could no longer sense the violation of those rights. (citation omitted).

118 Dworkin, *supra* n. 70, at 13–14 (stating that right depends on evidence of "an actual past decision contemplating the circumstances the patient is now in"). Despite this formulation, Dworkin apparently believes it would be sufficient to invoke the right of autonomy if "we have good reason to think he would have made that request [to be kept alive] if he had thought it necessary." **Dworkin,** *supra* n. 72, at 50. Of course there does come a point where the inference of a choice from an expressed preference is so strong that it counts as a choice from an expressed preference. There is room for disagreement on precisely when this point is reached. I understand Dworkin to mean that his test should be applied in all cases where the inferred preference is not that strong.

119 **Dworkin,** *supra* n. 72, at 48–9.

120 *Id.* at 47.

121 *Id.*

122 *See* **Ronald Dworkin, Law's Empire** 225 (1986).

123 *See* **Thomas Nagel, Mortal Questions** 24–38 (1979).

124 In deploring the tormenting of animals, Bentham wrote: ". . . [t]he question is not, Can they *reason?* nor, Can they *talk?* but, Can they *suffer.*" **Jeremy Bentham, An Introduction to the Principles of Morals and Legislation** 283 n.b. (J. H. Burns and H. L. A. Hart, eds., 1970).

14

Fetal-maternal conflicts

HOLLY M. SMITH

Since the early 1970s a great deal of attention has been paid to what we might term "conflicts of interest" between a fetus and the woman carrying it. The most dramatic of these conflicts occurs when pregnancy is unwanted and the woman desires to have an abortion. However, conflicts can arise even when the pregnancy is wanted and the fetus brought to term. Improvements in medical knowledge and technology, combined with alterations in women's social roles and expectations, have revealed or created a broad range of potential clashes between the well-being of the mother and that of the fetus. Fetal-maternal conflicts of this type can occur in the following kinds of cases:

1. The pregnant woman has the choice of introducing a substance into her body that would have differential effects on herself and the fetus. Salient examples include cases in which the woman consumes alcohol, coffee, tobacco, cocaine, or heroin. Other cases include the woman's medications during pregnancy or delivery (for example, aspirin, anticonvulsant and anticoagulant medications, drugs to relieve morning sickness, or drugs to reduce pain during labor and delivery) that may be necessary for her own health or comfort, but deleterious to the health of the fetus. Conversely, the woman may take – or refuse to take – medications or substances that improve the prospects of the fetus but compromise her own health or comfort. An example of this is provided by a PKU mother who must choose whether to undertake a burdensome and unpleasant low-phenalylanine diet during pregnancy in order to avoid severe mental retardation, microcephaly, and congestive heart disease in her fetus.

2. The pregnant woman has the choice of undergoing surgery that would have differential effects on her own and the fetus's well-being. She may choose – or reject – delivery by Caesarian section, or intrauterine surgery on fetal abnormalities. Such surgery would improve the fetus's chances of unimpaired survival but expose the mother to the risks, discomforts, and disabilities brought on by major abdominal surgery. Similarly the woman may choose – or reject – interventions that would improve her own health or longevity but compromise fetal health or longevity.

3. The pregnant woman may choose to behave in a manner that risks

physical impairment or death for the fetus. Sustained bedrest and avoidance of sexual intercourse may be necessary to avoid miscarriage in certain high-risk pregnancies; extremely vigorous exercise may induce premature labor in normal pregnancies; lack of sufficient exercise may render delivery more difficult and dangerous to the fetus; while certain physically dangerous pursuits, such as ice-skating or hang-gliding, may jeopardize the fetus's health or life.

4. The pregnant woman may choose to expose the fetus to environmental dangers. Holding a job in a workplace containing substances hazardous to fetal health may expose the fetus to risk of miscarriage and death or to a variety of disabilities and malformations. Living in a household with a heavy tobacco-using spouse may expose the fetus to the effects suffered by "passive smokers." Residing in a community with polluted water or soil may expose the fetus to chemical fetotoxins.

Most pregnant women want what is best for their children and choose their behavior accordingly. However, patterns of social behavior and actual individual incidents involving maternal-fetal conflicts of the kinds described have been widely reported over the last ten years. An estimated one baby out of ten is born with some illicit drug in its blood; babies born to mothers on crack suffer severe and often permanent neurological defects.[1] Women who use drugs during pregnancy have been charged with child abuse, and in at least one case, with the felony of delivering drugs to the baby.[2] Courts in Michigan and Illinois have held that a child can sue his or her mother for actions which may have adversely affected the child's development prior to birth. The Michigan case involved a mother who took tetracycline during pregnancy and thereby allegedly stained the teeth of her baby.[3] By 1987 courts in at least eleven states had ordered women to undergo Caesarean sections against their will.[4] Dramatic advances in fetal intrauterine surgery have occurred in the last several years; most recently a San Francisco surgeon successfully repaired a diaphragmatic hernia in a 24-week-old fetus who survived to normal birth. The availability of such remedies places increasing pressure on pregnant women to make use of them, even though they may involve the traumas to the mother of major abdominal surgery, and in some cases may promise only slight or low-probability benefits for the fetus. Although the fetal hernia repair was necessary to save the fetus's life, the surgeon who performed it cites the fact that intrauterine surgery leaves no scarring as a reason to correct such defects before rather than after birth in cases where either is possible.[5] In the case of workplace hazards, women are often not being permitted to make the choice for themselves. A number of important firms, including DuPont, General Motors, B.F. Goodrich, Olin, Gulf Oil, Allied Chemical, Monsanto, and American Cyanimid, have adopted employment policies excluding all fertile women from reproductively hazardous jobs. These policies have resulted in several notorious cases in which women have had themselves sterilized rather than lose their jobs or be transferred to safer but less well-paying positions.[6] Finally, some states have considered adopting a very broad approach to fetal-maternal conflicts: in 1987 Arkansas voters narrowly defeated a proposed constitutional amendment to make it a state responsibility to protect "every unborn child from conception to birth."[7]

Fetal-maternal conflicts arise because the pregnant woman and the fetus are physically linked in such a way that what affects the one may unavoidably affect the other as well. But family ties that bind parents to their children *after* birth may operate in much the same manner, giving rise to comparable conflicts of interest. The above cases form a continuum with ones in which conflict arises after the child's birth. A parent's smoking in the house poses a threat to other family members; crack-using parents often abuse and neglect their children[8]; parents who fail to buy smoke detectors expose their children to risk of death or injury by fire; parents who uproot the family to pursue career goals may subject children to disruption of important social ties or inferior schools; parents who fail to use an automobile child restraint system increase the child's chance of being killed or maimed in an accident; parents who reside in heavily polluted areas expose their children to the associated health risks; parents who purchase a lightweight fuel-efficient car increase the child's chance of being killed or disabled in an accident.

These cases remind us that there is an extremely general problem about the duties of parents in general, including pregnant women, to their children. In this paper I shall initially focus on only one component of this problem, the duties of a pregnant woman to her fetus when no abortion is planned. In examining this problem, I shall phrase the issue as follows: Does a fetus have a right that its mother engage in conduct that will maximize its chances of leading a healthy and unimpaired existence? In asking whether a fetus has such a *right,* I shall mean a *strong moral claim,* the kind that ought (at least prima facie) to be enforced by society, if necessary through the use of the criminal code. We can also express this question by asking whether the mother has a *duty to the fetus* to conduct herself so as to maximize the fetus's chances of leading a healthy and unimpaired existence.

I

In approaching this question, we must recognize two different kinds of case: those in which maternal conduct would either risk or result in fetal death, and those in which maternal conduct would either risk or result in less grave fetal impairment or ill-health. From a practical point of view it is somewhat artificial to separate these two kinds of cases since many forms of maternal conduct that risk one kind of result may risk the other as well. However, since the moral issues raised by the two kinds of case are importantly different, they must be considered separately. In this paper I shall focus primarily on maternal conduct that may affect the fetus's health or functioning, but not affect its chance of survival. In addition, I shall only consider cases in which the fetus retains sufficient health and level of functioning so that its postnatal life is worth living. Cases in which the fetus survives, but would be better off dead than in its resulting condition, require a different analysis.

What I shall call lethal fetal injury involves fetal death before the normal term of the pregnancy. *Nonlethal fetal injury,* the type we shall consider here, involves injuries that do not cause fetal death. Nonlethal fetal injury might involve fetal suffering or discomfort while the fetus is still *in utero.* However, most nonlethal fetal injuries primarily involve suffering for the fetus after it is born – the suffering of pain, disability, cosmetic deformity, ill-health, mental retardation, or a shortened lifespan. I shall restrict my attention to cases involving postnatal injuries of this sort.

Does a fetus have a right not to suffer such postnatal, nonlethal injuries? Strictly speaking, the fetus does not, because it is not the fetus but rather the child or adult whom it becomes that would suffer the evil of these injuries. But if the fetus survives, then the child or adult which it becomes *does* have a right not to suffer from pain and disability. Any action which wrongfully inflicts these evils on the child or adult violates a duty not to cause pain and suffering, *even though that action only causes this suffering by first affecting the fetus.* The mere fact of a gap in months or years between the time of the injurious action and the resultant suffering does not undermine the duty not to cause this suffering. Consider a terrorist who plants a time bomb that detonates and injures someone ten years later. This terrorist's act is morally no better than the act of a second terrorist who pushes the plunger and detonates his bomb immediately, causing an instant similar injury to a second victim. Assuming the two terrorists have equally certain knowledge of the consequences of their acts, the moral quality of the acts is the same, despite the difference in rapidity with which the consequences occur. Consider a third terrorist, who plants a bomb that explodes ten years later, injuring a child who was still *in utero* at the time the bomb was planted. His act is just as heinous as the acts of the first two terrorists. The reason for this is that the child has a right not to suffer, and *this* right is violated by the action of the terrorist ten years earlier – even though the child was still a fetus at that time.[9] Such a duty would be a duty to the child or adult which the fetus would become. It would not be a duty to the fetus itself, since it is not the fetus but rather the child or the adult who would experience the suffering. By the same token, any such right would be a right possessed by the child or the adult, not by the fetus. However, for brevity of exposition I shall allow myself in such cases to speak loosely of a duty to the fetus, or a right of the fetus, with regard to nonlethal injury.

If this is correct, then in considering any action which involves less-than-lethal postnatal injury to a fetus, we must view the fetus as though it were a child or adult, because it will develop into a child or adult whose rights may be violated by our action. From this point of view we can see that the conflicts of interest between a pregnant woman and her fetus are more closely allied to the conflicts of interest between a parent and a child after birth than we may initially have supposed. But acknowledging this parallel does not, in itself, tell us what the mother's duty to the fetus (on behalf of its future selves) is. In the next section I shall sketch three different approaches to the problem and argue that one of them provides the best framework for determining what a pregnant woman's concrete duties to her fetus are. I shall discuss the apparent implications of this framework for certain kinds of concrete cases, without attempting a definitive resolution of these cases.

II

One way of ascertaining the woman's duty to the fetus is by doing a utilitarian calculus. According to this approach, the woman is morally obliged to choose the alternative, among those open to her, that would have the least bad net effect on the welfare of everyone involved. Let us take the example of a pregnant woman who is considering whether or not to remain in a job where fetotoxins pose significant hazards to the health of her fetus. To determine her duty according to a utilitarian calculus, one details the possible consequences of her retaining the hazardous job: damage to the well-being of the child or adult that the fetus would become, secondary suffering of the immediate family, financial drain on society, and so forth – counterbalanced to some degree by the benefits of the mother's retaining a productive and remunerative job. One then details the possible consequences of her various alternatives. For example, the consequences of her quitting work might include financial strain and emotional stress affecting the entire family, possible health damage to the fetus from inadequate nutrition if the woman cannot find alternative employment, social loss of a productive worker, and so forth – counterbalanced to some degree by birth of a baby whose well-being has not been compromised by workplace fetotoxins. These various effects are assigned values, weighted by their probabilities of occurrence, and the resulting sums for each of the mother's alternatives are compared. If the net effect of the pregnant woman's retaining the job is worse than the effect of quitting, then she has a duty to quit; if the reverse is true, then she has a duty to remain on the job, even though doing so imperils the fetus.

If one can carry out such a utilitarian calculus, one can derive a definite answer to the question of whether or not the pregnant woman has a duty in any particular case to avoid activity that threatens the fetus's well-being. However, it is notorious that the answers provided by utilitarianism are often unsatisfactory. The reasoning behind this dissatisfaction might be expressed as follows: "Suppose it turns out that the woman ought to keep the job, even at a severe cost to the health of the fetus. Then the fetus (or the child it becomes) is being directly harmed in order to secure benefits for other people, for example, self-esteem for the woman, a higher standard of living for the family, cheaper manufactured goods for society. In starker terms, the fetus is *being sacrificed* for them. But it is immoral to sacrifice one person in order to benefit others, even when the gain for them outweighs the loss for the victim. Utilitarianism misses this point, and so goes astray in this case as in many others."

This objection rests on a view about morality that provides the foundation for the second and third approaches to our central question. According to this view, there is an important moral distinction between harming another person and failing to help that person. People have a *right* not to be harmed, and this right creates a strict duty on the part of others. But generally speaking people have no right to be helped, and there is no *duty* to assist others, although it may be morally admirable to do so. Thus, you have a duty not to harm another person by stealing his money, but you have no duty to help him out by giving him your money. Similarly, you have a duty not to injure someone with your car, but you have no duty to assist the victim of an accident caused by someone else. Helping people in need is an act of Good Samaritanism which morality commends but generally speaking does not require. The latter qualification is necessary because some people feel that there is a duty to help others *if the cost of doing so would be minimal.* On this view there may be a duty to help the accident victim by some minimally costly act, such as calling an ambulance, but there is no duty to help the victim by providing artificial respiration for forty-five minutes until the paramedics arrive. But the duty not to harm others holds whether or not the cost of avoiding harm would be minimal: even if the cost to you is major, you have a duty not to steal, and a duty not to injure someone with your car. One sign of the difference between harming and failing to help is the fact that it is appropriate for society to forbid harmful acts and to enforce this prohibition by imposing criminal sanctions, but, by and large, it is not appropriate for society to use criminal penalties to compel acts of assistance or charity. The predominant exceptions to the latter involve acts of assistance that would involve minimal cost to the agent, or acts that occur within relationships of trust, such as the family.[10]

There is currently a good deal of philosophical controversy about the view that causing harm is morally worse than failing to help. However, the view is deeply entrenched in ordinary moral consciousness and informs much of our common and statutory law. It will repay us to ask how the distinction applies to the problem of the fetus's right vis-à-vis the mother. Clearly (on this view) a woman has a strict duty not to positively harm her fetus by, for example, shooting it while it is still *in utero* and causing it to be paralyzed. On the other hand, there may be acts of assisting it which even as a parent she has no strict duty to perform. For example, if the fetus's intelligence could be raised twenty points by a series of prenatal treatments, she has no strict duty to undertake the treatments. Indeed, if the cost to her is high – if, for instance, the treatments are extremely painful to the mother, or if financing them would require her to give up her own college education – the moral pressure on her to undertake the treatments is minimal or nonexistent.

In order to trace the implications of this moral perspective for maternal-fetal conflicts, we must know what kind of conduct on the part of a pregnant woman counts as "positively harming" her fetus, and so is prohibited. There seem to be two possible approaches to answering this question. I shall call these approaches the "Simple Causal View" and the "Contextual View." According to the Simple Causal View, whether or not an act counts as harming someone simply depends on the causal nature of the act. If the agent *actively produces* the injury, then he counts as having harmed the victim. If, on the other hand, the agent does not intervene to prevent already existing conditions from producing an injury, or if he does not actively produce an improvement in the victim's situation, then he counts as merely having failed to assist the person. Thus, a person who shoots a child harms him, but a person who passively stands by while another individual shoots the child, fails to assist him.

On the Simple Causal View, the mother's ingesting toxic substances such as drugs or alcohol counts as positively harming the fetus, because she acts in a way that positively produces fetal injury. Similarly, her undergoing surgery that benefits herself but injures the fetus, or her engaging in damaging physical activity such as overly vigorous exercise or hang-gliding, would count as positively harming the fetus. By the same token, the mother's exposing a fetus to toxic workplace chemicals would appear to count as positively harming it. Of course exposing a fetus to toxins in the workplace is not, in terms of causal structure, precisely like firing a gun at it. But it is not necessary personally to pull the trigger in order to actively produce a gunshot wound: It would be sufficient to carry the victim onto a military target range where he is hit by the gunfire of others. Carrying someone within range of firing guns actively produces a situation in which the person will be injured, and so counts as harming the person. On the Simple Causal View, carrying a fetus into a hazardous workplace is analogous to carrying the child onto a firing range. When the fetus suffers, the mother has harmed it. On this view, since the fetus has a right not to be so harmed, the mother has a strict duty not to undertake work that is hazardous to it.[11] Since maternal activities such as smoking crack, drinking excessively, undergoing surgery beneficial to herself but harmful to the fetus, or exposing it to a hazardous workplace count as *harming* it, a pregnant woman has a strict duty not to engage in these activities, however burdensome the avoidance of these activities may be to her personally. At least up to certain extreme limits, she evidently cannot justify the pursuit of these activities by pointing out the personal sacrifices by her forgoing them.

The Simple Causal View is initially plausible, and many writers on fetal-maternal conflicts have assumed it is correct. For example, John A. Robertson and Joseph Schulman, in discussing PKU mothers who refuse to follow a diet necessary to preserve the fetus's health, refer repeatedly to "The mother's . . . behavior occurring during pregnancy [that] directly injures babies who could be born healthy," her "harmful conduct," more generally to "obligations to refrain from harming children by prenatal actions," and to "women who will not or cannot comply with proper conduct [who] will wind up injuring a child who could be born healthy."[12] Similarly Dawn Johnsen states that "pregnant women make countless decisions that pose some threat to their fetuses," and says they "should not and cannot make . . . decisions solely on the basis of what is most likely to reduce the chance of harming the fetus."[13] The Simple Causal View has a strong grip on our initial understanding of fetal-maternal conflicts. However, I think this understanding is faulty. There is another way of interpreting the situation that results in a different judgment, and that seems to me more adequate. This approach, which I call the "Contextual View," maintains that whether or not an act counts as harming does not depend solely on the causal structure of the act. It also depends on the context, or background conditions, in which the act takes place. When this is taken into account, our understanding of fetal-maternal conflicts is altered. To see how contextual factors affect the question of whether or not an act counts as a harming, let us consider the following two cases.

In the first case a motorist, driving through an uninhabited desert, comes upon the figure of a woman sprawled by the roadside. Inspection reveals that she has been bitten in the leg by a rattlesnake, has lapsed into unconsciousness, and will certainly die if not given expert medical aid. The motorist cannot render this aid, and there is no probability that anyone else will pass by in time to save the snakebite victim. The only way to save her life is to transport her to the nearest hospital, which involves going several hundred miles out of the motorist's way. Most motorists would undoubtedly be happy to perform this service. But according to the tradition that helping is morally optional, there is no strict duty to do so. Note that since the snakebite victim is unconscious, no hope of rescue would be raised in her mind by the motorist's arrival or dashed by his unfeeling departure: If the motorist decides not to rescue the victim, or abandons a rescue effort at some stage, he leaves her no worse off than she would have been had he never come along. Let us imagine, however, that humanitarianism moves the motorist to take the snakebite victim to the hospital. On his arrival, the doctor informs him that their facilities are limited; although they will be able to save the victim's life, they will not be able to prevent gangrene from necessitating amputation of her leg. In another community there is a hospital possessing adequate facilities to save both the victim's life and leg, but unfortunately the local ambulance has broken down. In fact the only way for the victim to get to the second hospital would be for the motorist to transport her an additional hundred miles out of his way. Does the fact that the motorist has undertaken to render *some* assistance to the snakebite victim mean that he is now obliged to render her *further* assistance – to prevent her losing her leg as well as prevent her losing her life? It seems clear that there is no strict duty to render this second act of assistance any more than there was to render the first one. We might not admire a motorist who refuses to render this higher level of aid, but the snakebite victim has no *right* to it.

Now consider a second case. The scenario is much the same: if the motorist takes the snakebite victim to a hospital several hundred miles away, the victim's life will be saved. Seeing the victim's plight, the motorist places her in the car and starts for the hospital. However, he realizes that the shortest route to the hospital involves traversing an extremely rough stretch of road, and that the inevitable jolting will traumatize the victim's leg, causing it become gangrenous and ultimately to require amputation. There exists an alternative route over a smoother road, but taking this route would send the motorist an additional hundred miles out of his way. Does he have a strict duty to take the longer route and avoid loss of the victim's leg?

There is an obvious sense in which the motorist's taking the shorter route would *cause* the victim to lose the leg. If we rely solely on this fact, as the Simple Causal View does, we must say that the motorist who takes the shorter route positively *harms* the victim, and so is morally required to take the longer route to the hospital if he attempts to rescue the victim at all. But in fact the motorist's taking the shorter route to the hospital seems morally on a par with his failing to take the victim to the second hospital in the first case described. In the first case, rendering the lower level of aid merely involves ceasing efforts on behalf of the victim, while in the second case, it involves physically injuring the victim in the process of rescuing her. But because in both cases the victim is better off than she would have been if no assistance had been rendered at all, we cannot say her rights have been violated. Thus, the Simple Causal View presents *too* simple a picture of what harming consists in. Certain acts that would count as harming when looked at from a purely causal point of view are not harms when they take place within a context of rendering aid, and indeed qualify as *ways* of rendering aid. Then they count merely as rendering a lower level of aid than would have been possible. Since rendering aid at the highest possible level is not required, such acts are morally permissible. It is just as permissible in the second case for the motorist to take the shorter, rougher route as it was in the first case for him to refuse to take the victim to the second hospital.[14]

The lesson to be learned from these two cases is this. Just as a person's rights are not violated by failure to render her aid, so her rights are not violated by provision of aid at less than the optimal level. Sometimes rendering a less-than-optimal level of aid involves ceasing one's efforts on her behalf, but sometimes it involves treating the person, in the course of the rescue effort, in a manner that would otherwise constitute harming her. But in this context the treatment does not count as harming her – rather it merely counts as rendering her a lower level of aid, and so does not violate her rights.

Let us apply this lesson to the problem of fetal-maternal conflicts in which the pregnant woman can choose to act in a manner that would result in postnatal nonlethal fetal injury. To do so, we must first recognize that a pregnant woman is someone who is *benefiting* or *assisting* her fetus.[15] She is providing it with the use of her body for shelter and nourishment while it develops. Her act of carrying the child to term should be seen as morally parallel to the act of donating a kidney to someone dying of renal disease. Special considerations aside, the pregnant woman is not morally required to provide this assistance, just as the donor is not morally required to donate his kidney.

The pregnant woman is therefore morally on a par with the motorist engaged in saving the life of the snakebite victim by transporting him to the hospital. If the woman acts in a manner that results in postnatal fetal injury, for example, if she exposes the fetus to toxic substances in her workplace, her act is parallel to the motorist's act of transporting the victim to the hospital by the shortest, but rough, route. Just as there is an obvious sense in which the motorist's act causes the victim to lose his leg, so there is an obvious sense in which the woman's act causes her fetus to suffer disability or ill-health.[16] But, just as the victim is better off overall to have been rescued in this fashion than not to have been rescued at all, so the fetus is better off overall to have been given life under these circumstances than not to have been given life at all. Because the woman is engaged in a course of assisting the fetus, her act of exposing it to workplace toxins does not count as harming it. Instead the act counts as providing the fetus with a lower level of aid. Hence, no right of the fetus is violated by this act.

On the Contextual View, as I have outlined it, it appears that a fetus has no right that its mother avoid activities that would result in postnatal nonlethal injury to the fetus. Such activities should be construed as the mother's rendering the fetus a lower level of aid than she might have done. But since she is not morally required to render aid at all (at least if doing so would require significant personal cost), she is certainly not required to render the highest possible level of aid. Hence, these activities are morally permissible, and

violate no right of the fetus. Earlier in this section I pointed out that the duty
not to harm another person holds even when the cost of avoiding harm would
be heavy: Whether one has a duty not to harm another does not vary with the
cost to oneself of fulfilling such a duty. But one only has a duty to assist
another person in circumstances where the cost of carrying out that duty
would be minimal. Hence, if a pregnant woman's activities that risk nonlethal
injury to her fetus are understood as *failures to assist* the fetus, rather than as
harms to the fetus, the moral quality of these activities alters considerably. If
these activities harm the fetus, she cannot justify pursuing them by citing the
cost to her of foregoing the activities. From this point of view, Robertson's
and Schulman's contention that fetal-maternal conflicts are to be resolved by
"a careful balancing of the offspring's welfare and the pregnant woman's
interest in liberty and bodily integrity" makes little sense.[17] No such balancing
is appropriate. But if these activities merely fail to assist the fetus at the
highest possible level, then the pregnant woman can justify pursuing them by
citing the cost to her of failing to do so. Adopting the Contextual View, rather
than the Simple Causal View, has a dramatic effect on the kinds of moral
judgments we can render in cases of fetal-maternal conflict.

III

I believe the conclusion reached in the last section is correct in its essentials.
However, it needs qualification, and it must be defended against certain
apparently plausible objections. In this section I will revisit the case of pregnancy and develop a more adequate application of the Contextual View to the
duties of the pregnant woman towards her fetus. In the following section I will
refine the Contextual View to rule out certain unacceptable conclusions that
might seem to follow from the analysis so far.

   An immediate objection to my conclusion about the pregnant woman's duty
toward her fetus might be stated as follows: "So far you have drawn a strict
parallel between the case of the motorist and the case of the pregnant woman.
But there is a glaring disparity between them: The motorist is a complete
stranger to the snakebite victim, while the pregnant woman is the *parent* of
her fetus. And parenthood is a paradigmatic example of a *fiduciary relationship* that generates strict duties to render assistance in circumstances where
such duties would not hold among strangers. A parent is morally bound to
help his children, for example to feed and clothe them – something no mere
stranger is obligated to do for them. According to the analysis so far, a
pregnant woman's subjecting her fetus to nonlethal injury, for example, by
exposing her fetus to toxic substances in the workplace, counts as (merely)
failing to help it. But because parents are strictly obligated to help their
children, it appears the pregnant woman has a strict duty to avoid subjecting
her fetus to these injuries after all."

I believe, however, that the fact of parenthood does not imply the pregnant woman is strictly prohibited from subjecting her fetus to these injuries. It is certainly true that parents have the duty to aid their children. However, they do not have the duty to aid their children in every conceivable way or at the highest possible level. A parent is required to feed his child, but not required to give him steak – to educate his child, but not required to send him to Harvard, even though he can afford to do so. Similarly, a parent is morally required to provide medical care for his child. But there are limitations to this duty too: He is not required to move from his community, severing all his ties and giving up his job with no prospect for another, in order to secure a greater level of medical expertise and a greater chance of curing the child of debilitating symptoms. How much a parent is required to do for a child seems to depend partly on the benefit to the child, and partly on the cost to the parent. Similarly, how much a pregnant woman – as a parent – may be required to do for her fetus may depend partly on the benefit to the fetus, and partly on the cost to the woman.[18] The presence of the parental relation in the fetal hazard case seems not to radically alter the analysis we arrived at by comparing it to the motorist case. What it shows is that at some level of potential benefit to the fetus, and some level of personal cost to the mother, it becomes the woman's duty not to subject the fetus to nonlethal harms, because to do so would be to fall below the level of aid that parents are required to provide their children. But at other levels the woman's failure to aid her fetus at the highest possible level remains morally optional.

What this implies for particular kinds of injurious activities the pregnant woman might undertake varies from case to case. In the case of workplace toxins that might injure the fetus, whether or not the mother should (say) quit her job will depend on the level of risk for the fetus and the alternatives available for the mother. If avoiding exposing her fetus to nonlethal hazards requires the mother to quit her job, when that job is the sole or a major support for the family, and when no other job is likely to be available either now or at the end of the pregnancy, this option seems to be on a par with leaving one's community to increase the chance of finding a cure for one's ailing child. If the latter is not morally required, neither is the former (which is not to say that many parents would not choose these courses of action).[19] On the other hand, if the mother can procure another decent and hazardless job, then she may be morally required to do so in order to avoid injuries to the fetus. The case of the mother's consuming fetotoxic substances is more complex. If the mother, in order to sustain her own health, must take medications, such as anticonvulsant drugs, that could be injurious to the fetus, then this activity appears morally permissible.[20] Parents are not morally required to undergo substantial harms to their own bodies or health in order to assist their children.[21] But what about the case of the mother who takes illegal drugs or drinks significant quantities of alcohol that risk serious detriment to the fetus?[22] A pregnant woman who is already a drug addict will suffer significant anguish from the withdrawal process if she quits in order to protect her fetus. From this point of view the cost to her of benefiting the fetus in this way is substantial. On the other hand, most of us would want to say that the mother would be objectively better off to rid herself of the addiction, even though the process of doing so is temporarily painful. The mother herself may even agree with this judgment, at least when the process is completed. From this broader perspective there is no *net cost* to the mother, but rather a *net benefit,* of acting in a manner that best promotes the health of her fetus. If we look at it this way, the mother has a moral duty to quit using drugs, because doing so significantly benefits her fetus without any net cost to herself.

But is this a moral duty of the kind with which we began: one which ought (at least prima facie) to be enforced by society, if necessary through the use of the criminal code? This is a difficult issue that cannot be adequately addressed here. However, several relevant considerations can be pointed out. On the one hand, it is clear that although we feel strongly that parents have certain duties to aid their children, we have historically been reluctant to incorporate more than a bare minimum of these duties into our criminal code. On the other hand, possession or use of illegal drugs is by definition illegal in itself, whether or not the user is pregnant. Hence, there should be no bar to enforcing this prohibition on pregnant women. But ought society – or may society – take stronger measures to enforce such a prohibition on pregnant women than it takes to enforce the prohibition on other citizens? For example, may society incarcerate pregnant women who are convicted of drug use during their entire pregnancy to keep them drug-free, despite the fact that similarly harsh preventative measures are not employed on men convicted of drug use?[23] We do not impose such restrictive measures on drug-addicted parents of minor children, even though their activities are likely to impose significant harms on their children. However, perhaps we cannot draw any conclusions from this fact, because the two kinds of case are not strictly parallel: The threatened children can always be removed from the care of the parents, whereas the threatened fetus cannot be removed from its mother.[24] On the other hand, a woman who is incarcerated in order to protect her fetus is thereby forced to suffer a very high cost – the restrictions, indignities, discomforts, risks, and disruptions of incarceration itself – in order to benefit her fetus. Her case is very unlike the case of the woman who is persuaded to quit drugs voluntarily. The latter woman does something that is arguably in her own interest in order to benefit her fetus. The incarcerated woman is forced to pay a very high price in order to benefit her fetus. My sense here is that we may not morally require parents to pay this high a price to benefit their children. If this is correct, then society may not impose this price on them. Society may and should strive to persuade drug-addicted pregnant women to give up drugs, but it may not impose substantially harsher drug-prevention measures on them than it does on men or on women who are not pregnant. Finally, we must keep in mind that enforcing a legal prohibition on most of the activities with which we are concerned would be extraordinarily intrusive: It would invade, in the most objectionable manner, the conduct of ordinary private life. Thus even if we conclude that pregnant women have a moral duty, for example, not to smoke and not to drink alcoholic beverages, we need not conclude that smoking and drinking should be made illegal during pregnancy.[25] Enforcing such prohibitions would necessitate invasions in the lives of private citizens that most of us are not prepared to tolerate. If pregnant women have a moral duty not to drink or smoke, we should conclude that there is a *prima facie* claim, but no more than a *prima facie* claim, that society ought to enforce this duty. Because this prima facie claim is overridden by claims of citizens to protection from intolerable invasions by the state into their private life, we would reject the conclusion that society ought *all things considered* to enforce this claim.

IV

We now need to refine the notion of failing to render a higher level of aid. In Section II, I stated that a woman has a strict duty not to shoot her fetus *in utero* and cause it to be paralyzed in later life, because doing so would count as positively harming the fetus. However, the Contextual View seems to imply that *any* maternal conduct detrimental to the fetus, so long as it leaves the fetus better off alive than dead, merely counts as failing to render it the highest possible level of aid, and so as potentially permissible (so long as the parental duty to aid a child would not prohibit such conduct). But it seems absurd to say that a woman shooting her fetus *in utero* is simply failing to render the highest level of aid – more needs to be said to distinguish this case from the case of a mother who exposes her fetus to workplace toxins or who drinks and causes the fetus to suffer from Fetal Alcohol Syndrome.

To deal with this problem we must elaborate the Contextual View. Let us turn to a new snakebite example. Suppose the scenario is the same as in the Rough Route case, with adequate facilities for saving the victim's life available at the nearest hospital several hundred miles away. The motorist starts to town with the victim. However, in this version, the motorist is a sadist, who uses the opportunity of having a helpless person in his grasp to beat the victim cruelly. He then continues to town. The victim's life is saved, but she loses her leg as a direct consequence of the motorist's beating. It seems intuitively clear that the sadistic motorist *harms* the victim, and violates a strict duty, by beating her. But nothing that has been said so far rules out an interpretation of the Contextual View according to which the sadistic motorist simply renders the victim a lower level of aid than he might have done, because his overall course of action leaves the victim better off than she would have been if the motorist had not rescued her at all. Hence, the view seems to imply that the beating cannot count as harming the victim, and so is perfectly permissible.

Fortunately, we can avoid this unwanted result. There are important differences between the Rough Route case and the Sadistic Motorist case that make it appropriate to say in the former that the motorist simply renders a lower level of aid, while in the latter that the motorist harms his victim. The difference between the two cases can be brought out by noticing that in the Sadistic Motorist case, but not in the Rough Route case, we can say that the motorist *uses* the victim to enhance his own welfare. Why is this true in the one case but not in the other? A full analysis of this difference exceeds the scope of this paper, but two relevant features of the cases may be mentioned here. First, in the Rough Route case, the action that causes the leg injury – transporting the victim over a rough road – is *a way* of rescuing the victim, just as calling an ambulance or flagging down another motorist might be ways of rescuing someone. But in the Sadistic Motorist case, the action that causes the leg injury – beating the victim – is *not* a way of rescuing the victim. Rather it is an adjunct activity made possible by the victim's plight and the occurrence of the rescue. Second, if we compare the benefits the two motorists gain by taking courses of action that are inferior from the point of view of the victim, it is clear that these benefits arise in structurally different ways in the two cases. In the Rough Route case, the motorist who takes the rough route gains a relative benefit (taking a shorter route) that would have been available to him whether or not he interacted with the victim; indeed whether or not the victim even existed. But in the Sadistic Motorist case, the motorist who beats the victim gains a relative benefit (the pleasure of sadism) that is *only* available to him because he interacts with the victim; indeed is only available to him because of the existence of the victim. It is these kinds of features that make it appropriate to view the Rough Route motorist as merely rendering a lower level of aid, and by contrast to view the Sadistic motorist as *using* the victim, and so as harming her by beating her on the way to the hospital.

Comparison of these two cases shows that we can distinguish between a rescuer's harming the person in need of aid versus his merely rendering the needy person a lower level of assistance. The latter may be permissible, but the former is morally prohibited. Clearly, the pregnant woman who exposes her fetus to workplace toxins is parallel to the Rough Route motorist rather than to the Sadistic motorist. She does not use her fetus to enhance her own welfare. Her working in the hazardous job is a way of continuing to rescue the fetus, since it involves continuing to support and nurture the fetus. And the benefits she gains by continuing to work rather than quitting her job (her salary, fringe benefits, and so on) are ones available to her whether or not she "interacts" with the fetus; indeed whether or not the fetus exists at all. Hence, we may understand her as merely rendering the fetus a lower level of aid. Similar remarks hold for the woman who drinks while pregnant and causes her fetus to suffer from Fetal Alcohol Syndrome.

But what about the woman who shoots her fetus *in utero* and causes it to be paralyzed? Of course it is difficult to imagine a realistic case of this sort. But let us imagine that the woman was raped by her estranged boyfriend. As the resulting pregnancy progresses, the woman comes to hate her ex-boyfriend and is possessed by an overwhelming desire to punish him for the rape. Since she cannot reach her ex-boyfriend, in a confused state of mind she decides to punish him by injuring his offspring, and so shoots the fetus.

In this case, it seems to me that she must be understood as *using* the fetus to accomplish her ends, and so as harming it, rather than merely as rendering it a lower level of aid. Her shooting the fetus is an adjunct activity to her continuing the pregnancy, not a way of continuing the pregnancy. Moreover, in shooting the fetus she gains a relative benefit (satisfaction at "punishing" her ex-boyfriend) that she can only gain by interacting with the fetus. Indeed, this particular benefit is only available to her because of the existence of the fetus. For these reasons her shooting the fetus counts as harming it. What she does is morally impermissible.

There are other versions of the case in which this would not be so. If the woman regularly engages in target practice as a matter of sport, and shoots herself in the abdomen by accident while practicing, we should view her shooting the fetus as her rendering it a lower level of aid. She was merely engaged in what was for her a normal activity, so that her shooting was not an adjunct activity to her continuing the pregnancy. She gained no relative benefit from the fact that the fetus as well as herself was injured by the shot. This woman does not wrongfully use her fetus to advance her own welfare. Rather she fails to render the higher level of aid she could have provided by avoiding engaging in a dangerous activity during pregnancy. The contrast between these two versions of the shooting case supplies further support for the central theme of this paper, namely that a simple causal account of an activity cannot demonstrate whether or not it is a case of causing harm. The shootings in these two cases have the same causal structure, but they are morally quite different. The context as well as the causal structure of the activity must be taken into account in order to assess its moral quality.

V

This paper has examined the question of whether or not a pregnant woman has a strict moral duty to avoid conduct that would subject her fetus to nonlethal postnatal injuries. If such a duty exists, it is a duty to the child or adult the fetus would become, rather than a duty to the fetus itself. I rejected a utilitarian answer to this question in favor of a traditional approach that draws an important moral distinction between harming another person and failing to assist another person. This approach holds that there is a strong moral duty not to harm another, but no such duty to assist others (at least if the cost of doing so is nontrivial). I then asked what kind of conduct on the part of a pregnant woman counts as harming her fetus. Using the snakebite cases I argued that the Simple Causal answer to this question must be rejected in favor of a Contextual View that takes into account the context in which an action occurs as well as its causal structure. Combining the Contextual View with the assumption that a woman who carries a fetus to term must be understood as benefiting the fetus, I argued that many cases in which a pregnant woman's activities risk nonlethal injury to her fetus must be seen as ones in which the woman's activities count, not as harming her fetus, but rather merely as rendering it a lower level of aid. Whether or not the woman has an obligation to avoid those activities depends on what kind of duty of aid a parent owes his or her children, a matter that seems to depend on the potential benefit to the child as well as on the level of personal sacrifice required of the parent in order to provide that benefit. Using this approach, we can see the continuity between cases in which a pregnant woman smokes, drinks, uses cocaine, or exposes her fetus to workplace toxins, and cases in which parents fail to install smoke detectors in their houses or child restraint devices in their cars, or refuse to move their families from residential areas contaminated by toxic chemicals. In all these cases, the parent fails to render the highest possible level of care for his or her child: the remaining issue is what level of care is morally required of parents – and what level of parental care can be legally compelled.[26]

Notes

1 "Cocaine Use Linked to Infant Brain Defects," *The Arizona Daily Star,* Monday, January 19, 1987; and "Crack Addiction Can Make Parent Shun Child, Experts Say," *The Arizona Daily Star,* Sunday, March 18, 1990, 10A.
2 "Mother of Addicted Baby Faces Felony Drug Charge," *The Arizona Daily Star,* December 17, 1988, 22A.
3 Dawn Johnsen, "A New Threat to Pregnant Women's Autonomy," *The Hastings Center Report* 17 (November 1987): 34.
4 "The Troubling Question of 'Fetal Rights'," *Newsweek,* December 8, 1986, 87; and Johnsen, *op. cit.,* 34.
5 John Barbour, "Surgery's New Frontier," *The Arizona Daily Star,* August 11, 1990, 5B.
6 Ronald Bayer, "Women, Work, and Reproductive Hazards," in *The Hastings Center Report* (August 1982): 15. In *International Union et al. v. Johnson Controls* the

Supreme Court unanimously struck down a policy imposed since 1982 by Johnson Controls, Inc., which barred fertile women from potentially risky jobs involving the handling of lead in auto battery manufacture. Against company advice, some women had themselves sterilized in order to retain their jobs. Males working in the company also face the possibility of reproductive compromise from exposure to lead. *Arizona Daily Star,* March 21, 1991, 1A.

7 "The Troubling Question of 'Fetal Rights'," *Newsweek,* December 8, 1986, 87.

8 "Crack Addiction Can Make Parent Shun Child, Experts Say," *The Arizona Daily Wildcat,* Sunday, March 18, 1990, 10A.

9 Clearly, the act of someone who causes the *death* of a fetus cannot be analyzed in the same way. We cannot say that it violates the right of the adult into which the fetus will develop, because when the fetus dies, that adult never comes into existence. Hence, there never is a future right which is violated by the act which causes death now.

Note that because the fetus has not yet been born, there is realistically some uncertainty as to whether it will survive to term and eventually live long enough for the bomb to injure it. Thus, actions that have the potential to injure a child or adult into whom a fetus develops may always be somewhat less heinous than actions that immediately injure a child or adult, because the former actions involve risk rather than certainty.

10 For a general discussion of these issues, see Joel Feinberg, *Harm to Others* (Oxford: Oxford University Press, 1984), chapter 4.

11 Of course in many cases the pregnant woman who harms her fetus by carrying it into a hazardous workplace helps others at the same time, namely other children in the family, who benefit from her wages. It is unclear how the moral view we are assuming must deal with this fact. It certainly must recognize that occasionally it is morally necessary to harm one person in order to fulfill obligations to others.

12 John A. Robertson and Joseph D. Schulman, "Pregnancy and Prenatal Harm to Offspring: The Case of Mothers with PKU," *The Hastings Center Report* 17 (November 1987): 24–6.

13 Dawn Johnsen, *op. cit.,* 36.

14 Another way to analyze this situation would be to say that the motorist who takes the rougher route in the second case *both* harms *and* helps the victim. If harming a person is not absolutely prohibited, and can be morally overridden by simultaneously assisting that person, then we would still get the conclusion that the motorist acts permissibly in taking the shorter route, even though doing so results in the victim's losing her leg. This kind of analysis could be applied, *mutatis mutandis,* to fetal-maternal conflicts. However, in some of these cases the "harming" action and the "helping" action are so intertwined that it is difficult to clearly distinguish them in the way this analysis requires. Moreover, the principle that harming a person is permissible so long as one simultaneously assists that person is obviously too simple to be acceptable: The relation between the harming and the helping must be tighter than mere simultaneity. In view of these considerations, I prefer the approach taken in the text.

15 The view that the pregnant woman benefits her fetus, or acts as a Good Samaritan towards it, has been defended on somewhat different grounds by Judith Jarvis

Thomson, "A Defense of Abortion," in Joel Feinberg, ed., *The Problem of Abortion* (Belmont, California: The Wadsworth Publishing Co., 1973), 121–39; and by Donald Regan, "Rewriting *Roe v. Wade*," *Michigan Law Review*, 77 (August 1979), 1569–1646.

16 We should not forget that many such activities on the part of the pregnant woman *risk*, but do not *actually result in*, injuries to the fetus.

17 John A. Robertson and Joseph D. Schulman, *op. cit.*, 32.

18 We should note that the maternal-fetal relationship is different in significant ways from the more usual parent-child relationship. Because of the fetus's incomplete development, its relationship to the mother bears few of the normal hallmarks of a child's relation to its parents: for example, the ties of affection and bonds of reliance that normally characterize these relationships are utterly absent. Such features surely play a role in underpinning the moral duty of a parent to aid its child. From this point of view, the relationship of the fetus to its mother is closer to that of the snakebite victim to the motorist: since the fetus has little if any sentient life, and no awareness of any special relationship to its mother, her failure to assist it would not violate any expectations of help. On the other hand, we are primarily concerned with suffering experienced by the child or adult into whom the fetus develops. This child or adult will certainly be able to understand, and possibly condemn, its mother's failure to provide it with the highest possible level of aid.

19 Of course there is a larger policy issue here: Perhaps the best solution is for the employer to be required to provide a workplace free from toxic hazards. Most discussions of reproduction hazards in the workplace have focused on this kind of question, rather than the one which is central to this paper. I believe it is difficult to settle the obligations of the employer before having settled the obligations of the pregnant worker. However, one should not allow focus on the woman's obligations to distract one's attention from what may be even heavier obligations of society or the employer.

20 Support for this conclusion is provided by the recommendations of the National Commission for the Protection of Human Subjects of Biomedical and Behavioral Research. The Commission recommended that in the case of *therapeutic* research directed towards the pregnant woman, the health of the woman takes priority over that of the fetus. Treatment that would be harmful to the fetus is permitted so long as it is necessary to the health of the woman. The Commission further recommended that the woman be prohibited from undergoing *nontherapeutic* research that poses greater than minimal risk to the fetus. (*Federal Register*, November 30, 1978). One obvious difference between these two types of research involves the costs to the woman of forgoing them. In the case of forgoing therapeutic research, the woman's health will suffer, whereas in the case of nontherapeutic research, she will only suffer minor pecuniary loss, or perhaps frustration of her desire to participate in a project designed to benefit humanity. Because these latter losses are relatively minor, she may be prohibited from undergoing nontherapeutic research; because the losses to health may be major, she may not be prohibited from undergoing therapeutic research.

21 In *McFall v. Shimp* (1978), a court refused to order a man to donate bone marrow to save his cousin's life, on grounds that "to *compel* the Defendant to submit to an

intrusion of his body would change every concept and principle upon which our society is founded. To do so would defeat the sanctity of the individual . . ." Quoted in Dawn Johnsen, *op. cit.*, 37–8. More recently an Illinois judge refused to order 3-year-old twins to undergo tests that would determine if they could donate bone marrow to their leukemia-stricken half-brother, saying the tests would be an invasion of privacy. "Judge Refuses to Order Marrow Tests for Twins," *Arizona Daily Star,* July 19, 1990, 14.

22 The parallel here, in terms of the original snakebite cases, would be a motorist who has been drinking prior to his discovery of the snakebite victim, and who continues to drink even after placing the snakebite victim in his car and driving to the nearest hospital in order to save her life. His inebriated driving jolts her leg, hastens the onset of gangrene, and results in her losing her limb. We would not admire such a motorist as much as we admire the motorist who exercises maximum care in his rescue effort, but nonetheless it is true that the inebriated motorist merely offers a lower level of aid than he might have done. He has not violated any right of the victim, since she has no right to a higher level of aid. She is still better off than she would have been if he had offered no aid at all, an option that was morally available to him.

23 In 1984, an Illinois judge ruled that a pregnant heroin user was abusing her fetus, made it a ward of the state, and sent the mother to a drug-rehabilitation center. "The Troubling Question of 'Fetal Rights'," *Newsweek,* December 8, 1986, 87. A pregnant woman convicted of second-degree theft was sentenced by a Washington, D.C. superior court judge to jail to protect her fetus from her alleged drug abuse (*U.S. v. Vaughn*). "The Latest Word," *Hastings Center Report,* 18 (October/November 1988): 55.

24 A New York Family Court judge ordered a pregnant woman with an alleged history of child abuse and neglect to surrender her baby at birth; he subsequently indicated that the mother could regain custody by meeting several conditions, including passing drug screening tests. *In the matter of Unborn Baby Beruiti,* cited in "The Latest Word," *Hastings Center Report,* 18 (October/November 1988): 55.

25 In this context we should remember that the potential fetal harms from smoking and drinking are much less severe, and much less certain, than the potential harms caused by other activities, for example using illegal drugs.

26 An embryonic version of this paper was presented to the Occupational Health and Safety Meeting at the Hastings Center in fall of 1981. Research for that version was supported by grants to the Hastings Center (Institute of Society, Ethics, and the Life Sciences) from the National Science Foundation-EVIST Program and the National Foundation/March of Dimes. For later support I am grateful to the National Endowment for the Humanities. I am also grateful to Allen Buchanan and Donald Regan for helpful comments.

15

Benign and malign morality

HYMAN GROSS

For me this is an opportunity to celebrate a quarter century of deeply rewarding friendship. It is not the place to talk of personal things, so I shall say of
Joel only that in ways that matter most my life would have been poorer
without the many things we have enjoyed together. There is much in his work
that has affected my own thinking, and certainly among the pieces that have
had a lasting influence is "The Expressive Function of Punishment."

Joel has told me of his own experience of crime and punishment in the
army, when an act of kindness while guarding prisoners resulted in his finding
himself among the condemned. Though this must bring to mind the celebrated
remark of Clemenceau that military justice is to justice as military music is to
music, it reminds me of how easily any of us might cross the great divide that
separates "us" from "them." This, I think, should be a source of moral
inspiration.

I

Taken at face value there is little to dispute in the proposition that punishment
for crime is right. It is right, and indisputably right, in the same way that war
is right to defend against armed aggression, or custodial restraint is right to
prevent dangerous madmen from harming others. But differences begin to
appear almost at once. In the case of war and in the case of madness it is
normal to look for some alternative that avoids the need for measures that are
recognized as terrible evils. With punishment it is otherwise.

Most people most of the time think that in general it is a good thing to
punish crime. People who concern themselves professionally about the justification of punishment generally take this line and treat punishment as something morally worthy so long as the person punished is guilty and the punishment fits the crime. It is true that there are different degrees of enthusiasm
here. Some theorists think punishment is good in the same way that all
instances of justice are good. It is cause for abiding satisfaction to know that

I am grateful to Peter Lipton and John Thompson for their very helpful comments.

justice has been done and a guilty person punished. Others show less enthusiasm and see punishment as a moral duty whose discharge is on the whole unpleasant. Still, doing one's duty is taken to be a good thing, and perhaps even better when it is unpleasant.

Both of these views of punishment stress its moral worthiness, and stand in sharp contrast to prevailing attitudes toward war. A war that is justifiable is morally tolerable, but not more than that. When we must fight to defend ourselves or to prevent a catastrophic loss, we do so with great regret and only when we are convinced that there is no way of avoiding the bloodshed and misery of war without giving in to the aggressor. But no matter how just the cause, the war is still the parade of horrors that makes all wars a matter of moral depravity. Those who wage the just war are exempt from the moral disgrace that is the lot of those who made waging it necessary. But under views that now prevail we regard the glorification of war as a moral sickness. During wartime there is a measure of rejoicing in the glory of war. Bravery, heroism, and self-sacrifice are extolled, and hearty approval is expressed for those who do their duty for their country. All of this seems right if it is necessary to help ensure a successful outcome and to console the nation for the terrible losses that are suffered. In other circumstances the glorification of war is rightly condemned as a species of moral pathology.

The moral development that marks our progress in civilization is not uniform in all areas of communal life. Perhaps because the threat of crime is continuous and close at hand we turn a blind eye to the evil of punishment, and so philosophers, no less than less reflective types, give it robust support. Only philosophers, however, think they must take pains to tell us why. Considerable ingenuity is devoted to philosophical justifications and to bolstering the notion that some worthy purpose is being served. What I wish to suggest is that eulogies for punishment are as great a moral mistake as praise for the virtues of war.

II

Why then is punishment right?

The need for punishment as part of a system of criminal law seems inescapable. We might have laws that were enforceable only by a procedure to adjudicate alleged violations, followed by solemnly recorded decisions of guilt or innocence. International law provides some interesting examples of this sort of thing. But in the ordinary context of domestic criminal law, it is only reasonable to expect that under such a system many people would choose to break the law to take advantage of appealing opportunities that required such transgression. In such a world some might still wish to continue to abide by the law, but even those most dedicated to such a policy would soon find that in order to survive they were forced to take, or to arrange for, measures outside the law to protect themselves from others who chose to disregard the law. In a world of mere token enforcement the law itself would be held in contempt when it failed utterly to provide the protection for which it existed and left everyone to depend upon self-help. Crime would certainly provoke further crime in the form of retaliation, revenge, or protection from further harm. Zealous self-help, unrestrained and unguided by due process of law, would regularly result in miscarriages of vengeance destroying wholly innocent lives.

It is hardly necessary to examine life in such a world in great detail to make the point. But it is worth mentioning one further feature that would affect law enforcement as we know it now. Without any possibility of imposing the extended detention that is the standard form of punishment for someone convicted of serious crime, it would be hard to justify arrest and detention pending adjudication of the charges. Why, after all, should anyone be held in custody at all by the police if what is going on is nothing more important than a procedure to determine and record whether or not *this* person committed *that* crime. And without the threat of arrest and detention, even a policeman at one's elbow would not have much of an inhibiting effect.

In fact everyone feels a measure of anger, even outrage, when a serious crime is committed – most immediately when one is the victim, but even at a distance simply by hearing an account of it. Accompanying the anger – indeed, even psychologically prior to it – there is fear; and for the victim, humiliation. Everyone feels helpless, inadequate, and in need of protection from criminal threats to one's person or property. There are also the more numerous, though less prominent, crimes that are invented as tools of government regulation and that in many instances likewise entail life-shattering terms of imprisonment. These crimes produce resentment rather than anger, and no fear at all unless (as is rarely the case) such a crime admits of the identification of an individual victim who suffers some palpable harm. But these crimes, no less than those crimes that do produce fear and anger, must be punishable if the law is to be taken seriously both by those who will break the law if they think they can get away with it, and those who abide by the law as a matter of conscience.

If crimes were not punishable those who committed crimes would always be allowed to get away with their crimes as far as the law was concerned. This general impunity would perhaps be the least tolerable of all of the consequences of the abolition of punishment, and the principal cause of the social chaos that would then prevail. Without the possibility of punishment, the law would be unable to provide the remedy for feelings that above all else is the immediate reason for having a system of enforceable laws.

Feelings, then, come first, and the failure to address them effectively through measures of law enforcement will result in unacceptable social consequences.

It may be, of course, that these speculations are unsound, and that the awful consequences that I have suggested would not come about. I would be delighted to learn that this was the case since we would then be free to develop much better ways than we now have of responding to crime. In the meantime, punishment seems an indispensable part of our system of law enforcement.

III

The grim necessity that apparently keeps us from doing away with punishment does not require us to be indifferent to what punishment consists of. It is clear enough that only what is necessary in punishment is justified, because more than that is the wanton infliction of suffering. With the notable exception of Bentham, philosophers usually pay little attention to these matters. Bentham's concern may be thought somewhat obsessive in its practical detail as well as in its guiding theory, but at least Bentham understood that the proper subject at hand is people rather than ideas about them, and that how these people are to be treated must be at the heart of moral concerns about punishment.

Philosophical concern seems unfortunately to be directed more to questions of interest to philosophers than to questions arising from the troubling nature of punishment. The philosopher's questions are concerned with such things as definitions that correctly distinguish punishment from other things, whether the person being punished is the same person over time as the person who committed the crime, how to calculate punishment correctly, and whether those who are punished are in some illicit way being used for some supposed social benefit. Because concern about the justification of punishment is recognized to be an urgent moral concern, and since punishment as it is in the real world must weigh heavily in dealing with that concern, it seems important that philosophers who work on this problem concern themselves with the facts of punishment and not simply with ideas about it.

Like war, punishment is a parade of horrors. Prison experience is a composite of unrelenting humiliation, waste and abuse. It breeds brutality, bitterness and despair. Although some prisons are better than others, and some countries more enlightened than others in the building and operation of their prisons, no experience in prison can make the whole episode of the crime and its consequences into a positive affair morally. If there is to be any progress in that direction money must be spent to create a decent physical environment and decent amenities of life, with a program for each day that seems to make life worth living, and an institutional regime that preserves respect for personal autonomy. This surely is where moral enthusiasm has a place and where moral ideals need to be asserted. In the midst of the misery we must inevitably create because we do not yet know how to live without punishment, we have ample opportunity to treat with humanity those who we must punish because we cannot let them get away with their crimes. Just as we have a moral responsibility to wage war as humanely as possible, so we also have a moral responsibility to treat in as humane a way as we can those whom we must punish.

A further opportunity for benign morality is presented when the day of reckoning comes and a sentence is to be passed. Sufficient on that day is a sentence that is seen not to be letting the perpetrator get away with his crime. If any good reasons exist for reducing the sentence from what the criminal conduct itself would indicate, those reasons should be given their full effect so long as a point of impunity is not reached. In this way only unavoidable misery will be produced by punishment. What counts as a good reason is not self-evident, for there are many varieties that need to be investigated, each having credentials of a different sort. Neither is it easy to tell when the point of impunity is reached and a sentence is tantamount to letting the perpetrator get away with his crime. In fact both of these considerations are constantly in play and sentencing decisions are reached under their influence in criminal courts throughout the world every day. Philosophers can make a useful contribution in all of this by making clear what we ought to do when we do what we must, and why.

Next there is the matter of alternatives to punishment. Both legislators and judges ought to think of effective law enforcement as a *threat* of punishment that may *when necessary* produce a sentence of punishment to prevent impunity. But when punishment is not necessary to prevent impunity the same objective ought to be accomplished by enforcing the law in some other way. The question then arises what counts as punishment and what does not. There is no point in pursuing conceptual niceties here. Punishment in essence means imprisonment. Various noncustodial dispositions are substitutes for punishment that import a measure of condemnation and shame, but still represent enforcement of the law. What we ought to seek in a morally enlightened community are more ways to avoid the shattering of lives through punishment when the need arises to enforce the law, while still not compromising the very important business of enforcing the law.

Finally, a morally robust community will consider carefully whether any particular activity ought really to be made the subject of criminal liability. Though we may strongly disapprove of certain conduct, that alone can never be enough. Even when some activity is properly enrolled as criminal, we must exercise morally sensitive judgment in deciding whether to seek to impose criminal liability on any particular occasion when we think that activity has taken place. We need not and should not enforce the law on each such occasion, because often the purpose for which the law exists would not be served, and so the horrific experiences of the criminal process could be avoided. To carry out a morally enlightened policy requires a point of view about the law that is at odds with many prevailing views. The law needs to be seen not as a set of rules whose transgressions are *ipso facto* crimes, but rather a set of rules to guide members of the community in what they do and to provide limits for the imposition of criminal liability by officials who have the responsibility for enforcing the law when that *needs* to be done.

IV

Certain morally questionable practices appear even in philosophical discussions of punishment.

It is a fundamental principle of criminal justice that criminal liability be imposed only for what was done and not because of the sort of person the person who did it has shown himself to be. When it comes time to decide what sort of disposition to make at the sentencing stage, it is then proper to consider many things about the person. One class of considerations are those that enlighten us about how he saw the crime when he was committing it and how he now sees it in retrospect. This is not a quest to retrieve thoughts and feelings, but an attempt to get a sense of how committed, or inclined, a person is to certain kinds of behaviour.

In the hands of some writers this concern is given a different twist. The crime itself is taken to be a sign of moral deficiency in the person who commits it, and punishment is justified by the bad character for which the crime stands as evidence. The worst sort of prejudices may be indulged by judges who adopt such a view, and it is one of the main objectives of any enlightened sentencing policy to prevent that from happening. Philosophical convenience, however, often seems served by this view of a person convicted of crime. Indeed in the more passionate (though by no means uncommon) form of retributive argument, it is not unusual to take some particularly horrific crime, and then to treat the crime and the person who committed it as the very paradigm of criminality, and the test case for justifying punishment. Prisons may now in fact be filled with perpetrators of drug related crimes, but for the philosopher in his philosophical investigation Hitler is a more useful example of the criminal, and some almost unimaginable horror a more useful example of crime. In reality these horrors are part of the criminal process only because civilized standards of the modern world require us to accord them the protection of a legal system. Their true interest lies elsewhere either as pathology or moral depravity where they are illuminated by investigations outside the law. As philosophical paradigms, however, they create in the audience the mood of fear, rage, and even loathing that makes punishment such a popular business. Though clothed in the respectability of philosophical argument it is a kind of philosophical dirty trick and discreditable in much the same way as the dirty tricks that politicians play when they select an emotive incident in the annals of criminal justice to denigrate the people in power when it occurred.

A second feature of malign morality is this. Everyone agrees that punishment should be deserved and that subjecting anyone to undeserved punishment is wrong. This means that the innocent should not be punished, and that the guilty should not receive more punishment than they deserve. Not infrequently, however, it is taken to mean that a full measure of punishment must be inflicted to exact full payment for the crime. No one has ever found out how that full measure is to be determined, though presumably it is as much as is not undeserved, but no less. In any case, though matching and measuring can only be an empty pretense, the attitude behind it is morally insensitive and very much at odds with standard civilized practice. Having determined how serious was the crime for which the perpetrator is to be punished, we should then consider what good reasons there might be for passing a lighter sentence than we otherwise would, so long as in the end we do not pass a sentence that lets the perpetrator get away with his crime. The stern exacting of the right penalty, not a day more, not a day less, insists that we leave out of account everything that matters except the extremely lean version of the crime that concerns the law. It is of course quite proper that the law should circumscribe the object of its concern as it does, so that only those matters of conduct that make it appropriate to have criminal liability in the first place are considered when a determination of criminal liability is being sought. But in sentencing there is no reason to limit consideration to those matters that bear only on liability. Anything that affects those feelings which make it necessary to have criminal liability in the first place are properly considered in order to prevent any greater deprivation and suffering than is necessary.

Following on from this there is a final point of moral weakness. When the whole story is told as a novelist, a journalist, or a dramatist might tell it, there are many things that give the entire criminal episode a moral dimension that transcends the legal proceedings and what they are capable of embracing. Why do philosophers not address the problems of punishment with that moral imagination and breadth of moral vision instead of insisting on the simple elements of the crime? Concern then is not only about the criminal and his crime, but about the full panoply of events that produced it and about its consequences, not only for the victim, but for many others, including those whose lives are entangled with that of the perpetrator. This adventure in moral exploration requires a certain boldness and a willingness to give up the comfortable assumptions that philosophical simplicity affords. It is not easy to take on board life as it is in all its complexity. But the larger moral investigation that requires this is far more rewarding, and the only way to achieve genuine moral progress. Its secret is the growth of conscience.

Publications by Joel Feinberg

1   "Does Nixon Play the Game?" *The Nation* 190 (1960): 448–50.
2   "On Justifying Legal Punishment." In *Nomos III: Responsibility,* ed. by C. J. Friedrich, 152–67. New York: Liberal Arts Press, 1960.
3   "Supererogation and Rules," *Ethics,* 71 (1961): 276–87. Reprinted in *Ethics,* ed. by J. J. Thomson and G. Dworkin. New York: Harper & Row, 1968. In *Philosophical Ethics,* ed. by Tom L. Beauchamp. New York: McGraw-Hill, 1982. In *Introduction to Ethical Theory,* ed. by Kenneth F. Rogerson. New York: Holt, Rinehart, and Winston, Inc., 1989.
4   "Problematic Responsibility in Law and Morals." *Philosophical Review* 71 (1962): 340–51.
5   "Justice and Personal Desert." *Nomos VI: Justice,* ed. by Carl J. Friedrich and John W. Chapman, 69–97. New York: Atherton Press, 1963. Reprinted in the Bobbs-Merrill Reprint Series in Philosophy, 1969.
6   "On Being 'Morally Speaking a Murderer,'" *Journal of Philosophy* 61 (1964): 158–71. Reprinted in *Ethics,* ed. by J. J. Thomson and G. Dworkin. New York: Harper & Row, 1968.
7   "Wasserstrom on Human Rights." *Journal of Philosophy* 61 (1964): 641–5. Reprinted in *Philosophy and the Black Revolution,* ed. by Ronald Santoni. Indianapolis: Bobbs-Merrill, 1972.
8   "Action and Responsibility." In *Philosophy in America,* ed. by Max Black, 134–60. London: George Allen & Unwin, Ltd., 1965. German translation, Frankfurt: Suhrkamp Verlag, 1978. Reprinted in *The Philosophy of Action,* ed. by Alan R. White. Oxford: Oxford University Press, 1968.
9   *Reason and Responsibility.* Edited with six section introductions. Belmont, Cal.: Wadsworth Publishing Company, 1965. Second Edition, 1971. Third Edition, 1975. Fourth Edition, 1978. Fifth Edition, 1981. Sixth Edition, 1984. Seventh Edition, 1988. Eighth Edition, 1992.
10 "Psychological Egoism," published in *Reason and Responsibility.* Reprinted in *Moral Philosophy: Problems of Theory and Practice,* ed. by James Rachels. Belmont, Cal.: Wadsworth Publishing Company, 1976. In *Reason at Work,* ed. by Steven M. Cahn, Patricia Kitcher, and George Sher. San Diego, Cal.: Harcourt, Brace, Jovanovich, 1984. Also in *Ethical Theory,* ed. by Louis P. Pojman. Belmont, Cal.: Wadsworth, 1987.
11 "The Expressive Function of Punishment," *The Monist.* 49 (1965): 397–423. Reprinted in *Philosophical Perspectives on Punishment,* ed. by Gertrude Ezorsky.

New York: State University of New York Press, 1972. In *Criminal Law and Its Processes,* Third Edition, ed. by Sanford Kadish and M. G. Paulsen. Boston: Little Brown & Co., 1975. In *Sentencing,* ed. by Hyman Gross and Andrew von Hirsch. New York: Oxford University Press, 1980. Also in 50.

12 Review of *The Death Penalty in America* by Hugo Bedau. *Ethics* 76 (1965): 63–6.

13 "Duties, Rights, and Claims." *American Philosophical Quarterly* 3 (1966): 1–8. Reprinted in *Philosophy and Law,* ed. by Edward A. Kent. New York: Appleton-Century-Croft, 1970.

14 Review of *Psychotherapy and Morality* by Joseph Margolis. *Princeton Alumni Weekly* 17 (1966).

15 "Causing Voluntary Actions." In *Metaphysics and Explanation* (The Proceedings of the 1964 Oberlin Colloquium in Philosophy), ed. by W. H. Capitan and D. D. Merrill, 29–47. Pittsburgh: University of Pittsburgh Press, 1966.

16 "Rejoinders to Professors Donnellan and Lehrer." *Ibid.,* 55–61.

17 "Analytical Jurisprudence." In *Encyclopedia of Philosophy,* ed. by Paul Edwards, 109–11. New York: Macmillan, 1967.

18 "The Forms and Limits of Utilitarianism." *Philosophical Review.* 76 (1967): 268–81.

19 "Collective Responsibility," *Journal of Philosophy* 65 (1968): 674–88. Reprinted in *Collective Responsibility,* ed. by Larry May and Stacey Hoffman. Totowa, N.J.: Rowman and Littlefield, 1991, and in 45, First Edition.

20 Review of *An Introduction to Ethics* by J. D. Mabbott. *University Review* (October, 1969).

21 *Moral Concepts,* edited with an introductory essay (pp. 1–17), Oxford Studies in Philosophy series (Oxford: Oxford University Press, 1970). Spanish language edition published by Fondo Cultura Economica de Mexico (1989).

22 "Crime, Clutchability, and Individuated Treatment," presented to the Western Division of the American Philosophical Association, May, 1967. Published in 25 below. Reprinted in J. G. Murphy, ed., *Punishment and Rehabilitation,* ed. by J. G. Murphy. Belmont, Cal.: Wadsworth Publishing Company, 1973. Also in *Biomedical Ethics,* ed. by Thomas A. Mappes and Jane S. Zembaty. New York: McGraw-Hill, 1980.

23 "What Is So Special About Mental Illness?", presented to the Symposium on Responsibility at Cleveland State University, May, 1968. Published in 25. Reprinted in 9, Fourth Edition, and in *Readings in Philosophy of Law,* ed. by John Arthur and William Shaw. Englewood Cliffs, N.J.: Prentice-Hall, 1983.

24 "Sua Culpa," presented to the Chapel Hill Colloquium in Philosophy, University of North Carolina, October, 1969. Published in 25. Reprinted in *Ethical Issues in the Use of Computers,* ed. by Deborah G. Johnson and John W. Snapper. Belmont, Cal.: Wadsworth, 1984 and in 45.

25 *Doing and Deserving, Essays in the Theory of Responsibility.* Princeton, N.J.: Princeton University Press, 1970. Contains revised versions of 3, 4, 5, 6, 8, 11, 15, 16, 19, 21, 22, and 23. Revised paperback edition, 1974.

26 "The Nature and Value of Rights," *The Journal of Value Inquiry* 4 (1970): 243–57. Reprinted in *Concepts in Social and Political Philosophy,* ed. by Richard E.

Flathman. New York: Macmillan, 1973. In *Moral Problems in Medicine,* ed. by Samuel Gorovitz. Englewood Cliffs, N.J.: Prentice-Hall, 1976. In *Contemporary Issues in Bioethics,* ed. by Tom L. Beauchamp and Leroy Walters. Belmont, Cal.: Wadsworth, 1978. In *Bioethics and Human Rights: A Reader for Health Professionals,* ed. by B. and E. Bandman. Boston: Little, Brown, 1978. In *Rights,* ed. by David Lyons. Belmont, Cal.: Wadsworth, 1978. In 45, Second Edition. In *Philosophical Ethics,* ed. by Tom L. Beauchamp. New York: McGraw-Hill, 1982. In *Making Ethical Decisions,* ed. by Norman E. Bowie. New York: McGraw-Hill, 1985. In *Ethical Theory,* ed. by Louis P. Pojman. Belmont, Cal.: Wadsworth, 1987. In *Introduction to Ethical Theory,* ed. by Kenneth F. Rogerson. New York: Holt, Rinehart, and Winston, 1989. In *Contemporary Political Theory,* ed. by Philip Pettit. New York: Macmillan, 1989. In *The International Library of Essays in Law and Legal Theory,* ed. by Tom D. Campbell. Aldershot: Dartmouth Publishing Company, 1991. In the Bandman volume the article includes a Postcript. (See 56.)

27 "Commentary on Carl Wellman's 'Reasons for Breaking the Law'". *The Journal of Value Inquiry* 4 (1970): 269–72.

28. "Commentary on Jan Narveson's 'Utilitarianism and Moral Norms'". *The Journal of Value Inquiry* 4 (1970): 282–5.

29 "Comments on 'Moral Progress,'" *Society, Revolution, and Reform* (The Proceedings of the 1969 Oberlin Colloquium in Philosophy), ed. by Robert Grimm and Alfred Mackay, 19–31. Cleveland: Case Western Reserve University Press, 1971.

30 "Legal Paternalism." *Canadian Journal of Philosophy* 1, no. 1 (1971): 105–24. Reprinted in *Today's Moral Problems,* ed. by Richard A. Wasserstrom. New York: Macmillan, 1974. In *Readings for an Introduction to Philosophy,* ed. by Charles Reagan. New York: Macmillan, 1976. In *Paternalism,* ed. by Rolf Sartorius. Minneapolis: University of Minnesota Press, 1984. In *Philosophy of Law,* Second Edition, ed. by Edward A. Kent;. Englewood Cliffs, N.J.: Prentice-Hall, 1983. In *The Value of Life,* ed. by Joseph Grcic. St. Paul, M.N.: West Publishing Co., 1989. Also in *The International Library of Essays in Law and Legal Theory,* ed. by Tom D. Campbell. London: Dartmouth Publishing Co., 1992.

31 Review of *Responsibility* by Jonathan Glover. *Philosophical Review* 81 (1972): 237–40.

32 "Justice, Fairness, and Rationality," *The Yale Law Journal* 81 (1972): 1004–32. Reprinted in part in *Reading Rawls: Critical Studies on 'A Theory of Justice,'* ed. by Norman Daniels. New York: Basic Books, 1975. Also in *Readings in Jurisprudence and Legal Philosophy,* ed. by Cohen and Cohen, revised by Philip Schuchman. Boston: Little, Brown, 1977.

33 "'Harmless Immoralities' and Offensive Nuisances." *Issues in Law and Morality* (The Proceedings of the 1970 Oberlin Colloquium in Philosophy), ed. by Norman Care and Thomas Trelogan, 83–106. Cleveland: Case Western Reserve University Press, 1973. Reprinted in *Philosophical Ethics,* ed. by Tom L. Beauchamp. New York: McGraw-Hill, 1982. Also in *Aids: Ethics and Public Policy,* ed. by Donald VanDeVeer. Belmont, Cal.: Wadsworth, 1987.

34 "Rejoinder to Professor Bayles." *Ibid.,* 127–40.

35 *Social Philosophy.* Englewood Cliffs, N.J.: Prentice-Hall, 1973. Portuguese translation *Filosofia Social.* Rio de Janeiro: Zahar Editores, 1974. Japanese translation by Ho Kassegawa for Baifukan Publishing Company pending. Chinese translation by Wang Showchang. Guangzhou, Guangdong: GuiZhou Peoples Publisher, 1992. Sections are reprinted in *Ethics and Public Policy*, ed. by Tom L. Beauchamp. Englewood Cliffs, N.J.: Prentice-Hall, 1975. In *Ethics in Perspective*, ed. by K. J. Struhl and P. R. Struhl. New York: Random House, 1975. In *Philosophical Issues in Law*, ed. by Kenneth Kipnis. Englewood Cliffs, N.J.: Prentice-Hall, 1977. In *Social Ethics: Morality and Social Policy*, ed. by Thomas A. Mappes and Jane S. Zembaty. New York: McGraw-Hill, 1977. In *Contemporary Issues in Bioethics*, ed. by Tom L. Beauchamp and Leroy Walters. Belmont, Cal.: Wadsworth, 1978. In *Freedom of Expression*, ed. by Fred R. Berger. Belmont, Cal.: Wadsworth, 1979. In *Moral Problems*, Third Edition, ed. by James Rachels. New York: Harper & Row, 1979. In *Philosophy for a New Generation*, Fourth Edition, ed. by Arthur Bierman and James A. Gould. New York: Macmillan, 1980. In *Right Conduct: Theory and Applications*, ed. by Michael Bayles and Kenneth Henley. New York: Random House, 1982. In *Philosophical Ethics*, ed. by Tom L. Beauchamp. New York: McGraw-Hill, 1982. In *Readings in the Philosophy of Constitutional Law*, ed. by R. N. Bronaugh, C. B. Hoffmaster, and S. B. Sharzer. Dubuque, Iowa: Kendall, Hunt Publishing Co., 1983. In *Readings in the Philosophy of Law*, ed. by John Arthur and William Shaw. Englewood Cliffs, N.J.: Prentice-Hall, 1983. Also in *Ethical Theory*, ed. by Louis P. Pojman. Belmont, Cal.: Wadsworth, 1987.

36 "The Idea of a Free Man." In *Educational Judgments*, ed. by James F. Doyle, 143–69. London: Routledge & Kegan Paul, 1973.

37 "Some Conjectures About the Concept of Respect." *The Journal of Social Philosophy* 3 (1973): 1–3.

38 "Insane or Guilty?" A taped conversation between Alan Dershowitz and Joel Feinberg. Produced by the Council for Interdisciplinary Communication in Medicine, Ltd. under a grant from Smith, Kline & French Laboratories. Copyright © 1973, Council for Interdisciplinary Communication in Medicine, Ltd.

39 "Duty and Obligation in the Non-Ideal World." *The Journal of Philosophy*, 70 (1973): 263–75. Reprinted in part in *Reading Rawls: Critical Essays on 'A Theory of Justice'* ed. by Norman Daniels. New York: Basic Books, 1975.

40 *The Problem of Abortion*, ed. with an introductory essay, 1–9. Belmont, Cal.: Wadsworth, 1973. Second Edition, 1983.

41 "Noncomparative Justice." *The Philosophical Review* 83 (1974): 297–338. Reprinted in *Justice*, see 45 and 65.

42 "The Rights of Animals and Unborn Generations," in *Philosophy and Environmental Crisis*, ed. by William T. Blackstone, 43–68. Athens, Georgia: University of Georgia Press, 1974. Reprinted in part in *Animal Rights and Human Obligations*, ed. by Thomas Regan and Peter Singer. Englewood Cliffs, N.J.: Prentice-Hall, 1975. In *Social Ethics: Morality and Social Policy*, ed. by Thomas A. Mappes and Jane Zembaty. New York: McGraw-Hill, 1977. In *Today's Moral Problems*, Second Edition, ed. by Richard A. Wasserstrom. New York: Macmillan, 1979. In *Ethical Theory and Business*, ed. by Tom L. Beauchamp and

Norman Bowie. Englewood Cliffs, N.J.: Prentice-Hall, 1979. In *Responsibilities to Future Generations,* ed. by Ernest Partridge. Buffalo, N.Y.: Prometheus Books, 1980. In *Values and Ethics in Human Development Professions,* ed. by T. R. Vallance. Dubuque, Iowa: Kendall-Hunt, 1984. In *Moral Dilemmas,* ed. by Richard L. Purtill. Belmont, Cal.: Wadsworth, 1984. In *Philosophical Issues in Human Rights,* ed. by Patricia H. Werhane, A. R. Gini, and David Ozar, (N.Y.: Random House, 1985). In *Ethics: Theory and Practice,* ed. by Manuel Velasquez and Cynthia Rostankowski. Englewood Cliffs, N.J.: Prentice-Hall, 1985. In *Virtue and Values,* ed. by Joshua Halberstam. Englewood Cliffs, N.J.: Prentice-Hall, 1988. In *Contemporary Issues in Bioethics,* Third Edition, ed. by Tom L. Beauchamp and LeRoy Walters. Belmont, Cal.: Wadsworth, 1989. In *Contemporary Moral Problems,* Third Edition, ed. by James E. White. St. Paul, M.N.: West Publishing Company, 1991. In *Ethics for Modern Life,* ed. by Ragiel Abelson and Marie-Louise Frieguegnon. New York: St. Martin's Press, 1991. In *Ethical Issues: Perspectives for Canadians,* ed. by Eldon Soifer. Peterborough, Ontario: Broadview Press, 1992. Also in 64. German translation in *Okologie Und Ethik,* ed. by Dieter Birnbacher. Stuttgart: Reclam, 1979. Italian translation in *Diritti Degli Animali,* ed. by S. Castignone. Bologna: Societa'ditric iI Mulino, 1984. Japanese translation in the journal *Gendai-shicho,* by Keyiro Unoki. Chiba University, 1991.

43 "Human Duties and Animal Rights." In *The Fifth Day: Animal Rights and Human Ethics,* ed. by Richard K. Morris and Michael W. Fox, 45–69. Washington, D.C.: Acropolis Books, 1978. Preprinted in Proceedings of the Creighton Club: New York State Philosophical Association, 1974. Polish translation in *ETYKA: Reports on Philosophy.* Published by the Institute of Philosophy, Jagiellonian University of Cracow. Warsaw-Cracow, Poland: Polish Scientific Publishers, 1979.

44 "Limits to the Free Expression of Opinion," presented at Ithaca College, N.Y., November 1973. Published in 45, 135–51.

45 *Philosophy of Law,* co-edited with Hyman Gross, with extended introductions to parts II ("Liberty"), III ("Justice"), and V ("Punishment"). Belmont, Cal.: Wadsworth, 1975. Separate paperback editions of *Responsibility* and *Punishment* published in 1976. Separate paperback editions of *Law in Philosophical Perspective, Liberty* and *Justice,* each with additional materials and revised introductions, published in 1977. Second Edition, 1980. Third Edition, 1986. Fourth Edition, 1990.

46 "Is There a Right to be Born?" In *Moral Philosophy: Problems of Theory and Practice,* ed. by James Rachels, 346–57. Belmont, Cal.: Wadsworth, 1976.

47 Review of *The Conscience of the Courts: Law and Morals in American Life* by Graham Hughes, in *New York University Law Review* 51 (1976): 903–10.

48 "Wollaston and his Critics." *Journal of the History of Ideas* 28 (April, 1977): 345–52.

49 "Harm and Self-Interest." In *Law, Morality, and Society: Essays in Honour of H.L.A. Hart,* ed. by P. M. S. Hacker and J. Raz, 289–308. Oxford: Clarendon Press, 1977. Spanish translation in a volume on Analytic Legal Philosophy, ed. by Martin D. Farrell and Carlos S. Nino. Buenos Aires: Eudeba, 1984.

50 *Moral Philosophy: Classic Texts and Contemporary Problems,* co-edited with Henry West, with extended Introductions to Part I, "Three Classical Theories," Part IV, "Rights, Justice, and Punishment," and Part VI, "Egoism and the Ethics of Character." Belmont, Cal.: Wadsworth, 1977.

51 "Justice." In *Encyclopedia of Bioethics,* ed. by Warren T. Reich. New York: Macmillan, 1978.

52 "Freedom and Behavior Control." *Encyclopedia of Bioethics,* ed. by Warren T. Reich. New York: Macmillan, 1978.

53 "Rights," *Encyclopedia of Bioethics,* ed. by Warren T. Reich. New York: Macmillan, 1978.

54 "The Interest in Liberty on the Scales." In *Values and Morals: Essays in Honor of William K. Frankena, Charles L. Stevenson, and Richard B. Brandt,* ed. by Alvin I. Goldman and Jaegwon Kim, 21–35. Dordrecht, The Netherlands: Reidel, 1978.

55 "Voluntary Euthanasia and the Inalienable Right to Life," *Philosophy and Public Affairs,* 7 (Winter, 1978): 93–123. Reprinted in *The Tanner Lectures on Human Values,* Vol. 1 Salt Lake City: University of Utah Press, 1980. Also in *Medicine and Moral Philosophy,* ed. by Marshall Cohen, Thomas Nagel, and Thomas Scanlon. Princeton, N.J.: Princeton University Press, 1982. Abridged and reprinted as "Suicide and the Inalienable Right to Life." In *Suicide,* ed. by M. Pabst Battin and David J. Mayo. New York: St. Martin's Press, 1980.

56 "Postscript to 'The Nature and Value of Rights'." In *Bioethics and Human Rights: A Reader for Health Professionals,* ed. by Bertram and Elsie Bandman. Boston: Little, Brown, 1978. Reprinted in 45, Second Edition, and in 65.

57 "Abortion." In *Matters of Life and Death,* ed. by Thomas Regan, 182–217. New York: Random House, 1979. Reprinted in part as "The Concept of a Person." In *Contemporary Issues in Bioethics,* Second Edition, ed. by T. Beauchamp and L. Walters. Belmont, Cal.: Wadsworth, 1982. In *Moral Issues,* ed. by Jan Narveson. Oxford University Press, 1983, and in 40, Second Edition. The revised version in the second edition of the Regan book contains a four page "Postscript". Swedish translation in a volume on Ethical Aspects of Abortion, ed. by Thomas Anderberg and Ingmar Perrson. Lund, 1985. Japanese translation in a volume on Bioethics, ed. by Hisatake Kato and Nobuyuki Iida. Tokyo: Tokai University Press, 1987.

58 "The Idea of the Obscene," The Seventeenth Annual Ernest H. Lindley Lecture, 1979. Lawrence, Kansas: The University of Kansas Press, 1979.

59 "Pornography and the Criminal Law." *The University of Pittsburgh Law Review* 40, no. 4 (1979): 567–604. Reprinted in *Pornography and Censorship: Scientific, Philosophical, and Legal Studies,* ed. by Susan Wendall and David Copp. Buffalo, N.Y.: Prometheus Books, 1984.

60 "Civil Disobedience in the Modern World." *Humanities in Society* 2, no. 1 (Winter, 1979): 37–59, and in 45, Third Edition. Reprinted in *Civil Disobedience,* ed. by Paul Harris. University Press of America, 1989. Also in *Morality and the Law,* edited by R. M. Baird and Stuart Rosenbaum. Buffalo, N.Y.: Prometheus Books, 1989.

61 "Absurd Self-fulfillment." In *Time and Cause, Essays Presented to Richard Tay-*

lor, ed. by Peter van Inwagen, 255–81. Dordrecht, The Netherlands: Reidel, 1980. Reprinted in 62, Second Edition.

62 *Philosophy and the Human Condition,* co-edited with Tom L. Beauchamp and William T. Blackstone, with extended introductory essays to Chap. 1, "The Nature of Philosophy," Chap. 4, "The Sanctity of Life," Chap. 7, "Love and Sexuality," and Chap. 10, "The Meaning of Life." Englewood Cliffs, N.J.: Prentice-Hall, 1980. Second Edition, 1988.

63 "Legal Moralism and Free-floating Evils." *Pacific Philosophical Quarterly* 61, nos. 1 & 2 (1980): 130–63. Reprinted in *The Philosopher's Annual,* Vol. 4. Ridgeview Publishing Co., 1981.

64 "What Is Philosophy?." In *Reason and Responsibility,* Fifth Edition. Belmont, Cal.: Wadsworth, 1981.

65 *Rights, Justice, and the Bounds of Liberty.* Princeton, N.J.: Princeton University Press, 1980. Contains numbers 13, 26, 30, 33, 34, 36, 41, 42, 43, 46, 48, 49, 54, 55, and 56.

66 "The Child's Right to an Open Future." In *Whose Child? Children's Rights, Parental Authority, and State Power,* ed. by William Aiken and Hugh LaFollette, 124–53. Totowa, N.J.: Rowan and Littlefield, 1980. Reprinted in *Ethical Principles for Social Policy,* ed. by John Howie, 202–46. Carbondale, Ill.: Southern Illinois University Press, 1982.

67 "Obscenity, Pornography, and the Arts: Sorting Things Out." In *Contemporary Value Conflicts* ed. by Burton M. Leiser. New York: Macmillan, 1981.

68 "Protecting a Way of Life." In *Absolute Values and the Search for the Peace of Mankind,* Vol. I, 185–201. New York: The International Cultural Foundation Press, 1981.

69 "Sentiment and Sentimentality in Practical Ethics." Presidential Address, Pacific Division, American Philosophical Association, 1982. Published in *Proceedings and Addresses of The American Philosophical Association* 56, no. 1 (Sept., 1982).

70 "Autonomy as Personal Sovereignty" and "Privacy as Autonomy." The Eleventh Annual Lectures on Civil Rights, The University of Notre Dame Law School, 1982. Published as "Autonomy, Sovereignty, and Privacy: Moral Ideals in the Constitution?" in *The Notre Dame Law Review* 58 (1983): 445–92. Reprinted in *Liberalism,* ed. by Richard J. Arneson. London: Edward Elgar Publishing, Ltd., 1991.

71 "Noncoercive Exploitation." In *Paternalism,* ed. by Rolf Sartorius, 201–35. Minneapolis: University of Minnesota Press, 1983.

72 "Obscene Words and the Law." *Law and Philosophy* 2 (1983).

73 "The Moral and Legal Responsibility of the Bad Samaritan." *Criminal Justice Ethics* 3 (1984): 56–68. Reprinted in the *Proceedings* of the 11th World Congress on Philosophy of Law and Social Philosophy. Wiesbaden: Franz Steiner Verlag, 1985. Also in *The Spectrum of Responsibility,* ed. by Peter A. French. New York: St. Martin's Press, 1991.

74 *Harm to Others.* New York: Oxford University Press, 1984. Volume I of *The Moral Limits of the Criminal Law.* Paperback edition, 1986. Partially reprinted in

The Metaphysics of Death ed. by John Martin Fischer. Stanford, Cal.: Stanford University Press, 1992, as "Environmental Pollution and the Threshold of Harm" in the *Hastings Center Report*, June 1984, and in *Ethical Theory and Business*, ed. by Tom L. Beauchamp and Norman Bowie (Englewood Cliffs, N.J.: Prentice-Hall, 1988).

75   *Offense to Others.* New York: Oxford University Press, 1985. Volume II of *The Moral Limits of the Criminal Law.* Paperback edition, 1987. Reprinted in part as "The Mistreatment of Dead Bodies." *The Hastings Center Report*, February, 1985. Reprinted in part as "Obscenity as Pornography" in *Philosophical Problems in the Law*, ed. by David M. Adams, 275–90. Belmont, Cal.: Wadsworth, 1992.

76   *Harm to Self.* New York: Oxford University Press, 1986. Volume III of *The Moral Limits of the Criminal Law.* Paperback edition, 1988. Reprinted in part in *The Inner Citadel, Essays on Individual Autonomy*, ed. by John Christman, 27–53. New York: Oxford University Press, 1989.

77   *Harmless Wrongdoing.* New York: Oxford University Press, 1988. Volume IV of *The Moral Limits of the Criminal Law.* Paperback edition, 1990.

78   "The Argument from the Moral Gradation of Punishments." *Social Sciences Review.* Universidad de Valparaiso, Chile (1987). Special issue dedicated to the work of H. L. A. Hart, in Spanish.

79   "Wrongful Conception and the Right Not to be Harmed." *Harvard Journal of Law and Public Policy* 8 (1985): 57–77.

80   "Victims' Excuses: The Case of Fraudulently Procured Consent." *Ethics* 96 (1986): 330–45.

81   "Harm to Others: A Rejoinder." Symposium on Joel Feinberg's *Harm to Others*, *Criminal Justice Ethics*, 5 (1986): 16–24.

82   "Wrongful Life and the Counterfactual Element in Harming." *Social Philosophy and Policy* 4 (1986): 145–78.

83   "Some Unswept Debris from the Hart-Devlin Debate." *Festschrift* for Kurt Baier. *Synthese* (August, 1987): 249–75.

84   "The Paradox of Blackmail." *Ratio Juris*, I (1988).

85   "Liberalism, Community, and Tradition." *Tikkun* (May, 1988).

86   "The Right to Disobey." Review of *Conflicts of Law and Morality* by Kent Greenawalt. *Michigan Law Review* 87 (1989).

87   "Responsibility for the Future." *Philosophy Research Archives* 14 (1989).

88   "Responsibility Tout Court." *Philosophy Research Archives* 14 (1989).

89   "Harm and Offense" *Encyclopedia of Ethics*, edited by Lawrence C. Becker. Garland Publishing Co., 1991.

90   "The Social Importance of Moral Rights." *Philosophical Perspectives*, Volume 6 *Ethics*, ed. by James E. Tomberlin. (1992).

91   "Law and Morals." *The Encyclopedia of Language and Linguistics*. Aberdeen: The Pergamon Press, 1992.

92   Review of Robert Goodin's *No Smoking* in *Bioethics*, (1991).

93   "A Youthful Reminiscence," in *The Becoming of a Philosopher*, ed. by David D. Karnos and Robert G. Shoemaker (New York: Oxford University Press, 1993).

94   "The Classic Debate" (over "Punishment") in 45, Fourth Edition, 646–50 (1990).

95   "Overlooking the Merits of the Individual Case: An Unpromising Approach to the Right to Die," *Ratio Juris,* Vol. 4, No. 4, 1991. Reprinted in 97.

96   "In Defence of Moral Rights," *Oxford Journal of Legal Studies,* (1992), 149–69.

97   *Freedom and Fulfillment.* Princeton, N.J.: Princeton University Press, 1992. Contains revised versions of 44, 57, 60, 61, 66, 69, 73, 82, 90, 95, 96.

98   "The Constitutional Relevance of Moral Rights" in 97.

99   "Seven Modes of Reasoning that Can Justify Overlooking the Merits of the Individual Case – When the Facts are Right," in 97.

100   "The Absurd and the Comic: Why Does Some Incongruity Please?" in 97.

101   Review of Fred Berger's *Freedom, Rights, and Pornography in Ethics* (1992).